MANAGEMENT ACCOUNTING

CORINE T. NORGAARD, Ph.D., C.P.A.
University of Connecticut

MANAGEMENT
MANAGEMENT
MANAGEMENT ACCOUNTING
ACCOUNTING
ACCOUNTING

PRENTICE HALL, INC., Englewood Cliffs, N.J. 07632

Library of Congress Cataloging in Publication Data

NORGAARD, CORINE T.
   Management accounting.

   Includes index.
   1.–Managerial accounting. I.–Title.
HF5635.N775–1985   658.1′511   84-13363
ISBN 0-13-548488-X

Material from Uniform CPA Examination Questions and Unofficial Answers, Copyright © 1970, 1972, 1973, 1974, 1976, 1977, 1978, 1979, 1980, 1981 by the American Institute of Certified Public Accountants, Inc., is reprinted or adapted by permission.

Materials from the Certificate in Management Accounting Examinations, Copyright © 1980, 1979, 1978, 1977, 1975, 1974 by the National Association of Accountants are reprinted and/or adapted with permission.

Editorial/production supervision: Sonia Meyer
Interior design: Lee Cohen/Sonia Meyer
Cover design: Lee Cohen
Manufacturing buyer: Ray Keating

Printed in the United States of America

10 9 8 7 6 5 4 3 2 1

ISBN 0-13-548488-X 01

PRENTICE-HALL INTERNATIONAL, INC., *London*
PRENTICE-HALL OF AUSTRALIA PTY. LIMITED, *Sydney*
EDITORA PRENTICE-HALL DO BRASIL, LTDA., *Rio de Janeiro*
PRENTICE-HALL CANADA INC., *Toronto*
PRENTICE-HALL OF INDIA PRIVATE LIMITED, *New Delhi*
PRENTICE-HALL OF JAPAN, INC., *Tokyo*
PRENTICE-HALL OF SOUTHEAST ASIA PTE. LTD., *Singapore*
WHITEHALL BOOKS LIMITED, *Wellington, New Zealand*

To my husband, son, and babysitter in appreciation
of their patience and support throughout
this long project.

CONTENTS

six   Product Cost Accumulation Systems II—Process Cost Accounting   185

SECTION II   USING ACCOUNTING DATA FOR PLANNING AND CONTROL

seven   The Budgetary Process and the Mechanics of Budget Preparation   223

eight   Responsibility Accounting Systems   293

nine   Using Flexible Budgets and Standard Costs for Controlling Direct Material and Direct Labor   352

ten   Using Flexible Budgets and Standard Costs for Controlling Manufacturing Overhead   393

eleven   Controlling Revenues, Expenses, and Investment   437

SECTION III   USING ACCOUNTING DATA IN SPECIAL ANALYSIS FOR DECISION MAKING

twelve   Cost-Volume-Profit Analysis   490

thirteen   Analysis for Short-Term, Nonroutine Decision Making   534

fourteen **Capital Budgeting Preliminaries: Present-Value Concepts and Income Tax Implications of Investment Decisions   581**

fifteen **Evaluation of Capital Expenditure Projects   620**

PREFACE

One aim of this text is to convey to the reader my enthusiasm for managerial accounting. I believe that this topic is one of the most useful that a student will explore. Whether a person is working for a profit-making institution, a government entity, a nonprofit organization, a service organization, a large enterprise or a small one, many of the concepts and techniques described here will surface and prove useful again and again.

To help the reader see how it all fits together, the text is organized around three major uses of accounting data: (1) for costing products and services, (2) for planning and control, and (3) for analysis. Many of the examples use products and services with which students are familiar—beanbag chairs, walkmans, and running shoes, for example—and the numbers are realistic. The relevance of the concepts and techniques discussed to service and nonprofit organizations is woven into each chapter to make the reader aware of their wide range of applicability.

Each chapter ends with at least 20 questions, 15 exercises, and 15 problems. Overall more than 750 such items have been included. The exercises and problems relate to manufacturing entities and service organizations, to profit and nonprofit institutions, to large enterprises and to individuals. This is done to stimulate interest and emphasize the broad usefulness of managerial accounting.

Illustrations from practice are included throughout the text. These are based on real company and organization examples, using the true company names. Forms and procedures used by these companies are shown and described so that the reader can see how the topics discussed are applied outside the classroom.

The text is designed for use in a one-semester introductory course in managerial accounting and assumes that the reader is familiar with elementary financial accounting concepts. A supplementary solution manual gives a detailed solution to each question, exercise, and problem. The solution manual includes teaching notes for each chapter, describing how I approach the teaching of the materials in that chapter. An introduction to and a summary of each section of the text is included in the solution manual as well as a model assignment sheet listing topics and suggesting problem assignments on a day by day basis. These aid the instructor in conveying the logical arrangement of the materials to the students. A study guide, test bank, and transparencies of selected illustrations also are available.

Acknowledgments

I would like to express my appreciation to the following individuals and companies who discussed their managerial accounting procedures with me, gave me samples of their forms, and described the techniques they use: Heath Fitzsimmons at Aetna Life and Casualty, Celeste Michalski at American Can, Ron Budnick at American Thread, Guy Boyle at Brand Rex, Emhart, Robert Nelson of General Electric, the National Tooling and Machining Association, Richard Helms of Uniroyal, Don Altieri of Xerox, and Richard Cody (formerly of Xerox).

My appreciation goes also to the American Institute of CPAs and the National Association of Accountants, who permitted me to use or to adapt for use problems from past Certified Public Accountant Examinations and the Certificate in Management Accounting Examinations. These problems are designated AICPA and CMA adapted, respectively. My thanks also to Dun and Bradstreet, Standard & Poor's, and Gleim Publishing, who also allowed me to use some of their copyrighted materials.

Many scholars at other campuses have provided extensive reviews of early drafts. My thanks go to James T. Bristol, Suffolk University in Boston; Jackson F. Gillespie, University of Delaware; Robert E. Hansen, University of Toledo; Catherine T. Jeppson, California State University, Northridge; W. Elbert Jones, University of South Carolina; Denis P. Neilson, University of San Francisco; Mary E. Tanner Pedersen, Highline Community College, Seattle; Howard R. Toole, San Diego State University; Srinivasan Umapathy, Boston University; and Harry I. Wolk, Drake University.

Finally, I would like to thank Gail Bruhn, who helped me prepare this manuscript, and my special thanks go to my assistant, Barbara Melady, who spent endless hours typing, proofing, and otherwise helping put the manuscript together.

Corine T. Norgaard

chapter one

INTRODUCTION TO MANAGERIAL ACCOUNTING

THE NATURE OF MANAGERIAL ACCOUNTING

The purpose of managerial accounting is to generate data which are useful to persons managing a firm—internal users rather than outsiders. An effective managerial accounting system helps managers achieve the organization's goals.

What kind of information do managers need? The answer depends on the manager's level and the purpose for which the information will be used. Managers make a wide variety of decisions, such as:

1. What should be the selling price for our product?
2. Is the data processing department being managed effectively and efficiently?
3. Should we buy a new piece of equipment?
4. Are we collecting our receivables rapidly enough?

Managerial accounting data are tailored to meet specific needs. The same data that would help a manager set a proper selling price for the company's product would not help him or her decide whether to buy a new piece of equipment.

Many types of managerial accounting data are useful to a wide variety of organizations. The budgetary process, for example, is useful to the manager of both profit and nonprofit organizations, to large businesses such as General Motors and to smaller ones such as a local doughnut shop. However, a well-developed managerial accounting system is probably most important to the large business, where sheer size makes the manager's job more complex. For example, the owner/manager of the local doughnut shop is on the scene and observes the operations of the business on a day-to-day basis. Suppose that the owner/manager opens a second doughnut shop: what happens to his or her job? It becomes more difficult! More people are involved, and the owner/manager cannot physically be at both shops at once to see what is happening. Instead, he or she will probably depend more on financial information, such as sales figures, and on the use of specified procedures to insure that both doughnut shops are being operated efficiently and in a way which will achieve the owner/manager's objective—to generate a profit.

Imagine the difficulties of being the chief executive officer (CEO) of a company such as General Electric with thousands of employees, a large number of locations both inside and outside the United States, and a multitude of managers supervising day-to-day operations, making decisions, and planning for the future. How can operations be controlled so that all parts of the organization are moving toward the company's goals? The managerial accounting system is a critical link in this process.

A managerial accounting system helps an organization accomplish its goals in the following ways:

1. It provides a way to communicate expectations to managers throughout the organization.
2. It provides feedback which enables a manager to monitor the day-to-day operations of the part of the company for which he or she is responsible. If operations depart significantly from expectations, the manager is alerted, can look for causes, and can take corrective actions.
3. It enables managers removed from an operation to evaluate the performance of a subcomponent of the organization, such as a department or division, and the performance of the manager of that subcomponent.
4. It provides a set of prescribed tools and techniques for use in nonroutine decision making which give an organizationwide coherence to this process. For example, a number of techniques can be used in deciding whether a particular long-term asset should be acquired. A properly functioning managerial accounting system insures that these decisions are approached similarly throughout the company and evaluated in terms of the same set of parameters.

FINANCIAL VERSUS MANAGERIAL ACCOUNTING

Financial accounting differs from managerial accounting in a number of ways:

FINANCIAL ACCOUNTING	MANAGERIAL ACCOUNTING
Methods used in generating the data are prescribed by generally accepted principles.	Data can be generated to fit the manager's needs
Data are historical in nature.	Both historical and future data are used.
Data are based on accrual accounting concepts.	Data generated are based on both accrual and cash accounting concepts, depending on how the data are being used.
Data are produced at predetermined intervals, cover set time periods (usually a quarter or a year), and often are mandatory.	Data are produced as needed and have different time horizons, depending on the purpose for which they will be used.
Employee behavior is generally not a prime consideration in the design, gathering, and use of the data.	Employee behavior is often an important consideration affecting the design, gathering, and use of the data.

There are two major reasons for these differences:

1. The types of decisions being made by persons external to the firm are different from those being made by the firm's managers.
2. Persons external to the organization receive a limited amount of information, and that information is produced by management.

Those external to the firm use accounting data as an aid in making investment and disinvestment decisions. These persons—stockholders and creditors—are not involved in the day-to-day operations of the business, its planning for the future, or its nonroutine decision making. Instead, they are concerned with the results of these processes, and this is the information they receive—historical data describing the results of a company's operations and its financial position at a particular point in time.

Those external to the firm are not using financial accounting data to motivate employees, to encourage them to act in ways congruent with the organization's goals, or to evaluate individual performance at various levels throughout the organization. Managerial accounting data are used for all of these purposes, and so the data's behavioral dimensions become significant.

Because external users are not a part of the firm generating the data, they have limited access to such data. If each company could produce accounting data for external consumption any time it wished and using any set of reporting conventions it liked, external users would have difficulty interpreting the data. While one can argue about the ability of generally accepted accounting principles to produce useful information for investors, their use does mean that external users have some knowledge of how numbers presented in the financial statements were generated, and they do receive periodic reports.

The data bases for financial and managerial accounting are not separate; rather, they overlap. Some of the same information used by the manager is used also by the external investor, though it may be presented in a different form. For example, the sales figure reported externally is the same one used internally to compare actual performance with expectations, as expressed in the company's budget. However, for internal purposes the sales figures may be broken down and stated in terms of sales territories, salespersons, product lines, and customers.

THE TRANSITION FROM FINANCIAL ACCOUNTING TO MANAGERIAL ACCOUNTING

In financial accounting your perspective of the firm was quite limited. You recorded *actual* transactions, and you prepared reports which summarized those transactions in the form of income statements, balance sheets, and statements of changes in financial position. The view of the firm which you will take in managerial accounting is greatly expanded. Besides looking at the actual transactions that a company engaged in, you will be developing data that express a company's plans and that help management make decisions, such as what a selling price should be, whether a product line should be added or dropped, and whether a long-term investment in fixed assets should be made. You will learn how results of operations can be expressed in different forms to help management evaluate the performance of subcomponents of the organization, decide whether corrective actions are needed, and evaluate the performance of other managers.

THE STRUCTURE OF MANAGERIAL ACCOUNTING

This text envisions the following primary uses of management accounting data:

1. For costing products and services for purposes of decision making and financial reporting (income determination and asset valuation).
2. For planning, controlling day-to-day operations, and evaluating the performance of managers and organizational subcomponents.
3. For special analysis as an aid in making short-run and long-run nonroutine decisions.

Each of these uses is described in more detail below.

Costing Products and Services

Managerial accounting is concerned with the determination of the cost of products produced or services rendered for at least two purposes: (1) making decisions and (2) in the case of tangible products, deciding what amount of costs should be attached to units sold and to those still on hand as inventory.

In a decision-making context, managers need to know costs for price-setting purposes and in choosing between alternative courses of action. How do we know what constitutes an appropriate selling price if we don't know what it costs us to produce that product? Or how do we decide whether to make more of Product A and less of Product B, or whether to drop Product B altogether, unless we have relevant cost data?

We must also attach costs to units produced to determine the cost of units sold, so that income for financial reporting purposes can be calculated. In addition, we must assign a cost to units still on hand so that assets on the company's externally circulated balance sheet can be valued. Generally, in managerial accounting, there are no rules imposed by outside authoritative bodies as to how we generate the data we use, how we manipulate the data, or how we arrange them. However, since the way we cost products affects an organization's externally circulated financial statements, we are constrained in this area and must determine product costs in keeping with generally accepted accounting principles (GAAP). In contrast, in using product costs in a decision-making context, we may wish to use cost figures that are not in keeping with GAAP.

Planning, Controlling, and Evaluating

The functions of a manager have often been described as planning and controlling. *Planning* is the process of setting goals and objectives for the future and deciding what activities are consistent with them. Managerial accounting provides the quantitative expression of those plans, most commonly in the form of budgetary data.

Controlling is concerned with keeping the organization's activities consistent with its plans and ensuring that progress is being made toward its longer-run goals and objectives. The managerial accounting system generates data which enable the responsible manager to monitor operations. A common control activity which relies on management accounting data is the comparison of actual results with budget data. This comparison tells the manager where expectations differed from actual results and, since this difference is expressed in dollar terms, gives some indication as to how significant that difference is. The manager must decide whether corrective actions are necessary to bring actual performance closer to anticipated performance.

Evaluation can be thought of as part of the control process, although we have listed it as a separate activity. Evaluation is the process of determining how well a part of the organization or the manager of some part of the organization has performed relative to predetermined standards. The appropriate measure of performance differs with the nature of the activities which the manager oversees. For example, the performance of some managers and some organizational units is best measured by how well costs are controlled. In contrast, the chief executive officer's performance and that of the company as a whole may be measured by a number of different standards, such as the market price of the firm's stock or its return on invested assets. Managerial accounting provides much of the quantitative data used in evaluation.

Special Analysis

Not only are managers interested in planning, controlling, and evaluating with respect to daily operations, but they need to assess the impact of making changes. To remain effective and efficient, organizations must respond to changing conditions, such as the demand for their goods or services, or to technological innovations.

Managerial accounting provides a set of tools and techniques which are useful to the manager in doing special analysis and quantifying the effects of nonroutine decisions. For example, suppose that a college is considering closing one of its branch campuses, or a profit-making institution is trying to determine whether it should make a long-term capital commitment in the form of a building and equipment. Managerial accounting provides techniques which can be used to quantify the impact of these decisions.

This textbook is organized in major parts, which correspond to the structure of managerial accounting just described.

THE MANAGEMENT ACCOUNTANT

The term "management accountant" has not yet developed a distinctive image. The term has been applied to anyone who performs accounting work within a firm, and it encompasses persons performing activities which range from (1) posting customers' receivable accounts to (2) doing financial analysis for decision making to (3) making high-level decisions such as those made by the financial vice-president of a large organization. No particular academic or professional accomplishments have been associated with the term.

Recognizing the problem, the National Association of Accountants (NAA) formed the Institute of Management Accounting (IMA) to offer and administer an examination leading to the Certificate in Management Accounting (CMA) designation. The purposes of developing the designation were:

1. To establish an objective measure of an individual's knowledge and competence in the field of management accounting.
2. To establish management accounting as a recognized profession by identifying the role of the management accountant and the underlying body of knowledge and by outlining a course of study by which such knowledge can be acquired.
3. To foster higher educational standards in the field of management accounting.

The CMA designation is awarded to persons who successfully complete the CMA examination by passing all five parts within a six-consecutive-exam period and who have relevant work experience. To sit for the examination, candidates must:

1. Be of good moral character.
2. Satisfy *one* of the following requirements:
    a. Hold a baccalaureate degree—in any area—from an accredited college or university
    b. Achieve a score satisfactory to IMA on either the Graduate Record Examination or the Graduate Management Admission Test.
    c. Be a Certified Public Accountant or hold a professional designation comparable to CMA or CPA issued in a foreign country.
3. Be, or expect to be, employed in management accounting.

The work experience required before the CMA is awarded is two years of professional experience in management accounting, which can be completed at any time prior to or within seven years of having passed the CMA examination. Professional experience is defined as full-time continuous experience at a level where judgments are regularly required that employ management accounting principles.

The CMA examination is currently given twice each year in June and December. It requires $17\frac{1}{2}$ hours to complete and covers the following primary areas and subareas:

Part I: *Economics and Business Finance ($3\frac{1}{2}$ hours)*
            Microeconomics
            Macroeconomics
            Working-capital finance
            Capital-structure finance
            International economics
            Government regulations

Part II: *Organization and Behavior, Including Ethical Considerations ($3\frac{1}{2}$ hours)*
            The planning process
            The organizing process
            The directing process
            The controlling process
            Ethical considerations

Part III: *Public Reporting Standards, Auditing, and Taxes ($3\frac{1}{2}$ hours)*
            Financial accounting
            Auditing
            Reporting to government
            Taxes

Part IV: *Periodic Reporting for Internal and External Purposes ($3\frac{1}{2}$ hours)*
            Financial statements
            Ratio analysis
            Cost accounting
            Budgeting and responsibility accounting
            CVP analysis

Part V: *Decision Analysis, Including Modeling and Information Systems ($3\frac{1}{2}$ hours)*
            Capital budgeting
            Statistics
            Models
            Electronic data processing and management information systems

A brief comparison of the Certified Public Accountant (CPA) designation and the CMA designation is given in Illustration 1-1. While the CPA designation has become a widely accepted indication of professional competence in the practice of public accounting, the history of the CMA designation is short. Its ability to imply a certain level of professional achievement in the field of managerial accounting is not yet fully tested.

ILLUSTRATION 1-1

Selected CMA and CPA examination data

	CMA	CPA
Sponsoring organization and membership	National Association of Accountants (90,000)	American Institute of Certified Public Accountants (175,000)
Passing score	70%	75%
Average pass rate by exam part	45%	30%
Year examination was first administered	1972	1916
Major exam sections and length[a]	1. Economics and Business Finance ($3\frac{1}{2}$ hours) 2. Organization and Behavior, Including Ethical Considerations ($3\frac{1}{2}$ hours) 3. Public Reporting Standards, Auditing, and Taxes ($3\frac{1}{2}$ hours) 4. Periodic Reporting for Internal and External Purposes ($3\frac{1}{2}$ hours) 5. Decision Analysis, Including Modeling and Information Systems ($3\frac{1}{2}$ hours)	1. Auditing ($3\frac{1}{2}$ hours) 2. Business Law ($3\frac{1}{2}$ hours) 3. Accounting Theory ($3\frac{1}{2}$ hours) 4. Accounting Practice (9 hours)
Length of exam	$17\frac{1}{2}$ hours	$19\frac{1}{2}$ hours
Candidates sitting for exam in 1982	4,538[a]	138,677[a]

SOURCE: Adapted from Irvin N. Gleim and Dale L. Flesher, *CMA Examination Review* 2nd edition, vol. 1, Outlines and Study Guides, © Accounting Publications, Inc,. Gainesville, Florida, 1984, p. 13.
[a] Total number of candidates sitting for two examinations; substantial numbers are repeats.

COMPANY EXAMPLES

Throughout this book you will find descriptive materials printed in special boxes and labeled "Illustration from Practice." These materials are based on information provided by real-world companies. They are provided to help you see how the concepts and techniques being discussed in the text are applied in practice.

On some of the forms shown in this text which are used by real-world companies there may be parts or sections which you do not understand completely. This should not concern you at this point in your career. When confronted with such forms when you are employed by a company, you will be able to obtain either a written or oral explanation of the parts you do not understand.

chapter two

COST CLASSIFICATIONS AND COST FLOWS

OBJECTIVES

After studying this chapter, you should be able to answer the following questions:

- Why is it important to know the cost of an organization's output?
- What is a "cost objective"?
- In what ways can the term "cost" be further defined?
- How do costs flow through:
  a. A simple manufacturing company?
  b. A simple service organization?
- How is the Cost of Goods Manufactured Statement prepared?
- What is the relationship of the Cost of Goods Manufactured Statement to the Income Statement?

INTRODUCTION

In this chapter we discuss why entities need to know the cost of their output—the products they make or the services they render. Also we introduce terminology basic to managerial accounting and to understanding different definitions of the term "cost." Finally, the chapter describes and illustrates how costs flow through manufacturing and service enterprises from the time they are incurred until they reach the financial statements—the Income Statement and the Balance Sheet.

THE IMPORTANCE OF KNOWING COST OF OUTPUT

Different types of enterprises have different kinds of output. For the manufacturing company the output is a tangible product. We are all familiar with large manufacturers such as the "big three" auto makers: Chrysler, Ford, and General Motors. Retailing establishments such as Sears and J.C. Penney provide goods and some limited services. Some enterprises provide services only—for example, your doctor, dentist, or CPA.

Enterprises may be either profit-making or nonprofit. If they are profit-making enterprises, one of their primary objectives is to operate at a profit. In contrast, the nonprofit organization has as its primary objective something other than making a profit—for example, providing a service such as rehabilitation for alcoholics. You should not confuse *service* enterprises with *nonprofit* enterprises. While nonprofit enterprises are generally providers of service, many service enterprises, such as banks, stockbrokers, and CPA firms, are profit-making organizations.

Why do organizations need to understand their cost structure? For profit-making enterprises the answer seems especially clear. One of their primary objectives is to make a profit, and this means generating revenues which exceed their expenses. To properly set their prices at a level to insure a profit for the entity as a whole, they must know what their costs are. In making decisions, such as adding new products or dropping old products, knowledge of what costs are and hence how profits will change with various alternatives is essential.

For a nonprofit institution, knowing cost is also important. Such knowledge helps it to determine what level of funding is needed to provide the programs and services which are its objective. In addition, knowing costs of various programs and services helps management decide what kinds of activities the organization can engage in most efficiently.

DETERMINING THE COST OBJECTIVE

To many of us whose contacts are mostly with retail establishments, "cost" is an unambiguous concept. We see something we want, look at the price tag, and this is the cost. In terms of managing an enterprise, the term "cost" can assume a number of different meanings, all useful for different purposes.

From a managerial accounting point of view, the key question in defining cost is defining the cost objective. By *cost objective* we mean *the purpose for which costs are being measured*. For example, we might be interested in knowing how much it costs to *manufacture* a product. This cost does not represent the total costs which a company must recover if it is to operate at a profit; other costs also are involved. Some are related to selling the product—selling expenses—and still others, which we classify as general and administrative expenses, are incurred in keeping an enterprise functioning but are not directly related to either the manufacturing or selling functions.

Instead of wanting to know the cost of manufacturing a product or selling it, we as a manager might wish to know the cost incurred in a particular department, such as maintenance or data processing. Or we might be seeking information about the cost of a particular decision, such as dropping a product line. Thus we can see quite clearly that in using the term "cost" we need to define the purpose for which we are making the measurement: we must define our *cost objective*.

In the first part of the text we are concentrating on product costing rather than the use of costs for other purposes, such as for control and special analysis. Within this context of product costing we must understand some different definitions of costs.

COST TERMINOLOGY

Manufacturing Versus Nonmanufacturing Costs

We shall first distinguish manufacturing from nonmanufacturing costs. *Manufacturing costs* are those costs related to factory operations which are essential to the completion of the product. We usually further subclassify manufacturing costs as direct material costs, direct labor costs, and manufacturing overhead.

Direct materials are the materials which are the major components of the finished product and can be clearly identified with it.

Direct labor is the labor which is used in actually producing the product—for instance, that of the assembly-line worker.

Manufacturing overhead consists of all other costs related to the *manufacturing process* but not classified as either direct materials or direct labor—for example, depreciation of the equipment used in the manufacturing process.

All other costs of running the business and selling the product are *nonmanufacturing costs* and may be classified very broadly as either selling expenses or general and administrative expenses.

Two other terms relevant to manufacturing operations can be introduced at this time: prime costs and conversion costs. *Prime costs* are direct material and direct labor costs. *Conversion costs* are those costs necessary to convert raw material into finished products—that is, direct labor and manufacturing overhead.

Let's look at a simple example to illustrate some different concepts of the term "cost." A company manufactures and markets high-fashion plastic molded "organizers" for convenient storage of items such as cosmetics and toiletries. One of its product lines is an attractive wall unit known as a "Blower-Storer," which holds a blow dryer, cord, and accessories. To keep our example simple, we are going to assume that the company has only this one product line, that it had no beginning inventories, and that during the month of June it manufactured 500 of these units. Let us further assume that during the month of June the company incurred the following costs:

Direct materials	$400
Direct labor	525
Manufacturing overhead	900
Selling expenses	475
General and administrative expenses	550

We can make a number of different calculations of cost, depending on what our cost objective is. The cost of manufacturing a Blower-Storer during the month of June can easily be calculated as follows:

Direct materials	$400
Direct labor	525
Manufacturing overhead	900
Total manufacturing costs	$1,825
Cost per unit: $1,825/500 units	$3.65

Based on our example, it is obvious that the company cannot look just at the $3.65 in determining an appropriate selling price. If the company is to operate at a profit, the selling price must also cover the nonmanufacturing costs. We refer to this combination of manufacturing and nonmanufacturing costs as the *full cost* of the product produced. In our example, full cost would be

Manufacturing costs	$1,825
Selling expenses	475
General and administrative expenses	550
Total costs for the month	$2,850
Full cost per unit: $2,850/500 units	$5.70

Based on our data, we can see the relationship of manufacturing and nonmanufacturing costs to full cost. Full cost is the sum of the manufacturing costs and the nonmanufacturing costs. This relationship is shown graphically in Illustration 2-1.

Period Versus Product Costs

Another important classification of costs is that of period costs versus product costs. *Period costs* are those costs which we treat as expenses during the accounting period—in other words, those costs which appear on the income statement in the period incurred and are used in determining the results of operations. Using traditional definitions, period costs are the nonmanufacturing costs—selling expenses and general and administrative expenses.

ILLUSTRATION 2-1

Manufacturing, nonmanufacturing, and full costs

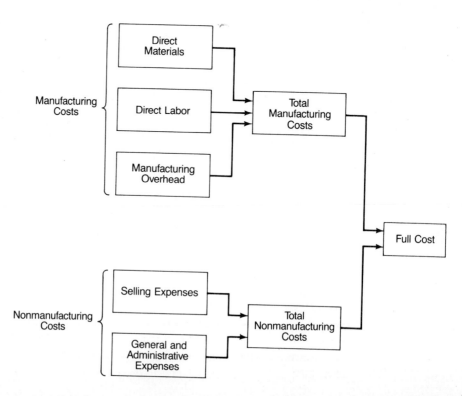

ILLUSTRATION 2-2

Product costs versus period costs

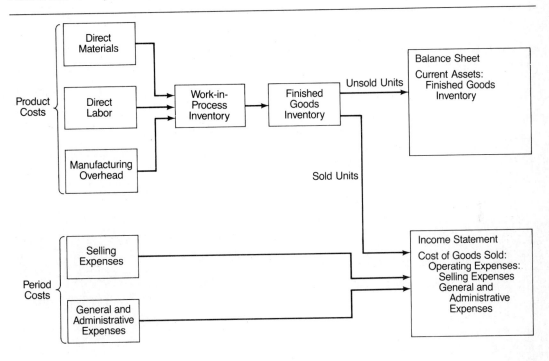

Product costs, in contrast, are those which attach to the products produced and will reach the income statement as an expense in the period during which the goods to which they attach are sold. The costs of units which are unsold at the end of the accounting period do not have any impact on the profits (or losses) of the period. Instead they are identified as inventory costs and are shown on the period's balance sheet as an asset. Only when the units are sold do these costs reach the income statement. Traditionally, product costs have been defined as manufacturing costs. The distinction between product costs and period costs is shown graphically in Illustration 2-2.

The word "traditionally" has been used when talking about product and period costs because not all accountants and those interested in accounting agree that only nonmanufacturing costs—selling and general and administrative expenses—should be treated as period costs. This point will be discussed fully in Chapter 4, when the concepts of absorption costing and variable costing are explained.

To make our discussion of product and period costs clearer, let us refer back to our example involving the "Blower-Storer." Assume the same costs as previously given:

Direct materials	$400
Direct labor	525
Manufacturing overhead	900
Total manufacturing costs	$1,825
Selling expenses	475
General and administrative expenses	550
Total costs	$2,850

Further assume that the company sold only *400* of the 500 units which were manufactured. That is, it has an ending inventory of 100 finished units which have not been sold as of the end of the accounting period.

To prepare an income statement for the month of June, we must divide the manufacturing costs between those units which were sold and those still on hand. Our income statement would appear as follows, based on an assumed selling price of $7 per unit:

Sales, 400 units units @ $7		$2,800
Cost of sales:		
Beginning inventory	$ 0	
Cost of 500 units manufactured @ $3.65	1,825	
Goods available for sale, 500 @ $3.65	1,825	
Ending inventory, 100 @ $3.65	365	
Cost of sales		1,460
Gross profit		$1,340
Operating expenses:		
Selling expenses	475	
General and administrative expenses	550	1,025
Net income		$ 315

A statement of financial position (balance sheet) as of the end of June would show finished goods inventory of $365, representing the manufacturing costs of the 100 unsold Blower-Storers still on hand.

The company's period costs were the selling and general administrative expenses which appeared in total on the income statement. If the level of these expenses were the same and only 300 units were sold, or all 500 units were sold, the income statement still would show $475 of selling expenses and $550 of general and administrative expenses.

In contrast, the product costs—the costs of manufacturing the Blower-Storer—appeared on the income statement as a cost only when the product to which they attached was sold. When 100 units were unsold at the end of the period, these costs were not charged against revenues but instead were carried to the balance sheet as an asset, finished goods inventory.

Indirect Versus Direct Costs

Another way of classifying costs is between direct and indirect costs. *Direct costs* are those which can be clearly identified with the cost objective. *Indirect costs* are those which (1) cannot be clearly identified with the cost objective, or which (2) it is not practical to trace to a cost objective, or which (3) management does not wish to trace to a cost objective. When these last two aspects of what constitutes an indirect cost are left off, it may be difficult to understand the direct/indirect distinction. When we remember that a cost may be identified as indirect simply because of practical considerations, such as cost versus benefit, or management policy, the classification between direct and indirect becomes easier to understand.

To illustrate, suppose for a manufacturing firm our cost objective is to measure the cost of the products being produced. In a manufacturing operation which produces jogging shoes, the nylon fabric from which the shoes are made is clearly identifiable as a direct material cost. What about the glue necessary to assemble the shoes or the shoelaces? Both are necessary ingredients of the manufacturing process, and the shoelaces are visibly identifiable with the product. Yet both the glue and the shoelaces *may* be considered indirect materials costs and treated as a part of manufacturing overhead, simply because, in the case of the glue, identification is impracticable and, in the case of both the shoelaces and the glue, the cost per unit is probably insignificant and thus may not warrant treatment as a direct material cost.

For both labor and materials, we frequently find both direct and indirect costs. Commonly *direct material costs* are those raw material costs which are the major components of the finished products and can be clearly identified with the product being produced. *Direct labor costs* are the costs of labor which was used directly in the manufacturing process. Indirect materials and indirect labor used in the manufacturing process are also necessary for the completion of the product being produced, but because of the factors cited above—difficulties of tracing these costs to the products, impracticalities of tracing these costs to the products, or lack of desire on the part of management to trace these costs—they are considered a part of manufacturing overhead.

Especially in the area of labor a number of costs may be treated logically as either direct or indirect, and treatment varies from company to company. These include the costs of idle time, premiums paid for overtime, and fringe benefits. *Idle time* arises when labor is available but, because of factors such as equipment breakdowns or bottlenecks in the production process, there is no product on which work can be performed. The problem with treating either idle-time or overtime costs as direct labor costs is that this treatment may cause the products being produced at a particular time to have a higher unit cost than identical products produced at some other time. If they are treated as overhead costs, overtime premiums and idle time generally will be allocated to all products produced during the accounting period rather than to a particular batch of goods produced.

On the other hand, it seems more appropriate to treat fringe-benefit costs the same way as the wages to which they relate are treated. Thus, if the fringe benefits relate to work which is classified as indirect labor, they are considered indirect labor costs; if they relate to wages classified as direct labor, they are considered direct labor costs. This position is based on the idea that actual wage rates do not describe the compensation of a worker. Fringe benefits are an important part of the total compensation package in the modern corporation.

ILLUSTRATION FROM PRACTICE:
THE FRINGE-BENEFIT PACKAGE OF AMERICAN THREAD

American Thread is a subsidiary of a large British Company called Tootal Group, PLC. It produces thread and yarn products for both industrial and consumer consumption. If you are near a display of thread or yarn, check to see the American Thread label. In addition, much of the thread used to stitch jeans is made by American Thread. Its revenues are more than $130,000,000 annually.

American Thread budgets and accounts for the following package of fringe benefits for one of its thread mills:

Retirement pay
Termination pay
Vacation pay
Holiday pay
Bereavement pay
Jury duty
Group life insurance
Hospitalization insurance
Compensation insurance
Payroll taxes
Pension plan

This total package averages almost 44% of direct labor costs.

If our objective is to measure manufacturing costs and we want to look at direct versus indirect manufacturing costs, we tend to classify those raw materials which are the major components of the finished products as direct materials costs. Direct labor would be the cost of the labor used directly in the manufacturing process. All other manufacturing costs would be indirect costs. Keep in mind, however, that managerial judgment is used in deciding which costs are accounted for as direct costs and which as indirect.

In our Blower-Storer example, the plastic from which the product is molded represents a direct material cost. The wage costs of those persons who worked on the molding machines would be classified as direct labor costs. Wages paid to maintenance personnel, screws and glue used to assemble the product, cost of electricity to run the machines and light the factory, heating costs, and depreciation of the factory building and the manufacturing equipment are indirect costs and are accounted for as elements of overhead.

Thus far, we have been assuming that our cost objective is to measure the manufacturing costs of units of output. If our cost objective—the purpose for which we are measuring costs—were different, our classification of direct and indirect costs would also differ. For example, if our cost objective were to measure the costs of a division of a company, such as the Chevrolet Division of General Motors, direct costs would be all those costs which could be clearly associated with the operations of that division—or, as some management accountants would say, those costs which would disappear if the division were discontinued. In this part of the text we will be looking at direct and indirect costs in terms of determining *product costs* rather than with respect to other cost objectives.

Period and Product Costs and Direct and Indirect Costs for the Nonmanufacturing Organization

Can we apply the same cost concepts to the nonmanufacturing firm which we apply to the firm engaged in producing a tangible product? The answer is, "Sometimes." The concepts of period and product costs are not meaningful for service types of enterprises. Such organizations do not have inventories of finished services equivalent to the finished goods inventory of a manufacturer, which can be carried over to subsequent accounting periods. Hence all the costs of providing a service are recognized as an expense on the income statement of the period in which revenue was earned or other inflows were recognized for performing the service. Practically, then, we can say that for the service enterprise all costs of providing the service are period costs and flow directly to the income statement.

On the other hand, service enterprises may find it useful to use the concept of direct and indirect costs, direct costs being those which can be most clearly identified with the service being performed or which represent the major costs of the service being performed. Consider two examples. For an X-ray department in a hospital, we might consider the costs of the X-ray films and the salary earned by the person who runs the X-ray machine to be the direct costs of the service being provided to persons needing X-rays. Indirect costs include items such as electricity, heat, depreciation, and costs for the general administration of the hospital.

Another example involves the CPA firm preparing a tax return. The salary or salaries earned by persons directly involved in completing the tax return constitute direct costs. Indirect costs include, besides the administrative costs of the firm, items such as the costs of maintaining an adequate library of tax materials and the costs of having the tax form typed and reproduced in its final form.

This classification of costs into direct and indirect components may be helpful to service enterprises in setting appropriate rates for their services. Price can be based on direct costs plus an allowance to cover all the items of indirect costs (overhead) and, in the case of the profit-making enterprise, a contribution to profits. How large the allowance to cover indirect costs must be depends on the entity's forecast of the level of its revenues or other inflows from services rendered and the forecasted amount of each element of its direct and indirect costs. Our CPA firm, based on its forecast of revenues, expenses, and desired level of profit, may decide to bill for the tax return at a rate of $40 per hour plus 60% of the hourly rate to cover indirect costs and contribute to profit. If the firm spent 20 hours on the tax return, its bill would be calculated as:

20 hours @ $40 per hour	$ 800
$800 × 60%	480
Total charge	$1,280

Variable Versus Fixed Costs

At this point we have looked primarily at the way costs are treated for financial reporting purposes. Are they manufacturing costs and thus product costs, affecting both the income statement and the balance sheet, depending on whether the units to which they attach are still on hand or are sold during the accounting period? Or are they nonmanufacturing costs, which are period costs and will be expensed out as incurred?

In management accounting the impact of costs on financial statements is just one of our areas of concern. We are also interested in costs as a basis for decision making and control. Thus, we find additional cost classifications useful. A classification often used in management accounting is based on how a cost is affected by changes in the level of activity to which it is related. This classification is said to be based on cost behavior, and we designate costs as being either variable or fixed.

Some costs vary directly or almost proportionately with the level of activity—in a manufacturing operation, with the number of units produced. For example, in our Blower-Storer example, the amount of raw material used will vary with the number of units produced. In contrast, if we are using straight-line depreciation for our manufacturing equipment, the depreciation charge will be the same regardless of the number of

Blower-Storers produced. This first type of cost we refer to as a *variable cost*—a cost which varies in direct proportion to the activity level but is fixed when expressed on a per-unit basis.

In contrast, a *fixed cost* is fixed in total within a relevant range of activity for a period of time but varies when expressed on a per-unit basis.

To illustrate, based on the figures we previously used in our Blower-Storer example, direct material costs were $.80 per unit ($400/500 units). When we produced 500 units, our material costs were $400; if our production doubled, total material costs would also be expected to double. Hence, if we produced 1,000 units, we would anticipate direct material costs of $800 (1,000 × $.80).

On the other hand, assume that our depreciation charge for manufacturing equipment is $100 per month. In June, when we produced 500 units, depreciation expense expressed on a per-unit basis was $.20 ($100/500 units). If production doubled, depreciation expense per unit would be reduced to $.10. We can see, then, that the more units we produce, the lower our manufacturing cost per unit will be, because we have a larger base over which to spread the same amount of total fixed costs. On the other hand, if production decreased, unit manufacturing costs would increase, as we would have the same amount of fixed costs but fewer units of output over which to spread them.

To illustrate the impact of fixed costs on unit product costs, let us assume that a company had direct material cost of $1 per unit, direct labor of $2 per unit, and manufacturing overhead—all of which was fixed—of $12,000 for the period. Unit costs for four different levels of production—3,000, 4,000, 5,000, and 6,000 units—are shown below:

	VOLUME LEVEL			
	3,000	4,000	5,000	6,000
Unit costs:				
Direct material	$1	$1	$1	$1
Direct labor	2	2	2	2
Manufacturing overhead	4[a]	3[b]	2.40[c]	2[d]
Cost per unit	$7	$6	$5.40	$5

[a] 12,000/3,000 units.
[b] 12,000/4,000 units.
[c] 12,000/5,000 units.
[d] 12,000/6,000 units.

The important thing to note from this exhibit is: *a particular cost per unit of output is relevant only for a stated production volume.* To say that the goods we produce cost us $5 per unit is appropriate only so long as we are producing at a volume of 6,000 units. Because of the impact of fixed costs, unit costs decline as production increases and increases as production declines.

Our definition stated that fixed costs are fixed within a relevant range of production. If the machine we use to produce Blower-Storers can produce at a rate of 1,000 units per month, our depreciation cost per month will be $100 so long as we don't go over 1,000 units. If we wanted to produce more than 1,000 units, we would have to add a new machine. Depreciation would still be fixed if calculated on the straight-line basis, but it would be fixed at a higher level once the new machine was added, because we would be depreciating two machines rather than one.

This concept is not limited to manufacturing costs; nonmanufacturing costs also may be classified as variable or fixed. For example, if a company pays its salespersons on a commission basis, commissions are variable costs. However, the activity base with which they vary is sales, rather than production.

Some costs are a combination of variable and fixed components; we call these costs either *semivariable* or *semifixed*. Some utilities price electricity in such a way to industrial consumers that there is a flat charge for a certain level of usage and an additional charge per kilowatt-hour for consumption beyond that level. For a manufacturing operation which uses electricity priced this way, part of their costs would be fixed and part would be variable.

For purposes of managerial accounting analysis we assume that any costs which are a combination of variable and fixed components can be broken down into these components. Although a number of different types of costs may not be entirely variable or entirely fixed, we *assume* for purposes of analysis that they behave in a pure fashion.

When looking at manufacturing activities, we cannot equate direct costs with variable costs and indirect costs with fixed costs. Direct costs such as direct materials and direct labor are variable; however, some components of indirect manufacturing such as indirect materials and utility costs may be variable with the level of productive activity. In our example involving the jogging shoes, the costs of shoelaces were treated as indirect material costs. Yet, it is clear that the costs of these shoelaces will vary directly with the number of pairs of shoes produced.

When we were discussing period and product costs, we noted that this concept was not relevant for the service enterprise. In addition, the classification of costs as direct and indirect was modified when applied to the service organization. With fixed and variable costs, these concepts are applied in the same way to service enterprises as they are to manufacturers and are of equal relevance.

FLOW OF COST TO PRODUCTS

In our example involving the Blower-Storer we assumed that assigning costs incurred to the product being produced was a simple process. This is true with respect to direct costs, which by their very definition are those costs which can be specifically associated with the product being produced.

With indirect costs, however, the process becomes more complex. Two issues relate to the flow of indirect costs to products:

1. Which costs shall we deem to be indirect manufacturing costs as opposed to nonmanufacturing costs?
2. How shall we allocate indirect costs to the products produced?

With respect to the first issue there is no clear-cut answer. For example, what shall we do with the salary paid to the vice-president of manufacturing? Should all or part of this amount be assigned to the products being produced? How do we treat the cost of the data processing department which provides services to manufacturing? Should some of this department's costs represent a part of the cost of the products being produced?

In reality there is a great deal of management discretion with respect to the costs assumed to be part of indirect manufacturing overhead. Whether part of the salary of the vice-president of manufacturing or the cost of the data processing department becomes a part of the cost of the products being produced depends in large part on how management wants these costs treated. Practices vary from company to company as to what is defined as a product cost.

The issue of allocating indirect costs to products arise in situations such as the following. Suppose that more than one product line is being manufactured in the same facility. How should costs such as heating, lighting, and depreciation on the building be divided among the different types of products being produced? Or suppose a company carries on all its functions in the facility—manufacturing, selling, and the general administration of the business. How shall costs be divided among these different functions? The answer is that costs must be allocated on some logical basis. For example, depreciation on a building which houses all the activities of the business may be allocated among functions on the basis of square feet occupied by that function. This question of allocation will be discussed more fully in Chapter 3.

The point is that determining product costs is not a precise process. Different decisions about the classification of costs as manufacturing costs or nonmanufacturing costs or about an appropriate means of allocating indirect costs among product lines and company functions will lead to different definitions of what the cost of a product is.

A COST ACCUMULATION SYSTEM

We are now going to illustrate how costs flow through the accounting system for a manufacturing enterprise. This process is shown graphically in Illustration 2-3. Note that the manufacturing costs—direct materials,

**ILLUSTRATION
2-3**

Manufacturing-
cost flows

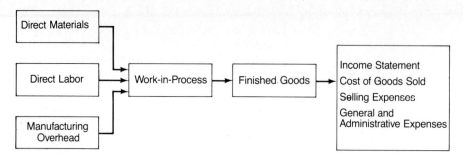

direct labor, and manufacturing overhead—are charged (debited) to an
inventory account called Work-in-Process. All manufacturing costs are
collected in this account. As goods are completed, the cost of those items
is taken out of the Work-in-Process Inventory account and moved to the
Finished Goods Inventory account. As goods are sold, costs are removed
from the Finished Goods Inventory account.

The company in our example, Shirts, Unlimited, manufactures cotton
tee-shirts in three sizes. These tee-shirts are then sold to companies which
imprint them with a variety of patterns and logos. Product specifications
are as follows:

Materials: One and one-half yards of cotton knit per shirt at $.50 per yard.
Direct Labor: 20 minutes per shirt at $5.40 per hour.

The transactions of Shirts, Unlimited, for the month of May, during
which 2,400 tee-shirts were made, are described below along with the
journal entry which would be required to record the transaction.

a. Purchased 4,000 yards of fabric at a cost of $.50 per yard.

Raw Materials Inventory	$2,000	
Accounts Payable		$2,000

b. Requisitioned during the month, 3,600 yards of material and put it into the manufacturing
process (2,400 tee-shirts × 1½ yards per tee-shirt, ignoring any spoilage).

Work-in-Process	$1,800	
Raw Materials Inventory		$1,800

c. To manufacture the 2,400 tee-shirts 800 hours of direct labor time were used at a cost of $5.40
per hour. (Based on labor specifications of 20 minutes per shirt, three can be completed each
hour. Thus, 2,400 shirts would require an input of 800 hours.)

Work-in-Process	$4,320	
Wages Payable		$4,320

d. Other indirect manufacturing costs (overhead) were as follows:

Indirect Labor (factory supervision)	$700
Indirect Materials	100
Depreciation	300
Utilities	200
Other	140

Manufacturing Overhead	$1,440	
Indirect Materials Inventory		100
Wages Payable		700
Accumulated Depreciation		300
Cash (Utilities and Other)		340

e. Charged overhead costs into production.

Work-In-Process	$1,440	
Manufacturing Overhead		$1,440

f. During the month, the 2,400 finished tee-shirts were transferred to Finished Goods Inventory.

Finished Goods Inventory	$7,560	
Work-in-Process Inventory		$7,560[a]

[a] $1,800 materials + $4,320 labor + $1,440 overhead = $7,560.

g. During the month, 2,000 tee-shirts were sold at $5 each.

Accounts Receivable	$10,000	
Cost of Goods Sold	6,300[a]	
Sales		$10,000
Finished Goods Inventory		6,300

[a] Unit costs = $7,560/2,400 units = $3.15; cost of goods sold = 2,000 units at $3.15 each.

h. Selling expenses amounted to $800 for the month, while general and administrative expenses were $1,500. (To simplify our illustration, we shall assume that all these expenses were paid in cash. Realistically, a number of different types of expense accounts would be debited—selling salaries, depreciation on office equipment, etc.; and various accounts would be credited—payables, accumulated depreciation, etc., as well as cash.)

Selling Expenses	$ 800	
General and Administrative Expenses	1,500	
Cash		$2,300

       Selected transactions described and recorded above are shown in T-account form in Illustration 2-4.

At the end of the month the company can prepare two statements which describe its operations during the month—A Schedule of Cost of Goods Manufactured and an Income Statement—as shown below.

SHIRTS, UNLIMITED
Cost of Goods Manufactured
for the Month of May

Direct Material Usage:		
Beginning Inventory	0	
Purchases	$2,000	
Available for Use	2,000	
Ending Inventory (400 yd @.50)	200	
Raw Material Used during the month		$ 1,800
Direct Labor		4,320
Manufacturing Overhead:		
Indirect Materials	100	
Indirect Labor	700	
Utilities	200	
Depreciation	300	
Other	140	1,440
Total Manufacturing Costs this period		7,560
Work-in-Process, Beginning Inventory		0
Total Cost in Process		7,560
Less: Work-in-Process, Ending Inventory		0
Cost of Goods Manufactured, 2,400 units @		
$3.15		$ 7,560

SHIRTS, UNLIMITED
Income Statement
for the Month of May

Sales, 2,000 @ $5		$10,000
Cost of Goods Sold, 2,000 @ $3.15		6,300
Gross Profit		3,700
Operating Expenses:		
Selling Expenses	$ 800	
General and Administrative	1,500	2,300
Net Income		$ 1,400

Let's look back at the new terms we have introduced in describing the flow of costs to products produced. We have three different types of inventory accounts: Raw Materials, Work-in-Process, and Finished Goods. The first of these, *Raw Materials Inventory*, is used to collect information as to the cost of materials acquired which will be used in the manufacturing process. In our simplistic example, there was only one type of raw material; for a large manufacturer there will be many different types of Raw Materials Inventory accounts, one for each of the major classes of raw materials which the company needs. As we noted from the entries given above and the flow of costs through the accounts shown in Illustration 2-4, the Raw Materials Inventory account is debited to reflect acquisitions

**ILLUSTRATION
2-4**

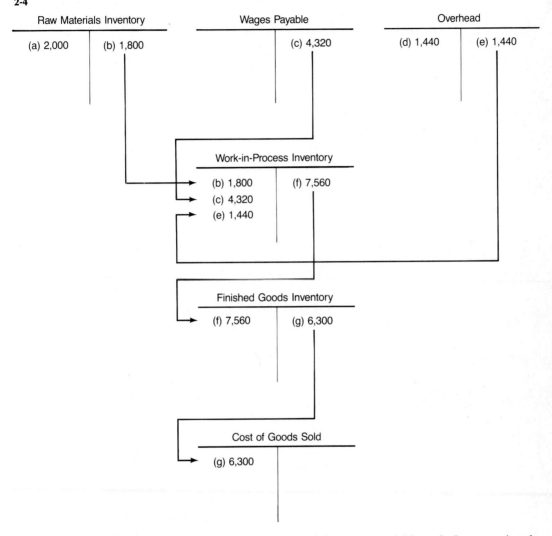

of raw materials. As raw materials are requisitioned for use in the manufacturing process, the Raw Materials account is credited. The balance in the account at the end of an accounting period should represent the costs of the raw material units which are still on hand and will be classified as a current asset on the balance sheet.

The *Work-in-Process Inventory* account is the account in which manufacturing activities are summarized. It is debited for the components of the manufacturing process: direct materials put into production, direct labor, and the other elements essential to the manufacturing process known collectively as manufacturing overhead. As units of product are completed, the Work-in-Process Inventory account is credited for the costs of those units. At the end of the accounting period, any balance in this account should represent the costs to date of units which are still in process—that is, in some stage of completion. The determination of just how much costs to associate with those units which are still in production is discussed in Chapters 5 and 6. The balance in the Work-in-Process account will be shown on the balance sheet as a current asset.

As units are physically completed and transferred into storage awaiting subsequent sale, *Finished Goods Inventory* should be debited for the costs of those units which have been completed. It is credited for the cost of goods which are sold by the company during the accounting period. The balance in Finished Goods Inventory at the end of an accounting period should represent the costs of goods which are awaiting sale and are still on hand at that time. As with our Raw Materials and Work-in-Process Inventory accounts, the balance at the end of period in Finished Goods Inventory is a current asset on the balance sheet.

Looking at the Cost of Goods Manufactured Statement, we note that it shows the various inputs to the manufacturing process: direct materials, direct labor, and manufacturing overhead. All these inputs taken together represent *manufacturing costs* for the period. This will be different from *cost of goods manufactured* if the company had any beginning or ending work-in-process. If it has a beginning Work-in-Process Inventory balance, this is added to total manufacturing costs; the ending balance of Work-in-Process Inventory is subtracted. The resulting figure—Cost of Goods Manufactured—represents the costs of goods which were *finished* during the period and transferred to Finished Goods Inventory.

For manufacturing enterprises, Finished Goods is increased as goods are completed in the factory and transferred into the Finished Goods Inventory. In a retailing enterprise, there would be no cost of goods manufactured, and the use of the adjective "finished goods" to describe inventory is not necessary, since all inventory is goods which are ready for sale. Instead, increases in inventory are represented by purchases, and the account is described as simple "Inventory" or "Merchandise Inventory." The changes in the Finished Goods Inventory account of a manufacturer versus those of the inventory account of a retailing establishment are shown in Illustration 2-5.

In addition, on the balance sheet of the manufacturer, current assets would include three types of inventories, while the retailer would have only one.

Manufacturer	Retailer
Current Assets: Inventories: 　Raw Materials 　Work-in-Process 　Finished Goods	*Current Assets:* Inventory

ILLUSTRATION
2-5

Changes
in inventory
of goods
awaiting sale,
manufacturer
and retailer

MANUFACTURER	RETAILER

Finished Goods Beginning Inventory
  + Cost of Goods Manufactured
	Beginning Inventory
	  + Purchases

Goods Available for Sale − Cost of
  Goods Sold
	Goods Available for Sale − Cost of
	  Goods Sold

Finished Goods Ending Inventory	Ending Inventory

COST OF GOODS SOLD ON THE COST OF GOODS MANUFACTURED STATEMENT

Some companies show the calculation of cost of goods sold on the Cost of Goods Manufactured Statement. Such a statement would appear as follows. All numbers on the statement illustrated below are *assumed and do not relate to the examples given in the chapter.*

ACME PRODUCTS
Cost of Goods Manufactured and Sold
for the Year Ended December 31

Direct Materials	$1,000
Direct Labor	2,000
Manufacturing Overhead	800
Total Manufacturing Costs this period	$3,800
Add: Beginning Work-in-Process	400
Total Costs in Process	$4,200
Less: Ending Work-in-Process	500
Cost of Goods Manufactured	$3,700
Add: Finished Goods Beginning Inventory	1,000
Goods Available for Sale	$4,700
Less: Finished Goods Ending Inventory	700
Cost of Goods Sold	$4,000

COST FLOWS FOR A SERVICE ORGANIZATION

Let us now compare the cost flows for a service organization with those of a manufacturer. For the manufacturer we measure the cost of its output by measuring the costs of the products being produced. For the service organization our objective is to measure the cost of its output—but what is that output? Because of the difficulties of defining the output, many service enterprises, including some very large organizations, have done little in terms of developing a management accounting system. The result is that such organizations have problems in setting prices, in measuring efficiency, and in controlling operations.

To illustrate how product costing concepts used by a manufacturer can be adapted to the needs of a service enterprise, let us take a simple example involving a lawyer. Our lawyer needs some perspective within which to view her costs so that she can decide what represents an appropriate charge for her services. Suppose she prepares a will for an individual: what should she charge? A local department store offers her $200 per month to represent it in small claims court to collect delinquent accounts; does this represent adequate compensation?

The lawyer and other service organizations need some logical measure of output to which their costs can be attached or related. For lawyers, CPAs, and consultants, billable hours or service hours is often a useful measure of output. For a hospital the number of beds maintained, or laboratory tests performed, or persons seen in its emergency room may be useful measures of output for some of the service departments it maintains. A university may want to measure costs in terms of students enrolled or hours of instruction.

Returning to our example of the lawyer, let us assume that she wants to withdraw $1,500 for her salary and estimates that she will average 80 hours of billable time each month. Her estimated monthly costs are as follows:

Personal salary	$1,500
Paraprofessional's salary	750
Office rent	450
Telephone	80
Supplies	150
Depreciation	70
Miscellaneous	100
Total costs	$3,100

Based on the estimated output and monthly costs, our lawyer's billing rate would have to be approximately $39 ($3,100/80 billable hours = $38.75) plus any additional direct costs incurred in servicing the client, such as the cost of travel to and from the client's premises or the courts.

The lawyer could take an approach which is more like that of the manufacturer by classifying her expenses as direct and indirect. What constitutes "direct" and "indirect" in this context is largely a matter of judgment. She might consider only her salary to be a direct cost of the services provided, or she might classify only part of her salary as a direct cost because not all her time is spent on work which contributes directly to revenues. As a means of attracting additional clients, for example, she may attend meetings of the local Chamber of Commerce as part of her workday. She might also define some of the paraprofessional's salary as direct. Let's assume that she considers only the salary which she wants to pay to herself as a direct cost. On this basis, her cost per billable hour could be computed in this way:

Direct Cost: Personal salary, $1,500/80 = $18.75	$18.75
Indirect Costs: All others, $1,600^a/80	20.00
	$38.75

^{a} ($3,100 − 1,500 = $1,600)

She could think in terms of an overhead rate, as discussed earlier in the chapter. Based on the estimated cost and number of billable hours, the overhead rate would be $20 per billable hour.

The cost flows of the service enterprise are compared to those of the manufacturing enterprise in Illustration 2-6. Note that with the service enterprise the concept of period and product cost is not meaningful. While relating costs to measures of output can serve a useful purpose, as in setting appropriate prices and making other decisions, it is not relevant in terms of allocating costs between the income statement and the balance sheet. Since there are no inventories in the service company equivalent to those of the manufacturing enterprise, all the expenses related to the services rendered during the period are period costs and appear directly on the income statement.

With manufacturing organizations, manufacturing costs are allocated to the products produced and reallocated between the income statement and the balance sheet, depending on whether units of product have been sold or are still on hand. In addition, manufacturing costs related to units sold do not appear directly on the income statement but are encompassed by the account "Cost of Goods Sold."

Service organizations face the problem of how much they should refine a measure of output. For example, should our lawyer have a billable rate for court-related as opposed to non-court-related work, such as preparing wills? In a university, should we measure costs simply on the basis of students enrolled or should we further refine this on the basis of graduate versus undergraduate students or full-time versus part-time students?

As is so often the case in management accounting, there is no right or wrong answer to this issue of how much refinement should take place when establishing a measure of output for a service organization. Instead, the question is: Does additional refinement serve a useful purpose to the extent that the benefits of further refinements justify the costs? In addition, it should be pointed out that the more narrowly the measure of output is defined, the more allocations (many of which can be highly arbitrary) must be made. If, in a university, looking at costs in terms of students enrolled is our objective, we can divide the university's total budget by the number of students. If we want costs defined in terms of graduate and undergraduate enrollees, we must start making allocations between these measures of output for professional salaries, building occupancy costs, and the costs of maintaining university libraries. Allocation is discussed in detail in Chapter 3.

**ILLUSTRATION
2-6**

Cost flows of a manufacturer
compared
to those of a service enterprise

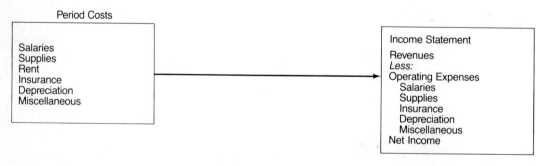

chapter highlights

In this chapter we have pointed out that before costs can be measured, the cost objective—the purpose for which costs are being measured—must be defined. In the managerial accounting environment the term "cost" used alone is ambiguous and needs to be further defined before a proper meaning can be attributed to it. For example, are we interested in manufacturing costs per unit or full cost per unit? Do we want to look at costs in terms of their behavior and classify them as either variable or fixed?

In this chapter and in the next four the focus is on measuring the costs assigned to the output of manufacturing and service organizations. In the manufacturing process we define output as units of product produced. The term "product costs" is used to refer collectively to the direct material, direct labor, and all other manufacturing-related costs (commonly called manufacturing overhead) which are necessary to get a product to its finished state. Only those product costs which attach to units sold reach the income statement for the period. The costs of unsold units appear on the balance sheet as an asset. Selling and general and administrative expenses incurred by a manufacturer are termed period costs and are matched with revenue in the period incurred.

The measure of output for a service enterprise is not so well defined. Before we can think of assigning costs to output, we must decide what an appropriate measure of output is. This measure can take many forms, such as hours of service or number of persons served. Although we can think of the costs of a service enterprise as attaching to the measure of output, there is a critical difference between the manufacturer and the service organization. The costs of the service organization are not inventoriable but flow directly to the income statement in the period incurred.

questions

1. Define the term "cost objective."
2. Distinguish between the terms in the following sets:
   a. Manufacturing and nonmanufacturing costs.

    b. Indirect and direct costs.

    c. Indirect manufacturing and direct manufacturing costs.

    d. Manufacturing and full costs.

    e. Fixed and variable costs.

    f. Period and product costs.

3. What three inputs are required to manufacture a product?

4. Distinguish between a direct material cost and an indirect material cost and give an example of each for a company which manufactures bicycles.

5. Define the term "manufacturing overhead" and give five examples of costs which could be considered as manufacturing overhead.

6. How does the manufacturing cost of a product differ from its full cost?

7. List three reasons why a service organization needs to measure the cost of its output.

8. Some companies treat fringe benefits paid to factory assembly-line workers as direct labor costs; other companies consider these benefits to be part of overhead. Justify each position.

9. Explain why the classification of costs as product costs and period costs is not relevant for the service organization.

10. The text states that there is a great deal of management discretion in determining which costs should be treated as overhead costs and hence assigned to the products being produced as opposed to being treated as period costs and charged out in the period incurred. Give three examples of costs where management may use its discretion in determining whether these are product costs or period costs.

11. What are the major differences on the financial statements of the merchandising organization as opposed to those of the manufacturing entity?

12. Distinguish between: Raw Material Inventory, Work-in-Process Inventory, and Finished Goods Inventory.

13. What is the relationship of the Cost of Goods Manufactured Schedule to the Income Statement of a manufacturer?

14. Under what circumstances will Cost of Goods Manufactured be the same as Total Manufacturing Costs on a Cost of Goods Manufactured Schedule?

15. What are some measures of output which could be used for a commercial bank?

16. Your text states that problems of allocation arise as service organizations attempt to define their measures of output more finely. What does this mean?

17. Distinguish between the terms "prime cost" and "conversion cost."

18. A company purchased 100 units of raw material at a cost of $5 per unit. Describe the possible accounts in which this $500 of cost could be at the end of the accounting period and describe the circumstances under which it would be in each particular account.

19. A member of management of a manufacturer made the following statement: "Our unit cost of making and selling our product (full cost) amounted to $15. We're anticipating a 10% rise in all elements of cost

next year. This year we produced and sold 10,000 units; next year we expect to produce and sell 13,000 units. Our selling price was $20 per unit this year; to keep the same margin of $5 per unit, we'll have to raise our selling price next year to $21.50." Do you agree with what the manager has said? Why or why not?

20. Why would a nonprofit organization be interested in determining the cost of services which it provides, since profit making is not one of its objectives?

exercises

2—1. *Defining the cost objective.* An article in a local paper stated that the cost of attending State University next year would be approximately $10,500. An article in another local paper quoted the Admissions Director as saying that the estimated cost of attending State University next year would be $5,800.

REQUIRED: Explain why these quoted figures could vary so materially. Relate your answer to the concept of cost objectives.

2—2. *Relating cost to differing cost objectives.* A company manufactures ceramic mugs. Costs for one month of operations, during which all units produced were sold, are as follows:

Direct materials	$100,000
Direct labor	150,000
Manufacturing overhead:	
Indirect materials	10,000
Indirect labor	18,000
Depreciation	22,000
Utilities	8,000
Selling expenses	27,000
General expenses	54,000

REQUIRED: Calculate total costs if your cost objective is to measure:

1. Manufacturing costs.
2. Conversion costs.
3. Prime costs.
4. Nonmanufacturing costs.
5. Full costs.
6. Product costs.
7. Period costs.

2—3. Referring back to the data in Exercise 2—2, assume that during the month 200,000 mugs were produced and 180,000 of them were sold.

REQUIRED: Calculate the company's Cost of Goods Sold for the period and its Finished Goods Ending Inventory.

2—4. *Defining product costs.* The following costs were incurred by a company which produced 10,000 units of product and sold 7,000 of them at a price of $20 per unit during the month of August. Assume that it had no beginning or ending inventories of finished goods, raw materials, or work-in-process.

Direct material cost	$20,000
Direct labor cost	50,000
Indirect material cost	6,000
Indirect labor cost	10,000
Factory utilities	3,000
Depreciation on factory and manufacturing equipment	5,000
Company cafeteria (net of receipts)	4,000
Annual company picnic	2,000
Manufacturing vice-president's salary	10,000
Selling expenses	15,000
Other general and administrative expenses	30,000

REQUIRED: Calculate the cost of producing a unit this period, the net income for the month, and the balance-sheet valuation for Finished Goods Inventory under each of the following assumptions:

1. The company treats company cafeteria costs, annual company picnic costs, and the manufacturing vice-president's salary as product costs.
2. The company allocates 75% of company cafeteria and annual company picnic costs to the costs of products being produced, since 75% of the company's employees are engaged in the manufacturing function. In addition, it treats the entire amount of the manufacturing vice-president's salary as a period cost.

2—5. *Period versus product costs*

REQUIRED: Classify the following costs as either period costs or product costs.

1. Advertising expense.
2. Salary of the president of the company.
3. Research and development costs.
4. Sales commissions.
5. Salary paid to factory foreman.
6. Depreciation—office equipment.
7. Depreciation—factory equipment.
8. Wages paid to workers on the assembly line.
9. Fringe benefits paid to factory workers.
10. Overtime payment to assembly-line workers.

11. Freight costs on finished goods sent to customers.
12. Freight costs on raw materials for the manufacturing process.
13. Fees paid to the company's board of directors.
14. Rent on building (50% of the building is used for manufacturing operations).

2—6. *Determining costs in a nonprofit organization.* The Recreation Department of the town of Greenberg has been asked by the Town Council to prepare a proposal showing the cost of a summer parks recreation program. Children 6 through 12 years of age could participate. There are four parks in the town where the programs would be run. The Recreation Department has prepared the following data preliminary to coming up with the requested cost figures:

Anticipated daily attendance	50 children, each park
Recreation directors needed	3 for each 50 children, at a cost for the 40-day program of $800 for each director
Snacks for the children	$.50 per child per day
Equipment (balls, bats, etc.)	$600 per location
Craft supplies	$8 per child for the 40-day period

REQUIRED:
1. Based on the data provided, calculate the cost per child per day for the 40-day period.
2. Does your answer to part 1 above represent the *full cost* of the program? Why or why not?
3. One member of the recreation department believes that the estimated enrollment figures are too high and that a more likely level would be 40 children at each of the four locations. Based on this enrollment projection and assuming that three recreation directors per park would still be needed, what would be the cost per child per day?
4. Why do your results in parts 1 and 3 differ?

2—7. *The impact of fixed manufacturing costs on unit product costs.* Refer back to the information in Exercise 2—2. Assume that during the month for which these data are provided, 200,000 mugs were produced. Assume indirect materials and utilities are variable costs, while the other elements of manufacturing overhead are fixed.

REQUIRED: Calculate:

1. The variable cost *per mug* at the following production levels:
   a. The present level.
   b. 250,000 mugs.
   c. 100,000 mugs.
2. The fixed costs per mug at each of the above production levels.
3. The total manufacturing cost per mug at each of the above production levels.

2—8. *The impact of fixed costs on full cost per unit.* During the month of June, Brew-Right anticipates producing and selling 10,000 automatic coffee makers. The company has no beginning or ending inventories. At a production level of *10,000* coffee makers, Brew-Right's unit manufacturing costs are estimated as follows:

Direct materials	$3.30
Direct labor	2.50
Manufacturing overhead:	
Variable	1.00
Fixed	1.90

Its estimated selling and general administrative expenses expressed on a per-unit basis at a volume of 10,000 units are:

Selling expenses:	
Variable	$ .50
Fixed	.80
General and administrative expenses	1.10
(all fixed)	

REQUIRED: **1.** If the company wishes to make a profit of $3 per unit, what should its selling price be?

2. Assume that the company anticipates producing and selling 15,000 coffee makers and wishes to make a profit of $3 per unit. At what level must it set its selling price?

3. Why do your answers to parts 1 and 2 differ?

2—9.   *The flow of costs.* A company incurred the following salary and wage costs for the accounting period:

Direct labor	$700,000
Indirect factory labor	200,000
Sales salaries	150,000
All other salaries	300,000

The company produced 100,000 units of product and still has 20,000 of these units on hand. It has no beginning or ending work-in-process inventory.

REQUIRED: **1.** What amount of salary and wage cost will appear on the income statement for the period? Specify how it will be classified.

2. What amount of salary and wage costs will appear on the balance sheet for the period? Specify the accounts in which it will appear.

2—10.   *Determining costs for services rendered.* The Willowbrook Bank has five tellers who serve customers between 9 and 2 P.M. five days each week. The average salary of the tellers is $9,600 per teller per year. Supplies used by the customers—money wrappers, deposit and withdrawal forms for savings accounts, and similar types of items—are estimated to average $.10 per customer visit. Of the general overhead cost of operating the bank, such as the president's salary, heating, lighting, and insurance, the bank's accountant believes $120,000 per year should be associated with serving customers directly through tellers.

The bank estimates that it serves approximately 1,000 customers each week based on a 50-week year.

REQUIRED: **1.** Calculate the full cost of teller services per customer visit.

2. Does the number calculated tell you the cost of providing teller services to a particular customer, for example, Rosita Gonzales, for a year? Why or why not?

3. Management of the bank has noted that Mondays and Fridays are the peak times when teller services are used. They are considering terminating two full-time tellers and replacing them with two part-time tellers who would receive $6 per hour for working 8–3 on Mondays and Fridays. Assuming a 50-week period, what impact would this change have on the cost of a customer visit?

4. In your opinion, should the company take the actions described in part 3 above? Justify your position.

2—11. *Nonquantitative exercise involving the determination of a charge for services by a nonprofit institution.* The Contemporary American Artists Museum is a nonprofit institution which for many years has provided free admission to its patrons. Funds to operate the institution have been provided by appropriations from the state in which it is located. In addition to providing a place where contemporary art can be viewed, the museum also provides an education function. Three times each week a class and guided tour are provided for school children throughout the state or for other groups, such as clubs or service organizations. The class and tours are conducted by members of the art department at the campus of the state university, which is located in the same town as the museum. The tour and lecture take approximately 3 hours, and the professors are paid at the rate of $300 for each class and tour which they conduct.

Owing to an extremely tight state budget, a number of state legislators have advocated user charges for organizations such as the museum. It has been suggested that an admission charge and a charge to groups using the special class and tour be made.

REQUIRED: As a staff aid to a member of the legislature, you have been asked to write a memo describing the steps which should be taken in determining an appropriate fee for the two services the museum provides. Your memo should note the sources of information which should be used in developing the fee structure.

2—12. *Defining cost at different production levels.* The Agostino Company manufactures fountain pens. Total costs for *February*, when 100,000 pens were produced and sold, follow:

Direct materials	$ 53,200
Direct labor	125,000
Manufacturing overhead:	
Indirect materials	7,000
Indirect labor	13,400
Depreciation	6,000
Utilities	7,400
Selling expenses	18,000
General and administrative expenses	31,000

During *March,* 75,000 pens were produced and 60,000 of these were sold. All manufacturing overhead costs are variable except depreciation and $3,000 of the utilities expense.

REQUIRED: Calculate:

1. The variable manufacturing costs per pen at the 100,000 and 75,000 production levels and total variable costs at the two levels.
2. The fixed manufacturing costs per pen at the same two production levels and total fixed costs at the two levels.
3. The total manufacturing cost per pen at each of the two production levels.
4. The cost of goods sold for each period and Finished Goods Ending Inventory. Assume the company costs its inventory using the LIFO method.

2—13.   *Calculating unit costs, net income, and ending inventory.*   Jasper Jones, Inc., produces fishing poles. During the last quarter the company produced 80,000 poles and sold 68,000 at $4 per unit. Direct material costs were $2 per unit; total direct labor cost for the period was $71,000; and indirect labor cost was $5,300. In addition, indirect material costs were $.55 per unit. Fixed manufacturing costs for the period included depreciation on factory equipment of $5,000 and utilities expense of $2,700. Selling and general and administrative expenses were $.20 per unit variable and $18,700 fixed. Assume no beginning or ending inventories for raw materials, finished goods, or work-in-process.

REQUIRED: 1. Calculate the cost of producing a fishing pole during the quarter.
2. Calculate net income or loss for the quarter.
3. Calculate the valuation for Finished Goods Ending Inventory.
4. Assume Jasper Jones had hoped to make a $1.50 profit per unit. What selling price should have been set, assuming the current level of production and sales?

2—14.   Lightner Manufacturing produces disposable flashlights. Information regarding the company's first month of operations (the month of October) is given below:

a. Purchases of direct materials inventory for cash, $7,000.
b. Purchases of indirect materials inventory for cash, $800.
c. Direct materials put into production, $5,000 of direct materials.
d. Direct labor costs incurred and paid in cash, $3,000.
e. Factory overhead costs incurred and charged to production:
   (1) Indirect materials used, $600.
   (2) Indirect labor, paid in cash, $1,000.
   (3) Utilities, paid in cash, $200.
   (4) Depreciation, $800.
f. 10,000 flashlights were finished during the month and transferred to Finished Goods Inventory. There was no Work-in-Process Ending Inventory.
g. 9,000 flashlights were sold for $1.80 each.
h. Selling expenses of $1,100 were paid in cash.
i. General and administrative expenses amounted to $1,500. Of this amount, $500 was depreciation. Of the other general and administrative expenses, $600 were paid in cash and the remainder were incurred on account.

REQUIRED: 1. Give the general journal entries required to record the information described above for the month of October.
2. Prepare a Cost of Goods Manufactured Statement for October.
3. Prepare an Income Statement for the month of October, assuming a 50% tax rate.
4. Determine the carrying value of the Raw Materials Ending Inventories and the Finished Goods Inventory on a balance sheet prepared as of October 31.

2—15. *Developing an appropriate charge for services rendered.* Anthony Katz is planning to run a lawn service as a means of making money during his summer vacation. He estimates that he will incur the following costs during the summer:

Lawn mower	$400
Other garden equipment—edger, rakes, etc.	150
Maintenance of equipment and miscellaneous	100
Gasoline and oil for his father's pickup truck	250

Anthony's next-door neighbor has asked how much Anthony would charge to provide lawn service. Anthony believes that he could mow and edge the lawn in 3 hours. He wants to earn, after all expenses, $6 per hour for his time and recover fully the cost of the lawn mower and other equipment.

REQUIRED: 1. What additional information must Anthony have before he can quote a rate to his neighbor?
2. Anthony cannot charge for time spent traveling from one job to another. He hopes, however, that he will be able to work 6 billable hours each day, 5 days each week, for a 12-week period. Based on this assumption, what rate should Anthony quote to his neighbor?
3. After developing the estimates shown in part 2 above, Anthony concludes that he should plan to work only 4 days per week because he needs to be tutored over the summer in calculus. Without doing any calculations, how will the change to a 4-day work week affect the billing rate per hour? Why?
4. In determining whether the rate developed in part 2 is reasonable, what major factors should Anthony consider?

problems

2—16. *Preparation of journal entries and financial statements.* The Paper Supplies Company incurred the following transactions during the month of February, when it produced 200,000 spiral notebooks each containing

100 sheets of paper:

Feb. 1:   Purchased raw materials inventory consisting of paper, cardboard backing sheets, and wire spirals costing $25,000.

Feb. 2–28:   a. Put into production raw materials costing $20,000.
            b. Incurred direct labor costs for the period of $16,000.
            c. Incurred factory overhead costs of $10,000, of which $8,000 were cash expenditures and $2,000 was accumulated depreciation, and charged these costs to production.
            d. Transferred the completed notebooks to Finished Goods Inventory.
            e. Sold 170,000 of the spiral notebooks at $.50 each. The company uses a perpetual inventory system.
            f. Incurred and paid selling expenses of $7,000 for the month and general and administrative expenses of $12,000.

REQUIRED: 1. Prepare the general journal entries required to record summary information for the month of February.
               2. Prepare a Statement of Cost of Goods Manufactured for the month of February.
               3. Prepare an Income Statement for the month of February.
               4. What will be the valuation of the Finished Goods Inventory on the balance sheet prepared as of February 28?

2—17.   *Cost of Goods Manufactured Schedule*

REQUIRED: For each of the cases shown below, supply the missing amount.

	Case A	Case B	Case C	Case D
Raw Materials Beginning Inventory	$ 20,000	$ 65,000	$ 10,000	$ 5,000
Purchases	100,000	180,000	300,000	?
Raw Materials Available for Use	?	245,000	310,000	25,000
Raw Materials Ending Inventory	15,000	?	?	7,000
Raw Materials Used	105,000	195,000	302,000	?
Direct Labor Costs	?	300,000	190,000	29,000
Manufacturing Overhead	60,000	170,000	?	11,000
Total Manufacturing Costs	?	665,000	602,000	?
Work-in-Process Beginning Inventory	28,000	?	?	5,000
Total Cost in Process	373,000	750,000	?	?
Work-in-Process Ending Inventory	?	50,000	125,000	4,000
Cost of Goods Manufactured	356,000	?	587,000	?

2—18.   *Cost terminology.*   Outdoors, America, Inc., manufactures small backpacks designed for use by hikers on day trips or by students to carry books and supplies. Product costs per unit at a production level of 20,000 packs and selling and general and administrative expenses expressed in per-unit terms, based on the production and sale of 20,000 packs are:

Direct materials	$2.00
Direct labor	3.25
Variable manufacturing overhead:	
Indirect materials	.80
Indirect labor	.75
Other	.05
Fixed manufacturing overhead:	
Indirect labor	.50
Depreciation	.30
Utilities	.10
Other	.12
Selling expenses:	
Variable	.15
Fixed	1.25
General and administrative:	
(all fixed)	1.40

REQUIRED: **1.** Calculate the following amounts based on the current production level:

    a. Full cost per unit.

    b. Manufacturing cost per unit.

    c. Conversion cost per unit.

    d. Prime cost per unit.

    e. Fixed manufacturing cost per unit.

    f. Variable manufacturing cost per unit.

    g. Selling price per unit, assuming the company wishes to set the selling price at 150% of full cost.

  2. Calculate the amounts called for in (a)–(g) above, assuming that the company's production and selling level was 15,000 rather than 20,000 units. (Round all costs to the nearest cent.)

2—19. *Preparation of Cost of Goods Manufactured Statement and Income Statement.* Use the data given in Problem 2—18 and assume a production level of 20,000 units but a sales level of 12,000 units at a selling price of $18.95. In addition, assume that variable selling expenses vary with units sold, not with units produced.

REQUIRED: **1.** Prepare a Schedule of Cost of Goods Manufactured for the period. There were no beginning or ending inventories of raw materials or work in process.

  2. Prepare an Income Statement for the period.

2—20. *Cost concepts applied to a nonprofit service entity.* The Navarro Hospital operates a mental health clinic which charges users on a cost basis; that is, the fee is based on estimated costs of operating the clinic. Patients have been referred to the clinic and are provided psychiatric services at a set rate per hour based on estimated costs for the period. For the past accounting period the fee charged to users for each hour of service was $58, based on the following estimated costs:

Direct costs:	
Salaries and fringe benefits of 5 psychiatrists	$350,000
Salaries of receptionist and secretary	22,000
Telephone and utilities	7,000
Total direct costs	$379,000
Indirect costs:	
Overhead charge by Navarro for maintenance, accounting, and other services provided, assessed at 10% of the mental health clinic's direct costs	$ 37,900
Total Costs of mental health clinic	$416,900

There were no significant differences between the actual level of costs incurred by the mental health clinic and the estimated level of those costs. During the year, 6,500 hours of patient care were provided by the psychiatrists on the clinic's staff.

REQUIRED: 1. How many hours of service to patients did the clinic *estimate* it would provide for the period? (Round to nearest whole hour.)

2. Did the clinic recover both its direct and indirect costs for the period? Why? Support your answer with an income statement.

3. Assume that costs are expected to stay substantially the same next period as they were this period. The clinic does not wish to raise its fee charged per hour above $58. What alternatives are available to it if it wants to cover all its direct and indirect costs?

4. What is your opinion of the fairness of the *method* used to levy a charge against the clinic for services rendered by Navarro Hospital?

5. If the clinic staff could increase the hours of service which were actually rendered by 10%, what fee per hour would be required to cover the clinic *direct costs* only? (Round to the nearest dollar.)

2—21. *Effects of different definitions of product costs on financial statements.* The following costs were incurred by a company which produced 10,000 units of its product and sold 7,000 of them at $20 per unit. It had no beginning inventories and no ending inventories of either raw material or work-in-process. In addition, it had no beginning finished goods inventory.

Direct material cost	$20,000
Direct labor cost	50,000
Indirect material cost	6,000
Indirect labor cost	10,000
Factory utilities	3,000
Depreciation on factory and manufacturing equipment	5,000
Quality control testing	2,000
Modifications in dies and molds	6,000
Raw materials spoilage	1,000
Company cafeteria (net of receipts)	3,000
Annual factory workers' picnic	1,000
Manufacturing vice-president's salary	10,000
Machinery repairs	3,000
Selling costs	5,000
General and administrative expenses	30,000
Total	$155,000

REQUIRED: Calculate the company's net income for the period and the valuation of its finished goods inventory under these two differing assumptions:

1. The company considers all the costs listed above except selling and general and administrative expenses to be product costs.
2. The company capitalizes the costs of quality control testing and modifications in dies and molds. One-third of the cost of the company cafeteria is considered to be related to use by nonmanufacturing personnel. The manufacturing vice-president's salary is treated as a period cost.

2—22. *Costing output for service organizations.* Cindy Ruland, a consultant in managing job-related stress, makes the following estimate of her average operating expenses for a month. Not included are costs directly related to a particular job, such as travel; these are billed to each client directly.

Office rent	$500
Telephone	200
Utilities	120
Secretary	800
Supplies	150
Office equipment depreciation	90
Insurance and miscellaneous	100
	$1960

Ms. Ruland estimates that she works 100 billable hours each month.

REQUIRED: **1.** If Ms. Ruland wants to withdraw $3,000 from the business each month, what must she charge on the average for each hour of billable service which she renders?
2. A local school district would like her to run a series of workshops for its elementary-school teachers. The series would be scheduled for 2 hours per week for 10 weeks. They have offered her $800 for the series plus her direct costs, which include travel to the school and the preparation of workbooks for the participants.

  a. Assume that she is currently rendering only about 80 hours of service during the month to other clients and she believes this pattern will continue during the next year because of economic conditions, which are causing companies to spend less on services by outside consultants. Based on quantitative factors, should she take the $800-per-month assignment? Support your answer with relevant calculations.
  b. What nonquantitative factors may influence her decision with respect to accepting this job?
3. If Ms. Ruland could render 120 hours of billable service during the month, rather than 100, by what amount could she reduce her billing rate per hour?

2—23. *Cost concepts applied to a retail operation.* Norma Olsen owns a self-service gasoline station which provides no services. It does maintain a small inventory of oil, windshield cleaner, cigarettes, and candy. Ms. Olsen has prepared the following estimated income statement for the coming year:

Revenues from sale of gasoline, 600,000 gallons @ $1.20 average selling price per gallon net of state and federal taxes	$720,000
Revenues from sale of miscellaneous products	18,000
Total revenues	$738,000
Expenses:	
Cost of gasoline, $1 per gallon for 600,000 gallons	600,000
Cost of miscellaneous products sold, averaging approximately 60% of the retail price ($18,000 × .60)	10,800
Salaries, 1 person each shift for 3 eight-hour shifts 365 days per year @ $5 per hour	43,800
Heat, light, and utilities	12,400
Maintenance of pumps and facility	7,500
Taxes, insurance, and miscellaneous	11,000
Depreciation of building and equipment (straight-line basis)	9,000
Accounting services	2,400
Total expenses	$696,900
Income before taxes	$ 41,100

REQUIRED:

1. What is the gross margin (selling price less cost of goods sold) on each gallon of gasoline sold?

2. Assume that, other than the cost of the products themselves, the amount of expenses incurred in providing the miscellaneous products is insignificant. What is the before-tax profit margin (revenues less full cost per gallon) on a gallon of gasoline pumped? (Round to the nearest cent.)

3. Ms. Olsen is concerned about competition from a discount gas distributor nearby. Prepare an estimate of her annual income before taxes, assuming the average price she receives per gallon has to be cut to $1.17. The price of gasoline supplied to her would remain at $1 per gallon.

4. Ms. Olsen is considering a different strategy: cutting the price of the gasoline she sells below that of her competitor. This would mean lowering the retail price to $1.15 per gallon. She believes that if she did this, she could raise volume by 15%.

   a. Calculate the full cost of providing a gallon of gasoline. Assume that (1) other than the cost of the products themselves, the amount of expenses incurred in providing the miscellaneous products is insignificant, (2) the cost of gasoline supplied to Ms. Olsen will remain at $1, and (3) the level of other costs will not change materially. (Round to the nearest cent.)

   b. Should Ms. Olsen adopt the strategy described in part (a)? Support your answer with calculations.

5. Assume that the actual selling price and cost per gallon of gas were as estimated, but only 550,000 gallons were sold. All other costs and revenues were as estimated.

   a. By what amount did the actual full cost of pumping a gallon of gasoline exceed the estimated full cost per gallon? (Round all amounts to the nearest cent.)

   b. Why?

2—24. *Comprehensive cost-flow problem for two months.* The Quick Start Shoe Company makes running shoes for adults which are sold at discount stores for $22.95 per pair. The price charged by Quick Start to the discount stores is $18.50. Cost data for Quick Start for the months of April and May are as follows:

	APRIL	MAY
Raw materials purchases:		
Direct materials—nylon fabric, composition materials for sole	$226,000	190,000
Indirect materials—eyelets, glue, etc.	29,000	25,000
Direct labor	480,000	400,000
Direct materials put into process	216,000	180,000
Overhead:		
Variable:		
Indirect materials put into process	24,400	19,400
Utilities—variable portion	3,600	3,000
Repair and maintenance supplies	12,000	10,000
Fixed:		
Indirect labor	50,000	50,000
Depreciation	36,000	36,000
Maintenance	18,000	18,000
Utilities—fixed portion	12,000	12,000
Insurance and Taxes	15,600	15,600
Selling expenses:		
Variable	110,000	95,000
Fixed	126,000	126,000
General and administrative expenses	300,000	308,000
Units completed	120,000	100,000
Units sold	110,000	95,000
Estimated tax rate	45%	45%

As of April 1 there were no beginning inventories of raw materials, work-in-process, or finished goods. As of April 30 and May 31, there were no ending inventories of work-in-process. Quick Start uses a perpetual inventory system.

REQUIRED:

1. Prepare general journal entries to record the transactions described above for Quick Start for the months of April and May. Assume the company costs its Finished Goods Inventory on a LIFO basis.
2. Prepare a Schedule of Cost of Goods Manufactured for each of the two months and calculate the cost of producing a unit in each of the two months.
3. Prepare an Income Statement for each of the two months.
4. Explain why the cost of producing a unit in April differed from that in May.
5. What would the Raw Materials and Finished Goods Inventory accounts show as of May 31?

2—25. *Nonquantitative problem: defining costs.* You are planning to renovate a van and outfit it in such a way that you can operate a grill from it. You plan to drive it to the college campus each weekday and service students and faculty at lunch. You have decided to limit your menu to hamburgers, cheeseburgers, and hot dogs along with various flavors of soda. You will also offer prepackaged items such as potato chips, corn chips, and cupcakes. You are going to be seeking a loan to give you initial financing and want to prepare a projected income statement for your potential lender.

REQUIRED:
1. What kinds of variable costs would you anticipate? List types, do not specify amounts.
2. What kinds of fixed costs would you anticipate? List types, do not specify amounts.
3. What will you have to do before you can estimate an appropriate level for your variable costs?

2—26. *Costing services of a nonprofit organization.* The Happy Scholar Preschool, an exclusive prekindergarten program, has developed the following data with respect to its operations for the coming year:

Number of children	20 four-year-olds
	24 three-year-olds
Teachers	2 @ $8,600 each for the 9-month period
Teachers' aides	2 @ $4,000 each for the 9-month period
Rental of facility	$500 per month including utilities
Books and supplies	$80 per child
Snacks	$35 per child
Services of a specialist to teach reading	$100 per month + $8 per child per month for 9 months
Services of creative movement teacher	$6 per child per month for 9 months
Payroll taxes on teachers' salaries, including aides	10% of annual salary
Insurance and miscellaneous	$900
Field trips, cost of bus and miscellaneous	5 @ $80 per trip
Advertising of school's program	$300
Miscellaneous sources of revenues:	
School tag and bake sale	$350
School fair and crafts sale	$500

The Happy Scholar Preschool operates as a nonprofit organization. It does try to price its services at an amount which will provide a year-end surplus (contingency fund) of $1,500. Although the facility rented will be in use only 9 months, the school must pay for 12 months of rent. For payroll purposes, the reading specialist and the creative movement teacher are considered independent contractors. Hence, the school does not pay payroll taxes on the earnings of these two persons.

REQUIRED:
1. What measure of output should be used for the school; i.e., on what basis should they calculate unit costs?
2. Based on the measure of output you have recommended, which costs are variable?
3. Project the annual tuition charge which the school should make for the next year. Round to the nearest $100.
4. The school's board believes that two disadvantaged children should be given a

full scholarship. The board believes it can raise sufficient donations to support these two children. What is the minimum amount per child the board should raise?

5. If the school could increase enrollment by 10 students without changing the level of any of its fixed costs, what should its tuition charge for next year be? Assume no disadvantaged children would be enrolled.

2—27. *The effects of volume on profits.* Sunrise, Inc., manufactures goosedown pillows. Their accounting department has prepared the following schedule of costs based on the production and sale of 7,500 pillows in a one-month period:

Prime costs	$120,000
Conversion costs	81,750
Direct materials	60% of prime costs
Selling expenses	12,250
General administrative	8,500

Additional data:

Manufacturing overhead includes fixed costs of $11,250.

Selling expenses include fixed costs of $10,000. The variable portion varies with sales.

General and administrative expenses are all fixed costs.

There were no beginning or ending raw materials inventories.

Sunrise expects a gross profit margin of 30% of sales.

REQUIRED:
1. Calculate the selling price Sunrise should charge, based on the data given. (Round your answer to the nearest dollar.)
2. Assume that owing to a strike in the factory, only 5,300 pillows were manufactured and sold. Unit variable costs were at the level estimated by the accounting department, and fixed costs remained at the level estimated by the accounting department. Prepare an income statement under these conditons.
3. Was the 30%-of-sales gross profit margin achieved. If not, why not? Support your answer with calculations. Use the selling price you calculated in part 1 and a volume of 5,300 pillows.

2—28. *Calculation of Ending Work-in-Process Inventory.* (AICPA adapted) On June 30 a flash flood damaged the warehouse and factory of Padway Corporation, completely destroying the work-in-process inventory. There was no damage to either the raw materials or finished goods inventories. A physical inventory taken after the flood revealed the following valuations:

Raw materials	$ 62,000
Work-in-process	-0-
Finished goods	119,000

The inventory on January 1 had consisted of the following:

Raw materials	$ 30,000
Work-in-process	100,000
Finished goods	140,000
	$270,000

A review of the books and records disclosed that the gross profit margin historically approximated 25% of sales. The sales for the first six months of the year were $340,000. Raw material purchases were $115,000. Direct labor costs for this period were $80,000, and manufacturing overhead has historically been 50% of direct labor.

REQUIRED: Compute the value of the Work-in-Process Inventory lost at June 30. Show supporting computations in good form. [*Hint:* First prepare a partial Income Statement to find the cost of goods manufactured, then prepare a Cost of Goods Manufactured Statement to find ending Work-in-Process.]

2—29.   *Preparation of Cost of Goods Manufactured after finding unknowns.* (AICPA adapted)   The following information was taken from the records of a manufacturing concern:

		BEGINNING	ENDING
Raw materials		$11,000	$12,100
Work-in-process		14,800	12,900
Finished goods		16,100	18,800
Cost of goods sold	$227,400		
Direct labor	90,000		
Factory overhead costs	79,500		

REQUIRED: 1. Prepare the Cost of Goods Sold section of the Income Statement.
2. Prepare the Cost of Goods Manufactured Statement.

2—30.   *Straightforward preparation of Cost of Goods Manufactured Statement and Income Statement.* (AICPA adapted)   The following items pertain to the Engle Co. for the year 19X2 (in thousands of dollars):

Work-in-process, Dec. 31 19X2	$ 2	Selling and administrative expenses (total)	$70
Finished goods, Dec. 31, 19X1	40	Direct materials purchased	80
Accounts receivable, Dec. 31, 19X2	30	Direct labor	70
Accounts payable, Dec. 31, 19X1	40	Factory supplies	6
Direct materials, Dec. 31, 19X1	30	Property taxes on factory	1
Work-in-process, Dec. 31, 19X1	10	Factory utilities	5
Direct materials, Dec. 31, 19X2	5	Depreciation—plant and equipment	21
Finished goods, Dec. 31, 19X2	12	Indirect labor	20
Accounts payable, Dec. 31, 19X2	20	Sales	350
Accounts receivable, Dec. 31, 19X1	50	Miscellaneous factory overhead	10

REQUIRED: 1. Prepare a combined Cost of Goods Manufactured and Sold Statement.
2. Prepare an Income Statement.

2—31. *Finding unknown amounts.* (CMA adapted) Selected data concerning the past fiscal year's operations (000 omitted) of the Televans Manufacturing Company are presented below:

INVENTORIES

	Beginning	Ending
Raw materials	$75	$ 85
Work-in-process	80	30
Finished goods	90	110

Other data:

Raw materials used	$326
Total manufacturing costs charged to production during the year (includes raw materials, direct labor, and factory overhead, which was 60% of direct labor cost)	686
Cost of goods available for sale	826
Selling and general expenses	25

REQUIRED: Determine:

1. The cost of raw materials purchased during the year.
2. Direct labor costs charged to production during the year.
3. The cost of goods manufactured during the year.
4. The cost of goods sold during the year.

chapter three

ALLOCATING COSTS TO PRODUCTS AND SERVICES

OBJECTIVES

After studying this chapter, you should:

- Be able to define the terms: cost center, production center, service center, mission center, and support center.
- Know the difference between the step-down method and the direct method for allocating service (support) center costs to producing (mission) centers.
- Understand the steps in allocating costs to products and services.
- Be able to complete an allocation problem for either a manufacturer or a service enterprise.
- Be aware of the difficulties in allocating costs and the limitations of the resulting cost data.

INTRODUCTION

In Chapters 2 through 6 we are attempting to answer the questions: What did it cost to produce a product? to render a service? In Chapter 2 we determined the cost of *manufacturing* a Blower-Storer and the *full cost* of that product, which included manufacturing as well as nonmanufacturing costs. This example of cost determination was simple because we were dealing with a single type of output—a unit of product.

Suppose that the company which makes the Blower-Storer manufactures other products using the same manufacturing facility. How much depreciation on the factory building should be allocated to the Blower-Storer and how much to other product lines? In a nonprofit setting, such as a university, if we want to know the cost of the MBA program, how much of the facility, library, and administrative costs, for example, should we allocate to this program?

In such situations we are faced with a *difficult* and *recurring* problem in managerial accounting—the allocation (assignment) of indirect costs to cost objectives. In this chapter we shall describe (1) two commonly used methods for making allocations to cost objectives, and (2) the problems of allocation and the limitations of the resulting cost figures.

INDIRECT VERSUS DIRECT COSTS

As discussed in Chapter 2, direct costs are those which can be traced to a particular cost objective. If our objective is to measure the cost of a product's being produced, then direct costs are those which can be traced to the product. In contrast, indirect costs are those (1) which cannot be specifically traced to the objective for which costs are being measured, (2) which it is not practical to trace to a cost objective, or (3) which management does not wish to trace to a cost objective.

What represents a direct cost or an indirect cost depends on our cost objective. It may be to measure the cost of a product being produced or a service rendered, or we may wish to measure the costs incurred in a particular department, such as data processing, or by a particular function, such as selling. In addition, management makes decisions as to which costs should be accounted for as direct costs and which as indirect costs.

Since we are concerned here with the costs of products and services, we are looking at direct and indirect costs in terms of products and services being produced by an organization rather than in terms of other cost objectives, such as departments or functional areas. However, the allocation techniques described in this chapter can be used for allocating cost to other cost objectives.

COMMON COSTS AND COSTS OF SERVICE AND SUPPORT CENTERS

When the cost objective is to determine the cost of producing a product or rendering a service, often two allocation processes are required: (1) to allocate *common costs* to cost centers, and (2) to allocate costs of *service centers* or *support centers* to *production* or *mission centers*.

A *cost center* is any subcomponent of the organization for which management wants to accumulate and measure costs. It may be, among other things, a department, a part of a department, or an entire function, such as research and development. With a cost accounting system, costs are first accumulated in cost centers and then assigned to other cost objectives.

In this chapter we use the term *common cost* to mean costs that are shared by more than one cost center. For example, if two departments are housed in the same building, building depreciation is a common cost to the two departments. In manufacturing entities, cost centers may be classified as production centers or service centers. A *production center* is actually producing the product which the company makes and sells. A *service center* is providing support through the performance of various services to other parts of the organization, which may include both producing departments and other service departments. The accounting, personnel, and data processing departments are service departments.

In service enterprises, since the output is in the form of service, the terminology used in manufacturing is revised. The term "production center" may be replaced by the term *mission center* and "service center" by *support center*. A *mission center* is a part of the organization which is directly involved in providing the services rendered by the organization. *Support centers* are all other organizational components for which costs are accumulated. In a school of business, the marketing department may be viewed as a mission center while the school library may be considered a support center.

To illustrate the two-step allocation process described above—(1) the allocation of common cost to cost centers and (2) the allocation of service- and support-center costs to production or mission centers—let's assume a hospital has organized its management accounting system around five cost centers: (1) general administration, (2) regular patient care, (3) intensive patient care, (4) cafeteria, and (5) housekeeping and maintenance. Assume that our cost objective is to measure the cost of providing a bed for a patient in (a) regular care and (b) intensive care for a single day.

First we must deal with common costs, such as those of heating and lighting the hospital facility, which are shared by the five cost centers. We will allocate such costs among the five cost centers, using some rational allocation basis. At this point we have not achieved our final cost objective, but rather we have allocated common cost to an *intermediate cost objective*— an objective other than the final objective.

Next, to determine the full (total) cost of providing a bed for a patient in the hospital for a day in regular care and intensive care we would have to allocate the costs of the three support centers—general administration, cafeteria, and housekeeping and maintenance—to our final cost objective, the two mission centers. This process will become clearer through two examples which are given later in the chapter.

DEVELOPING AN ALLOCATION BASE

There should be a logical relationship between the method used for allocating a cost and the cause of the cost. For example, if we are trying to allocate the cost of a company cafeteria to various departments within an organization, we might use as an allocation basis the number of employees in each department served by the cafeteria. It would probably not be logical to allocate such costs on the basis of the feet of floor space occupied by each department, as there is no cause-and-effect relationship between floor space and costs in the cafeteria.

Some examples of costs which may require allocation and some commonly used bases for allocating them are shown in Illustration 3-1.

ILLUSTRATION 3-1

Commonly used bases for allocating costs

TYPE OF COST	ALLOCATION BASIS
Utilities	Floor space
Data processing	Minutes used, number of documents processed
Personnel department	Number of employees
Advertising	Sales dollars
Telephone	Number of instruments
Medical facilities	Number of cases handled
Purchasing	Number of orders processed
Buildings and grounds	Floor space, number of employees
Engineering	Service hours rendered
Accounting	Service hours rendered
Materials handling	Number of units or orders processed

ILLUSTRATION FROM PRACTICE:
FINDING A BASIS FOR ALLOCATING PERSONNEL
DEPARTMENT COSTS AT BRAND REX

Brand Rex was for many years a subsidiary of Akzona. Recently it was offered for sale by its parent and is being acquired by a group of its upper-echelon managers in a management buy-out. Brand Rex consists of eight operating divisions with nineteen manufacturing facilities in the United States, Canada, the United Kingdom, and Switzerland. It produces a number of industrial products including electrical and electronic wire and cable, connectors, flexible printed circuits, power cords, and electrical interconnecting assemblies. Its sales are more than $260 million annually.

Brand Rex maintains its corporate headquarters and one of its wire-producing plants in the same facility. The corporate headquarters and the producing plant are served by a single personnel department. The company wished to allocate the costs of the personnel department between corporate headquarters and the manufacturing facility and decided that time inputs was a logical way of making the allocation.

Brand Rex asked all members of the personnel department to keep records of how they spent their time for a period of several days, classified between corporate- and manufacturing-related activities. Based on an analysis of these time records, the company allocates personnel department costs between the two functions. At periodic intervals the personnel department is asked to again keep records of how it spends its time to determine whether the allocation base being used is consistent with the department's current activities.

STEPS IN THE ALLOCATION PROCESS

The steps in allocating costs to a cost objective are:

1. Define the cost objective—the reason for which costs are being measured.
2. Determine an appropriate basis for allocating common costs to intermediate cost objectives.
3. Allocate common costs to the intermediate cost objectives.
4. Determine an appropriate basis for allocating service or support center costs to producing or mission centers consistent with the final cost objective.
5. Allocate the service- or support-center costs.
6. If relevant to the cost objective, divide the total costs associated with the cost center by the output of the cost center (i.e., units produced, hours of service rendered, X-rays performed).

Step 6 is stated in terms of "if relevant" to take account of different definitions of the cost objective. If we want to know the cost of operating a department, this last step is not needed. If our objective is to find the cost of units produced by that department, we would have to divide departmental costs by the number of units produced.

STEP-DOWN VERSUS DIRECT ALLOCATION

Some service (support) centers serve not only production (mission) departments but also other service centers. For example, suppose that a bank wants to determine the cost of making a commercial loan. The loan department is supported by the data processing department and the accounting department, which in turn also provide service to each other.

In such cases we must decide whether we are going to use step-down allocation or direct allocation. With *step-down allocation*, service (support) department costs are allocated to production as well as other service departments and then reallocated to the production (mission) departments. A decision must be made as to which service department to start with, and this department will not have any other service department costs allocated to it. The decision as to where to start is frequently a matter of judgment, although it should be based on which service department provided the greatest dollar amount of services to other service departments. When we use step-down allocation the implication is that we are trying to determine as accurately as possible the total costs of operating a service department. By beginning with the service department which provided the greatest dollar amount of services to other service departments we are more closely approximating the total costs of those other service departments. To clarify, assume the following data:

	SERVICE DEPARTMENT		
	A	B	C
Direct costs	$200,000	$400,000	$600,000
Percent of total services rendered to other service departments	20%	20%	20%

We should begin our allocation process with Service Department C since the amount of allocation to other service departments is of a more significant amount ($600,000 × 20% = $120,000) than would be true if we began our allocation with any other service department. The costs of Service Department B, including those allocated from Department C, would be allocated next, and Service Department A's costs would be allocated last.

Suppose in our bank example we begin the allocation process with the accounting department. With step-down allocation we would allocate the accounting department costs to data processing, to the commercial loan department, and to other mission departments. Then in our final allocation we would allocate the data processing department costs, which include some allocated accounting department costs, to the commercial loan and other mission departments. This process will be clarified by illustrations later in the chapter.

With *direct allocation*, service- or support-center costs are not allocated to other service or support departments; instead they are allocated immediately to the final cost objective—in our example, the commercial loan department and other mission centers.

ILLUSTRATION—MANUFACTURER

Our first illustration of the allocation process involves a company which manufactures wire. In one of its production departments it makes a plastic-coated steel-alloy type wire. Copper wire is manufactured in its other production department. These manufacturing operations are housed in the same facility along with all other company functions, such as selling and the general administration of the business.

To keep our example of manageable size, we shall lump a number of cost centers together. Let's assume that our company through its cost accounting system has defined the following cost centers: one for the manufacture of plastic-coated wire, one for the manufacture of copper wire, one for maintenance, one for personnel, and the other for all other parts of the organization. Financial data with respect to the company and its cost centers are shown below. We have simplified our illustration by lumping what may actually be many different cost centers into the category "Selling and Corporate Administration."

DIRECT COST BY COST CENTER

Production Department—Plastic-Coated Wire	$150,000
Production Department—Copper Wire	320,000
Maintenance Department	50,000
Personnel Department	90,000
Selling and Corporate Administration	300,000

In addition we are going to illustrate the allocation of common costs using only one of many types of such costs. These costs, which we are referring to collectively as building-related costs, are as follows:

BUILDING-RELATED COSTS

Depreciation	$40,000
Utilities	25,000
Insurance, Property Taxes, and Other	30,000
Total	$95,000

Assume production in the two manufacturing departments for the period was:

Plastic-Coated Wire Department   280,000 feet
Copper Wire Department   400,000 feet

Step 1: Define the cost objective.   Our cost objective is to determine the cost of *manufacturing* a foot of plastic-coated wire and the cost of *manufacturing* a foot of copper wire. With this definition of cost objective, we will not allocate any of the selling and corporate administrative costs to the two producing departments, because these are nonmanufacturing costs.

Step 2: Determine an appropriate basis for allocating common costs to intermediate cost objectives.   In our simplified illustration we have only one category of common cost to allocate to all the cost centers which share a common facility. These we have described as "building-related." It would appear that a logical basis for making the allocation would be the number of feet of floor space occupied by each cost center.

Let's assume that occupying percentages (feet occupied by a department/total number of feet in the building) for our five cost centers are as follows:

COST CENTER	PERCENT OF TOTAL SPACE OCCUPIED BY EACH COST CENTER
Plastic-Coated Wire Production	45%
Copper Wire Production	30
Selling and Corporate Administration	17
Maintenance	5
Personnel	3
	100%

Step 3: Allocate common costs to the intermediate cost objectives.   Using the percentages of floor space shown above, the $95,000 of building-related costs will be allocated to the five cost centers. For example, $42,750 ($95,000 × 45%) will be allocated to the plastic-coated wire production department. The complete results of this allocation process are shown in Illustration 3-2.

Step 4: Determine an appropriate basis for allocating service-center costs to producing centers consistent with the final cost objective; and Step 5: Allocate the service-center costs.   Since our objective is to determine the cost of manufacturing wire in the two producing departments, the costs accumulated in the Selling and Corporate Administration cost center will not be allocated.

Let's assume that the Maintenance and Personnel Departments serve each other as well as the other three departments. Thus, we must decide whether we will use the step-down allocation process or direct allocation.

ILLUSTRATION 3-2

Allocation of common costs and step-down allocation of service department costs

| | PRODUCTION DEPARTMENTS | | | | SERVICE DEPARTMENTS | | | | OTHER COST CENTERS | | TOTAL COSTS |
| | Plastic-Coated Wire | | Copper Wire | | Maintenance | | Personnel | | Selling and Corporate Administration | | |
	Costs	Allocation Percent	Costs	Allocation Percent	Costs	Allocation Percent	Costs	Allocation Percent	Costs	Allocation Percent	
Direct costs	$150,000		$320,000		$ 50,000		$ 90,000		$300,000		$ 910,000
Building-related costs	42,750	45%	28,500	30%	4,750	5%	2,850	3%	16,150	17%	95,000
	192,750		348,500		54,750		92,850		316,150		$1,005,000
Personnel Department	18,570	20%	18,570	20%	9,285	10%	(92,850)		46,425	50%	
					64,035						
Maintenance Department	25,614	40%	28,816	45%	(64,035)				9,605	15%	
Total costs	$236,934		$395,886						$372,180		$1,005,000
Output	280,000	feet	400,000	feet							
Manufacturing cost per foot	$.846[a]		$.990[a]								

[a] Rounded to three decimal places.

For illustrative purposes we will do both: the results of the step-down process are shown in Illustration 3-2 and those of direct allocation in Illustration 3-3.

Step-down allocation.   With the step-down approach we must determine which service department's costs we will allocate first. Let's assume an analysis shows that the Personnel Department provided more service to Maintenance than Maintenance provided to it. Our first allocation will be that of the Personnel Department to the other four departments. No Maintenance Department costs will be allocated to Personnel.

We will use the number of employees in each department as the basis for allocating Personnel costs to the other four cost centers. Employment records show the following data:

DEPARTMENT	NUMBER OF EMPLOYEES
Plastic-Coated Wire	6
Copper Wire	6
Selling and Corporate Administration	15
Maintenance	3
Personnel	4
Total Employees	34

The Personnel Department has 4 employees; however, since this is the department whose costs we are allocating, we will not include those employees when coming up with our allocation percentages, which are calculated as follows:

DEPARTMENT	NUMBER OF EMPLOYEES	PERCENT OF EMPLOYEES
Plastic-Coated Wire	6	20%
Copper Wire	6	20
Selling and Corporate Administration	15	50
Maintenance	3	10
	30	100%

As you can see in Illustration 3-2, after the original allocation of the building-related costs, there are now $92,850 of costs in the Personnel Department which must be allocated to the other four departments. Of this amount, the Plastic-Coated Wire Department will receive $18,570 ($92,850 × 20%). Other allocations are shown in Illustration 3-2.

Our final allocation is the Maintenance Department cost of $64,035, which consists of the following parts:

Direct costs of the Maintenance Department	$50,000
Share of common building-related costs	4,750
Share of Personnel Department costs	9,285
Maintenance Department costs to be allocated	$64,035

ILLUSTRATION 3-3

Allocation of common costs and direct allocation of service-department costs

| | PRODUCTION DEPARTMENTS | | | | SERVICE DEPARTMENTS | | | | OTHER COST CENTERS | | TOTAL COSTS |
| | Plastic-Coated Wire | | Copper Wire | | Maintenance | | Personnel | | Selling and Corporate Administration | | |
	Costs	Allocation Percent	Costs	Allocation Percent	Costs	Allocation Percent	Costs	Allocation Percent	Costs	Allocation Percent	
Direct costs	$150,000		$320,000		$ 50,000		$ 90,000		$300,000		$ 910,000
Building-related costs	42,750	45%	28,500	30%	4,750	5%	2,850	3%	16,150	17%	95,000
	192,750		348,500		54,750		92,850		316,150		$1,005,000
Personnel Department	20,427	22%	20,427	22%	—		(92,850)		51,996	56%	
Maintenance Department	21,900	40%	24,638	45%	(54,750)		—		8,212	15%	
Total costs	$235,077		$393,565		0		0		$376,358		$1,005,000
Output	280,000 feet		400,000 feet								
Cost per foot	$.840*		$.984								

* Rounded to three decimal places.

Assume we have determined that a logical allocation of Maintenance Department costs to the other three cost centers is on the basis of direct labor hours of service provided to each of these departments. Although Maintenance did provide service to Personnel, this is not relevant because we have already allocated Personnel Department costs.

Suppose we have the following information about service rendered to the two production departments and to Selling and Corporate Administration.

DEPARTMENT	PERCENT OF DIRECT LABOR HOURS OF SERVICE RENDERED TO EACH DEPARTMENT[a]
Plastic-Coated Wire	40%
Copper Wire	45
Selling and Corporate Administration	15
	100%

[a] Number of hours rendered to a particular department/total number of hours of service rendered.

Based on these relationships, $25,614 of Maintenance Department costs will be allocated to the department producing plastic-coated wire ($64,035 total Maintenance costs × 40%).

Direct allocation. If we use the direct method of allocating service departments costs to other cost centers, no Personnel costs will be allocated to Maintenance and vice versa. Instead, the costs of these two departments will be split three ways, based on the allocation methods selected between Plastic-Coated Wire, Copper Wire, and Selling and Corporate Administration.

Personnel is allocated on the basis of the number of employees. Relevant data are as follows:

DEPARTMENT	NUMBER OF EMPLOYEES	ALLOCATION PERCENT
Plastic-Coated Wire	6	22%
Copper Wire	6	22
Selling and Corporate Administration	15	56
	27	100%

Based on these relationships, Plastic-Coated Wire would be allocated $20,427 [($90,000 direct personnel costs + $2,850 allocated common building-related costs) × 22%].

With direct allocation, the allocation percents previously developed for the Maintenance Department using the step-down method will be the same, because with the step-down method no maintenance costs were allocated to Personnel. However, the amount of costs to be allocated is only $54,750 (versus $64,035 with step-down), since no Personnel costs have been allocated to this department ($50,000 of direct costs + $4,750 of allocated common building-related costs). Thus, Plastic-Coated Wire would be allocated $21,900 of Maintenance Department costs ($54,750 × 40%).

The complete results of the direct method of allocating the service department costs to other cost centers are shown in Illustration 3-3.

Step 6: Divide the total costs associated with the cost center by the output of the cost center. Since our objective is to determine the cost of manufacturing a foot of wire in each of the two producing departments, our final procedure is to divide the costs accumulated in each department by the production of that department.

Step-down allocation. With this method we have now collected costs totaling $236,934 in the Plastic-Coated Wire Department and $395,886 in the Copper Wire Department. These amounts will be divided by the 280,000 feet of wire produced by the Plastic-Coated Wire Department and the 400,000 feet produced by the Copper Wire Department:

Plastic-Coated Wire: cost per foot   = $236,934/280,000

= $.846 per foot

Copper Wire: cost per foot   = $395,886/400,000

= $.990 per foot

Direct allocation. As can be seen from Illustration 3-3, with direct allocation our results are very similar because the costs accumulated in the two service departments were relatively small. Thus, with direct allocation, cost per foot in the two departments is:

Plastic-Coated Wire: $235,077/280,000 = $.84 per foot

Copper Wire: $393,565/400,000 = $.984 per foot

ILLUSTRATION—SERVICE ORGANIZATION

The Oakdale Clinic is a community-sponsored nonprofit organization, established to provide limited health-care services to an economically depressed area of the city in which it is located. Its management accounting system collected the following information for the clinic's six cost centers for a typical month:

	PEDIATRICS	INTERNAL MEDICINE	MENTAL HEALTH	RADIOLOGY	LABORATORY	GENERAL ADMINISTRATION
Direct costs:						
Salaries	$42,000	$218,000	$23,000	$15,000	$18,000	$22,000
Supplies	6,000	12,000	1,000	8,000	10,000	6,000
Other	8,000	14,000	5,000	7,000	8,000	10,000
	$56,000	$244,000	$29,000	$30,000	$36,000	38,000

Costs not directly associated with the six cost centers (common costs) are as follows:

Building rental	$6,000
Utilities	1,500
Insurance	1,000
Other	3,000
	$11,500

Step 1: Define the cost objective. The administrator of the Oakdale Clinic wants to know the average cost of providing a minute of patient care by the physicians in the three departments which are considered mission departments—Pediatrics, Internal Medicine, and Mental Health. (Although Radiology and Laboratory could be treated as mission departments, the clinic treats them as service departments.)

Physicians were asked to keep records of the amount of time spent with each patient during the month for which the data shown above were gathered. An analysis of the data reveals the following:

DEPARTMENT	TOTAL MINUTES PHYSICIANS SPENT IN PATIENT CARE
Pediatrics	22,500 Minutes
Internal Medicine	75,000
Mental Health	17,000
	114,500

Step 2: Determine an appropriate basis for allocating common costs to intermediate cost objectives, and Step 3: Allocate the common costs. To keep our example simple, we shall assume that the $11,500 of common costs which need to be allocated will be charged to the various cost centers on the basis of space occupied. In addition, we shall assume that the percentage of total space occupied by each cost center is as follows:

DEPARTMENT	PERCENT OF FLOOR SPACE
Pediatrics	20%
Internal Medicine	20
Mental Health	10
Radiology	15
Laboratory	20
General Administration	15
	100%

Using these allocation percents, Pediatrics would be allocated $2,300 ($11,500 × 20%) of the common costs. The complete results of this allocation process are shown in Illustration 3-4.

ILLUSTRATION 3-4

Allocation of common costs and support-center costs—service organization

| | MISSION DEPARTMENTS | | | | | | SUPPORT CENTERS | | | | | | TOTALS |
| | Pediatrics | | Internal Medicine | | Mental Health | | Radiology | | Laboratory | | General Administration | | |
	Costs	Allocation Percent	Costs	Allocation Percent	Costs	Allocation Percent	Costs	Allocation Percent	Costs	Allocation Percent	Costs	Allocation Percent	
Total direct costs	$56,000		$244,000		$29,000		$30,000		$36,000		$38,000		$433,000
Allocated common costs	2,300	20%	2,300	20%	1,150	10%	1,725	15%	2,300	20%	1,725	15%	11,500
Total	58,300		246,300		30,150		31,725		38,300		39,725		$444,500
Allocation of radiology	9,518	30%	22,207	70%	—	—	(31,725)		—		—		
Allocation of laboratory	7,660	20%	30,640	80%	—	—			(38,300)		—		
Allocation of general administration	13,904	35%	19,862	50%	5,959	15%					(39,725)		
Total costs	$89,382		319,009		36,109		0		0		0		$444,500
Minutes of physician/patient contact	22,500		75,000		17,000								
Cost per minute	$3.97		$4.25		$2.12								

66

Step 4: Determine an appropriate basis for allocating support-center costs to mission centers consistent with the final cost objective, and Step 5: Allocate the support-center costs.   Since the cost objective is to determine the cost of a minute of contact time between physician and patient in the three mission departments—Pediatrics, Internal Medicine, and Mental Health—the costs of Radiology, Laboratory, and General Administration will be allocated. A decision must be made as to whether step-down or direct allocation will be used. In our example, we shall use direct allocation.

In looking for a basis for allocating the cost of the three support centers to the mission centers, assume that the following bases were selected as being most logical:

General Administration—Number of physicians in each mission department.
Laboratory—Number of laboratory reports rendered to each department.
Radiology—Number of X-rays performed for each department.

Based on these allocation approaches, the following cost allocation percents were developed:

	GENERAL ADMINISTRATION	LABORATORY	RADIOLOGY
Pediatrics	35%	20%	30%
Internal Medicine	50	80	70
Mental Health	15	—	—
	100%	100%	100%

Using these percents, Pediatrics will be assigned $13,904 of General Administration costs ($39,725 × 35%), $7,660 of Laboratory costs ($38,300 × 20%), and $9,518 of Radiology Department costs ($31,725 × 30%). The results of allocations of the support centers to mission centers are shown in Illustration 3-4.

Step 6: Divide the total costs associated with the cost center by output of the cost center.   Our objective is to find the cost of providing a minute of physician care to a patient in each of the three mission departments. Our final step is to take the costs we have accumulated in the three departments and divide by the measure of output: the number of minutes of physician service rendered in each department. As we can see from Illustration 3-4, cost per minute of patient contact ranges from a low of $2.12 in Mental Health to $4.25 in Internal Medicine.

USES OF DATA DEVELOPED THROUGH ALLOCATION

In our first illustration, we developed a cost for a foot of wire produced by two production departments. In our second illustration, we calculated the cost of a minute of patient care rendered by physicians in three mission centers. How can these data be used?

Costing Inventory

For tangible products such as the wire we must be able to calculate manufacturing costs so that we can properly value inventory and determine the cost of goods sold. For example, suppose that the company making the plastic-coated wire had no beginning inventory of that product and that 250,000 feet of the 280,000 feet produced were sold during the year. In Illustration 3-2 we calculated a cost per foot for the wire of $.846. We can use this figure to value the company's finished goods ending inventory: 30,000 feet × $.846 = $25,380. We can establish cost of goods sold for the period by multiplying the 250,000 feet of wire sold by the cost per foot.

Costing as a Basis for Pricing

Cost data are frequently the starting point for determining a price for products or services. To be profitable, a profit-making organization must recover over time something above its total costs. The nonprofit organization that charges for its services must charge in a manner which will enable it to recover its costs, or costs less funds provided by other sources such as grants and donations.

One method used in coming up with the first approximation of a selling price, sometimes referred to as a *target price*, is to use a general markup formula:

$$\text{markup percentage} = \frac{\begin{array}{c}\text{desired profit on product or service +} \\ \text{selling and administrative expenses}\end{array}}{\text{volume in units} \times \text{unit cost to manufacture}}$$

Let's see how we could apply this formula to the data generated for our wire producer shown in Illustration 3-3. The relevant data from that illustration are:

	PLASTIC-COATED WIRE	COPPER WIRE
Direct costs	$150,000	$320,000
Total *manufacturing* costs	$235,077	$393,565
Feet of wire produced	280,000	400,000
Cost per foot of wire	$0.84	$0.984
Selling and corporate administration		$376,358

Since we have two product lines, before we can apply the general markup formula shown above we must allocate selling and administrative expenses between the two production departments. Suppose that we do this on the basis of feet of wire produced in each department. Based on this allocation assumption, Selling and Corporate Administration costs of

$376,358 will be split as follows:

Plastic-Coated Wire:	280,000 ft/680,000 ft × $376,358	= $154,971
Copper Wire:	400,000 ft/680,000 ft × $376,358	= $221,387

We use the markup formula given above to provide a beginning point for setting a selling price for plastic-coated wire; then, if the company wants to make a profit of $40,000 on this product line,

$$\text{markup} = \frac{\$40,000 + 154,971}{\$235,077 - \text{manufacturing cost of 280,000 feet}} = \begin{array}{l} \text{approximately 83\% (.8294)} \\ \text{on manufacturing costs} \end{array}$$

Based on the profit assumption, applying the markup percent would yield an initial selling price of $1.47 calculated as follows:

Manufacturing cost per foot	$ .84
83% markup on manufacturing cost ($.84 × 83%)	.70
Target selling price	$1.54 per foot

Note that the manufacturer of the wire cannot just adopt this price of $1.54 per foot. Factors such as price of competing products, the general state of the economy, and industry conditions and practices will have to be considered. In addition, the $.84 of manufacturing cost per foot is based on a particular assumption about volume—the production of 280,000 feet. Because of fixed costs, this manufacturing cost per unit is valid only at that volume level. The price of $1.54 is based on a specified profit objective for the product line—$40,000 of profit—which may not be realistic considering industry conditions.

The general markup formula can be modified to permit the expression of a target selling price in terms of a markup on cost constructions other than manufacturing cost. Two of these other ways of expressing markup are illustrated below:

$$\frac{\text{Markup based on full cost}}{\text{(manufacturing + nonmanufacturing cost)}} = \frac{\text{desired profit}}{\text{full cost for product line}}$$

$$\text{Plastic-Coated Wire} = \frac{\$40,000}{\$235,077 + 154,971 \text{ (allocated selling and administrative)}}$$

$$= 10.3\% \text{ markup on full cost}$$

Full cost per foot ($390,048/280,000 feet)	$1.39
Markup on full cost ($1.39 × 10.3%)	.14
Target selling price	$1.53[a]

[a] Differs slightly from target price based on markup on manufacturing cost due to rounding.

$$\text{Markup based on direct cost} = \frac{\text{desired profit} + \text{allocated costs}}{\text{(including selling and administrative)}}{\text{direct cost}}$$

$$\text{Plastic-Coated Wire} = \frac{\$40,000 + \$240,084^*}{\$150,000}$$

$$= 187\% \text{ markup on direct costs}$$

Direct cost per foot ($150,000/280,000 feet)	$ .54
Markup on direct cost ($.54 × 187%)	1.01
Target selling price	$1.55[a]

[a] Differs slightly due to rounding.

Other Analysis and Decision Making

Besides being used in pricing decisions, cost-based data can also be used for other purposes such as measuring efficiency. For example, we can compare the cost to manufacture a foot of plastic-coated wire or the cost to provide a minute of physician care for a pediatrics patient with standards such as the budgeted costs of these products or services, data from external sources available from trade associations and professional organizations, and historical data—the cost of producing these goods or services in past periods.

We can use information of the type developed to determine what product lines or service lines are most profitable or which services or programs we can offer most cost-effectively, given limited resources. As a result we might discover that we are spending too much effort on products or services which yield poor returns.

Uses of cost information will be discussed in more detail later in this text.

PROBLEMS AND LIMITATIONS OF COST ALLOCATION

It is sometimes difficult to find a clear-cut cause-and-effect relationship to serve as a basis for allocating indirect cost to cost objectives. When no such basis exists, allocation may be done on an arbitrary basis. A different decision regarding the proper method of allocating costs between cost objectives could lead to a significantly different set of costs for those cost objectives.

* From Illustration 3-3:		
	Allocated building-related costs	$42,750
	Allocated personnel costs	20,427
	Allocated maintenance costs	21,900
Selling and administrative (previously calculated)		154,971
		$240,048

In addition, the finer we want to partition our data, the more subjective the resulting information may become. For example, for the Oakdale Clinic, the direct costs by definition were clearly associated with the various cost centers recognized by the clinic's accounting system. However, since we wanted to associate all clinic costs with time that physicians spent with patients, we had to allocate costs not directly associated with the three mission departments to those departments. Also, since we wanted a cost per minute, the amount of minutes spent in contact with the patients during the period had to be estimated by the physicians or others. If these estimates are inaccurate or atypical, the resulting cost figures are inaccurate.

Despite these problems, we must often make allocations. To the extent that allocations are required in determining product costs, we have no choice, because these numbers are needed for financial reports to establish inventory valuation and cost-of-goods-sold figures. In a decision-making context, we should ask whether the data resulting after allocation provide a better basis for the decision than data directly associated with the cost objective. This point will be discussed in more detail later.

MECHANICS OF ALLOCATION

Once an initial decision has been made as to which costs to allocate, to what cost objectives, and the allocation basis, the time devoted to making such allocations can be minimized and computational errors eliminated through the use of the computer. A program which will allocate costs to a defined set of cost objectives is relatively simple to develop and can be used on personal as well as larger computers.

chapter highlights

Determining the cost of a good or service may require the allocation of common costs or the costs of service or support centers. The key to allocation is developing a cause-and-effect relationship between the cost objective and the costs which must be allocated.

Two methods widely used for allocating cost of service (support) centers to production (mission) centers are the step-down method and the direct method. With the step-down method, service-department costs are allocated initially to production and to other service departments. With direct allocation, service-department costs are not allocated to other service departments.

The choice of a different allocation basis or the use of step-down rather than direct allocation can lead to different assignments of costs to cost objectives. While allocations may be required to establish inventory valuation, in a decision-making context the decision maker should always consider the question: "Will allocation (or further allocation) improve the data on which the decision is being based?"

questions

1. For what three reasons may a cost be classified as indirect?

2. Give an example of an indirect cost based on the following cost objectives:
   a. The cost objective is to measure the cost of shoes being manufactured.
   b. The cost objective is to measure the cost of operating the data processing department for the shoe manufacturer.
   c. The cost objective is to measure the cost of the western division of the shoe manufacturer.

3. What are examples of indirect costs which are incurred by many kinds of manufacturing companies if our objective is to measure the costs of the products they produce?

4. Two companies are manufacturing identical products and have identical costs. Why may the cost which they inventory for their product differ between the two companies?

5. What is a cost center? Give three examples of different ways in which a cost center may be defined.

6. Define the following terms:
   a. Production center.
   b. Service center.
   c. Mission center.
   d. Support center.

7. What is meant by the term "cost objective"? Give three examples of what the cost objective might be for a town's recreation department.

8. Define the term "common cost"; give three examples of common costs in a school of business which has as its cost objective the measurement of the cost of educating undergraduates, students in the MBA program, and students in the Ph.D. in Business program.

9. A school of business in a large university has the following departments for which it wants to measure costs: Accounting, Computer Science, Finance, Management, and Marketing. On what basis would you suggest allocating the following costs between these five departments:

   a. The salary of the dean of the school.

   b. The cost of books for the school's business library.

   c. The cost of running a computer facility which is used by students and faculty within the school.

   d. The cost of the school's job placement department.

10. A school of business is undertaking a study to determine the costs of educating its students. A committee composed of faculty and students has been established to formulate policy as to how the costs should be measured. One professor on the committee contends that costs should be measured for the following types of output:

    Undergraduates—full time

    Undergraduates—part time

    MBA students

    Ph.D. students

    Another professor states that there should be only one measure of output. That is, there should be only one cost figure defined for all types of students. Give the advantages and disadvantages of each position. What key question should you ask in deciding between the two positions?

11. A company has two production departments which are manufacturing products. *All costs of the company have been allocated to these two departments,* resulting in a unit cost for Department A of $10 and for Department B of $14. Will units produced in these two departments be put into Finished Goods Inventory at those amounts? Why or why not?

12. A company carries out all its functions—manufacturing, marketing, and administration—in the same facility. Common costs include items such as heat, light, insurance, property taxes, and maintenance. The company has followed the practice of allocating these costs among the three functions. A member of management suggests that this practice be stopped and that such costs should all be charged to the manufacturing function. The manager states that this approach will save time and effort and that the results will be just as meaningful as those that are currently developed using allocation procedures. Do you agree with the manager? Justify your position.

13. A town-supported nonprofit clinic used by disadvantaged residents of the town has five different areas of service: pediatrics, internal medicine, orthopedic, gynecology, and mental health. The clinic has an accounting system which does not measure costs by area of service. For example, the system will tell you how much was spent for physicians' salaries, but not how much was spent for physicians' performance of services. As administrator of the clinic you have suggested the development of a system which would provide you with the cost of a patient visit to each service area. The cost of revising your current information system to generate this information is estimated to be $5,000. A town council member claims that spending the $5,000 would be a waste of money. How would you reply?

14. Define the term "target price."

15. List three different ways that a markup percentage on cost can be calculated and show how each is calculated.

16. A company which makes unpainted bookcases has calculated a target price for its product of $40 for the two-shelf model. Why may the actual selling price which the company sets be different from its target price?

17. What are some problems with costs which are allocated as opposed to costs which can be directly identified with a cost objective?

18. Distinguish between the direct method and the step-down method for allocating service-department costs to production departments.

19. If a college or university is trying to determine the cost of teaching an elementary-level course in managerial accounting, list five examples of indirect cost allocations which will have to be made.

20. The manager of the assembling department of a manufacturing operation states that maintenance costs should be allocated between his department and that of the finishing department on the basis of the dollar costs of the machinery maintained in each department. The manager of the finishing department argues that allocation of maintenance-department costs should be based on the number of employees in each department. With which manager, if either, do you agree and why?

exercises

3—1. For each of the following types of costs, indicate a basis which might be appropriate for allocating that cost.

a. Heating.
b. Janitorial services department.
c. Data processing department.
d. Property taxes.
e. Personnel-department costs.
f. Building depreciation.
g. Company cafeteria.
h. Company picnic.
i. Cost of operating a library at the university to serve the various schools and colleges within the university.
j. Security-force salaries.
k. Repair and maintenance department.
l. Company doctor and nurse's salaries.
m. Purchasing department.

3—2. The Mallory Company manufactures frisbees and jumping ropes in the same facility. The following costs have been accumulated for these operations:

	FRISBEE PRODUCTION	JUMPING ROPE PRODUCTION
Units produced	500,000	300,000
Direct materials	$ 50,000	$ 15,000
Direct labor	375,000	60,000
Manufacturing overhead which can be directly identified with each production process (for example, indirect materials)	25,000	21,000
Total	$450,000	$ 96,000

Common costs of the factory:	
Depreciation	$40,000
Factory superintendent's salary	55,000
Utilities	18,000
Other factory costs	21,000
Total common costs	$134,000

REQUIRED:
1. Calculate the cost of producing a unit in each department, assuming common costs are allocated between the two departments on the basis of floor space occupied. The Frisbee Department occupies 40% of the manufacturing space, the Jumping Rope Department 60%. (Round your unit cost to the nearest cent.)
2. Suppose, instead, that Mallory allocated common costs on the basis of the number of units produced. How would your answer to part 1 change? (Round your unit costs to the nearest cent.)

3—3. Sports Topics Publishing engages in two activities. First, they publish a series of paperback books on topics such as well-known figures in the sports world and how to participate in sports activities, such as how to windsurf. Second, they publish a monthly magazine, *Sports Topics.* The company has a marketing staff, an accounting and data processing staff, and publication staffs which are responsible for the content of the organization's publications. Printing is contracted out to another firm. The company has never tried to relate costs to its two different publishing activities. However, they believe that it would be worthwhile to do so, as the company's profits have been shrinking. There are two different production managers, one for each of the publishing activities, and each claims to be largely responsible for any profits which the company is making.

REQUIRED: You have been hired to design a system which will accumulate the costs for each of the two publishing functions. List the steps you would go through to set up such a system. Be specific in describing your activities.

3—4. After allocation of common costs on an appropriate basis, the data shown below are available for four cost centers which Atlas Insurance Company recognizes as part of its information system:

	LIFE INSURANCE PRODUCTS	PROPERTY AND CASUALTY PRODUCTS	ACCOUNTING, PERSONNEL, AND INFORMATION SYSTEM SUPPORT (APIS)	GENERAL CORPORATE ADMINISTRATION
Direct costs	$800,000	$1,500,000	$500,000	$600,000
Allocated common costs	150,000	180,000	80,000	240,000
Total cost identified with each cost center	$950,000	$1,680,000	$580,000	$840,000

Atlas wishes to determine the cost of writing $1 of insurance coverage for each of the two product lines shown. As a preliminary to doing this, it must allocate service center costs to the two product lines. The company believes that step-down allocation should be used and should begin with general corporate administration, since it provides more overall service to accounting, personnel, and information systems than is provided to it. A decision has been made to allocate General Corporate Administration on the basis of the number of employees and to allocate the costs of the other service center (APIS) on the basis of dollars of sales by each product line. The following data have been collected:

	LIFE	PROPERTY/ CASUALTY	APIS	ADMINISTRATION
Number of employees	50	70	30	40
Percent of total dollars of sales made by the two product lines	35%	65%		

REQUIRED: 1. Calculate the total costs which will be associated with each of the two product lines using step-down allocation for the two service centers. Round allocation percents to the nearest whole percent.

2. Assume that $2,100,000 of life insurance policies and $3,900,000 of property/casualty policies were written, and calculate the cost of writing $1 of insurance coverage for each of the two product lines.

3—5. Refer to the information provided in Exercise 3—4.

REQUIRED: 1. Determine the total costs which will be associated with the two product lines assuming the use of direct, rather than step-down, allocation for the service centers' costs.

2. Assume that $2,100,000 of life insurance policies and $3,900,000 of property/casualty policies were written, and calculate the cost of writing $1 of insurance coverage for the two product lines.

3—6.   For the coming year, when the Rest-Easy Waterbed Company expects to produce and sell 5,000 waterbeds, the following cost estimates have been made.

Direct materials	$250,000
Direct labor	150,000
Manufacturing overhead	50,000
Selling expenses	125,000
General administration	200,000

REQUIRED:
1. Assuming the company wants to make a profit of $50 on each waterbed, calculate the markup percentage based on the following (round your answer to the nearest whole percent):

  a. Full costs.

  b. Product costs.

  c. Direct manufacturing costs.

2. Show calculations to prove that the target selling price will be the same regardless of which of the three markup percentages you used. (Your results may be slightly different owing to rounding.)

3—7. Refer to the data in the table below.

REQUIRED: Calculate the missing amounts. (Round markup percents to the nearest whole percent and other amounts to the nearest dollar.)

	CASE A	CASE B	CASE C
Direct materials	$100,000	$ 7,000	?
Direct labor	$300,000	$ 6,000	$500,000
Manufacturing overhead	$200,000	$10,000	$300,000
Selling expenses	$120,000	$12,000	$400,000
Administrative expenses	$250,000	$ 5,000	$200,000
Units produced and sold	10,000	100	100,000
Selling price per unit	?	?	$40
Desired profit per unit	$15	?	$17
Markup based on full cost	?	25%	?
Markup based on product costs	?	?	?
Markup based on prime costs	?	?	?

3—8. Communications, Inc., collects costs for three departments which are all housed in the same facility—two production departments and a maintenance and repair department. The company makes pushbutton telephones in one production department and cordless phones in the other. The following are the estimated costs including allocated common costs of the three departments for the coming year:

	PUSHBUTTON	CORDLESS	MAINTENANCE AND REPAIR
Estimated costs	$2,800,000	$3,200,000	$600,000

To determine product costs in the two production departments, maintenance costs have traditionally been allocated between the two on the basis of the number of employees in each. The manager of the Cordless Department is advocating a change in method based on the floor space occupied by each producing department. Allocating percents under both plans are shown below:

	PUSHBUTTON	CORDLESS
Percent ot total employees in two departments	40%	60%
Percent of total floor space occupied	65%	35%

Anticipated production is:

Pushbutton telephones	140,000 units
Cordless telephones	64,000 units

Communications, Inc., pays a bonus to managers of producing departments who are judged to have controlled cost for the period effectively.

REQUIRED:
1. Calculate the effect on unit costs of each of the two allocation methods for each producing department.
2. Do you believe that, in judging the effectiveness of the managers in the two producing departments, the allocated costs of the Maintenance and Repair Department should be included? Why or why not?
3. Can you suggest an allocation method or methods which you believe would be more equitable than allocation based either on number of employees or on space?

3—9. The Reef View Hotel collects costs in terms of the following three cost centers:

	ROOMS	FOOD SERVICES	GENERAL ADMINISTRATION
Cost for the current period	$864,000	$280,000	$280,000

The Reef View Hotel has traditionally allocated the costs designated General Administration to the cost center related to overnight accommodations for guests—rooms—and to food service on the basis of the revenues generated by each type of activity. The purpose of making this allocation is to determine full costs for each of the two classes of revenue-producing activities, apply a markup percentage to these costs, and use the result as a first estimate of charges which should be made next year. For example, in pricing a room, the first estimate of an appropriate charge is last year's costs of maintaining a room plus a markup percentage set by management. Revenues for the past two years generated by the two revenue-producing functions are as follows:

	CURRENT YEAR	LAST YEAR
Revenues provided by room rental	$1,500,000	$1,350,000
Revenues provided by food services	500,000	250,000

The doubling in revenues produced by food services was due largely to the efforts of a new manager, who was able to attract a large increase in banquet, wedding, and other special party types of food services.

REQUIRED: 1. Assume that the cost of General Administration did not differ significantly last year from this year. Calculate the amount of General Administration costs allocated to the two revenue-producing functions for last year and the current year. Round your allocation percents to the nearest whole percent.
2. Do you believe that the result of the allocation process based on sales revenues is equitable in this case? Explain the basis for your answer.

3—10.   A computer center has been servicing the needs of three state agencies: the Education Department, the Department of Traffic Services, and the Department of Consumer Services and Environmental Protection. In the past, the computer center has been a special item in the state budget, and none of its costs have been considered as costs of the state agencies which it serves. A state legislator says that the costs of the computer center should be allocated to the three agencies and not considered a separate item, so that interested parties can see the total costs of the three agencies. Another legislator agreed with her colleague but wanted the process taken a step further. Each state agency which uses the computer center should be charged a fee for services rendered that would cover the costs of the computer center and generate a profit.

REQUIRED: Discuss the advantages and disadvantages of the following:

1. The present system.
2. The proposal to allocate cost to users.
3. The proposal to make a charge above cost to users.

3—11.   The Youth Activities Service Association is a nonprofit organization founded to provide activity programs for teenagers (ages 14 to 18) in the town in which it is located. The organization offers three activities—a swimming program, a basketball program, and an exercise and gymnastics program. Charges are made to participants in the program on a cost basis. A program lasts six weeks; the facility is closed four weeks each year.

Each year staff members of the association develop a budget of expected costs for the coming year, estimate the number of participants in each program for the year, and calculate a charge for each participant in a program. The schedule of charges is reviewed by a board of directors composed of town citizens who serve on a voluntary basis. Charges actually put into effect are approved by the board. The following data have been collected:

	SWIMMING PROGRAM	BASKETBALL PROGRAM	EXERCISE AND GYMNASTICS PROGRAM
Direct costs	$50,000	$12,000	$18,000

Indirect costs of the Youth Activities Service Association are:

Building-related, including heat, light, and water	$60,000
General administration	$80,000
Publication and advertising	$12,000

The indirect costs are allocated as follows:

Building-related—30% is allocated immediately to swimming because of the high costs of heating and maintaining the pool. After deducting this amount, the remainder is allocated on the basis of floor space. Swimming and basketball each occupy 40% of the total space; the remaining space is associated with exercise and gymnastics.

General administration—allocated on the basis of the number of participants in each program.

Publication and advertising—allocated equally to the three programs.

The number of participants in each program last year was:

Swimming	3,700
Basketball	1,840
Exercise and gymnastics	2,800
Total	8,340

The staff of the association believes that with the exception of exercise and gymnastics there will be a 10% decrease in the number of participants because of a declining population in the 14–18 age bracket. The exercise and gymnastics program has proved extremely popular with teenage girls and is expected to have an enrollment equal to last year's.

REQUIRED:

1. Calculate the rate which should be charged for a participant in each of the programs based on the projected cost and number of participants. (Round any allocation percents to the nearest whole percent and calculate the participant's fee to the nearest dollar.)

2. A member of the association's board of directors claims that participation in programs is decreasing because of the level of fees charged. He observes also that economically disadvantaged teens, who might benefit most from the programs, cannot afford to participate. What alternatives are available to the association to enable it to lower its fees?

3—12. A CPA firm, Chatfield and Corcoran, classifies its services as of three types: audit, management services, or taxes. The firm maintains six cost centers, for which the following data, including allocated common costs for the coming year, have been estimated:

	AUDIT	TAXES	MANAGEMENT SERVICES	FIRM ADMINISTRATION	ACCOUNTING AND INFORMATION SYSTEMS	WORD PROCESSING, REPRODUCTION, AND CLERICAL ASSISTANCE
Costs	$300,000	$250,000	$180,000	$220,000	$80,000	$100,000

The firm is trying to set an appropriate billing rate for next year. They believe a markup of 40% on the full cost of the three mission centers—audit, management services, and taxes—is appropriate. Support-center costs are to be allocated on the following bases:

SUPPORT CENTER	BASIS OF ALLOCATION	PERCENT ALLOCATED TO		
		Audit	Taxes	M/S
Firm Administration	Number of clients expected to be served	30%	60%	10%
Accounting and Information Systems	Number of professional staff in each mission center	40%	40%	20%
Word Processing, Reproduction, and Clerical Assistance	Hours of service expected to be rendered	40%	45%	15%

REQUIRED:
1. Calculate the cost associated with each mission center after support-center costs have been allocated. Use the direct method of allocation.
2. Comment on the allocation basis for Firm Administration. Do you believe it is a good one? Why or why not?

3—13. Refer back to the data in Exercise 3-12. Assume the CPA firm concludes that the costs of all support centers should be allocated to mission centers on the basis of hours of billable time expected to be rendered by each mission center. Estimates of hours of billable time are:

Audit	12,000 hours
Taxes	15,000 hours
Management Services	3,000 hours
Total hours	30,000 hours

REQUIRED:
1. Calculate the full cost of rendering an hour of billable service in each of the three mission centers. Round your result to the nearest dollar.
2. Based on management's desired markup of 40% of full cost, develop a schedule of fees to be charged for each billable service hour rendered by the three mission departments. Round your result to the nearest dollar.

3—14. The following data have been accumulated for the cost centers maintained by the Robertson Computer Company for one of its factory operations:

	GAME-TYPE COMPUTERS	EDUCATIONAL COMPUTERS	FACTORY CAFETERIA	INDUSTRIAL RELATIONS AND HUMAN RESOURCES
Direct costs	$780,000	$540,000	$150,000	$210,000
Number of employees	15	20	4	5
Hours of service rendered by Industrial Relations and Human Resources	4,000	3,000	200	—

Factory cafeteria costs are allocated on the basis of the number of employees in each department. Costs of the Industrial Relations and Human Resources Departments are allocated on the basis of the number of hours of service rendered by that department to other departments.

REQUIRED:
1. After allocating the costs of the Factory Cafeteria and the Industrial Relations and Human Resources cost centers, will you know the *full cost* of game-type computers and educational computers produced? Why or why not?
2. Using the step-down method of allocating the cost of the two service centers, determine the costs which should be associated with units of each type of computer produced this period. Begin with the factory cafeteria. (Round your allocation percents to the nearest whole percent.)

3—15. You are tutoring a student in managerial accounting who is very confused about allocation. He tells you that he has no trouble with the arithmetic but does have the following questions:

1. What do cost centers have to do with allocation?
2. How many cost centers should an organization have?
3. What does allocation have to do with the amount of costs which you assign to a unit of production—that is, with product costs?
4. If the objective of your allocation process is to calculate the full cost of a unit manufactured, will you get the same results as you would if your cost objective were to determine the manufacturing cost of a unit?
5. Since service enterprises don't manufacture goods, how does allocation relate to such organizations?

REQUIRED: Draft a response to the questions posed by the confused student.

problems

3—16. *Allocating service-department cost to producing departments—direct method.*   The Alloy Wire and Cable Company has two producing departments housed in the same facility along with a maintenance and janitorial department and an industrial engineering department. One of the producing departments makes plastic-coated wiring; the other, copper-coated wiring. Cost figures for the two manufacturing departments and the two service departments, along with some costs which are common to the four departments but have not yet been allocated, are shown below.

	COMMON COSTS	PLASTIC WIRING DEPT.	COPPER WIRING DEPT.	MAINTENANCE AND JANITORIAL DEPT.	INDUSTRIAL ENGINEERING DEPT.
Direct materials	$	$ 80,000	$120,000	$ 5,000	$ 3,000
Direct labor		140,000	290,000	25,000	90,000
Other direct costs		70,000	40,000	15,000	25,000
Building depreciation	$ 50,000				
Heating and utilities	36,000				
Food and health service	90,000				
Other	12,000				
Totals	$188,000	$290,000	$450,000	$45,000	$118,000

REQUIRED: 1. Allocate the common costs to the four departments, assuming that depreciation and heating and utilities are allocated on the basis of floor space. Food and health services and other common costs are allocated to each department on the basis of the number of employees in each department. Relevant data are as follows:

DEPARTMENT	SQUARE FEET	NUMBER OF EMPLOYEES
Plastic Wiring	17,000	8
Copper Wiring	20,500	11
Maintenance	5,000	4
Engineering	7,500	2

(Round allocated amounts to the nearest $100.)

2. Allocate the costs of the two service departments, maintenance, and industrial engineering to the two manufacturing departments on a direct basis. Maintenance is to be allocated on the basis of square feet, Industrial Engineering on the basis of dollars of direct material usage. Industrial Engineering does not provide any service to maintenance, but Maintenance does provide service to Industrial Engineering. (Round allocated amounts to the nearest $100 and allocation percents to the nearest whole percent.)

3. Assuming that each of the two production departments made 1 million feet of wire during the period, what was the cost of making a foot of wire in each department?

3—17.   *Allocating service-department costs to producing departments—step-down allocation.*   Refer to the data in Problem 3—16.

REQUIRED: Do the three requirements of Problem 3—16, assuming that the step-down method of allocating service-department costs is used rather than the direct method. Begin the allocation of service-department costs with the Maintenance Department. Round allocated amounts to the nearest $100 and allocation percents to the nearest whole percent.

3—18. *Allocating common costs.* Gourmet Foods maintains two operations: a catering service and a take-out service. It wants to know the costs of each. Some costs are incurred for the benefit of both operations, and Gourmet wishes to allocate these on an equitable basis. Relevant data are:

	DIRECT COSTS	
	Catering	Take-out
Food costs	$300,000	$550,000
Labor	100,000	150,000
Other direct costs	50,000	80,000
Total	$450,000	$780,000

	COMMON COSTS	PROPOSED ALLOCATION BASIS
General manager's salary	$ 35,000	Equally
Rent	60,000	Floor space
Utilities	30,000	Floor space
Clerical and secretarial	20,000	Equally
Advertising	15,000	Sales
Insurance	8,000	Equally
Other	12,000	Equally
Total	$180,000	

REQUIRED:

1. The manager of the catering service states that he does not believe any common costs should be allocated. What arguments can be offered in support of this position? What arguments can be offered to refute this position?

2. The manager of the take-out service argues that allocating clerical and "other" costs on an equal basis is not equitable and that she is being charged with more than her fair share of costs. The major portion of the $12,000 "Other" cost is for accounting-related services. Do you agree with the manager? Why or why not?

3. Calculate costs for the two operations using the proposed allocation basis, assuming catering occupies 60% of the floor space and had sales of $600,000, while take-out occupied the other 40% of the floor space and had sales of $1,200,000.

4. Assume that the catering operation prepared meals to serve approximately 55,000 persons, while the take-out operation prepared meals for approximately 220,000 customers. Calculate the unit cost of a meal for each division after all costs have been allocated to the two divisions.

5. Based on the number of meals described in part 4, recalculate the unit cost of a meal, assuming that all the common costs are allocated on the basis of sales generated by each operation.

3—19. *Cost allocations required to determine overhead; entries to record transfers between two departments.* (AICPA adapted) The Zeus Company makes stands which hold stereo components and has two production departments (Fabrication and Finishing) and a Service Department. Service Department expenses are allocated to the production departments as follows:

EXPENSE	ALLOCATION BASE
Building maintenance	Space occupied
Timekeeping and personnel	Number of employees
Other	Half to Fabrication, half to Finishing

The following data were taken from the Fabrication Department's records for December:

Direct materials	$147,800
Direct labor costs	$154,000
Departmental overhead	$132,000

Service Department expenses for December, not included in departmental overhead above, were:

Building maintenance	$ 45,000
Timekeeping and personnel	27,500
Other	39,000
	$111,500

Other information for December includes:

	SQUARE FEET OF SPACE OCCUPIED	NUMBER OF EMPLOYEES
Fabricating	75,000	180
Finishing	37,500	120

The stereo stands are fabricated in the Fabrication Department and then transferred to the Finishing Department. After work is complete in the Finishing Department, they are transferred to Finished Goods Inventory.

REQUIRED:
1. Compute the cost of overhead for the Fabrication Department for December.
2. Compute the cost of processing a unit in the Fabrication Department, assuming 45,000 units were completed during the period. (Round to the nearest cent.)
3. Give the journal entries to transfer the 45,000 units from the Fabrication Department to the Finishing Department and from the Finishing Department to Finished Goods Inventory, assuming the cost incurred in the Finishing Department to complete a unit was $5.20.
4. Assume the company wants to make a profit of $10 per unit and estimates its selling and administrative expenses to be $360,000.
   a. Calculate a markup percent based on manufacturing costs.
   b. Calculate the estimated selling price.

3—20. *Allocating of costs in a service enterprise and pricing of services.* The National Institute of Legal Education (NILE) (1) develops and sponsors seminars for its members and (2) provides a reference service for its members. The organization is a nonprofit institution. Seminars are supposed to be priced at cost. The reference-service cost is covered by membership dues. NILE needs to determine what it should charge for each day of education to seminar participants and also to review its current membership fee of $50 per year to see if it is adequate. The following data have been gathered:

	SEMINARS	REFERENCE SERVICE
Direct costs	$567,000	$1,575,000

COST TO BE ALLOCATED		ALLOCATION BASIS
Staff salaries not directly identifiable with one of the service functions	$170,000	Effort expended: 40% to seminars, 60% to reference service
Institutional advertising	$ 60,000	Participants in each type of service: 6,000 in seminars, 30,000 in reference service
Information systems	$ 85,000	Direct costs
Facility costs	$100,000	Floor space: 50% to seminars, 50% to reference service

REQUIRED: **1.** Allocate the costs to the two service functions and

a. Estimate the charge to be made for one day of education, assuming 6,000 participants.

b. Determine whether the current membership dues are adequate to cover next year's estimated costs, assuming membership enrollment is 35,000. This varies from participation in the reference service, as not all members make requests in a particular year. (Round all allocation percents to the nearest whole percent.)

2. Assume that all the *direct costs* associated with seminars are *variable* and the allocated costs are fixed. If participation in seminars could be increased by 1,000 persons without increasing the fixed costs allocated to the seminar function, what could NILE charge? (Round to the nearest dollar.)

3. Give some examples of the types of costs which would be direct costs for an organization such as NILE which offers seminars to its members.

4. Staff salaries not directly associated with either function were to be allocated on the basis of effort expended. How would you go about measuring "effort expended"?

3—21. *Review of cost concepts; pricing.*   Brown Electronics is a major producer of tapes used in video recorders. It has developed the following cost estimates for the coming year based on anticipated production and sale of 500,000 tapes.

Direct materials	$1,250,000
Direct labor	850,000
Manufacturing overhead:	
Variable	450,000
Fixed	600,000
Selling expenses:	
Variable	500,000
Fixed	450,000
Administrative expenses (fixed)	650,000
Total	$4,750,000

The company believes it can sell the tapes at a price which will yield a before-tax profit of $6 per tape.

REQUIRED: 1. What is the anticipated selling price for the tapes for next year?

2. If the company wants to express its selling price in terms of markups, calculate the appropriate markup percent based on:

   a. Prime costs.
   b. Product cost.
   c. Variable costs.

   Prove that the markups you calculated will all yield the same selling price. You will have slight differences due to rounding.

3. Ignore your results in parts 1 and 2 above. The company believes that if it could offer tapes at $12.50 per tape, it could increase its sales volume by 15%. Brown Electronics has discovered a new production process which it estimates will enable it to cut direct labor costs by 10%. In addition, it is streamlining its operations and expects to be able to eliminate $180,000 of fixed selling and administrative expenses. Other fixed costs will be unaffected by the increased volume and the cost-cutting operations. Based on the anticipated actions described, determine by what amount total before-tax profits would increase or decrease from the original estimate of $6 per tape.

3—22. *Allocation to determine overhead and journal entries for a manufacturer.* The Big-Tote Company makes two kinds of bags—canvas carrying bags which can be used for a variety of purposes such as carrying books and groceries, and a bag used by travelers to carry garments. The following data have been collected during the accounting period for the two departments, which share the same manufacturing facility:

	CANVAS BAGS	GARMENT BAGS
Direct materials	$100,000	$480,000
Direct labor	245,000	880,000
Manufacturing overhead which can be specifically identified with each department	175,000	672,000

Allocation of the following common manufacturing costs is required:

COST TO BE ALLOCATED		ALLOCATION BASIS
Building-related	$280,000	Square feet occupied: 35% by canvas bags; 65% by garment bags
General factory administration	$306,000	Employees in each department: 32 in canvas bags; 48 in garment bags

Production and sales data for the period were:

Canvas bags	100,000 produced;	93,000 sold at $15
Garment bags	160,000 produced;	142,000 sold at $25

Selling and administrative expenses for the period amounted to $1,354.000. The tax rate is 46%.

REQUIRED: 1. Calculate the total amount of manufacturing overhead for each product line for the period.

2. Calculate the cost of producing a unit in each of the two departments.

3. What would you have to do if you wanted to calculate the *full cost* of each product?

4. Prepare summary journal entries for canvas bags which were made to record (a) manufacturing costs put into process, (b) the transfer of units completed to Finished Goods Inventory, and (c) the sale of units.

5. Prepare an income statement which shows the gross margin by product line and the overall company profit after taxes.

3—23.   *Allocation to obtain product cost versus allocation to obtain full cost; direct allocation.*   Polanski, Incorporated, manufactures western-style boots and saddles. These manufacturing functions, along with all other functions, are housed in the same facility. The company has collected the following estimated data for the coming year.

	BOOT PRODUCTION	SADDLE PRODUCTION	BUILDING AND GROUNDS	HUMAN RESOURCES
Direct costs	$4,500,000	$9,250,000	$890,000	$1,800,000
Number of employees	40	80	15	10
Floor space occupied	6,000 feet	8,000 feet	500 feet	2,500 feet
Production and sales volume	300,000 pairs of boots	50,000 saddles	—	—

	SELLING	GENERAL CORPORATE ADMINISTRATION
Direct costs	$4,110,000	$2,740,000
Number of employees	30	50
Floor space occupied	2,000 feet	4,000 feet

Building and Grounds and Human Resources are considered by management to be service centers where costs should be fully allocated to the other cost centers using the direct method. Management believes *a portion* of Building and Grounds and Human Resources costs should be considered a part of manufacturing overhead. To make any required allocations, the company's management thinks the following are appropriate:

Building and Grounds	Space occupied
Human Resources and General Corporate Administration	Number of employees
Selling	Direct costs

REQUIRED: 1. Calculate the following:

    a. The cost of *manufacturing* a pair of boots this period.

    b. The cost of *manufacturing* a saddle this period. Round any allocation percents to the nearest whole percent.

2. Historically, as a first approximation of selling price (target price) the company has used the following markup based on *full cost*: boots—60%, saddles—50%. Calculate target prices for the two product lines for the coming year. (Round all amounts to the nearest cent.)

3—24. *Allocation to obtain product cost versus allocation to obtain full cost using step-down allocation for service centers.* Refer to the data in Problem 3—23.

REQUIRED: 1. Rework requirements 1 and 2 of Problem 3—23, assuming that the costs of the two service centers are allocated to other cost centers using step-down allocation. Management has concluded that Human Resources should be allocated first. In doing requirement 2 to obtain full costs, Selling and General Corporate Administration should be allocated directly to the two product lines. (Round all allocation percents to the nearest whole percent.)

2. Assume that actual results for the period were exactly equal to estimated results. Calculate the ending inventory valuations for boots and for saddles if 20,000 pairs of the boots and 3,000 of the saddles produced during the period were unsold.

3—25. *Allocation and calculation of cost of service rendered.* The town of Johnsonville operates an Employment Services Agency (ESA), which has two primary functions—job placement and job training. Job placement is provided at no cost to participants. Job training is offered at cost to participants in the various six-month programs such as typing, basic mechanics, and computer programming. ESA is preparing its budget request to the town council of Johnsonville. Costs are accumulated for four cost centers within the agency, and the following estimates have been made of costs for the coming budget period for each of those centers:

	JOB PLACEMENT	JOB TRAINING	AGENCY ADMINISTRATION	AGENCY ACCOUNTING AND RECORD KEEPING
Costs directly identified with each department	$2,800,000	$2,300,000	$1,300,000	$600,000

ESA estimates that it will have approximately 4,800 persons enrolled in its job training programs and will offer employment placement services to approximately 6,000 persons. ESA's Job Placement Department has a staff of 50, while ESA staff in the Job Training Department is 25.

REQUIRED:

1. Based on direct costs only, what amount should a participant in the job training program pay next year? (Round to the nearest dollar.)

2. Based on direct costs only, what is the estimated cost of offering job placement services to an individual for the budget period? (Round to the nearest dollar.)

3. A member of the Johnsonville Town Council believes that persons participating in the job training program should pay the full cost of that program, rather than just direct costs. Assume that ESA management believes that Agency Administration should be allocated to Placement and Training on the basis of the number of employees in each department and that Accounting and Record Keeping should be allocated on the basis of the number of persons served. Using direct allocation for the support center, calculate:

   a. The amount which should be charged to participants in the job training program based on the full cost of this service. (Round to the nearest dollar.)

   b. The estimated full cost of serving a job placement candidate for the coming year. (Round to the nearest dollar.)

4. Suppose that almost all the cost of ESA is fixed. If Job Training could obtain an outside grant of $500,000 and could also increase its enrollment by 500 persons without increasing costs, what charge would it have to make to participants, assuming the charge was sufficient to cover direct costs plus allocated Agency Administration and Accounting and Record Keeping. (Round to the nearest dollar.)

3—26. *Allocation, calculation of manufacturing overhead and product costs, income statement.*   The Cashin Manufacturing Company makes stuffed animals. It has two producing departments; one makes washable animals suitable for very young children, the other makes stuffed animals depicting popular cartoon and comic characters and is designed for older children and adults. The following data have been collected for the two departments and for service centers which provide service related to the manufacturing process.

	WASHABLE ANIMALS	CARTOON CHARACTERS
Direct materials	$150,000	$180,000
Direct labor	300,000	336,000
Manufacturing overhead directly identifiable with each department:		
Indirect materials	45,000	60,000
Supervisory salaries	30,000	48,000
Repairs and depreciation of equipment	60,000	72,000

The following common manufacturing costs for the two product lines must be allocated between the two departments on the basis indicated:

COST TO BE ALLOCATED		ALLOCATION BASIS
Heat, light, and other utilities	$ 65,000	Space occupied: 60% washable animals, 40% cartoon characters
Supervisory and other salaries	180,000	Number of employees: 45% washable animals, 55% cartoon characters
Depreciation of building, taxes, and insurance	96,000	Space occupied

During the year, 150,000 washable animals were produced and 135,000 sold at an average markup on *manufacturing cost* of 50%. There was a beginning inventory of 8,000 washable animals, which had cost $4.85 each to produce. During the year 120,000 cartoon characters were produced and 110,000 were sold at an average markup of 60% on *product cost*. There was no beginning inventory of these stuffed items. The company costs its inventory on a FIFO basis. Selling and administrative expenses amounted to $383,000 for the year. The company's tax rate is 46%.

REQUIRED:
1. Calculate the total manufacturing overhead for each of the two departments.
2. Calculate the average cost of manufacturing (a) a washable animal and (b) a cartoon character this period. (Round to the nearest cent.)
3. Prepare an Income Statement for the period. Your Income Statement should be prepared in a format that will show the *gross margin* from each product line and the net income for the company as a whole.
4. Calculate the ending inventory valuations for each of the two product lines.

3—27. *Allocation, general journal entries, Cost of Goods Manufactured Statement, and Income Statement.* Cosmos Manufacturing Company makes a low-priced telescope. It had the following transactions during the first year of its operations.

a. Purchased direct raw materials inventory $1,010,000 and indirect raw materials inventory of $280,000. Purchases were made for cash.
b. Used $960,000 of direct raw materials and $240,000 of indirect raw materials in the manufacturing process to make 48,000 telescopes.
c. Incurred direct labor costs of $1,200,000 and indirect labor costs in the manufacturing process of $336,000. All labor costs were paid in cash.
d. Incurred the following additional manufacturing overhead costs which could be directly identified with the production process:

Depreciation	$20,000
Repairs and maintenance, all paid in cash	83,000
Miscellaneous, all paid in cash	86,080

e. The costs of the Personnel Department were $230,000, of which $215,000 was paid in cash and the other $15,000 represented depreciation. Since this department serves three functions—manufacturing, selling, and administra-

tion—management allocates Personnel Department costs between these functions on the basis of effort expended. The manager of the Personnel Department
believes the department's efforts were expended as follows:

Manufacturing	65%
Selling	15
Administration	20
	100%

Make two entries to record this data. First record the department's expenses
using a summary account entitled "Personnel Department Expenses Summary."
Then transfer these expenses to the three functions using the following entry:

```
Manufacturing Overhead Summary
Selling Expenses
Administrative Expenses
        Personnel Department Expense Summary
```

f. The costs of the Information Systems Department were $306,000, of which
$260,000 was for cash, $20,000 was on account (account payable), and the
remainder was for depreciation. This department also serves manufacturing,
selling, and administration and its costs are allocated between these three
functions based on number of employees. On this basis the following allocation
percentages have been developed:

Manufacturing	55%
Selling	20
Administration	25
	100%

Make two entries to record these data, similar to the system used above for the
Personnel Department.

g. Transferred manufacturing overhead expenses from the Manufacturing Overhead Summary Account to Work-In-Process.

h. Transferred 48,000 telescopes to Finished-Goods Inventory. There was no
ending Work-in-Process Inventory.

i. In addition to expenses allocated to it, selling expenses amounted to $288,000,
of which $240,000 was paid in cash, $30,000 was on account and $18,000
represented depreciation.

j. Administrative expenses in addition to allocated expenses amounted to
$433,000. Of this amount, $350,000 was paid in cash, $30,000 was on account,
and $53,000 represented depreciation.

k. During the period 40,000 telescopes were sold for cash at $100 each. The
company uses a perpetual inventory system and records cost of goods sold and
updates its inventory account at the time of sale.

REQUIRED: **1.** Prepare the journal entries to record the transactions described above. Record
all manufacturing overhead costs in a Manufacturing Overhead Summary
account, then transfer the total to Work-in-Process.

2. Prepare a Cost of Goods Manufactured Statement.

3. Prepare an Income Statement and prepare the journal entry to record taxes at
a 46% rate.

4. Calculate the ending inventory valuation which will be shown on Cosmos's end-of-the-period balance sheet.

3—28. *Nonquantitative problem—purpose of, and problems with, cost allocation.* The First Security Bank of Adenville's record-keeping system is designed in such a way that costs are classified by type, rather than in terms of service functions. For example, the bank knows how much it pays to employees and how much depreciation it records on its plant and fixtures. It has not attempted to measure salary costs or depreciation expense associated with the three basic types of customer services it offers—checking accounts, savings accounts, and loans. As the banking business has become more competitive, First Security has become convinced that it needs to know more about the cost of the services it offers. Currently, for instance, it charges customers who maintain less than $1,000 average balance in their accounts a $3 monthly fee plus $.20 for every check they write. The bank is unsure whether this charge is appropriate. You have been hired as a consultant to provide some advice to the bank with respect to improving their information system so that management would have a better understanding of bank costs for various services rendered.

REQUIRED: Draft a memo to the management of First Security Bank which responds to the following issues.

1. If First Security Bank wants to determine costs of the three different types of services it offers, what steps must it take? Be specific.
2. List three costs which will probably be common costs for the three service functions and suggest an allocation basis for each.
3. For service enterprises we use the terms "mission center" and "support center." Name two possible support centers which First Security may establish as part of a new managerial accounting system.
4. Distinguish between the direct method of allocating costs of service centers or support centers and the step-down method.
5. Suppose that as the result of the managerial accounting system established by First Security it is determined that it costs the bank $400 per year to service the "average" checking account.
    a. Should the bank institute a charge or set of charges on all checking accounts which will yield the bank this amount each year? Why or why not?
    b. What limitations do you see associated with the $400 cost figure which has been developed?

3—29. *Service cost allocation.* (AICPA adapted) The Parker Manufacturing Company has two production departments (Fabrication and Assembly) and three service departments (General Factory Administration, Factory Maintenance, and Factory Cafeteria). A summary of costs and other data for each department prior to allocation of service-department costs for the year appears below.

	FABRICATION	ASSEMBLY	GENERAL FACTORY ADMINISTRATION
Direct labor costs	$1,950,000	$2,050,000	$90,000
Direct material costs	$3,130,000	$ 950,000	—
Manufacturing overhead costs	$1,650,000	$1,850,000	$70,000
Direct labor hours	562,500	437,500	31,000
Number of employees	280	200	12
Square footage occupied	88,000	72,000	1,750

	FACTORY MAINTENANCE	FACTORY CAFETERIA
Direct labor costs	$82,100	$87,000
Direct material costs	$65,000	$91,000
Manufacturing overhead costs	$56,100	$62,000
Direct labor hours	27,000	42,000
Number of employees	8	20
Square footage occupied	2,000	4,800

The costs of the General Factory Administration Department, Factory Maintenance Department, and Factory Cafeteria are allocated on the basis of direct labor hours, square footage occupied, and number of employees, respectively. (Round all final calculations to the nearest dollar.)

REQUIRED:
1. Assuming that Parker elects to use the direct method to allocate service-department costs to production departments, calculate the amount of Factory Maintenance Department costs which would be allocated to the Fabrication Department.
2. Assuming the same method of allocation as in part 1, calculate the amount of General Factory Administration Department costs which would be allocated to the Assembly Department.
3. Assuming that Parker elects to use the step-down method to distribute service-department costs (starting with the service department with the greatest total direct costs), calculate the amount of Factory Cafeteria Department costs which would be allocated to the Factory Maintenance Department.
4. Assuming allocation as in part 3, calculate the amount of Factory Maintenance Department costs which would be allocated to the Factory Cafeteria.

3—30. *Allocation of overhead expenses and service-department costs.* (AICPA adapted) Thrift-Shops, Inc., operates a chain of three food stores in a state which recently enacted legislation permitting municipalities to levy an income tax on corporations. The legislation establishes (1) a uniform tax rate which the municipalities may levy, and (2) regulations which provide that the tax is to be computed on income derived within the taxing municipality after a reasonable and consistent allocation of general overhead expenses. General overhead expenses for Thrift-Shops, Inc., have not been allocated to individual stores previously and include warehouse, general office, advertising, and delivery expenses. Each of the municipalities in which Thrift-Shops, Inc., operates a store has levied the corporate income tax as provided by state legislation, and management is considering two plans for allocating general overhead expenses to the stores. Operating results for the past year before general overhead and taxes for each store were as follows:

	STORE			
	Ashville	Burns	Clinton	Total
Sales, net	$416,000	$353,600	$270,400	$1,040,000
Less: Cost of sales	215,700	183,300	140,200	539,200
Gross margin	200,300	170,300	130,200	500,800
Less: Local operating expenses:				
Fixed	60,800	48,750	50,200	159,750
Variable	54,700	64,220	27,448	146,368
Total	115,500	112,970	77,648	306,118
Income before general overhead and taxes	$ 84,800	$ 57,330	$ 52,552	$ 194,682

General overhead expenses were as follows:

Warehousing and delivery expenses:		
Warehouse depreciation	$20,000	
Warehouse operations	30,000	
Delivery expenses	40,000	$ 90,000
Central office expenses:		
Advertising	18,000	
Central office salaries	37,000	
Other central office expenses	28,000	83,000
Total general overhead		$173,000

Additional information includes the following:

1. One-fifth of the warehouse space is used to house the central office, and depreciation on this space is included in other central office expenses. Warehouse operating expenses vary with quantity of merchandise sold.

2. Delivery expenses vary with distance and number of deliveries. The distances from the warehouse to each store and the number of deliveries made were as follows:

STORE	MILES	NUMBER OF DELIVERIES
Ashville	120	140
Burns	200	64
Clinton	100	104

3. All advertising is prepared by the central office and is distributed in areas in which stores are located.

4. As each store was opened, the fixed portion of central office salaries increased $7,000 and other central office expenses increased $2,500. Basic fixed central office salaries amount to $10,000 and basic fixed other central office expenses amount to $12,000. The remainder of central office salaries and the remainder of other central office expenses vary with sales.

REQUIRED: 1. For each of the following plans for allocating general overhead expenses, compute the income of each store that would be subject to the municipal levy on corporation income:

a. *Plan 1:* Allocate all general overhead expenses on the basis of sales volume.

b. *Plan 2:* First, allocate central office salaries and other central office expenses evenly to warehouse operations and each store. Second, allocate the resulting warehouse operations expense, warehouse depreciation, and advertising to each store on the basis of sales volume. Third, allocate delivery expenses to each store on the basis of delivery miles times number of deliveries.

2. Comment on the results you obtained in part 1.

chapter four

ASSIGNING MANUFACTURING OVERHEAD TO PRODUCTION

OBJECTIVES

After completing this chapter, you should be able to answer the following questions:

- Why do many companies use a predetermined overhead rate in costing products rather than actual overhead?
- How is a predetermined overhead rate developed?
- What is meant by "overapplied" or "underapplied" overhead?
- What factors cause overhead to be over- or underapplied?
- When a predetermined overhead rate is used, how are both actual and applied overhead recorded by the accounting system?
- How does variable (direct) costing differ from absorption costing?
- What is meant by a "contribution-margin format income statement"?
- What is the difference between the following concepts of product costing: an actual absorption system, an actual/applied absorption system, an actual variable costing system, and an actual/applied variable costing system?

INTRODUCTION

The primary things we do in this chapter are:

1. Show how a predetermined rate is calculated.
2. Illustrate the journal entries which are made when predetermined overhead rather than actual overhead is assigned to production.
3. Discuss why a company may use predetermined overhead in costing its output rather than actual overhead.

In addition, an alternative concept of applying costs to production is introduced—the concept of a variable costing system which treats all fixed manufacturing overhead as a period, rather than a product, cost. The impact of variable costing on income determination and inventory valuation is illustrated.

THE CONCEPT OF PREDETERMINED OVERHEAD

In Chapter 2 we illustrated how direct material, direct labor, and other manufacturing costs, known collectively as manufacturing overhead, attached to products manufactured. In Chapter 3 we looked at a more complex situation, where, to determine the amount of manufacturing overhead which should attach to production, allocation of common costs and service-department costs was required. In both of these chapters we attached to the units produced *actual* manufacturing overhead costs. In reality, many companies cost their products on the basis of a predetermined *overhead rate* based on an *estimate of what actual overhead costs will be* and an *estimated level of production*.

What the use of a predetermined overhead rate (also called an *applied overhead rate*) means is that Work-in-Process will be charged with actual direct material costs, actual direct labor costs, and estimated manufacturing overhead costs. The unit cost of products transferred from Work-in-Process to Finished Goods Inventory will be based on actual direct material and labor cost but estimated overhead costs.

To calculate an overhead rate for an annual period, each component of overhead costs for the year is estimated. This total is then divided by some measure of input, such as the hours of direct labor used, and applied to units on this basis. For example, assume total overhead costs for the coming year are estimated at $600,000. The company wishes to apply overhead to production on the basis of direct labor hours, which it estimates for the period as 100,000. The predetermined or applied overhead rate will be $6 per direct labor hour ($600,000 estimated overhead/100,000 direct labor hours), and a unit of production which required 2 hours of direct labor time would bear $12 of manufacturing overhead (2 hours × $6 predetermined overhead rate). This process is described in more detail later in this chapter.

Throughout this text, if a company attaches cost to units produced on the basis of *actual direct material and direct labor costs* and *applied (predetermined)* overhead, we are going to say it uses an *actual/applied* product costing system. If it attaches costs to units on the basis of *actual direct material, actual direct labor*, and *actual manufacturing* overhead, we are going to refer to its costing system as an *actual* product costing system.

WHY A PREDETERMINED OVERHEAD RATE IS USED

Why do companies use a predetermined (applied) overhead rate? There are three good reasons. First, when actual overhead costs are used, the company may not have the data it needs on a timely basis. When does a company know how much the products produced during the fiscal year actually cost? Or, putting it another way, when can total actual overhead costs for the year be determined? The answer is, "At some time after the end of the year." Yet, during the year, or before the year begins for which costs are being measured, the company has to make decisions such as pricing its products, taking special orders, and offering discounts.

Second, if we tried to calculate actual overhead costs more frequently, say, on a monthly basis rather than waiting till the end of the year, this could lead to distortions because of different levels of costs between months. For example, heating costs could affect the unit costs of items produced during cold months.

Finally, because of different production levels in different months, product costs could vary greatly, depending on which month of the year they were produced. To illustrate, assume that fixed manufacturing overhead totals $12,000 per month. Also, because of seasonal demand factors, in the highest month of production 6,000 units are produced, but only 4,000 units in the slowest month. If actual overhead costs were used to calculate a unit cost for each month's production, in the month when 6,000 units were produced, fixed overhead cost per unit would be $2 ($12,000/6,000). In the month when 4,000 units were produced, fixed overhead cost per unit would be $3 ($12,000/4,000).

CALCULATING A PREDETERMINED OVERHEAD RATE

If a company decides to use a predetermined overhead rate, how does it go about calculating this rate? The steps in the process are as follows:

1. The activity level for the period is estimated as a basis for estimating overhead costs.

2. An estimate is made of anticipated overhead costs at that level of activity.

3. A rate is calculated by dividing estimated overhead by some measure of input.

Selection of an Activity Level

Before we can estimate our total anticipated overhead costs for the year, we must first determine at what level we shall be producing. If our overhead costs were all fixed, this would not be necessary, since they would not vary with the activity level. However, since some overhead costs are variable—that is, they vary in total directly with the number of units produced—we cannot estimate these costs until we have estimated our production or activity level.

Different theories exist as to how the activity level should be selected. The two most common approaches are known as the *annual-capacity concept* and the *normal-capacity concept*. With the annual-capacity concept, we view each annual accounting period as separate from other periods and calculate a new rate for each period. With the normal-capacity concept we take a longer-run perspective and estimate activity for a number of periods based on an average (normal) level for those periods. This concept is based on the assumption that there will be activity swings within a period of years but underlying those swings is a normal level of activity.

To illustrate the difference between the two concepts, assume the following anticipated levels of production for a five-year period:

19X1	10,000 units
19X2	11,000
19X3	12,000
19X4	10,000
19X5	11,000
19X6	12,000

If we calculated an overhead rate based on annual capacity, in 19X1 it would be based on output of 10,000 units, in 19X2 11,000 units, and in 19X3 12,000 units. Because of the presence of fixed costs, even if the total amount of fixed overhead costs were the same for the three-year period, the rate per unit would differ for each of those three years.

On the other hand, if we look for the underlying level of production, using the normal-capacity concept, we can see that the company is producing on the average 11,000 units. We would calculate a rate based on 11,000 units, knowing that in some years the rate would be too low (when we produced only 10,000 units) and in some years too high (when we produced 12,000 units). But, in general, the rate based on 11,000 units would apply our normal level of overhead cost to units produced.

In this text we are going to assume the use of *annual capacity* and calculate an overhead rate each year based on that year's anticipated activity level.

MECHANICS OF CALCULATING AN OVERHEAD RATE

We shall now illustrate how an applied overhead rate is calculated based on the steps previously described.

Step 1: Estimate the activity level for the period for which an overhead rate is being calculated.   Let us assume that a radio manufacturing company estimates it will make 10,000 radios next year, each requiring $1\frac{1}{2}$ hours of direct labor.

Step 2: Estimate each element of overhead costs at the level of activity at which the company is expected to operate.   Suppose that we make the following estimates:

Variable overhead costs:	
Indirect materials	$1.00 per unit
Utilities—variable portion	.50
Other miscellaneous	.30
Total variable costs	$1.80
Fixed overhead costs:	
Indirect labor	$10,000 per year
Depreciation	15,000
Utilities—fixed portion	8,000
Other miscellaneous	6,000

Notice that we classify overhead costs as being either variable or fixed. This is necessary in order to calculate total overhead costs correctly, because some elements of overhead (variable costs) will vary directly with the activity level. Let us now make out an estimated schedule of total overhead costs for the coming year.

In addition, keep in mind that to come up with the estimated costs shown above, it may be necessary to use the allocation procedures described in Chapter 3. If there are common costs or service-department costs which management considers to be part of manufacturing overhead, these costs will have to be estimated and allocated to production departments to calculate total estimated overhead.

ESTIMATED TOTAL OVERHEAD

Anticipated production in units	10,000
Estimated direct labor hours (10,000 units × $1\frac{1}{2}$ hr)	15,000
Variable overhead costs:	
Indirect materials (10,000 × $1)	$10,000
Utilities (10,000 × $.50)	5,000
Other (10,000 × $.30)	3,000
Total variable overhead	18,000
Fixed overhead costs:	
Indirect labor	$10,000
Depreciation	15,000
Utilities	8,000
Other	6,000
Total fixed overhead	$39,000
Total overhead	$57,000

Remember our discussion of the effect of activity level on unit costs. Regardless of the production level, our variable costs totaled $1.80 per unit. Our fixed costs per unit and hence total overhead cost per unit will vary, depending on how many units are produced. When 10,000 units are produced, *fixed* overhead costs are $3.90 and *total* overhead costs per unit $5.70 ($1.80 + $3.90). If we had estimated our production at 12,000 radios, fixed overhead costs would drop to $3.25 per unit and total overhead costs per unit to $5.05 ($1.80 + $3.25).

Step 3: Select a measure of input and divide estimated overhead by that amount to come up with an applied overhead rate.   Assume that we believe overhead should be applied on the basis of direct labor time. Remember that each radio requires $1\frac{1}{2}$ direct labor hours. The rate at which overhead will be applied to the radios produced is:

$57,000 total estimated overhead/$1\frac{1}{2}$ hours $\times$ 10,000 radios

$$= \$57,000/15,000 \text{ direct labor hours}$$

$$= \underline{\underline{\$3.80}} \text{ per direct labor hour}$$

This means that to each radio we will attach $5.70 of manufacturing overhead ($3.80 of overhead per direct labor hour $\times$ $1\frac{1}{2}$ hours required to make each radio).

If we actually made 10,000 radios next year and used 15,000 direct labor hours, Work-in-Process Inventory would be debited for $57,000 of overhead. Each radio that was transferred from Work-in-Process to Finished Goods Inventory would carry with it $5.70 of manufacturing overhead.

USE OF AN INPUT MEASURE FOR APPLYING OVERHEAD

Looking at our example, you could ask, "Why not use the number of units—that is, radios produced—as the basis for allocating overhead to production rather than using some input measure such as direct labor?" This is certainly one of the more confusing aspects of using a predetermined overhead rate. If actual units were used, we could divide $57,000 by 10,000 units and come up with the same amount of overhead—$5.70 per unit—as we calculated when we based the rate on the number of direct labor hours used. Why do we need to bother with some measure other than units as a means of allocating overhead to the products manufactured?

The use of units produced is perfectly logical for a company which produces only one type of product and which has no ending Work-in-Process Inventory. However, because companies do produce different types of products and have ending Work-in-Process, which by definition is incomplete units, a rate based on some measure of input is needed.

Different Types of Products

To illustrate the need for calculating an overhead rate based on a measure of input rather than units produced, suppose that a company produces either different product lines or identifiable batches of products—say, three different product lines using the same manufacturing facility: an inexpensive AM/FM radio, an AM/FM clock radio combination, and a combination AM/FM radio and cassette player and recorder. The company produced the following quantities:

AM/FM radios	5,000 units
AM/FM clock radios	3,000
AM/FM radio/cassette	2,000

If we took the $57,000 of total overhead and divided it by 10,000 units, we would assign to each unit, regardless of what type of unit, $5.70 of overhead. Yet, our models vary in sophistication and consequently in production costs. We could try to come up with a separate rate for each product line, but this would entail allocating all overhead costs among the various product lines. This is a costly process which involves judgments and perhaps highly arbitrary decisions as to how much of each of our elements of manufacturing overhead should be assigned to each product line. For example, depreciation of the factory building, heating, lighting, property taxes, and insurance would have to be allocated to each product line, as illustrated in Chapter 3.

To overcome these problems, accountants have chosen to use an averaging process whereby they try to relate overhead to some measure of productive input. As a result, those products which have the greatest amount of the input measure used to allocate overhead will be assigned the greatest amount of overhead.

For our purposes let us suppose that direct labor hours is chosen as our method of assigning overhead to units produced and that direct labor inputs and production of our three products are estimated as follows:

AM/FM radio	1.5 hours for 5,000 units =	7,500 hours
AM/FM clock radio	2.0 hours for 3,000 units =	6,000
AM/FM radio/cassette	3.5 hours for 2,000 units =	7,000
	Total hours	20,500

Referring back to our original example, the estimated overhead for next year is $57,000. Expressing the rate in terms of direct labor hours would result in a rate per hour of approximately $2.78 ($57,000/20,500 hours). Or we could say that overhead will be applied at the rate of $2.78 per direct labor hour. Thus each AM/FM radio would be charged with 1.5

hours × \$2.78 = \$4.17 of overhead. The more complex product—the AM/FM radio/cassette combinaton—would be assigned overhead of \$9.73 per unit (3.5 hours × \$2.78 per hour).

Work-in-Process Inventory

The use of a predetermined overhead rate is also helpful when there are incomplete units in process at the end of an accounting period; that is, the company has an ending Work-in-Process. We must attach some cost to those units still in process.

If we are using an overhead rate based on actual units, to value ending inventory we will have to estimate the degree of completion of the units still in process and make some assumption as to when overhead costs are incurred in the production process. If we use a predetermined overhead rate, we can look at some other input to the production process and on the basis of this input assign overhead to the units still in process.

For example, assume that at the end of an accounting period we have 200 AM/FM radios in various degrees of completion. If we know how many hours of direct labor have been put into these units which are still in process, we can calculate the related overhead quite easily. Suppose our records show that as of the end of the accounting period 150 hours of direct labor have been used on the units still in process. We will attach \$417 of overhead to the Work-in-Process Inventory (\$2.78 per hour × 150 direct labor hours = \$417).

SELECTING AN INPUT MEASURE

In our example, we assume that manufacturing overhead would be applied to units produced on the basis of direct labor hours. While this is a commonly used basis for applying overhead, overhead could be applied instead on the basis of factors such as direct material units used, machine hours used, direct labor costs, or direct material costs.

In determining which of the possible bases to use, an attempt should be made to see if one is more logical than the other. Is there any relationship between the types of overhead costs being incurred and direct labor, for example? That is, does having people engaged in the manufacturing process cause a significant portion of the overhead? Practically, a company may not be able to make such an association, and the choice of a base for applying overhead is largely arbitrary.

There is a problem with using dollar measures of input rather than physical measures of input such as hours or raw material units. When dollar measures are used, the amount of overhead allocated to products is affected by changes in prices rather than changes in the level of activity.

Assume, for example, that we estimate overhead for the next two years as $600,000 each year. We have two products, for which the following data have been accumulated:

	PRODUCT #101	PRODUCT #102
Year 1: Raw material inputs	10,000 units @ $2	20,000 units @ $3
Year 2: Raw material inputs	10,000 units @ $2	20,000 units @ $3.50

If we develop a single overhead rate for the company based on raw material *usage*, in both years overhead allocation will be as follows:

Overhead rate	$600,000/30,000 raw material units = $20 per raw material unit
Product #101 overhead	10,000 × $20 = $200,000
Product #102 overhead	20,000 × $20 = $400,000

If overhead were allocated on the basis of raw material *costs* rather than usage, in year 2 Product #102 would have a larger proportion of overhead allocated to it, not because of a change in the number of units produced but because of an increased price for the raw materials used in production.

Based on raw material costs, overhead allocation would be as follows:

	Year 1
Overhead rate	$600,000/(10,000 × $2) + (20,000 × $3) = $7.50 per dollar of raw material
Product #101 overhead	$20,000 × $7.50 = $150,000 = 25% of total overhead ($150,000/600,000)
Product #102 overhead	$60,000 × $7.50 = $450,000 = 75% of total overhead ($450,000/600,000)

	Year 2
Overhead rate	$600,000/(10,000 × $2) + (20,000 × $3.50) = $6.67 per dollar of raw material
Product #101 overhead	$20,000 × $6.67 = $133,400 = 22% of total overhead ($133,400/600,000)
Product #102 overhead	$70,000 × $6.67 = $466,600[a] = 78% of total overhead ($466,600/600,000)

[a] This figure is adjusted so that overhead sums to 600,000. The $6.67 figure is a rounded figure.

USE OF MULTIPLE OVERHEAD RATES

In our example with three types of radios and radio combinations being produced, we developed one overall overhead rate for factory operations. The same rate per direct labor hour was applied to the three different product lines.

A company may instead use multiple overhead rates. Such rates could be developed, for example, on the basis of (1) different rates for different product lines, (2) different rates for different departments through which a product passes, or (3) different rates depending on the plant in which a product is manufactured. The radio manufacturer, then, rather than having a single rate, could have had a different rate for each of the three products. Or suppose that each radio passed through two departments—an assembly department and a finishing department; there could be different overhead rates for these two departments. Or suppose that half the radios were made in an old factory facility in Gary, Indiana,

ILLUSTRATION FROM PRACTICE: CLASSES OF OVERHEAD AT AMERICAN THREAD

For one of its finishing mills, American Thread recognizes the following classes of variable and fixed (period) overhead:

VARIABLE OVERHEAD	PERIOD OVERHEAD
Routine repair labor	Overhead salaries
Other overhead labor	Overhead labor
Mill supplies	Office and mill supplies
Processing supplies	R & R and general mill repair supplies
Ticketing and labeling	Travel and entertainment
Packing and shipping supplies	Industrial relations
Routine repair supplies	Taxes
Electricity	Insurance
Fuels	Depreciation
All other	Telephone and telegraph
	Electricity
	All other

Based on its budget, American Thread assigns variable overhead to production; that is, based on the budget they estimate a variable cost per unit of production. This cost per unit for variable overhead is assigned to the units produced. A predetermined rate based on direct labor costs is used in assigning period overhead (fixed overhead) to production. In a recent period the predetermined rate used in assigning fixed overhead to production in this finishing mill was equal to 47.77% of direct labor costs.

Fringe-benefit costs are treated as a separate element of overhead, and a separate predetermined rate based on direct labor cost is used to assign them to production. This rate was recently 43.64% of direct labor costs.

and the other half in a new facility in Arlington, Texas; the company might choose to use two different overhead rates for the same product being produced in two different facilities.

One reason for using multiple rates is that one overhead rate may not result in equitably allocated overhead. For example, one product line may be raw materials intensive (i.e., the major cost is raw materials), another labor intensive, and a third, machine-hour intensive. Use of the same overhead rate base—for example, direct labor hours—could result in poorly defined product costs.

The decision on how many different overhead rates to use should be based on managerial judgment after consideration of the costs of using different rates versus the benefits of doing so. There is a great deal of variation in practice.

RECORDING ACTUAL AND PREDETERMINED OVERHEAD IN THE ACCOUNTS

To show how actual and predetermined overhead are recorded in the accounts of a company which uses an actual/applied costing system, let's return to our original example in which the company manufactured only one type of radio. Relevant data for the year just completed are as follows:

	ESTIMATED DATA	ACTUAL DATA
Production in units	10,000	10,000
Direct labor hour usage	15,000	15,000
Variable overhead costs:		
Indirect materials	$10,000	$10,800
Utilities	5,000	5,500
Other	3,000	2,800
Total variable overhead	$18,000	$19,100
Fixed overhead costs:		
Indirect labor	$10,000	$11,100
Depreciation	15,000	15,000
Utilities	8,000	8,700
Other	6,000	6,100
Total fixed overhead	$39,000	40,900
Total overhead	$57,000	$60,000
Predetermined overhead rate per direct labor hour ($57,000/15,000)	$3.80	

To record manufacturing overhead, an account with the title "Manufacturing Overhead Summary" (or a similar title) is used. Actual manufacturing overhead expenses are first recorded in the usual way by debiting an expense account and crediting cash, inventory, payable, or another appropriate account. Then these expense accounts are closed out to (summarized in) the Manufacturing Overhead Summary account.

At periodic intervals, based on the company's record-keeping system, Manufacturing Overhead Summary is credited for predetermined overhead based on the predetermined rate times the number of direct labor hours used. Thus, at the end of the accounting period, the Manufacturing Overhead Summary account will show, on the debit side, actual manufacturing overhead and, on the credit side, applied manufacturing overhead:

Manufacturing Overhead Summary
| Actual Overhead | Applied Overhead |

To clarify this discussion, entries to record the information given for the manufacturer of radios are shown below:

Journal entries made during the year are as follows:

a. To record *actual* overhead:

Indirect Materials	10,800	
Indirect Materials Inventory		10,800
Utilities Expense ($5,500 + $8,700)	14,200	
Cash (Payable)		14,200
Miscellaneous Expenses	8,900	
(Other $2,800 + $6,100)		
Cash (Payable)		8,900
Indirect Labor Expense	11,100	
Cash (Salaries and Wages Payable)		11,100
Depreciation Expense	15,000	
Accumulated Expenses		15,000

b. To summarize actual manufacturing overhead in the Manufacturing Overhead Summary Account:

Manufacturing Overhead Summary	60,000	
Indirect Materials		10,800
Utilities Expense		14,200
Miscellaneous Expense		8,900
Indirect Labor Expense		11,100
Depreciation Expense		15,000

c. To charge Work-in-Process Inventory with predetermined overhead:

Work-in-Process (15,000 hours × $3.80)	57,000	
Manufacturing Overhead Summary		57,000

OVER- AND UNDERAPPLIED OVERHEAD

When a predetermined overhead rate is used during the period, products being produced are charged with a predetermined amount of overhead. At the same time the accounting system will be collecting actual overhead cost for the period. Seldom will overhead applied and actual overhead cost incurred be exactly equal. We shall have either charged to the products being produced more overhead than was actually incurred (we have overapplied overhead) or charged to the products being produced less overhead than was actually incurred (we have underapplied overhead).

It is not difficult to understand why actual and applied overhead generally differ in amount. Remember the process we used to develop an overhead rate. We had to *estimate* our activity level for the period and *estimate* the cost of each individual element of overhead for the period to provide a basis for the rate. In addition, by using a measure of input, such as direct labor hours, to apply overhead to production we made an *assumption* that there was a *causal relationship* between the input measure and the occurrence of overhead costs. In other words, we assumed that the use of direct labor (or whatever input measure we used) *caused* overhead costs to be incurred.

Based on the entries shown above, our Overhead and Work-in-Process accounts looked as follows at the end of the accounting period:

Manufacturing Overhead Summary

Actual	$60,000	Applied	$57,000

Work-in-Process Inventory

Applied	$57,000	

Notice that the charge to the Work-in-Process Inventory account was for the applied overhead, not the actual. In our illustration we have charged this account for $3,000 less than the actual amount of overhead incurred. Our Manufacturing Overhead Summary has a debit balance, indicating that actual overhead exceeded applied overhead.

There are three different ways that we can dispose of the $3,000 balance in the Manufacturing Overhead account. The most common and the easiest approach is to adjust cost of goods sold for this amount. What we assume in this case is that the cost of goods which we sold was understated by $3,000 because we had charged too little overhead to the units being produced.

Conceptually you can see that if we charge off all the underapplied overhead to cost of goods sold, this is correct only so long as we have no Work-in-Process Ending Inventory and no goods which were manufactured this period and are still in Finished Goods Inventory. If the actual situation is otherwise, then theoretically a better disposition of the underapplied overhead would be to allocate it on a proportional basis between the units which are still in process, the units which are still in Finished Goods Inventory, and the units which were made this period and have been sold. This approach should be used in situations where significant cost distortions would occur if overhead were charged off to cost of goods sold.

A third alternative is to carry over the over- or underapplied overhead to the next accounting period. This is consistent with the idea (the normal-capacity concept) that overhead application should be based on a cycle longer than that represented by the annual accounting period. When the normal-capacity concept is used, it is assumed that in some years actual overhead will be greater than applied overhead, in some years it will be less, but over some cycle of time applied and actual overhead will be equal.

For purposes of this text we will assume that over- or underapplied overhead is immaterial in amount and will be charged off as an adjustment to cost of goods sold.

THE CAUSES OF OVER- OR UNDERAPPLIED OVERHEAD

The predetermined overhead rate is a function of two factors: (1) the estimated level of overhead and (2) the estimated level of the input measure. In the illustration given, the predetermined overhead rate was based on estimated overhead costs of $57,000 and the estimated use of 15,000 direct labor hours.

If actual results differ from either of these factors or a combination of them, overhead will be over- or underapplied. Based on the data just given, direct labor hours *actually* used (15,000) was exactly equal to the *estimated* number of direct labor hours (15,000). The reason overhead was underapplied was that actual overhead costs exceed estimated overhead costs.

Assume that, instead, actual overhead costs were $57,000 and were exactly equal to estimated overhead costs, but 15,500 direct labor hours were used to achieve the production of 10,000 units. The amount of overhead applied to production (charged to Work-in-Process) would have been:

$3.80 per direct labor hour $\times$ 15,500 direct labor hours = $\underline{\underline{\$58,900}}$

Since we are assuming that actual overhead was $57,000, in this case overhead would have been overapplied by $1,900.

It is not unusual for both factors on which overhead is based— estimated overhead costs and a measure of input—to differ from the actual level. The result will be over- or underapplied overhead.

ILLUSTRATIVE PROBLEM

To illustrate the flow of overhead and other manufacturing costs through the accounts and the disposition of over- or underapplied overhead, let us assume the following estimated cost data for Casual Comfort, Inc., a company which produces beanbag chairs:

Forecasted production		20,000 chairs
Direct materials:		
Plastic covering @ $4 per unit		$ 80,000
Filler @ $2 per unit		40,000
Total direct materials @ $6 per unit		$120,000
Direct labor @ 2 hours per unit, @ $4 per hour = $8 per unit × 20,000 units		$160,000
Manufacturing overhead:		
Variable manufacturing overhead:		
Indirect materials	$6,000	
Supplies	3,000	
Other	1,000	
Total variable manufacturing overhead @ $.50 per unit		$ 10,000
Fixed manufacturing overhead:		
Indirect labor	$20,000	
Utilities	5,000	
Depreciation	15,000	
Total fixed manufacturing overhead @ $2 per unit		$ 40,000
Total cost at a production volume of 20,000 chairs @ $16.50 per unit		$330,000

Before continuing our example, note from the above schedule of estimated costs that the $16.50 per unit is the *anticipated cost at a level of production of 20,000 chairs*. Why? Remember our discussion of the impact of fixed overhead on the cost of units produced. If our fixed overhead is truly fixed, it will remain at $40,000 regardless of the number of chairs produced within a relevant range. Thus, the $2 of fixed overhead *per unit* will change if our output changes. For example, what if we produced 40,000 chairs? Our direct materials would still be $6 per unit, our direct labor $8, and our variable overhead $.50. But our fixed overhead of $40,000 could now be spread over 40,000 chairs, thus reducing fixed overhead on a *per-unit* basis to $1; the cost of producing a beanbag chair would now be $15.50 rather than the $16.50 forecasted for a production level of 20,000 chairs.

Next let us calculate our predetermined manufacturing overhead rate, assuming that we are basing it once again on the number of direct labor hours. It would thus be $10,000 variable + $40,000 fixed/40,000 direct labor hours (2 hours per unit × 20,000 units) or $1.25 per hour and $2.50 per unit, since each unit consumes 2 hours of direct labor time.

Now let's look at actual results. We'll assume that 20,000 chairs were produced by Casual Comfort, Inc., and that direct material and direct labor costs and usage were exactly as estimated. (Later in the text we'll look at situations where estimated data in the form of budgets and actual data differ—a more realistic situation and see how we can analyze the differences.) Actual variable overhead and fixed overhead exceeded estimated levels and were as follows:

Actual variable manfacturing overhead:		
Indirect materials	$ 6,800	
Supplies	3,200	
Other	1,000	$11,000
Actual fixed manufacturing overhead:		
Indirect labor	$20,900	
Utilities	5,600	
Depreciation	15,000	$ 41,500
Total actual overhead		$ 52,500

Sales amounted to 17,000 chairs at a price of $25 each. Selling and general and administrative expenses amounted to $100,000.

Here are the journal entries which would have been made during the year to record Casual Comfort, Inc.'s transactions.

a. To record the use of raw materials:

Work-in-Process, 20,000 @ $6	$120,000	
Raw Materials Inventory—Plastic, 20,000 @ $4		$ 80,000
Raw Materials Inventory—Filler, 20,000 @ $2		40,000

b. To record the use of direct labor:

Work-in-Process, 20,000 @ 2 hours, @ $4 per hour	160,000	
Wages Payable		160,000

c. To charge Work-in-Process with the predetermined overhead:

Work-in-Process, 40,000 hours @ $1.25 per hour	50,000	
Manufacturing Overhead		50,000

d. (i) To record actual overhead incurred during the year:

Indirect Materials	6,800	
Supplies Expense	3,200	
Other Expenses	1,000	
Indirect Labor Expense	20,900	
Utilities Expense	5,600	
Depreciation	15,000	
Indirect Materials Inventory		6,800
Accumulated Depreciation		15,000
Cash		30,700[a]

[a] We've assumed that supplies, other expenses, indirect labor, and utilities were paid for in cash.

(ii) To transfer actual manufacturing overhead costs for the period to the Manufacturing Overhead Summary account:

Manufacturing Overhead Summary	52,500	
Indirect Materials		6,800
Supplies Expense		3,200
Other Expenses		1,000
Indirect Labor Expense		20,900
Utilities Expense		5,600
Depreciation		15,000

e. To transfer the 20,000 completed units to Finished Goods Inventory:

Finished Goods Inventory	$330,000[a]	
Work-in-Process Inventory		$330,000

[a]
Direct Materials	$120,000
Direct Labor	160,000
Applied Overhead	50,000
Total Cost of 20,000 chairs	$330,000
Cost per chair, $330,000/20,000 =	$16.50

f. To record the sale of 17,000 units and cost of goods sold:

Accounts Receivable, 17,000 @ $25	$425,000	
Cost of Goods Sold, 17,000 @ $16.50	280,500	
Sales		$425,000
Finished Goods Inventory		280,500

g. To record selling expenses and general and administrative expenses:

Selling and General and Administrative Expenses	$100,000	
Various Credits (Cash, Accumulated Depreciation, Payables, Prepaids)		$100,000

h. To close underapplied overhead to cost of goods sold:

Cost of Goods Sold	$ 2,500[a]	
Manufacturing Overhead		$ 2,500

[a]
Applied (Entry c)	$ 50,000
Actual (Entry d)	52,500
Underapplied	$ 2,500

Overhead is underapplied because we had set the rate based on estimated overhead costs totaling $50,000. Actual overhead costs were

$52,500. We applied $2,500 less overhead to the products produced than we should have.

Selected entries shown above are given in T-account form in Illustration 4-1. A Cost of Goods Manufactured Schedule is shown below along with an Income Statement for the year.

CASUAL COMFORT, INC.
Cost of Goods Manufactured
for the Year Ended December 31

Direct materials:		
Plastic	$ 80,000	
Filler	$ 40,000	$120,000
Direct Labor		160,000
Overhead Applied		50,000
Total Manufacturing Costs		$330,000
Add: Work-in-Process, Beginning Inventory		0
Total		$330,000
Less. Work-in-Process Ending Inventory		0
Cost of Goods Manufactured, 20,000 units @		$330,000
$16.50 per unit		

CASUAL COMFORT, INC.
Income Statement
for the Year Ended December 31

Sales		$425,000
Cost of Goods Sold, 17,000 @ $16.50	$280,500	
Add: Underapplied Overhead	2,500	
Adjusted Cost of Goods Sold		283,000
Gross Margin		$142,000
Selling and General and Administrative		
Expenses		100,000
Net Income		$ 42,500

We have charged all the underapplied overhead to cost of goods sold. As discussed previously, it would be theoretically more correct if we had allocated it to all units in the production process this period. Since there are no goods in process, using this system we would have allocated it as follows:

$$\text{Finished Goods Inventory, } 3{,}000/20{,}000 \times \$2{,}500 = \$\ \ 375$$
$$\text{Cost of Goods Sold, } 17{,}000/20{,}000 \times \$2{,}500 \ \ \ = \$2{,}125$$

It should be emphasized that in our illustration, applied overhead and actual overhead were different because estimated overhead differed from actual overhead. In reality, this is just one of a number of reasons or combinations of reasons why the two amounts may differ.

**ILLUSTRATION
4-1**

Flow of Manufac-
turing Costs
through the
Accounts

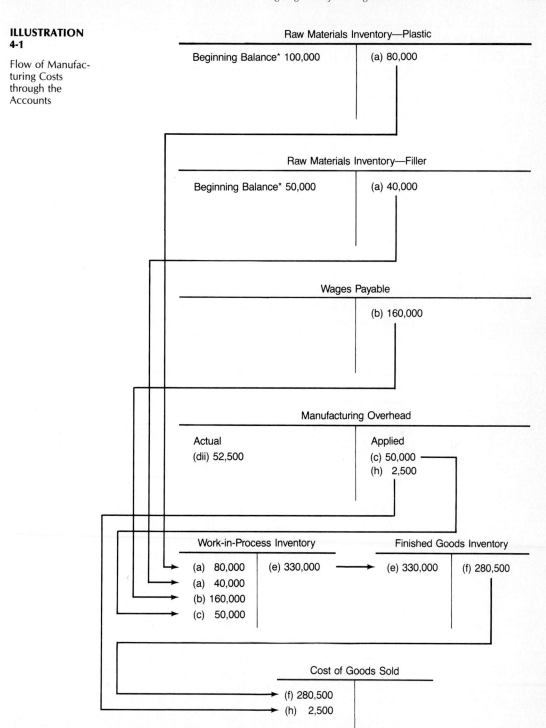

*The beginning balance for the raw materials inventory accounts are assumed figures
and cannot be derived from the data provided.

USE OF PREDETERMINED OVERHEAD RATES BY SERVICE ORGANIZATIONS

As illustrated in the previous chapter, the development of an overhead rate can be useful to a service organization when setting prices for its services or in other situations which require the assignment of indirect costs to output or organizational subcomponents. However, as we have discussed, the concept of product cost as opposed to period cost is not relevant to the service enterprise. Hence the concept of the predetermined overhead rate as a way of avoiding costing outputs at different or inappropriate rates because of changes in the production level, or because of incurring of costs at different levels due to differing conditions within the same accounting period, has no real significance.

Remember that with the service organization there are no work-in-process or finished goods inventories. There are no decisions to make as to the disposal of over- or underapplied overhead for the service organization. Expenses of the service organization appear on the income statement when incurred to be matched with the related revenues or other inflows.

VARIABLE (DIRECT) VERSUS ABSORPTION COSTING

We have pointed out earlier that the cost of the units produced in a particular period will vary, depending on the number of units produced during that period. The reason is the fixed component of manufacturing overhead. The method of attaching cost to units which we have been using is known as *absorption costing*. With absorption costing, each unit produced bears a portion of direct material, direct labor, variable manufacturing overhead, *and fixed manufacturing overhead* incurred in the production process. Critics of absorption costing note that increased profits can result not from selling more units nor cutting costs but simply from making more units. This economically illogical outcome can be avoided by the use of a variable (frequently referred to as a direct) costing system.

With a *variable (direct) costing system*, the only costs which are considered to be product costs and thus attach to the goods produced are variable manufacturing costs—direct materials, direct labor, and *variable manufacturing overhead*. Advocates of this approach consider fixed manufacturing overhead costs to be the cost of being prepared for production. These costs are incurred regardless of the production level achieved and hence should be thought of as period costs rather than product costs. With our traditional absorption cost accounting system both fixed and variable manufacturing costs are assigned to the output of the production process.

To illustrate, let's assume the following data for a company:

	YEAR 1	YEAR 2
Beginning inventory (units)	0	2,000
Unit sales	8,000	8,000
Unit production	10,000	8,000
Production costs:		
Variable per unit	$ 5	$ 5
Fixed	40,000	40,000
Selling expenses:		
Variable ($1 per unit)	8,000	8,000
Fixed	4,000	4,000
General and administrative expenses	16,000	16,000
Selling price per unit	$ 15	$ 15

Unit manufacturing costs under the two systems for the two years would be as follows:

Absorption Costing System

Year 1: Manufacturing cost per unit = $ 5 + $40,000/10,000 units
= $ 9

Year 2: Manufacturing cost per unit = $ 5 + $40,000/8,000 units
= $10

Variable Costing System

Year 1: Manufacturing cost per unit = $ 5
Year 2: Manufacturing cost per unit = $ 5

With the absorption costing system, the cost per unit changed by $1 owing to changes in the production level. With the variable costing system, cost per unit was the same, since under this concept no fixed costs are assigned to units produced and as a consequence changes in the production level will have no influence on unit costs.

Income statements for the two periods under the absorption costing system appear in Illustration 4-2, while income statements for the two one-year periods using variable costing are shown in Illustration 4-3. A FIFO (first-in, first-out) costing flow is assumed for the absorption costing illustration. Since unit costs do not differ between the two years under the variable costing system, the cost-flow assumption is irrelevant.

Observe Illustrations 4-2 and 4-3 carefully and consider the following points:

1. The company reported the greatest amount of net income in both years under the absorption costing system.
2. Even though the company sold the same number of units in both years and the unit selling price did not change, it reported higher profits in Year 1 than it did in Year 2 using absorption costing.

ILLUSTRATION 4-2

Income statement using absorption costing

	YEAR 1	YEAR 2
Sales, 8,000 @ $15	$120,000	$120,000
Cost of Goods Sold	72,000[a]	78,000[b]
Selling Expenses	12,000	12,000
General and Administrative Expenses	16,000	16,000
Total Operating Expenses	$100,000	$106,000
Net Income	$ 20,000	$ 14,000

[a] Cost of Goods Sold: 8,000 units @ $9 = $72,000.
[b] Cost of Goods Sold: Beginning Inventory, 2000 units @ $9 = $18,000
    Produced and Sold this Period,
      6,000 @ $10   =   60,000
    Total   = $78,000

3. Under variable costing, when the sales level was the same and there were no changes in variable manufacturing cost per unit, selling price per unit, and total fixed manufacturing costs, the same amount of profit was reported.

Observing Illustration 4-2, you can see why critics of absorption costing point out that increasing production without increased sales or reducing costs can result in higher net income.

Our illustration is designed to make a point and is overly simplistic. Although unit manufacturing costs can be reduced under an absorption costing system by increased production, holding large amounts of inventory is a costly process. Not only are there the cost of handling, warehousing, insuring, and otherwise maintaining inventory in a salable state, but some of the company's working capital is tied up in that inventory. In times of high interest rates, excess inventory can represent a significant cost.

How can we reconcile the $20,000 of first-year profit under absorption costing with the $12,000 resulting from the use of the variable costing system; or the $2,000 more of net income reported in year 2 under absorption costing in comparison to net income using variable costing?

ILLUSTRATION 4-3

Income statement using variable costing (income statement prepared in the contribution-margin format)

	YEAR 1	YEAR 2
Sales, 8,000 @ $15	$120,000	$120,000
Cost of Goods, Sold, 8,000 @ $5	40,000	40,000
Variable Selling Expense, 8,000 @ $1	8,000	8,000
Total Variable Expenses	$ 48,000	$ 48,000
Contribution Margin	$ 72,000	$ 72,000
Fixed Costs:		
Fixed Manfacturing Overhead	$ 40,000	$ 40,000
Selling Expenses	4,000	4,000
General and Administrative Expenses	16,000	16,000
Total Fixed Costs	$ 60,000	$ 60,000
Net Income	$ 12,000	$ 12,000

To answer this question we must remember where product costs go. They are allocated to either the income statement or the balance sheet, depending on whether the units to which they attach are still on hand or have been sold. We can reconcile net income differences by looking at the related balance-sheet carrying values for inventories:

Absorption Costing Balance Sheets

Year 1: 2,000 units @ $9 = $18,000
Year 2: 2,000 units @ $10 = $20,000

Variable Costing Balance Sheets

Year 1: 2,000 units @ $5 = $10,000
Year 2: 2,000 units @ $5 = $10,000

The $8,000 more of net income reported for Year 1 under absorption costing is due to the fact that fixed manufacturing cost of $4 per unit has been inventoried and is on the balance sheet. In Year 2, an additional $1 of fixed costs was put into inventory. The $10,000 of additional profit shown for the two year period under absorption costing consists of $5 of fixed overhead spread over the 2,000 units in ending inventory. Under variable costing, by defining *product cost* as being only *variable* costs, the fixed manufacturing overhead is treated as a period cost and expensed out in its entirety in the period incurred. Under absorption costing, product cost is defined as consisting of both variable and fixed manufacturing costs. Under this latter concept, the only fixed manufacturing cost reported on the income statement is that which is attached to the units sold. The flow of costs through an absorption costing system is compared to that through a variable costing system in Illustration 4-4.

In concluding our discussion of absorption versus variable costing systems, we should make two points. First, since we do not have inventories in service organizations, the issue of absorption costing versus variable costing has no significance.

Second, while numbers generated by a variable costing system may be meaningful internally to the firm (and this is why we discuss variable costing), this method is not in keeping with generally accepted accounting principles (GAAP) and cannot be used for externally circulated financial statements, which must be prepared in keeping with GAAP. While advocates of variable costing systems may point to distortions in net income which could be avoided if variable costing were used, the prevailing view is that the resulting balance-sheet inventory valuation is not appropriate. Defenders of absorption costing point out that fixed manufacturing costs are just as essential to the production process as variable manufacturing inputs and that each unit of output should bear a proportional part of these costs. Later in this text we will discuss the usefulness of variable costing concepts in decision making.

ILLUSTRATION 4-4

Cost Flows Using Absorption and Variable Costing Systems

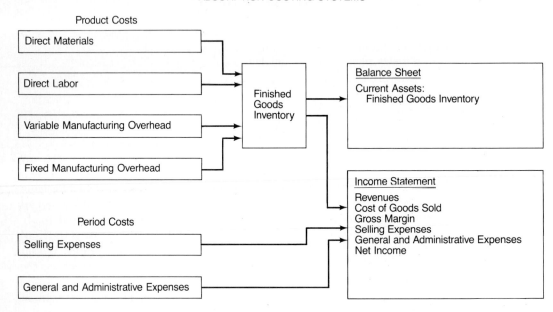

ABSORPTION COSTING SYSTEMS

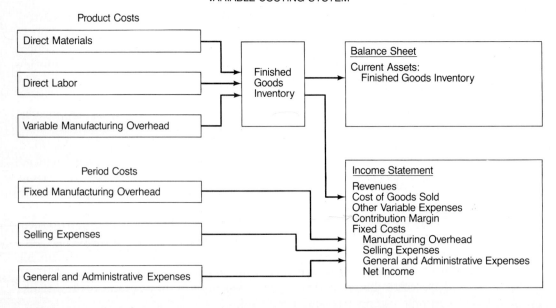

VARIABLE COSTING SYSTEM

CONTRIBUTION-FORMAT INCOME STATEMENT

Referring back to Illustration 4-3, the income statement has been prepared in a different format from the usual one shown in Illustration 4-2, which makes no distinction between variable and fixed costs. The format used in preparing the income statement in Illustration 4-3 is called a *contribution-format income statement*.

Contribution margin is defined as the difference between revenues and *all* variable expenses. Contribution margin is the amount available to cover fixed costs and generate a profit for the organization. An income statement which shows total variable costs subtracted from revenues to obtain the contribution margin is termed a contribution-format income statement.

Don't become confused with the form of the income statement and what costs are put into inventory. Although any variable selling or administrative expenses are subtracted from revenues to determine contribution margin when a contribution-format income statement is prepared, no part of these costs is inventoried under either absorption or variable costing. Only manufacturing costs are product costs.

We shall be using the concept of contribution margin and contribution-margin format income statements in subsequent chapters of this text.

COSTING SYSTEMS—SUMMARY OF TERMINOLOGY

Up to now we have discussed two basic concepts for attaching cost to units produced:

1. Absorption costing—each unit is assigned a portion of direct materials, direct labor, variable manufacturing overhead, *and* fixed manufacturing overhead (the method required for GAAP accounting).
2. Variable (direct) costing—each unit is assigned a portion of direct materials, direct labor, and variable manufacturing overhead. No fixed manufacturing overhead is assigned to the units produced.

Using these two concepts of attaching costs to units, we have also discussed two variations:

1. An actual cost system—*actual* direct materials, direct labor, and manufacturing overhead are assigned to units produced.
2. An actual/applied system—actual direct material and direct labor and *applied* (predetermined) overhead are assigned to units produced.

Either of these two variations can be used with absorption costing or variable costing. Keep in mind, however, that with variable costing, if we used an actual/applied system, the applied relates to variable manufacturing overhead only.

   In summary, costs may be applied to units produced in the following ways:

1. *Actual absorption costing*—actual direct materials, direct labor, and both variable and fixed manufacturing overhead are attached to output.
2. *Actual/applied absorption costing*—actual direct materials, actual direct labor, and applied manufacturing overhead (including both fixed and variable components) are attached to units produced.
3. *Actual variable (direct) costing*—actual direct materials, direct labor, and variable manufacturing overhead are assigned to production.

ILLUSTRATION 4-5

Systems for Attaching Costs to Units Produced

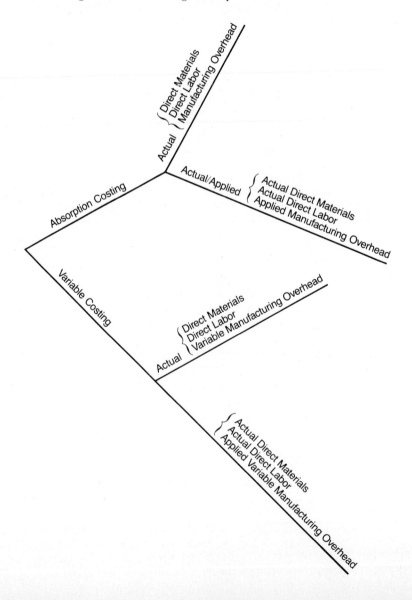

4. *Actual/applied variable (direct) costing*—actual direct materials, actual direct labor, and applied variable manufacturing overhead are assigned to production.

These different concepts of which costs should be assigned to units produced are shown in Illustration 4-5. Later in this text we will introduce another costing system—standard costing.

chapter highlights

Many companies assign a predetermined amount of overhead, rather than actual overhead, to units produced. We have termed this type of product costing system an actual/applied system in contrast to an actual system, which attaches actual overhead costs to units produced. This system is used because managers need to determine unit costs before the end of an annual period when the total amount of actual manufacturing overhead costs are known.

Assigning overhead to units on the basis of actual costs collected for some shorter period of time, such as a month, can lead to distortions in unit costs. Certain overhead costs may be much higher in one month than in another, resulting in higher unit costs in those months when an actual cost system is used. Also, if the number of units produced from month to month varies, assigning actual overhead costs to units on a monthly basis will result in varying unit costs over the year. This is true because of the fixed overhead component of product costs.

A predetermined overhead rate is developed by (1) selecting a measure of activity for the period for which overhead costs are being estimated, (2) estimating overhead costs at that level of activity, and (3) calculating a rate based on the relationship of estimated overhead costs to some measure of input such as direct labor hours or direct material usage.

When a predetermined overhead rate is used, predetermined rather than actual overhead is charged into the production process. When actual overhead exceeds applied overhead, overhead is said to be underapplied, meaning that the goods passing through the production process for the period bear an overhead charge which is too small. If applied overhead exceeds actual overhead, overhead is said to be overapplied, and products in the production process in this period have been charged with too much overhead. A commonly used method of disposing of over- or underapplied overhead if the amounts are not material is to adjust cost of goods sold.

Even though variable cost per unit may not change from one period to the next and fixed costs may not change in total from one period to another, unit costs can vary from period to period because of changes in the level of production. Since fixed costs are fixed in total, when expressed in per-unit terms they will vary with the production level. For this reason some people advocate a system called variable costing, whereby the only costs inventoried are variable manufacturing costs. Fixed manufacturing costs are treated as period costs and charged off in total in the period incurred. While variable costing results in changes in income when changes in sales volume occur rather than when changes in production volume occur, this method is not accepted as being in keeping with generally accepted accounting principles. Instead, absorption costing must be used, and each unit produced is assigned a proportional share of both variable and fixed manufacturing overhead. While not acceptable for financial reporting purposes, the concepts of variable costing can be very useful in a decision-making context.

questions

1. What are the steps in establishing a predetermined overhead rate?
2. What are the major reasons for calculating an annual predetermined overhead rate rather than assigning to the products produced actual overhead on a month-by-month basis?
3. Differentiate between the concept of normal capacity and that of annual capacity.
4. In estimating overhead for a particular period, why do we have to classify our various components of overhead as being either variable or fixed?
5. How do changes in the level of production affect unit cost of the output and why?
6. Explain what is meant by the terms overapplied overhead and underapplied overhead.
7. In what way is the cost of a unit of production misstated if manufacturing overhead is "overapplied" for the period during which the unit was produced?
8. List the three different ways in which we can dispose of over- or underapplied overhead. From a theoretical point of view which method is best and why?
9. Describe the difference between an absorption costing system and a variable costing system.

10. Why is a variable costing system not in keeping with generally accepted accounting principles?

11. A company in its *first year* of operations produced 10,000 units of its product and sold 7,000 units. Under which costing system—absorption or variable—will its income statement show the greatest amount of profit and its balance sheet show the highest inventory valuation. Why?

12. How does a contribution-margin format income statement differ from an income statement prepared in the traditional form?

13. What is the relationship of allocation, which was discussed in the previous chapter, to the development of an overhead rate?

14. A member of management in a firm stated: "An easy way to cut our unit production cost is to produce more units." Is the manager correct in her statement? Why or why not?

15. The Wang Company makes three different product lines. Traditionally it has used a single overhead rate in assigning overhead to these three product lines. What are the disadvantages, if any, of the use of a single overhead rate? What are the advantages?

16. What factors can cause overhead to be over- or underapplied?

17. When an income statement is prepared in a contribution-margin format, variable manufacturing, selling, and administrative expenses are subtracted from revenues to obtain a contribution margin. Does this mean that variable selling and administrative expenses are being inventoried—i.e., considered a part of product cost? Explain.

18. Variable costs are said to vary directly with activity level. Do variable manufacturing and variable selling expenses vary with the same activity level? Explain.

19. If variable costing cannot be used for financial reporting purposes because it is not in keeping with generally accepted accounting principles, why is it a part of the subject matter taught in managerial accounting?

20. Distinguish among the following types of product costing systems:

   a. Actual absorption costing system.
   b. Actual/applied absorption costing system.
   c. Actual variable costing system.
   d. Actual/applied variable costing system.

exercises

4—1. A company which produces small appliances showed the following estimate of overhead for its coming accounting period based on an anticipated production level of 180,000 units and the use of 120,000 direct labor hours.

Indirect materials	$150,000
Indirect labor	285,000
Repairs and maintenance	63,000
Depreciation—equipment	135,000
Rent—factory building	74,000
Utilities	96,000
Taxes and insurance	49,000
Total	$852,000

Variable overhead costs include indirect materials, repairs and maintenance, and one-half of the utilities.

REQUIRED: 1. Calculate a predetermined overhead rate for the company based on:

   a. Estimated direct labor hours to be used of 120,000 hours. (Round to the nearest cent.)

   b. Estimated dollars of direct materials to be used of $5 per unit. (Round to the nearest cent.)

   2. If variable overhead cost per unit is equal to the estimated costs per unit, and fixed overhead cost in total is equal to the estimated level of fixed overhead, and the company produced 120,000 units using 80,000 direct labor hours, will manufacturing overhead be over or underapplied? How do you know?

4—2.   Refer back to the information in Exercise 4—1. Assume that the company used an applied overhead rate in costing its products and based its overhead rate for the current period on estimated direct labor hours of 120,000. During the current accounting period it used 122,000 hours to produce the 180,000 units. There was no beginning inventory of finished goods, and, of the 180,000 units produced this period, 15,000 were still unsold as of the end of the accounting period. There was no ending inventory of work in process. Assume that both variable and fixed overhead were actually exactly equal to the total dollar amounts shown in Exercise 4—1.

REQUIRED: 1. Give the entries to record actual overhead (assume indirect materials are taken out of inventory and with the exception of depreciation all other expenses are paid out of cash) and overhead applied.

   2. Give the entry to close out any over- or underapplied overhead to the cost of goods sold account.

   3. What would the adjustment to cost of goods sold have been if the company elected to allocate over- or underapplied overhead between finished goods, work in process, and cost of goods sold? (Round to the nearest dollar.)

4—3.   A company estimates its variable cost per unit of product for next year as follows:

Direct materials	$4
Direct labor	6
Variable manufacturing overhead	2

Its estimated fixed manufacturing overhead *per month* for the year is estimated to be $48,000.

REQUIRED: Assume that during July and August actual variable costs per unit were exactly equal to estimated variable costs per unit, and that total actual fixed costs were exactly equal to estimated total fixed costs. During July 20,000 units of product were produced while during August only 17,000 units were produced.

1. Calculate the cost of producing a unit in July and that of producing a unit in August. (Round unit costs to the nearest cent.)
2. Why do the unit costs for the two months differ?
3. How can the company avoid unit costs which vary from month to month as production varies?

4—4. Refer to the information in Exercise 4—3. Suppose the company estimates that for the coming year it will produce a total of 262,000 units at the costs described in Exercise 4—3. It decides to use a predetermined overhead rate based on direct labor costs to assign overhead *costs* to the units produced.

REQUIRED: 1. Calculate the predetermined overhead rate for the company. (Round to the nearest cent.)
2. Calculate the cost of a unit produced in July when 20,000 units were produced and the cost of a unit produced in August when 17,000 units were produced.

4—5. A company's variable manufacturing costs amount to $10 per unit; based on a production level of 25,000 units, its fixed manufacturing costs amount to $5 per unit. A new recruit to the company's management training program tells the company that it can be more profitable at its *current sales level* simply by producing more units.

REQUIRED: 1. Is what the new recruit is telling the firm true? Explain.
2. Assume that the company's selling price is $25 per unit and that it currently sells 20,000 units a year. By what amount would the company's gross profit change if it produced 30,000 units rather than 25,000 but still sold 20,000 units?

4—6. Refer back to the information in Exercise 4—5. Suppose the company uses a variable costing system rather than an absorption costing system. Its variable selling expenses are $2 per unit sold, while its fixed selling expenses for the year are $25,000 and its general and administrative expenses, all of which are fixed, amount to $50,000.

REQUIRED: Prepare income statements in the contribution-margin format assuming:

1. 25,000 units were produced and 20,000 units sold for $25 each.
2. 30,000 units were produced and 20,000 were sold for $25 each.

4—7. Figuera Products estimates the following costs associated with its principal product for June:

Direct materials	$12 per unit
Direct labor	9 per unit
Variable manufacturing overhead	4 per unit
Fixed manufacturing overhead (total)	$1,125

Estimated production is 225 units and a *predetermined overhead rate, based on direct labor costs, is used* to assign manufacturing overhead costs to production. During June actual variable costs were at their estimated per-unit level. Actual fixed costs in June were $1,125. Actual labor costs for the month were $9 per unit.

REQUIRED: 1. Assuming actual production of 250 units, calculate the cost assigned to a unit produced in June.

2. Give the entry to close out any over- or underapplied overhead to the cost of goods sold account.

3. Assuming actual production of 215 units, how would the answers to parts 1 and 2 differ?

4—8. (AICPA adapted) JV Company began its operations on January 1, uses an actual cost system, and produces a single product that sells for $7 per unit. During the year 100,000 units were produced and 80,000 units were sold. Manufacturing costs and selling and administrative expenses were as follows:

	FIXED COSTS	VARIABLE COSTS
Raw materials	—	$1.50 per unit produced
Direct labor	—	1.00 per unit produced
Factory overhead	$150,000	.50 per unit produced
Selling and administrative	$ 80,000	.50 per unit sold

REQUIRED: 1. In presenting inventory on the balance sheet at December 31, calculate the total cost under absorption costing and under variable costing.

2. Prepare income statements for the year under absorption costing and variable costing. Use the contribution-margin format for the variable costing income statement.

3. Explain any difference in net income under the two costing methods.

4—9. Alpine, Inc., manufactures cross-country skis. Its estimated cost of production for the year at a volume of 120,000 pairs of skis was:

Direct materials	$1,200,000
Direct labor, 240,000 hours @ $6	1,440,000
Manufacturing overhead:	
Variable:	
Indirect materials	720,000
Repairs and utilities	250,000
Fixed:	
Indirect labor	960,000
Depreciation	300,000
Insurance and property taxes	80,000
Miscellaneous	240,000

Actual costs for the period when 120,000 pairs of skis were produced were:

Direct materials	$1,250,250
Direct labor, 246,000 hours @ $6	1,476,000
Manufacturing overhead:	
Variable:	
Indirect materials	726,000
Repairs and utilities	246,000
Fixed:	
Indirect labor	963,000
Depreciation	300,000
Insurance and property taxes	82,000
Miscellaneous	248,000

Direct materials costing $1,500,000 and indirect materials costing $800,000 were purchased for cash. There were no beginning inventories of either on hand. Direct labor costs for the period were paid in cash. Alpine had no beginning finished goods inventory and sold 108,000 pairs of skis during the year at $150 per pair. Selling and administrative expenses for the year amounted to $7,638,000.

REQUIRED:

1. Prepare an income statement which shows income before taxes for the period, assuming Alpine uses an *actual/applied* product costing system and adjusts Cost of Goods Sold for any over- or underapplied overhead. The predetermined overhead rate is based on estimated direct labor hours and was applied on the basis of the actual hours used. Carry the overhead rate you develop to three decimal places.

2. Calculate income before taxes for the period, assuming Alpine uses an *actual* product costing system. (Round cost per unit to the nearest cent.)

3. Why do the net income figures you calculated differ in parts 1 and 2? Where will this difference be reported for financial reporting purposes?

4. Can you think of any reason why it might be particularly desirable for a company such as Alpine to use a predetermined overhead rate?

4—10. Use the data in Exercise 4—9.

REQUIRED: Assuming Alpine uses an actual/applied costing system, prepare the journal entries to record the period's transactions. The company uses a perpetual inventory system. Except for depreciation and indirect materials, all manufacturing overhead costs were paid in cash. Of the selling and administrative expenses, all were paid in cash except for $600,000 of depreciation. In calculating the overhead rate, use three decimal places.

4—11. Use the data in Exercise 4—9.

REQUIRED:

1. Prepare an income statement in the contribution-margin format, assuming that Alpine uses an actual variable costing system for costing its production and that 30% of the selling and administrative costs are variable. (Round the cost of a unit produced to the nearest cent.)

2. Without making any computations, if Alpine had used an actual absorption costing system, would its net income have been more or less than what you calculated in part 1? How do you know?

4—12. Cheng Lee, an architect, wants to use the concept of an overhead rate as a basis for developing a billing rate for his clients. Cheng estimates his costs for the coming year as follows:

Office rent	$ 6,000
Depreciation of equipment	1,200
Utilities	2,400
Part-time clerical assistance	4,800
Supplies	3,000
Dues in professional organizations	1,800
Total	$19,200

Cost which can be directly associated with services rendered to a client will be added to the overhead rate per hour, which will be based on the costs described above. Cheng Lee estimates that he will be able to provide 1,200 hours of billable service during the coming year.

REQUIRED:

1. What is Cheng Lee's estimated overhead rate per billable hour for the coming year?

2. Assume that Cheng Lee needs $30,000 for his personal needs. How much per hour will he have to charge above any direct costs incurred to realize the $30,000?

3. Owing to depressed economic conditions, Cheng Lee was able to provide only 900 hours of billable service during the year.

   a. If his indirect costs were exactly as estimated, how much before-tax profit did Cheng realize for the year? Assume his charge per hour was the rate you computed in part 2.

   b. If he had correctly estimated the hours of billable service as 900 hours, to realize the $30,000 for his personal needs, what billing rate should he have set? (Round to the nearest dollar.)

4. How does the concept of an overhead rate for Cheng Lee differ from that for a manufacturing entity?

4—13. The Independent Paper Products (IPP) Company manufactures two types of calendars—bound booklets which will fit into pocket or purse and can be used to record appointments on a week-by-week basis and wall-style calendars which are used for decorative purposes. IPP estimates the direct costs which it can associate with each product line as follows:

	APPOINTMENT CALENDARS	WALL CALENDARS
Estimated production	500,000	300,000
Direct materials	$ 250,000	$ 90,000
Direct labor	1,000,000	600,000
Manufacturing overhead directly identified with each product line	100,000	75,000

The following estimates of manufacturing overhead costs common to the two product lines have been made. The basis on which each is allocated to the two product lines is also indicated.

Estimated
Common
Manufacturing
Costs

ITEM	AMOUNT	ALLOCATION BASIS
Building depreciation and utilities	$100,000	Square feet of space; 60% to appointment calendars, 40% to wall calendars
Factory superintendent's salary and office costs	$ 90,000	Number of employees in each department: 55% to appointment calendars, 45% to wall calendars

REQUIRED: **1.** Calculate the total estimated manufacturing overhead for each product line.
2. Assume that a unit of production requires a half-hour of direct labor time in either department. Calculate an overhead rate for each department based on direct labor hours. (Round to the nearest cent.)
3. Management calculates a target selling price for appointment calendars based on a markup on estimated manufacturing costs of 70%. Calculate the target price for the coming year. (Round to the nearest cent.)

4—14. One of the lines of products made by Quality Office Products is a standard model stapler. Last year, when 600,000 staplers were made and sold, unit manufacturing, selling, and administrative costs were as follows:

Direct materials	$1.00
Direct labor	1.80
Variable manufacturing overhead	.30
Fixed manufacturing overhead	.40
Variable selling expenses	.50
Fixed selling expenses	.15
Administrative expenses—all fixed	.45
Full cost per unit	$4.60

Quality Office Products estimates that direct material and variable manufacturing overhead costs will increase by 10% next year. Direct labor costs will increase by 15%. Variable selling expenses will decrease by 10%. All fixed expenses will remain at the same total level as they were last year. The anticipated selling price for the stapler for the coming year is $9.95, and Quality expects to produce and sell 660,000 staplers, each of which will require on the average one-third hour to complete. Quality Office Products uses an actual/applied absorption costing system and applies overhead to production on the basis of the dollar value of direct materials used.

REQUIRED: **1.** Calculate an overhead rate for Quality for the coming year. (Round to the nearest cent.)
2. What is the estimated gross margin on each stapler produced next year?
3. What is the estimated contribution margin on each stapler produced next year?

4—15. Refer back to the data in Exercise 4—14. Assume that for the current year, except for manufacturing overhead, all costs were exactly as estimated and 660,000 staplers were produced, of which 600,000 were sold at $9.95 each. The company's actual variable manufacturing overhead was $.35 per unit and its fixed overhead $250,000. Quality Office Products uses a perpetual inventory system.

REQUIRED:

1. Give the general journal entries to record the company's transactions for the current year. In recording actual manufacturing overhead and selling and administrative expenses, entitle the credit part of the entry "Various credits," as sufficient detail is not provided to make the actual credits. Assume that over- or underapplied overhead is treated as an adjustment to Cost of Goods Sold. (Round the overhead rate you calculate and the unit product cost to the nearest cent.)

2. Prepare an income statement and the journal entry to record the company tax liability based on a rate of 46%.

3. Calculate the balance-sheet valuation of the 60,000 staplers which are unsold as of the end of the period.

problems

4—16. *Straightforward calculation and use of a predetermined overhead rate.* Timers, Inc., manufactures a digital stopwatch. It uses an actual/applied overhead system and estimates its overhead costs for the coming year, when it expects to manufacture 200,000 watches, as:

Variable manufacturing overhead:	
Indirect materials	$200,000
Other variable costs	60,000
Fixed manufacturing overhead:	
Indirect labor	400,000
Depreciation	100,000
Utilities	80,000
Other	40,000
Total estimated overhead for production of 200,000 watches	$880,000

Timers applies overhead on the basis of direct labor hours and estimates that each watch takes 2 hours of direct labor time. Actual production did amount to 200,000 stopwatches, and 400,000 hours of direct labor were used. However, actual overhead costs were as follows:

Variable manufacturing overhead:	
Indirect materials	$202,000
Other variable costs	61,000
Fixed manufacturing overhead:	
Indirect labor	407,000
Depreciation	100,000
Utilities	78,000
Other	43,000
Total actual overhead	$891,000

Indirect materials used during the period were taken from inventory. All other overhead costs except depreciation were paid in cash.

REQUIRED: 1. Calculate a predetermined overhead rate for Timers, Inc.

2. Give the entries to record the application of overhead and actual overhead.

3. Suppose that direct material costs per unit are $4 and direct labor costs per unit are $10. During the year 183,000 of the watches produced were sold.

   a. If over- or underapplied overhead is accounted for as an adjustment to Cost of Goods Sold, what amount of Cost of Goods Sold including the overhead adjustment will be shown on the company's income statement for the period?

   b. Give the entry to adjust Cost of Goods Sold and close Manufacturing Overhead Summary.

   c. What will be the balance-sheet carrying value of Timer's Ending Finished Goods Inventory?

4. What caused overhead to be underapplied? What else could have occurred which would have caused it to be underapplied?

4—17.   *Straightforward calculation and use of a predetermined overhead rate.* Decorative Mirrors assembles and sells large mirrors, which it purchases and puts into ornate gold frames. The company uses an actual/applied overhead system and applies overhead on the basis of direct labor hours. Decorative Mirrors estimates its unit overhead costs for the coming year as follows, based on anticipated production of 400,000 mirrors:

Variable manufacturing overhead:	
Indirect materials	$1.00
Rework and repairs	.20
Utilities—variable portion	.15
Fixed manufacturing overhead:	
Indirect labor	2.15
Depreciation	.55
Utilities—fixed portion	.20
Miscellaneous	.25
Total estimated overhead costs	$4.50

Each mirror takes $1\frac{1}{2}$ hours of direct labor time.

During the year, owing to economic conditions, the demand for mirrors began to decline. Decorative Mirrors cut its production and produced only 350,000 mirrors, each of which used $1\frac{1}{2}$ hours of direct labor time. Variable overhead *costs per unit* were exactly as estimated, and fixed manufacturing overhead was at the same *total level* as the company had estimated. Each mirror produced cost $55 for direct materials and $12 for direct labor.

REQUIRED: 1. Calculate the predetermined overhead rate for Decorative Mirrors based on estimated direct labor hours for a production level of 400,000 mirrors.

2. Calculate the amount of over- or underapplied overhead for the period. Indicate whether the amount you calculated is over- or underapplied, and explain why this occurred.

3. Suppose that each mirror had a selling price of $125 and that 320,000 of the 350,000 mirrors produced were sold. Calculate Decorative Mirrors' gross margin for the period, assuming Cost of Goods Sold is adjusted for any over- or underapplied overhead.

4. What is the carrying value of the ending inventory on Decorative's balance sheet?

5. If Decorative had used an actual cost system rather than an actual/applied cost system, what would the carrying value of the ending inventory have been?

6. If the company had been able to anticipate production of only 350,000 mirrors, what would its predetermined overhead rate have been?

4—18.   *Importance of a predetermined overhead rate.*   The manual typewriter division of Superior Office Equipment Company makes the following estimates of its production costs for the coming year.

Variable Costs
per Typewriter

Raw materials	$12.00
Direct labor (2 hours per typewriter)	16.00
Variable overhead:	
Indirect materials	5.00
Indirect labor	6.00
Other	.50

Fixed Overhead
Costs per Month

Indirect labor	$25,000
Depreciation	10,000
Other	18,000

Superior estimates that its production for a three-month period will be as follows: June—5,000 typewriters; July—5,500 typewriters; August—4,200 typewriters.

REQUIRED: 1. Calculate the estimated cost of producing a typewriter for each of the three months, June, July, and August. (Round all dollar amounts to the nearest cent.)

2. Why does the cost per typewriter differ among the three months?

3. How can the company overcome the problem of assigning identical products different unit costs depending on the month in which the unit was produced?

4—19.   *Calculating a predetermined overhead rate.*   Use the costs data given in Problem 4—18.

REQUIRED: 1. Calculate a predetermined overhead rate for the company based on direct labor hours to be used. The company estimates that it will average using 10,000 direct labor hours each month.

2. Calculate a predetermined overhead rate based on direct labor costs, which are estimated to average $80,000 per month.

3. Assume that Superior uses the predetermined overhead rate which you calculated in part 1. During the current year the company actually used 125,000 direct labor hours to manufacture 62,500 typewriters. Variable costs per unit were as estimated, and total fixed cost did not vary from the original estimate.

a. Using the predetermined overhead rate you calculated in part 1, determine the cost of a unit.
b. Calculate the actual cost of a unit produced during the period.
c. Why do your answers to (a) and (b) differ?
d. Was overhead over- or underapplied and by what amount?

4—20. *Journal entries using a predetermined overhead rate and the preparation of a schedule of cost of goods manufactured.* The Chocolate Enterprises of America Company manufactures a milk chocolate bar for which they have made the following cost estimates:

Estimated Costs per Unit Based on a Monthly Production Volume of 800,000 Bars

Primary ingredients (raw materials)	$.04
Direct labor	.03
Manufacturing overhead:	
Variable:	
Packaging materials	.015
Indirect labor	.02
Utilities and other	.01
Fixed:	
Depreciation	.01
Indirect labor	.005
Insurance and taxes	.005
Utilities and other	.005
Cost per bar at a volume level of 800,000:	$.140

Chocolate Enterprises estimates that it will require 5,000 direct labor hours to produce at the 800,000 volume level. As of the beginning of September the company had on hand raw materials costing $10,000 and 20,000 bars of milk chocolate which had been produced in previous periods at a cost of $.135 per bar. There was no beginning work-in-process inventory. The following summarized transactions occurred during the month of September:

a. Purchased $40,000 of raw materials.
b. Placed into process raw materials sufficient to make 800,000 milk chocolate bars at a cost of $.04 per bar.
c. Incurred direct labor costs for the month at the rate of $5 per hour for 5,000 hours.
d. Applied overhead to production based on actual direct labor hours used.
e. Actual overhead costs for the period were as follows:

Packaging	$11,500
Indirect labor	16,000
Utilities and other variable costs	7,800
Depreciation	8,000
Insurance and taxes	4,500
Indirect labor	4,300
Utilities—fixed portion	5,000

f. Transferred to finished goods inventory 800,000 milk chocolate bars.

g. During the month 780,000 milk chocolate bars were sold. The company costs its inventory on a LIFO basis. The selling price per box of 50 bars was $10.95. The company uses a perpetual inventory system.

h. The company incurred selling expenses during the month of September of $16,000 and general and administrative expenses of $20,000. For the credit part of the entry, simply use the term "various credits."

i. Chocolate Enterprises closed any balance in over- or underapplied overhead to cost of goods sold.

j. The company recorded its estimated taxes for the period at a rate of 50%.

REQUIRED:

1. Calculate a predetermined overhead rate for the company based on estimated direct labor hours.

2. Prepare general journal entries to record all the transactions for the month of September.

3. Prepare a schedule of Cost of Goods Manufactured for the period ended September 30.

4. Prepare an Income Statement for the period ended September 30.

5. What balances for Raw Materials and Finished Goods Inventory will appear on a Balance Sheet prepared as of September 30?

4—21. *Calculating a predetermined overhead rate.* Estimated production costs for the Leroy Jones Company follow:

Variable Costs per Unit:	
Raw materials	$ 8.00
Direct labor (1.5 hr per unit)	10.50
Overhead—variable	
Indirect materials	3.50
Indirect labor	7.00
Other	1.25
Fixed Overhead Cost per Quarter:	
Indirect labor	$17,700
Depreciation	16,000
Other	18,500

REQUIRED:

1. Calculate a predetermined overhead rate for the company based on direct labor hours to be used. The company anticipates using 18,000 direct labor hours per month.

2. During the current quarter Jones Company manufactured 45,500 units, using 70,000 direct labor hours. Variable cost per unit as well as total fixed costs were as originally estimated.

   a. Determine the cost per unit, using the predetermined overhead rate calculated above. (Round unit cost to the nearest cent.)

   b. Determine the actual cost of a unit produced during the period. (Round unit cost to the nearest cent.)

   c. Determine the amount of any under- or overapplied overhead. Explain the reason for its existence.

4—22. *Manufacturing costs—relationships.* The following incomplete data relate to operations of the Lyons Manufacturing Company for the past year:

| | INVENTORIES | | OTHER DATA |
	BEGINNING	ENDING	
Raw materials	$105	$115	
Work-in-Process	110	60	
Finished goods	120	141	
Raw materials used			$380
Total manufacturing costs charged to production during the year (raw materials, direct labor, and manufacturing overhead)			721
Selling and administrative expenses			35

REQUIRED: Assuming Lyons applies manufacturing overhead at a rate of 55% of direct labor cost, determine:

1. Cost of raw materials purchased during the year.
2. Direct labor costs during the year.
3. Manufacturing overhead applied.
4. Cost of goods manufactured.
5. Cost of goods available for sale.
6. Adjusted cost of goods sold, assuming actual overhead was $120 for the year and cost of goods sold is adjusted for any over- or underapplied overhead.
7. Net income, assuming sales were $1,000. (Ignore taxes.)

4—23. *Manufacturing costs—relationships, journal entries.* The following data are available for Bendur, Inc.'s *actual* manufacturing costs during its first year of operations:

Variable Cost per Unit:	
Raw materials	$ 7.50
Direct labor (3 hr per unit)	28.50
Indirect materials	3.25
Indirect labor	4.00
Other overhead	.75
Fixed Costs for the Period:	
Indirect labor	$15,000
Depreciation	8,600
Other	22,000

Additional data:

1. Bendur estimated production for the first year at 3,000 units; 3,200 units were actually produced.

2. Ending inventories:

Raw materials	$ 2,250
Work-in-Process	9,300
Finished goods	10,200

3. Sales for the period were $175,000.

REQUIRED: Prepare all journal entries (with brief explanations) for the period to record the above cost data. Actual variable costs per unit were the same as estimated variable cost per unit, while actual total fixed costs were the same as estimated total fixed costs. The company uses an actual product costing system.

Note: To record the entries for the company you will have to calculate the following amounts:

Raw material purchases.
Direct materials, direct labor, and manufacturing overhead charged (debited) to work in process.
The cost of goods transferred from work in process to finished goods inventory.
The cost of goods sold.

4—24. *Development of an overhead rate, allocation required.* Dairy Delight makes a high-priced ice cream and packages it in gallon containers for sale to expensive restaurants and specialty grocery stores. All the company's operations—production, selling, and corporate administration—are housed in the same facility. Dairy Delight's accounting system collects costs for five different cost centers—Production, Selling, Corporation Administration, Buildings and Grounds, and Human Resources and Accounting. Dairy Delight believes that a portion of the Buildings and Grounds cost and Human Resources and Accounting costs should be treated as manufacturing overhead. Before the allocation of any of these costs, Dairy Delight made the following production cost estimates for the coming year:

Estimated
Production
Costs—180,000
Gallons

Direct materials	$108,000
Direct labor	90,000
Manufacturing overhead other than allocated costs	36,000

Estimated costs for the other cost centers are:

	SELLING	CORPORATE ADMINISTRATION	BUILDINGS AND GROUNDS	HUMAN RESOURCES AND ACCOUNTING
Costs	$103,000	$148,000	$96,000	$124,000

Dairy Delight uses an actual/applied product costing system and calculates a predetermined overhead rate on the basis of milk used in the production process. For every gallon of ice cream a half-gallon of milk is used.

Allocation of the costs of Buildings and Grounds and Human Resources and Accounting is based on the following allocation percents; the percent in the case of Buildings and Grounds is related to space occupied and in the case of Human Resources and Accounting is on the basis of number of employees.

	BUILDINGS AND GROUNDS	HUMAN RESOURCES AND ACCOUNTING
Production	50%	35%
Selling	20	40
Corporate Administration	30	25
Total	100%	100%

REQUIRED:
1. Calculate a predetermined overhead rate for Dairy Delight for the coming year.
2. Calculate the estimated cost of producing a gallon of ice cream during the coming year.
3. Dairy Delight would like to earn a profit before taxes of $1 per gallon. Based on this objective, at what level should its selling price be set? (Round cost per unit to the nearest cent.)
4. Suppose that actual overhead costs were exactly as estimated, that 180,000 gallons of ice cream were produced and 95,000 gallons of milk were used. Will overhead be over- or underapplied? Why?

4—25. *Development of a predetermined overhead rate; preparation of an income statement.* The Little Giant Refrigerator Company uses an actual/applied product costing system for assigning costs to the refrigerators it makes. These refrigerators are popular with students, who put them in their dormitory rooms, and for office use. Little Giant estimated its overhead, which it applies on the basis of direct labor hours, as follows for a period in which it anticipated producing 480,000 refrigerators:

Indirect materials	$2,400,000
Indirect labor	1,440,000
Depreciation	1,848,000
Repairs and maintenance	960,000
Utilities	1,200,000
Miscellaneous	720,000
Total estimated overhead	$8,568,000

Little Giant makes two lines of refrigerators—one having a very small, two-tray freezing compartment, the other having a very small refrigeration area and an automatic ice-maker. These products are referred to as "the standard model" and "the ice-maker," respectively. Little Giant plans to make 300,000 of the standard model and 180,000 of the ice-maker next year. Labor requirements are 3 hours for the standard model and $3\frac{1}{2}$ hours for the ice-maker. The company uses the same overhead rate for both models. Actual data for the period are shown below:

	STANDARD MODEL	ICE-MAKER
Direct materials	$9,000,000	$6,120,000
Direct labor:		
905,000 hours	$7,240,000	
633,000 hours		$5,064,000
Units produced	300,000	180,000
Selling price	$135	$150
Units sold	285,000	160,000

Actual
Manufacturing
Overhead

Indirect materials	$2,405,000
Indirect labor	1,370,000
Depreciation	1,850,000
Repairs and maintenance	966,000
Utilities	1,203,000
Miscellaneous	718,000
Total actual overhead	$8,512,000

Selling expenses amounted to $10,206,000, administrative expenses to $8,703,000.

REQUIRED:

1. Calculate the predetermined overhead rate for Little Giant.
2. Calculate the unit costs attached to each of the two models manufactured during the period. (Round to the nearest cent.) Overhead was applied to units produced on the basis of the predetermined rate times actual hours used.
3. By what amount was overhead over- or underapplied for the period? Why?
4. Assume that over- or underapplied overhead is disposed of by making an adjustment to Cost of Goods Sold. Calculate the balance-sheet carrying value of ending inventory for each of the two product lines which Little Giant has on hand at the end of the period.
5. Prepare an income statement for the period. Use a tax rate of 46%.
6. What additional steps would you have had to take if Little Giant had wanted to develop a separate overhead rate for each of the two product lines?

4—26. *Preparation of journal entries.* Use the data in Problem 4—25 along with the following additional information:

1. Purchases of direct materials inventory and indirect materials inventory, all for cash, amounted to $18,000,000 and $3,200,000, respectively.
2. All direct labor costs were paid in cash.
3. With the exception of indirect materials, which were taken from inventory and depreciation, all other overhead costs were paid in cash.

4. All sales were for cash. The company records cost of goods sold and updates its inventory at the time units are sold.

5. Of the selling expenses, $400,000 were depreciation and the remainder were paid in cash. Of the administrative expenses, $550,000 were depreciation and the remainder were paid in cash.

6. Over- or underapplied overhead is treated as an adjustment to Cost of Goods Sold.

REQUIRED: Prepare all the journal entries required to record the transactions of the Little Giant Refrigerator Company. Maintain separate Work-in-Process and Finished Goods Inventory accounts for the two product lines. You do not have to prepare the journal entry to accrue income taxes for the period.

4—27.   *Effect of actual versus applied overhead on product cost; disposal of over- or underapplied overhead.*   The following data relate to the operations of Sparkle-Lots Jewelry, which makes rings using simulated diamonds.

	ESTIMATED DATA FOR THE PERIOD	ACTUAL DATA FOR THE PERIOD
Production in units	500,000 rings	500,000 rings
Direct materials	$15,000,000	$15,000,000
Direct labor hours	$1\frac{1}{4}$ hr/ring	625,000 hr
Direct labor costs	$3,750,000	$3,750,000
Manufacturing overhead	5,400,000	5,510,000
Sales in units	450,000	450,000

Sparkle-Lots uses an actual/applied costing system and applies overhead to rings produced on the basis of direct labor hours.

REQUIRED: 1. Calculate the predetermined overhead rate which was used by Sparkle-Lots in costing its ring production for the period.

2. Calculate cost of goods sold for the period, assuming that over- or underapplied overhead is considered an adjustment to cost of goods sold.

3. Calculate the carrying value of the ending Finished Goods Inventory.

4. Assume that Sparkle-Lots allocated over- or underapplied overhead to the appropriate accounts rather than treating it as an adjustment to Cost of Goods Sold. Calculate:

   a. Cost of Goods Sold.

   b. Ending Finished Goods Inventory.

5. Assume that Sparkle-Lots used an actual costing system rather than an actual/applied system. Calculate:

   a. Cost of Goods Sold.

   b. Finished Goods Inventory.

6. Compare the answers you obtained in parts 4 and 5 and comment.

4—28. *Absorption costing versus variable costing.* The following information was taken from the records of the Garcia Company.

	LAST YEAR	CURRENT YEAR
Beginning inventory (units)	-0-	2,000
Unit sales	8,000	8,000
Unit production	10,000	8,000
Production costs:		
Direct materials	$1	$1
Direct labor	$2	$2
Variable manufacturing overhead	$1	$1
Fixed manufacturing overhead	$40,000	$40,000
Selling expenses:		
Variable	$2	$2 per unit sold
Fixed	$24,000	$24,000
Administrative expenses (all fixed)	$16,000	$16,000
Selling price per unit	$20	$20

The company uses LIFO costing.

REQUIRED:
1. Prepare income statements for the two years using absorption costing.
2. Prepare income statements for the two years using variable costing. Prepare the income statements in the contribution margin format.
3. Determine the ending Finished Goods Inventory at the end of each year under the two costing methods and explain any differences.

4—29. *Absorption versus variable costing.* The Petix Company uses an actual absorption cost system. Selling and administration expenses are treated as period costs. The company costs its inventory using a LIFO basis and as of June 30 had on hand 400,000 units @ $2.25 per unit. The company's monthly sales volume, production, and costs for June, which was a *typical* month, are as follows:

Sales (400,000 units at $3)		$1,200,000
Costs of 400,000 units		
Raw material	$200,000	
Direct labor	400,000	
Manufacturing overhead:		
Variable	100,000	
Fixed	200,000	
Cost of goods manufactured and sold	$900,000	
Selling expense		
($40,000 + $.20 per unit sold)	$120,000	
General and administrative expense		
($30,000 + $.10 per unit sold)	70,000	
Total selling and administrative expenses	$190,000	
Total costs		$1,090,000
Net Income		$ 110,000

In July, sales soared to 500,000 units, but because of a strike production fell to only 200,000 units.

REQUIRED:

1. Prepare an income statement for the month of July based on absorption costing concepts. Assume that Petix was unable to cut back on any of its fixed costs.
2. Prepare an income statement based on absorption costing concepts showing what profits would have been in July if Petix could have produced all 500,000 units which it sold during the period without any increases in fixed costs.
3. Prepare an income statement for the month of July in the contribution format assuming the use of variable costing. Assume the 400,000 units on hand at the end of June are carried at variable cost of $1.75 per unit.
4. Prepare an income statement for the month of July in the contribution format assuming the use of variable costing and the production of 500,000 units.
5. Comment on the different results you obtained in parts 1 through 4.

4—30. *Converting a variable-costing-basis income statement to an absorption-costing-basis income statement.* The Vice-President for Sales of Mason Corporation has received the Income Statement for January. The statement has been prepared on a variable costing basis and is reproduced below. The firm has just adopted a variable costing system for internal reporting purposes.

MASON CORPORATION
Income Statement
for the Month of January
($000 omitted)

Sales	$2,400
Less: Variable Cost of Goods Sold	1,200
Manufacturing Margin	$1,200
Less: Fixed Manufacturing Cost	600
Gross Margin	$ 600
Less: Fixed Selling and Administrative costs	$ 400
Net Income Before Taxes	$ 200

The controller attached the following notes to the statements:

The unit sales price for January was $24.
Production for January was 50,000 units in excess of sales.

REQUIRED: The Vice-President of Sales is not comfortable with the variable costing basis and would like to know what net income would have been under the absorption costing basis.

1. Prepare the January Income Statement on an absorption costing basis.
2. Reconcile and explain the difference between the variable costing and absorption costing net income figures.

chapter five

PRODUCT COST ACCUMULATION SYSTEMS I:

Job Order Costing

OBJECTIVES

After you finish studying this chapter, you should be able to answer the following questions:

- Why do we need more sophisticated cost accumulation systems than those previously discussed?
- When is a cost accumulation system based on the concept of job order costing appropriate in contrast to a process cost system?
- What documentation underlies a job order costing system?
- What journal entries and accounts are required when a job order costing system is used?
- How can a job order costing system be applied by a nonmanufacturing entity?

INTRODUCTION

Many kinds of organizations wish to associate costs with specifically identifiable measures of output—for example, a unit of product, a contract, or a customer. In managerial accounting terminology, these identifiable measures of output are referred to as *jobs*. This chapter describes how costs can be identified with and attached to jobs completed by both manufacturing and service enterprises.

THE NEED FOR PRODUCT COST ACCUMULATION SYSTEMS

In earlier chapters, when we were illustrating journal entries and accounts used to assign costs to products being manufactured, we made at least two simplifying assumptions:

1. We assumed that our manufacturing process was producing homogeneous products.
2. We assumed that all the units begun in the productive process were completed as of the end of the accounting period.

Suppose that instead of only one type of product, such as beanbag chairs, we are producing products of different types in identifiable lots—for example, we are producing nuclear submarines under a contract with the United States Navy. Is it likely that we will have no submarines under construction at the close of our accounting period? Or suppose that we are producing plastic in a continuous production process from petroleum. In the first situation, we will want to identify costs with various lots being produced. In both situations we will want to assign a value to our ending work-in-process inventory. We need more sophisticated cost accumulation systems than those we have previously used. Two such systems are job order costing and process costing.

JOB ORDER COSTING VERSUS PROCESS COSTING

Job order costing and process costing are uniquely suited to different types of costing situations. Job order costing is suitable for organizations which process or service identifiable units or groups of units. For example, the Sikorsky Division of United Technologies is producing helicopters under different contracts. A job order costing approach is well suited to this situation, where it is desirable to collect costs by contract. Each contract represents a different job order. The use of job order costing is not limited to manufacturers. Think of the place where you have your automobile repaired; repair costs are collected for each automobile being serviced. In a hospital, a patient may represent a job order for whom costs are collected.

In contrast to an entity which is producing or servicing identifiable units or groups of units, other enterprises have a homogeneous outflow of product and there is no reason to try to separate one set of outputs from another which is identical. For this type of organization a process cost accounting system is suitable. Examples include chemical processors, flour mills, and petroleum refineries.

OBJECTIVES OF A JOB ORDER COSTING SYSTEM

When a company chooses to use a job order costing system, it is indicating that it wants to identify its output in terms of individual units or homogeneous groups of units. The assumption is that these units of output or groups of units of output can be distinguished, one from the other.

UNDERLYING DOCUMENTATION FOR A JOB ORDER COSTING SYSTEM

The transactions described in an organization's accounts and then summarized in its financial statements are generally supported by a flow of paper known as *documentation*. For example, what evidence do we have that a company made a particular sale? We could look for a purchase order from the customer, a record that goods were shipped, and a copy of the invoice (bill) which was sent to the customer.

With a job order cost system we also have a system of underlying documentation on which the transactions to be recorded are based. Common types of supporting documentation for the costs incurred in completing a particular job include:

Materials requisitions: These documents are used when materials are withdrawn from inventory. They describe the types and amounts of materials and the jobs on which they are going to be used.

Time cards, tickets, or records: These documents are designed to show how much time was used and what type of labor was performed on various jobs.

Job order cost sheets: These records summarize all the costs associated with a particular job.

ILLUSTRATION 5-1

Documents and accounts used in a job order cost accounting system

---

DOCUMENTS

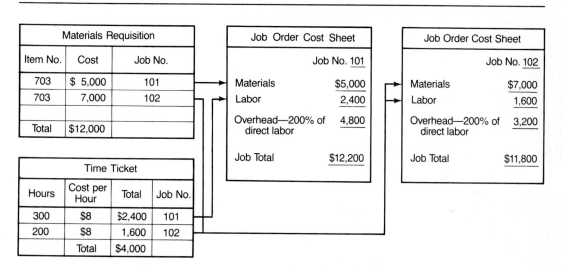

Materials Requisition		
Item No.	Cost	Job No.
703	$ 5,000	101
703	7,000	102
Total	$12,000	

Job Order Cost Sheet	
	Job No. 101
Materials	$5,000
Labor	2,400
Overhead—200% of direct labor	4,800
Job Total	$12,200

Job Order Cost Sheet	
	Job No. 102
Materials	$7,000
Labor	1,600
Overhead—200% of direct labor	3,200
Job Total	$11,800

Time Ticket			
Hours	Cost per Hour	Total	Job No.
300	$8	$2,400	101
200	$8	1,600	102
	Total	$4,000	

GENERAL LEDGER ACCOUNTS	SUBSIDIARY LEDGER—WORK-IN-PROCESS

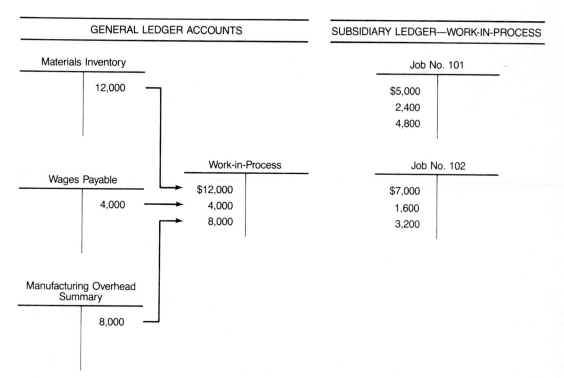

Materials Inventory

12,000

Wages Payable

4,000

Manufacturing Overhead Summary

8,000

Work-in-Process

$12,000
4,000
8,000

Job No. 101

$5,000
2,400
4,800

Job No. 102

$7,000
1,600
3,200

The accounts used in conjunction with a job order costing system are the same that we have discussed already—Raw Materials Inventory, Work-in-Process Inventory, Finished Goods Inventory, and Manufacturing Overhead Summary. Manufacturing costs are collected in the Work-in-Process Inventory account; as jobs are finished, their costs are transferred from Work-in-Process to Finished Goods.

Withdrawals of materials from inventory as reflected on materials requisition forms represent credits to the Raw Materials Inventory account(s) in the general ledger and debits to Work-in-Process. The record of time used, as shown on time cards, provides the basis for debiting Work-in-Process for direct labor costs and crediting wages payable or cash. Most job order costing systems use predetermined overhead, and the recording of the amount of overhead applied as a credit in the Manufacturing Overhead Summary account is offset by a debit to Work-in-Process. Actual overhead costs are summarized on the debit side of the Manufacturing Summary Account, and differences between actual and applied overhead represent under- or overapplication.

Besides a general ledger account, Work-in-Process, a subsidiary ledger is maintained which supports this account and is composed of the various jobs in process. The subsidiary ledger may consist of the job order cost summary sheets described above. If all the amounts shown on individual job cost records in the subsidiary ledger were totaled, this amount should be equal to the total cost shown in the general ledger account, Work-in-Process.

A simplified set of documents and the related general ledger and subsidiary ledger accounts used in a job order costing system are shown in Illustration 5-1 on page 147. We look next at a set of documents actually used for job order costing.

ILLUSTRATIVE JOB ORDER COST DOCUMENTATION

Illustrations 5-2, 5-3, 5-4, and 5-5 are job order cost documents adapted from forms developed by the National Tooling and Machining Association for use by job order machining and tool companies.

Illustration 5-2 shows a job order cost estimate sheet. This sheet may be prepared as a means of coming up with a price quotation for a particular job. It also provides the data that can be used in comparing the actual cost of a job which is completed with the costs anticipated when the job was undertaken.

Note that the form in Illustration 5-2 provides for estimates of direct materials, special tools and supplies, subcontracting (work done by others), and direct labor. The form is designed for the use of a predetermined overhead rate, and thus it does not include a section to summarize the various separate elements of manufacturing overhead.

For a manufacturing entity, as discussed in Chapter 2, manufacturing costs are not the total costs. It, like other types of companies, has selling expenses and general and administrative expenses. Before the company can make a profit on a job, it must cover not only manufacturing costs but also selling and general and administrative expenses. Thus, the estimate sheet provides for the assignment of these costs, which the form terms "general and administrative overhead," to the job to be processed using a predetermined rate, just as is done for manufacturing overhead. In management accounting terminology, the form provides for the calculation of the *full costs* of the job rather than just the *manufacturing costs*.

Note that the estimate sheet is used to help develop a proper price quotation and as a means of comparing anticipated results with actual results. Although it shows the general and administrative overhead being assigned to the products manufactured, for financial reporting purposes this would not be done. Only the manufacturing costs would be assigned to the products being made and carried over into inventory if the products were not sold. The selling and general and administrative expenses would be treated as period costs and would appear on the income statement of the period in which they were incurred.

A company which prepares an estimate sheet similar to the one illustrated can use the cost figures to calculate a suitable selling price. The price may be based on a markup on materials associated with the order plus an additional profit element, or it may simply be based on all cost elements, such as 120% of total costs. The form illustrated assumes that the freight will be charged directly to the purchaser and thus will be added to costs-plus-profit to come up with an estimated price

A material requisition form is shown in Illustration 5-3. Note that it provides for removing the materials from the company's own storage—parts crib or steel storage—or for ordering from an outside vendor. The top half of the form is for acquisition of materials from an outside vendor, the bottom half for the issuance of materials from the company's own storage areas. The key identification element on the requisition is the job number, which allows the company to identify materials put into process with a particular unit of production or batch of units for which it is accumulating costs.

Illustration 5-4 shows the underlying documentation for direct labor inputs. Again the key element is the job number, which permits the identification of labor inputs with a particular job. The form illustrated also provides for the segregation of time into straight time, overtime, and double time. Many companies, such as the machining shops which use these forms, break their labor down into various types of operations. For example, a machining shop might identify the following types of operations: mill, lathe, steel grind, jig, engineering, assemble and groom,

ILLUSTRATION
5-2

Estimate sheet

CUSTOMER _____

PART NAME _____

CUSTOMER'S PART NO. _____

PART DESCRIPTION _____

_____

TOTAL UNITS REQUIRED _____

NUMBER OF UNITS	DELIVERY DATE
_____	_____
_____	_____
_____	_____
_____	_____

ESTIMATE NO. _____

DATE REQUEST RECEIVED _____

DATE ESTIMATE REQUIRED _____

EXACT REPEAT ☐ ⎫
MODIFICATION ☐ ⎬ SEE JOB NO.
NEW ☐ ⎭ _____
CHANGE ORDER ON JOB IN PROCESS ☐

HOW QUOTED: FIRM PRICE ☐
TIME & MATERIAL ☐
TIME & MATERIAL OVERTIME ☐
DISASSEMBLE & QUOTE ☐
ESTIMATED COST ☐

CUSTOMER DRAWING NO. _____

OUR DRAWING NO. _____

JOB NO. _____ (IF AWARDED)

DELIVER TO: _____ VIA: _____ FOB: _____

INSPECTION PROCEDURES: _____

_____

DIRECT MATERIAL

ITEM NO.	MATERIAL SPECIFICATIONS	DATE REQUIRED	ORDER DATE	QUANTITY	PRICE	AMOUNT
					TOTAL	

SPECIAL SUPPLIES AND TOOLS

ITEM NO.	DESCRIPTION	DATE REQUIRED	ORDER DATE	QUANTITY	PRICE	AMOUNT
					TOTAL	

ILLUSTRATION
5-2 (cont'd)

Subcontracting

SUBCONTRACTING

ITEM NO.	DESCRIPTION	DATE REQUIRED	ORDER DATE	QUANTITY	PRICE	AMOUNT
					TOTAL	

DIRECT LABOR

OPERATION NO.	OPERATION	DEPT. NO.	MACHINE NO.	HOURS	RATE	AMOUNT
					TOTAL	

ESTIMATE SUMMARY

EXPENSE	AMOUNT
DIRECT MATERIAL	
SPECIAL SUPPLIES AND TOOLS	
SUBCONTRACT	
DIRECT LABOR	
TOTAL DIRECT COST	
MANUFACTURING OVERHEAD	
GENERAL AND ADMINISTRATIVE OVERHEAD	
TOTAL ESTIMATED COST	
MARK-UP ON MATERIAL @_____%	
PROFIT @_____%	
FREIGHT CHARGES	
ESTIMATED PRICE	
ADJUSTMENTS	
QUOTED PRICE	
NET PROFIT*	

REMARKS:

NET PROFIT AS % OF QUOTED PRICE

_____ %

*QUOTED PRICE MINUS TOTAL ESTIMATED COST AND FREIGHT CHARGES

DATE	PREPARED BY	CHECKED BY	DATE QUOTED

**ILLUSTRATION
5-3**

Material
requisition

ORDER FROM: PARTS CRIB ☐ STEEL STORAGE ☐ OUTSIDE ☐

DATE _____

JOB NO. _____ DEPT. NO _____

DATE REQUIRED _____

VENDOR _____

ADDRESS _____

_____

DATE ORDERED _____

DELIVERY DATE _____

REVISED DELIVERY _____

ITEM	QUANTITY	DESCRIPTION	UNIT PRICE	AMOUNT

REQUESTED BY _____   PURCHASE ORDER NO. _____

APPROVED BY _____ DATE _____ ORDERED BY _____

APPROVED BY _____

ISSUED FROM: PARTS CRIB ☐ STEEL STORAGE ☐

ITEM	QUANTITY	ALL?	SHORT	REMARKS:	ISSUED BY
		☐			
		☐			
		☐			
		☐			
		☐			
		☐			
		☐			
		☐			
		☐			
		☐			

inspection, repair and rework, and "other," assigning a number to each. Using this system, the type of labor input is described on the time record.

The material and labor inputs are summarized for a particular job on a job cost record sheet such as that shown in Illustration 5-5. The materials requisitioned for a particular job are posted from the materials requisition form to the job cost sheet. Direct labor costs are initially recorded on the job operation tickets and then summarized on the job cost sheet. Any subcontracting costs for a particular job are also entered on this summary form. The section called the Completed Job Report summarizes total direct material, special supplies and tools, subcontracting costs, and direct labor costs. Then manufacturing overhead is applied, using the predetermined rate. The result is the total *manufacturing cost* of the job.

In addition, with the form illustrated, a portion of all nonmanufacturing expenses are assigned to the job to come up with what the form terms "total costs" and which we refer to as "full cost." Any freight and miscellaneous charges which are billed directly to the customer are added to the total costs, and this figure is compared with the amount for which the customer is billed—the invoice price—to obtain the net profit on the job. The form also has a column under the section entitled Completed Job Report for entering all the estimated figures previously developed on the estimate sheet. Thus, the manager can quickly compare what he or she had anticipated for costs and revenues with what those figures actually were.

ILLUSTRATION 5-4

Job operation ticket

EMPLOYEE ______________ EMPLOYEE NO. ______________

JOB NO. ______________ JOB DESCRIPTION ______________

OPERATION NO. ______________ OPERATION ______________

DEPT. NO. ______________

MACHINE NO. ______________

TIME	
START	
STOP	
ELAPSED	

LABOR COST	HOURS	RATE	AMOUNT
STRAIGHT TIME			
OVERTIME			
DOUBLE TIME			
TOTAL			

ILLUSTRATION 5-5 Job cost sheet

CUSTOMER _____

PART NAME _____

CUSTOMER'S PART NO. _____

CUSTOMER'S PURCHASE ORDER NO. _____

PART DESCRIPTION _____

SEE _____ BEFORE STARTING

JOB NO. _____

DATE STARTED _____

EXACT REPEAT ☐
MODIFICATION ☐ } SEE JOB NO. _____
NEW ☐
CHANGE ORDER ON JOB IN PROCESS ☐

HOW QUOTED:
FIRM PRICE ☐
TIME & MATERIAL ☐
TIME & MATERIAL OVERTIME ☐
DISASSEMBLE & QUOTE ☐
ESTIMATED COST ☐

NUMBER OF UNITS REQUIRED	DELIVERY DATE	NUMBER OF UNITS DELIVERED	SHIPPING DATE

DELIVER TO: _____ VIA: _____ FOB: _____

INSPECTION PROCEDURES: _____

NUMBER OF UNITS REQUIRED	DELIVERY DATE	NUMBER OF UNITS REQUIRED	SHIPPING DATE

DIRECT LABOR

DATE	OPN. NO.	OPERATION	[CHECK IF COMPLETED]	EMP. NO.	DEPT. NO.	MACH. NO.	STRAIGHT TIME HR.	STRAIGHT TIME RATE	OVERTIME HRS	OVERTIME RATE	DOUBLE TIME HRS	DOUBLE TIME RATE	TOTAL HOURS	AMOUNT	CUMULATIVE AMOUNT
			☐												
			☐												
			☐												
			☐												
			☐												
			☐												
			☐												
			☐												
			☐												
			☐												
														TOTAL	

ILLUSTRATION 5-5 (cont'd)   Direct material

DIRECT MATERIAL

DATE RECEIVED	DATE ORDERED	ITEM NO.	DESCRIPTION	PURCHASE ORDER NO.	QUAN.	PRICE	AMOUNT	CUM. AMOUNT
							TOTAL	

SUBCONTRACT

DATE RECEIVED	DATE ORDERED	ITEM NO.	DESCRIPTION	PURCHASE ORDER NO.	QUAN.	PRICE	AMOUNT	CUM. AMOUNT
							TOTAL	

COMPLETED JOB REPORT

EXPENSE	ESTIMATE	ACTUAL
DIRECT MATERIAL		
SPECIAL SUPPLIES AND TOOLS		
SUBCONTRACT		
DIRECT LABOR		
TOTAL DIRECT COST		
MANUFACTURING OVER HEAD		
GENERAL & ADMINISTRATIVE		
TOTAL COST		
FREIGHT & MISC. CHARGES		
INVOICE PRICE		
NET PROFIT		

ESTIMATED DIRECT LABOR HOURS _____

ACTUAL DIRECT LABOR HOURS _____

REMARKS

NET PROFIT AS % OF INVOICE PRICE [____] %

The record keeping inherent in a job order cost accounting system is easily adaptable to computer technology. Rather than making entries on the various forms manually, we can have this done directly by computer. For example, terminals at various work stations in a large manufacturing enterprise allow the worker to enter (or have entered by someone at the terminal) the time a worker began an operation on a particular job and the time the operation was completed. Requisitions of raw materials can be entered directly onto computer-maintained job order records at the time the raw materials are withdrawn from inventory.

BENEFITS OF A WELL-DESIGNED JOB ORDER COST SYSTEM

When we look at the sample documentation which underlies a well-designed job order cost accounting system, some of its benefits should be apparent. One thing it does is related to financial accounting. It provides a basis for attaching costs to the items being produced and thus facilitates the proper determination of cost of goods sold and inventory valuation.

However, an important additional benefit is the control such a system provides. For example, materials cannot be removed from storage without proper supporting documentation in the form of a materials requisition. Labor and materials used on various jobs and in various operations on those jobs are recorded. Knowing when and where costs were incurred permits the assigning of responsibility to the proper individuals.

If an estimation sheet, such as that shown in Illustration 5-2, is used, a basis for comparing actual and estimated results is provided. Significant deviations from expected performance can be noted and investigated to determine the cause.

THE WORK-IN-PROCESS INVENTORY ACCOUNT

In our previous illustrations we assumed that there was no beginning or ending Work-in-Process Inventory. With a job order costing system it is easy to visualize how ending work-in-process (which is beginning work-in-process for the next accounting period) is collected. Job order cost sheets serve as the collection mechanism for a job order costing system. Those which relate to jobs that have not been finished as of the end of the accounting period provide the data necessary to cost ending Work-in-Process Inventory.

FLOW OF COSTS THROUGH A JOB ORDER COSTING SYSTEM

To illustrate how costs are collected and flow through the accounts of an organization which uses a job order cost system, we are using a small contracting firm, Whitworth Machines, which specializes in manufacturing grinding machines.

During the current accounting period the company worked on five different jobs. The transactions of the company are described below, together with the related journal entries which would be required to record these transactions. At the beginning of the accounting period Whitworth had one job in process on which the following costs had been incurred:

Job #101	
Direct Materials	$10,000
Direct Labor	15,000
Overhead @ 80% of Direct Labor	12,000
	$37,000

a. There was no raw materials beginning inventory. During the period, $75,000 of raw materials were purchased.

Raw Materials Inventory	75,000	
Accounts Payable		75,000

b. Direct materials requisitioned for the jobs in process at the beginning of the period and jobs started during the current period were as follows:

Job #101	$ 8,000
Job #102	17,000
Job #103	12,000
Job #104	20,000
Job #105	4,000
	$61,000

Work in Process	61,000	
Raw Materials Inventory		61,000

Note: In the individual job order cost records in the subsidiary ledger, the direct material, direct labor, and manufacturing overhead inputs would be recorded as the Work-in-Process Control account in the general ledger is debited for the summarized amounts of these inputs.

c. Direct labor costs incurred for the job in process at the beginning of the accounting period and jobs started during the current period were as follows:

Job #101	$ 4,000
Job #102	12,000
Job #103	8,000
Job #104	16,000
Job #105	7,000
	$47,000

Work-in-Process	47,000	
Wages Payable		47,000

d. Overhead is applied to jobs on the basis of 80% of direct labor costs.

Job #101	$ 4,000 × .80 =	$ 3,200
Job #102	12,000 × .80 =	9,600
Job #103	8,000 × .80 =	6,400
Job #104	16,000 × .80 =	12,800
Job #105	7,000 × .80 =	5,600
		$37,600

Work-in-Process	37,600	
Manufacturing Overhead Summary		37,600

e. Actual overhead costs for the year amounted to $35,000.

Manufacturing Overhead Summary	35,000	
Cash, Wages Payable, Accumulated Depreciation, and		35,000
various other accounts		

Note: To shorten the illustration, we have combined two steps—recording the actual overhead in individual expense accounts and then closing those expense accounts to Manufacturing Overhead Summary.

f. Jobs #101, 102, and 104 were completed during the period, while Jobs #103 and 105 were still in process at the end of the period.

Finished Goods Inventory	139,600	
Work-in-Process Inventory		139,600

	JOB #101	JOB #102	JOB #104	TOTAL TO FINISHED GOODS
Costs inputs last period	37,000	—	—	
Materials	8,000	17,000	20,000	
Labor	4,000	12,000	16,000	
Overhead	3,200	9,600	12,800	
Totals	$52,200	$38,600	$48,800	$139,600

g. Jobs #101 and 104 were sold at 150% of their manufacturing costs.

Accounts Receivable	151,500	
Cost of Goods Sold	101,000	
Sales		151,500
Finished Goods Inventory		101,000

	COST OF GOODS SOLD			SALES
Job #101	$ 52,200	×	150%	$ 78,300
#104	$ 48,800	×	150%	$ 73,200
	$101,000			$151,500

h. Overapplied manufacturing overhead was closed out to Cost of Goods Sold.

Manufacturing Overhead Summary	2,600[a]	
Cost of Goods Sold		2,600

[a] 37,600 applied − $35,000 actual = $2,600 overapplied.

General Ledger Accounts

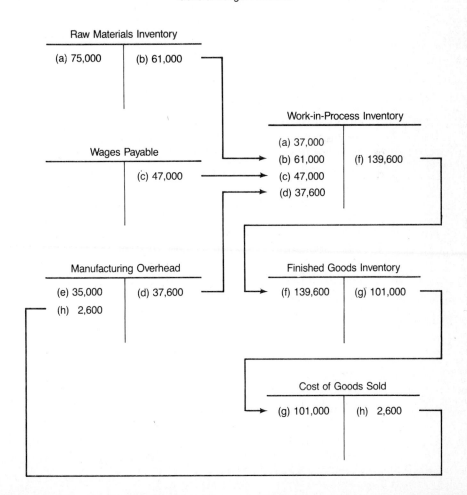

Subsidiary Ledger—Work-in-Process

Job #101	
Beg. Bal. 37,000	(f) 52,200
(b) 8,000	
(c) 4,000	
(d) 3,200	

Job #102	
(b) 17,000	(f) 38,600
(c) 12,000	
(d) 9,600	

Job #103	
(b) 12,000	
(c) 8,000	
(d) 6,400	

Job #104	
(b) 20,000	(f) 48,800
(c) 16,000	
(d) 12,800	

Job #105	
(b) 4,000	
(c) 7,000	
(d) 5,600	

In looking at these entries the concept of control and subsidiary accounts should be reviewed. The journal entries illustrated show the debits and credits to the Work-in-Process control account only. A subsidiary ledger composed of the various jobs must also be maintained because one of our objectives is to identify the costs incurred with the various jobs being completed. Thus when raw materials are put into process not only is the Work-in-Process control account debited, but each of the job order cost records is updated to reflect the material inputs to each job. The same process is followed with respect to direct labor. The control account, Work-in-Process, is debited with the total direct labor inputs for the period. The labor inputs on each job are entered on the job order cost records.

In this illustration we have assumed the use of a predetermined overhead rate based on direct labor costs. As jobs are completed and transferred to finished goods at the end of each accounting period, overhead is calculated based on the labor inputs for each job and entered on that job order cost record. The total overhead charge is debited to the Work-in-Process control account.

As is true of other control accounts which summarize the detail contained in supporting subsidiary accounts, the balance of the control account should be equal to the sum of the balances in the subsidiary accounts. During the accounting period, as completed jobs are transferred into finished goods, the control account, Work-in-Process, is credited for the total costs of the jobs being transferred. At the end of the accounting period the inputs of direct materials, direct labor, and overhead on each individual job should be equal to the balance—that is, the ending inventory—of Work-in-Process.

At the end of its accounting period the company will prepare a Cost of Goods Manufactured Schedule and an Income Statement. For Whitworth Machinery, based on the data contained in the illustration, the Cost of Goods Manufactured Schedule would appear as follows:

WHITWORTH MACHINERY
Cost of Goods Manufactured
for the Year Ended December 31

Direct Materials	$ 61,000
Direct Labor	47,000
Manufacturing Overhead Applied	37,600
Total Manufacturing Costs this period	$145,600
Add: Work-in-Process Beginning Inventory	37,000
Total Manufacturing Costs	$182,600
Less: Work-in-Process Ending Inventory	43,000
Cost of Goods Manufactured	$139,600

Assuming the company had selling expenses of $18,000 and general and administrative expenses of $17,000, its Income Statement for the period is shown below.

WHITWORTH MACHINERY
Income Statement
for the Year Ended December 31

Sales		$151,500
Cost of Goods Sold	$101,000	
Less: Overapplied Overhead	(2,600)	98,400
Gross Margin		$ 53,100
Operating Expenses:		
Selling Expenses	18,000	
General and Administrative	17,000	35,000
Net Income		$ 18,100

Cost of Goods Sold was calculated by taking the costs associated with the two jobs which were sold during the period. Looking at the subsidiary ledger accounts for these two jobs, we can see that the cost of manufacturing Job #101 was $52,200 and that of Job #104 was $48,800, summing to our Cost of Goods Sold figure before the adjustment for overapplied overhead.

Our balance sheet will show the following amounts and types of inventories:

Raw Materials Inventory	$14,000
Work-in-Process	43,000
Finished Goods Inventory	38,600

Work-in-Process consists of two jobs not completed during the accounting period: Job #103, on which costs of $26,400 have been accumulated, and Job #105, on which costs of $16,600 have been incurred, as of the end of the accounting period. Finished Goods Inventory consists of one job which was started and finished during the period—Job #102, which cost the company $38,600 to make.

ANOTHER LOOK AT APPLIED OVERHEAD

Our illustration can be used to point out again the usefulness of using a predetermined overhead rate. Whitworth Machinery worked on only five jobs during the accounting period. But each job was unique. Imagine the cost and problems of allocating costs such as factory depreciation, utilities, and supervisory salaries to these various jobs—and yet there were only five jobs in process during the period. Such an allocation would require detailed records, or the allocations would be quite arbitrary. With a predetermined overhead rate these problems and costs are avoided.

In addition, in pricing its various jobs or in negotiating with customers for contracts, the company must be able to come up with an estimate of the costs of producing the job. Rather than trying to determine the indirect costs associated with a particular job, the company can use a predetermined overhead rate to provide a cost estimate readily.

JOB ORDER COSTING AND THE SERVICE ENTERPRISE

The service enterprise does not have an inventory of products which it has produced nor does it encounter problems in assigning a proper amount of costs to products which are still in process at the end of the accounting period. Yet the concepts of a job order costing system are very useful to many types of service enterprises. These organizations want to know how much it costs them to perform a certain service for a customer and what kind of price they should quote to realize a profit. Thus they, too, need a system whereby they can associate costs with a particular job.

Consider a company, Seminars International, which offers a number of programs to various kinds of enterprises. Seminars International provides materials and a qualified instructor for the seminar participants. Assume the company is contacted by Bostick Plastics and asked to quote a price for an all-day seminar for thirty middle-level managers on stress management. The seminar will be held at Bostick Plastics' headquarters.

Seminars International could use an estimate sheet just as a manufacturing firm does to develop the data needed for a suitable price quotation. If Seminars International has a job order cost accounting system and gets the job from Bostick, it will track its various costs which are associated with the seminar on stress management. The job order cost accumulation form shown in Illustration 5-6 could be used by a firm such as Seminars International to summarize the costs which can be directly associated with a particular program and to allocate a portion of all other costs to the seminar. The costs which are allocated and termed "general overhead" on the form include items such as selling expenses and costs related to the general administration of Seminars International.

Hospitals, CPA firms, dentists, doctors, lawyers, and repair shops are examples of service enterprises which commonly employ the basic idea of a job order costing system—that is, to accumulate costs for an identifiable job, be it patient, client, or automobile. Other types of service enterprises may not find the job order costing approach applicable. For example, a customer of a bank may maintain a checking account, a savings account, a safety deposit box, and a bank charge card. Rather than trying to determine the cost of serving this particular customer, the bank would probably try to develop an accounting system which would enable the bank to determine the cost of serving checking and savings accounts of various sizes, of maintaining safety deposit boxes, and of providing a charge card service.

ILLUSTRATION 5-6

Seminars International job cost summary sheet

Company Name _____

Company Address _____

Seminar Dates _____ Location _____

Instructor _____

Number of Participants _____

Direct Costs:

    Participants' materials $_____

    Instructional costs:

        Instructor's fee $_____
        Transportation   _____
        Hotel   _____
        Meals   _____
        Other   _____

    General Overhead   _____

    Total costs   _____

    Invoice price   _____

    Profit   _____

chapter highlights

A job order cost accounting system is suitable for a company producing goods and services which can be specifically identified, either individually or in groups. As raw materials and labor are used in the productive process, the inputs of each are associated with jobs in process during the period.

Generally, a predetermined overhead rate is used to assign overhead to each job. As jobs are completed, they are transferred into finished goods. Ending Work-in-Process Inventory consists of those jobs which are still in process at the conclusion of the accounting period. Finished Goods Inventory covers those jobs which have been finished during the period but have not been sold.

questions

1. For what types of enterprises is a job order cost accounting system suitable?
2. What is the primary objective of a job order cost accounting system?
3. Give three examples involving service types of enterprises for which a job order costing system may be appropriate.
4. Distinguish between a control account and a subsidiary account.
5. Give three examples of situations where a control account supported by subsidiary accounts may be used.
6. How does using a predetermined overhead rate simplify the record keeping for a company which uses job order cost accounting?
7. List the three inventory accounts which will appear on the balance sheet of a manufacturing company which uses a job order costing system and give a brief description of what will be included in the ending balance of each account.
8. Will Cost of Goods Manufactured during a period be equal to Cost of Goods Sold for that period? Why or why not?
9. A company applied $85,000 of manufacturing overhead during an accounting period and had actual overhead costs of $80,000. Assuming the company adjusts Cost of Goods Sold for over- or underapplied overhead,

what effect will the difference between actual and applied overhead have on Cost of Goods Sold?

10. How is a predetermined overhead rate useful in setting prices for a company which uses job order costing?

11. A company made an error in recording the costs of some raw materials which were purchased. The company uses a job order costing system. The error was not discovered during the accounting period. What accounts of the company will probably be misstated because of the error?

12. What items are debited to the Work-in-Process account during the period, and when is it credited, if a job order cost accounting system is used?

13. An accountant maintained that a transaction which had been recorded was supported by appropriate documentation. What does this mean?

14. What are three major types of documents used to support the transactions recorded when a job order costing system is in use? Describe briefly how each is used.

15. We have discussed the use of a predetermined overhead rate in product costing. Why do companies which use job order costing systems sometimes develop a rate for associating all other company costs (selling and administrative expenses) with individual jobs? What effect does the use of such a rate have on the costs of jobs for inventory valuation purposes?

16. In a job order costing system, what major pieces of information would you expect to find on a materials requisition?

17. The costs recorded on job order cost sheets for jobs which were incomplete as of the end of the accounting period total $586,000. Where else should this number be found in the company's accounting records?

18. Will total manufacturing costs incurred in an accounting period be equal to the Cost of Goods Manufactured for that period? Why or why not?

19. What is the relationship of Cost of Goods Manufactured to Finished Goods Inventory?

20. At the end of an accounting period a company found that it had underapplied manufacturing overhead. What does this mean about the costs of jobs on which the company worked during the period?

exercises

5—1. A company engaged in the following transactions (which have been summarized) during its accounting period. It uses a job order cost accounting system.

a. Purchased raw materials, 10,000 units @ $2 per unit. The company had no beginning inventory of raw materials.

b. Put into process 8,000 units of raw materials, distributed among jobs as follows:

Job #67	3,000 units
Job #68	4,000
Job #69	1,000

c. Direct labor inputs, which cost the company $7 per hour, were as follows:

Job #67	200 hours
Job #68	400
Job #69	100

d. Manufacturing overhead is applied at the rate of $5 per direct labor hour. Actual manufacturing overhead costs amounted to $3,000.

e. Job #67 was begun last period and had $1,200 of costs put into it during that period. It was completed during the current period and sold for $12,000.

f. Job #68 was completed during the period and is still unsold, while Job #69 is in process as of the end of the accounting period.

REQUIRED: Calculate the following amounts:

1. Raw Materials Ending Inventory.
2. Work-in-Process Ending Inventory.
3. Finished Goods Ending Inventory.
4. The Gross Margin on the sale of Job #67.

5—2.   Use the information in Exercise 5—1.

REQUIRED: Prepare a Schedule of Cost of Goods Manufactured for the period.

5—3.   Use the information in Exercise 5—1 and assume that the company incurred Selling and Administrative Expenses of $1,800 and adjusted Cost of Goods Sold for over- or underapplied overhead.

REQUIRED: Prepare an Income Statement for the company.

5—4.   Use the information in Exercise 5—1.

REQUIRED: 1. Set up general ledger T-accounts for Raw Materials Inventory, Work-in-Process Inventory, Finished Goods Inventory, Manufacturing Overhead, and Cost of Goods Sold and record the transactions described in Exercise 5—1 in these accounts. Also set up a subsidiary Work-in-Process ledger which has an account for each job. Begin your recording by entering the beginning balances described in transaction (e). Close any balance in manufacturing overhead to Cost of Goods Sold.

2. Provide calculations which indicate that the subsidiary ledger for Work-in-Process is in agreement with the control account in the General Ledger for Work-In-Process at the end of the accounting period.

5—5.   Quality Service Auto Repair wants to use a predetermined overhead rate in conjunction with its job order cost accounting system. It estimates its overhead cost for the period at $80,000 and wishes to apply overhead to each repair job on which it works on the basis of direct labor hours. It etimates that, during the period, it will use 20,000 direct labor hours at a cost of $8.50 per hour.

REQUIRED:
1. Calculate the predetermined overhead rate for Quality.
2. In repairing an automobile designated as Job #3,028, $35 of parts and 5 hours of direct labor were used. If Quality wants to charge the customer its costs of repairing plus 70% of those costs, for what amount should it bill the customer?
3. At the end of the period, Quality's actual overhead costs amounted to $78,000. However, Quality did use 20,000 direct labor hours during the period. Determine whether overhead was over- or underapplied and by what amount.

5—6. Given below are some general ledger accounts for Kitrell Manufacturing Company. For each account, describe the nature of the transactions which will cause the account to be debited or credited. The first account is filled in as an example.

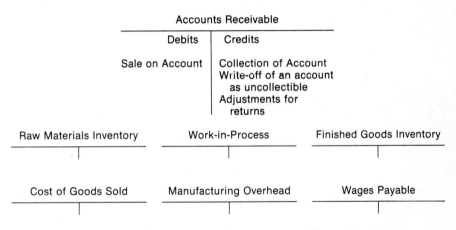

Accounts Receivable	
Debits	Credits

Sale on Account	Collection of Account
	Write-off of an account
	   as uncollectible
	Adjustments for
	   returns

Raw Materials Inventory	Work-in-Process	Finished Goods Inventory

Cost of Goods Sold	Manufacturing Overhead	Wages Payable

5—7. (CMA adapted) The following data apply to the Chen Company.

Department 203
Work-in-Process
Beginning of Period

JOB NO.	MATERIAL	LABOR	OVERHEAD	TOTAL
1376	$17,500	$22,000	$33,000	$72,500

Department 203
Costs for the Year

INCURRED BY JOBS	MATERIAL	LABOR	TOTAL
1376	$ 1,000	$ 7,000	$ 8,000
1377	26,000	53,000	79,000
1378	12,000	9,000	21,000
1379	4,000	1,000	5,000

NOT INCURRED BY JOBS	MATERIALS	LABOR	OTHER	TOTAL
Indirect materials and supplies	$15,000	—	—	$15,000
Indirect labor	—	$53,000	—	53,000
Employee benefits	—	—	$23,000	23,000
Depreciation	—	—	12,000	12,000
Supervision	—	20,000	—	20,000

Department 203
Overhead Rate
for the Year

Budgeted overhead		
Variable—Indirect materials		$16,000
	Indirect labor	56,000
	Employee bene-	
	fits	24,000
Fixed—Supervision		20,000
	Depreciation	12,000
	Total	$128,000
Budgeted direct labor dollars		$ 80,000
Rate per direct labor dollar		160%
($128,000 ÷ 80,000)		

REQUIRED: 1. Calculate actual overhead for Department 203 for the year.
2. Calculate any over- or underapplied overhead for the period.

5—8. The Computer Services Division of a large bank uses a job order cost accounting system. In setting up a predetermined overhead rate, the division estimated total overhead costs for the upcoming quarter at $64,800. Overhead is applied on the basis of direct labor costs, which are anticipated as 1,200 direct labor hours for the quarter at a newly negotiated labor rate of $15 per hour.

REQUIRED: 1. Calculate the charge to the Trust Department for a job which required 2.5 hours of direct labor and required $10 worth of paper.
2. It was determined at the end of the quarter that the Computer Services Division had incurred $68,000 in overhead costs and had used 1,200 direct labor hours during the period. Explain how this difference between actual and anticipated results would be accounted for.

5—9. The Woo Company uses a job order costing system and a predetermined overhead rate to apply overhead to individual job orders. Jobs are processed through two departments, and overhead is applied on the basis of machine hours in Department A and on the basis of direct labor hours in Department B. A budget prepared at the beginning of the period showed the following estimates:

	DEPARTMENT A	DEPARTMENT B
Direct labor hours	75,000	150,000
Machine hours	260,000	27,000
Direct labor cost	$900,000	$1,650,000
Manufacturing overhead	$793,000	$630,000

Job #210 has accumulated the following costs:

	DEPARTMENT A	DEPARTMENT B
Direct labor cost	$13,500	$ 6,200
Direct materials	$18,000	$34,000
Machine hours	1,800	50
Direct labor hours	500	290

REQUIRED: **1.** Determine the predetermined overhead rate for Department A and Department B.

2. Determine the total overhead cost of Job #210.

3. What is the total cost of Job #210?

5—10. (AICPA adapted) Tillman Corporation uses a job order cost system and has two departments, M and A. Budgeted manufacturing costs for the year were as follows:

	DEPT. M	DEPT. A
Direct materials	$700,000	$100,000
Direct labor ($10/hr)	200,000	800,000
Manufacturing overhead	600,000	400,000

Tillman applies manufacturing overhead to production orders on the basis of direct labor cost, using departmental rates predetermined at the beginning of the year based on the annual budget. Actual material and labor costs charged to Job #432 during the year were:

	DEPT. M	DEPT. A
Direct material		$25,000
Direct labor:		
Dept. M	$8,000	
Dept. A	————	$12,000

REQUIRED: **1.** Calculate predetermined overhead rates for Departments M and A.

2. Calculate the total manufacturing cost associated with Job #432.

3. Assume Tillman applies manufacturing overhead on the basis of direct labor hours. Calculate the total manufacturing overhead cost attributed to Job #432.

5—11. Novelty Printing makes wall posters. Some of its business is done under contract; other printings are made for inventory in anticipation of future orders. Novelty uses a job order costing system, and its records show the following information for the period:

	JOB #708	JOB #709	JOB #710	JOB #711
Put into process last period	$11,000	4,000	—	—
Added during the current period:				
Direct materials and direct labor	$12,000	$15,000	$14,000	$ 7,000
Direct labor hours used	1,000	1,400	1,000	600

Estimated manufacturing overhead for the period was $60,000. Overhead is applied to jobs on the basis of direct labor hours, which were estimated to be 4,000 for the period.

Jobs #708 and #709 were finished during the period and transferred to Finished Goods Inventory. Job #709 was sold at a markup of 50% of its manufacturing costs.

REQUIRED: 1. At what rate per direct labor hour was overhead applied to jobs during the period?

2. Calculate the following amounts:

   a. Beginning Work-in-Process Inventory.
   b. Ending Work-in-Process Inventory.
   c. Ending Finished Goods Inventory.

3. Prepare the journal entries to record:

   a. The transfer of finished jobs out of Work-in-Process Inventory.
   b. The sale of Job #709 for cash. Assume the company records Cost of Goods Sold and updates its inventory records as inventory is sold.

5—12.   Custom Craftsmen accumulated the following costs and data for the past accounting period:

	JOB #556	JOB #557	JOB #558	JOB #559
Beginning Work-in-Process	$12,000	—	—	—
Added this period:				
Direct materials	15,000	$23,000	$24,000	$13,000
Direct labor	20,000	16,000	19,000	15,000
Applied Overhead	12,000	9,600	11,400	9,000

Additional data:

a. Beginning Direct Materials Inventory amounted to $17,000. Purchases of direct raw materials for the period amounted to $76,000 and were paid in cash.

b. The average cost of an hour of direct labor time during the period was $10. All direct labor costs were paid in cash.

c. Actual overhead amounted to $47,000, of which all but $17,000 of depreciation was paid for in cash.

d. At the end of the period Job #558 is still in process.

e. At the beginning of the period Job #554 was on hand. The job had cost $45,000 to complete. At the end of the period, Job #557 is still in finished goods inventory.

f. Selling and administrative expenses for the period amounted to $78,000, of which $12,000 was depreciation, $8,000 was incurred on account, and the remainder was paid in cash.

g. The jobs which were sold were sold for cash at a markup of 100% of manufacturing costs.

REQUIRED: 1. The estimated direct labor hours on which the overhead rate was based was exactly equal to the number of direct labor hours actually used. At what rate per direct labor hour was overhead applied to production during the period?

2. Give the journal entries to record the transactions described above. Account for any over- or underapplied overhead as an adjustment to Cost of Goods Sold.

3. Prepare an income statement for the period and record the accrued income taxes for the period at a rate of 24%.

4. Calculate the balance-sheet carrying values of all ending inventories.

5—13. The following relates to the Merrimac Co., which manufactures custom-designed golf carts. It uses a job order costing system and a predetermined overhead rate in costing its products (000 omitted from all data).

WIP Beginning Inventory, Job #200	$ 800
Finished Goods Beginning Inventory, Job #190	$5,000

Inputs during the period:

	JOB #200	JOB #201	JOB #202
Direct materials	$2,000	$1,600	$1,600
Direct labor	1,400	1,800	1,200

Overhead is applied on the basis of 150% of direct labor costs. Actual overhead amounted to $6,200.

REQUIRED:
1. Give the general journal entry to record this period's inputs for materials, labor, and overhead. Materials were taken from inventory, and labor costs were paid in cash.

2. Give the general journal entry to transfer Jobs #200 and #201 to finished goods.

3. Assuming the company sells Job #201 for $8,500, calculate the company's gross margin, assuming any over- or underapplied overhead is treated as an adjustment to cost of goods sold.

4. Calculate:

a. Ending Work-in-Process Inventory.

b. Ending Finished Goods Inventory.

5—14. Larry and Lynn Smith are opening a catering service which will provide decorations, food, and drinks for a variety of social events, ranging from formal weddings to poolside cook-outs. They have come to seek your advice on a number of issues.

REQUIRED: Provide answers to the following questions which Larry and Lynn have posed to you:

1. How do they go about developing a system which will allow them to quote a price for a particular event? Be specific.

2. How can they be sure that the price they quote covers not only the costs directly associated with the event but a proportional share of all other costs of running the business plus a profit margin? Be specific.

3. What would be an effective way for them to keep records with respect to the events they are catering?

5—15. Reflections, Inc., is a vanity press. Anyone who has written a book may have it published in a hardcover form and run in minimum quantities of 1,000 copies by Reflections, Inc. The output cannot be distinguished from books published by commercial publishers unless one is familiar with the name, Reflections, Inc. Reflections has developed the following estimated average cost data:

	BOOKS WITH LESS THAN 150 PAGES	BOOKS WITH 150 TO 300 PAGES
Direct materials per book	$ 5	$ 8
Direct labor	12	14

Overhead costs related to book production are estimated to total $330,000 for the coming year and are to be applied on the basis of direct material costs. Reflections hopes to publish 30,000 copies of books which have fewer than 150 pages and 50,000 copies of books which are longer.

REQUIRED:

1. Calculate the estimated unit publishing cost for the two lengths of books which Reflections publishes.

2. An accounting professor has written a manuscript entitled *Applying Nonparametric Statistics to Decision Problems of Bicycle Manufacturers.* Since he has been unable to find a commercial publisher for his manuscript, he asks Reflections for a price quotation for 5,000 copies. The book in published form will be approximately 280 pages in length.

   a. How much of Reflections' total estimated overhead costs associated with production would be applied to this production run?

   b. Reflections estimates that company costs not related directly to production of the books (selling and administration) will amount to $5 per book. If Reflections wants to make a profit of $3 per book, what price will it have to quote the professor for the publishing job?

3. What steps are necessary before a figure for nonproduction costs per book can be calculated?

problems

5—16. *Straightforward job order cost, one period of transactions.* During the month of May the Lightner Manufacturing Company engaged in the following transactions:

a. Purchased 50,000 units of raw materials on account at a cost of $3 per unit. It had a beginning inventory of raw materials of 10,000 units at $2 per unit and uses a LIFO system in costing out its units.

b. During May the company put into process 48,000 units of raw materials, distributed among the following jobs:

Job #789	10,000 units
Job #790	15,000
Job #791	12,000
Job #792	4,000
Job #793	7,000

c. Direct labor hours put into each job during the period at a cost of $6 per hour were as follows:

Job #789	2,000 hours
Job #790	3,500
Job #791	1,800
Job #792	1,400
Job #793	600

d. Manufacturing overhead is applied at the rate of 95% of direct labor costs.
e. Actual manufacturing overhead costs were:

Indirect labor	$18,000
Depreciation	12,000
Indirect materials	7,000
Utilities	13,000
Other	5,000

Except for depreciation, all overhead costs were paid for with cash.

f. Job #789 was in process at the beginning of the period and had accumulated $13,000 of costs during the previous period. During the month of May that job and Jobs #790 and #791 were transferred to Finished Goods.

g. At the beginning of May Job #786 was on hand. It had cost the company $32,000 to complete. Jobs #786 and #790 were sold at 170% of the manufacturing costs on each job. The company uses a perpetual inventory system. The sales were for cash.

h. Selling and general administrative costs for the month were $18,000 and $25,000, respectively. Of these amounts $10,000 was depreciation; the other costs were paid in cash.

Additional information: Any over- or underapplied overhead is considered as an adjustment to Cost of Goods Sold at the end of each month.

REQUIRED:
1. Record the transactions described above in general journal form.
2. Prepare the necessary T-accounts for the data described above and enter the proper amounts in each account. You should set up a subsidiary ledger of work-in-process with a T-account for each job.
3. Prepare a Schedule of Cost of Goods Manufactured for the month of May.
4. Prepare an Income Statement for the month of May.
5. List the inventory accounts with appropriate balances which the company will show on its May 31 balance sheet.

5—17. *Two departments.* The Songbird Company makes birdhouses of several different styles. It produces some units for inventory but produces generally under contract. It uses a job order costing system which has the contract as the unit of accountability. In other words, each contract is considered a job order. Songbird maintains two departments; one saws the birdhouses out of redwood, the other assembles the houses. Data for the two departments are as follows for the month of September:

Sawing
Department

	Contract No.				
	205	206	207	208	209
August inputs	$800				
September inputs:					
Raw material units					
used	100	150	217	75	142
Direct labor hours					
used	80	120	160	50	74

Manufacturing overhead in the Sawing Department is applied at the rate of $.75 per direct labor hour. Raw material unit costs average $2, while direct labor costs average $5 per hour.

Assembling
Department

	Contract No.				
	203	205	206	207	208
August inputs:					
Sawing	$1,040				
Assembling	300				
September:					
Costs transferred in	?	?	?	?	?
from Sawing					
Direct labor hours	100	120	180	240	160

Direct labor costs in the Assembling Department average $6 per hour, and manufacturing overhead is applied at the rate of 30% of direct labor costs.

Additional information: Contract No. 209 was still in process in Sawing at the end of September, while Contract No. 208 was still in process in the Assembling Department at the end of September. Contract Nos. 203, 205, and 207 were sold for 200% of manufacturing costs. Contract No. 206 was put into inventory.

REQUIRED: 1. Give the journal entry to record all the inputs into Contract #206 in the Sawing Department during September.
2. Calculate the gross profit on Contract #203. Assume there was no over- or underapplied overhead.
3. Calculate the total work-in-process ending inventory for the Songbird Company as of September 30.
4. Calculate the finished goods ending inventory for Songbird as of September 30.

5—18.   *Cost of Goods Manufactured Statement*

REQUIRED: Calculate the amounts necessary to complete the Cost of Goods Manufactured Statements in each of the following cases.

	CASE A	CASE B	CASE C	CASE D
Direct Materials Usage:				
Beginning inventory	$?	$ 80,000	$ 50,000	$ 150,000
Purchases	90,000	?	300,000	400,000
Available for Sale	100,000	340,000	350,000	?
Ending Inventory	?	90,000	75,000	100,000
Direct Materials Used	92,000	?	?	450,000
Direct labor	200,000	110,000	225,000	370,000
Manufacturing Overhead	100,000	140,000	300,000	?
Total Manufacturing Costs	?	500,000	?	1,020,000
Beginning Work-in-Process	80,000	?	230,000	?
Total	472,000	680,000	?	?
Less: Ending Work-in-Process				
Inventory	?	120,000	?	130,000
Cost of Goods Manufactured	372,000	?	850,000	940,000

5—19. *Costing services.*   The Memorial Hospital is trying to determine an appropriate cost at which to bill patients who are not in any of its special care units. It has developed the following estimated annual data:

Nursing staff salaries	$900,000
Depreciation of equipment	300,000
Maintenance and repairs	450,000
Utilities	290,000
Depreciation of building	100,000
Other	250,000

REQUIRED: 1. What kind of costs can be assigned directly to a patient?
2. Which of the costs listed above, if any, are variable?
3. What other data are required before a billing rate can be determined?
4. Assume that the hospital decides to develop a billing rate based on the cost data provided, the number of beds, an assumed occupancy rate, and a return over costs of 100% to contribute toward covering other hospital costs. Memorial Hospital maintains 150 beds and estimates an 80% occupancy rate based on a 360-day year. On this basis calculate the proposed billing rate per bed per day for Memorial. (Round to the nearest dollar.)
5. Jack Lamont was a patient in Memorial for 6 days. Drug and other costs which were billed directly to Jack for the 6-day period amounted to $732. Calculate the total amount for which Jack will be billed.

5—20. *Job order costing for two periods.*   Relevant data for the Douglas Manufacturing Company, a custom producer of cabinets, for the months of October and November are as follows.

			Job No.		
	1001	1002	1003	1004	1005
September inputs	$ 5,000				
October inputs:					
Materials	$10,000	$ 7,000	$13,500	—	—
Direct labor	21,000	12,000	18,000	—	—
November inputs:					
Direct Materials			—	$18,000	$23,000
Direct Labor			4,000	21,000	17,000

Additional data:

1. Jobs 1001 and 1002 were finished in October and transferred to finished goods. Jobs 1003 and 1004 were finished and transferred to finished goods in November.
2. Manufacturing overhead is applied at the rate of 80% of direct material costs.
3. Job 1001 was sold at 200% of its manufacturing costs during October, and Jobs 1002 and 1003 were sold for 200% of their manufacturing costs during November.
4. There was no Finished Goods Inventory on hand as of September 30.
5. Actual overhead was equal to applied overhead.

REQUIRED: 1. Calculate the following amounts:

   a. Beginning Work-in-Process Inventory for October 1 and November 1.
   b. Cost of Goods Sold for November.
   c. Finished Goods Inventory as of October 31 and November 30.

2. Prepare an Income Statement for the two-month period, assuming that for the two months selling expenses totaled $10,000 and general and administrative expenses $25,000.

5—21. *Job order: journal entries, Cost of Goods Manufactured Schedule.* (AICPA adapted)   The Jackson Company uses a job order cost system. The following data were obtained from the company's cost records as of June 30. No jobs were in process at the beginning of June, all costs listed being incurred during the month.

JOB ORDER NO.	DIRECT MATERIALS	DIRECT LABOR HOURS	DIRECT LABOR COST
1,001	$ 4,320	1,300	$ 1,600
1,002	9,150	3,700	7,250
1,003	11,275	8,200	14,325
1,004	3,225	1,500	2,800
1,005	6,500	3,200	6,100
1,006	2,750	980	1,650

Manufacturing overhead costs are charged to jobs on the basis of $1.50 per direct labor hour. The actual manufacturing overhead cost for the month totaled $30,350. During June, Jobs 1001, 1002, 1004, and 1005 were completed. Jobs 1001 and 1002 were shipped out, and the customers were billed $9,000 for Job 1001 and $20,000 for Job 1002. Selling and administrative expenses for the month totaled $3,800.

REQUIRED:
1. Prepare general journal entries to record the above information.
2. Prepare a Schedule of Cost of Goods Manufactured.
3. Compute the gross margins on Job 1001 and 1002 before any adjustment for over- or underapplied overhead.

5—22. *Job order costing: Statement of Cost of Goods Manufactured.* (AICPA adapted)   The Helper Corporation manufactures one product and accounts for costs by a job order cost system. You have obtained the following information for the year ended December 31 from the corporation's books and records:

Total manufacturing cost added during the year (sometimes called cost to manufacture) was $1,000,000, based on actual direct material, actual direct labor, and applied factory overhead on actual direct labor dollars.

Cost of goods manufactured was $970,000, also based on actual direct material, actual direct labor, and applied factory overhead.

Factory overhead was applied to work-in-process at 75% of direct labor dollars. Applied factory overhead for the year was 27% of the total manufacturing cost.

Beginning work-in-process inventory, January 1, was 80% of ending work-in-process inventory, December 31.

REQUIRED: Prepare a formal Statement of Cost of Goods Manufactured for the year ended December 31 for Helper Corporation. Use actual direct material used, actual direct labor, and applied factory overhead. Show supporting computations in good form.

5—23. (CMA adapted)   The Stevenson Works is a medium-sized manufacturing plant in a capital-intensive industry. The corporation's profitability at the moment is very low. As a result, investment funds are limited and hiring is restricted These stringencies have placed a strain on the plant's repair and maintenance program. The result has been a reduction in work efficiency and cost-control effectiveness in the repair and maintenance area.

The assistant controller proposes the installation of a maintenance work order system to overcome these problems. This system would require a work order to be prepared for each repair request and for each regular maintenance activity. The maintenance superintendent would record the estimated time to complete a job and send one copy of the work order to the department in which the work was to be done. The work order would also serve as a cost sheet for a job. The actual cost of the parts and supplies used on the job as well as the actual labor costs incurred in completing the job would be recorded directly on the work order. A copy of the completed work order with the actual costs would be the basis of the charge to the department in which the repair or maintenance activity occurred.

The maintenance superintendent opposes the program on the grounds that the added paperwork will be costly and nonproductive. The super-intendent states that the departmental clerk who now schedules repair and maintenance activities is doing a good job without all the extra forms the new system would require. The real problem, in the superintendent's opinion, is that that department is understaffed.

REQUIRED: **1.** Discuss how such a maintenance work order system would aid in cost control.
2. Explain how a maintenance work order system might assist the maintenance superintendent in getting authorization to hire more mechanics.

5—24. *Job order costing—journal entries.*   The Gregoropoulis Scientific Company employs a job order cost system. The Work-in-Process Inventory at *January 1* consisted of the following jobs:

JOB NO.	MATERIALS	LABOR	MANUFACTURING OVERHEAD
101	55,000	73,000	36,500
104	62,000	60,000	30,000
107	51,000	56,000	28,000

Other accounts include:

Raw Materials and Supplies	$240,000
Finished Goods, Job #98	360,000

Data for the year:

a. Raw materials and supplies purchased on account, $450,000.
b. Actual overhead costs were: depreciation, $40,000; utilities, $12,000; miscel-laneous, $18,000.
c. Direct materials requisitioned for Job #101, $120,000; Job #104, $75,000; Job #107, $140,000.
d. Labor costs paid in cash were: Job #101, $150,000; Job #104, $140,000; Job #107, $190,000; indirect labor, $165,000.
e. Overhead is assigned to Work-in-Process on the basis of direct labor costs at the same rate as in the previous year.
f. During the year, Jobs #101 and #104 were completed.
g. Jobs #98 and #101 were sold during the period for $1,500,000 cash.

REQUIRED: **1.** Prepare all journal entries necessary to record the above data, including the adjustment of Cost of Goods Sold for under- or overapplied overhead.
2. Calculate the ending balance in Job #107, Finished Goods Inventory, Work-in-Process Inventory, and Raw Materials and Supplies Inventory accounts.

5—25. *Job–order costing for three periods.* The Johnson Company uses a job order costing system. Data relevant to their fourth quarter of operation follow:

	Job No.			
	205	206	207	208
September inputs, including overhead	$10,000			
October inputs:				
Materials	7,000	$20,000		
Direct Labor	10,500	7,000		
November inputs:				
Materials		1,000	$ 8,000	$18,000
Direct Labor		500	11,000	7,000
December inputs:				
Materials		9,000	7,500	4,500
Direct Labor		7,500	2,000	3,200

Additional data:

1. Job #205 was finished in October and transferred to Finished Goods. Jobs #207 and #208 were started November 1. Jobs #206 and #207 were finished and transferred to Finished Goods in December.
2. Manufacturing overhead is applied at the rate of 75% of direct labor costs.
3. Job #205 was sold for 150% of its manufacturing cost on November 15, and Job #207 was sold for 150% of its manufacturing cost in December.
4. Selling and general and administrative expenses totaled $32,000 for the quarter.
5. Actual overhead for the quarter was $37,000. Over- or underapplied overhead is treated as an adjustment to Cost of Goods Sold.

REQUIRED:
1. Calculate beginning and ending Work-in-Process Inventories for Oct. 1, Nov. 1, and Dec. 1.
2. Calculate Finished Goods Inventory at Oct. 31, Nov. 30, and Dec. 31.
3. Prepare a Quarterly Income Statement.

5—26. *Determination of overhead rate; calculating cost of jobs.* Patio Products makes three different styles of picnic tables—a round table, Table #1; an oblong table with detached benches, Table #2; and an oblong table with benches attached, Table #3. It accounts for each different type of table on a job order basis. Prior to the beginning of the current period, Patio Products made the following estimate of manufacturing overhead costs:

Indirect materials	$138,000
Indirect labor	180,000
Depreciation	70,000
Utilities	36,000
Other	116,000
Total estimated overhead	$540,000

It estimated that it would produce 12,000 tables of each of the three different styles. Estimated direct labor requirements were:

TABLE NO.	HOURS PER TABLE
1	3
2	$2\frac{1}{2}$
3	$3\frac{1}{2}$

Patio uses an actual/applied costing system and predetermines overhead on the basis of estimated direct labor hours. Actual results for the current period were collected as follows:

	TABLE #1	TABLE #2	TABLE #3
Tables produced	12,000	12,000	12,000
Direct materials	$360,000	$480,000	$600,000
Direct labor hours at a cost of $7 per hour	34,000	33,000	44,000
Beginning inventory of tables	4,000 @ $62	2,000 @ $69	3,000 @ $90
Sales in units	11,000	10,000	10,000

Other data:

Actual overhead for the period amounted to $550,000.
Selling price: 80% markup on production costs *rounded to nearest dollar.*
The company costs its inventory using LIFO.

REQUIRED:

1. Calculate a predetermined overhead rate for Patio Products.
2. Calculate the total costs associated with each of the three different jobs.
3. Calculate the gross margin per table for round tables (Table #1) before any adjustment for over- or underapplied overhead.
4. Calculate over- or underapplied overhead and explain why the difference between actual and applied which you computed occurred.
5. Calculate the ending inventory valuation for Table #3.

5—27. *Straightforward job-order costing, T-accounts, and income statements.* Anchors Away makes sailboats, some to customers' specifications and others for inventory and sale by the company. At the beginning of the period Anchors Away had beginning inventories as follows:

Raw Materials and Supplies	$18,000
Work-in-Process:	
Boat #854	14,000
Boat #856	10,000
Finished Goods:	
Boat #850	38,000
Boat #845	27,000

During the period, Anchors Away incurred the following costs in its production process:

	BOAT #854	BOAT #856	BOAT #858	BOAT #859
Direct Materials	$ 8,000	$7,000	$6,000	$18,000
Direct Labor	10,000	8,000	4,000	15,000

Additional information:

a. Overhead is applied to boats on the basis of 150% of direct labor. Cost of Goods Sold is adjusted for over- or underapplied overhead.

b. During the period Boats #854, #856, and #859 were completed.

c. Boat #854 and Boat #859 were built to order for two customers and were transferred to them for cash of $92,000 and $115,000, respectively. Boat #845 was sold at a markup of 200% on manufacturing costs.

d. Raw materials and supplies purchases for the period were $37,000.

e. Actual overhead totaled $54,000.

f. Selling and administrative expenses for the period were $41,000.

g. Anchors Away's earnings are taxed at a rate of 30%.

REQUIRED:

1. How much overhead should be charged to Boat #858?

2. Prepare the following T-accounts, enter any beginning balance, and show the entries made in them during the year: Raw Materials and Supplies Inventory, Work-in-Process Inventory, Finished Goods Inventory, Cost of Goods Sold, and Manufacturing Overhead Summary.

3. What was the company's gross margin on Boat #854? (Ignore any over- or underapplied overhead.)

4. What is the carrying value on the end-of-period balance sheet of the company's:

    a. Raw Materials and Supplies Inventory?

    b. Work-in-Process Inventory?

    c. Finished Goods Inventory?

5. Prepare an income statement for Anchors Away for the period. Over- or underapplied overhead is considered an adjustment to cost of goods sold.

5—28. *Straightforward job-order costing, T-accounts, journal entries.* Yokomota Machinery makes heavy equipment which is used in the textile industry. It maintains a job-order costing system, and its records for the period show the following information:

	INPUTS LAST PERIOD	INPUTS THIS PERIOD Direct Materials	INPUTS THIS PERIOD Direct Labor
Job #743	$80,000	$ 20,000	$ 30,000
Job #744	10,000	25,000	80,000
Job #745	—	32,000	61,000
Job #746	—	54,000	92,000
Job #747	—	26,000	44,000
Totals	$90,000	$157,000	$307,000

Additional information:

a. Overhead is applied at the rate of 180% of direct materials costs.

b. All labor costs were paid in cash.

c. Actual overhead for the period amounted to $293,600.

d. Raw Materials Inventory at the beginning of the period amounted to $60,000. Raw material purchases for the period were $148,000.

e. Finished Goods Inventory at the beginning of the period consisted of:

Job #740	$185,000
Job #742	209,000

REQUIRED: 1. Give the journal entries to record:

a. The purchase of raw materials for cash.

b. All the inputs into the manufacturing process this period.

c. Actual overhead for the period. For the credit part of the entry assume all costs were for cash except $80,000 of depreciation.

d. The transfer of all the jobs except #747, which is still in process at the end of the period, to Finished Goods.

e. The sale of jobs #740, #742, #744, and #746 at 180% of their manufacturing costs. Yokomota records cost of goods sold and updates its inventory at the time of sale. The sales were for cash.

f. The disposal of under- or overapplied overhead as an adjustment to cost of goods sold.

2. Post the journal entries you prepared in part 1 to the following T-accounts: Raw Materials Inventory, Work-in-Process Inventory, Finished Goods Inventory, Manufacturing Overhead Summary, and Cost of Goods Sold. Be sure to enter beginning balances. Determine the ending balance in each of the three inventory accounts.

3. For Work-in-Process and Finished Goods Inventories, reconcile the balances you computed in part 2 with the balances associated with the jobs still in process and in Finished Goods Inventory.

5—29. *Comprehensive problem: allocation of costs, determination of overhead, product costing with a job-order system.*   American Manufacturing, Inc., makes snowmobiles under various contracts with companies who then attach their brands to the product. Manufacturing costs are accumulated by contracts. The following information relates to the operations of American Manufacturing.

Cost Estimates Made Prior to the Beginning of the Period

1. Before the beginning of the current period, American estimated that its manufacturing overhead before allocation of service-department costs would be $5,971,000.

2. Two service departments serve manufacturing, and their estimated costs for the coming year and allocation bases for those costs were:

Human Resources: $680,000;

allocation basis: number of employees;

50% to manufacturing,

30% to selling,

20% to corporate administration.

Information Systems: $740,000;

allocation basis: service hours rendered;

45% to manufacturing,

20% to selling,

35% to corporate administration.

3. American Manufacturing applies manufacturing overhead on the basis of direct labor hours and estimates that 1,208,000 hours will be used during the period.

Actual Data for the Period

1. The following data were collected with respect to manufacturing activities.

		INPUTS THIS PERIOD		
	INPUTS LAST PERIOD	Direct Materials	Direct Labor	
			Dollars	Hours
Job #69	$2,500,000	$ 100,000	$1,700,000	170,000
Job #70	—	900,000	2,250,000	225,000
Job #71	—	1,800,000	4,500,000	450,000
Job #72	—	900,000	2,250,000	225,000
Job #73	—	800,000	1,400,000	140,000
Totals	$2,500,000	$4,800,000	$12,100,000	1,210,000

2. At the end of the period Job #73 was still in process.
3. Actual overhead, including allocated amounts, totaled $6,650,000.
4. Selling expenses before allocation of service-department costs amounted to $3,920,000. Expenses of Human Resources and Information Systems were exactly as estimated.
5. There was no beginning or ending finished goods inventory, as manufacturing is done to order only.
6. The contract price for Job #69 was $8,850,000.

REQUIRED:

1. Calculate the predetermined overhead rate for American Manufacturing, Inc.
2. Calculate the manufacturing costs associated with each of the jobs as of the end of the accounting period.
3. Prepare the journal entry to transferred finished jobs out of work in process.
4. Calculate the carrying value of the ending Work-in-Process Inventory.
5. Calculate the amount of over- or underapplied overhead for the period and explain the reason for the over- or underapplication.
6. Calculate the gross margin on Job #69. Does the figure you computed represent the profit on that contract? Ignore any over- or underapplied overhead.
7. Calculate the *total* amount of selling expenses which should appear on the period's income statement.

5—30. *Straightforward job-order costing.* Basu Manufacturing produces motors which are sold to makers of small appliances such as blenders and fans. Basu accounts for its manufacturing costs using a job-order costing system, because most of its business is done under contracts. Basu's accounting records show the following data:

Raw Materials Beginning Inventory	$ 35,000
Beginning Work-in-Process: Job #212	95,200
Finished Goods Inventory: Job #210	106,000

Basu uses a predetermined overhead rate for costing its production and applies overhead at the rate of 90% of direct material costs.

Direct Material and Direct Labor inputs into the production process for the period were:

	JOB #212	JOB #213	JOB #214	JOB #215
Direct Materials	$ 7,000	$30,000	$75,000	$52,500
Direct Labor	24,000	38,000	95,000	66,000

Raw Material purchases during the period were $170,000.

Actual overhead for the period amounted to $149,800.

Job #212, #213, and #214 were completed during the period. Selling and administrative expenses amounted to $308,000.

Revenues from Jobs #210, #212, and #214, which were delivered to customers during the period, amounted to $1,064,000. Job #213 was placed in Finished Goods Inventory.

REQUIRED: 1. Calculate ending inventories for Raw Materials, Work-in-Process, and Finished Goods.

2. Give the entry which was made when Job #212 was completed and transferred to Finished Goods.

3. Prepare an income statement for the period. Earnings are taxed at a 46% rate, and Cost of Goods Sold is adjusted for over- or underapplied overhead.

PRODUCT COST ACCUMULATION SYSTEMS II:

PROCESS COST ACCOUNTING

OBJECTIVES

After you complete this chapter, you should be able to answer the following questions:

- When should an organization use a process cost accounting system?
- What is meant by an equivalent unit of production?
- How is an equivalent unit of production calculated for materials and for labor and overhead?
- What journal entries and accounts are used in a process cost accounting system?

USEFULNESS OF PROCESS COST ACCOUNTING SYSTEMS

As described in Chapter 5, process cost accounting is suitable for organizations which produce homogeneous products in a continuous flow. With job order costing our emphasis was on a unit of product or a group of products which constituted a "job." With process cost accounting our objective is to develop a unit cost for the homogeneous units being produced.

Process cost accounting provides a logical approach to allocating costs between units which have been completed and transferred to finished goods and either are still on hand or have been sold and units which are still in the productive process as part of work-in-process inventory. With job order costing we looked at the cost of material and labor accumulated for jobs which were incomplete as of the end of the accounting period and assigned an appropriate amount of overhead on a predetermined basis. The cost of all jobs in process at the end of the accounting period constitutes our ending work-in-process inventory.

Imagine, for instance, a thread mill where wool yarn is being produced as continuous output. The productive process does not stop at the end of the accounting period, with all wool which is in process being completely processed before the end of the day. Instead, the production period ignores the end of the accounting period. Wool which is being transformed into knitting yarn is at various stages of completion. How do we determine work-in-process ending inventory in this situation?

THE CONCEPT OF EQUIVALENT UNITS

In situations such as the one just described, accountants have developed the concept of equivalent units of production as a way of estimating a carrying value for work-in-process inventory.

Equivalent units of production can be defined as the number of units which could have been completed *entirely* with the inputs as of the end of the current period. This idea will become clearer when we look at some examples.

A confusing aspect here is that we may use as a basis for calculating unit costs different measures of equivalent units of production for materials, for labor, and for overhead. For example, we may use one number of equivalent units in calculating direct material costs per unit and a different number in calculating direct labor or overhead costs per unit. This occurs because direct materials, direct labor, and manufacturing overhead may be put into the production process according to different patterns. It is not uncommon, for instance, for all direct materials to be added at the beginning of the production process. Labor and overhead, on the other hand, may be added throughout the production process.

Illustration

Let's consider a company, Grow Fast, Inc., which produces liquid fertilizer used by commercial growers. The fertilizer is mixed in the Processing Department, then transferred to the Bottling and Sealing Department and from there to the company's warehouse. Output is measured in terms of gallons, and each gallon requires the following inputs:

Raw materials—3 pounds per gallon of output at an estimated cost of $1 per pound.
Direct labor—$6 per hour. Each gallon takes $\frac{1}{4}$ hour of direct labor.
Manufacturing overhead—applied on the basis of $2 per direct labor hour.

During the accounting period 450,000 gallons of liquid fertilizer were transferred from the Processing Department to the Bottling and Sealing Department; 60,000 are still in process at the end of the accounting period. The work-in-process account showed the following inputs during the period:

Work-in-Process—Processing Department

Materials: 1,530,000 lb @ $1/lb	$1,530,000
Direct labor: 120,000 hours @ $6/hour	720,000
Overhead: Applied on the basis of $2 for each direct labor hour	240,000
Total inputs	$2,490,000

Now at the end of the accounting period we confront the problem of deciding how much cost to transfer out of Processing into Bottling representing the cost of the 450,000 gallons which were completed during the period, and how much cost to leave in the work-in-process account representing the cost of the 60,000 gallons which are still in process at the end of the accounting period.

Equivalent Units

This is where we need the concept of equivalent units. We need to calculate the number of whole units we could have completed with our inputs as of the end of the period. The 60,000 gallons which are still in process are in various degrees of completion. It would not be worthwhile and could not be justified on a cost/benefit basis to try to estimate the degree of completion for each gallon still in process. Instead what we do is come up with an average degree of completion for the total amount of work still in process.

Before we make this estimate, we must know how inputs are put into production during the period. Is the raw material added at the beginning of the process, evenly throughout the process, or at the end of the process? We need to ask the same questions for labor and overhead. We shall assume for our example that raw materials are added in their entirety at the beginning of the production process and that labor and overhead are used evenly through the process. Now we are ready to estimate our degree of completion and then calculate equivalent units of production. Let us make an assumption which is common in production processes such as this one—that the units still in process are 50% complete as to labor and overhead. Since the raw materials go in at the beginning of the process, they are 100% complete as to materials. Thus we will need two schedules of equivalent units of production—one for materials and one for labor and overhead. An Equivalent Units of Production and Related Costs Schedule based on our example is shown in Illustration 6-1.

ILLUSTRATION 6-1

Grow Fast, Inc.—Processing Department Equivalent Units of Production

	TOTAL UNITS	MATERIALS		LABOR AND OVERHEAD	
		Degree of Completion	Equivalent Units	Degree of Completion	Equivalent Units
Units transferred out	450,000	100%	450,000	100%	450,000
Ending Work-in-Process	60,000	100%	60,000	50%	30,000
Equivalent Units for Period			510,000		480,000
Material Cost per Gallon:			$1,530,000/510,000 = $3		
Labor and Overhead Cost per Gallon:			$960,000/480,000 = $2		

Based on the estimated degree of completion, our cost per unit for this period was $5: $3 for materials and $2 for labor and overhead. Now we can determine the valuation for our work-in-process ending inventory and also determine how much costs should be transferred to the Bottling and Sealing Department. Since 450,000 gallons were completed, we will transfer $2,250,000 (450,000 gallons × $5 per gallon) out of work-in-process of the Processing Department into the next department. Our work-in-process ending inventory valuation can be calculated in two different ways:

1. Total inputs into Work-in-Process $2,490,000
    Cost of 450,000 gallons transferred to Bottling   2,250,000
    Work-in-Process Ending Inventory—
       Processing $ 240,000

2. Materials, $3 per unit × 60,000 units (units in
    process have received all their materials
    inputs) $ 180,000
    Labor and Overhead, $2 per unit × 60,000
    units which are 50% complete ($2 ×
    60,000 × 50%)   60,000
    Work-in-Process Ending Inventory—
    Processing Department $ 240,000

TRANSFERS TO OTHER DEPARTMENTS

Many types of goods require processing by more than one department.
If this is the case and a process cost accounting system is used, as goods
are transferred to a department, previous department costs are attached
to them and moved on to the next department. To illustrate, let us
continue with our Grow Fast example. Chemical fertilizer is transferred
from the Processing Department into the Bottling Department, where it
is put into one-gallon containers before it is transferred to finished goods.
The Bottling Department received from the Processing Department
450,000 gallons which already had costs inputs of $5 per unit (referred
to as "prior department costs"), or a total of $2,250,000. Assume that the
bottling department had no beginning inventory and completed the
bottling of 400,000 gallons during the current period. The remaining
50,000 gallons are still in the process of being bottled and are estimated
to be 50% complete. The work-in-process account of the Bottling and
Sealing Department showed the following inputs for the period:

Work-in-Process—Bottling and Sealing Department

Prior department costs from Processing: 450,000 @ $5	$2,250,000
Materials	127,500
Labor: 42,500 hours @ $5 per hour	212,500
Manufacturing overhead: applied at the rate of $1 per direct labor hour	42,500
	$2,632,500

In this department, raw materials are the containers and the caps which
seal the containers. Since the containers are used immediately in this
department and the capping process is the final step, it is assumed for
costing purposes that raw materials are added evenly throughout the
process. Hence, we need not calculate a separate Equivalent Units of
Production Schedule for materials. That schedule for the bottling and

sealing department is as follows:

Materials, Labor, and Overhead

	UNITS	DEGREE OF COMPLETION	EQUIVALENT UNITS
Units transferred out	400,000	100%	400,000
Units still in process	50,000	50%	25,000
Equivalent units produced			425,000

We can now calculate the unit costs of the Bottling and Sealing Department. Materials costs per unit are $.30 ($127,500/425,000 equivalent units), and labor and overhead costs are $.60 ($255,000/425,000). In addition, each unit already bears $5 of costs from the Processing Department.

The transfer of costs to finished goods inventory is calculated as follows:

Prior Department Costs:	
$5 × 400,000 units	$2,000,000
Materials Costs:	
30¢ × 400,000	120,000
Labor and Overhead Costs:	
60¢ × 400,000 units	240,000
Total Costs:	
400,000 units @ $5.90	$2,360,000

The balance of work-in-process can be found by subtracting the amount transferred from the total inputs:

Inputs	$2,632,500
Transferred to Finished Goods	2,360,000
Work-in-Process Inventory	$ 272,500

This balance can be verified as follows:

Prior Department costs on 50,000 units still in process: 50,000 × $5	$250,000
Materials, Labor, and Overhead: $.90 × 50,00 units 50% complete (.90 × 50,000 × 50%)	22,500
Work-in-Process Ending Inventory	$272,500

Journal Entries and T-Accounts

The transactions described for Grow Fast would be recorded in journal form as follows. We have also assumed the purchase of raw materials:

a. Purchased 1,800,000 pounds of chemicals for use in fertilizer by the Processing Department at a cost of $1 per pound and $150,000 of containers and seals for use in the Bottling and Sealing Department.

Raw Materials—Chemicals	$1,800,000	
Raw Materials Inventory—Bottles and Seals	150,000	
Accounts Payable		$1,950,000

b. Requisitioned raw materials into the production process as follows:

Processing Department: 1,530,000 lb @ $1 per lb		$1,530,000
Bottling and Sealing		
Department		127,500
Work-in-Process—Processing	$1,530,000	
Work-in-Process—Bottling and Sealing	127,500	
Raw Materials—Chemicals		$1,530,000
Raw Materials—Bottles and Seals		127,500

c. Incurred direct labor costs as follows:

Processing Department: 120,000 hours @ $6		$720,000
Bottling & Sealing Department: 42,500 hours @ $5		212,500
Work-in-Process—Processing	$720,000	
Work-in-Process—Bottling and Sealing	212,500	
Wages Payable		932,500

d. Applied Overhead at the rate of $2 per direct labor hour in the Processing Department and $1 per direct labor hour in the Bottling and Sealing Department.

Work in Process—Processing	$240,000	
Work in Process—Bottling and Sealing	42,500	
Manufacturing Overhead Summary		$282,500

e. Actual overhead costs for the period totaled $284,000.

Manufacturing Overhead Summary	$284,000	
Various credits including cash, payables,		
accumulated depreciation		$284,000

f. 450,000 gallons of fertilizer were transferred to the Bottling and Sealing Department from the Processing Department.

Work-in-Process—Bottling and Sealing		
(450,000 gal. @ $5)	$2,250,000	
Work-in-Process—Processing		$2,250,000

g. 400,000 gallons were bottled and sealed and transferred to Finished Goods by the Bottling and Sealing Department.

Finished Goods Inventory		
(400,000 gal. @ $5.90)	$2,360,000	
Work in Process—Bottling and Sealing		$2,360,000

A Cost of Goods Manufactured Statement for the Grow Fast, Inc., is shown below.

GROW FAST, INC. Cost of Goods Manufactured	
Processing Department:	
Raw Materials Used	$1,530,000
Direct Labor	720,000
Manufacturing Overhead Applied	240,000
Total Manufacturing Inputs—Processing	$2,490,000
Add: Beginning Work-in-Process	0
Deduct: Ending Work-in-Process	(240,000)
Cost of Goods Transferred to Bottling	$2,250,000
(450,000 gallons @ $5)	
Bottling Department Inputs:	
Raw Materials Used	127,500
Direct Labor	212,500
Manufacturing Overhead Applied	42,500
Total Manufacturing Inputs	$2,632,500
Add: Beginning Work-in-Process	0
Deduct: Ending Work-in-Process	(272,500)
Cost of Goods Transferred to Finished	
Goods (400,000 gallons @ $5.90)	$2,360,000

Let us further assume that during the period the company sold 350,000 gallons of liquid fertilizer at $11.95 per gallon. It had no beginning inventory of finished goods. Assume also that any over- or underapplied overhead is treated as an adjustment to cost of goods sold and that selling expenses were $550,000, while general and administrative expenses amounted to $725,000. Income is taxed at a rate of 46%. The entries to record this additional information are as follows:

h. Sale of 350,000 gallons at $11.95 per gallon.

Cash	$4,182,500	
Cost of Goods Sold		
(350,000 gal. @ $5.90)	2,065,000	
Sales		$4,182,500
Finished Goods Inventory		2,065,000

i. Adjustment of Cost of Goods Sold for underapplied overhead (Actual overhead, $284,000, less Applied Overhead, $282,500 = $1,500).

Cost of Goods Sold	$1,500	
Manufacturing Overhead Summary		$1,500

j. Record selling expenses and general and administrative expenses of $550,000 and $725,000 respectively.

Selling Expenses	$550,000	
General and Administrative Expenses	725,000	
Cash, Payables, and various other credits		$1,275,000

k. Record taxes based on income as calculated in the illustrated income statement.

Tax Expense	$386,860	
Taxes Payable		$386,860

The Income Statement for Grow Fast, Inc., is shown below.

GROW FAST, INC.
Income Statement

Sales (350,000 gal. @ $11.95)		$4,182,500
Cost of Goods Sold		
(350,000 gal. @ $5.90)	$2,065,000	
Underapplied Overhead	1,500	2,066,500
Gross Profit		2,116,000
Operating Expenses:		
Selling	550,000	
General and Administrative	725,000	1,275,000
Income Before Taxes		841,000
Income Taxes @ 46%		386,860
Net Income		$ 454,140

The entries described above are recorded in T-accounts in Illustration 6-2.

**ILLUSTRATION
6-2**

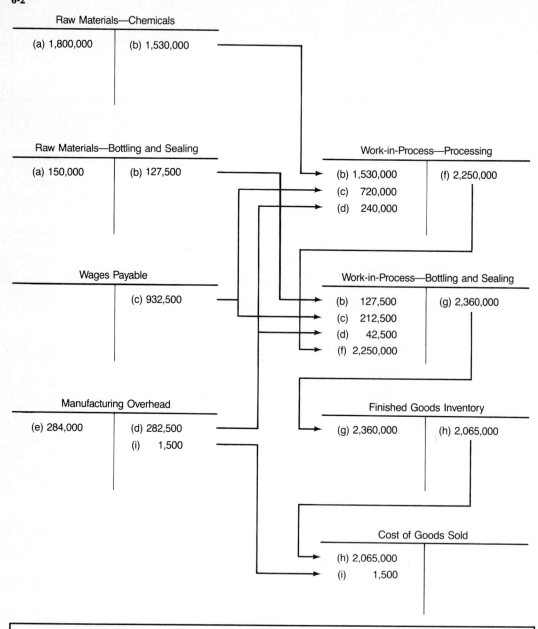

Raw Materials—Chemicals	
(a) 1,800,000	(b) 1,530,000

Raw Materials—Bottling and Sealing	
(a) 150,000	(b) 127,500

Wages Payable	
	(c) 932,500

Manufacturing Overhead	
(e) 284,000	(d) 282,500
	(i) 1,500

Work-in-Process—Processing	
(b) 1,530,000	(f) 2,250,000
(c) 720,000	
(d) 240,000	

Work-in-Process—Bottling and Sealing	
(b) 127,500	(g) 2,360,000
(c) 212,500	
(d) 42,500	
(f) 2,250,000	

Finished Goods Inventory	
(g) 2,360,000	(h) 2,065,000

Cost of Goods Sold	
(h) 2,065,000	
(i) 1,500	

EQUIVALENT UNITS WITH A BEGINNING
WORK-IN-PROCESS

Because this concept of equivalent units of production is so fundamental to an understanding of process cost accounting, let us continue our example and look at what happened in the next accounting period in the

Processing Department. The Ending Work-in-Process Inventory, consisting of 60,000 gallons which were complete as to materials and 50% complete as to labor and overhead, becomes the beginning inventory of the current period.

Let us further assume that 600,000 additional gallons were begun during the current period. This means that we must account for 660,000 gallons (60,000 beginning inventory + 600,000 started). During the period 610,000 gallons were completed and transferred out. The Work-in-Process Inventory account would show the following information for the period, assuming that amounts and costs of inputs did not change from last period.

Work-in-Process Inventory

Beginning Inventory:		Transferred Out:	
Materials	$ 180,000	610,000 gal @ $5	$3,050,000
Labor and Overhead	60,000		
	240,000		
Current Inputs:			
Materials: 1,800,000 lb			
@ $1 per lb	$1,800,000		
Direct Labor: 151,250			
hours @ $6 per			
hour	907,500		
Overhead: Applied on			
the basis of $2 per			
direct labor hour	302,500		
Total	$3,250,000		

The related Equivalent Units of Production Schedule is shown in Illustration 6-3.

ILLUSTRATION 6-3

Equivalent Units of Production and Unit Costs

	TOTAL UNITS	MATERIALS Degree of Completion	Equivalent Units	LABOR AND OVERHEAD Degree of Completion	Equivalent Units
Units transferred out during the period	610,000	100%	610,000	100%	610,000
Ending Work-in-Process	50,000	100%	50,000	50%	25,000
Equivalent Units of Production			660,000		635,000
Material Cost Per Unit:					
Material Cost in Beginning Inventory				$ 180,000	
Added during the period				1,800,000	
				$1,980,000/660,000 units = $3	
Labor and Overhead:					
Labor and Overhead Costs in Beginning Inventory				$ 60,000	
Added during the period				1,210,000	
Total Cost Per Unit				$1,270,000/635,000 units = $2	
				$5	

THE COST OF PRODUCTION REPORT

Companies which use process cost-accounting systems may prepare a Cost of Production Report similar to that shown in Illustration 6-4. The report is divided into five parts. The first part shows how many units must be

ILLUSTRATION 6-4

Grow Fast, Inc. Cost of Production Report—Processing Department

PHYSICAL UNITS					
Units to Be Accounted for:					
Units in Beginning Inventory	60,000				
Units Started during the period	600,000				
Units to Be Accounted for	660,000				

		EQUIVALENT UNITS			
		Materials		Labor and Overhead	
	PHYSICAL UNITS	Degree of Completion	Units	Degree of Completion	Units
Units Accounted for:					
Units Completed and Transferred Out	610,000	100%	610,000	100%	610,000
Units in Process at the End of the period	50,000	100%	50,000	50%	25,000
Units Accounted for	660,000		660,000		635,000

	TOTAL	MATERIALS	LABOR AND OVERHEAD
Costs to Be Accounted for:			
Work-in-Process Beginning Inventory	$ 240,000	$ 180,000	$ 60,000
Inputs for the period	3,010,000	1,800,000	$1,210,000
Costs to Be Accounted for	$3,250,000	$1,980,000	$1,270,000
Unit Costs (Costs to Be Accounted for divided by Equivalent Units):	$5	$3	$2
Costs Accounted for:			
Transferred Out	$3,050,000[a]	$1,830,000[a]	$1,220,000[a]
Ending Work-in-Process	200,000	150,000[b]	50,000[c]
Costs Accounted for	$3,250,000	$1,980,000	$1,270,000

[a] 610,000 Units @ $5 = 3,050,000; Materials: 610,000 × 3 = $1,830,000; Labor and Overhead: 610,000 × $2 = $1,220,000.
[b] 50,000 Equivalent Units @ $3 = $150,000.
[c] 25,000 Equivalent Units @ $2 = $50,000.

accounted for—that is, how many units were in beginning inventory and how many were transferred in or started by the department during the period.

The second part of the Cost of Production Report actually accounts for the units; in other words, it answers the question: Where are the units for which the department is accountable at the end of the period? It shows how many are still in the department and how many have been transferred out. The number of units to be accounted for from the first part of the report should agree with the units actually accounted for in the second part. It also translates the actual physical units into equivalent units of production. In our example, since materials are not put into the process evenly, as are labor and overhead, we will have two separate schedules of equivalent units of production—one for materials and one for labor and overhead.

The bottom half of the Cost of Production Report is concerned with costs. The first part in this half—the third part of the whole report—describes the costs to be accounted for by the department. These include any costs which were in process at the beginning of the period, costs which were transferred into the department from a prior department, and the cost inputs (materials, labor, and overhead) of the department itself. In our example, for the Processing Department we do not have any prior department costs, and Illustration 6-4 shows only beginning-of-the-period costs and the inputs during the period.

The fourth part of the report calculates unit costs, which is the major objective of our process cost accounting system. Total material costs are divided by equivalent material units of production. Conversion cost per unit (labor and overhead) is found by dividing total labor and overhead costs for the period by equivalent units of production for labor and overhead. To get the unit costs for the period at which goods will be transferred out of the department we must sum material unit costs ($3 in our example) and labor and overhead costs per unit ($2). We cannot directly divide all costs for the period by the total actual units, because the units have not all been finished and are in different degrees of completion as to materials and conversion costs.

The final section of the report describes where the costs for which the department is accountable are at the end of the period. That is, it shows which costs are still in process and constitute Work-in-Process Ending Inventory for the department and which costs have been transferred out of the department into another processing department or into Finished Goods Inventory. The costs for which the department is accountable as described in the third part of the report should agree with the total costs of Work-in-Process Inventory for the department and the costs that were transferred out of the department when physical units were transferred out.

In our illustration we assumed that costs did not change from one accounting period to the next. Let us assume instead the following information about labor and overhead:

Beginning Work-in-Process Inventory:
Physical units: 60,000, half-complete
as to labor and overhead $60,000   costs
Units started this period: 600,000
Labor input this period: 151,250 hours
@ $6.25 $945,312.50
Overhead this period: $2 per direct
labor hour $ 302,500.00
Total labor and overhead this
period $1,247,812.50

Ending Work-in-Process Inventory:
Physical units: 50,000, half-complete
as to labor and overhead

Labor costs in the previous period were $6 per hour. They have risen to $6.25 per hour in the current period. This change in cost will have a different effect on unit costs depending on how we decide to cost units moving out of work-in-process into finished goods. For purposes of this text, we are going to assume that an average costing approach is used; hence we will merge last period's labor and overhead costs with this period's and come up with an average cost per unit.

Based on our assumption we would have:

Units transferred out:
Beginning inventory   60,000
Units started   600,000
Total units in process   660,000
Ending inventory   50,000
Units transferred out   610,000
Equivalent units:
Transferred out 610,000, 100%
complete   610,000
Ending Inventory 50,000, 50%
complete   25,000
Equivalent units   635,000
Unit costs for labor and overhead:

$$\frac{\$60,000 \text{ in beginning inventory} + \$1,247,812.50 \text{ added this period}}{635,000 \text{ equivalent units}} = \$2.06^a \text{ per unit}$$

^{a} Rounded to the nearest cent.

Our results would have been different if we had assumed a FIFO flow out of Work-in-Process. Under this assumption we would have segregated the cost of units which were in our beginning inventory from the costs of goods which were started and completed this period. These batches would have been transferred into finished goods at different unit costs, because an equivalent of 30,000 labor and overhead units had been put in on the beginning inventory when labor costs were $6 per hour rather than $6.25. How a FIFO basis for transferring costs works is shown in the appendix to this chapter.

The calculation of equivalent units can be much more complex than we have presented here, owing to factors such as lost or spoiled units. But for those who are not planning to be accountants, what is needed is a thorough understanding of the concept rather than of the various complexities which can arise.

PROCESS COSTING AND SERVICE ORGANIZATIONS

The concept of equivalent units is not applicable to the service organization, as it does not have services in various degrees of completion as the manufacturing concern may have. Also, the service organization does not have the problem of allocating costs incurred during the period among Work-in-Process Inventory, Finished Goods Inventory, and Cost of Goods Sold.

However, the idea of trying to find unit costs, based on some measure of output, for various types of services rendered may be an objective of the service organization's managerial accounting system. A bank, for example, may wish to determine how much it costs to maintain a checking account for a customer or to provide a credit card service.

The problems relevant to determining costs of this type are those of allocation described in Chapter 3. To determine the costs of maintaining a checking account, the bank would have to calculate the direct costs associated with providing this service and then allocate a proportional share of indirect costs to it. Picture a bank with which you do business or with which you are familiar and the numerous types of activities in which it engages, and you can perceive the complexities of cost determination for its various service functions.

Once costs have been determined, expressing them in unit terms is a straightforward process. The costs associated with the service are divided by the specified units of output—in the banking illustration, the number of checking accounts serviced by the bank.

---

chapter highlights

Process costing accounting is best suited to those organizations which have a continuous outflow of homogeneous products. Fundamental to a process costing system is the concept of the equivalent unit of production. Since process costing is used when units are homogeneous, it is difficult and generally not practical to identify specific units or lots of units as we did in job order costing. This lack of identification makes determining how much costs should be attached to goods as they pass through the production process more difficult.

The equivalent-units-of-production concept is based on the question: How many units could we have completed entirely with our inputs as of the end of the period? The answer is the equivalent units of production. Different inputs—materials, labor, and overhead—may require different calculations of equivalent units of production, since these inputs may be put into production following different patterns.

Once we have calculated the appropriate equivalent units of production, we can find the cost of the input per unit and hence the cost of units moving through the production process.

chapter six appendix

USE OF FIFO COSTING IN A PROCESS COST ACCOUNTING SYSTEM

In this chapter we used an average costing system, and we merged units which were in production at the beginning of the period with units which were begun during the period. This method is described as average costing.

A company may wish to separate the costs of units which were in process at the beginning of the period and the costs of completing those units from the costs of units which were begun during the period. Such a company would be using FIFO (first-in, first-out) costing.

To illustrate how FIFO works, assume the following:

	UNITS	MATERIALS		LABOR AND OVERHEAD	
		Percent Complete	Cost Inputs	Percent Complete	Cost Inputs
Beginning Work-in-Process	60,000	100%	$ 210,000	40%	$ 52,800
Units Started in Production during the Period	600,000		$2,340,000		$1,502,500
Units in Production	660,000				
Units Transferred Out	610,000				
Ending Work-in-Process	50,000	100%		30%	
Total Costs			$2,550,000		$1,555,300

With FIFO, we want to know the cost of making a unit this period and do not want to combine costs in the beginning inventory with cost inputs made during the period. Our Equivalent Units of Production Schedule would appear as follows:

EQUIVALENT UNITS OF PRODUCTION—FIFO COSTING

	Materials	Labor and Overhead
Units Completed and Transferred Out	610,000	610,000
Deduct: Equivalent Units in Beginning Inventory:		
Materials: 60,000 × 100%	(60,000)	
Labor and Overhead: 60,000 × 40%		(24,000)
	550,000	586,000
Add: Equivalent Units in Ending Inventory:		
Materials: 50,000 × 100%	50,000	
Labor and Overhead: 50,000 × 30%		15,000
Equivalents Units of Production *This Period*	600,000	601,000

Unit costs incurred *This Period* are:

Materials: $2,340,000/600,000 = $3.90

Labor and Overhead: $1,502,500/601,000 = $2.50

We can now calculate the cost of the units in beginning inventory which were transferred out during the period:

Cost of 60,000 Units in Beginning Work-in-Process Inventory

Cost of Materials:	
60,000 units 100% complete as of the beginning of the period	$210,000
Cost of labor and overhead:	
Put in last period to complete 24,000 equivalent units (60,000 × 40% complete) (Beginning Work-in-Process)	52,800
Labor and overhead added this period to complete 36,000 equivalent units (60,000 × 60%) × $2.50	90,000
Cost of 60,000 units @ $5.88	$352,800

Note that we had to add enough labor and overhead to complete 36,000 equivalent units. Since the 60,000 units in beginning inventory were 40% complete as of the beginning period, we had to add 60% of the labor and overhead at this period's unit cost of $2.50.

We both started and completed 550,000 units this period, calculated as follows:

Units transferred out this period	610,000
Deduct: Units transferred out which were in beginning Work-in-Process Inventory	(60,000)
Units both started and completed this period	550,000

The costs of these units is:

$$550,000 \times (\$3.90 \text{ materials cost} + \$2.50 \text{ labor}$$
$$\text{and overhead}) = 550,000 \times \$6.40 \qquad \underline{\$3,520,000}$$

Work-in-Process Ending Inventory would be costed as follows:

Cost of 50,000
Units in Ending
Work-in-Process
Inventory

Cost of materials for 50,000 units 100% complete as to materials = 50,000 × $3.90	$195,000
Cost of labor and overhead for 15,000 equivalent units (50,000 units 30% complete) = 15,000 × $2.50	37,500
Cost of Work-in-Process Ending Inventory	$232,500

We could have calculated the cost of Work-in-Process Ending Inventory this way:

Beginning Balance in Work-in-Process ($210,000 materials + 52,800 labor and overhead)		$ 262,800
Inputs this period:		
Materials	$2,340,000	
Labor and overhead	1,502,500	$3,842,500
Total		$4,105,300
Transferred out:		
60,000 units @ $5.88	$ 352,800	
550,000 units @ $6.40	3,520,000	3,872,800
Ending Balance in Work-in-Process		$ 232,500

The Work-in-Process Inventory and the Finished Goods Inventory accounts for the period are shown below:

Work-in-Process Inventory			Finished Goods Inventory	
		Transferred:		
Beginning:		60,000 @ $5.88	60,000 @ $5.88	
Materials	210,000	= $352,800	= $352,800	
Labor and Overhead	52,800	550,000 @ $6.40	550,000 @ $6.40	
Current inputs:		= $3,520,000	= $3,520,000	
Materials	2,340,000			
Labor and Overhead	1,502,500			

The company's accounts show that unit costs have risen. Specifically, material costs last period were:

$210,000/60,000 equivalent units in beginning inventory = $3.50 per unit

For the current period, material costs were $3.90. Labor and overhead costs for last period were:

$52,800/24,000 equivalent units in beginning inventory = $2.20 per unit

In contrast, the current period's unit costs for labor and overhead are $2.50.

If the company had been using an average costing system, the 610,000 units transferred to Finished Goods Inventory would have been transferred at the same average price based on equivalent units calculated as follows:

Equivalent Units
of Production—
Average Costing

	MATERIALS	LABOR AND OVERHEAD
Units Completed and Transferred Out:	610,000	610,000
Equivalent Units in Ending Inventory:		
Materials: 50,000 × 100%	50,000	
Labor and Overhead: $50,000 × 30%		15,000
Equivalent Units of Production:	660,000	625,000

When we used FIFO costing, our Equivalent Units of Production Schedule was labeled Equivalent Units of Production *This Period*. With average costing we are not concerned with the fact that of the 660,000 equivalent material units shown on the schedule above, 60,000 were completed last period, and for labor and overhead of the 625,000 equivalent units, 24,000 were completed last period.

Unit cost under average costing would be calculated as follows:

Materials:	Beginning Inventory	$ 210,000
	Current Inputs	2,340,000
	Total	$2,550,000/660,000 equivalent units = $3.86[a]
Labor and Overhead:	Beginning Inventory	$ 52,800
	Current Inputs	1,502,500
	Total	$1,555,300/625,000 equivalent units = $2.49[a]
	Average Unit Cost	$6.35

[a] Rounded

Using average costing, all 610,000 units transferred to Finished Goods Inventory would be transferred at the same unit price, unlike FIFO costing, which resulted in the transfer of the 610,000 units in two batches at two different unit costs. With average costing, the cost transfer to Finished Goods Inventory would be:

610,000 units @ $6.35 = $3,873,500

questions

1. For what types of organizations is a process cost accounting system suitable?

2. Define the term equivalent units of production.

3. Under what circumstances is it necessary to calculate different schedules of equivalent units of production for materials, labor, and overhead?

4. What is meant by the term prior department costs?

5. In what way is accounting under a job order cost accounting system similar to accounting under a process cost accounting system?

6. How does the primary focus of process cost accounting differ from that of job order cost accounting?

7. What kind of estimates are necessary to use a process cost accounting system?

8. Distinguish between physical units in production and equivalent units of production.

9. Contrast the entry involved in the transfer of inventory from work-in-process to finished goods in a job order system versus a process costing system.

10. How does the application of direct labor and material rates differ in job order and process costing systems?

11. Into what four major sections is a cost of production report generally divided?

12. What is the purpose of preparing a cost of production report such as that shown in Illustration 6-4?

13. Peerless Products started 10,000 units in the production process during the current period. Where may they be at the end of the accounting period?

14. Explain how service institutions adapt the concept of process cost accounting to provide information which managers may need.

15. In what ways are job order costing and process costing similar?

16. The process cost accounting system described in the chapter uses an average cost flow assumption. What does this mean?

17. A unit of raw material was purchased for $2. Describe the different places where that $2 may be found at the end of the accounting period.

The following questions are based on the Appendix to Chapter 6.

18. What is the difference between using an average cost flow assumption and a FIFO cost flow assumption in a process costing accounting system?

19. Under what circumstances would you obtain the same unit cost regardless of whether you used an average cost flow assumption or a FIFO cost flow assumption?

20. A company started the period with a balance in Work-in-Process of $12,000. If you are to use a FIFO costing approach, what additional information must you have with respect to that piece of data?

exercises

6—1. Ajax Bottling provided you with the following information for the accounting period ended December 31.

	MIXING DEPARTMENT	BOTTLING DEPARTMENT
Beginning Inventory	1,000 units 50% complete as to materials; 25% complete as to labor and overhead	600 units 100% complete as to materials; 60% complete as to labor and overhead
Units *Started* and *Completed* This Period	40,000	35,000
Ending Inventory	1,400 units 50% complete as to materials; 20% complete as to labor and overhead	1,000 units 100% complete as to materials: 50% complete as to labor and overhead

REQUIRED: Calculate the equivalent units of production for each of the two departments, assuming the beginning inventory was completed during the period.

6—2. Assume that the Work-in-Process account of Ajax Bottling referred to in Exercise 6—1 above for the Mixing Department showed the following:

Work-in-Process—Mixing

Beginning Inventory:	
Materials	$ 500
Labor and Overhead	750
Inputs for the Period:	
Materials	41,200
Labor and Overhead	123,090

REQUIRED:
1. Calculate the cost of each unit which was transferred to the Bottling Department during the period, assuming that unit costs are accounted for on an average basis.
2. Calculate the carrying value of the Work-in-Process Ending Inventory for the Mixing Department two different ways.

6—3. The accounting records of the Grinding Department of the Miller Manufacturing Company showed the following information for the month of April:

Units in Beginning Inventory, April 1	8,000
Units Started and Completed during April	40,000
Units in Ending Inventory, April 30	5,000

REQUIRED: Calculate equivalent units of production for materials under each of the following assumptions:

1. All raw materials are added at the beginning of the manufacturing process.
2. Raw materials are added 50% at the beginning of the manufacturing process and 50% at the end of the manufacturing process.

6—4. When yarn enters the Dyeing Department of the Finest Thread Company, it already carries a cost of $20 per 100 pounds. Records of the Dyeing Department for the month of March provide the data given below:

	UNITS	COST IN DYEING DEPARTMENT
Beginning Inventory	20,000 pounds 50% complete	
Started and Completed during March	300,000 pounds	$16,750
Ending Inventory	30,000 pounds 50% complete	

Additional information: Materials, labor, and overhead are added evenly throughout the process. An average cost system is used. The yarn is assembled in packages of 100 pounds.

REQUIRED: 1. Calculate the costs of each 100-pound lot which was transferred to Finished Goods Inventory during the period.

2. Calculate the Ending Work-in-Process Inventory for March 31 for the Dyeing Department of Finest Thread.

6—5. Quality Milling accumulated the following information for the month of September:

	UNITS	PERCENT COMPLETED	
		Case A	Case B
Beginning Inventory	20,000	40%	60%
Units Started This Period	200,000		
Ending Inventory	32,000	30%	80%

REQUIRED: Use the data given above to complete the following schedule of physical units and equivalent units:

	CASE A	CASE B
Units to be accounted for:		
Units in Process, September 1	?	?
Units started in Process during September	?	?
Total Units to be accounted for	220,000	220,000
Units accounted for as follows:		
Transferred out during September	?	?
Units in process, ending	?	?
Total Units accounted for	220,000	220,000
Computation of Equivalent Units:		
Units transferred out during September		
Equivalent Units in ending inventory, September 30		
Equivalent Units		

6—6. Use the data in Exercise 6—5 for *Case A* for Quality Milling. Assume that material costs for August were $2.20 per unit, while in September they were $2.30 per unit. Labor and Overhead costs per unit were $7 in August and $7.25 in September.

REQUIRED:
1. Calculate the September 1 beginning balance of Work-in-Process.
2. Give the entry to transfer completed units into Finished Goods, assuming that the company uses an average costing method in accounting for its production costs. (Round unit cost to the nearest cent.)
3. Calculate the September 10 ending balance in Work-in-Process.

6—7. (AICPA adapted) Information concerning Department B of the Toby Company is as follows:

	UNITS	TOTAL COSTS
Beginning Work-in-Process	5,000	$ 6,300
Units transferred in	35,000	58,700
	40,000	$65,000
Units completed	37,000	
Ending Work-in-Process	3,000	

Composition of Total Costs Shown Above

	PRIOR DEPARTMENT COSTS TRANSFERRED IN	MATERIALS	CONVERSION	TOTAL COSTS
Beginning Work-in-Process	$ 2,900	$ —	$ 3,400	$ 6,300
Current Period to Inputs	17,500	25,500	15,700	58,700
	$20,400	$25,500	$19,100	$65,000

Conversion costs were 20% complete as to the beginning work-in-process and 40% complete as to the ending work-in-process. All materials are added at the end of the process. Toby uses the average method.

REQUIRED:
1. Calculate the cost per equivalent unit for conversion costs. (Round to the nearest cent.)
2. Calculate the portion of the total cost of ending work-in-process which is attributable to transferred in cost from prior departments.

6—8. (AICPA adapted) On April 1 the Collins Company had 6,000 units of work-in-process in Department B, the second and last stage of their production cycle. The costs attached to these 6,000 units were $12,000 of costs transferred in from Department A, $2,500 of material costs added in Department B, and $2,000 of conversion costs added in Department B. Materials are added in the beginning of the process in Department B. Conversion was 50% complete on April 1. During April 14,000 units were transferred in from Department A at a cost of $28,000; and material costs of $3,500 and conversion costs of $3,400 were added in Department B. On April 30, Department B had 5,000 units of work-in-process 60% complete as to conversion costs.

REQUIRED: **1.** Using the average method, calculate the equivalent units for the month of April.

2. Calculate the cost per equivalent unit for conversion costs.

3. What will be the carrying value of Ending Work-in-Process?

6—9. (AICPA adapted) Information for the month of May concerning Department A, the first stage of Wit Corporation's production cycle, is as follows:

	MATERIALS	CONVERSION COSTS
Work-in-process, beginning	$ 4,000	$ 3,000
Current cost inputs	20,000	16,000
Total costs	$24,000	$19,000
Goods completed		90,000 units
Work-in-process, ending inventory		10,000 units

Material costs are added at the beginning of the process. The ending work-in-process is 50% complete as to conversion costs.

REQUIRED: Calculate total costs and show how they would be distributed between units transferred out and units still in process at the end of the period.

6—10. (AICPA adapted) Read, Inc., instituted a new process in October. During October, 10,000 units were started in Department A. Of the units started, 8,000 were transferred to Department B, and 2,000 remained in work-in-process at October 31. The work-in-process at October 31 was 100% complete as to material costs and 50% complete as to conversion costs. Material costs of $27,000 and conversion costs of $45,000 were charged to Department A in October.

REQUIRED: What were the total costs transferred to Department B?

6—11. (AICPA adapted) Sussex Corporation's production cycle starts in the Mixing Department. The following information is available for the month of April:

	UNITS
Work-in-process, April 1 (50% complete)	40,000
Started in April	240,000
Work-in-process, April 30 (60% complete)	25,000

Materials are added at the beginning of the process in the Mixing Department.

REQUIRED: **1.** Calculate equivalent units of production using the average costing method for materials and for conversion costs.

2. Assume instead that materials are added evenly throughout the process and that the beginning inventory was 60% complete and the ending inventory 30% complete. Calculate the equivalent units of production for April.

6—12. The Fresh Mouthwash Company processes its product through two departments—a Processing Department and a Bottling Department. The following information relates to the operations of those two departments for the period.

	PROCESSING DEPARTMENT	BOTTLING DEPARTMENT
Prior Department Costs in Beginning Inventory	—	$54,400
Beginning Inventory	100,000 pints 50% complete	160,000 pints, 50% complete as to materials, 25% complete as to labor and overhead
	Materials $9,000	Materials $18,400
	Labor and Overhead $8,000	Labor and Overhead $8,000
Started in Process this Period	1,000,000 pints	?
Cost inputs this period	Materials $175,500	Materials $213,900
	Labor and Overhead $156,000	Labor and Overhead $184,000
Ending Inventory	150,000 pints, 50% complete	200,000 pints, 50% complete as to materials, 25% complete as to labor and overhead

Mouthwash is mixed in the Processing Department, then transferred to the Bottling Department, where it is put into 16-ounce (pint) plastic containers, capped, and transferred to Finished Goods Inventory.

REQUIRED: 1. How many pints of mouthwash were started in process during the period in the Bottling Department?

2. For each department calculate equivalent units of product for the period, assuming the use of an average costing system.

3. For each department, calculate the average unit cost for the period for a pint of mouthwash.

4. Calculate the unit cost of a bottle of mouthwash transferred to Finished Goods.

5. For each department, calculate the carrying value of the ending work-in-process inventory.

6. Did unit cost for the Processing Department differ this period compared to last period? How do you know?

6—13. The Thunderbird Co. uses a process cost-accounting system to account for manufacturing cost of a thirst-quenching drink for athletes. The following costs are relevant to the *conversion cost* for a department of that company for the month of February:

CONVERSION COSTS

Work-in-Process, beginning	6,000 units ⅓ complete, $13,000
New units started during the period	70,000
Ending Work-in-Process	8,000 units ⅛ complete
Conversion costs incurred during February	$448,610
Material cost per unit	$1

Materials are added at the beginning of the process.

REQUIRED: Calculate the following amounts:

1. Equivalent units of production with respect to conversion cost for the month of February.
2. The cost of a unit which is transferred to finished goods during February, assuming the use of an average costing system.
3. Ending Work-in-Process Inventory.

Exercises 6-14 and 6-15 relate to the Appendix to Chapter 6.

6—14.   Use the information provided for the Thunderbird Company in Exercise 6—13.

REQUIRED:
1. Prepare an Equivalent Units of Production Schedule, assuming that Thunderbird uses an FIFO costing system.
2. Assume FIFO costing and that material cost for all units was $1 per unit. Give the journal entries to transfer units to Finished Goods (a) that were in process at the beginning of the period, (b) that were both started and completed during the period. (Round unit costs to the nearest cent.)
3. What were conversion costs per unit last period?
4. What is the carrying value of ending Work-in-Process Inventory?

6—15.   (AICPA adapted) Walton, Incorporated, had 8,000 units of work-in-process in Department A on October 1. These units were 40% complete as to conversion costs. Materials are added in the beginning of the process. During the month of October, 34,000 units were started. Walton had 6,000 units of work-in-process on October 31. These units were 80% complete as to conversion costs.

REQUIRED:
1. How many equivalent units would you use in computing material cost per unit and conversion costs if the company used an average costing system?
2. How many equivalent units would you use in computing material cost per unit and conversion cost per unit if the company used the FIFO approach?

---

problems

6—16.   *Straightforward calculation of equivalent units and unit costs; journal entries.* Crossgrove Chemical records show the following information for the month of October.

a. Beginning Work-in-Process Inventory, 8,000 units, complete as to materials, 50% complete as to labor and overhead. Material cost to date of the units, $8,960; labor and overhead costs, $15,000.

b. Finished Goods Inventory, October 1, 12,000 units @ $4.75 = $57,000. Raw Materials Beginning Inventory, $15,000.

c. The following transcations occurred during the month of October:

(1) 40,000 units were started in process.

(2) Raw materials costing $60,000 were purchased and $44,800 were put into process. All raw materials are added at the beginning of the process.

(3) Labor inputs for the period amounted to $96,750 while overhead applied amounted to $57,000. Actual overhead amounted to $56,400.

(4) During the month 42,000 units were transferred to finished goods. The units remaining in process at the end of the period were 50% complete as to labor and overhead.

(5) During the period 44,000 units were sold on account at a price of $7.50 per unit. The company costs its Finished Goods Inventory on a LIFO basis and adjusts Cost of Goods Sold for over- and underapplied overhead.

(6) Selling expenses for the period were $23,000 and general and administrative expenses $57,000. The company's tax rate is 50%.

REQUIRED:

1. Calculate the equivalent units of production for October for materials and for labor and overhead.

2. Calculate the unit cost for materials and for labor and overhead, assuming that the company uses an average cost system for costing its production.

3. Give the journal entries to record the company's transactions for the month of October.

4. Calculate ending inventories of: Work in Process and Finished Goods.

5. Prepare an Income Statement for the month of October for Crossgrove.

6—17. *Calculation of equivalent units and unit costs.* Quality Milling Company's records for the month of January provide the data shown below:

	PHYSICAL UNITS	MATERIALS		LABOR AND OVERHEAD	
		Percent of Completion	Cost	Percent of Completion	Cost
January 1 Inventory	50,000	80%	$174,000	60%	$234,000
Started in January	280,000	—			
January 31 Inventory	40,000	80%		50%	

Additional information:

Material costs put into production for the month of January totaled	$1,268,560
Labor and overhead costs charged into process in January totaled	$2,215,000

REQUIRED:

1. Calculate equivalent units of production.

2. Give the journal entry to transfer completed units from Work-in-Process to Finished Goods. Assume that production is costed at average costs.

3. Calculate ending Work-in-Process Inventory using two different methods.

4. Were raw material costs higher or lower in January than in the previous month? Explain how you know.

6—18. *Prior department costs.* Mid Central Brewing accumulated the following data for one of its departments, the Blending Department. Before reaching the Blending Department the product passes through the Mixing Department. From the Blending Department, the brew goes into the Kegging Department.

Additional information:

1. The Blending Department started the period with 100,000 gallons of brew on hand, which had prior department costs of $208,000. This inventory was estimated to be 50% complete as to materials, labor, and overhead with respect to Blending Department costs. The Blending Department had incurred material, labor, and overhead costs with respect to this inventory of $75,000 in the prior period.
2. During the period, 2,500,000 additional gallons of brew were transferred into Blending. The unit costs transferred into Blending from the Mixing Department were $2.08 per gallon.
3. The Blending Department incurred material costs totaling $1,746,500 during the period and labor and overhead costs of $2,495,000.
4. At the end of the period, 110,000 gallons were still in process, which are estimated to be 50% complete as to materials, labor, and overhead.

REQUIRED: 1. Prepare a schedule which shows the equivalent units of production for the period.
2. Calculate the cost of goods transferred to the Kegging Department during the period. (Round unit costs to the nearest cent.)
3. Calculate the cost of ending Work-in-Process Inventory using two different methods.

6—19. *Cost of Production Report.*

REQUIRED: Calculate the missing amounts for the January Cost of Production Report for Swanee Chemicals.

Units to be accounted for:		
Units in process, January 1	15,000	
Units started in process in January	?	
Total Units to be Accounted for	?	
Units accounted for as follows:		
Transferred out during January	110,000	
Units in Process, January 31	?	
Total Units Accounted for	?	

	Materials	Labor and Overhead
Computation of equivalent units:		
Units transferred out during January	?	?
Equivalent units, January 31	?	10,000
Equivalent units	?	?

Cost to be accounted for:	
Work-in-Process, January 1	
Materials	$?
Labor and Overhead	75,000
January inputs:	
Materials	138,000
Labor and Overhead	?
Total Cost to Be Accounted for	$?
Cost accounted for as follows:	
Transferred out	?
Work in Process January 31	
Materials	?
Labor and Overhead	?
Total Cost Accounted For	$?

Additional information:

1. Materials are added at the beginning of the period; labor and overhead are added evenly throughout the production process.
2. Units in process at the end of each period are estimated to be 50% complete as to labor and overhead.
3. Material costs and labor and overhead costs per unit were the same last period as they are in the current period.

6—20. *Calculation of equivalent units, preparation of a Cost of Production Report.* Quiet Nights makes a patented cough suppressant. The following information describes operations in the Compounding Department, where the medication is mixed. From there the product is passed to the Finishing Department, where it is bottled, capped, and labeled.

a. Beginning Work-in-Process Inventory, 10,000 gallons, 70% complete as to materials, and 60% complete as to labor and overhead. Material costs in the beginning inventory, $11,200. Labor and overhead costs in the beginning inventory, $15,360.
b. During the period 300,000 gallons were started in process.
c. Material inputs for the period amounted to $480,960.
d. Labor and overhead inputs for the period were $769,024.
e. At the end of the period 12,000 gallons were still in process, which were 80% complete as to materials and 70% complete as to labor and overhead.

REQUIRED: Prepare a Cost of Production Report for the Compounding Department for the period.

6—21. *Calculation of equivalent units, journal entries, and Income Statement.* Gramling Manufacturing uses a process cost accounting system to account for the cost of heavy cable which it produces. The following data have been accumulated for the period.

a. Beginning Work-in-Process Inventory, 100,000 feet, 60% complete as to materials, labor, and overhead. Cost in beginning inventory: Materials, $360,000;

Labor and Overhead, $660,000. All the beginning Work-in-Process Inventory was complete during the period.

b. Finished Goods Inventory (costed using the LIFO method), 1,500,000 feet @ $16.70 = $25,050,000.

c. Raw Materials: Beginning Inventory, $6,000,000. Purchases for Cash, $34,000,000.

d. During the period 5,500,000 feet of cable were *started and completed.*

e. Ending Work-in-Process Inventory: 200,000 feet, 70% complete as to materials, labor, and overhead.

f. Manufacturing Inputs for the period: Materials, $34,080,000; Labor and Overhead, $62,480,000. The company does not use a predetermined overhead rate.

g. Sales amounted to 5,500,000 feet at $30 per foot. Sales were for cash.

h. Variable selling expenses were $1 per foot sold. Fixed selling expenses amounted to $4,320,000 and administrative expenses totaled $17,600,000. (For the credit part of this entry simply use the term "various credits.")

REQUIRED:
1. Calculate the equivalent units of production for the period.
2. Prepare the journal entries to record Gramling Manufacturing's transactions for the period. In cases where insufficient data are provided to record the credit part of an entry, use the term "Various credits." The company uses a perpetual inventory system.
3. Prepare an Income Statement for the period and the journal entry to record Gramling's income tax liability at a rate of 46%.
4. Calculate ending inventory valuations which will appear on the balance sheet.

6—22. *Equivalent units: various cost constructions and cost behavior—complex problem.* The Gleam Company makes laundry detergent. In the Processing Department the necessary ingredients are combined. The detergent is then transferred to the Boxing Department, where it is put into 5-pound boxes and sent to Finished Goods Inventory. Gleam has prepared the following *estimated* data for the coming year for the Boxing Department:

Variable Manufacturing Cost per 5-pound box:
Direct Materials	$.08
Direct Labor	.13
Variable manufacturing overhead	.04
Fixed Manufacturing Costs for the Period:	$6,125

Work-in-Process at the beginning of the period amounts to 20,000 boxes, complete as to materials and 50% complete as to labor and overhead. Work-in-Process Ending Inventory is estimated to be 15,000 boxes, complete as to materials and 50% complete as to labor and overhead. Material cost in Work-in-Process Beginning Inventory, $1,400. Labor and Overhead cost in Work-in-Process Beginning Inventory, $2,000.

The Gleam Company estimates that 600,000 pounds of detergent will be transferred to the Boxing Department during the period. A pound of detergent coming into the Boxing Department for the period has an estimated cost of $.38. Last period's cost was $.36 per pound.

The company expects to have variable selling costs of $.04 per box of detergent, fixed selling expenses and administrative expenses $12,500. It anticipates keeping Finished Goods Inventory at its current level.

REQUIRED:
1. Calculate the estimated average cost of boxing a 5-pound box of detergent in the Boxing Department. (Carry your answer to three decimal places.)
2. Calculate the average cost of a box of detergent transferred to Finished Goods during the period. Carry your answer to three decimal places. Why does this answer differ from what you got in part 1?
3. If the company wants to set a target selling price which represents a 40% markup on the *full cost* of a 5-pound box of detergent, what will that selling price be? Assume a sales volume of 125,000 boxes.

6—23. *Equivalent units; inventory valuation.* The Pest-Away Company manufactures a pesticide powder designed to kill snails, slugs, ants, and other pests which live in the ground. Earthworms are not affected by the use of the powder. Pest-Away uses a process cost accounting system to account for the manufacture of the pesticide. The chemical formula is mixed in the Formulation Department and put into 1-pound boxes in the Packaging Department. The following data relate to the operations of the Formulation Department for the accounting period.

Work-in-Process Beginning Inventory	50,000 pounds in process, 45% complete as to all inputs, costing: Materials, $15,750; Labor and Overhead, $16,425
Pounds started in process during the period	1,000,000 pounds
Cost inputs during the period	Materials, $739,125; Labor and Overhead, $778,545
Work-in-Process Ending Inventory	60,000 pounds, 30% complete as to all inputs

The pesticide is put into 1-pound containers in the Packaging Department and then transferred to Finished Goods. Costs incurred in packaging a container during the period averaged $.25. At the end of the period the Packaging Department had 12,000 containers in process, which were 60% complete. The selling price of a container of pesticide is $3.25. Of pesticide completed this period, 28,000 containers are still on hand. There was no beginning Finished Goods Inventory.

REQUIRED:
1. Calculate equivalent units of production in the Formulation Department.
2. Give the journal entry to transfer completed units out of the Formulation Department. (Round unit costs to the nearest cent.)
3. What was the gross margin on a container of pesticide sold during the period?
4. Calculate the following ending inventory valuations:
   a. Work-in-Process—Formulation.
   b. Work-in-Process—Packaging.
   c. Finished Goods.

6—24. *Computation of equivalent units/inventory valuation.* (AICPA adapted) You are engaged in the audit of the December 31 financial statements of Spirit Corporation, a manufacturer of a digital watch. You are attempting to verify the costing of the ending inventory of work-in-process and finished goods, which were recorded on Spirit's books as follows:

Ending Inventory

	UNITS	COST
Work in process December 31 (50% complete as to labor and overhead)	300,000	$660,960
Finished goods	200,000	1,009,800

Materials are added to production at the beginning of the manufacturing process, and overhead is applied to each product at the rate of 60% of direct labor costs. There was no finished goods inventory on January 1. A review of Spirit's inventory cost records disclosed the following information:

	UNITS	COSTS Materials	COSTS Labor	COSTS Overhead
Work-in-Process January 1 (80% complete as to labor and overhead)	200,000	$ 200,000	$ 315,000	$ 189,000
Units started in production	1,000,000			
Material costs		$1,300,000		
Labor costs			$1,995,000	
Overhead costs				$1,197,000
Units completed	900,000			

REQUIRED: **1.** Prepare schedules as of December 31 to compute the following:

  a. Equivalent units of production using the average method.
  b. Unit costs of production of materials, labor, and overhead.
  c. Costing of the finished goods inventory and work-in-process inventory.

2. Calculate any differences between inventory valuation based on your audit and inventory valuation per the books.

6—25. *Cost of Production Report.* (AICPA adapted) The Dexter Production Company manufactures a single product. Its operations are a continuing process carried on in two departments—Machining and Finishing. In the production process, materials are added to the product in each department *without increasing the number of units produced.* For the month of June the company records indicated the following production statistics for each department:

	MACHINING DEPARTMENT	FINISHING DEPARTMENT
Units in process, June 1	0	0
Units transferred from preceding department	0	60,000
Units started in production	80,000	0
Units completed and transferred out	60,000	50,000
Units in process, June 30	20,000	10,000
Percent of completion on units in process, June 30		
Materials	100%	100%
Labor	50%	70%
Overhead	25%	70%

Cost records showed the following charges for the month of June:

	MACHINING DEPARTMENT	FINISHING DEPARTMENT
Materials	$240,000	$ 90,000
Labor	140,000	142,500
Overhead	65,000	25,650

REQUIRED: For both the Machining and Finishing Departments, prepare in good form a Cost of Production Report for June. (Round all computations to the nearest cent.)

6—26. *Equivalent units/cost allocation—complex.* (AICPA adapted) In the course of your examination of the financial statements of the Zeus Company for the year ended December 31 you have ascertained the following concerning its manufacturing operations:

a. Zeus has two production departments (Fabricating and Finishing) and a Service Department. In the Fabricating Department polyplast is prepared from miracle mix and bypro. The Service Department provides services to both production departments.

b. The Fabricating and Finishing Departments use process cost accounting systems. Actual production costs, including overhead, are allocated monthly.

c. Service Department expenses are allocated to production departments as follows:

EXPENSE	ALLOCATION BASE
Building maintenance	Space occupied
Timekeeping and personnel	Number of employees
Other	50% to Fabricating, 50% to Finishing

d. Work-in-process is priced on an average basis.

e. The following data were taken from the Fabricating Department's records for December:

Quantities (units of polyplast):

In process, December 1	3,000
Started in process during month	25,000
Total units to be accounted for	28,000
Transferred to finishing department	22,000
In process, December 31	6,000
Total units accounted for	28,000

Cost of work-in-process, December 1:

Materials	$ 13,000
Labor	17,500
Overhead	21,500
	$ 52,000
Direct labor costs, December	$154,000
Departmental overhead, December	$130,550

f. Polyplast work-in-process at the beginning and the end of the month was partially completed as follows:

	MATERIALS	LABOR AND OVERHEAD
December 1	66⅔%	50%
Docembor 31	100%	75%

g. The following data were taken from raw materials inventory records for December: (FIFO pricing is used).

	MIRACLE MIX Quantity	Amount	BYPRO Quantity	Amount
Balance, December 1	62,000 @ $1.00	$62,000	265,000 @ $.07	$18,550
Purchases:				
December 12	39,500 @ $1.25	49,375		
December 20	28,500 @ $1.20	34,200		
Fabricating Department usage	83,200		50,000	

h. Service Department expenses for December (not included in departmental overhead, above) were:

Building maintenance	$ 45,000
Timekeeping and personnel	27,500
Other	39,000
	$111,500

i. Other information for December is presented below:

	SQUARE FEET OF SPACE OCCUPIED	NUMBER OF EMPLOYEES
Fabricating	75,000	180
Finishing	37,500	120
	112,500	300

REQUIRED: 1. For the Fabricating Department compute the equivalent number of units of polyplast, with separate calculations for materials and conversion cost (direct labor plus overhead), manufactured during December.
2. Compute the following items to be included in the Fabricating Department's production report for December, with separate calculations for materials, direct labor, and overhead. Prepare supporting schedules.

   a. Total material costs to be accounted for and total conversion costs to be accounted for.

   b. Unit costs for equivalent units manufactured.

   c. Transfers to Finishing Department during December and work-in-process at December 31. Reconcile your answer to part 2a.

6—27. *Equivalent production unit costs: two departments.* (AICPA adapted) Poole, Inc., produces a chemical compound by a unique chemical process which Poole has divided into two departments, A and B, for accounting purposes. The process functions as follows: The formula requires 1 pound of Chemical X and 1 pound of Chemical Y. In the simplest sense, 1 pound of Chemical X is processed in Department A and transferred to Department B for further processing, where 1 pound of Chemical Y is added evenly throughout the process. When the processing is complete in Department B, the finished chemical compound is transferred to Finished Goods. The process is continuous, operating 24 hours a day.

In Department A conversion costs are incurred uniformly throughout the process. Materials are added at the beginning of the process in Department A.

Poole's unit of measure for Work-in-Process and Finished Goods Inventories is pounds.

The following data are available for the month of October:

Unit Data		
	DEPARTMENT A	DEPARTMENT B
Work-in-Process, October 1	8,000 pounds	10,000 pounds
Stage of completion of beginning inventory (one batch per dept.)	75%	30%
Started or transferred in	50,000 pounds	?
Transferred out	46,500 pounds	50,000 pounds
Work-in-Process, October 31	?	?
Stage of completion of ending inventory (one batch per dept.)	20%	20%

Cost Data

	DEPARTMENT A	DEPARTMENT B
Costs in Beginning Work-in-Process Inventory:		
Materials	$ 25,200	$ 6,150
Conversion Costs	26,580	5,400
Prior Department Costs	—	75,870
Costs Added During October:		
Materials	160,400	101,430
Conversion costs	193,020	92,220
Totals	$405,200	$281,070

1. Prepare schedules computing equivalent pounds of production (materials and conversion costs) for Department A and for Department B for the month of October using the average method for inventory costing.
2. Calculate the cost of a unit transferred from Department A to Department B in October. Round to the nearest cent.
3. Calculate the cost of a unit transferred from Department B to Finished Goods during October. Round to the nearest cent.

6—28. *Reconstructing costs inputs and inventory valuations.* Sumner Company employs a process cost system. A unit of product passes through two departments—Assembly and Finishing—before it is completed. The following activity took place in the Finishing Department during May:

	UNITS
Work-in-Process Inventory, May 1	1,400
Units transferred in from the Assembly Department	14,000
Units transferred out to Finished Goods Inventory	11,200

Raw material is added at the beginning of the processing in the Finishing Department. The Work-in-Process Inventory was 40% complete as to conversion on May 1 and 70% complete as to conversion costs on May 31.

Sumner Company employs the average costing method. The cost per equivalent unit of production for each cost factor has been very stable and is as follows:

	COST PER EQUIVALENT UNIT
Cost of prior department	$5.00
Raw materials	1.00
Conversion cost	3.00
	$9.00

REQUIRED: 1. Determine the cost of production transferred to the Finished Goods Inventory.
2. Determine the cost of Work-in-Process Inventory on May 31.
3. Calculate the total amount of cost put into production in the Finishing Department in *May* for (a) materials and (b) conversion costs. Do not include costs which were put in during prior periods.
4. What was the carrying value of beginning Work-in-Process in the Finishing Department May 1?
5. Calculate the total costs transferred into the Finishing Department from prior departments during May.

6—29.   *Cost of Production Report; calculation of inputs.* (CMA adapted) West Corporation is a divisionalized manufacturing company. A product called Aggregate is manufactured in one department of the California Division. Aggregate is transferred upon completion to the Utah Division, where it is used in the manufacture of other products.

The raw material for Aggregate is added at the beginning of the process. Labor and overhead are added continuously throughout the process. In the California Division all departmental overhead is charged to the departments and divisional overhead is allocated to the departments on the basis of direct labor hours. The divisional overhead rate for the year is $2 per direct labor hour.

The following information relates to production during November:

a. Work-in-process, November 1 (4,000 pounds—75% complete):

Raw material	$22,300
Direct labor @ $5 per hour	$24,650
Departmental overhead	$12,000
Divisional overhead	$ 9,860
Total	$68,810

b. Raw material:

Inventory, November 1, 2,000 @ $5.000	$10,000
Purchases, November 3, 10,000 @ $5.10	$51,000
Purchases, November 18, 10,000 @ $5.15	$51,500
Put into production during November, 14,000 lb	

c. Direct labor costs @ $5.00/hour, $103,350.
d. Direct departmental overhead costs, $52,000.
e. Transferred to Utah Division, 15,000 lb.
f. Work-in-process, November 30: 3,000 lb, $33\frac{1}{3}$% complete.
g. The *FIFO* method is used for materials inventory valuation and the average method is for work-in-process inventories.

REQUIRED: Prepare a Cost of Production Report for the department of California Division producing Aggregate for November, presenting:

1. The equivalent units of production by cost factor of Aggregate (e.g., raw material, direct labor, and overhead).
2. A calculation of the equivalent unit cost for each cost factor of Aggregate.

Problems 6—30 and 6—31 are based on the Appendix to Chapter 6.

6—30.   *Equivalent units and FIFO costing.* Refer to the data provided in Problem 6—23 for the Pest-Away Company. Assume the company uses FIFO rather than an average costing assumption.

REQUIRED: 1. Prepare an Equivalent Units of Production Schedule.
2. Calculate the cost of a pound of pesticide that was in the beginning inventory in the Formulation Department and which is transferred to Packaging. (Round unit cost to the nearest cent.)
3. Calculate the cost of the pesticide which was both started and completed in the Formulation Department during the period and which is transferred to Packaging. (Round unit cost to the nearest cent.)
4. Determine the carrying value for the Work in Process ending inventory for the Formulation Department.

6—31.   *Equivalent units of production and units costs, FIFO costing asumption—two departments.* Use the data provided in Problem 6—27. Assume that Poole, Inc., used a *FIFO costing assumption* in conjunction with its process cost accounting system.

REQUIRED: 1. Prepare Equivalent Units of Production Schedules for the two departments for October.
2. Prepare journal entries to record the transfer of units which were in process at the beginning of the period to Department B and the transfer of units which were started and completed during the period to Department B. (Round all unit costs to the nearest cent.)
3. Calculate the unit costs of the two batches of units transferred from Department B to Finished Goods—i.e., those units which were in process at the beginning of the period and those units which were started and completed during the period. (Round all unit costs to the nearest cent.)
4. Calculate ending inventory valuations for Work-in-Process in both departments.

chapter seven

THE BUDGETARY PROCESS AND THE MECHANICS OF BUDGET PREPARATION

OBJECTIVES

After you have completed this chapter, you should be able to answer the following questions:

- What are the three types of management and control processes and how is each defined?
- How does a responsibility budget differ from a program budget?
- What is a responsibility center?
- What major factors should be considered in preparing a forecast of sales (or activity) for the budget period?
- What are the primary components of the budget package (the master budget) and how are they related to each other?
- Why is preparation of the sales or activity budget generally the first step in the budgetary process?
- How are the various schedules which make up the master budget prepared?
- How does the cash budget differ from the budgeted income statement?
- Why is the cash budget so critical to most organizations?

INTRODUCTION

This chapter describes what managers do and how those activities can be classified consistent with various management levels within the organization. The importance of the budget and the process by which it is developed are described. Finally, the mechanics of putting together an operating budget and a financial budget are illustrated.

THE MANAGEMENT PROCESS

Organizations, whether profit-making or nonprofit, whether manufacturing or service entities, are formed to accomplish a certain purpose or purposes. The local Chamber of Commerce has as one of its objectives to promote the business interests of the municipality in which it is located. The local McDonald's restaurant wants to make a profit by offering fast food service.

The persons who decide on the purposes or goals of an organization and who make decisions and play a leadership role within the organization are known collectively as *managers*. The authority and responsibilities of a particular manager vary with the philosophy of the employing entity and with the manager's level within the organization.

The function of the manager—the management process—is frequently broken down into two activities: planning and control. In very broad general terms, *planning* is concerned with determining what will be done within an organization, how it will be done, and who will do it. When a factory foreman assigns a worker to a particular job, this is an outcome of the planning process. IBM's decision to offer a personal computer as part of its product line is another example of the application of the planning function.

Control is the process by which a manager attempts to assure that the organization's direction and the activities of its people are in keeping with its plans. The use of time cards on which an employee's arrivals and departures are recorded is an example of the exercising of control. When the Board of Directors of an organization asks the Chief Executive Officer to explain why profits were less for the current year than for the past year, this too is an example of the control function at work.

TYPES OF PLANNING AND CONTROL PROCESSES

Robert Anthony[1] has identified three types of planning and control processes: (1) strategic planning, (2) management control, and (3) operational control.

Strategic planning is carried on at the highest levels of the organization and is the process of deciding on organizational goals and the strategies that should be used in achieving them. Policy setting, the definition of broad corporate goals, and the planning of major additions to or reductions in the company's products and facilities are encompassed by the strategic planning process. Planning for a new product line and deciding to acquire another company are activities consistent with the strategic planning function. The planning function, as opposed to the control function, tends to be emphasized at those levels of the organization where strategic planning is done.

Management control is concerned with carrying out the organizational strategies effectively and efficiently. The preparation of the budget, one of the best-known and widest-used managerial control tools, is done at this level. Examples of management control types of activities are (1) deciding on the purchase of a new machine, or (2) deciding what type of advertising is consistent with the corporate goals defined at the strategic planning level.

The control function is most important in the third planning and control process—*operational control.* This is defined as the process of assuring that specific tasks are carried out effectively and efficiently. Activities that are part of the operational control function include determining whether credit should be granted to a customer, deciding the sequence of jobs which are to be worked on, and determining whether workers are on the job.

In reality the three types of planning and control processes are integrated with one another. We cannot look at an organization and say, "This is where strategic planning ends and operational control begins," or, "This is operational control and this is management control."

In this text we are most concerned with the management control process. We will generally assume that an organization has defined its goals and developed appropriate strategies. How can the organization assure that those strategies are applied effectively and efficiently? One of the major tools developed for doing so is the budget, and we shall be discussing budgets and budgeting in this and the next three chapters.

---

[1] Robert N. Anthony, *Planning and Control Systems: A Framework for Analysis* (Boston: Division of Research, Graduate School of Business Administration, Harvard University, 1965).

PURPOSES OF BUDGETING

Once a company has defined its objectives as part of the strategic planning process, it must develop plans consistent with meeting those objectives. A budget is the quantitative expression of those plans—it describes in dollars the results of the planning process. However, it is not only the end product of the budgeting process which is important, but the process itself. The budgeting cycle makes a major contribution to an organization in the following areas: planning, communication, motivation, and control.

Planning

A budget is by definition an expression of an entity's future plans. While many people think of a budget in control terms—a means of limiting expenditures—one of the most important and helpful outcomes of budget preparation is that it forces managers in an organization to think about the future and its implications in an orderly manner. How many hospital beds will be needed? Can the raw materials for our product be obtained and at what cost? Will there be sufficient cash to pay our bills? How many salespersons do we need to meet our volume objectives?

The planning required for budget preparation focuses the attention of all managers on the common goals of the organization and the contribution of each manager to those goals. It leads to a consideration of current problems and of problems which may develop in the future and the formulation of appropriate strategies for coping with them.

Communication

The budgeting process fosters communication—both from the bottom of the organization upward to the top and from the top downward to the bottom. In terms of upward communication, the budgeting process provides the mechanism whereby a manager can communicate his or her needs to higher levels within the organization. For example, consider the manager of a claims department within an insurance company which is expected to process 100,000 claims during the next budget cycle. How many claims adjusters will be needed consistent with this volume of business, and what related expenses will be incurred to service those claims? The manager of the claims department communicates his or her estimate of these needs as part of the budget process.

In the downward communication process—from the higher levels of management to the lower—as an initial step in the budget process the organization's goals and objectives must be spelled out. In addition, the specific expectations of the organization with respect to a particular manager are communicated to that manager. For example, after considering the budget request of the manager of the claims department previously referred to and negotiating with that manager to develop budgetary figures agreeable both to him or her and to the overall organization, top management sets the budget. The budget figures communicate to the claims department manager the organization's expectations for the budget period.

Motivation

Most persons have achievement needs; that is, they need to have goals they are working toward and which they can meet. If the goals defined by the budget are realistic, they should serve as a means of challenging the manager and those persons whom the manager supervises. Also, since the budget expresses the plans of the organization, it tends to insure that employees are motivated to work toward the organization's goals rather than toward their own individual goals.

Control

The budget serves as a control device in a number of ways. First, the budgeting process requires the review of estimated future inputs and outputs to see if they are reasonable and consistent with goals of the entity. Second, the budget serves as a benchmark against which actual results of operations can be measured and performance of individual managers evaluated. Significant variations of actual results from planned results will require explanation and perhaps corrective actions by the responsible manager. Third, the budget focuses and directs the activities of employees toward the goals of the organization.

RESPONSIBILITY VERSUS PROGRAM BUDGETS

For the complex organization there are two outputs of the budget process— a program budget and a responsibility budget. Both parts come up with the same final figures, but they present budget data in different forms. A *program budget* focuses on the plans of an entity in terms of major classes of activities. What constitutes a program for budget purposes is defined by the management of the organization preparing the budget. A manufacturing concern may define a program as a particular product line— television sets, washing machines, and refrigerators. A CPA firm may budget in terms of auditing services, management consulting services, and tax services. A university may budget by departments.

A *responsibility budget* relates budgeted amounts to a specific manager who is the head of a responsibility center. A *responsibility center* is *an*

ILLUSTRATION
7-1

Program Budget

CONSUMER PRODUCTS, INC
Budgeted Income Statement
Black and White Televisions
for the Month of February

Sales		$3,565,000
Cost of Goods Sold	$1,085,000	
Selling Expenses	945,000	
General and Administrative Expenses	769,000	2,799,000
Product-Line Income		$ 766,000

Responsibility Budget

Assembly Department Supervisor's Budget
Black and White Televisions
for the Month of February

Controllable Costs:	
Raw materials	$ 153,000
Direct Labor	321,000
Controllable Manufacturing Overhead	89,000
Budgeted Controllable Costs	$ 563,000

organizational subcomponent headed by a manager who is charged with accomplishing defined organizational goals and performing specified activities.[2] The responsibility budget for each manager's responsibility center should contain those amounts which are controllable by that manager and for which he or she is responsible. The responsibility budget for the manager of the data processing department, for instance, should show those costs of the department for which that manager is being held accountable by persons at higher levels in the organization.

At the highest management level of an entity (the chief executive officer) the responsibility budget and the program budget will be the same, because the head of the organization is responsible for all the programs of the company. At upper-level managerial positions a program budget and the responsibility budget will be the same if the manager has responsibility for a particular program. This point is clarified by Illustration 7-1, which shows a summarized program budget and a summarized responsibility budget. If the company in the illustration, Consumer Products, Inc., is organized in such a way that a manager is responsible for the revenues and expenses relevant to black-and-white television sets, the

[2] A full discussion of responsibility centers is provided in the next chapter.

program budget which describes anticipated transactions for this particular product line and the responsibility budget by which that manager's performance is evaluated may be the same.

On the other hand, the performance of managers who are involved with black-and-white television sales and production at lower levels cannot be evaluated by use of the program budget. Instead, a responsibility budget such as that shown for the Assembly Department Supervisor must be developed as a basis for evaluating performance. Note that this responsibility budget contains a statement of controllable costs only. The concept of controllable costs will be discussed in the next chapter. The budgeted cost of the manager of the Assembly Department are just a part of the cost of goods sold for the product-line budget—for several reasons: (1) Other departments are involved in the production of black-and-white sets. (2) The cost of goods manufactured and subsequently sold includes all manufacturing costs, not just those controllable by a particular manager. (3) All or part of the television sets on which the Assembly Department will work during February may go into inventory, and thus their costs would not be included as part of budgeted cost of goods sold.

THE BUDGETARY PROCESS

The process by which the budget is developed is described graphically in Illustration 7-2. At the highest levels of the organization—where strategic planning is done—the broad goals, policies, and strategies are set. These are the foundation on which the budgeting process is based. What kind of organization do we want to be? Is the organizational objective to be the largest in terms of revenues? Do we want to be the dominant firm in a particular product area? Do we want to be known as the company which produces the most exclusive product or the highest-quality product? How an organization defines itself is critical in setting more specific goals and objectives. This type of goal setting tends to be continuous, rather than a specific step in the budgeting process.

The first step characterizing the budget process tends to be the development of critical assumptions relative to the budget period. The persons involved in this process are asking: "What factors significantly influence our operations? What will happen to these factors during the budget period?" For example, interest costs may be critical to a company. If the company preparing a budget is engaged primarily in the construction of homes, the assumed level of interest costs for the budget period will have a major impact on defining the volume of business. In most circumstances it would be unrealistic for such a company to budget a large increase in volume if it had as one of its critical assumptions high interest costs. Other examples of variables which may be critical to planning for the budget period include the rate of inflation, demographic characteristics

**ILLUSTRATION
7-2**

The budgetary
process

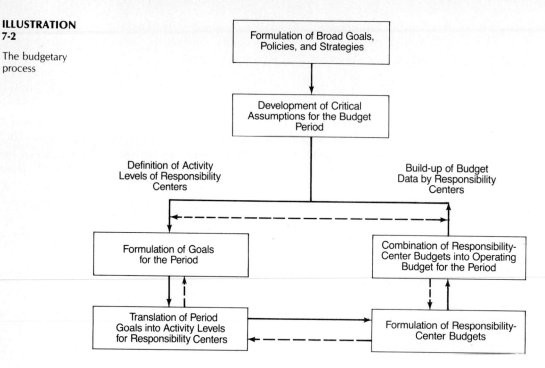

and trends, availability and costs of raw materials, and the level of personal income.

ILLUSTRATION FROM PRACTICE:
A CRITICAL BUDGET VARIABLE FOR BRAND REX

Brand Rex was described briefly in an earlier chapter. Copper is an important component in many Brand Rex products. As a result, at the highest level of the organization a price per pound for copper for the budget period is forecast. This price is communicated to managers involved in the budgetary process, and they are required to use it in developing their budget input.

The second step in the budgetary process is to define the goals for the budget period, taking into consideration the critical assumptions developed to begin this process. These goals may originally be stated in terms such as increasing the contributions of individuals to a charitable organization by 10%, increasing sales volume by 15%, or yielding a return on invested assets of 20%. To make these goals operational, however, they will have to be translated into activity levels—for example, units of product to be sold, dollar volume of services to be rendered, or dollar amounts of funds to be raised from various sources.

These period goals expressed as activity levels will in turn be restated as responsibility-center goals. To illustrate, to achieve its profit goals a company may have to produce and sell 10,000 units. How many of these units will be the responsibility of the manager of the Ohio factory and how many the responsibility of the manager of the Mississippi factory?

Next, responsibility-center goals will be translated into responsibility-center budgets. The setting of an activity level enables a responsibility-center manager to determine an appropriate level of costs. If the manager of the Ohio factory, for example, knows that he or she is expected to produce 4,000 units during the budget period, appropriate cost for the production of those units can be projected.

The combination of the responsibility-center budgets into a whole for the organization is the final step in the budgetary process, and the result is the organization's operating budget. As you will note from looking at Illustration 7-2, the goal-setting aspects of the budgetary process are viewed as primarily flowing from the top to the bottom of the organization, while the build-up of the budget figures, once goals have been assigned to responsibility centers, is a bottom-to-top-of-the-organization process. It should be stressed that both in goal setting and in formulation of budget figures, there should be two-way communication—from the top to the bottom and from the bottom to the top of the organization. This flow of communication is indicated in Illustration 7-2 by dotted lines. For example, the manager of the Ohio factory should participate in making the decision that 4,000 units of production represents a realistic goal for the budget period.

In the build-up of the budget figures, two way communication is also critical. In the final formulation of the operating budget there is negotiation between the responsibility-center manager and higher-level managers. This negotiation process is central to an effective responsibility accounting and budgeting system. The responsibility budget represents a major tool in evaluating the performance of a particular manager. If it is to be used successfully, the manager being evaluated must be committed to that budget and believe it is realistic. This commitment results from negotiation, whereby the budgetee and his or her organizational superior agree to an appropriate budget level for the period. Both parties agree that the budget is realistic and thus represents an acceptable yardstick against which actual performance can be measured.

To illustrate, the manager of the Ohio factory may develop a set of cost figures for the production of 4,000 units and calculate a unit cost of $12. This figure will be reviewed by the next highest level of the organization—say, the Vice-President of Manufacturing. The Vice-President of Manufacturing may contend that $12 is somewhat high, based on the profit objectives of the company. He or she may discuss with the factory manager cost-cutting measures which could be employed. The final result may be an agreement between the Vice-President and the factory manager that an appropriate level of unit costs for the budget period is $11.90. At the conclusion of the negotiation process, the factory manager should be committed to the production of 4,000 units at that unit cost.

ILLUSTRATION FROM PRACTICE:
THE BUDGET CALENDAR FOR AMERICAN CAN COMPANY

American Can is a diversified company primarily engaged in three businesses: packaging, specialty retailing, and financial services.

The packaging sector manufactures metal cans for the food, beverage, and specialty metal markets. This sector also manufactures single layer and complex multilayer plastic tubes and bottles, as well as providing plastics packaging such as flexible film, wrappers, food, liners, and pouches.

American Can's Fingerhut subsidiary is one of the largest direct-mail marketing companies in the United States, selling a broad line of general merchandise and serving more than eight million customers. Fingerhut's success is largely due to careful market definition and use of sophisticated computer technology. Another important contributor to the specialty retailing sector is the Musicland Group, including Sam Goody. With approximately 400 specialty retailing stores, Musicland is the world's largest retailer of prerecorded music products.

The newest and fastest growing business of American Can is the financial services sector, which includes several insurance companies, a mutual funds management firm with close to $5 billion in assets under management, and a brokerage firm. The insurance companies form the fastest growing insurance operation in the country. Combined "new sales" of the insurance subsidiaries would rank American Can in the top five of the 1800 life insurance companies nationwide in terms of "new business booked."

American Can has over 88,000 shareholders and more than 35,000 employees worldwide. Revenues in 1982 totaled $4.1 billion and assets at year-end were $2.6 billion.

	CURRENT YEAR
Long-range plan review completed and financial objectives established for budget	Aug. 15
Budget Instructions Issued	Sept. 1
Preliminary Budgets and Operating Overview letters from Business Units due at Corporate.	Oct. 21
Corporate Controller briefs Executive Committee on Consolidated Budget and significant issues	Nov. 15
Sector Budget review meetings with the Executive Committee; issues addressed and revisions made as agreed.	Nov. 16–23
Executive Committee meets to review final Budget.	Dec. 10
Board of Directors Budget Review	Dec. 13
	BUDGET YEAR
Income Statement Budget calendarization due at Corporate.	Jan. 10
Balance sheet and cash flow Budget calendarization due at Corporate.	Jan. 15

COMPONENTS OF THE MASTER BUDGET

Manufacturers

All the outputs of the budgetary process are known collectively as the *master budget* or the *comprehensive budget*. Budget terminology and classifications differ from company to company, but for purposes of this text we will think of the master budget for a manufacturing concern as consisting of these major components.

1. Operating budget—budgeted income statement supported by these major schedules:
   a. Sales budget.
   b. Production and inventory budget supported by:
      (1) Direct materials purchases and usage budget.
      (2) Direct labor budget.
      (3) Manufacturing overhead budget.
   c. Cost of goods sold budget.
   d. Selling expense budget.
   e. General and administrative expense budget.
   f. Financial income and expense budget.
2. Financial budget—budgeted balance sheet supported by these major schedules:
   a. Cash budget.
   b. Budgeted statement of changes in financial position (not illustrated in the chapter).
3. Capital expenditures budget (not illustrated in the chapter).

The *operating budget* summarizes the results of an organization's anticipated transactions for the budget period normally a year. The *budgeted income statement*, as can be seen from the outline above, is supported by a series of related budgets which provide the detail data for the budgeted revenues and expenses.

The *budgeted balance sheet* shows the company's anticipated financial position at the end of the accounting period consistent with the transactions described in the budgeted income statement. The estimated level of each at the balance-sheet date is supported by the *cash budget*, which provides details of cash inflows and outflows.

The *capital expenditures budget* describes the anticipated timing and outlays for longer-term projects, such as the acquisition of new equipment or the introduction of a new product line. Because of the longer time horizon for capital projects, the capital expenditures budget may project expenditures for a more extended period than one year, such as three, five, or even ten years.

Illustration 7-3 shows the relationship among the parts of the master budget.

Nonmanufacturing entities.   The basic structure of the master budget for nonmanufacturing organizations will be similar to that for the manufacturer. There will be an operating budget which describes sources of

ILLUSTRATION 7-3

The relationship of budget components

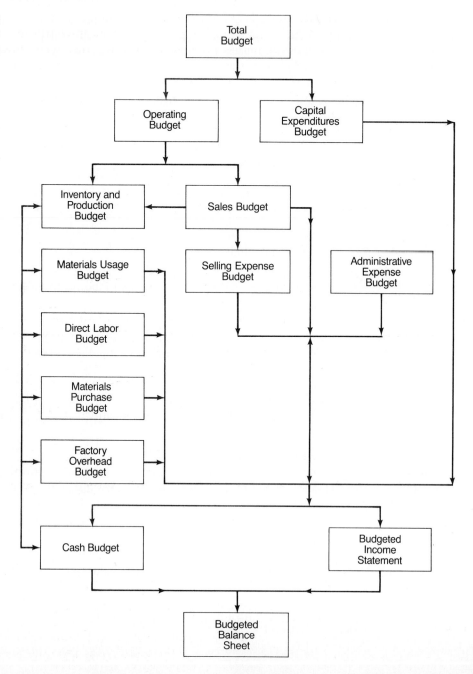

revenues or, for the organization which does not sell goods or services, sources of funding. In addition, expenses will be estimated and included in the operating budget. A budgeted statement of financial position accompanied by a cash budget and a captial expenditures budget would complete the budget package. However, the nature of the individual parts of the operating budget may differ from those described for the manufacturer.

For the nonmanufacturing firm, revenues may come from sources other than sales. A bank may budget revenues from sources such as interest, trust and agency fees, customer service fees, and trading account profits. A school system may have as sources of funds (revenues) town appropriations, state and federal grants, and special grants.

The manufacturing organization's expense budgets described are based on functional income statement classifications consistent with its activities: manufacturing, selling, and general administration. For retailers or service organizations there will be no production and inventory budget supported by a direct materials purchases and usage budget, a direct labor budget, and a manufacturing overhead budget, because manufacturing is not one of the functions of these organizations. Instead, budget expense categories will be derived consistent with the way the organization wants to classify its costs. For example, one brokerage firm prepares expense budgets based on the following classifications: officer and employee compensation and benefits, occupancy and equipment costs, communications costs, clearance and floor brokerage fees, interest, and miscellaneous and taxes. A museum budgets for the following types of expenses, among others: curatorial, education, financial and administration, public information, development and editorial, and membership services.

Regardless of what the individual parts of the master budget package are called (sales or sources of funding, for instance), a complete set of budgets for an organization will describe the anticipated financial results of its activities during the period (the operating budget), its financial position at the end of the period, and its anticipated capital expenditures. Not all organizations prepare a complete set of budget documents; some may omit the budgeted balance sheet or the capital expenditures budget.

IMPORTANCE OF DEFINING THE ACTIVITY LEVEL

We use the term *activity level* to describe the amount of output that an organization or a part of that organization produces for a period. While sales is a very common definition of activity for budget purposes, entities other than manufacturers and retailers may use some other measure of activity. For example, the definition of activity level may be service hours, number of customers, number of beds occupied, number of accounts maintained, or number of students enrolled. However the activity level is defined, its establishment is generally the starting point of the budget process, because many expenses, cash flows, the balance-sheet position, and in the long-run capital expenditure requirements are directly related to the level of output for the entity for the period.

As you can see from Illustration 7-3, much of the budget package is related directly to the sales budget. How many units we need to produce is determined by what we anticipate selling. The number of units to be produced determines the level of direct materials purchases and usage, the direct labor budget, and manufacturing overhead. Variable selling expenses are defined by the number of units sold, and all other selling expenses and administrative expenses are influenced by our sales volume. A large part of cash flows described in the cash budget are related to sales volume. Cash collections will depend on sales; cash outflows for raw materials, labor, overhead, and selling and administrative expenses are related to volume. In preparing the budgeted balance sheet, the level of cash, receivables, and inventories will depend on the budgeted sales volume. What kinds of capital expenditures we will make and the subsequent reflection of these in our budgeted balance sheet and cash budget depends on our longer-term volume expectations.

The activity level is also a major determinant of expense levels, financial position, and, in the longer term, capital expenditure requirements for the nonmanufacturing organization. The estimation of how many students will be enrolled, how many clients will require service, or how many hospital beds are needed will influence the level of many expenses for organizations who measure their activity level in these terms and is the starting point for the budget process.

FORECASTING THE ACTIVITY LEVEL

An extended discussion of the forecasting of the activity level for an organization is beyond the scope of this course. However, we do want to point out some of the more important aspects of the forecasting process.

The formulation of a forecast may be based primarily on judgment of knowledgeable persons within the organization, on the use of statistical or econometric models, or a combination of the two. Whatever method is used, consideration should be given to:

1. General economic conditions and those economic factors critical to the organization.
2. Industry conditions and outlook.
3. Managerial plans for the future.
4. Historical data and historical relationships.

General Economic Conditions and Critical Factors

An organization's volume of activity is influenced by the general state of the economy and by some specific economic factors critical to the firm. Will the economy be in a recession? Will the country be at war or at peace?

To assess the economic outlook, a large organization may have its own staff that develops economic data. For many organizations this is beyond the scope of their resources, but fortunately many outside sources report on the state of the economy. These range from U.S. Government publications such as *Economic Indicators, The Federal Reserve Bulletin*, and *Survey of Current Business* to nongovernment publications such as the National Industrial Conference Board's *The Conference Board's Business Record*, Chase Manhattan Bank's *Business in Brief*, and the First National City Bank of New York's *Business and Economic Conditions*. In addition, widely read periodicals such as the *Wall Street Journal* and *Business Week* contain economic information.

Easily accessible printed sources of economic and other data useful in the forecasting process continue to be important. However, with modern computer technology, especially the advent of the small or personal computer, the person needing information can access it directly and have it displayed on a screen or printed out in his or her office.

A so-called "on-line data-base industry" has emerged. This industry sells data-bank access to users. These data banks may include a variety of information ranging from very general to very specific. For example, one could get:

1. A forecast of the inflation rate for the coming quarter or year.
2. Sales by the major producers of a particular product such as automobiles.
3. The anticipated demand for a product such as colored television in a part of the country, for example, Alabama.
4. The profit margins of different-size companies in an industry for a period of years.

The current problem for many organizations is not the lack of data but rather the decision as to which sources are most relevant and can be justified on a cost/benefit basis.

Generally organizations find that certain critical economic factors also influence their activity level. As part of the forecasting process it is essential that we know (1) which specific economic factors are most important, (2) how these economic factors will be defined for the budget period, and (3) the effects of these factors on our performance. Specific economic factors which may be critical include short- and long-term interest rates, the rate of inflation, the unemployment rate, and tax rates. To give an example, consider a company which is engaged primarily in building homes. The availability and rate of mortgage funds is critical. It would probably be unrealistic for such a firm to forecast a large increase in its volume in the face of either a shortage of mortgage funds or high costs for such funds. Information on these critical economic factors is available from the sources previously listed for general economic information.

Industry Conditions

An organization, as part of its forecasting process, needs to consider what is happening to the industry of which it is a part. Is it a growing industry where new competitors are entering? What kinds of actions that will influence our volume can we anticipate from our competitors—new product lines? lower prices? What is the anticipated total output of the industry?

Industry assumptions, like general economic assumptions, can be based on data generated by the forecasting firm or data developed by external sources. Various trade association publications provide information of this type. One of many sources, Standard & Poor's, issues a series of Industry Surveys covering 45 industries, consisting of a *Basic Analysis*, usually issued annually, followed by supplementary sections entitled *Current Analysis and Outlook*. A sample page is shown in Illustration 7-4. In addition, more and more industry-related information is available from data-base firms and accessible directly on the computer.

Management's Plans for the Future

Another factor which must be considered in formulating a forecast is management's plans for the future. What changes are being anticipated which will cause a volume change? These could include things such as:

1. Changes in channels of distribution.
2. Price, quality, or packaging changes.
3. Introduction of new products.
4. Dropping of old products.
5. Changes in the type of advertising or the expenditure level.

Historical Data and Relationships

The starting point in most forecasting processes is what happened in the past. What was the volume for a particular product? How did the sales of Product A influence those of Product B? What is the trend in demand for a particular good or service? What was our market share?

Taking an overly simple illustration, which incorporates general economic conditions, the industry outlook, management's plans, and historical data into a judgment-based forecast, a manager might reason as follows:

Historical data and relationships:	We sold 10,000 units last year at $2.50 each, which represented 30% of the total market for this product.
General economy conditions and critical factors:	Business conditions are improving. The inflation rate for the budget period is expected to be less than 4%. Short-term borrowing rates will fluctuate between 9 and $10\frac{1}{2}$%.

Industry outlook:

The improved state of the economy will be translated into a 10% volume increase in industry sales. Because of the low inflation rate, costs will increase only slightly and sales prices will probably be raised by less than 5%.

A new competitor will be selling our product line, which means new strategies on our part to retain our market share.

Management plans:

Changing the credit terms which we are extending will help us retain our volume and not be too costly, based on the outlook for interest rates.

Translation into forecast figures:

The total market will increase by 10% and we shall retain our 30% share. Therefore, our projected sales are 10,000 × 1.10 = 11,000; Raising prices by 4% will give us a sales price of $2.60 ($2.50 × 1.04 = $2.60). Our projected sales = 11,000 × $2.60 = $28,600.

PARTICIPATION IN THE FORECAST PROCESS

There is a great deal of variation between companies as to who participates in the sales (activity-level) forecasting process and the nature of that participation. Some firms see forecasting as confined to highest-echelon line managers, while others entrust it to a staff unit. Some firms use their salespersons as a major source of forecast information, as these persons are assumed to be closest to the user and thus better able to assess future demand. Product-line managers may be considered a primary source of input to the forecasting process.

Whoever participates, the organization should provide the participants with the relevant information and assumptions described previously: information as to the state of the economy, the critical economic factors for the company and what the future expectation for those factors is, management's plans, and historical data. Some organizations develop a data package which contains some or all of this information and give it to participants in the forecast process. This is essential if all participants are to start at the same place with the same view of the world. Forms which structure forecast data are usually desirable if there is extended participation in the process by individuals with different backgrounds and skills. This structuring is necessary so that data can be combined into a meaningful form by those charged with mechanically putting the forecast together.

Regardless of how the forecast is generated, the final step in the process is the acceptance of the forecast by the highest-level line manager in the organization; it may even require approval by the board of directors. Implied in this acceptance is the commitment of the organization and its resources to achieving the forecast.

If managers at middle and upper levels are to be committed to the forecast, negotiations in formulating the final version should have taken

ILLUSTRATION 7-4 Sample Data from Standard & Poor's Industry Surveys

COLA REMAINS NO. 1 FLAVOR
(In Percent—1980)

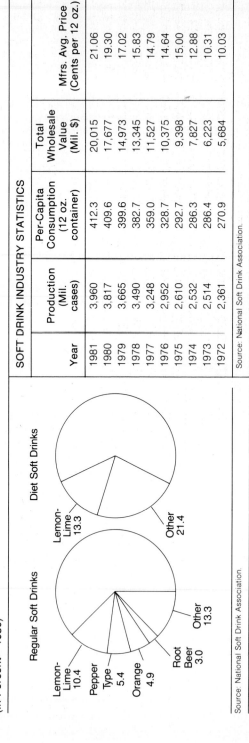

Regular Soft Drinks

Lemon-Lime 10.4
Pepper Type 5.4
Orange 4.9
Root Beer 3.0
Other 13.3

Diet Soft Drinks

Lemon-Lime 13.3
Other 21.4

Source: National Soft Drink Association.

SOFT DRINK INDUSTRY STATISTICS

Year	Production (Mil. cases)	Per-Capita Consumption (12 oz. container)	Total Wholesale Value (Mil. $)	Mfrs. Avg. Price (Cents per 12 oz.)
1981	3,960	412.3	20,015	21.06
1980	3,817	409.6	17,677	19.30
1979	3,665	399.6	14,973	17.02
1978	3,490	382.7	13,345	15.83
1977	3,248	359.0	11,527	14.79
1976	2,952	328.7	10,375	14.64
1975	2,610	292.7	9,398	15.00
1974	2,532	286.3	7,827	12.88
1973	2,514	286.4	6,223	10.31
1972	2,361	270.9	5,684	10.03

Source: National Soft Drink Association.

CONSUMPTION OF SOFT DRINKS BY BRAND

Company and Brand	1976 Million Cases	1976 % Market	1977 Million Cases	1977 % Market	1978 Million Cases	1978 % Market	1979 Million Cases	1979 % Market	1980 Million Cases	1980 % Market	1981 Million Cases	1981 % Market	1980–81 % Change
Coca-Cola Co.													
Coca-Cola	1,190.0	24.3	1,290.0	24.5	1,335.0	24.3	1,365.0	23.9	1,425.0	24.3	1,463.0	24.2	2.7
Sprite	130.0	2.7	150.0	2.8	158.0	2.9	165.0	2.9	171.0	2.9	178.0	2.9	4.1
Tab	125.0	2.6	137.0	2.6	149.0	2.7	170.0	3.0	188.0	3.2	216.0	3.6	14.9
Fanta	112.0	2.3	119.0	2.3	112.0	2.0	107.0	1.9	98.0	1.7	88.0	1.5	−10.2
Mr. Pibb	37.0	0.7	45.0	0.9	46.0	0.8	43.0	0.8	39.0	0.7	34.0	0.6	−12.8
Fresca	31.0	0.6	28.0	0.5	27.0	0.5	25.0	0.4	26.0	0.4	24.0	0.4	−7.7
Others	10.0	0.2	15.0	0.3	19.0	0.4	61.0	1.1	75.0	1.2	79.0	1.3	5.3
Total	1,635.0	33.4	1,784.0	33.9	1,846.0	33.6	1,936.0	34.0	2,022.0	34.4	2,082.0	34.5	3.0

PepsiCo, Inc.													
Pepsi-Cola	830.0	17.0	903.0	17.2	969.0	17.6	1,022.0	17.9	1,056.0	17.9	1,104.0	18.3	4.5
Mountain Dew	73.0	1.5	100.0	1.9	130.0	2.4	156.0	2.8	169.0	2.9	179.0	3.0	5.9
Diet Pepsi	90.0	1.9	109.0	2.1	127.0	2.3	142.0	2.5	154.0	2.6	173.0	2.9	12.3
Pepsi Light	25.0	0.5	27.0	0.5	22.0	0.4	24.0	0.4	24.0	0.4	29.0	0.5	20.9
Teem	12.1	0.2	12.5	0.2	14.0	0.3	15.0	0.3	15.0	0.3	14.0	0.2	−6.7
Others	15.3	0.3	20.3	0.4	19.0	0.3	18.0	0.3	17.0	0.3	16.0	0.2	−5.9
Total	1,045.4	21.4	1,171.9	22.3	1,281.0	23.3	1,377.0	24.2	1,435.0	24.4	1,515.0	25.1	5.6
*Seven-Up Co.													
7-Up	305.8	6.3	315.0	6.0	322.0	5.9	320.0	5.6	317.0	5.4	301.0	5.0	−5.0
Diet 7-Up	60.0	1.2	62.3	1.2	63.0	1.1	63.6	1.1	64.0	1.1	70.0	1.2	9.4
Dixie Cola	10.0	0.2	10.5	0.2	10.2	0.2	10.0	0.2	9.0	0.2	8.0	0.1	−11.1
Howdy Flavors	1.3	—	1.2	—	1.0	—	1.0	—	1.0	—	1.0	—	—
Total	377.1	7.7	389.0	7.4	396.2	7.2	394.6	6.9	391.0	6.7	380.0	6.3	2.8
Dr Pepper Co.													
Dr Pepper	243.0	5.0	278.0	5.3	299.5	5.4	311.5	5.5	323.0	5.5	326.0	6.4	0.9
Sugar Free Dr Pepper	39.0	0.8	52.0	1.0	60.5	1.1	62.9	1.1	69.1	1.2	79.5	1.3	15.1
Total	282.0	5.8	330.0	6.3	360.0	6.5	374.4	6.6	392.1	6.7	405.5	6.7	3.4
Royal Crown Cos.													
Royal Crown	162.2	3.3	168.0	3.2	164.0	3.0	159.0	2.8	163.0	2.8	154.0	2.5	−1.1
Diet Rite Cola	40.6	0.8	40.6	0.8	40.2	0.7	38.0	0.7	40.5	0.7	52.0	0.8	28.4
Nehi and Others	55.6	1.2	53.0	1.0	53.5	1.0	53.0	0.9	50.0	0.8	43.0	0.7	−14.0
Total	258.4	5.3	261.6	5.0	257.7	4.7	250.0	4.4	253.5	4.3	249.0	4.1	−1.8
Crush International													
Hires, Crush, etc.	R136.4	R2.8	R150.7	R2.9	R169.6	R3.1	R180.0	R3.4	186.3	3.2	193.6	3.2	3.9
Sun Drop	R19.5	R0.4	R23.0	R0.4	R24.0	R0.4	R25.0	R0.5	25.9	0.4	26.4	0.4	1.9
Total	R155.9	R3.2	R173.7	R3.3	R193.6	R3.5	R205.0	R3.9	212.2	3.6	220.0	3.6	3.7
Total (6 companies)	R3,753.8	R76.8	R4,112.6	R78.2	R4,337.5	R78.9	R4,540.0	F79.6	4,705.8	80.1	4,851.5	80.4	3.1
Others	R1,136.2	R23.2	R1,147.4	R21.8	R1,162.5	R21.1	R1,160.0	F20.4	1,169.2	19.9	1,183.5	19.6	1.2
Grand Total	4,890.0	100.0	5,259.0	100.0	5,500.0	100.0	5,700.0	100.0	5,875.0	100.0	6,035.0	100.0	2.7

*Subsidiary of Phillip Morris Inc. as of June 1978. R—Revised.
Source: Beverage Industry and John C. Maxwell.
Source: Standard & Poor's Industry Surveys, 1982.

place. The result should be a general feeling throughout the organization that the goals implied by the forecast are realistic.

ILLUSTRATIVE EXAMPLE

To illustrate how the budget is put together once the sales forecast has been made, we are going to use a company, the New Frontiers Company, which makes fiberglass canoes. To keep our example within manageable limits we will assume the company makes only one type of canoe, which it sells to retailers at $300. Budget data are presented for a three-month period, rather than for the annual period that is the normal budget cycle.

An organization chart for New Frontiers is shown in Illustration 7-5. The levels within the organization have been kept to a minimal number. Two Vice-Presidents, one of Operations and the other of Administration and Finance, each have two persons reporting to them. The Vice-President of Operations oversees the work of the Production Manager and the Sales Manager. The Vice-President of Finance and Administration has reporting to him or her the Manager of Accounting and Data Processing and the Personnel Manager.

The Balance Sheet for New Frontiers as of the beginning of the budget period is shown in Illustration 7-6. The numbers in this illustration have been assumed and cannot be recalculated by the user.

For each component of the budget, the process used by New Frontiers to derive the data is described below. The process described is just one approach which could be used; it is presented for illustrative purposes rather than as representing the only way this information can and should be formulated.

ILLUSTRATION 7-5

New Frontiers, Inc.,
Organization Chart

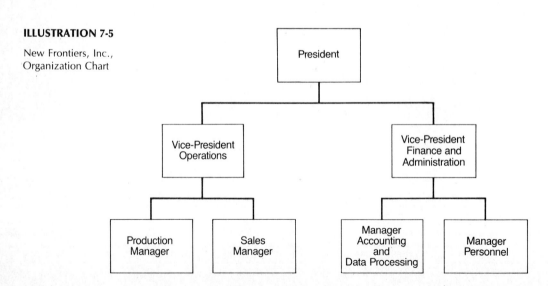

ILLUSTRATION
7-6

NEW FRONTIERS
Balance Sheet
as of January 1
(the beginning of the budget period)

Current Assets		*Current Liabilities*	
Cash	$ 17,000	Accounts Payable	$ 22,500
		Accrued Interest	
Accounts Receivable	120,000	Expense	4,000
Marketable Securities	30,000	Taxes Payable	38,500
Inventories:[a]			
Raw Materials[b]	3,975	Long-Term Debt	
Work-in-Process	0	Currently Due	100,000
Finished Goods[c]	10,400		
		Total Current	
Total Current Assets	$181,375	Liabilities	$165,000
Property, Plant and			
Equipment	$853,000	12% Mortgage Payable	200,000
Less: Accumulated			
Depreciation	218,820	Total Liabilities	$365,000
Net Property, Plant and		*Stockholders' Equity*	
Equipment	$634,180	Common Stock	250,000
		Paid-in Capital in	
		Excess of Par	100,000
		Retained Earnings	100,555
		Total Stockholders'	
		Equity	$450,555
		Total Liabilities and	
Total Assets	$815,555	Stockholders' Equity	$815,555

[a] A LIFO costing assumption is used for both Raw Materials and Finished Goods Inventories.
[b] On hand were 159 units which cost $25 each.
[c] On hand were 80 canoes which cost $130 each to produce.

The following budget schedules are illustrated:

Schedule 1: Sales Budget and Schedule of Cash Collections
Schedule 2: Production Budget
Schedule 3: Direct Materials Budget and Schedule of Cash Disbursements for
Raw Materials
Schedule 4: Direct Labor Budget
Schedule 5: Manufacturing Overhead Budget
Schedule 6: Budgeted Cost of Goods Manufactured Statement
Schedule 7: Selling and Administrative Expenses Budget
Schedule 8: Cash Budget
Schedule 9: Financial Income and Expenses Budget
Schedule 10: Budgeted Income Statement
Schedule 11: Budgeted Balance Sheet

The Sales Budget

The sales budget for New Frontiers for the months of January, February, and March is shown in Schedule 1. The sales forecast on which the budget is based was developed judgmentally. Salespersons were provided with historical volume figures for the past three years. In addition, each was provided with a forecast of spending for recreational equipment per household for the budget year in those parts of the country where New Frontiers markets its canoes. The Vice-President of Finance uses his personal computer to access data on recreational spending from an on-line data base service to which the firm subscribes.

Using the data provided, each salesperson was asked to project volume for the budget period for his or her territory. The Sales Manager reviewed these projections and felt that in general they were overly conservative—because the sales force wanted to insure that sales quotas represented by the final budget would be met. He revised them upward, except where he believed the salesperson had been completely realistic.

Schedule 1

NEW FRONTIERS
Sales Budget and Schedule of Cash Collections
for the Quarter Ending March 31

	January	February	March	Quarter Total
Expected sales in units	800	750	900	2,450
Selling price per unit	$ 300	$ 300	$ 300	$ 300
Total Sales	$240,000	$225,000	$270,000	$735,000

Schedule of Expected Cash Collections[a]

	January	February	March	Quarter Total
Collection of beginning balance in Accounts Receivable	$120,000			
January Sales ($240,000)	144,000	$ 96,000		
February Sales ($225,000)		135,000	$ 90,000	
March Sales ($270,000)			162,000	
Total Cash Collections	$264,000	$231,000	$252,000	$747,000

[a] Assumptions re. cash collections, Schedule 1:
1. All sales are on account.
2. For purposes of simplification, no bad-debt losses are incurred.
3. Sixty percent of sales are collected in the month of sale, the other 40% in the following month.

The Sales Manager's projections were reviewed in a meeting between the Vice-President of Operations, the Vice-President of Administration and Finance, and the President. A meeting was held with the Production Manager to determine productive capabilities and the effects of increased volume. Discussions resulted in the figures reflected in Schedule 1, which were approximately 15% higher than the previous year's actual volumes for January, February, and March. The projected volume increases were based primarily on (a) the assumption that the inflation rate would decrease from 12% to 10% during the budget period, (b) evidence of increasing interest in canoeing as a sport, (c) a forecasted increase in spending for recreational equipment, and (d) a new advertising program.

The sales prices reflected in the sales budget were not finally set until budget estimates of production and other costs were developed. New Frontiers has found historically that to obtain the profit margin they desire, selling prices must be set at about 210% of manufacturing costs. This necessitated a $20 rise in selling prices over those of the previous period. The chief causes of the price increase were discussed with the sales manager, who in turn discussed the increase with salespersons to gauge customer reaction. Prices of chief competitors were also reviewed. As a result of this process, the $300 budget price was considered to be realistic based on profit objectives and consistent with volume expectations.

Schedule of Expected Cash Collections. New Frontiers makes all sales on account. To simplify this illustration, an assumption was made that there would be no uncollectible accounts. Historically, New Frontiers has collected about 60% of the month's sales in the month of sale, since their credit terms are net/15—the account is due within 15 days of receipt of the invoice. New Frontiers is not anticipating any change in their credit policies, nor will they be selling to new types of customers during the budget period. Economic conditions are stable. Hence, New Frontiers' management believes that historical collection patterns will prevail—60% collected in the month of sale; 40% in the month following sale—and has prepared the schedule of cash collections accordingly.

The providing of information as to historical collection patterns and the development of the data in this schedule was done by the Manager of Accounting and Data Processing.

The Production Budget

The Production Budget for New Frontiers is shown in Schedule 2. It is a product of (a) the level of beginning Finished Goods Inventory, (b) expected sales, and (c) management's policies as to the appropriate ending inventory level. Last year New Frontiers reviewed its policy with respect to an appropriate level for inventory. As a result they decided to maintain minimal inventory levels both of raw materials and finished goods. For the past three months, on a trial basis, they have been keeping these inventories at 10% of the next month's needs.

The major reason for the inventory policy review, which was instituted by the Vice-President of Administration and Finance, was short-term interest costs of approximately 17% per year. Money tied up in inventories cannot be used for other purposes. After studying economic forecasts of interest costs for the budget period, which showed rates varying from 12% to 20%, it was concluded that an appropriate short-term rate (which seemed to be the modal rate being forecast) to use for projection purposes was 15%. This anticipated rate was a primary factor in management's decision to continue keeping inventory at the 10% level for the budget period.

Schedule 2

NEW FRONTIERS
Production Budget
for the Quarter Ended March 31

	January	February	March	Total
Expected sales (Schedule 1)	800	750	900	2,450
Add: Desired ending inventory of finished goods[a]	75	90	100[b]	100[b]
Total needs	875	840	1,000	2,550
Less: Beginning inventory of finished goods[c]	80	75	90	80
Units to be produced	795	765	910	2,470

[a] Set by management policy at 10% of next month's sales.
[b] Assumed April sales, 1,000 units
[c] Units on hand at the beginning of the period—see the January 1 Balance Sheet.

The Direct Materials Budget

New Frontiers prepares the Direct Materials Budget in a format which displays the costs of raw materials to be purchased during the budget period, the costs of raw materials to be used during the budget period, and a schedule of cash disbursements for raw materials inventory purchases. The first step in determining these amounts is to calculate usage in unit terms.

New Frontiers communicates to the Production Manager the sales forecast for the budget period. Using the Production Budget in conjunction with the number of units of raw material required for a unit of output, the Production Manager can determine how many units are needed for current production. Allowance should be made for raw material units which will be spoiled or lost in the production process. Since lost or spoiled raw materials will cause the units being produced to be more costly, the allowance built into the budget for these items is carefully reviewed by the Vice-President of Operations.

The number of raw material units to be purchased is determined by current production needs and the levels of beginning and ending raw materials inventories. As discussed previously, New Frontiers managerial policy is to keep all inventories at 10% of next month's needs. In the case of raw materials, inventory is kept at 10% of the total number of units required by next month's production budget.

The person responsible for purchasing will provide major input as to anticipated costs of raw materials for the budget period. Such an estimate will be based on quotes provided by the suppliers from whom the company usually buys in quantity lots of the size normally purchased. If alternate vendors are available, quotes from these organizations should also be reviewed to insure that the purchase price is as low as possible based on quality requirements and the ability of the vendor to supply the materials readily.

As part of the planning process at the highest levels of the organization, a long-run perspective should prevail. Questions as to the future availability of raw materials at prices which the firm can afford should be considered.

New Frontiers has a contract with its suppliers which lasts through June of the budget period which specifies a delivered price of $25 per sheet of fiberglass. The units of raw materials used will differ from those of raw materials purchased because of changes in the inventory levels.

Schedule of Cash Disbursements for Raw Materials Inventory Purchases. To develop the cash budget, cash disbursements for raw materials purchases must be calculated. Based on the terms granted by its suppliers and on historical patterns, New Frontiers estimates that it will pay for 50% of any month's purchases in that month and for the other 50% in the following month. No change in this pattern is forecast, since New Frontiers believes that its collections will follow historical patterns. If collections were slowing down, New Frontiers might try to slow down its outgo for purchases, consistent with retaining its credit rating and taking advantage of any savings through discounts for early payments. If New Frontiers were changing suppliers, a review of the credit policies of those new suppliers could affect the historical payment pattern. For example, if discounts were not available for early payment from old suppliers but were available from new suppliers, New Frontiers would have to make an analysis to decide whether the amount of discount could justify speeding up its payment process.

Direct Labor Budget

The process followed in developing the Direct Labor Budget is very similar to that in formulating the Direct Materials Budget except that there are no inventories to consider. Consistent with the production schedule, the different kinds of labor required for the period's output will have to be specified and appropriate labor rates applied. The labor required to efficiently perform an operation or complete a unit may be based on engineering estimates, historical patterns, or the work of time-and-motion experts.

New Frontiers is unionized and has a contract calling for cost-of-living adjustments tied to the inflation rate as measured by the Consumer Price Index. Budgeted hourly increases are based on an assumed inflation rate of 10%. This rate was adopted by the upper-echelon managers and communicated to the Production Manager as part of her budget instructions. New Frontiers believes that satisfied workers are productive workers. In support of this philosophy they have adopted a number of policies and procedures, including (1) discounting food costs in the factory cafeteria,

---

Schedule 3

NEW FRONTIERS
Direct Materials Budget and Schedule of Cash Disbursement for Raw Materials
for the Quarter Ended March 31

	January	February	March	Total
Units to be Produced (Schedule 2)	795	765	910	2,470
Raw Material Needs per unit, 2 sheets fiberglass	×2	×2	×2	×2
Needed for Current Production	1,590	1,530	1,820	4,940
Desired Ending Inventory of Raw Materials[a]	153	182	205[a]	205[a]
Total Needs	1,743	1,712	2,025	5,145
Less: Beginning Inventory of Raw Materials	159[b]	153	182	159
Raw Materials to be Purchased	1,584	1,559	1,843	4,986
Raw Material Cost per unit Purchased	$ 25	$ 25	$ 25	$ 25
Cost of Raw Materials Purchased	$39,600	$38,975	$46,075	$124,650
Cost of Raw Materials Used:				
Needed for current production (see above)	1,590	1,530	1,820	4,940
Cost per unit[c]	$ 25	$ 25	$ 25	$ 25
Cost of Raw Materials Used	$39,750	$38,250	$45,500	$123,500

Schedule of Cash Disbursement for Raw Materials Inventory Purchases[d]

	January	February	March	Total
Payment of Beginning Balance in Accounts Payable	$22,500			
January Purchases ($39,600)	19,800	$19,800		
February Purchases ($38,975)		19,488	$19,487	
March Purchases ($46,075)			23,038	
Total Cash Payments for Inventory Purchases	$42,300	$39,288	$42,525	$124,113

[a] Management policy is to keep raw material ending inventory at 10% of next month's production. Assumed April production is 1,025 units.
[b] See the beginning-of-the-period balance sheet.
[c] The January 1 beginning raw materials inventory also had a cost of $25 per unit.
[d] Inventory purchases are paid for 50% in the month purchased and 50% in the following month.

(2) soliciting suggestions for improved operations and giving cash rewards for suggestions which are used, and (3) promoting to higher-level positions almost exclusively from within the firm. In addition, during the coming year New Frontiers is sending all departmental supervisors in its factory to a special seminar on human resource motivation and management. The cost of this seminar is reflected in the "Other Fixed Overhead" item of Schedule 5, which details the Manufacturing Overhead Budget.

Schedule 4

NEW FRONTIERS
Direct Labor Budget
for the Quarter Ended March 31

	January	February	March	Quarter Total
Units to be Produced (Schedule 2)	795	765	910	2,470
Direct Labor Hours per unit	×2	×2	×2	×2
Total Direct Labor Hours	1,590	1,530	1,820	4,940
Cost Per Direct Labor Hour[a]	$ 15	$ 15	$ 15	$ 15
Total Direct Labor Costs	$23,850	$22,950	$27,300	$74,100

[a] This cost per hour included fringe benefits such as pensions and health insurance.

Manufacturing Overhead Budget

To prepare the Manufacturing Overhead Budget, which is illustrated in Schedule 5, manufacturing overhead costs must be classified as either variable or fixed. Those which are variable will vary with the production level, while those which are fixed will not. For each variable element a rate must be projected, and the level of each fixed cost must be estimated. To illustrate, each canoe requires a piece of metal stripping to go around its top. New Frontiers considers this to be an indirect material cost, and it is obvious that the amount of metal stripping will vary with the output. Thus, it is a variable overhead cost. Based on the production of 795 canoes in the month of January (see Schedule 2), and an estimated cost for the metal stripping for each canoe of $4, $3,180 of indirect materials costs for this item should be budgeted (795 × $4 = $3,180). In February, costs of the metal stripping will be only $3,060, because fewer units— 765—will be produced (765 × $4 = $3,060).

On the other hand, New Frontiers calculates depreciation on factory plant and equipment on a straight-line basis. The depreciation cost for last year, adjusted for depreciation on new acquisitions or retirements, will be the budget level for the current quarter. This is a fixed overhead cost and will not vary from month to month with changes in the level of production.

New Frontiers uses an applied overhead system. This discussion of the Manufacturing Overhead Budget provides an opportunity for us to review and reinforce our understanding of how such a system works. Remember the steps in the process of setting a predetermined overhead rate:

1. Estimate the activity level.
2. Estimate each element of overhead cost at that activity level.
3. Divide the estimated overhead costs by some measure of input.

The budget reflects an activity level based on production for the period, with each element of variable overhead cost being estimated consistent with that level. Each fixed overhead cost is projected in total for the budget period. New Frontiers applies overhead on the basis of direct labor hours used. We have shortened the budget process to a quarter. In a real situation we would have the annual overhead budget and would divide it by the annual inputs for direct labor. In our example, we will divide the quarterly total by the quarterly input of direct labor hours to get the budgeted predetermined rate of $30 per direct labor hour ($148,200 total overhead costs/4,940 estimated direct labor hours).

Schedule 5

NEW FRONTIERS
Manufacturing Overhead Budget
for the Quarter Ended March 31

	January (DLH 1,590)	February (DLH 1,530)	March (DLH 1,820)	Quarter Total (DLH 4,940)
Variable Overhead:				
Indirect materials	$ 7,155	$ 6,885	$ 8,190	$ 22,230
Indirect labor	11,925	11,475	13,650	37,050
Utilities	2,385	2,295	2,730	7,410
Repairs and maintenance	4,770	4,590	5,460	14,820
Other	2,385	2,295	2,730	7,410
Total Variable Overhead	$28,620	$27,540	$32,760	$ 88,920
Fixed Overhead:				
Supervisory salaries	4,940	4,940	4,940	14,820
Supplies	2,470	2,470	2,470	7,410
Depreciation	7,410	7,410	7,410	22,230
Utilities	2,223	2,223	2,223	6,669
Insurance and Taxes	977	977	977	2,931
Other	1,740	1,740	1,740	5,220
Total Fixed Overhead	$19,760	$19,760	$19,760	$ 59,280
Total Overhead	$48,380	$47,300	$52,520	$148,200

Note the importance of this predetermined rate. Fixed overhead costs are, by definition, assumed to be the same for each of the three months. However, the anticipated production requirements vary. If we did not use an applied rate, the cost of producing a canoe in January would differ from the cost of producing one in February or March; this situation can be illustrated as follows:

MONTH	BUDGETED PRODUCTION	FIXED OVERHEAD	FIXED OVERHEAD COST PER UNIT
January	795	$19,760	$24.86
February	765	19,760	25.83
March	910	19,760	21.71

With an applied overhead system, New Frontiers will charge each unit of production, regardless of the month in which it was produced, with $60 ($30 per direct labor hours × 2 direct labor hours per unit) of manufacturing overhead.

Budgeted Cost of Goods Manufactured Statement

The Budgeted Cost of Goods Manufactured Statement shows the budgeted inputs of direct materials, direct labor, and *applied* overhead. As explained above, the use of an applied overhead rate results in the same budgeted unit costs for each month in the quarter. If actual overhead had been charged to production, each month's production would have had a different cost per canoe produced because of fixed manufacturing overhead and the different production volumes for the three months. These budgeted costs per unit are the expected costs which will attach to the units produced.

Schedule 6

NEW FRONTIERS, INC.
Budgeted Cost of Manufactured Statement
for the Quarter Ended March 31

	January	February	March	Quarter Total
Direct Labor Hours	1,590	1,530	1,820	4,940
Direct Material (Schedule 3)[a]	$ 39,750	$ 38,250	$ 45,500	$123,500
Direct Labor (Schedule 4)	23,850	22,950	27,300	74,100
Manufacturing Overhead Applied ($30 per Direct Labor Hour)	47,700	45,900	54,600	148,200
Total Manufacturing Cost	$111,300	$107,100	$127,400	$345,800
Add: Beginning Work-in-Process	0	0	0	0
Less: Ending Work-in-Process	0	0	0	0
Cost of Goods Manufactured	$111,300	$107,100	$127,400	$345,800
Units Produced	795	765	910	2,470
Budgeted Unit Cost	$ 140	$ 140	$ 140	$ 140

[a] This figure is based on materials used, not materials purchased.

Selling and Administrative Expenses Budget

To prepare the Selling and Administrative Expenses Budget, costs must be classified as either variable—varying in total with some activity level—or fixed in total for the period. The variable expenses shown on New Frontiers' budget are assumed to vary with the number of units sold, unlike the variable manufacturing overhead costs, which varied with a different activity level—the number of units produced.

If we look at this budget relative to the organization chart shown in Illustration 7-5, it becomes clear how a budget prepared in terms of responsibility centers differs from one prepared to describe expectations for programs—in our case, the production and sale of canoes. What you see in Schedule 7 is the combination of a number of budgets prepared by responsibility centers. The Managers of Accounting and Data Processing and of Personnel would have prepared budgets for their operations which would then have progressed to the next level and have become a part of the Vice-President of Administration and Finance's budget. The Sales Manager's budget would have become part of the budget of the Vice-President—Operations. There would have been a responsibility budget for the President's office. Presented in program budget style, all their different responsibility budgets have been combined into a schedule which details selling and administrative expenses for the entire company by class of expenditure, rather than by the manager who is responsible.

Schedule 7

NEW FRONTIERS, INC.
Selling and Administrative Expenses Budget
for the Quarter Ended March 31

	January	February	March	Quarter Total
Variable Expenses:				
Sales Commissions	$12,000	$11,250	$ 13,500	$ 36,750
Clerical	3,600	3,380	4,050	11,030
Supplies	4,800	4,500	5,400	14,700
Other	1,200	1,120	1,350	3,670
Total Variable Expenses	$21,600	$20,250	$ 24,300	$ 66,150
Fixed:				
Advertising	12,500	12,500	12,500	37,500
Sales Salaries	14,000	14,000	14,000	42,000
Administrative Salaries	25,000	25,000	25,000	75,000
Insurance	2,500	2,500	2,500	7,500
Depreciation	11,000	11,000	11,000	33,000
Taxes	4,600	4,600	4,600	13,800
Utilities	7,200	7,200	7,200	21,600
Total Fixed Expenses	$76,800	$76,800	$ 76,800	$230,400
Total Selling and Administrative Expenses	$98,400	$97,050	$101,100	$296,550

After the sales volume for the budget period has been set, the Sales Manager projects variable selling expenses. The sales commission rate has remained constant for several years and is 5% of sales. As part of the budget process the Sales Manager reviews this rate each year with the Vice-President of Operations. No change was made for the current budget period, since the rate is consistent with what competing firms are paying their sales force. The Sales Manager also considers it to be sufficiently high to encourage the salespersons to try hard to make sales. The other elements of variable expenses were projected based on historical data adjusted for the anticipated 10% inflation rate.

Advertising is a discretionary expense—that is, an expense the level of which is set by management decision. The advertising campaign for the coming year has been agreed to and contracts relative to that plan have already been signed. These contracts call for equal monthly payments to the advertising vendors over the budget period.

Salaries are projected on a person-by-person basis using the current salary level plus the increments which have been awarded for the coming year. Depreciation is calculated on a straight-line basis. The only uncertainty in projecting this amount is the portion related to new equipment acquisitions. The depreciation charge on items to be acquired during the budget period is based on their expected costs as reflected in the Capital Expenditures and Cash Budgets.

New Frontiers has reviewed its insurance coverage as part of the budgetary process and believes it to be adequate. Insurance costs are based on policy rates provided by its insurance carriers. New Frontiers knows its approximate electrical usage but is uncertain as to rates because of rate hearings which its supplier has pending. Using his microcomputer, the Manager of Accounting and Data Processing consulted a data bank, which showed historical trends in rates and a projection of a 10% average rise for the coming year. This 10% rate increase was reflected in New Frontiers' budget.

The Cash Budget

Importance of the Cash Budget.   The Cash Budget is a very important element in the budgeting process because cash management is so critical to a firm. To stay in business an organization must be able to pay its employees, replenish its inventories, pay interest on its debts, and satisfy the claims of other creditors. Inadequate cash planning is often a major cause of business failure.

A well-prepared Cash Budget shows a company (a) when it is going to need additional cash, (b) when it is going to have excess cash, and (c) for what period of time these conditions will exist. Knowing when it is going to need cash enables management to review alternative sources of cash, decide which is best, and take whatever actions are necessary to obtain that cash—for example, to negotiate a loan.

Schedule 8

NEW FRONTIERS, INC.
Cash Budget
For Quarter Ended March 31

	January	February	March	Quarter Totals
Cash Receipts from Operations:				
Cash sales	0	0	0	0
Collections on Account (Schedule 1)	$264,000	$231,000	$252,000	$747,000
Total Cash Receipts from Operations	264,000	231,000	252,000	747,000
Cash Disbursements for Operations:				
Raw Material Purchases (Schedule 3)	42,300	39,288	42,525	124,113
Direct Labor (Schedule 4)[a]	23,850	22,950	27,300	74,100
Manufacturing Overhead (Schedule 5)[b]	40,970	39,890	45,110	125,970
Selling and Administrative (Schedule 7)[c]	87,400	86,050	90,100	263,550
Income Taxes[d]	38,500	—	—	38,500
Total Cash Disbursed for Operations	233,020	188,178	205,035	626,233
Cash Generated (Used) by Operations	30,980	42,822	46,965	120,767
Other Sources of Cash:				
Sale of Assets[e]	30,000	—	—	30,000
Issuance of Stock[f]		100,000		100,000
Beginning-of-the-Period Cash Balance	17,000	17,980	15,552	17,000
Total Cash Available	77,980	160,802	62,517	267,767
Other Uses of Cash:				
Purchase of Plant and Equipment[g]	70,000	—	—	70,000
Payment of Dividends	—	—	4,000	4,000
Long-Term Debt Retirement and Interest[h]	—	106,000	—	106,000
Minimum Cash Balance Required	15,000	15,000	15,000	15,000
Total Other Uses	85,000	121,000	19,000	195,000
Cash Excess or (Deficiency)	(7,020)	39,802	43,517	72,767
Calculation of Ending Cash Balance:				
Financing:				
Loans required to cover deficit and minimum balance requirements[i]	10,000			10,000
(Loan Repayments and Interest)[j]		(10,250)		(10,250)
Investment[k]				
Available for Investment	—	(29,000)	(43,000)	(72,000)
Cash Earnings on Investments	—	—	—	—
Net Inflows (Outflows) from financing and Investing	10,000	(39,250)	(43,000)	(72,250)
Add (Deduct) Cash Excess or (Deficiency)	(7,020)	39,802	43,517	72,767
Add: Minimum Cash Balance	15,000	15,000	15,000	15,000
Ending Cash Balance	$ 17,980	$ 15,552	$ 15,517	$ 15,517

Assumptions:
[a] Direct labor costs are paid in the month incurred.
[b] All manufacturing overhead costs, except depreciation, which is a noncash expense, were paid in the month incurred.
[c] All selling and administrative expenses, except depreciation, which is a noncash expense, were paid in the month incurred.
[d] Income taxes are paid the fifteenth of the month following the end of the quarter. Taxes paid in the month of January are those shown on the beginning-of-the-period balance sheet.
[e] The company liquidated marketable securities shown on its beginning-of-the-period balance sheet at book value.
[f] The company sold stock for $100,000 to help liquidate long-term debt shown on the beginning-of-the-period balance sheet and one-half year's interest at 12% per annum.
[g] The company purchased on January 2 new equipment costing $70,000.
[h] The company owes $100,000 plus six months interest at 12% due on February 28; The company sold stock to help liquidate long-term debt shown on the beginning-of-the-period balance sheet and one-half year's interest at 12% per annum.
[i] The company can borrow in multiples of $10,000 at 15% per year.
[j] Short-term borrowing plus interest of $250 is repaid at the end of February. It is assumed that the $10,000 short-term borrowing was made January 1.
[k] The company will make short-term investments in multiples of $1,000 with excess cash. Investment will take place at the end of the month, and the projected earnings rate is 15% per year. Interest collections will take place at maturity. None of the investments mature during the budget quarter.

On the other hand, when excess cash is available it needs to be used. The Cash Budget enables the company to see what amounts of cash are expected to be available and for what periods of time. Thus the company can consider alternative uses for the cash and decide which is best. For example, if cash is available for only a short period, investments in marketable securities such as U.S. Treasury bills may be a good use of the funds. On the other hand, if excess cash is being generated on a long-term basis, management could decide to increase dividends or make a long-term investment in the stock of another company.

In addition, the budgetary process itself helps a firm to better manage its cash. For example, New Frontiers has a quarterly tax payment due in the month of January. It also plans to invest $70,000 in new equipment and maintain a minimum cash balance of $15,000. Looking at cash from operations, it is clear that cash from that source is insufficient to meet these needs. As the budget is stated, New Frontiers apparently has decided to finance part of these costs by selling off its marketable securities, which represent a temporary use of idle cash, and obtain a short-term loan from the bank. It might instead have decided to defer the investment in equipment until the following month. Or New Frontiers could have deferred liquidating the marketable securities and financed the equipment entirely through borrowing either long- or short-term or through leasing. Putting the budget together forces a company to think about its needs and make decisions as to how those cash needs can best be satisfied.

Format of the Cash Budget.   Many formats can be used in preparing a Cash Budget. New Frontiers has chosen to use one which can be especially helpful to management in evaluating its cash position. This format separates *cash from operations* from other sources and uses of cash. By cash from operations we mean cash which flows in and out as a result of the normal business activities of the firm—in our example, making and selling canoes.

Why is this format desirable? Think for a minute about where a company can get cash. Cash comes primarily from (a) operations, (b) selling ownership rights (stock), (c) borrowing, and (d) liquidating assets. It is obvious that if the company wants to stay in business, it cannot depend on selling its assets as a constant source of cash. In addition, borrowing and selling of shares of stock is limited by availability of funds and the market's ability to absorb new security offerings. Borrowing may also be restricted because of the cost of the funds. This means that companies which are going to stay in business must be able to generate cash from operations. There may be periods when operations use cash rather than generate it, but these should be offset by periods when operations do generate cash.

The Budgeted Income Statement is based on accrual accounting concepts and thus does not tell management the cash consequences of its transactions. The Cash Budget format adopted by New Frontiers clearly separates cash generated or used by operations from other sources of cash.

Cash Budget Mechanics.   As noted earlier, New Frontiers, like many organizations, uses an accrual basis for recognizing revenues and expenses. As a result, its budget schedules for manufacturing overhead and selling and administrative expenses do not reflect cash outlays. In addition, since the company sells its products on account and buys its raw materials on account, neither the sales nor purchases budgets show cash inflows and outflows.

The inflows from collections on account and outflows for raw materials purchases have already been discussed in conjunction with Schedules 1 and 3. For the various elements of manufacturing overhead and selling and administrative expenses, the cash budget will be the result of the company's contracts, agreements, policies, and assumptions regarding payment of expenses. For example, cash flows for wages and salaries are estimated based on when payment is called for by contracts and agreements with employees. The cash flow for utilities such as electricity and telephone is based on assumptions as to when the bills will be received and how soon after receipt the company will make payment.

Depreciation expense is not included as part of the Cash Budget because it does not represent required cash outlays. Cash outlays relative to plant and equipment are made as part of the acquisition process, not the depreciation process. This can be seen in the "Other Uses of Cash" section of the New Frontiers' Cash Budget. The cash outflow for equipment to be purchased (or at least paid for) in January is reflected in that month's cash budget.

Other sources and uses of cash in the Cash Budget generally reflect management policies and decisions or the cash consequences of contracts. To illustrate, the amount and timing of dividend distributions is set by managerial decision or policy. The payment of interest on borrowed funds and the repayment of those funds is set by contract with the lender.

Frequently management has a policy as to the minimum cash balance which it wants to have on hand at the end of each month. Last year New Frontiers had a minimum balance policy of $20,000. The President, in consultation with and upon the recommendation of the Vice-President of Administration and Finance, has decided to lower that balance to $15,000. This recommendation was reviewed in light of agreements with long-term lenders that require a minimum amount of working capital to be maintained by New Frontiers. Because of forecasted high interest rates, the company is anxious to maintain as little idle cash as possible. This was the major reason for cutting back the minimum cash balance requirement.

The ending cash balance for one month becomes the beginning cash balance for another month. The Cash Budget format adopted by New Frontiers shows the amount of cash which must be borrowed to satisfy monthly needs and to meet minimum balance requirements. The amount of cash available for investment at the end of each month is also depicted in the budget. New Frontiers is planning to buy U.S. Treasury notes with excess cash and believes the earnings rate of these securities will be 15% per year.

Financial Income and Expenses Budget

Schedule 9 shows projected borrowing costs on an accrual basis and projected earnings on investments which will be made from excess cash. These expenses and revenues are also projected on a cash basis on the schedule. For debt which is already on the books, the interest rate is known and can be used to project the interest costs and related cash flows. For the short-term borrowing which will be required, New Frontiers, after consultation with its bank from whom it will seek the loan, is projecting an interest cost of 15% per year.

Based on the schedule of cash flows for the year, of which we have only the first quarter, New Frontiers has decided to invest cash available at the end of February and March in U.S. Treasury Notes, from which it expects to earn a return of 15%. This results in budget income for

---

Schedule 9

NEW FRONTIERS, INC.
Financial Income and Expenses Budget
for the Quarter Ended March 31

	January	February	March	Quarter Total
Interest Expense:				
Long-Term Debt Due 2/28	$1,000	$1,000	$ —	$2,000
12% Mortgage	2,000	2,000	2,000	6,000
Short-Term Borrowing[a]	125	125		250
Total Interest Expense	$3,125	$3,125	$2,000	$8,250
Interest Income:				
Short-Term Investments[b]	—	—	363	363

Schedule of Cash Flow for Financial Income[c] and Expense

	January	February	March	Quarter Total
Interest Expense:				
Long-Term Debt Due 2/28		6,000[d]		6,000
12% Mortgage	—	—	—	—
Short-Term Borrowing	—	250		250
Cash Required for Interest Payments	—	$6,250	—	$6,250

[a] $10,000 \times 15\% \times \frac{1}{12} = \$125$.
[b] $29,000 investment $\times 15\% \times \frac{1}{12}$ (investment made at the end of February) = $363.
[c] No cash income will be received during the budget period on investments.
[d] $100,000 \times 12\% \times \frac{6}{12}$. As of the beginning of the budget period, $4,000 had already been accrued (see January 1 Balance Sheet).

February's investment. No cash receipts from the firm's investments are shown, because, although interest has been earned, it will not be collected during the budget period.

The Budgeted Income Statement

Once the supporting schedules have been completed, the Budgeted Income Statement, given in Schedule 10, is for the most part a compilation of the appropriate budgetary schedules. Sales, as reflected on the income statement, for example, reflect the figures initially derived and presented in Schedule 1. Cost of Goods Sold in the illustrated income statement is not supported by a separate schedule but is easily derived. The company uses a LIFO costing system and does not liquidate any of its beginning-of-the-period inventory. Thus, Cost of Goods Sold is found by taking the number of units sold times the budgeted cost per unit calculated on the Budgeted Cost of Goods Manufactured Schedule.

The income tax rate which New Frontiers uses in its budget is based on the current tax rates, adjusted for any changes which have been legislated by Congress for the budget year or which management anticipates. To simplify our illustration, the assumption is made that book income and taxable income are the same amounts, hence tax expense shown on the quarterly income statement is reflected as taxes payable in the budgeted end-of-the-quarter balance sheet.

Schedule 10

NEW FRONTIERS, INC.
Budgeted Income Statement
for Quarter Ended March 31

	January	February	March	Quarter Total
Unit Sales	800	750	900	2,450
Sales (Schedule 1)	$240,000	$225,000	$270,000	$735,000
Cost of Goods Sold[a]	112,000	105,000	126,000	343,000
Gross Margin	$128,000	$120,000	$144,000	$392,000
Selling and Administrative (Schedule 7)	98,400	97,050	101,100	296,550
Operating Income	$ 29,600	$ 22,950	$ 42,900	$ 95,450
Interest Expense (Schedule 9)	(3,125)	(3,125)	(2,000)	(8,250)
Interest Income (Schedule 9)	—	—	$ 363	$ 363
Income Before Taxes	$ 26,475	$ 19,825	$ 41,263	$ 87,563
Income Taxes @ 50%	13,237	9,913	20,631	43,781
Net Income	$ 13,238	$ 9,912	$ 20,632	$ 43,782

[a] Since New Frontiers uses LIFO costing, Cost of Goods Sold is based on sales volume × budgeted unit costs of $140.

The Budgeted Balance Sheet

New Frontiers' end-of-the-quarter balance sheet, given in Schedule 11, reflects the results of the transactions already described in other budget schedules. The following brief comments describe the source of the budgeted figure:

1. *Cash and Marketable Securities.* These balances tie in with those shown in the Cash Budget as the end-of-the-period cash balance and the level of investments in marketable securities projected in that budget. Marketable securities on hand January 1 were liquidated during January.
2. *Accounts Receivable.* This balance is based on the assumption described in Schedule 1 that 40% of a month's sales will not be collected until the following month. This figure represents 40% of March sales ($270,000 × 40% = $108,000).

Schedule 11

NEW FRONTIERS, INC.
Budgeted Balance Sheet
for the Quarter Ended March 31

Current Assets:		*Current Liabilities:*	
Cash	$ 15,517	Accounts Payable	$ 23,037
Marketable Securities	72,000	Accrued Interest Expense	6,000
Accounts Receivable	108,000	Taxes Payable	43,781
Inventories		Total Current Liabilities	72,818
Raw Materials	5,125	12% Mortgage Payable	200,000
Work-in-Process	—		
Finished Goods	13,200		
Accrued Interest Receivable	363	Total Liabilities	$272,818
Total Current Assets	$214,205		
Property, Plant and		Stockholders' Equity:	
Equipment	923,000	Common Stock	330,000
Less: Accumulated,		Paid-in Capital in Excess	
Depreciation	274,050	of Par	120,000
Net Property, Plant and			
Equipment	$648,950	Retained Earnings	140,337
		Total Stockholders'	
		Equity	$590,337
Total Assets	$863,155	Total Liabilities and	
		Stockholders' Equity	$863,155

---

3. *Inventories.* Management's policy is to try to maintain ending inventories of both raw materials and finished goods at 10% of next period's needs. The company uses LIFO costing procedures. Raw materials costs did not change from last period but remained at $25. Thus raw materials ending inventory is calculated as follows: Ending Inventory (Schedule 3) of 205 × $25 per unit = $5,125.
    Finished Goods Inventory consists of two layers: the one on hand at the

beginning of the period and the new units added during the current period:

Beginning of the period:	
80 canoes @ $130	
(Jan. 1 Balance Sheet)	$ 10,400
Added to inventory during the budget period:	
20 @ $140 (Schedules 2 & 6)	2,800
Budgeted Ending Inventory	$ 13,200

4. *Property, Plant and Equipment, and Accumulated Depreciation.* The budgeted balances in these accounts were calculated as follows:

Property, Plant and Equipment, Jan. 1	$853,000
Add: January acquisitions (See Cash Budget, Schedule 8)	70,000
Budgeted Ending Balance	$923,000
Accumulated Depreciation, Jan. 1	$218,820
Add: Depreciation in manufacturing overhead (Schedule 5)	22,230
Depreciation—Selling and Administrative (Schedule 7)	33,000
Budgeted Ending Balance	$274,050

5. *Accounts Payable.* Accounts Payable are liquidated 50% in the month they are incurred and 50% in the following month. The balance in this account is based on 50% of March purchases ($46,075 × 50% = $23,037) as shown in Schedule 3.

6. *Accrued Interest Expense and Long-Term Debt Currently Due.* The $4,000 of Accrued Interest Payable and the Long-Term Debt of $100,000 were both liquidated on February 28. The March 31 balance in Accrued Interest Expense is based on the 12% Mortgage Payable, on which interest is paid annually each December 31. Thus three months of interest expense ($6,000) has been incurred as of the end of the current quarter.

7. *Taxes Payable.* Taxes shown on the beginning-of-the-period balance sheet were paid in January. Taxes on the current quarter's earnings have been accrued (see the Budgeted Income Statement, Schedule 10) and appear on the March 31 Balance Sheet.

8. *Common Stock and Paid-In Capital in Excess of Par.* These account balances increased during the period by $80,000 and $20,000, respectively, when stock having a par value of $80,000 was sold for $100,000.

9. *Retained Earnings.* This balance is derived as follows:

Beginning of the period, Jan. 1	$100,555
Add: Budgeted Net Income (Schedule 10)	43,782
Total	$144,337
Less: Budgeted Dividends (Schedule 8)	4,000
March 31 Budgeted Balance	$140,337

ZERO-BASED BUDGETING

In response to the way that most budgets are put together, from time to time attention focuses on a different approach. One that has been advocated by a variety of public and private individuals or organizations (notably former President Jimmy Carter) is that of zero-based budgeting.

In the standard budget preparation process there is an implicit assumption that an organization and its budget units will continue engaging in the types of activities they have traditionally performed. As a result, the starting point for the development of the current period's budget is last year's budget and/or actual data. In other words, the status quo, but usually at a little higher level (more revenues, higher expenses), is incorporated into the current budget.

Zero-based budgeting is based on the idea that the manager should start each year at zero budget levels—zero revenues and expenses—and justify anything beyond that. To make this idea operational, the manager develops a series of decision packages which encompass all the activities of the budget unit. The manager then ranks these decision packages in terms of their importance and cuts out those which are less important. A public-sector example may clarify this process.

Assume that the Motor Vehicles Department of a state (1) administers driving tests and issues driver licenses, (2) issues registration plates for vehicles, (3) prepares publications on highway safety, (4) gives programs at schools and for other organizations on safety, and (5) checks vehicle inspection stations around the state to insure that they are operated properly. In a zero-based budgeting context, this department would have to associate all its costs with these activities and then rank the activities in terms of their importance. Those activities which were considered least important might be eliminated either by the department itself in its budget request or by the next higher level in the state's budgetary review chain.

While the zero-based budget approach trys to get the manager to decide what is important and justify his or her position, it is generally considered too time consuming and costly to be part of the annual budget process. Instead, zero-based budgeting might be applied on some cyclical basis, with a particular part of an organization undertaking this activity at periodic intervals—for instance, every five years.

SOME BEHAVIORAL ASPECTS OF THE BUDGETING PROCESS

As noted in Chapter 1, the amount, type, and timing of internal accounting data may be affected by and affect employee behavior. This fact is very apparent in the budgeting area. Some examples are given below.

Ideally each manager at every level in the organization develops budget data which properly describe the needs of his or her part of the organization consistent with the organization's goals. In turn, the next higher-level manager accepts the budget developed by the lower-level manager, knowing it represents efficient performance. Managers in the real world often depart from this ideal, and game playing becomes a part of the budget process.

In some entities, for example lower-level managers know from past experience that the budgets they submit will be cut by upper-echelon managers. Their response is to "pad"—to underestimate revenues and overestimate expenses. In turn, upper-level managers, knowing that lower-level managers pad their budgets, automatically raise the level of anticipated revenues for the budget unit and cut its budgeted expenses. Hence a vicious circle of counterproductive activity becomes part of the budget process.

Another phenomenon occurs frequently in organizations. As the budget period progresses, it becomes apparent that the organization's short-term goals such as return on investment or budgeted profits are not going to be met, and the company begins strenuous cost-cutting measures. It is not unusual to have upper-level management issue an edict to the effect that all areas must cut their costs relative to budget by some percent, say 10%. This can be extremely demoralizing to those parts of the entity which truly have no fat (excess resources). While upper-level management may perceive such a move as "fair," in reality it pays no attention to organizational differences and does not assign priorities consistent with the company's longer-run goals.

In addition, through the way the budget is used, upper-level management may be giving messages to other managers in the organization which they did not intend to send or which may be counter to the company's goals. For example, with the best intentions, a company could decide to start treating the data processing department (or some other service department) as a profit center and to charge its users in the organization. The intent is to make managers who are using data processing aware of the costs of the services they are getting. The actual outcome may be that user departments, to cut costs and stay within budget limits, may not use data processing to the extent they should consistent with efficient management.

In other kinds of situations, the budget may be set at a level which does not provide a part of the organization with the resources it needs to do its job efficiently. This is not an unusual occurrence at colleges and universities where support staff, in the form of secretarial assistance, and supplies and equipment are limited. What this means is that higher-paid personnel, generally professors, who should be using their time for other things, are typing exams, running the Xerox machine, and engaging in activities having high costs which are masked by the fact that these people (the professors) are already included in the budget and new personnel or equipment costs are not being incurred.

Budgets and the budgeting process can also focus too much attention on the short run at a high cost in the long run. Actions may be taken by managers in an attempt to stay within their budgets which will eventually be detrimental to the firm. For instance, in the private sector, lower-quality raw materials may be used in the company's product. This may mean the raw materials budget constraint is adhered to, but it could result in a lower-quality product that produces customer dissatisfaction and loss of business. In the public sector, the desires of legislators to keep the budget down may cause the deferral of expenditures for such needs as the upkeep of roads and public buildings—deferrals which may simply mean higher costs in the future.

The level at which budgets are set—be they either too high or too low—can adversely affect employee behavior. If a budget is set at a level which is impossible to attain, rather than inspiring the best efforts of company personnel, it may simply leave them demoralized. On the other hand, if the budget does not represent an efficient standard, there may be little incentive for members of the entity to perform efficiently. If resources, based on the budget, are provided beyond the needs of the budget unit, employees may see little need to do their job well or exercise proper control over the organization's assets. For example, padding one's expense account, leaving work early, or taking company supplies home may become acceptable practices.

The budget and the process by which it is developed can also lead to positive behaviors in the form of commitment to organizational goals, an esprit de corps, and efficient performance. Those involved in the budgetary process must be ever aware of the type of behavior which it is fostering throughout the organization.

chapter highlights

The major functions of managers are planning and controlling. The types of planning and control activities in which a manager engages are determined by the philosophy of the organization and the level in the organization which the manager occupies.

Planning and control activities may be classified as:

1. Strategic planning—the process of setting broad goals and defining strategies for the entity.
2. Management control—the process of assuring that organizational strategies are carried out effectively and efficiently.

3. Operational control—the process of assuring that specific tasks are carried out effectively and efficiently.

One tool which is part of the management control process is the budget. There are three types of budgets which an organization may need: an operating budget, a financial budget, and a capital expenditures budget.

The operating budget normally has two parts—a program budget, which focuses on the plans of the organization in terms of its major activities, such as products or services offered, and a responsibility budget, which shows the amounts for which a head of a responsibility center is responsible.

For both manufacturers and nonmanufacturers a complete set of budgets will consist of:

1. An operating budget showing estimated revenue or funding sources and expenses.
2. A financial budget depicting the organization's estimated financial position at the end of the budget period and supported by a budget of anticipated cash inflows and outflows.
3. A capital expenditures budget describing long-term capital acquisition plans.

The beginning of the budgetary process generally is the preparation of a forecast of activity for the period. For many firms this is a sales forecast. Service organizations may use other measures of activity such as the number of accounts maintained, clients served, or students enrolled. For the nonmanufacturing entity, as for the manufacturer, activity level, however it is defined, is a major determinant of expense levels, financial position, and, on a long-term basis, capital expenditure requirements.

The forecasting process should recognize the impact of general economic conditions, industry conditions, and management's plans on the organization's volume of activity. In addition, historical data and historical relationships provide a foundation on which most forecasts are based. Data as to general economic and industry conditions are available from a variety of sources, most recently from on-line database firms which provide data access by computer in the user's offices.

For a manufacturing firm, the sales budget and the inventory levels determine the production budget, which in turn provides the measure of activity necessary to prepare the direct materials, direct labor, and manufacturing overhead budgets. All these budgets along with the budget of selling and administrative expenses must be translated from the accrual to the cash basis so that a cash budget can be prepared.

The cash budget is extremely important to most firms because cash is such a critical element to the organization's operations. A cash budget enables a firm to see in advance when it will need additional cash or when it will have excess cash and for what periods of time. The cash budget format illustrated separates cash generated from and used by operations from other sources of cash, such as sale of stock or assets, and from other uses of cash, such as payment of dividends or liquidation of debt. This format is helpful in that management can see if its operations are providing cash.

The budgeted income statement and the budgeted balance sheet are in the same form as their historical counterparts. The budgeted income statement of a manufacturer will generally reflect expenses consistent with its major functions of manufacturing, selling, and general administration. The nonmanufacturer's budget expense categories can take a number of different forms and should be derived consistent with the way the organization wants to classify its costs.

questions

1. Differentiate between the planning and control functions of the management process, indicating what factors influence the type and degree of planning and control carried out by a manager.
2. What are the three planning and controlling processes described in the text? Give a brief description of each.
3. What is a budget?
4. What major purposes are served by the budgeting process?
5. List the major components of an operating budget for a manufacturing company.
6. List the primary factors that enter into the generation of a sales forecast. Give an example and source of information for each factor you list.
7. In what way is the process of formulating a sales forecast similar to that of formulating a budget?
8. How might a museum define its activity level, and what factors would influence its forecast for the coming period?
9. What are the advantages of using an on-line data-base system for retrieving information on economic and industry conditions?
10. Management's decision regarding ending inventory levels for finished

goods is important and requires careful review. What part does the ending inventory level play in the budgeting process, and why is management's decision about the proper inventory level important?

11. What length of time should be covered by the operating budget?

12. Why is applied overhead, rather than estimated actual overhead costs, used in calculating budgeted unit costs for each month of the budget period?

13. What part does the sales budget play in the budgeting process, and when should it be established?

14. The concept of a sales forecast and sales budget may not be relevant to the nonprofit organization. How do such organizations begin their budgetary process, and what major problems exist?

15. How do variable indirect manufacturing costs and variable selling and administrative expenses differ?

16. What effect, if any, does the pattern of collections from credit sales have on a firm's planned cash disbursements for raw materials purchases? What other factors might affect plans for a cash disbursement schedule?

17. Explain why the cash budget is a critical tool for management of a firm.

18. The owner of a printing firm had her CPA prepare a budgeted income statement on a monthly basis but did not wish to incur the additional expense of having a monthly cash budget prepared. The budgeted income statement for the month of January showed a profit of $13,000. Actual results exceeded this by $1,500. However, the owner's bank account at the end of January was very low, and she found that she would have to postpone payments to some of her creditors. She is puzzled by the difference between her profits and her cash balance. Explain to the owner the reason for this difference and give two examples of transactions which would be treated different in the two budgets.

19. The Breeze Manufacturing Company, which makes window fans, has been a very stable company in terms of its production and sales volume. The company maintained a finished goods inventory of 45,000 units and produced about 540,000 fans per year. Because of increasing costs, the company has decided to reduce its finished goods inventory level for the next budget period to 30,000 units.

   a. What are some costs of carrying inventory which Breeze is probably incurring?

   b. What budget schedule will be affected by the decision to reduce the level of finished goods inventory?

   c. Will the costs of producing a unit of product be affected by the decision to reduce the level of finished goods inventory for the coming budget period?

20. The text states that it may be desirable to prepare a cash budget in such a way that it shows cash from operations separate from cash from other sources and other uses.

   a. What is meant by the term "cash from operations"?

   b. What is the major advantage of preparing a cash budget in this format?

exercises

7—1. Ironside, Inc., manufactures and sells cast iron bathtubs which are reproductions of antique originals. Sales have increased steadily, owing to the growing interest in restoration of old homes.

The budget period for the firm begins on January 1, and Ironside's balance sheet as of that date is presented below with a partial income statement for the previous period. Based on a combination of factors, including past sales, industry outlook, and competitors' plans, management of Ironsides has prepared a sales forecast for the coming year which represents a 12% increase in unit sales per quarter over each of the previous year's quarters. Ironsides desires to maintain an average gross profit margin of 20% for the upcoming year but anticipates that variable manufacturing costs will be 5% higher, owing to a new labor contract and increased raw material costs, and fixed manufacturing costs will be 3% higher. Other management policies include:

1. The LIFO costing assumption is used for both raw materials and finished goods inventories.
2. Inventory is to be maintained at a level representing 9% of the next quarter's needs for finished goods and 10% for raw materials.

IRONSIDE, INC.
Balance Sheet
(as of beginning of period)

Current Assets:		Current Liabilities:	
Cash	$ 1,200	Accounts Payable	$ 1,350
Accounts Receivable	1,550	Accrued Salaries	
Inventories		Payable	800
Raw Materials ($1		Federal Income Taxes	
× 330 lb)	330	Payable	550
Work-in-Process	0		
Finished Goods[a]	1,616		
Total Current Assets	$ 4,696	Total Current Liabilities	$ 2,700
Property, Plant and			
Equipment	9,500		
Less: Accumulated		Common Stock	8,000
Depreciation	(3,000)	Retained Earnings	496
Total Property, Plant		Total Stockholders'	
and Equipment	$ 6,500	Equity	$ 8,496
Total Assets	$11,196	Total Liabilities and	
		Stockholders' Equity	$11,196

---

[a] Six units, all produced in the fourth quarter of previous year when there was no beginning inventory.

**Partial Budgeted Income Statement
(past 4 quarters)**

	1	2	3	4
Sales[a]	$17,500	$21,000	$17,150	$18,550
Cost of Goods Sold[b]	13,750	15,500	13,575	14,275
Gross Margin	$ 3,750	$ 5,500	$ 3,575	$ 4,275

[a] Selling price per unit = $350.
[b] Fixed manufacturing costs = $5,000 per quarter.

REQUIRED:

1. Prepare a sales budget by quarter for the year. Round unit sales to the nearest whole unit and the selling price to the nearest dollar.
2. Prepare a quarterly production budget for the year, assuming the desired level of ending inventory for the fourth quarter is 4 units.

7—2. Refer to the information in Exercise 7—1. Ironsides requires 50 pounds of iron for every bathtub produced. As of the beginning of the budget period, the delivered price per pound of iron is expected to rise from $1 to $1.25 per pound. In addition, 11.5 hours of direct labor are required per unit produced, and labor costs, which averaged $10 per direct labor hour in the past period, will increase to $10.75 per direct labor hour in the current period, owing to a new labor contract.

REQUIRED:

1. Prepare a quarterly direct materials budget for the year which shows raw materials to be purchased in units, the cost of raw materials purchased, and the cost of raw materials used. Assume the desired finished goods inventory for the fourth quarter is 4 bathtubs and the ending raw materials inventory for the fourth quarter is 300 pounds of iron.
2. Prepare a quarterly direct labor budget for the year which shows the number of direct labor hours which will be used and the quarterly cost of those hours.

7—3. The Stonemill Tile Manufacturing Company anticipates producing 800 batches, 850 batches, and 900 batches of tiles, respectively, in July, August, and September, the first quarter of the current period. They anticipate that it will continue to take 2 direct labor hours per batch of tiles. Indirect manufacturing costs and direct labor hours used during the last *quarter* of the previous year were as follows:

Direct labor hours	4,800 hours
Indirect materials (variable)	$ 8,160
Indirect labor (variable)	$12,000
Rent of factory (fixed)	$ 1,800
Repairs and maintenance (variable)	$ 3,840
Insurance (fixed)	$ 600
Factory supervision (fixed)	$ 9,600
Depreciation of factory equipment (fixed)	$ 4,200
Other (⅔ fixed, ⅓ variable)	$ 1,440

Stonemill uses an applied manufacturing overhead system based on direct labor hours used. They anticipate that current variable costs will be at the same rate as in the previous period and that fixed costs will remain the same, with the exception of depreciation. Stonemill purchased a new firing kiln at the beginning of the current period for $5,000. The kiln has a useful life of 10 years with a $200 salvage value. Stonemill uses the straight-line depreciation method.

REQUIRED:

1. Prepare a manufacturing overhead budget for Stonemill Tile Company for the quarter ending September 30 which shows the anticipated level of each element of manufacturing overhead.

2. Calculate a quarterly overhead rate for the period. (Round to the nearest cent.)

7—4. Refer to the information provided in Exercise 7—3. Stonemill Tile Company has budgeted 100 lb of clay for each batch of tiles produced in the upcoming period and has contracted with a local vendor who will deliver the clay at a cost of $5 per lb for the coming year, a cost increase of $0.30 per lb over the previous year. Direct labor cost is $15 per hour. Raw materials inventory at the beginning of the period included 5,000 lb of clay. There were no beginning or ending work-in-process inventories. Stonemill desires to maintain 10% of next month's production needs in raw materials inventory and anticipates producing 875 batches in October. *Assume* overhead will be applied at the rate of $8.50 per direct labor hour.

REQUIRED: Prepare a Budgeted Cost of Manufacturing Statement by month for Stonemill for the quarter ended September 30. Stonemill uses a LIFO costing approach for raw materials inventory.

7—5. The Clearview Manufacturing Company makes all sales on account, and their past history of accounts receivable indicates that 50% of sales are collected in the month of sale, 40% in the month following the sale, and 10% in the second month following the sale. Any amounts not collected by the end of the second month are written off at that time as uncollectible. Clearview's manager of accounting anticipates that this pattern will continue in the upcoming period. Clearview expects credit sales to consist of 400, 475, and 425 units respectively in April, May, and June of the forthcoming quarter at a unit price of $550. The accounts receivable balance at the end of March is $140,000, and $18,000 of that balance represents credit sales from February. All accounts receivable from months prior to February have been collected or written off.

REQUIRED:

1. Prepare a schedule of expected cash receipts for Clearview for the upcoming quarter, assuming all balances are collectible.

2. Clearview estimates that it will pay for 60% of any month's raw materials purchases in that month and 40% in the following month. Assuming that budgeted materials costs for April, May, and June are $265,000, $232,000, and $254,000, respectively, should management attempt to revise their cash disbursement schedule and why? The balance in accounts payable at the end of March was $97,000, all of which will be paid in April.

7—6. Some of the expenses of a manufacturing firm are listed below.

REQUIRED: Indicate whether the expenses listed represent variable or fixed costs. If variable, do they vary with units produced, with units sold, or with some other measure of activity?

a. Sales commissions.
b. Depreciation on delivery truck (based on miles driven).
c. Shipping expense.
d. Factory supervisor's salary.
e. Advertising expense.
f. Administrative salaries.
g. Depreciation on factory building (straight-line).
h. Insurance.
i. Direct materials.
j. Depreciation on word processing equipment (straight-line).
k. Labor to assemble the product.

7—7. Last year's sales for a line of jogging and athletic suits for Sports Fashions, Inc., during the quarter October 1–December 31 were as follows:

	OCTOBER	NOVEMBER	DECEMBER
Units sold	25,000	30,000	50,000

The rate of increase in unit sales from month to month in this quarter has been consistent for the past three years and is expected to continue during the budget period. (For example, November sales will be 120% (30,000/25,000) of October sales and December sales will be double those of October.) The average price per jogging suit sold was $35. Sports Fashions wishes to prepare three schedules of sales in units and in dollars as a preliminary step in their budgeting process. These schedules will be based on the following assumptions:

Optimistic: Owing to a new advertising campaign October sales will be 30,000. The sales price will be raised by $2.50 per unit.

Most Likely: October sales will be 28,000 units. Because of new competition, a sales price increase of only $1 per unit can be made.

Pessimistic: October sales will drop to 18,000 units, and the sales price will have to be maintained at last year's level. This forecast reflects an increase in competition and a lessening of consumers' interest in physical-fitness activities.

REQUIRED: Prepare sales forecasts which show unit and dollar sales for each month in the quarter and the quarter totals based on each set of assumptions.

7—8. Shown below is a Budgeted Units of Production Schedule.

	PRODUCT A	PRODUCT B	PRODUCT C	PRODUCT D	PRODUCT E
Forecasted Sales	100,000	?	500,000	300,000	?
Desired Ending Inventory	50,000	8,000	?	?	60,000
Units Required	?	88,000	512,000	350,000	760,000
Less: Beginning Inventory	?	?	17,000	?	?
Required Production	110,000	78,000	?	310,000	685,000

REQUIRED: Calculate the missing amounts.

7—9. (AICPA adapted) Varsity Co. is preparing its cash budget for the month of May. Of the sales on account 1% are never collected. The remainder are collected according to the following pattern:

Current month's sales	12%
Prior month's sales	75%
Sales two months prior to current month	9%
Sales three months prior to current month	4%

Credit sales are as follows:

May—estimated	$100,000
April	90,000
March	80,000
February	95,000

REQUIRED:
1. Calculate estimated accounts receivable collections for May.
2. Assume that actual results for Varsity's first six months of operation were as follows and calculate the June 30 ending cash balance.

Sales (90% collected)	$1,500,000
Bad debt write-offs	60,000
Disbursements for costs and expenses	1,200,000
Disbursements for income taxes	90,000
Purchases of fixed assets	400,000
Depreciation on fixed assets	80,000
Proceeds from issuance of common stock	500,000
Proceeds from short-term borrowings	100,000
Payments on short-term borrowings	50,000

7—10. (AICPA adapted) Patsy Corp. has estimated its activity for December. Selected data from these estimated amounts are as follows:

Sales	$350,000
Gross profit (based on sales)	30%
Increase in trade accounts receivable during month	$ 10,000
Change in accounts payable during month	$ 0
Increase in inventory during month	$ 5,000

Variable selling, general and administrative expenses (S, G & A) includes a charge for uncollectible accounts of 1% of sales.

Total S, G & A is $35,500 per month plus 15% of sales.

Depreciation expense of $20,000 per month is included in fixed S, G & A.

REQUIRED: **1.** On the basis of the above data, determine estimated cash receipts from operations for December.

2. Determine estimated cash disbursements from operations for December.

7—11. A number of activities for a manufacturing concern are listed below.

   a. Acquiring a new subsidiary.
   b. Determining whether credit should be granted to a customer.
   c. Deciding that the company should create a research and new-product-development function.
   d. Acquiring a new delivery truck.
   e. Scheduling production.
   f. Deciding to switch from radio advertising to television advertising.
   g. Deciding to fire the company president.
   h. Deciding to accept an advertising campaign developed by an advertising agency.
   i. Deciding to fire a production-line worker.
   j. Scheduling vacations for hourly workers.
   k. Preparing budgets.
   l. Checking workers as they leave the premises for company property.
   m. Deciding to lower the minimum inventory quantity the company maintains.
   n. Deciding to build a new plant.
   o. Defining characteristics which will be considered before credit is granted to a potential customer.

REQUIRED: For each activity, indicate whether it is part of the (1) strategic planning process, (2) management control process, or (3) operational control process.

7—12. The Gurleyville Preschool Day Care Center is a nonprofit organization funded primarily by the town of Gurleyville. Fees are set on the following sliding scale:

FAMILY ANNUAL INCOME	STUDENT FEE PER DAY
Less than $10,000	0
$10,000–$12,000	$1
$12,001–$15,000	$1.50
$15,001–$18,000	$2.00
$18,001–$20,000	$2.50

Children from families with incomes greater than $20,000 are not accepted in the program. Enrollment is limited to 100 children.

The Day Care Center employs 5 regular teachers who are paid $12,000 per year and 5 teachers aides who receive $6,500 per year. Children in the program are given a midmorning and midafternoon snack plus a hot lunch. Hot lunches are provided by a catering service at a cost of $1.25 per student per day; the estimated cost of the snacks provided during the day totals $.15 per day. The Center operates 230 days a year. Based on past data, supplies for the year are expected to cost $4,200. Facilities where the Center operates and the equipment are provided by the town.

Based on requests for a place in the program and the application of admission criteria, it appears that enrollments for the next year will be as follows:

CHILD'S FAMILY INCOME	PERCENT OF TOTAL ENROLLMENT
Less than $10,000	40%
$10,000–$12,000	20%
$12,001–$15,000	15%
$15,001–$18,000	15%
$18,001–$20,000	10%

REQUIRED:
1. Prepare a schedule of budgeted tuition income for the coming year.
2. The Center must make a request to the town of Gurleyville for the amount by which its financial needs exceed tuition generated. Prepare an operating budget which will show the amount of funds which must be requested from the town.

7—13. The Goodwell Printing Company prepared the following operating budget for the month of August:

Revenues:		
From printing	$28,000	
From subletting part of the building	300	$28,300
Operating Expenses:		
Paper and other supplies	9,000	
Salaries	7,000	
Depreciation of equipment	2,000	
Rent	1,000	
Insurance	200	
Miscellaneous	400	19,600
Income before taxes		$ 8,700
Estimated Taxes @ 30%		$ 2,610
Net Income		$ 6,090

Additional information for August:

1. Of receivables which were on the books August 1 for printing services, $2,000 will be collected. Of the $28,000 revenues from printing, 30% will be in the form of receivables at the end of the period.
2. During August paper and other supplies costing $11,500 will be purchased and paid for in cash.
3. The $300 rent from subletting was collected in June.
4. Rent for the remainder of the year must be paid on August 1. The rental rate is $1,000 per month.
5. Salaries and miscellaneous will be paid in cash.
6. The $200 of insurance represents a write-off of previously prepaid insurance.
7. No taxes are due in August.
8. A payment of $1,200 on printing equipment which was purchased earlier in the year is due August 15. The remaining balance due on the note, excluding the $1,200, is $4,000.

Mr. Goodwell, the owner of the printing company, is looking forward to paying off the remainder of the equipment note at the end of August, based on the projected net income figure for the month. The August 1 cash balance of Goodwell is $2,500.

REQUIRED: 1. Will Goodwell Printing be able to liquidate its note? Support your answer with a cash budget for the month of August.
2. Assume that your calculations show that Goodwell Printing will have a cash deficiency as of the end of August. What are some actions it may be able to take to prevent or lessen that cash deficiency?

7—14.   Gourmet-on-the-Go prepares gourmet meals which can be ordered in advance and picked up at three locations throughout the city. The company's accountant has prepared the following report, which shows actual results and the variance from budgeted results.

	ACTUAL	VARIANCE FROM BUDGET[a]
Meals served	39,700	(3,300)
Revenues	$230,260	($27,740)
Variable Expenses:		
Food	$ 77,415	$ 8,584
Supplies	20,644	856
Part-time labor	13,498	(598)
Fixed Expenses:		
Salaries	43,000	—
Depreciation of facilities	40,850	—
Utilities	8,720	(120)
Insurance	15,050	(2,150)
Other	9,750	1,000
Total Expenses	$228,927	$ 7,573
Income before taxes	$ 1,333	($20,167)

[a] Parentheses indicate an unfavorable variance.

REQUIRED: 1. How much income before taxes was Gourmet expecting when the budget was prepared?

2. Calculate the budgeted selling price per meal and the actual selling price per meal. By what amount did actual revenues differ from budgeted revenues because of this price difference?

3. How much *anticipated revenue* was lost because Gourmet sold 3,300 fewer meals than expected?

4. Calculate the budgeted total variable cost per meal and the actual total variable cost per meal. What effect did any differences between the two figures you have calculated have on income before taxes?

5. By what amount were anticipated total variable costs different from actual total variable costs owing solely to volume factors?

6. Calculate budgeted total fixed costs per meal and actual total fixed costs per meal. Explain any difference in results which you obtained.

7. If Gourmet had been able to accurately estimate the number of meals it would sell as 39,700, what amount of fixed costs would the company have included in its budget?

7—15.   The Golden Years Nursing Home is a profit-making organization which has a maximum capacity of 50 persons. Persons admitted must be mobile and able to attend to their personal needs. Golden Years has accumulated the following information in anticipation of preparing its operating budget for the coming year.

1. Charge per month for each patient, $1,200.
2. Anticipated costs of three meals per day for each occupant, $12.
3. Anticipated costs of various supplies per day for each occupant, $4.
4. Salaries for the budget year, $100,000.
5. Depreciation of building and equipment for the budget year, $85,000.
6. Estimated utility costs, $29,000.
7. Budgeted insurance and property taxes for the year, $27,000.
8. Accounting and bookkeeping services are estimated to cost $1,000 per month.
9. The Home offers a series of trips, parties, and other entertainments for which it anticipates spending $9,000 for the year.
10. The Home has a waiting list and expects to operate at capacity all 365 days of the budget year.
11. Earnings of the Home are taxed at a 46% rate.

The costs of medical services or personal services such as barbers or beauticians are billed directly to the patient and not included in the basic monthly fee.

REQUIRED: 1. Prepare a budgeted income statement for Golden Years. Use a contribution-margin format in preparing the budget. (Remember, contribution margin is found by comparing revenues with all variable costs. Fixed costs are then subtracted from the contribution margin to get the profit before taxes.)

2. Golden Years is thinking about opening another facility in another location. The costs and patient charge would be almost identical to those of its present facility. Management anticipates that during its first year of operations it would operate at an average capacity level of 60%. What first-year net income (or

loss) could be expected from the second facility? [*Hint:* Use the data from part 1 to calculate a contribution margin per patient.]

3. If Golden Years could increase the capacity of its present facility by 5 patients at an increase in fixed costs of $45,000, what effect would this have on its projected income before taxes?

problems

7—16. *Preparation of Budgeted Cost of Goods Sold Statement.*   The Matchless Products Company incurred the following costs for the year ended December 31, when 500,000 units of product were produced.

Direct Materials, 1,000,000 lb @ $2/lb		$ 2,000,000
Direct Labor, 3,000,000 hr @ $7/hr		21,000,000
Variable Manufacturing Overhead:		
Indirect Materials	$250,000	
Supplies	100,000	
Utilities	150,000	
Fixed Manufacturing Overhead:		
Depreciation	200,000	
Insurance	50,000	
Property Taxes on Factory Building	20,000	770,000
Total Actual Manufacturing Costs		$23,770,000
Cost per Unit		$47.54

For the coming year, the company has made the following budget estimates:

Production: 600,000 units.

Direct Materials: New production techniques are expected to cut raw material usage per unit of output by 5%, while the cost to acquire raw materials is expected to increase by 10 cents per pound.

Direct Labor: Input per unit of output and price per hour are expected to remain at last year's level.

Variable Manufacturing Overhead:

Indirect Materials: The cost of these materials used is expected to rise 10%.

Supplies: Input per unit of output and price for supplies are expected to remain at last year's level.

Utilities: 1,000,000 kilowatt-hours were used last year. The cost per kilowatt-hour is expected to increase by 15% over last year.

Fixed Manufacturing Overhead: The only anticipated change in these costs is a forecasted rise of $2,000 in property taxes.

REQUIRED: 1. Prepare a budgeted cost of goods manufactured schedule for Matchless based on the data provided. Assume there were no work-in-process inventories.
2. Calculate budgeted cost of goods sold, assuming the company uses a LIFO costing approach and expects to sell 550,000 units. (Round unit cost to the nearest cent.)
3. Compare last year's cost per unit of production with the budgeted unit cost, and comment on the results of your comparison.

7—17. *Preparation of Sales Budget and Schedule of Cash Collection of Receivables.* The Fast Start Bicycle Company has provided you with the following historical data:

1. January sales, 4,000 bikes. February sales are usually about 70% of January sales, while March sales exceed January sales by 25%.
2. Sales price per unit to retailers: $120.
3. Cash sales were 20% of total sales.
4. Approximately 8% of all credit sales were never collected. Of those which were collected, 30% was collected in the month of sale and 70% in the following month.

Fast Start has made the following assumptions for its upcoming quarterly budget:

1. January sales will be 20% higher than last year. The relationship of February and March sales to January sales will be in keeping with the historical trend.
2. Last year's sales price of $120 was 150% of product costs. Production costs for the budget period are expected to be 10% higher than last year. The company believes it should maintain a selling price which is 150% of production costs.
3. Cash sales will be only 15% of total sales for the budget period.
4. The collection pattern of 30% in the month of sale and 70% in the following month is expected to continue. However, because of tightened credit-granting and follow-up policies, Fast Start believes it should budget for only a 5% level of uncollectible accounts.

REQUIRED: 1. Prepare a sales budget for Fast Start for January–March which shows unit sales and dollar sales.
2. Prepare a schedule of expected cash collections for January–March. Assume the January 1 balance in Accounts Receivable, net of anticipated bad-debt losses, was $581,875, all of which was collected during January. (Round all amounts to the nearest dollar.)
3. Based on the January 1 balance in Accounts Receivable, estimate what unit sales were for the previous December.

7—18. *Comprehensive Cash Budget preparation with supporting schedules.* The Pratt Pickle Company would like to purchase new bottling equipment to be put into operation at the end of their next quarter (March). The company president has requested that you prepare a budget which will indicate the firm's cash position for the next three months, January–March, if the $75,000 equipment is purchased and paid for in equal installments during those three months. Other relevant data include:

1. Ending Cash Balance December 31, $2,750.
2. Expected Sales (units): January—200,000, February—180,000, March—197,000.
3. Expected Selling Price, $2/unit.
4. All sales are on account, and the January 1 beginning balance in Accounts Receivable was $127,000. Assume all $127,000 will be collected in January.
5. Fifty percent of sales will be collected in the month of sale, 40% in the following month, and 10% in the second month following the sale. Uncollectibles may be ignored.
6. Inventory of Finished Goods is to be maintained at 10% of the next month's sales. There were 15,000 units on hand at January 1, and April sales are anticipated to be 205,000 units.
7. Raw Materials Inventory is to be maintained at 10% of the next month's production, and April production is estimated to be 208,000.
8. Four pounds of raw materials at a cost of $.08 per pound are needed per unit produced. Raw material costs per unit are the same as last year's. Beginning Raw Materials Inventory at January 1 was 65,000 lb.
9. Raw material inventory purchases are paid for 50% in the month purchased and 50% in the following month. There was a $32,340 beginning balance in accounts payable at January 1, all of which was paid in January.
10. For each unit .25 direct labor hours are required. The cost per direct labor hour is $4, and labor costs are paid in the month incurred. Manufacturing overhead is equal to 20% of direct labor cost and is paid for with cash in the period incurred except for depreciation. The *annual* depreciation charge is $16,800.
11. Selling and administrative expenses excluding depreciation are expected to be $35,200, $37,600, and $33,400 in January, February, and March and will be paid in the month incurred.
12. Taxes for the previous quarter of $15,000 will be paid in January.
13. In January $35,000 is received from the sale of old bottling equipment.
14. The company can borrow in multiples of $5,000 at interest of 12% per year. Assume that any borrowing will take place on the first day of the month during which there will be a cash deficiency and will be repaid on the last day of the month during which cash becomes available.

REQUIRED: Is the purchase feasible in terms of availability of cash to pay for the machinery? Support your answer with a month-by-month cash budget for the quarter. To develop the cash-flow data you will need you should prepare a schedule of expected cash collections, a production budget, a direct materials budget, a schedule of cash disbursements for materials, and a direct labor budget. Round all amounts to the nearest dollar.

7—19. *Comprehensive Budgeting Problem.*   Tomorrow Today, Inc., manufactures a line of glass-top tables. Its balance sheet as of December 31 was as follows:

TOMORROW TODAY, INC.
Balance Sheet
as of December 31

Current Assets:		*Current Liabilities:*	
Cash	$ 34,000	Accounts Payable	$ 57,600
Accounts Receivable (net)	274,313	Other Payables (Manufacturing overhead)	8,600
Marketable Securities	60,000	Total Current Liabilities	66,200
		Long-Term Liabilities	0
Inventories:[a]			
Raw Materials	72,000[b]		
Work-in-Process	0		
Finished Goods	192,000[c]		
Total Current Assets	$ 632,313		
Noncurrent Assets:		*Stockholders' Equity:*	
Property, Plant and Equipment	1,700,000	Common Stock, 100,000 shares par $10	1,000,000
Less: Accumulated Depreciation	(436,000)	Capital in Excess of Par	800,000
Net Property, Plant and Equipment	$1,264,000	Retained Earnings	180,113
		Total Stockholders' Equity	$1,980,113
Other Assets	150,000		
Total Noncurrent Assets	$1,414,000		
Total Assets	$2,046,313	Total Liabilities and Stockholders' Equity	$2,046,313

[a] All inventory is costed out on a LIFO basis.
[b] 800 glass sheets @ $40 each + 800 brass bases @ $50 each = $72,000.
[c] 1,000 tables @ $192 each = $192,000.

Additional data:

a. The sales forecast for the first quarter of the coming budget period is as follows:

January	800 tables
February	700
March	1,000

The estimated selling price per table is $550.

b. One-quarter of total sales are normally cash sales. The other three-quarters are credit sales. On the average 5% of all credit sales prove to be uncollectible. Those that are collected are collected 30% in the month of sale and 70% in the month following sale.

c. The company likes to keep a finished goods inventory of 1,000 tables on hand.

d. The company's policy is to keep on hand raw materials sufficient to produce next month's required production volume. Each unit requires a sheet of glass and a brass base. The glass is cut on premises, but the brass base is purchased ready for assembly. The expected cost of each sheet of glass required to produce one table is $40, and the brass bases are expected to cost $50 each. April production is estimated at 800 tables.

e. Tomorrow Today, Inc., purchases all raw materials on account and pays for them 20% in the month of purchase and 80% in the following month.

f. Direct labor requirements for the tables are 4 hours per table at a cost of $10 per hour. Labor costs are paid entirely in the month incurred.

g. Variable manufacturing overhead costs are estimated at $20 per unit, while fixed manufacturing costs will be budgeted at $35,000 each month. With the exception of depreciation of $12,000 per month, all other variable and fixed overhead costs are assumed to be paid 80% in the month incurred and 20% in the following month. The amount owed for manufacturing overhead December 31 will be paid in January.

h. Sales commissions are set at 10% of the gross selling price. Other variable selling expenses are 2% of gross sales. Fixed selling expenses amount to $30,000 per month, of which $8,000 is depreciation. All selling expenses requiring cash are paid in the month incurred.

i. Administrative expenses other than bad-debt expense, all of which are fixed, per month are as follows:

Salaries	$28,000
Insurance	5,000
Depreciation	15,000
Utilities	9,000
Other	12,000

Those administrative expenses requiring cash outlays are paid in the month incurred.

j. Overhead is applied on the basis of direct labor hours.

k. The company plans to repurchase 10,000 shares of its stock from a disgruntled shareholder and estimates that the reacquisition price will be $45 per share. The repurchase is planned for February 1.

l. Marketable Securities shown on the December 31 balance sheet will be liquidated at their book value January 31.

m. The company has adopted a policy of maintaining a minimum balance of $30,000 for the budget period. Any excess cash can be invested in $1,000 multiples on the last day of the month at a rate of 10% per annum, with principle and interest receivable on the last day of the following month. Any excess cash for January will not be invested because of the anticipated share repurchase on February 1.

n. Any cash deficiency can be covered by short-term borrowing. Assume such borrowing will be done on the last day of the month for which the deficiency exists and is payable on the last day of the following month plus interest at the rate of 1% per month. Borrowing must be done in multiples of $1,000.

REQUIRED: Prepare the following budgets and accompanying schedules. Each should be designed to show figures for each of the three months in the quarter and for the quarter as a whole.

1. Sales budget with accompany schedule of cash flows from cash sales and credit sales. (Prepare a schedule of the type shown in the text in Schedule 1 and add an additional line for cash sales.) The December 31 balance in Accounts Receivable will be collected during January.
2. Production budget.
3. Direct materials budget which shows (a) the number of units and cost of direct materials to be purchased, the cost of raw materials used in production, and (b) an accompanying schedule showing cash disbursements for materials purchases. Accounts payable December 31 will be paid in January.
4. Direct labor budget.
5. **a.** Manufacturing overhead budget.
   b. Calculate an appropriate overhead rate for the year based on direct labor hours. Assume that the production patterns of the first quarter are reflected in the next three quarters.
6. Budgeted Cost of Goods Manufactured Statement.
7. Selling and administrative expenses budget.
8. Cash budget.
9. Budgeted Income Statement.
10. Budgeted Balance Sheet.

7—20. *Comprehensive Cash Budget, Budgeted Income Statement, and Balance Sheet.* The balance sheet for Deco, Inc., a retail clothing store as of June 30 is given below:

Cash	$ 40,000	Accounts Payable	$ 73,000
Accounts Receivable	45,000	Notes and Interest Payable	
		(due July 1)	30,000
Inventory	21,000	Common Stock	130,000
Property, Plant and Equipment	217,000	Retained Earnings	40,000
Less: Accumulated			
Depreciation	(50,000)		
Total Assets	$273,000		$273,000

Additional data include the following:

1. Collections of accounts receivable are expected to be 55% in the month of sale, 35% in the next month, and 10% in the following month. June 30 Accounts Receivable represents June sales. All earlier receipts have been collected.
2. Sales are budgeted at $185,000 in July, $200,000 in August, $190,000 in September, and $200,000 in October. All sales are on account. You may ignore uncollectible accounts.
3. The expected gross margin is 30% of sales.
4. All inventory purchases are made on account and paid for in the month after purchase. Inventory purchases were budgeted at $150,000 in July, $180,000 in August, and $150,000 in September. The $73,000 owed June 30 was paid in July.
5. Additional cash expenses for selling and administrative costs each month are expected to be $24,700.
6. Depreciation is $7,500 each month.

7. No required minimum cash balance has been set by the company.

8. On July 1, Deco will pay the note and interest.

9. During July Deco plans to declare and pay a $20,000 dividend.

10. Deco can borrow in $5,000 increments at a 15% annual interest rate for periods up to six months.

REQUIRED:

1. Prepare a cash budget for each month and show quarter totals.

2. Prepare a budgeted income statement for the quarter ending September 30. The income statement should show income statement data each month as well as quarter totals.

3. Prepare a balance sheet for the quarter ending September 30. (No monthly balance sheets are required.)

4. Compare net income each month with cash flows *from operations* each month and comment on the differences.

7—21.   *Cash Budget, Budgeted Income Statement, and Balance Sheet.   Projected* data are listed below for the Paine Manufacturing Company's *first quarter* of operations.

1. Collections for goods sold (40% of sales in first quarter), $236,000.

2. Gross Margin, 30% sales.

3. Second-quarter sales projected to be 10% higher than first quarter.

4. During the first quarter the company will purchase merchandise inventory sufficient to cover first-quarter sales and 20% of the sales anticipated in the second quarter. The *total* merchandise purchases made in the first quarter will require a cash payment in that quarter.

5. Cash disbursements for operating-expense payment for the quarter, $70,000. (Total operating expenses will be paid in cash.)

6. The anticipated income tax rate is 30%. No taxes will have to be paid until the second quarter.

7. Cash disbursement for purchase of depreciable fixed assets, $300,000.

8. Depreciation will be calculated on a straight-line basis at 1% per month.

9. Proceeds from issuing $10 par common stock, $400,000.

The company wants to end the first quarter with a cash balance of $21,000. It will finance any cash needs through a five-year note payable which bears interest at the rate of 12% per year payable annually. The company plans to borrow any amount it needs to finance its operations immediately and will borrow in multiples of $1,000.

REQUIRED:

1. Prepare a schedule of projected cash receipts and disbursements for the company for the first quarter which will indicate to management the amount it will have to borrow to finance operations.

2. Prepare a projected income statement for the company for its first quarter of operations. *Don't forget to include interest expense.*

3. Prepare a projected balance sheet as of the end of the first quarter.

7—22.   *Calculating budgeted cash flows based on credit terms and collection and payment history.*   (CMA adapted.) The Russon Corporation is a retailer whose sales are all made on credit. Sales are billed twice monthly, on the tenth of the month for the last half of the prior month's sales and on the twentieth of the month for the first half of the current month's sales. The terms of all sales are 2/10, net 30. Based upon past experience, the collection experience of accounts receivable is as follows:

Within the discount period	80%
On the thirtieth day	18%
Uncollectible	2%

The sales value of shipments for May and the forecast for the next four months are:

May (actual)	$500,000
June	600,000
July	700,000
August	700,000
September	400,000

Russon's average markup on its products is 20 percent of the sales price.

Russon purchases merchandise for resale to meet the current month's sales demand and to maintain a desired monthly ending inventory of 25% of the next month's sales. All purchases are on credit with terms of net 30. Russon pays for half of a month's purchases in the month of purchase and the other half in the following month. All sales and purchases occur uniformly throughout the month.

REQUIRED:

1. Determine how much cash Russon Corporation plans to collect from accounts receivable during July.
2. Determine planned collections in September from sales made in August.
3. Determine the budgeted dollar value of Russon's inventory at August 31.
4. Determine planned merchandise purchases for June.
5. Determine planned cash disbursements for merchandise payment in August.

7—23. *Preparation of a Cash Budget—nonprofit organization.* (CMA adapted) United Business Education, Inc. (UBE) is a nonprofit organization which sponsors a wide variety of management seminars throughout the United States. In addition, it is heavily involved in research into improved methods of educating and motivating business executives. The seminar activity is largely supported by fees and the research program from member dues. UBE operates on a calendar-year basis and is in the process of finalizing the budget for the coming year. The following information has been taken from approved plans, which are still tentative at this time.

Seminar Program

Revenue—The scheduled number of programs should produce $12,000,000 of revenue for the year. Each program is budgeted to produce the same amount of revenue. The revenue is collected during the month the program is offered. The programs are scheduled so that 12% of the revenue is collected in each of the first five months of the year. The remaining programs, accounting for the remaining 40% of the revenue, are distributed evenly through the months of September, October, and November. No programs are offered in the other four months of the year.

Direct Expenses—The seminar expenses are made up of three segments:

a. Instructors' fees are paid at the rate of 70% of the seminar revenue in the month following the seminar. The instructors are considered independent contractors and are not eligible for UBE employee benefits.

b. Facilities fees total $5,600,000 for the year. They are the same for each program and are paid in the month the program is given.

c. Annual promotional costs of $1,000,000 are spent equally in all months except June and July, when there is no promotional effort.

Research Program

Research Grants—The research program has a large number of projects nearing completion. The other main research activity this year includes the feasibility studies for new projects. As a result, the total grant expense of $3,000,000 for the year is expected to be paid out at the rate of $500,000 per month during the first six months of the year.

Salaries and Other UBE Expenses

Office Lease—Annual amount of $240,000, paid monthly at the beginning of each month.

General Administrative Expenses (telephone, supplies, postage, etc.)—$1,500,000 annually or $125,000 a month.

Depreciation Expense—$240,000 a year.

General UBE Promotion—Annual cost of $600,000, paid monthly.

Salaries and Benefits—

Number of Employees	Annual Salary (Paid Monthly)	Total Annual Salaries
1	$50,000	$ 50,000
3	40,000	120,000
4	30,000	120,000
15	25,000	375,000
5	15,000	75,000
22	10,000	220,000
50		$960,000

Employee benefits amount to $240,000 or 25% of annual salaries. Except for the pension contribution, the benefits are paid as salaries are paid. The annual pension payment of $24,000, based on 2.5% of salaries (included in the total benefits and the 25% rate), is due April 15.

Other information:

1. Membership Income—UBE has 100,000 members, each of whom pays an annual fee of $100. The fee for the calendar year is invoiced in late June. The collection schedule is as follows:

July	60%
August	30%
September	5%
October	5%
	100%

2. Capital Expenditures—The capital expenditures program calls for a total of $510,000 in cash payments to be spread evenly over the first five months of the budget year.
3. Cash and Temporary Investments at January 1 of the budget year are estimated at $750,000.

REQUIRED:

1. Prepare a budget of the annual cash receipts and disbursements for UBE, Inc., for the year.
2. Prepare a cash budget for UBE, Inc., for January.
3. Using the information you developed in parts 1 and 2, identify two important operating problems of UBE, Inc.

7—24. *Calculation of sales and manufacturing costs schedules.* (AICPA adapted) The Scarborough Corporation manufactures and sell two products, Thingone and Thingtwo. In July, Scarborough's budget department gathered the following data in order to project sales and budget requirements for the coming year:

Projected Sales

PRODUCT	UNITS	PRICE
Thingone	60,000	$ 70
Thingtwo	40,000	$100

Inventories—in units

PRODUCT	EXPECTED JANUARY 1	DESIRED DECEMBER 31
Thingone	20,000	25,000
Thingtwo	8,000	9,000

In order to produce one unit of Thingone and Thingtwo, the following raw materials are used:

		AMOUNT USED PER UNIT	
RAW MATERIAL	UNIT	Thingone	Thingtwo
A	lb	4	5
B	lb	2	3
C	units		1

Projected data for the budget year with respect to raw materials are as follows:

RAW MATERIAL	ANTICIPATED PURCHASE PRICE	EXPECTED INVENTORIES JANUARY 1	DESIRED INVENTORIES DECEMBER 31
A	$8	32,000 lb	36,000 lb
B	$5	29,000 lb	32,000 lb
C	$3	6,000 units	7,000 units

Projected direct labor requirements and rates are as follows:

PRODUCT	HOURS PER UNIT	RATE PER UNIT
Thingone	2	$3
Thingtwo	3	$4

Overhead is applied at the rate of $2 per direct labor hour.

REQUIRED: Based upon the above projections and budget requirements for Thingone and Thingtwo, prepare the following budgets:

1. Sales budget (in dollars).
2. Production budget (in units).
3. Raw materials purchase budget (in quantities).
4. Raw materials purchase budget (in dollars).
5. Direct labor budget (in dollars).
6. Budgeted finished goods inventory at December 31 (in dollars).

7—25. *Reconstructing the Budgeted Income Statement; effects of variances on operating results.* Total Sound manufactures a stereo radio and tape unit with earphones which can be worn on a belt or around the neck and is popularly known as a "walkman." Actual results and variances from budget for the company for the month of March are shown below:

	ACTUAL	VARIANCE FROM BUDGET[a]
Unit Sales	22,000	2,000
Sales	$2,310,000	$310,000
Cost of Goods Manufactured and Sold:		
Direct Materials	$ 221,760	$ (21,760)
Direct Labor	330,880	(30,880)
Variable Manufacturing Overhead	65,340	(5,340)
Fixed Manufacturing Overhead	181,500	(1,500)
Total Cost of Goods Manufactured and Sold	$ 799,480	$ (59,480)
Gross Margin	$1,510,520	$250,520
Operating Expenses:		
Variable Selling	$ 261,800	$ (21,800)
Fixed Selling	278,300	1,700
Fixed Administrative	460,000	0
Total Operating Expenses	$1,000,100	$ (20,100)
Income before taxes	$ 510,420	$230,420

[a] Parentheses indicate unfavorable variances.

REQUIRED: 1. Calculate the actual variable manufacturing overhead cost per unit and the budgeted variable manufacturing overhead cost per unit. Comment on how effective the company was in controlling this cost.

2. Calculate the actual fixed manufacturing overhead per unit and the budgeted fixed manufacturing overhead per unit. Explain any differences between the two figures and comment on the company's effectiveness in controlling this cost.

3. If variable costs *per unit* had been exactly as budgeted, would there have been any unfavorable variances? Explain your answer.

4. If Total Sound could have held all variable manufacturing costs *per unit* at the budgeted unit cost and fixed manufacturing overhead at the budgeted level, what amount of gross margin would the company have generated relative to actual sales?

5. How did the actual selling price per unit compare with the budgeted selling price?

6. Based on the budget, what was the anticipated contribution margin per unit? (Contribution margin = selling price less all variable costs.)

7. Assume that selling price and variable costs per unit are not expected to vary next year from those *budgeted* for the current year and that total fixed costs next year should be at this year's *budget* level. What effect would a drop in volume to 18,000 units have on next year's anticipated results? (Hint: use the contribution margin you calculated in your analysis.)

7—26. *Preparing a Budget for a Service Organization.* Carfiello Employment Service, which specializes in placing high-level executives, had the following operating results for the past year:

Revenues @ $3,000 per client		$900,000
Variable Expenses (vary with clients served)		
Supplies	$ 3,000	
Resume preparation	15,000	
Psychological and personality testing (done by an external consultant)	120,000	138,000
Contribution margin		$762,000
Fixed Expenses:		
Salaries	$250,000	
Rent	120,000	
Depreciation of furniture and equipment	60,000	
Entertainment	33,000	
Advertising	38,000	
Utilities	24,000	
Insurance	29,000	
Other	45,000	
Total fixed expenses		599,000
Income before taxes		$163,000

Carfiello wants to prepare two sets of budget figures—one an optimistic set based on an assumed, 20% increase in volume of clients, the other a pessimistic projection based on a 10% decline from the past year's volume. The following changes for the budget year are anticipated:

1. Supplies and resume preparation costs will increase by 10% per client.
2. The external consultant is raising her fee by $25 per client.

3. If business does increase by 20%, a new professional employment counselor will have to be hired at a salary of $60,000, and he or she will need a secretarial assistant at $18,000 per year. If business declines, one secretarial assistant at approximately $18,000 will be let go.

4. All salaries for persons currently on the payroll will be raised by 6%, which is the anticipated level of inflation. In addition, additional merit-related salary increases will total $10,000.

5. The costs of entertainment and advertising are expected to increase by 15%.

6. All other items included in the budget will stay at last year's levels. Fees will not be raised because of increasing competition in this field.

REQUIRED:

1. Prepare two sets of budgeted income statement figures—one based on a 20% increase in volume, the other on a 10% decrease in volume. Prepare the budgeted income statement in the contribution-margin format used above to report actual data.

2. Based on the budgeted data you have developed, calculate the contribution margin per client for each of the two volume assumptions.

3. Assume Carfiello could increase volume above that of the past year by 10% without any increase in personnel. What would budgeted profits be at this volume level? Begin your calculations with contribution margin per client. Compare your budgeted income before taxes with what you calculated for a 20% volume increase. Explain the difference.

7—27. *Budgeting with a process costing accounting system.*   White and Bright makes toothpaste and uses a process costing accounting system to account for its manufacture. Given below are data accumulated with respect to budget preparation for the Paste Making Department.

ACTUAL DATA

Actual Work-in-Process Ending Inventory (Beginning inventory for the budget period)	100,000 ounces complete as to materials, 60% complete as to labor and overhead
Costs in Work-in-Process:	
Materials	$2,000
Labor and Overhead	$4,400

ESTIMATED DATA

Ounces of toothpaste to be started in the Paste Department during the budget period	3,000,000
Ounces of paste expected to be in process at the end of the budget period	80,000
Degree of completion for Work-in-Process Ending inventory for budget period:	
Materials	100%
Labor and Overhead	60%
Estimated cost of toothpaste production:	
Direct Materials	$.02 per ounce
Direct Labor	$.03 per ounce
Variable Manufacturing Overhead	$.01 per ounce
Fixed Manufacturing Overhead	$44,820

REQUIRED: 1. Determine the amounts of direct materials and conversion costs which should be budgeted for the period. [*Hint:* Since unit costs are given, you will have to calculate equivalent units of production for the *budget period. Equivalent units* in the beginning inventory will not require direct materials and conversion costs inputs during the period.]

2. Assume that White and Bright uses an average system in attaching costs to units, and prepare a budgeted cost of goods manufactured statement. (Round unit costs to three decimal places.)

7—28. *Calculating the impact of differences between budgeted and actual results on profits.* Body Beautiful is an exercise salon which advertises a more beautiful body in just six months with their exercise program. The management of Body Beautiful has the following data comparing the company's performance with budgeted performance. Unfavorable variances are indicated by parentheses.

	ACTUAL	VARIANCE FROM BUDGET
Number of persons enrolled in six-month programs	400	(50)
Revenues	$232,000	($38,000)
Variable Expenses:		
Supplies	15,200	2,800
Part-time employees	23,200	1,550
Other	4,200	300
Fixed Expenses		
Salaries	82,000	(2,000)
Rent	18,000	—
Depreciation of Equipment	20,000	—
Utilities	7,600	400
Insurance	2,900	(900)
Advertising	12,000	1,000
Total Expenses	$185,100	$ 3,150
Income before taxes	$ 46,900	($34,850)

Management wants to understand more completely why actual results were not equal to expectations. To help them understand, answer the following questions:

REQUIRED: 1. What was the budgeted amount of income before taxes?

2. Calculate the budgeted fee charged and the actual fee charged for each enrollee.

3. How much of the revenue anticipated at the time the budget was developed was lost because Body Beautiful had 50 fewer enrollees than it had anticipated? What accounts for the remaining difference between actual and budgeted revenues?

4. Calculate the budgeted total variable cost per enrollee and the actual total variable cost per enrollee. What effect did any differences between the two figures you have calculated have on income before taxes?

5. By what amount were budgeted total variable costs different from actual total costs *owing solely to volume factors?*
6. Calculate budgeted total fixed costs per enrollee and actual total fixed costs per enrollee. Explain any difference in results which you have obtained.
7. Assume that fees for enrollment for the coming year will have to be decreased to $550 per enrollee because a new exercise salon has opened nearby which is charging the lower rate. Variable costs are expected to be equal to this year's actual level on a per unit basis and total fixed costs are expected to be the same as this year's actual. If enrollments can be held at this year's actual levels, how much income can Body Beautiful anticipate for next year.

7—29.   *Straightforward budgeting problem: preparation of Budgeted Income Statement and Cash Budget.*   The Hot Air Popcorn Popper Company makes a popper which does not require the use of oil. This product has proved very popular with calorie-conscious consumers. The company has made the following estimates for use in preparing its budget for the coming year.

ESTIMATED DATA

Selling Price	$24
Units sales	120,000
Desired level of ending finished goods inventory in units	30,000
Direct material costs per popper	$5
Direct labor costs per popper	$4.50
Variable manufacturing overhead costs per popper	$2
Total fixed manufacturing overhead	$357,500
Variable selling expenses per popper	$1.28
Fixed selling expenses	$302,400
Fixed administrative expenses	$412,800[a]

[a] Does not include bad-debt or interest expense.

Additional information:

1. Fifty percent of sales during the period will be for cash. Of the Accounts Receivable on the books as of the beginning of the budget period, $12,000 will be collected during the budget period. For poppers sold on account, 2% will represent bad debts. Of the collectible accounts, 80% will be collected during the budget period.
2. All direct materials are bought on account. Hot Air likes to keep a raw materials inventory of approximately 40,000 units. During the budget period, $30,000 of Accounts Payable on the books at the beginning of the period will be paid. For purchases made during the budget period, 15% will be unpaid as of the end of that period.
3. Depreciation included in manufacturing overhead and in fixed selling and fixed administrative expenses is $85,000, $29,000, and $74,000, respectively.
4. All other expenses except taxes will be paid in cash during the budget period.
5. In addition, during the budget period Hot Air plans to purchase some land for a future building site which will require a $25,000 cash outlay.

6. A $5,000 installment plus $500 interest incurred during the budget period is due on a note owed to the bank by the company.
7. The estimated tax on earnings is 46%. These taxes will be 60% paid during the budget period.

Actual data:

8. Finished Goods Beginning Inventory for the budget period, 20,000 poppers @ $14.
9. The company accounts for its Finished Goods Inventory on a FIFO basis.
10. Raw materials inventory, 50,000 units @ $5 per unit. Unit purchases made during the budget period are part of a contract calling for payments of $5 per unit for raw materials purchased. Each popcorn popper requires 1 unit of direct materials.
11. The company does not maintain a specific minimum cash balance. Its cash balance at the beginning of the budget period was $23,000.

REQUIRED:
1. Prepare a budgeted units of production schedule.
2. Prepare a budget which shows raw materials purchases in both units and dollar terms and the cost of raw materials which will be used in production.
3. Calculate the budgeted cost of manufacturing a popcorn popper.
4. Prepare a budgeted income statement.
5. Prepare a cash budget.

7—30. *Straightforward budgeting problem—service organization.* The Walton Word Processing Center offers two types of services: (1) copying of any type of printed materials and (2) typing of dissertations, theses, term papers, and resumes for students at Oakhurst College, located nearby. Actual results of operations for Walton for the past year are as follows:

Revenues: Copying, 3,000,000 copies		$300,000
Typing, 29,000 pages		87,000
Total Revenues		$387,000
Variable Expenses:		
Copying paper and supplies	$75,000	
Typing paper and supplies	29,000	
Depreciation on copying equipment (calculated on a per-copy-made basis)	45,000	
Fixed Expenses:		
Salaries	76,000	
Building and other equipment depreciation	37,000	
Utilities	12,000	
Advertising	7,000	
Insurance	2,000	
Other	6,000	
Total Operating Expenses		289,000
Income before Taxes		$ 98,000
Taxes @ 35%		34,300
Net Income		$ 63,700

The owner of Walton Word Processing has made the following estimates for the coming year.

1. The copying business will increase by 10%. The fee charged can also be increased by $.02 per page, since Walton is the only service near at hand to the college.

2. Enrollment in graduate programs has been declining, hence only 20,000 pages will be typed. Because there will be fewer theses and dissertations, which command a higher rate per page than term papers, the average charge per page will be approximately $2.85.

3. The cost of copying paper and supplies will increase $.01 per copy, while typing papers and supplies will increase by $.05 per copy.

4. Salaries will have to be raised by 9% to keep the employees happy and on the job.

5. Building depreciation and depreciation on noncopying equipment is calculated on a straight-line basis and will be at the past year's level.

6. Utility rates are expected to rise by 10%.

7. More advertising will be done in the college newspaper, which charges lower rates than the town paper. As a result, advertising expenditures will be held to $5,000.

8. Insurance and other costs will *each* increase by about $800.

9. Legislation reducing the tax rate will become effective for the budget period, lowering the rate to 33%.

REQUIRED:

1. Prepare a budgeted income statement for Walton in the contribution format. (Remember: Contribution margin = Revenues less Variable Expenses.)

2. If Walton could retain for the budget period the same volume of business for its typing service and charge the same rate per page as for the past year, by what amount would budgeted income before taxes change from the answer you got in part 1?

3. If Walton has a 10% decline from the past year's volume for its copying service, by what amount would budgeted income before taxes change?

chapter eight

RESPONSIBILITY ACCOUNTING SYSTEMS

OBJECTIVES

After you have completed this chapter, you should be able to answer the following questions:

- What are the objectives of a responsibility accounting system?
- How does a responsibility budget differ from a program budget?
- What four types of responsibility centers may an organization have?
- What is a performance report, and what kind of data should it contain?
- What is a transfer price?
- How should transfer prices be set?
- What are some of the problems in evaluating the performance of an investment center based on return-on-investment calculations?
- What is residual income, and in what ways may it be a better measure of performance than return on investment?

INTRODUCTION

In Chapter 7 we looked at the budget as a document describing an organization's expectations. In this chapter we relate the budgetary process to people. Our major subject here is the budget as a means of communicating with managers and as a measure of a manager's performance.

The chapter also explores two issues related to the use of the budget as a measure of performance: transfer pricing and the evaluation of performance relative to investment.

THE NEED FOR A MANAGEMENT INFORMATION SYSTEM

Consider a company such as IBM, which has more than 350,000 employees and operations scattered around the world. It is apparent that the chief executive officer of IBM cannot personally make all the decisions for that organization. Authority and responsibility must be delegated to lower-level managers, who will be held accountable for those activities within their sphere of authority. In any organization with operations beyond the scope of the chief executive officer, authority and responsibility should be delegated to lower-level managers.

Delegation carries with it these information needs:

1. Information *to the manager* describing the scope of activities for which he or she has authority and responsibility.
2. Information *for the manager* so that he or she will know when corrective actions are needed.
3. Information *from the manager* so that performance can be evaluated.

These information flows, described graphically in Illustration 8-1, are the essence of a management information system. The contribution that

ILLUSTRATION 8-1

Management Information Flows in an Organization

Higher-Level Management

Scope of Authority and Responsibility

Evaluation of Performance

Need for Corrective Actions

Lower-Level Management

managerial accounting makes to that information flow is a responsibility accounting system.

A RESPONSIBILITY ACCOUNTING SYSTEM

A *responsibility accounting system* generates accounting information for each responsibility center within an entity. Recall from Chapter 7 that a responsibility center is any organizational subcomponent headed by a manager who is charged with accomplishing defined organizational goals and performing specified activities. The objectives of a responsibility accounting system are:

1. To communicate to the manager of each responsibility center performance expectations—i.e., what is expected of him or her.
2. To provide the manager of a responsibility center with data which will indicate to him or her that corrective actions are needed.
3. To generate information useful in evaluating the performance of the manager of each responsibility center.

To clarify the concept of responsibility accounting, consider Illustration 8-2, a simplified organization chart for Western Manufacturing, Inc.

ILLUSTRATION 8-2

Western Manufacturing, Inc. Simplified Organization Chart

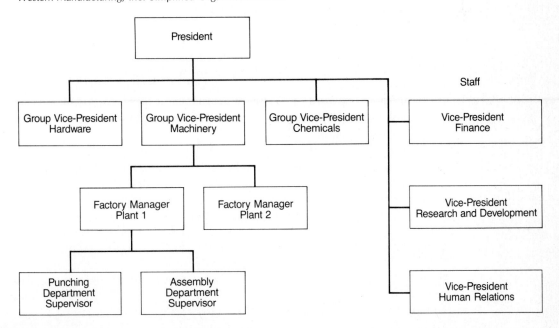

Authority and responsibility are delegated from the President to his or her various vice-presidents. The Group Vice-President—Machinery delegates to the managers of the two factories, who in turn delegate to the Punching and Assembly Department supervisors. Through the responsibility accounting system, each manager will be provided information as to expectations. In addition, the system will generate data which tells the manager when performance is deviating from expectations and corrective actions may be required. Finally, accounting data will provide significant input into the evaluation of the performance of each manager.

Study Illustration 8-2 and relate it back to our discussion of the three types of planning and control processes—strategic planning, management control, and organizational control. From Western Manufacturing's organization chart it should be clear that the major focus and scope of planning and control activities undertaken by the President will differ significantly from those of the factory manager of either of the plants.

RESPONSIBILITY CENTERS

Responsibility centers are commonly classified as expense (cost) centers, revenue centers, profit centers, or investment centers.

In an *expense center* the manager is held responsible for input only—that is, expenses. Heads of production departments and of staff units such as accounting or human resources are managers of responsibility centers, which are generally treated as expense centers. This means that the manager of that center is evaluated in terms of expenses incurred which he or she can significantly influence.

In a *revenue center* the manager is expected to generate revenues. He or she will likely be held responsible for expenses directly related to the responsibility center's activities, but the manager's primary responsibility is to provide revenues. Sales managers are typical examples of managers who head revenue centers. These managers may be held accountable for the level of expenses such as travel and entertainment incurred by sales personnel, but responsibility for expenses does not go beyond those related to the selling function.

In a *profit center* the manager is charged with responsibility both for revenues and for expenses incurred to earn those revenues. The manager of a profit center is motivated to engage in activities which will enhance the gap between revenues generated and expenses incurred.

The greatest amount of managerial responsibility is delegated when a manager is head of an *investment center*. In this type of responsibility center the manager is charged not only with managing revenues and expenses but also with controlling the investment base used to generate those revenues. Performance is commonly measured by looking at profits relative to the assets under the control of the responsibility center and computing a measure of return.

How many responsibility centers a company should have and whether a part of the organization headed by a manager is considered an expense center, a revenue center, a profit center, or an investment center is determined by (1) the nature of an organization's activities and (2) managerial policy based on the entity's goals and objectives. Refer back to the organization chart in Illustration 8-2. Because of the scope of their activities, staff functions and the factory operations of Plants 1 and 2 will probably be considered expense centers. To treat them otherwise would require some means of attributing revenues to them. While this could be done, the revenue figures would be artificially generated and not a part of the external financial accounting reporting system. Because of the difficulties of creating appropriate revenue figures and keeping the records involved in accounting for such amounts, the benefits of treating responsibility centers of this type as profit centers are frequently considered to be less than the costs.

On the other hand, the operations of the group vice-president of Western Manufacturing could be considered either a profit center or an investment center. This vice-president is charged with both manufacturing and selling machinery, functions consistent with profit determination. If assets can be identified with the machinery division and controlled by the Group Vice-President—Machinery, this responsibility center could be considered an investment center, and its manager will have his or her performance measured by return on investment.

The proper classification of a responsibility center is not always clear. For example, a division of a company manufactures and sells a product but because of the market structure cannot control the selling price. While this responsibility center does generate revenue, emphasis may be on cost control, and it could be treated as a cost center.

As another example, consider a company that has one responsibility center which makes and sells motors and another which makes and sells lawnmowers. What if most of the production of the motor center is transferred to the lawnmower center? Can the manager of the motor center exercise enough control over revenues to be treated as a profit center? By the same token, are the costs of the motors received by the lawnmower center controllable by that manager? If not, what effect should this have on how the responsibility center is classified? Issues related to transfers between profit or investment centers will be treated more fully later in this chapter when we discuss transfer pricing.

RESPONSIBILITY BUDGETING

We stated that with a responsibility accounting system each manager of a responsibility center is provided with information about what is expected of him or her. The manager will also be provided with data which indicate whether performance is deviating from expectations and whether corrective actions may be required. Finally, the responsibility accounting system provides data useful in evaluating the performance of a particular manager. The key element in this information flow is the responsibility budget.

In Chapter 7 we prepared a budgeted income statement which reflected the operating plans for a company for a three-month period. It showed budgeted revenues and expenses based on more detailed calculations contained in supporting budget schedules. The documents that we generated, however, are not presented in a form that can help us determine what a specific manager is responsible for, whether corrective actions should be taken by a manager, or whether that manager's performance is consistent with the organization's goals. For example, if budgeted income for the month of January is significantly less than was anticipated in the budget, we don't know whether that difference is due to factors which are controllable by a particular manager or group of managers or who, if anyone, should be held accountable. For these purposes we need a responsibility budget.

As stated in Chapter 7, a responsibility budget relates budgeted amounts to specific managers. The responsibility budget for each manager should contain those amounts which are controllable by the manager and for which he or she is held accountable. We consider an amount—revenue, expense or investment—to be *controllable* by a manager if that manager can significantly influence its level.

As the period for which the budget was prepared progresses, a manager can make comparisons of actual results with budgeted results and see where significant differences are occurring. These differences should be investigated to determine whether they are caused by factors which are controllable. If they are controllable, appropriate actions should be taken.

Not only the manager of a responsibility center but also his or her organizational superior has actual and budgeted performance data available. The higher-level manager uses the data (1) to assist the lower-level manager in deciding what, if any, corrective actions can be taken and (2) as a basis for deciding how well the lower-level manager is performing relative to the goals set for him or her.

BUDGET PREPARATION REVISITED

In describing responsibility budgeting we have not related the use of information provided by the budget to budget preparation. Although we looked first at the overall program budget for an organization in Chapter 7, the actual budgetary process is such that responsibility budgets are built up first rather than the reverse. Study Illustration 8-3, which was presented earlier (as Illustration 7-2) to depict the budgetary process.

Communication from lower-level to higher-level managers is part of

ILLUSTRATION 8-3

The Budgetary Process

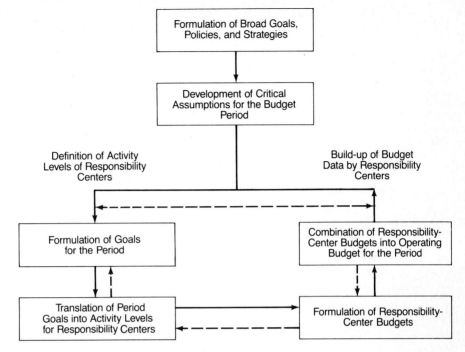

the process by which goals for the period are formulated. These goals are translated into activity levels for responsibility centers, again with two-way communication taking place. Both parties to budget negotiations—the budgetee and his or her organizational superior—should believe that the activity level on which budgeted dollars will be based is appropriate.

ILLUSTRATION FROM PRACTICE: THE PLANNING AND CONTROL PROCESS AT AMERICAN CAN COMPANY

American Can Company was briefly described in Chapter 7. Illustration 8-4 is a simplified diagram of the planning and control process at that company. As you can note, the planning phase begins with analysis of national factors and trends which are expected to impact on the company's performance and ends with the final approval and publication of the budget.

Control is exercised through the preparation of monthly reports which compare actual and budget and cover other relevant matters. Variances from budget and from the prior year are reviewed, and corrective action, if necessary, is formulated. Along with their monthly reports, managers forecast activity for the coming months if conditions have changed materially, making the budget figures outdated. Actual results in conjunction with the forecast are the basis upon which corrective action, if necessary, is taken. For future periods performance is compared not only with the original budget but with the revised expectations of the manager expressed in the form of a forecast.

ILLUSTRATION 8-4

Illustration from Practice: Simplified Diagram of the Planning and Control Process in American Can Company

	CORPORATE				DIVISIONS				
PREPLANNING	Senior Management	Strategic Planning	Treasurer	Controllers	Planning	Sales	Engineering	Manufacturing	Research and Development

1. Economic Evaluation of National Geographic and Industry Trends in consumer demands.

2. Analysis of company's past performance, competitive position, and potential in relation to trends.

3. Establishment and publication of objectives and policies

4. Development of summary operating and capital investment plans to accomplish objectives

5. Review and publication of summary operating and capital investment plans.

BUDGET PREPARATION

6. Preparation of operating programs for next year
   A) Sales
   B) Inventory
   C) Operating costs and expenses
   D) Research and development

7. Preparation of Financial program for next year
   A) Cash flow
   B) Capital investment
   C) Financial requirements
      F (short term, long term)

8. Translation into operating and financial budget

9. Consolidation into operating and financial budget summaries in management reporting format

10. Management review of financial consequences of operating and financial programs

11. Adjustments of programs to improve projected results.

12. Adjustments of budget summaries.

13. Final approval and publication

CONTROL OF OPERATIONS

14. Preparation of monthly reports which contain a forecast for the coming months

15. Review and explanation of variance from budget and prior year

16. Corrective action and revision of budget if necessary

Once activity levels have been established, the manager of each responsibility center can estimate the appropriate levels of expenses, revenues, and/or investment for that center. The final budgeted amounts are negotiated, and at the conclusion of the process each responsibility-center manager should be committed to the achievement of the goals expressed in his or her segment of the responsibility budget.

Responsibility budgets are combined and reexpressed in the form of a program budget for the company for the period. When all the parts of the budget are combined, if the final figures are not consistent with the goals of the organization—its profit objective, or, in the case of a nonprofit organization, available resources—either the organization's goals will have to be revised or modifications will have to be made in the budgets of the responsibility centers.

RELATING ORGANIZATIONAL STRUCTURE TO THE BUDGETARY PROCESS

Illustration 8-5 shows the relationship of the organization structure to the budgetary process for Western Manufacturing Company. Refer back to Illustration 8-2 for Western's organization chart. It is assumed that Western has defined its responsibility centers as follows:

Investment center—the entire company.
Profit centers—product-line segments headed by group vice-presidents.
Expense centers—plants headed by factory managers and departments headed by department supervisors.

The goal-setting part of the budgetary process for Western Manufacturing begins with the definition of a return on investment for the company as a whole. This must be translated into sales volumes for the various segments which will yield the overall return. The sales volumes required trigger production requirements for the plants and the departments within those plants.

The budget build-up begins with the definition of costs required to produce the volume of units required. These in turn are translated into unit costs and matched with forecasted revenues and selling and other expenses to yield the forecasted product-line segment incomes. Finally, the product segment incomes less all other expenses (staff costs and general corporate costs, such as the president's salary) result in a budgeted net income figure for the company as a whole. This budgeted income relative to the budgeted asset levels should result in the rate-of-return goal which was the starting point of the budgetary process. As the budgetary process progresses, it may become apparent that the original

ILLUSTRATION
8-5

Relation of
Organization
Structure to the
Budgetary
Process (Based
on Western
Manufacturing,
Illustration 8-2)

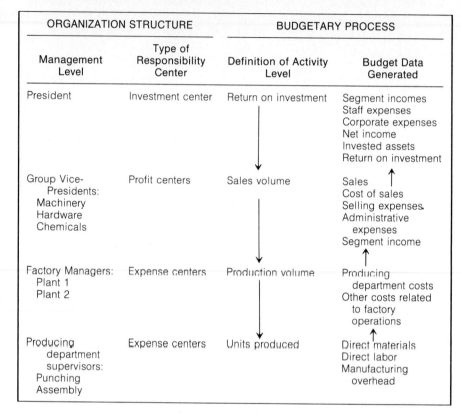

ORGANIZATION STRUCTURE		BUDGETARY PROCESS	
Management Level	Type of Responsibility Center	Definition of Activity Level	Budget Data Generated
President	Investment center	Return on investment	Segment incomes Staff expenses Corporate expenses Net income Invested assets Return on investment
Group Vice-Presidents: Machinery Hardware Chemicals	Profit centers	Sales volume	Sales Cost of sales Selling expenses Administrative expenses Segment income
Factory Managers: Plant 1 Plant 2	Expense centers	Production volume	Producing department costs Other costs related to factory operations
Producing department supervisors: Punching Assembly	Expense centers	Units produced	Direct materials Direct labor Manufacturing overhead

budget goal—in the case illustrated, return on investment—is unrealistic and must be revised. Or it may become apparent that the costs or revenues budgeted at various levels in the organization will not enable the company to meet its return-on-investment objective. Either of these outcomes would require revisions either in the goals or in the originally budgeted dollar figures. The final budget which is approved should tie back to and represent the plans for achieving the overall organizational goal or goals for the budget period.

RESPONSIBILITY BUDGETS AS A CONTROL DEVICE

We have seen how the budgetary process works and how responsibility budgets for managers of responsibility centers are developed. Our next step is to understand how these responsibility budgets are used for control purposes.

As discussed previously, the budget by which a manager's performance is going to be evaluated should be one which represents realistic goals for that manager and goals that he or she is committed to accomplishing. As the budget period progresses, actual data result from the transactions in which the entity engages. The actual results of the transactions relative to the assumed outcomes represented by the budget provide the data for evaluating performance and taking corrective actions. The actual data relative to the budget data represent the content of a responsibility report.

Illustration 8-6 is a simplified example of a responsibility reporting system for Western Manufacturing Company. A responsibility report can be designed in many ways. The one illustrated shows budget, actual, the variance between the two, and the variance expressed as a percent of the budget for the current month and on a year-to-date basis. Some alternative forms of presentation would include, among others:

1. Budget and variance only.
2. Current month and current year data relative to last year—that is, based on our example, March of this year relative to March of last year and current year-to-date relative to last year for the same three-month period.

What a responsibility report—also called a performance or control report—contains depends on what an organization wants it to contain. There is no one right way to prepare such a report. Note the president's report. For each of the product segments—machinery, hardware, and chemicals—sales, expenses, and segment income are given. This report might instead show only the segment income without any supporting detail.

CONTROLLABLE VERSUS NONCONTROLLABLE ITEMS

If the manager of a responsibility center is to be evaluated, at least in part, by the accounting data contained in a performance report, the performance report should either (a) contain only the expenses, revenues, and/or investment elements which he or she can control or (b) clearly segregate controllable from noncontrollable elements.

As one moves up the organization, the number of items which can be controlled increases. At the top of the organization all costs are considered to be controllable. However, the time span required for control may vary significantly between items. For example, investment in plant and equipment can be influenced by the top-level manager, but acquiring or disposing of such investment may require a significant period of time. On the other hand, a decision to spend or not spend funds for advertising may be executable almost immediately.

ILLUSTRATION 8-6

Simplified Example of Responsibility Reporting (In thousands of dollars)

President – – Responsibility Report for the Month of March

	Month				Year to Date			
	Budget	Actual	Variance*	%**	Budget	Actual	Variance	%
Machinery:								
Sales	2,880	2,860	(20)	(1%)	8,640	8,400	(240)	(3%)
Expenses	2,451	2,540	(89)	(4%)	7,367	7,449	(82)	(1%)
Segment Income	429	320	(109)	(25%)	1,273	951	(322)	(25%)
Hardware:								
Sales	1,200	1,224	24	2	3,800	3,917	117	3
Expenses	1,068	1,085	(17)	(2%)	3,400	3,508	(108)	(3%)
Segment Income	132	139	7	5	400	409	9	2
Chemicals								
Sales	3,600	3,420	(180)	(5%)	11,880	11,642	(238)	(2%)
Expenses	3.060	3,000	60	2	10,570	10,500	70	1
Segment Income	540	420	(120)	(22%)	1,310	1,142	(168)	(13%)
Total Segment Income	1,101	879	(222)	(20%)	2,983	2,502	(481)	(16%)
Corporate & Other Unallocated Expenses:								
Finance	43	45	(2)	(5%)	129	125	4	3
Research	55	53	1	2	170	170	–	–
Human Resources	65	66	(1)	(2%)	193	198	(5)	(3%)
Other	136	140	(4)	(3%)	415	423	(8)	(2%)
Total	299	304	(5)	(2%)	907	916	(9)	(1%)
Net Income	802	575	(227)	(28%)	2,076	1,586	(490)	(24%)
Annualized Return on Assets	18%	13%	(5%)	–	18%	14%	(4%)	–

*Unfavorable variances are indicated by ().   **Variance stated as a percentage of budget.

Group Vice President- -Machinery – – Responsibility Report for the Month of March

	Month				Year to Date			
	Budget	Actual	Variance	%	Budget	Actual	Variance	%
Sales	$2,880	2,000	(20)	(1%)	8,640	8,400	(240)	(3%)
Cost of Goods Manufactured and Sold:								
Plant #1*	749	730	19	3	2,247	2,209	38	2
Plant # 2	850	915	(65)	(8%)	2,550	2,615	(65)	(3%)
Selling Expenses	288	302	(14)	(5%)	870	910	(40)	(5%)
General & Administrative	564	593	(29)	(5%)	1,700	1,715	(15)	(1%)
Total Expenses	2,451	2,540	(89)	(4%)	7,367	7,449	(82)	(1%)
Segment Income	429	320	(109)	(25%)	1,273	951	(322)	(25%)

*To more clearly illustrate the tie in between reports, a simplifying assumption was made-that all units manufactured were sold.

Factory Manager- -Plant #1 – – Responsibility Report for the Month of March

	Month				Year to Date			
	Budget	Actual	Variance	%	Budget	Actual	Variance	%
Punching Department	$210	$ 215	($5)	(2%)	$ 630	$ 643	($13)	(2%)
Assembly Department	325	302	23	7	975	926	49	5
Factory Manager's Office:								
Salaries	180	178	2	1	540	529	11	2
Supplies	16	17	(1)	(6%)	48	51	(3)	(6%)
Telephone	6	4	2	33	18	17	1	5
Equipment Rental	2	2	–	–	6	6	–	–
Other	10	12	(2)	(20%)	30	37	(7)	(23%)
Total	$ 749	$ 730	$ 19	3%	$2,247	$ 2,209	$ 38	2%

Punching Department Supervisor – – Responsibility Report for the Month of March

	Month				Year to Date			
	Budget	Actual	Variance	%	Budget	Actual	Variance	%
Direct Material #301	$ 50	$ 55	(5)	(10%)	$ 150	$ 164	$ (14)	(9%)
Direct Material #425	28	27	1	3	84	86	(2)	2
Direct Labor	83	80	3	4	249	238	11	4
Indirect Materials	15	16	(1)	(7%)	45	48	(3)	(7%)
Indirect Labor	18	22	(4)	(22%)	54	62	(8)	(15%)
Supplies	5	5	–	–	15	13	2	13
Repairs and Maintenance	9	8	1	11	27	26	1	4
Other	2	2	–	–	6	6	–	–
Total	$ 210	$ 215	$ (5)	(2%)	$ 630	$ 643	$ (13)	(2%)

In thinking about this question of controllable versus noncontrollable, consider the performance report of the supervisor of the Punching Department shown in Illustration 8-6. This report does not include depreciation on equipment nor allocations of taxes, insurance, and other costs. *Some* costs which do not have to be allocated—for instance, depreciation on the equipment used by the Punching Department—and all costs which are allocated to a responsibility center are not subject to the influence of the manager of that center and hence should not be used in evaluating his or her performance.

Other costs are only partially controllable by a particular manager. Although they may be included in his or her performance report, care should be taken to assign responsibility only for the portion controllable by the manager. Direct material and direct labor costs are examples of costs which often are only partially controllable by the manager who oversees production. The costs of direct materials is probably the responsibility of another manager, the one in charge of purchasing. The wage rates paid for direct labor are frequently arrived at through union contract negotiations and are not controllable by the manager who oversees actual production. In addition, the amount of time which should be used for a particular operation may be determined by time-and-motion studies or engineering estimates.

However, in the case of both direct materials and direct labor, the manager overseeing production can exert some control over usage. For direct materials this is by activities such as safeguarding direct materials, motivating employees to perform in such a way that spoilage is minimized, and seeing that machines are properly set. Direct labor usage can be influenced through assigning and scheduling jobs, fostering efficiency on the part of the workers, and controlling idle time.

What this all means is that the items to be included in a particular manager's performance report should be carefully reviewed to determine whether that manager actually does have significant influence over them. In some cases variances of actual performance from budgeted performance may have to be further analyzed—for example, broken down into a cost and a usage component—with different managers being held responsible for the different parts of the variances. Analysis of variances is discussed in detail in the next three chapters.

From a behavioral point of view, when a manager's performance is being reviewed, the upper-level manager doing the review should allow the reviewed manager adequate opportunity to explain in full any significant variances of actual from budget. Arguments offered by lower-level managers in terms of their inability to influence a particular item for which they are being held accountable should be taken seriously, and an attempt should be made to decide whether the manager's position is justified.

Sometimes in practice a manager will be told something like this: "Oh, we're just including that item in your performance report because we have to put it somewhere. We don't really expect you to influence it and we won't hold you responsible for it." The problems with this approach are twofold. On the one hand, the manager may begin to doubt the seriousness with which performance reporting is viewed. On the other hand, an atmosphere of fear and distrust may be fostered, with the manager wondering whether only lip service is being paid to the fact that the item included in that manager's report is not controllable by him or her.

USING PERFORMANCE REPORTS

Suppose you are either the Punching Department Supervisor or the factory manager of Plant 1 and you are looking at the responsibility report for the Punching Department Supervisor shown in Illustration 8-6. With what items would you be concerned and why? If we look at the bottom line of the report, total variance is an unfavorable $5,000, and relative to budget the variance is only 2% for the month and the year to date. However, it is well to go beyond the bottom line, because significant variances in one direction—either favorable or unfavorable—may be offset by variances in the other direction. Unfavorable variances in the Punching Department actually totaled $10,000, but $5,000 of these were offset by favorable variances.

Usually each manager who is using a performance report has developed a policy as to what constitutes a significant variance, either in dollar terms, percent terms, or both. Whether the variance is favorable or unfavorable, if it is significant as defined by managerial policy it will be investigated further. You might think that an investigation should be caused only by an unfavorable variance. Not so, however, as favorable variances can signify problems or potential problems. For example, a favorable variance could be caused by budget standards which were not tight enough. Or, for expenses such as routine maintenance which may be postponed, a favorable variance may indicate a decision by a manager to "look good" relative to the budget in the short run—a decision which may be costly in the long run.

Let us suppose that in our role as Punching Department Supervisor or as factory manager of Plant 1 we have determined that any dollar variance of $4,000 or more and/or any percent variance of 8% or more warrants further study. Applying this standard to the performance report of the Punching Department Supervisor for the month of March, we note two items, both of which are unfavorable variances—direct material #301 and indirect labor. These two also represent the most out-of-line items on a year-to-date basis. We would attempt to determine whether they are caused by factors which can be controlled or by factors which are beyond our control.

We could analyze each of these two variances in more detail to determine whether the variance is related to price (cost) factors or to usage (efficiency) factors. This type of analysis will be discussed in detail in a subsequent chapter. For example, the variance for direct material #301 may be caused by the raising of prices by all suppliers of this item— a factor which is beyond our control. On the other hand, the difference may be due to factory workers' (a) spoiling raw materials units or (b) taking them home with them. For either of these situations actions can be taken to better control the item. If spoilage is the problem, we would look at things such as the workers' training, whether the machines used to process the materials are working properly, and the quality of the raw materials.

Now look at the responsibility report for the Group Vice-President— Machinery. Note that when a responsibility report contains both revenues and expenses, percentage variances which appear quite small may be magnified on the bottom line. Consider the sales variance of 1% and the total expense variance of 4%, both unfavorable. However, the segment income variance is 25%. This is true because segment income is the difference between revenues and expenses. An unfavorable revenue variance causes profits to decrease, and an unfavorable expense variance decreases profits even more.

ILLUSTRATION FROM PRACTICE:
PERFORMANCE REPORT FOR A MANAGER
AT AETNA LIFE AND CASUALTY

Aetna Life and Casualty is an insurance and financial service organization which sells almost all forms of insurance. It also maintains real estate development and technology-related enterprises. Aetna is the largest stock life insurer and is second largest in the casualty-property field. It has approximately 50,000 employees and earns revenues of more than $14 billion.

Illustration 8-7 shows the format of a report which Aetna Life Insurance and Annuity, a part of Aetna Life and Casualty, uses in evaluating the performance of its Vice-President of Marketing. This person's chief responsibility is to stimulate sales, and the report shows revenues generated by the various product lines relative to the previous year on a quarter basis and a year-to-date basis. In addition, results are compared on a year-to-date basis to the objective (budget). As you can see, when last year is compared to this year, differences are shown not in dollar amounts but in terms of percents. When the current results are compared to the objective, both the dollar difference and the percent difference are shown. The final column of the report shows the total objective for the current year.

ILLUSTRATION 8-7

Illustration from Practice:
Performance Report, Aetna Life Insurance and Annuity Company
Annualized Paid New Business—Annuities, Comparative Study ($000 omitted)

PRODUCT LINES	QUARTER ENDING 9/30			YEAR TO DATE 9/30			COMPARISON OF RESULTS TO OBJECTIVES				
							Where We Should Be After 9 Months	Where We Are After 9 Months	How We're doing		Total 1985 Objectives
	1984	1985	% DIFF	1984	1985	% DIFF			$ DIFF	% DIFF	
Corporate/MAP											
IRA											
Other PSS											
Pens. & Prof. Shar. Total											
TDA Total											
Deferred Comp. Total											
Estate & Bus. Anal. Total											
PSS Total											
Grand Total											

GENERAL PROBLEMS WITH RESPONSIBILITY ACCOUNTING

A number of problems occur with a responsibility accounting system; the more significant ones are discussed below.

Classifying Amounts As Controllable

Earlier we made two observations: (1) an amount is controllable by a particular manager if that manager can significantly influence the level of that amount; (2) a manager's performance should be judged on the basis of amounts which he or she can control. These statements appear logical but may be difficult to translate into practice.

Some amounts are clearly controllable—how much is spent, if any, on the company picnic. Expenses of this type are called *discretionary expenses*, because their level is strictly determined by management's decision. Some costs are controllable in the long run but not in the short run—depreciation on a piece of equipment. These costs are sometimes referred to as *committed* or *engineered costs*. Once the equipment is purchased, it is subject to depreciation, and the amount of that depreciation, unless it is based on use, is beyond the control of the manager.

Other costs are only partially controllable or may be controllable in part by more than one manager. For example, the costs incurred by the manager of maintenance and repairs are affected by the efficiency of the department and by the calls made on the department by other responsibility centers.

There is no simple answer to which costs are controllable and by whom. Significant expenses must be analyzed and judgment exercised in assigning them to a particular manager. Performance results must be evaluated in terms of the degree of influence which a manager can exert over a particular item included in his or her performance report.

Long-run Versus Short-run Performance

A serious and recurring problem in evaluating performance is related to long-run versus short-run results. Most performance-evaluation systems are geared to immediate results. The manager has a disincentive to take actions which will have a negative impact on today's performance but a positive effect on future periods' performance.

While this problem is most pronounced at higher management levels where decisions are being made about capital expenditures, research and development outlays, new product introduction, and acquisitions, it is not limited to these levels. Lowering the quality of the raw materials used or deferring maintenance may enhance short-run performance but be costly in the long run through lost customers and damaged machines.

Two appropriate responses can discourage short-run results at the cost of long-run results. First, managerial superiors must look carefully at areas where short-term performance-enhancing decisions can be made at the expense of the long run and insure that lower-level managers are acting appropriately. Second, reward systems such as bonuses can be geared to longer run results rather than short run. For example, some companies give bonuses to managers of profit centers which are based on three- to five-year performance and are only partially earned and awarded based on a single year's performance. Boards of directors need to be particularly cognizant of the long-run needs of a company and act in a manner consistent with those needs.

Budgeting at One Level and Performing at Another

The budgets we have looked at to date are geared to one activity level—the production of 10,000 motor boats, or the serving of 10,000 customers. It is not unusual for performance for a budget period to vary significantly from that anticipated when the budget was formulated.

Consider the simplified performance report of Debbie Thomas, who is manager of a group of clerical workers responsible for the billing operations of a department store:

	BUDGET	ACTUAL	VARIANCE	
Bills processed	100,000	85,000	15,000	
Salaries of five clerks	$ 5,000	$ 5,000	—	
Supplies—forms and envelopes	9,000	7,720	1,280	Favorable
Miscellaneous supplies	800	900	100	Unfavorable
Other	1,200	1,000	200	Favorable
Totals for the month	$16,000	$14,620	1,380	Favorable

Looking at this report, Debbie Thomas' performance report shows a favorable variance for the month. Should she be congratulated on her performance? The answer is that we don't know by looking at the report, because the budget was set for one level of performance and actual was at another—100,000 bills versus 85,000 bills processed.

Two issues would have to be addressed: (1) Why did the volume difference occur? (2) Was the actual volume processed efficiently? The first issue will require a study to determine whether only 85,000 needed to be processed this period or whether unprocessed bills remain, which may indicate inefficiencies in the operation or that the budget volume was not realistically set.

The second issue is whether Ms. Thomas processed the 85,000 bills efficiently. Envelopes and forms are a variable cost—the number used should vary with the volume of business. Let us also assume that the other two cost items—miscellaneous supplies and other—are also variable costs. We can restate the budget for the volume level achieved and then make a relevant comparison. The restated report would look as follows:

	BUDGET	ACTUAL	VARIANCE
Bills processed	85,000	85,000	
Salaries of five clerks	$ 5,000	$ 5,000	—
Supplies—forms and envelopes @ 9¢	7,650	7,720	70 Unfavorable
Miscellaneous supplies @ $.008	680	900	220 Unfavorable
Other @ $.012	1,020	1,000	20 Favorable
Total	$14,350	$14,620	$2,703 Unfavorable

We obtained the budget figures by finding the variable costs per unit based on the original budget data and applying this rate to the actual volume. For example, based on 100,000 bills, forms and envelopes were expected to cost $9,000. Thus the variable cost per unit is $9,000/100,000 = $.09. Applying this rate—$.09 × 85,000—we obtained our revised budget figure. Restating the costs in the budget for the volume actually achieved changed our interpretation of performance for the period. Rather than a favorable variance, the outcome is an unfavorable variance.

The response to situations such as this is the use of a flexible budget—a restatement of budgeted amounts based on the actual activity level achieved. Flexible budgets are discussed in detail in the next two chapters.

Note from this example that the concepts of responsibility budgeting, responsibility accounting, and performance reporting are not limited to manufacturing operations but can be applied whenever we can identify a responsibility center, regardless of the type of organization or the activities of the responsibility center.

Timing of Performance Reports

One issue that must be considered when the responsibility system is designed is how often performance reports or key elements in those reports should be generated. Consideration must be given to the significance of the items to the company, the time span required for corrective actions, and the costs of generating reports.

Some items may be so significant to a company and its profitability that it will want to look at them daily—for example, sales volume, raw material costs, or idle time. A weekly, monthly, or quarterly basis will be appropriate for other types of reports.

Some outcomes indicate problem areas which can and should be corrected quickly. Such information should be generated on a timely basis.

For example, a report of spoiled units may be required even more often than daily, if such spoilage is related to machines that are not properly functioning.

Finally, for all types of reports the cost of generating them must be weighed against the benefits. Can a weekly report be replaced by a monthly report without any loss of efficiency?

Extent of Analysis of Differences Between Actual and Budgeted Performance

Consider a company which makes ice cream and is setting up a responsibility accounting system which compares budgeted and actual data. When the system is being designed, this company needs to decide how much analysis of the data generated is needed.

For example, the reporting system could generate only one variance—actual profits versus budget profits. Or it could generate variances for revenues, cost of goods sold, and selling and administrative expenses. Within each category many additional types of variance can often be computed. With respect to revenues, for example, we could look at variances caused by volume versus variances caused by differences between anticipated and actual selling prices. We could do this analysis for different flavors of ice cream, for different sizes and types of containers, and for different classes of customers. Calculation of such detailed information has been enhanced by computer facilities, which, once programmed to produce a piece of data, can continue to do so rapidly and accurately.

The key question we must ask, when deciding how much analysis to do, is: What information does the additional analysis give that will lead to improved results in the future? If there is no clear relationship between future benefits and more detailed analysis, that analysis should not be done.

RESPONSIBILITY ACCOUNTING, SERVICE ORGANIZATIONS, AND NONPROFIT ORGANIZATIONS

Much of the basic philosophy which underlies a responsibility accounting system is equally applicable to manufacturing, retailing, and service organizations and to nonprofit as well as profit-making entities. In all these organizations, if responsibility and authority are delegated, a system is needed whereby a manager knows the extent of his or her responsibilities, has information which tells when corrective actions may be required, and which provides a basis for evaluation of managerial performance.

In addition, in all types of organizations, if managers are to be judged by budgetary data, they should participate in the development of that budget and be committed to meeting the goals it describes. The responsibility accounting system should help insure that individuals in an organization are acting in a manner consistent with the organization's goals.

For profit-making service organizations, the concept of responsibility centers in the form of expense, revenue, or profit centers is generally feasible. The concept of an investment center may not be relevant for some types of organizations, because investment in assets is not a significant activity. Consider a bank, insurance company, or CPA firm. While these organizations certainly maintain some fixed assets, their major costs and resources are personnel. As a result, they may not find the use of investment centers appropriate in a responsibility accounting system.

Nonprofit organizations can certainly apply the concept of cost centers, as these organizations have limited resources and cost control is important. Since they are not organized to make a profit, the concept of a profit center or an investment center is not directly relevant. These organizations may measure performance against goals not expressed in accounting terms. For example, an alcoholics rehabilitation center may measure performance in terms of how many persons have been "cured."

TRANSFER PRICING

A special problem of responsibility accounting for profit or investment centers is transfer pricing. A *transfer price* is the value assigned to goods being moved from one part of an organization to another for internal reporting purposes. Transfers of goods create problems when transfers take place between managers whose performance is being evaluated in terms either of profits or of profits relative to investment.

Consider the following example. The Motor Division of Household Products, Inc., makes motors, while the Fan Division makes fans which require a motor. Both divisions are treated as profit centers, and the general manager of each is charged with trying to maximize profits for his or her division.

If all or part of the motors made by the Motor Division are transferred to the Fan Division, conflict may arise as to an appropriate transfer price. Within the same organization, because the divisions are treated as profit centers, are two managers with competing goals. The manager of the Motor Division has as his goal transferring the motors at the maximum price. Since the price of the motor will be a cost to the Fan Division, the manager of the Fan Division has as her goal minimizing the transfer price.

Two possible alternative transfer prices come to mind: cost of the motors or the outside market price. Let's look at each of these alternatives using the following data:

	MOTOR DIVISION	FAN DIVISION
Expected production	100,000	60,000
Outside selling price per unit	$ 12.00	$ 50.00
Variable manufacturing costs	$ 4.20	$ 13.00—Excluding motor
Variable selling expenses	$ .80	$ 2.00
Fixed manufacturing expenses	$120,000	$252,000
Fixed selling and administrative expenses	$108,000	$180,000

Cost as a Transfer Price

Let's use *full cost* as the transfer price and see how the income statements of each division and the company as a whole would be affected if:

1. The Motor Division transfers 60,000 of its units to the Fan Division at full cost and sells the remaining 40,000 outside.
2. The Fan Division buys the motors it needs outside at $12 and the Motor Division sells its product to outside buyers.

The outcomes of these assumptions are shown in Illustration 8-8.

For the company as a whole, in this particular situation profits would be the same whether the motors were transferred or whether they were sold externally. However, for the division managers results looked significantly different depending on whether the transfer took place or not. Of

ILLUSTRATION 8-8
Alternative 1

60,000 motors are transferred to the Fan Division at full cost

	MOTOR DIVISION	FAN DIVISION	COMPANY AS A WHOLE
External Sales:			
40,000 @ $12	$480,000		
60,000 @ $50		$3,000,000	$3,480,000
Internal Sales:			
60,000 @ 7.28[a]	436,800		
	$916,800	$3,000,000	$3,480,000
Cost of Goods Sold	540,000[b]	1,468,800[c]	1,572,000[d]
	$376,800	$1,531,200	$1,908,000
Selling and Administrative	188,000[e]	300,000[f]	488,000
Income before taxes	$188,800	$1,231,200	$1,420,000

[a] Full cost = all costs = $4.20 + .80 + $\frac{\$120,000}{100,000} + \frac{\$108,000}{100,000}$ = $7.28 per unit.

[b] $4.20 var. mfg. × 100,000 = $420,000 + 120,000 fixed mfg. = $540,000.

[c] Cost of Motors = $436,800 + ($13 × 60,000) + 252,000 = $1,468,800.

[d] Cost of Goods Sold of two divisions less cost of motors transferred to Fan Division.

[e] ($.80 × 100,000) = $80,000 + 108,000 = 188,000. It is assumed variable selling expenses were incurred on the fans transferred.

[f] ($2 × 60,000) = $120,000 + 180,000 = $300,000.

**ILLUSTRATION
8-8**
Alternative 2

*The Motor
Division sells all
100,000 of its
fans outside
at $12, while the
Fan Division
purchases the
motors it needs
outside at $12*

	MOTOR DIVISION	FAN DIVISION	COMPANY AS A WHOLE
External Sales:			
100,000 @ $12	$1,200,000		
60,000 @ $50		$3,000,000	$4,200,000
Cost of Goods Sold	540,000ᵃ	1,752,000ᵇ	2,292,000
Gross Margin	$ 660,000	$1,248,000	$1,908,000
Selling and Administrative (same as Alternative 1)	188,000	300,000	488,000
Income before taxes	$ 472,000	$ 948,000	$1,420,000

ᵃ $4.20 var. mfg. × 100,000 = $420,000 + 120,000 fixed mfg. = $540,000.

ᵇ 60,000 × $12 for motors $720,000
Other Var. Mfg. Costs
$13 × 60,000   780,000
Fixed mfg. costs   252,000
                              $1,752,000

the 60,000 transferred at full cost of $7.28, the Motor Division received no profits, while the Fan Division was able to produce a product at a lower cost than if it had had to pay the outside price of $12. If the division managers are being judged on the basis of profits, assuming an outside market for all or part of the motors transferred to the Fan Division, a transfer price of cost is not equitable (nor would it be acceptable) to the Motor Division manager.

In this case, since some of the production of the Motor Division was being sold outside, the manager of the Motor Division still had an incentive to try to control cost. However, if all the division's production were simply transferred at cost, the incentive to control cost could be diminished.

Market Price as a Transfer Price

Now let's assume that market price will be used as a transfer price and look at results if:

1. The Motor Division transfers 60,000 of its units to the Fan Division at $12 and sells the remainder outside.
2. The Fan Division buys the motors it needs outside at $12, while the Motor Division sells its product to outside buyers.

It should be clear that with either of these alternatives we would get the same results for each division as we did with alternative 2 above. The profits of each division are the same whether the transfer takes place or not, because there is no difference between costs and profits with the two alternatives for each division and for the company as a whole, as can be seen from these calculations:

Motor Division:

Profit margin on internal sales = $12.00 − $7.28 full cost per unit = $4.72

Profit margin on external sales = $12.00 − $7.28 full cost per unit = $4.72

Fan Division:

Cost of motor from internal source = $12.00

Cost of motor from external source = $12.00

It might appear that we have found an answer to our dilemma—use the external market price as the transfer price. This is an appropriate solution so long as:

1. The production of the seller can be sold outside.
2. The buyer can buy the same product outside at the same price the seller is getting outside for its production.
3. The seller has no idle capacity—that is, it could not increase production without increasing its fixed manufacturing costs.

If these conditions are not met, market price may not be an appropriate transfer price. Let's consider two examples:

Example 1: Transfer pricing with idle capacity.   Assume that the Motor Division has idle capacity. It could increase its production from 100,000 motors to 120,000 motors without changing its fixed-cost structure. However, there is an outside market for only 100,000 motors. Should the extra motors be produced although there is no external market for them? If they are produced, what is an appropriate transfer price, since there is no external market for them?

Consider first the question of whether the motors should be produced. We have looked already at the results of producing 100,000 motors and selling them externally. Let's now see how results of the company *as a whole* would be affected if the Motor Division increased production to 120,000 motors, sold 100,000 externally and transferred the other 20,000 to the Fan Division. Those results are shown in Illustration 8-9.

Comparing the company's profits before taxes of $1,420,000, if the Motor Division makes only the 100,000 motors it can sell externally, with its profits of $1,560,000, if the 120,000 motors are made and 20,000 transferred to the Fan Division, the company benefits by $140,000 if the motors are made.

An appropriate transfer price for the transfer, however, is not clear. The manager of the Fan Division could argue that the motors should be transferred to her at cost because there is no external market. The manager of the Motor Division could contend, on the other hand, that

ILLUSTRATION 8-9

Assumption: Sale of 100,000 motors externally, transfer of 20,000 to Fan Division

Sales:		
100,000 motors @ $12		$1,200,000
60,000 fans @ $50		3,000,000
Total Revenues		$4,200,000
Cost of Goods Sold:		
Motors:		
120,000 @ $4.20 Variable cost	$504,000	
Add: Fixed Manufacturing cost	120,000	$ 624,000
Fans:		
Purchased motors, 60,000 − 20,000 = 40,000 × $12	480,000	
Other variable costs per fan, 60,000 × $13	780,000	
Fixed Manufacturing costs	252,000	1,512,000
Cost of Goods Sold		$2,136,000
Gross Margin		$2,064,000
Selling and Administrative Expenses:		
Motors, (.80 × 120,000)[a] + 108,000	$204,000	
Fans, ($2 × 60,000) + 180,000	300,000	504,000
Income before taxes		$1,560,000

[a] It is assumed that there were variable selling costs related to the motors transferred to the Fan Division.

since the transfer will enhance the profits of the Fan Division, some of this increase should be given to the Motor Division.

Example 2: Market-price differences and idle capacity. Assume that the Motor Division has capacity to produce 100,000 motors but has an outside market for only 40,000 of them at $12. It has submitted a bid to the Fan Division to supply the 60,000 motors it needs at a price of $12. However, the Fan Division has received a bid from another vendor offering a similar motor for $11.20.

The manager of the Fan Division will want to accept the outside bid. Should it be allowed to do so? The answer is "No," as can be seen by the effects on the company as a whole depicted in Illustration 8-10. In this situation what is best for the manager of one profit or investment center is dysfunctional for the company as a whole. In addition, not only will the whole organization be better off if the transfer takes place, but the Motor Division will be better off so long as it recovers any amount above its variable cost of $5 ($4.20 mfg. + .80 selling). Any such amount will contribute toward the fixed cost of the division.

This example exposes another dimension of the transfer-pricing problem. Since the company as a whole would be better off if the Fan Division bought from the Motor Division, should upper-level management step in and assure that this happens?

The idea of a profit center or investment center is to encourage the head of that center to use his or her initiative to enhance performance. The manager of the Motor Division was allowed to bid but did not bid successfully. The manager of the Fan Division has a better offer from outside. Will stepping in and forcing the transfer diminish the initiative

ILLUSTRATION 8-10

Assumptions

1. Productive capacity of Motor Division, 100,000 motors. Outside demand for 40,000 at $12. 2. Fan Division has a bid from an outside firm to supply 60,000 motors at $11.20

Effects of outside purchase of 60,000 motors on the company

Sales:		
Motors 40,000 × $12		$ 480,000
Fans, 60,000 × $50		3,000,000
Total Revenues		$3,480,000
Cost of Goods Sold:		
Motors:		
Variable Mfg. costs, $4.20 × 40,000	$168,000	
Fixed Mfg. costs	120,000	288,000
Fans:		
Motors, 60,000 × $11.20	$672,000	
Other Var. Mfg. costs, 60,000 × $13	780,000	
Fixed Mfg. costs	252,000	1,704,000
Total Cost of Goods Sold		$1,992,000
Gross Margin		$1,488,000
Selling and Administrative:		
Motors, (40,000 × $.80) + 108,000	$140,000	
Fans, (60,000 × $2) + 180,000	300,000	440,000
Income before taxes		$1,048,000

Effects of transfer of 60,000 motors on the company

Sales (same as above)		$3,480,000
Cost of Goods Sold:		
Motors:		
Variable Mfg. Costs, $4.20 × 100,000	$420,000	
Fixed Mfg. Costs	120,000	540,000
Fans:		
Cost of motors—included above		
Other Var. Mfg. Costs 60,000 × $13	780,000	
Fixed Mfg. Costs	252,000	1,032,000
Total Cost of Goods Sold		$1,572,000
Gross Margin		$1,908,000
Selling and Administrative		
Motors, (100,000 × $.80)[a] + 108,000	188,000	
Fans, (60,000 × $2) + 180,000	300,000	488,000
Income before taxes		$1,420,000

[a] Assumes $.80 of variable selling expenses on all motors including those transferred.

of the two managers in the future? Should the manager of the Motor Division "pay the price" for not bidding effectively? There is no simple answer to this question, and it must be viewed in context of the financial results which will occur without interference.

A Formula for Setting Transfer Prices

Some accountants have advocated a transfer-pricing system based on the following formula:

transfer price = incremental cost of unit

+ contribution margin lost on outside sales

This formula says that the minimum transfer price a manager can accept is the increase in costs which will occur with the production and transfer of a unit. Incremental costs tend to be the variable manufacturing costs plus any additional costs that result from the transfer. Recall that contribution margin equals revenues less variable expenses.

Using this rule, if there is an outside market for all the production of a profit or investment center, the transfer price will be that outside market price. Based on our data, and on the assumption that the variable selling expenses will not disappear if goods are transferred rather than sold outside, and applying the rule, the transfer price would be $12, calculated as follows:

$$\text{variable expenses} = \$4.20 + \$.80 = \$\ 5.00$$
$$\text{contribution margin} = \$12 - 5 \quad\quad = \underline{\ 7.00}$$
$$\underline{\$12.00}$$

If there were no outside market for the 60,000 motors transferred, the transfer price rule would yield a transfer price of $5:

$$\text{transfer price} = \text{variable costs} + \text{contribution margin lost}$$
$$= \$5 + 0 \ (\text{since there is no outside market})$$

However, it is not likely that this arrangement will be acceptable to the selling manager, who would show no profits on such transfers while the buying manager would have above-"normal" profits.

Negotiated Transfer Prices and Policies Regarding Transfer Prices

The practical answer to how a transfer price should be defined is that probably no single system is appropriate for all situations. In general, a transfer-price system should:

1. Cause managers to act in ways that enhance the overall welfare of the company, not just that of the responsibility center which they head.
2. Provide managers with incentives to operate efficiently.
3. Not undercut the authority and responsibility which have been delegated to the managers of the responsibility centers.

At a minimum a company should have a system which alerts upper-level managers to situations where overall company performance may be diminished when transfers do not take place. If management is aware of these situations, it can weigh the benefits of stepping in to assure that the transfer does take place against the costs of interfering with the managerial independence of the lower-level managers.

In situations where market price is not appropriate because of factors such as lack of outside demand or idle capacity, transfer prices may be set through negotiations between the buying and selling manager. The difficulty with this practice is that long and acrimonious debates may take place, because two highly competitive managers are each trying to enhance the performance of the part of the organization which they manage. Some companies have found it worthwhile to establish neutral negotiating committees either to do the negotiations directly or to aid in negotiations.

Still other companies have established either a set of transfer prices or a set of policies governing transfer prices when conflicts arise within the organization. For example, if there is no outside market for the production of the seller, the difference between the cost of producing the item and what the buyer would have had to pay outside may be determined and a predefined percentage (say, 50% to each) of the difference credited to the competing managers. Thus, an item costing $10 and having an outside market price of $18 would be transferred at $14 [$10 + (50% × $8)].

CALCULATING A RATE OF RETURN ON INVESTMENT

Calculating a rate of return is a special problem of responsibility accounting for investment centers. What distinguishes an investment center from a profit center is that in the former the manager is held responsible not only for profits but for the investment required to earn those profits. The most common way of looking at this relationship is calculating return on investment:

$$\text{return on investment (ROI)} = \frac{\text{income}}{\text{assets}}$$

While the formula looks simple, a number of issues must be resolved in measuring return on investment. These are discussed below, based on the following data for two divisions of Lindblom, Inc., a diversified manufacturer:

	HARDWARE DIVISION (000 omitted)	GLASS PRODUCTS DIVISION (000 omitted)
Sales	$18,000	$41,000
Operating Expenses	10,000	30,000
Divisional income before corporate expenses	8,000	11,000
Allocated Corporate Expenses	3,000	6,000
Division income	$ 5,000	$ 5,000
Gross Assets	$42,000	$42,000
Less: Accumulated Depreciation	12,000	8,000
Net Assets	$30,000	$34,000

Treatment of Allocated Corporate Expenses

A common argument between corporate headquarters management and management of operating units concerns the treatment of headquarters costs in evaluating performance. You can see the reason for this argument by looking at the Hardware Division and the Glass Products Division. Before the allocated corporate expenses, the Glass Products Division outperformed the Hardware Division in terms of income; after deducting the corporate charge, divisional income was the same.

Corporate headquarters staff are likely to argue that they provide a bundle of services to operating units and it is only fair that they bear the cost of these services. On the other hand, operating personnel are likely to contend that they have no control over those costs, they are not generally allowed to look for outside sources of any services provided by corporate staff, and the allocation tends to be arbitrary rather than based on any cause-and-effect relationship.

Ideally, operating units would have included in their measure of performance those costs which can be allocated to them on some reasonable basis. Practically, practice among companies will continue to be diverse in this area, and arguments continue to rage when such allocations are made.

Gross Assets versus Net Assets

Let's calculate ROI for the two divisions based on *divisional income* and (1) gross assets and (2) net assets.

	GROSS ASSETS	NET ASSETS
Hardware	$5,000/$42,000 = 12%	$5,000/$30,000 = 16.7%
Glassware	$5,000/$42,000 = 12%	$5,000/$34,000 = 14.7%

Both divisions look better with the net-asset figure, but the Hardware Division outperformed the Glassware Division when net assets were used. Divisions with older assets which are more fully depreciated will look better than divisions with newer assets if ROI is based on the use of net assets. Also divisions which are not replacing assets will look better on either a gross or net basis, assuming costs are rising.

The question of net versus gross assets is serious only so long as a company insists that all investment centers should have the same rate of return or that the manager of the investment center with the highest rate of return did the best job.

A company should simply make a decision as to whether they are going to use gross or net assets. If they decide to use net assets, expected ROIs should be set at a higher level than if the calculation is based on gross assets.

In addition, target ROIs should generally be based on the *potential* of a division negotiated in the budgetary process rather than an arbitrary figure applied to all divisions alike. Some operating units are in expanding markets, others in contracting markets. Some operating units need new equipment, others can continue to use older equipment. Some operating units may have an established reputation for their products and a customer base; others may be in a new field. It is not realistic to apply the same performance standards to operating units with significant differences in their potential.

Assets Controlled by Corporate Headquarters

Even though an organizational unit may be treated as an investment center, which implies control over assets, many companies limit the assets controlled by the investment center manager. The assets which are most likely to be controlled on a central basis are cash and accounts receivable. The reason is the value of liquid assets. While an operating unit may not have enough liquid funds to invest for a short period, all the operating units taken together may have a significant aggregate amount. One operating unit may have a cash shortage which can be covered by excess cash temporarily provided by another unit. (In addition, managers of operating units frequently do not have the time or expertise to engage in money management.)

Some organizations also manage inventories centrally. The question is, what happens to the investment base when some of the assets are centrally managed? There is a great deal of variance in practice. Some companies actually try to allocate to each operating unit for ROI calculations an appropriate share of assets which are controlled by corporate but associated with the transactions of the operating unit. Others simply look at ROI based on assets controlled by the investment center manager.

An Alternative Approach to Calculating ROI

Some firms prefer to calculate ROI indirectly using two other ratios:

$$\text{profit margin on sales} = \frac{\text{income}}{\text{sales}}$$

$$\text{asset turnover} = \frac{\text{sales}}{\text{assets}}$$

These two ratios can be combined to obtain ROI:

$$\text{ROI} = \text{profit margin on sales} \times \text{asset turnover}$$

or

$$= \frac{\text{income}}{\text{sales}} \times \frac{\text{sales}}{\text{assets}}$$

As you can see, when the two formulas are combined, sales can be canceled out, yielding the standard ROI formula of income/assets. However, by looking at ROI's component parts, operating units can obtain some additional insights into their strengths and weaknesses.

Suppose that we have the following industry data for companies which manufacture glass products similar to those made by Lindblom's Glass Products Division:

Profit margin on sales	14%
Asset turnover, (based on net assets)	1.2 times
ROI = 14% × 1.2	16.8%

We have already calculated the Glass Products Division's ROI based on net assets as 14.7%. Why does it vary by 2% from the industry average? We could look at the component parts of ROI and see whether Glass Products' profit margin differs significantly from that of the industry, whether its asset turnover is different, or whether both vary materially from the industry standard:

$$\text{profit margin (divisional income) on sales} = \$5,000/\$41,000 = 12.2\%$$

$$\text{asset turnover} = \$41,000/\$34,000 = 1.2 \text{ times}$$

Based on these two ratios, the return of the Glass Products Division seems to differ from that of the industry because of its failure to realize more of its sales dollars in profits. There are several places to look, once this piece of information is available: Is sales volume too low relative to the level of fixed costs to yield a satisfactory profit margin? Can costs be cut? Should sales prices be adjusted?

When ROI is calculated as a product of profit margin and asset turnover, the manager will have additional information which may aid him or her in improving performance.

Residual Income

Some organizations prefer to measure the return of an investment center in terms of residual income. *Residual income* is the profit generated after a specified rate of return on assets controlled by the investment center has been made.

To illustrate, referring to the information for Lindblom, Inc., assume that company management believes the minimum amount of return that a division should earn is 14% based on *net assets*. Managers of divisions will be evaluated in terms of how much beyond this minimum return they earn. Residual-income calculations for the Hardware and Glass Products Divisions are:

	HARDWARE	GLASS PRODUCTS
Divisional income	$5,000	$5,000
Minimum desired return:		
14% × $30,000	4,200	
14% × $34,000		4,760
Residual Income (Loss)	$ 800	$ 240

Advocates of the residual-income concept prefer this approach to measuring performance to standard ROI calculations for several reasons. First, it may encourage management to set different standards for investment centers with different potentials. For example, rather than setting a minimum return of 14% for both Hardware and Glass Products, 15% may be appropriate for Hardware, while, based on its particular circumstances, 12% may be more appropriate for Glass Products.

In addition, with residual income it is easy for management to set different rates of return on different types of assets which an investment center may control. For example, assume that the Hardware Division's net assets are composed of the following classes:

Current assets	$ 6,000
Noncurrent assets	24,000
Total net assets	$30,000

Lindblom's management may believe that a 15% return is sufficient on current assets. Because prices are rising and noncurrent assets are stated in old historical-cost dollars, a return of 20% is desired on this class of assets. Based on this set of assumptions, the residual income for the Hardware Division would be:

Divisional income		$5,000
Minimum desired returns:		
Current assets, $6,000 × 15%	$ 900	
Noncurrent assets, $24,000 × 20%	4,800	5,700
Residential Income (Loss)		$ (700)

Probably the strongest argument for residual income is that it encourages managers of investment centers to make investments which will enhance the overall return of the company. ROI may not do so. To illustrate, assume that Lindblom, Inc., as a company has an overall rate of return on its assets of 14% and sets as a minimum acceptable return 14%. Recall that the Hardware Division had a return of 16.7% on its net assets. Assume now that the Hardware Division is considering a project which will cost $10,000 and will generate a return of 14.5% or $1,450. Clearly the project is in the best interest of Lindblom as a whole because the return on the project exceeds the company's 14% rate of return.

Will the manager of the Hardware Division be motivated to accept the project? Consider the impact on his or her overall rate of return:

	CURRENT	WITH PROJECT
Divisional Income	$ 5,000	$ 5,000 + $1,450 = $6,450
Net assets	$30,000	$30,000 + $10,000 = $40,000
ROI	$5,000/$30,000 = 16.7%	$6,450/$40,000 = 16.1%

The return would be lowered. On the other hand, the project would contribute to the residual income of the investment center, and the manager would make the investment. Based on a desired rate of return of 14%, residual income would increase $400.

	CURRENT	WITH PROJECT
Divisional Income	$5,000	$6,450
Minimum Desired Return:		
14% × $30,000	4,200	
14% × $40,000		5,600
Residual Income	$ 800	$ 850

ILLUSTRATION FROM PRACTICE: XEROX CORPORATION'S CORPORATE ASSET CHARGE

The Xerox name is almost synonymous with "copying machine." Copying and duplicating machines (reprographics) are this company's major products. Paper for reprographic products is the other major industry segment of Xerox. It also produces other office-related products including electronic typing systems and computer-related equipment. Xerox's revenues are more than $6 billion, and it employs about 125,000 people.

At Xerox, strategic business-unit and product-line income statements of all operating groups prepared for reporting of actual results, outlooks, and business plans are required to include a corporate asset charge as a separate line item. The asset charge is an imputed amount for performance-reporting purposes only and is not reflected in the external financial statement.

The purpose of the corporate asset charge is to heighten the operating groups' awarenss of the importance of managing assets. While these groups are evaluated on an income basis rather than return on investment, upper-echelon management believes that they should be aware of the carrying cost of inventories, receivables, and fixed assets.

The asset charge is based on the following formula:

$$\text{asset charge rate} \times \text{average assets} = \text{asset charge}$$

The asset charge rate is intended to bear a reasonable relationship to the cost of borrowed funds and is modified to reflect longer-term trends in these rates. The average assets are defined as the average of beginning and ending gross assets.

International groups generally have borrowing power, and the cost of that borrowing is reflected on such a group's income statement. As a result, the formula is modified for those groups which do have borrowing authority as follows:

$$\text{asset charge rate} \times (\text{average assets} - \text{interest-bearing debt}) = \text{asset charge}$$

Thus, the asset charge does not charge international units twice—once for the interest expense paid on funds borrowed to finance assets and then again through the asset charge itself.

A reduction in its investment in assets by any business unit without any change in operating results will lead to an improved bottom line, as the asset charge will be reduced.

chapter highlights

When authority and responsibility are delegated, a system must be designed to (1) communicate to a manager what is expected of him or her, (2) provide information to let the manager know if corrective actions are needed, and (3) generate data useful in evaluating the performance of a manager. These are the primary functions that a responsibility accounting system fulfills, largely through the use of the responsibility budget.

As a preliminary step in the design of a responsibility accounting system, an organization must decide for what items the head of a responsibility center will be held accountable. There are four ways in which a responsibility center can be defined: as a cost center, a revenue center, a profit center, or an investment center.

Regardless of the form of the responsibility center, the responsibility budget should represent the commitment an individual manager has made toward achieving the goals of the organization and for which he or she is held accountable. Comparison of budget results and actual results will indicate whether deviations are occurring which may need correction and will provide data relevant to evaluation of the manager's performance.

If a manager of a responsibility center is being judged on the basis of either profits or return on investment and if goods or services are transferred from one such responsibility center to another within the same organization, transfer-pricing problems may arise. In situations where there is (1) external demand for the sellers output, (2) no difference between the prices received externally by the seller and those which the buying responsibility center pays outside, and (3) no idle capacity, the external market price is a valid transfer price. If these conditions do not exist, negotiated transfer prices or a predetermined system for assigning transfer prices is a practical solution.

For responsibility centers which are treated as investment centers, problems may arise as to how return relative to investment should be calculated. While no single solution to return-on-investment issues exist, at least two points should be kept in mind. First, the ROI calculated should be viewed in terms of the method used; for example, if net assets are used, a higher rate of return would be expected than if gross assets are used. Second, if the investment centers within an organization are significantly different in terms of their potential, different rates of return should be expected based on that potential and negotiated as part of the budgeting process.

questions

1. Distinguish between a program budget and a responsibility budget.
2. What purposes are served by the responsibility budget and the process of preparing it?
3. Are the program and responsibility budgets ever the same? Explain.
4. Define the term "responsibility center."
5. What primary purposes does a responsibility accounting system serve?
6. What four different types of responsibility centers may an organization have?
7. How does an expense center differ from a profit center and from an investment center?
8. Why are staff functions such as accounting and data processing generally treated as expense centers rather than profit or investment centers?
9. For a company engaged in producing soft drinks, what factors would have to be taken into account in developing assumptions relative to the budget period?
10. What part does commitment to a budget play in an effective responsibility accounting system?
11. What is meant by a controllable cost?
12. Define a responsibility report and state its purpose within an organization.
13. The budget for an expense center was based on a production volume of 10,000 units and total costs of $200,000. Actual results showed a volume of 9,500 units and total costs of $180,000. Did the manager of this expense center perform well? Explain your answer.
14. What is a transfer price?
15. Why can the setting of a transfer price be a problem?
16. Under what circumstances is the external market price the proper transfer price?
17. By what two formulas may return on investment be calculated?
18. What are some problems which arise in calculating return on investment for investment centers within an organization?
19. How is residual income calculated?
20. What are some perceived advantages of residual income rather than return on investment as a means of evaluating the performance of an investment center?

exercises

8—1. Hart Publishers anticipates the following sales figures and related expenses for its paperback book division for the month of June (currently, Hart is producing only one best-selling paperback):

Book sales	975,000 books
Selling price	$3.50 per book
Production costs:	
Variable	$2.00 per book
Fixed	$700,000
Selling and administrative expenses:	
Variable	$0.50 per book
Fixed	$150,000

REQUIRED:

1. Prepare a budgeted income statement for the paperback book division for the month of June. (Ignore taxes.)

2. Given the information in part 1, assume that Fred Grimes, Supervisor of the paperback assembly department, is responsible for controllable production costs which represent the division's variable production costs and 25% of its fixed production costs. Prepare a responsibility budget for Fred Grimes.

3. Assume that 1 million books were actually made during the period for which you prepared the responsibility budget in part 2 above and that variable production costs amounted to $1,988,000, while fixed production costs totaled $713,000. Prepare a report which will describe how well Fred Grimes performed for the period.

8—2. The following information pertains to the Envelope Division of the White Stationery Company for the month of March:

Anticipated sales	40,000,000 units
Selling price per 100 units	$2.00
Production costs:	
Raw materials	$0.40 per 100 units
Direct labor	$0.75 per 100 units
Manufacturing overhead	
Variable	$0.30 per 100 units
Fixed	$20,000 Total
Selling expenses	$55,000
General and administrative expenses	$72,000

REQUIRED:

1. Prepare a program budget for the division for the month of March.

2. Assume the Envelope Division is considered an investment center, and the assets identified with the division are valued at $900,000. How will the manager of the division be evaluated and what budgeted figure will be used to measure his performance?

8—3.   The Sunrise Motel maintains a coffee shop which serves lunch and light meals throughout the day. Its budget for the month of May was based on the assumption that it would serve 15,000 customers, each of whom would spend approximately $4.50. Food, beverage, and other variable costs were budgeted at 45% of sales revenue. Fixed costs were budgeted at $27,000. During the month of May the coffee shop actually served 16,000 customers and generated revenues of $68,000. Its food, beverage, and other variable costs were $29,000. Actual fixed costs totaled $28,500.

REQUIRED:
1. Prepare a schedule of budgeted income for the coffee shop based on the data provided.
2. Prepare a schedule of income actually produced by the coffee shop for the month of May.
3. Explain why a comparison of the budgeted schedule of income which you prepare with actual results *will not* show how efficiently the coffee shop operated for the month of May.
4. Prepare an analysis which will show how efficiently the restaurant operated during the month of May.

8—4.   Given below is a report which was used to evaluate the performance of the factory manager of the Finest Products Corporation for the month of October.

	BUDGET	ACTUAL	VARIANCE
Units produced	100,000	100,000	—
Direct materials	$100,000	$110,000	$10,000 U
Direct labor	400,000	395,000	5,000 F
Manufacturing overhead:			
Indirect materials	10,000	11,000	1,000 U
Indirect labor	14,000	14,000	—
Utilities	7,000	6,500	500 F
Depreciation	18,000	20,000	2,000 U
Insurance	3,000	3,000	—
Property taxes	2,500	2,800	300 U
Corporate headquarters' charge	25,000	32,000	7,000 U
Total factory costs	$579,500	$594,300	$14,800 U

Additional information:

1. The budget called for the use of 100,000 raw material units at a cost of $1. Actual usage was 100,000 units at a cost of $1.10. Purchasing is done centrally at corporate headquarters.
2. Direct labor hours budgeted amounted to 50,000 at a cost of $8 per hour. Actual labor hours amounted to 48,000 hours at an approximate average cost of $8.23. The $.23 per hour above budget cost was due to the settlement of a union contract at a rate higher than had been anticipated at the time the budget was developed.

REQUIRED: For each item listed, comment on the variance as a measure of how effectively the factory manager performed during the period. In other words, does the variance accurately describe the manager's performance? Why or why not?

8—5. The general manager of the North Central Division of Light and Tasty Beverages is evaluated on the basis of the return which the division she manages earns on assets. This past year the division earned 15%. Corporate headquarters can borrow funds at 10% per year which the North Central Division can use to finance new projects. The following projects are being considered for the coming year by the general manager:

PROJECT	ANNUAL NET INCOME	COST
A	$100,000	$1,000,000
B	$240,000	$2,000,000
C	$225,000	$2,500,000
D	$440,000	$4,000,000

REQUIRED: 1. Based on the fact that the general manager's performance is evaluated on the basis of return on investment, which projects, if any, will she choose? Justify your answer with appropriate calculations.
2. Using your solution to part 1, is the action which you anticipate the general manager taking in the best interest of the company? Why or why not?

8—6. The budgeted income statement for the U.S. division of Larson, Inc., is presented below for the quarter ending June 30. Actual results for the quarter were as follows:

Sales (548,000 units @ 7.60 per unit)	$4,164,800
Cost of Goods Manufactured and Sold:	
Akron Plant (25% fixed)	1,075,900
Dallas Plant (15% fixed)	725,700
Greensboro Plant (20% fixed)	1,089,300
Selling Expenses	389,600
General and Administrative Expenses	615,800

Budgeted Income Statement
U.S. Division
for the Quarter April 1–June 30

Sales (550,000 units @ $7.50)	$4,125,000
Cost of Goods Sold:	
Akron Plant (22% fixed) (158,000 units)	1,215,000
Dallas Plant (15% fixed)	712,000
Greensboro Plant (19% fixed)	1,010,000
Selling Expenses (fixed)	352,000
General and Administrative Expenses (fixed)	610,000
Division Income	$ 226,000

REQUIRED: 1. Prepare a responsibility report for the manager in charge of the U.S. Division, assuming he or she has control over all costs. The report should show budget, actual, variances of actual from budget, and the variances expressed as a percent of budget.

2. The Corporate President's office has determined that variances from budget greater than 8% should be investigated further. Apply this standard to the performance report above. Indicate which variances should be investigated and offer possible explanations for the variances.
3. Prepare a report showing budget, actual, and variance figures which more accurately reflects the efficiency of the Akron plant which produced 150,000 units during the period. (Round all variable expenses per unit to the nearest cent.)

8—7. The Royal Advertising Agency employs one sales executive to handle their account with the WXYZ Radio Station. The sales executive's salary is made up of a fixed portion of $1,000 per month plus a variable portion based on the dollar volume of advertising spot sales he makes during the month. His budgeted sales for the month of September along with budgeted expenses, all of which are variable with sales, are given below:

Sales	$50,000
Entertainment expenses	1,500
Travel expenses	500
Miscellaneous expenses	300

The sales executive's actual spot sales for the month totaled $45,000 and his expenses included $1,000 for entertainment, $500 for travel, and $275 for miscellaneous items.

REQUIRED:
1. Disregarding the reason for the discrepancy between actual and budgeted spot sales, what can you say about the sales executive's performance for the month and what method did you use to determine this?
2. Should the sales executive's salary depend so heavily on the volume of sales achieved, or should other factors be considered? Why?

8—8. (CMA adapted) Kane Corporation has a production capacity of one million units. The current year's budget was based on the production and sales of 700,000 units during the current year. Actual production for the current year was 720,000 units while actual sales amounted to only 600,000 units. The units are sold for $20 each and the contribution-margin ratio is 30%.

REQUIRED: Calculate the dollar amount which best quantifies the *marketing department's* failure to achieve budgeted performance for the current year.

8—9. A report summarizing the results of the Smoke Detection Devices Division of the Kray Corporation appeared as follows:

Divisional sales	$ 6,800,000
Divisional expenses	4,100,000
Allocated corporate expenses	1,300,000
Total expenses	$ 5,400,000
Divisional income	$ 1,400,000
Cash and accounts receivable controlled by corporate headquarters and allocated to the division	$ 6,000,000
Assets controlled by the division	21,000,000
Less: Accumulated depreciation	(7,000,000)
Net divisional assets	$20,000,000

REQUIRED: Calculate return on investment four different ways. Which one do you think should be used in evaluating the performance of the Smoke Detection Devices Division and why?

8—10. A comparison of selected data for the milk container industry and two companies in that industry are given below:

	INDUSTRY	COMPANY 1	COMPANY 2
Sales	$100,000,000	$20,000,000	$3,200,000
Profits	$ 15,000,000	$ 2,000,000	$ 480,000
Assets	$ 93,750,000	$18,692,000	$4,570,000

REQUIRED:
1. For the industry and the two companies, calculate return on investment.
2. For the industry and the two companies, calculate return on investment as the product of profit margin times asset turnover.
3. What are some things you would look at for each company in an effort to determine why the return on investment of each differed from that of the industry?
4. What are some questions you should ask with respect to the industry data?

8—11. The Ladies Shoe Division is a part of the General Shoe Manufacturing Company. General Shoe has a return on investment of 12% while the Ladies Shoe Division of that company has a return of 15% based on profits of $450,000 and an asset base of $3,000,000. The Ladies Shoe Division is considering the addition of more modern manufacturing equipment which it anticipates would cut cash operating costs by $104,000 per year. The cost of the new equipment is $800,000.

REQUIRED:
1. Assume that the manager of the Ladies Shoe Division is evaluated on the basis of return on investment. Will he or she be likely to purchase the equipment? Support your answer with appropriate calculations.
2. Assume that the manager of the Ladies Shoe Division is evaluated on the basis of residual income. Will he or she be likely to purchase the equipment? The current rate of return for General Shoe is the minimum return it expects from its divisions. Support your answer with appropriate calculations.
3. From the point of view of the company as a whole, should the investment in the new equipment be made? Support your answer with appropriate calculations.

8—12. Office Supplies Unlimited has three business units: one makes pencil sharpeners, one makes staplers, and the third makes hole punchers. Typical income and investment figures for the three business units are given below. Office Supplies Unlimited's minimum desired rate of return on assets is 10%. Corporate management is in the process of making a decision as to how performance of the managers of these business units should be measured. Three alternatives being considered are: profits, return on investment, and residual income.

	PENCIL SHARPENER UNIT	STAPLER UNIT	HOLE PUNCHER UNIT
Business unit profits	$ 480,000	$ 360,000	$ 240,000
Business unit investment	$6,000,000	$3,000,000	$2,000,000

REQUIRED: 1. Which measurement of performance will be favored by the manager of each of the three business units? Support your answer with calculations.

2. If management wants to rank performance of the three business units on one of the bases proposed, what important point may it be overlooking?

8—13. The Glass Container Division of Friedman United Company makes bottles of the type used by the Natural Fruit Juice Division of the Company. The Glass Container Division can make 1 million glass containers each month at a variable cost of $.02 and fixed cost of $.005 per bottle. Current external demand for these glass containers is 700,000 per month. The external selling price is $.05 per bottle. Selling and administrative costs of the division, all of which are fixed, total $8,500 per month.

The Natural Fruit Juice Division produces 400,000 bottles of fruit juice per month. It currently purchases all its bottles outside the company for $.05 per bottle. Cost incurred by this division in producing a bottle of fruit drink, including the cost of the bottle, is $.35. Bottles are sold for $.65 each. Variable selling and administrative costs per bottle are $.06. Fixed selling and administrative expenses total $40,000 per month. Divisions are treated as profit centers.

REQUIRED: 1. By what amount, if any, will the overall profits of the Friedman United Company increase if the Glass Container Division starts operating at full capacity of 1 million units and transfers those bottles which it cannot sell outside to the Natural Fruit Juice Division?

2. As the manager of the Glass Container Division, what is the minimum transfer price you will find acceptable for the bottles shipped to the Natural Fruit Juice Division if you can operate at full capacity?

3. As the manager of the Natural Fruit Juice Division, what is the maximum amount which you will be willing to pay for bottles shipped to you by the Glass Container Division?

8—14. Business units of Dunkirk Insurance are considered investment centers. They can either have their data processing done by Dunkirk's data processing center or have it done outside. The Variable Annuity Products Division of Dunkirk estimates that it needs 500 hours of computer services each month and has solicited bids for this service both internally and externally. The lowest external bid was $71,000 per month; Dunkirk's internal bid was $75,000 per month. Dunkirk's data processing center does not sell its services externally but it is treated as a profit center by the company for internal management accounting purposes. The center can provide the 500 hours per month of services needed by the Variable Annuity Products Division without increasing its fixed costs.

REQUIRED: **1.** What must the variable costs per hour for the Dunkirk data processing center be before it would be more profitable to the company as a whole for the Variable Annuity Products Division to have its computer work done internally rather than accepting the bid of $71,000?

2. Do you believe that Dunkirk's data processing center should be treated as a profit center and users given the option of going outside? What are the advantages and disadvantages of this treatment?

8—15.   Refer to the table below.

REQUIRED: Calculate the missing amounts: (*Note:* Amounts cannot necessarily be calculated in the sequence listed.)

	DIVISION 1	DIVISION 2	DIVISION 3	DIVISION 4
Sales	a	$200,000	$18,000	m
Operating income	$30,000	$ 16,000	i	$36,000
Assets	b	e	$27,000	$150,000
Minimum desired return on assets	18%	2%	6%	n
ROI	15%	f	j	24%
Residual income	c	$ 8,000	$ 1,080	$18,000
Profit margin on sales	20%	g	k	o
Asset turnover	d	h	l	2×

---

problems

8—16.   *Relationship of budget, actual and variances.*   A partially completed Schedule of Cost of Goods Manufactured for the Central City plant of the General Timekeeping Company is shown below.

	BUDGET	ACTUAL	VARIANCE[a]
Clocks Produced	40,000	40,000	—
Direct Materials	60,000	?	(2,000)
Direct Labor	?	?	3,000
Variable Overhead:			
Indirect Materials	20,000	21,000	?
Supplies	?	5,000	(800)
Electricity	?	2,500	?
Total Variable Manufacturing Costs	?	$287,500	(300)
Fixed Overhead:			
Indirect Labor	18,000	17,500	?
Depreciation	?	8,000	600
Insurance	?	?	?
Other	7,200	?	200
Total Fixed Costs	40,300	?	?
Cost of Goods Manufactured	?	?	(1,000 U)

[a] Parentheses indicate an unfavorable variance.

REQUIRED:
1. Supply the missing amounts in the schedule shown above, which compares budgeted cost of goods manufactured with actual cost of goods manufactured.
2. Does the information shown in the schedule which you have completed represent a control report suitable for judging the performance of the factory manager of the Central City plant? Explain your answer.

8—17. *Measuring performance and adjusting the budget to the actual activity level.* The performance of two divisions of Chemicals Company is shown below for the year ended December 31.

	NORTHERN DIVISION		SOUTHERN DIVISION	
	Budget	Actual	Budget	Actual
Sales in Units	100,000	103,000	80,000	75,000
Revenues	$300,000	$309,000	$240,000	$225,000
Cost of Goods Manufactured and Sold	150,000	156,560	120,000	111,000
Selling Expenses	60,000[a]	63,260[a]	52,000[a]	49,250[a]
Administrative Expenses	70,000[b]	70,500	55,000[b]	55,500
Total Expenses	$280,000	$290,320	$227,000	$215,750
Division Income	20,000	18,680	13,000	9,250
Division Assets	$250,000	$250,000	$ 80,000	$ 80,000

[a] Budgeted selling expenses include $40,000 of variable selling expenses for Northern and $32,000 of variable selling expenses for Southern. Actual fixed selling expenses were equal to budgeted fixed selling expenses for both divisions.
[b] Administrative expenses are assumed to be fixed.

REQUIRED:
1. If you were the manager of the Northern Division, would you prefer to have your division treated as a profit center or as an investment center based on current-year performance? Support your answer with appropriate computations.

2. Based on the figures supplied, calculate the variances between budget and actual for each division and comment on the shortcoming of the variances you have calculated.

3. Prepare an analysis of variable costs for each division which better describes its performance relative to expectations than that computed in part 2; i.e., adjust budgeted figures to the sales volume actually achieved and then compare with actual. Comment on each manager's performance relative to budget based on your calculations.

8—18. *Reconstructing the original budget; adjusting the budget to actual volume.* A summary of operating data for the Dover Division of Blake Manufacturing Company for last year (Year 1) and the current year (Year 2) are given below. The Dover Division is treated as a profit center for responsibility reporting purposes.

	YEAR 1 ACTUAL	YEAR 2 ACTUAL
Sales Volume (in units)	800	775
Selling Price	$125	$130
Production (in units)	800	775
Variable costs (per unit):		
Raw Material	$25	$23
Direct Labor	30	35
Overhead	10	12
Fixed costs (total):		
Rent	5,000	5,250
Supervisor's Salary	22,000	22,000
Selling and Administrative Expenses:		
Variable	$5/unit	$5.20/unit
Fixed	$ 3,500	$ 3,230

Additional information:

1. Year 2 sales were budgeted at 110% of the actual volume achieved in Year 1 with a budgeted selling price of $132 per unit. Budgeted production for Year 2 was equal to budgeted sales.

2. *Variable* manufacturing costs were budgeted at 105% of actual Year 1 costs, with the exception of variable manufacturing overhead which was budgeted at the rate of $11 per unit. Fixed manufacturing overhead for Year 2 was budgeted at the actual amount of fixed manufacturing overhead incurred in Year 1.

3. Year 2 variable selling and administrative expenses were budgeted at $5 per unit, while fixed selling and administrative expenses for Year 2 were budgeted at their actual level for Year 1.

4. Earnings are taxed at a 40% rate.

REQUIRED: 1. Reconstruct the Year 2 budgeted income statement for the Dover Division and calculate variances of actual from budget for Year 2.

2. Adjust the Year 2 budgeted income statement to a volume level consistent with that actually achieved in Year 2; i.e., 775 units produced and sold, compare the adjusted budget figures with actual, and comment on the performance of the Dover Division. (Round all amounts to the nearest dollar.)

8—19. *Responsibility accounting system.* As a consultant with the Addison Consulting Firm, you have been assigned a new client, the Longlife Pencil Company, which manufactures a uniquely designed pencil that lasts up to ten times longer than ordinary pencils. The president of Longlife has requested that you review the company's cost accounting system to help determine why costs have increased significantly in the last operating period. In addition, the president indicates that he feels the problem rests with the production supervisor, Al Sharp, who has not been able to keep actual production cost in line with budgeted operating costs and who has been complaining about his work load and contending that he is "doing all that he can do." In answer to your request, you have received the following data relating to Longlife's operations in the previous period:

Longlife Pencil Company Simplified Organization Chart

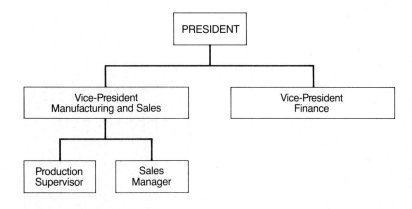

Additional data:

	BUDGET	ACTUAL
Sales (units)	600	625
Selling Price	$ 150	$ 152
Units Produced	600	625
Direct Material per unit	$ 35	$ 37
Direct Labor Hours per unit	4	4.10
Direct Labor Rate	$ 7.00	$ 7.00
Variable Overhead:		
Indirect Materials	$ 3.00	$ 3.05
Indirect Labor	10.50	10.75
Utilities	1.25	1.25
Set-up	2.50	2.65
Repairs and Maintenance	2.00	2.05
Fixed Overhead:		
Depreciation (straight-line basis)	3,000	3,000
Supervisor's Salary	4,000	4,175
Selling Expenses	$ 4 per unit	2,575
General and Administrative Expenses	$12,000	$11,500

Additional information:

1. All the units produced during a period are sold during that period.
2. The figures shown above for selling expenses and general and administrative expenses represent the portion of total expenditures for these items which are considered to be controllable by the Vice-President of Manufacturing and Sales. This Vice-President's performance is evaluated on the basis of profits.
3. The production supervisor is considered to be the head of an expense center for responsibility reporting purposes.

REQUIRED: Prepare the responsibility reports which should be used to evaluate the performance of the Production Supervisor and the Vice-President of Manufacturing and Sales and comment on the performance of each. (Round all amounts to the nearest dollar.)

8—20. *Responsibility accounting.* (CMA adapted) The Argon County Hospital is located in the county seat. Argon County is a well-known summer resort area. The county population doubles during the vacation months (May–August) and hospital activity more than doubles during these months. The hospital is organized into several departments. Although it is a relatively small hospital, its pleasant surroundings have attracted a well-trained and competent medical staff.

An administrator was hired a year ago to improve the business activities of the hospital. Among the new ideas he has introduced is responsibility accounting. This program was announced along with quarterly cost reports supplied to department heads. Previously cost data were presented to department heads infrequently. Excerpts from the announcement and the report received by the laundry supervisor are presented below.

"The hospital has adopted a '*responsibility accounting system.*' From now on you will receive quarterly reports comparing the costs of operating your department with budgeted costs. The reports will highlight the differences (variations) so you can zero in on the departure from budgeted costs (this is called 'management by exception'). Responsibility accounting means you are accountable for keeping the costs in your department within the budget. The variations from the budget will help you identify what costs are out of line, and the size of the variation will indicate which ones are the most important. Your first such report accompanies this announcement."

Additional information:

The annual budget for the year was constructed by the new administrator. Quarterly budgets were computed as one-fourth of the annual budget.

```
┌─────────────────────────────────────────────────────────────────────┐
│                      ARGON COUNTY HOSPITAL                            │
│              Performance Report—Laundry Department                    │
│                         July–September                                │
└─────────────────────────────────────────────────────────────────────┘
```

	Budget	Actual	(Over) Under Budget	Percent (Over) Under Budget
Patient Days	9,500	11,900	(2,400)	(25)
Pounds Processed—Laundry	125,000	156,000	(31,000)	(25)
Costs:				
Laundry Labor	$ 9,000	$ 12,500	$ (3,500)	(39)
Supplies	1,100	1,875	(775)	(70)
Water, Water Heating and Softening	1,700	2,500	(800)	(47)
Maintenance	1,400	2,200	(800)	(57)
Supervisor's Salary	3,150	3,750	(600)	(19)
Allocated Administration Costs	4,000	5,000	(1,000)	(25)
Equipment Depreciation	1,200	1,250	(50)	(4)
	$ 21,550	$ 29,075	$ (7,525)	(35)

Administrator's Comments: Costs are significantly above budget for the quarter. Particular attention needs to be paid to labor, supplies, and maintenance.

The administrator compiled the budget from an analysis of the prior three years' actual costs. For that three-year period costs were increasing from one year to the next with more rapid increases occurring between the second and third year. The administrator considered establishing the budget at an average of the prior three years' costs, hoping that the installation of the system would reduce costs to this level. However, in view of the rapidly increasing prices, he finally chose last year's costs less 3% for the current budget. The activity level measured by patient days and pounds of laundry processed was set at last year's volume, which was approximately equal to the volume of each of the past three years.

REQUIRED:
1. Comment on the method used to construct the budget.
2. What information should be communicated by variations from budgets?
3. Does the report effectively communicate the level of efficiency of this department? Give reasons for your answer.

8—21. *Performance reporting.* (CMA adapted) In late 1981 Mr. Sootsman, the official in charge of the State Department of Automobile Regulation, established a system of performance measurement for the department's branch offices. He was convinced that management by objectives could help the department reach its objective of better citizen service at a lower cost. The first step was to define the activities of the branch offices, to assign point values to the services performed, and to establish performance targets. Point values, rather than revenue targets, were employed because the department was a regulatory agency, not a revenue-producing agency. Further, the specific revenue for a service did not adequately reflect the differences in effort required. The analysis was compiled at the state office, and the results were distributed to the branch offices.

The system has been in operation since 1982. The performance targets for the branches have been revised each year by the state office. The revisions were designed to encourage better performance by increasing the target or reducing resources to achieve targets. The budget revisions incorporated noncontrollable events, such as population shifts, new branches, and changes in procedures.

The Barry County branch is typical of many branch offices. A summary displaying the budgeted and actual performance for three years is presented below.

Mr. Sootman has been disappointed in the performance of branch offices because they have not met performance targets or budgets. He is especially concerned because the points earned from citizens' comments are declining.

Barry County Branch Performance Report

	1982 Budget	1982 Actual	1983 Budget	1983 Actual	1984 Budget	1984 Actual
Population served	38,000		38,500		38,700	
Number of employees:						
Administrative	1	1	1	1	1	1
Professional	1	1	1	1	1	1
Clerical	3	3	2	3	1½	3
Budgeted Performance Points[a]						
1. Services	19,500		16,000		15,500	
2. Citizen comments	500		600		700	
	20,000		16,600		16,200	
Actual Performance Points[b]						
1. Services		14,500		14,600		15,600
2. Citizen comments		200		900		200
		14,700		15,500		15,800

Barry County Branch Performance Report (*Continued*)

	1982		1983		1984	
	Budget	Actual	Budget	Actual	Budget	Actual
Detail of Actual Performance[b]						
1. New driver licenses:						
a. Examination and road tests (3 pts.)		3,000		3,150		3,030
b. Road tests repeat—failed prior test (2 pts.)		600		750		1,650
2. Renew driver licenses (1 pt.)		3,000		3,120		3,060
3. Issue license plates (.5 pts.)		4,200		4,150		4,100
4. Issue titles:						
a. Dealer transactions (.5 pts.)		2,000		1,900		2,100
b. Individual transaction (1 pt.)		1,700		1,530		1,660
		14,500		14,600		15,600
5. Citizen comments:						
a. Favorable (+.5 pts.)		300		1,100		800
b. Unfavorable (−.5 pts.)		(100)		(200)		(600)
		200		900		200

[a] The budget performance points for services are calculated using 3 points per available hour. The administrative employee devotes half-time to administration and half-time to regular services. The calculations for the services point budget are as follows:

1982: $4\frac{1}{2}$ people × 8 hours × 240 days × 3 pts. × 75% productive time
       = 19,440 rounded to 19,500

1983: $3\frac{1}{2}$ people × 8 hours × 240 days × 3 pts. × 80% productive time
       = 16,128 rounded to 16,000

1984: 3 people × 8 hours × 240 days × 3 pts. × 90% productive time
       = 15,552 rounded to 15,500

The comments targets are based upon rough estimates by department officials in the state office.

[b] The actual point totals for the branch are calculated by multiplying the weights shown in the report in parentheses by the number of such services performed or comments received.

REQUIRED:
1. Does the method of performance measurement properly capture the objectives of this operation? Justify your answer.
2. The Barry County branch office came close to its target for 1984. Does this constitute improved performance compared to 1983? Justify your answer.

8—22. *Transfer pricing.* The Electronics Division of International Products, Inc., makes transistors of the type used by the Radio Division of that company. The Electronics Division has the capacity to produce 400,000 transistors a year and is currently working at 80% of that capacity because of lack of external demand for its transistors. The Radio Division makes 280,000 radios per year and is operating at full capacity.

Transistors are sold externally for $8. The cost of producing a transistor at *80% capacity* is as follows:

Direct materials	$1.50
Direct labor	2.00
Variable manufacturing overhead	.50
Fixed manufacturing overhead	.70

There are no variable selling or administrative expenses incurred by the Electronics Division. Selling and administrative expenses total $860,000 for that Division.

The manager of the Radio Division has offered to purchase 80,000 transistors from the Electronics Division at $4.50. The manager of the Electronics Division has rejected this offer. The Radio Division pays $8 for transistors it purchases externally. Total fixed manufacturing overhead of the Electronics Division is the same at 80% and 100% of capacity. The Radio Division sells its radios for $45. Manufacturing costs other than the cost of the transistor amount to $16 when the Division is operating at full capacity. Variable selling expenses amount to $3.50 per radio, while fixed selling and administrative expenses are $1,975,000.

REQUIRED:
1. Prepare income statements for the Electronics Division with and without the production of the additional transistors and their transfer to the Radio Division at $4.50.
2. Prepare income statements for the Radio Division with and without the transfer of the transistors at $4.50.
3. For the company as a whole calculate the impact on income of the transfer of the transistors to the Radio Division at $4.50.
4. Should upper-echelon management of International Products insist that the Electronics Division produce and transfer the 80,000 transistors to the Radio Division? Give the arguments pro and con.
5. What is the minimum amount at which the Electronics Division can afford to transfer the transistors to the Radio Division?
6. Would the company be better off if all the 280,000 transistors which the Radio Division needs were transferred to that Division by the Electronics Division rather than just the 80,000 which represent idle capacity of the Electronics Division?

8—23. *Responsibility accounting for a nonprofit organization.* The Western States Association of Medical Technicians, as one of its services, sponsors seminars for its members to help them keep up to date in technical matters and in laboratory management. The Association is a nonprofit organization and attempts to price its seminars at an amount which will generate a contribution to surplus that will be available for fixed-asset replacement. Actual results and variances from budget for the manager of the seminar division for the past fiscal period are shown below:

	ACTUAL	VARIANCE
Seminar participants	6,020	(1,380)
Number of seminars given	172	(13)
Revenues	$1,204,000	$(276,000)
Costs which vary with number of participants:		
Food	$ 49,665	$ 9,535
Materials—workbooks and handouts	264,880	45,920
Costs which vary with the number of seminars:		
Instructors' fees	137,600	10,400
Rental of sites	19,780	(1,280)
Equipment rental (overhead projectors, etc.)	6,880	(405)
Fixed costs of the seminar division Salaries of manager and assistants	104,000	(2,400)
Telephone	16,000	(580)
Promotion of seminars	93,000	8,000
General overhead of the association allocated to the seminar division	488,000	(13,000)
Total expenses	$1,179,805	$ 56,190
Surplus or (deficit) generated	$ 24,195	$(219,810)

All seminars last for one day and participants receive eight hours of continuing education credit, which they need to maintain their licenses. The manager's salary is $42,000, and it had been budgeted at this level.

REQUIRED:

1. Should the manager of the seminar division be held responsible for the number of participants who enroll in the Association's seminars? How, if at all, can he or she influence this figure?

2. Should the manager of the seminar division be held responsible for the number of seminars scheduled? How, if at all, can he or she influence this figure?

3. Comment on each item of cost which is listed and state to what extent, if any, it can be influenced by the manager of the seminar division.

4. How well did the manager of the seminar division control costs which vary with the number of participants in the seminars? Support your answer with computations. You do not have to analyze each element of cost separately.

5. How well did the manager of the seminar division control costs which vary with the number of seminars scheduled? Support your answer with computations. You do not have to analyze each element of cost separately.

6. The manager of seminars spent $8,000 less than was budgeted for promotion of seminars. Did this represent good cost control on the part of the manager? Explain your answer.

7. Prepare a report which better describes the performance of the manager for the budget period and decide which items need further investigation.

8—24. *Transfer pricing.* Burger Delight is well known for its quarter-pound hamburger that contains ¼ pound of ground beef and which sells for $1.50. Burger Delight has asked for bids for supplying the hamburger it needs. The lowest bid was for $.44 per pound. Burger Delight is part of Tastes Best Products, Inc. Burger Delight received a bid from another wholly owned subsidiary of the company, Meat Processors, Inc., to supply the hamburger at $.50 per pound. Burger Delight needs 150,000 pounds of hamburger per month. In addition to the meat costs, other variable costs related to preparing and serving a hamburger amount to $.48, while fixed costs per burger are $.04 at a monthly volume of 600,000 hamburgers. Selling and administrative expenses excluding advertising amount to $384,000 per month. Advertising costs are $.11 per hamburger.

Meat Processors, Inc., has a monthly volume of hamburger of 900,000 pounds. It is currently producing at that volume and supplying 200,000 pounds of hamburger made into hamburger patties at $.50 per pound to another fast-food chain. The other 700,000 pounds it is processing is sold in 100-pound packages to grocery stores, which then repackage it. The amount received per pound for the 100-pound packages is $.41 per pound. At full capacity, Meat Processors' cost per pound of hamburger is $.35, of which $.30 is variable. Making the hamburger into patties separated by a piece of paper increases the costs by $.01 per pound. Selling and administrative expenses of Meat Processors, Inc., all of which are fixed, amount to $56,000 per month.

For performance evaluation, Burger Delight and Meat Processors, Inc., are treated as investment centers. Assets of Burger Delight total $9,600,000, those of Meat Processors, Inc., $2,400,000. A monthly return-on-investment figure is calculated by dividing monthly income before any corporate charges by one-twelfth of the asset balance. The target monthly return on investment set by corporate management is 9% for Burger Delight and 11% for Meat Processors, Inc.

REQUIRED:

1. Prepare income statements for Burger Delight, Meat Processors, Inc., and to the extent possible for Tastes Best Products, assuming that Burger Delight accepts the contract from the outside vendor to supply the 600,000 pounds of hamburger it needs for the month. Calculate the monthly ROI for Burger Delight and Meat Processors, Inc., and Tastes Best Products.

2. Prepare income statements for Burger Delight, Meat Processors, Inc., and to the extent possible for Tastes Best Products, assuming that the 150,000 pounds are sold to Burger Delight by Meat Processors, Inc., at $.50. These 150,000 pounds represent ground beef which Meat Processors, Inc., is currently selling in bulk packages. Calculate the monthly ROI for Burger Delight, Meat Processors, Inc., and Tastes Best Products.

3. Is $.50 per pound an appropriate transfer price for the sale of the hamburger from Meat Processors to Burger Delight? Justify your answer.
4. What is the minimum selling price which Meat Processors could accept for the meat transferred to Burger Delight?
5. What is the maximum price which the manager of Burger Delight will be willing to pay to Meat Processors for the hamburger?
6. What nonquantitative factors should be considered in determining whether Meat Processors should become the supplier to Burger Delight?

8—25. *Issues in calculating return on investment; residual income.* The Green River Milling Company has the following, among other divisions. The Upholstery Fabrics Division produces materials which are used for covering chairs and couches and for making drapes. The Cotton Fabrics Division makes cloth which is used primarily in clothing and sheet manufacturing. Green River Milling Company treats these two divisions as investment centers. The following data have been assembled relative to the performance of each of the divisions.

	UPHOLSTERY FABRICS	COTTON FABRICS
Sales	$ 6,000,000	$24,000,000
Divisional operating expenses	4,000,000	18,000,000
Divisional income before allocation of corporate expenses	2,000,000	6,000,000
Allocated corporate expenses	1,100,000	3,800,000
Divisional income	$ 900,000	$ 2,200,000
Assets allocated to the division but controlled at corporate headquarters	$ 300,000	$ 1,800,000
Assets controlled by the division— gross	16,700,000	26,500,000
Less: Accumulated depreciation on division assets	(8,000,000)	(8,300,000)
Net assets	$ 9,000,000	$20,000,000

For Upholstery Fabrics, $600,000 of allocated corporate costs are based on services provided to the division. The other $500,000 of the allocated costs are allocated on the basis of sales of each division. The portion of Cotton Fabrics's allocated corporate costs based on services provided is $1,800,000.

Cash and accounts receivable are controlled at corporate headquarters. A detailed accounting system has been developed that allows corporate headquarters to trace the average investment in each of these assets to the various divisions. This average investment is the amount of assets allocated to the division. Divisions are not credited with any earnings on excess cash which they may generate and which is invested by corporate staff. They are charged for funds "borrowed" when they cannot meet their cash needs out of divisional funds, even though those borrowed funds may not come from an external source. These charges are part of the allocated corporate costs for services.

REQUIRED:

1. Calculate return on investment for the two divisions the following ways:

   a. Divisional income/net assets.
   b. Divisional income/gross assets.
   c. Divisional income before allocation/net assets.
   d. Divisional income before allocation/gross assets.
   e. Divisional income before allocation of corporate expenses less allocated expenses for services rendered/net assets.
   f. Divisional income before allocation of corporate expenses less allocated expenses for services rendered/gross assets.
   g. Divisional income before allocation of corporate expenses less allocated expenses for services rendered/net assets controlled by the division.
   h. Divisional income before allocation of corporate expenses less allocated expenses for services rendered/gross assets controlled by the division.

2. Assume that Green River Milling sets a minimum desired return on assets of 12%. Calculate residual income for each of the divisions defining assets as net assets and income as:

   a. Divisional income.
   b. Divisional income before allocation of corporate expenses.

3. Assume that Green River Milling has set a minimum return on liquid assets (cash and receivables) of 10% and a return of 15% on other net assets. Calculate residual income for each of the divisions defining income as divisional income.

4. Which measure of performance that you have computed do you think Green Milling should use? Why?

5. ROI computed for an investment center could be compared with (a) ROI for that same investment center on a historical basis, (b) ROI for other investment centers in the company, (c) budgeted ROI, and (d) ROI statistics from external sources. Comment on the advantages and disadvantages of each of these standards against which ROI for a division could be measured.

6. Calculate ROI for each based on:

$$\frac{\text{divisional income}}{\text{sales}} \times \frac{\text{sales}}{\text{net assets}}$$

What is the advantage, if any, of calculating ROI this way?

8—26. *Budget versus actual performance and different measures of performance for investment centers.* The Alaska Paper Company has a number of different investment centers, one of which is the Copying Paper business unit. The budgeted and actual performance for the business unit for the past year are shown below. Unfavorable variances are indicated by parentheses.

Copying Paper

	BUDGET	VARIANCE
Sales in 500-page reams	800,00	(20,000)
Revenues	$ 4,000,000	$ (61,000)
Cost of Goods Mfg,. and Sold:		
Direct Materials	$ 400,000	(13,400)
Direct Labor	$ 640,000	31,600
Variable Overhead	240,000	6,000
Fixed Overhead	160,000	(2,000)
Total	$ 1,440,000	22,200
Variable Selling Expenses	192,000	4,800
Fixed Selling Expenses	416,000	(2,500)
Administrative Expenses (fixed)	520,000	2,300
Total Expenses	$ 2,568,000	$ 26,800
Operating Income	$ 1,432,000	$ (34,200)

	BUDGET	ACTUAL
Assets Controlled by Business Unit	$10,410,000	$11,025,000
Less: Accumulated Depreciation	(1,460,000)	(1,473,000)
Net Assets of Business Units	$ 8,950,000	$ 9,552,000

REQUIRED: 1. *Based on the data presented,* which variances would you investigate further?
2. Using the data provided, calculate budgeted and actual ROI based on:
   a. Gross assets.
   b. Net assets.
3. Using the data presented, calculate budgeted and actual residual income, assuming the minimum return expected of the Copying Paper business unit on net assets is 14%.
4. Prepare a report for the business unit which restates budget data consistent with the actual number of units sold and which shows actual results and variances. Assume all paper manufactured during the period was sold.
5. Based on your calculations in part 4, which items do you think warrant further investigation?
6. Recalculate the measures of return you computed in parts 2 and 3; use your adjusted data and compare your measures of performance with those previously computed. Comment on the results of your comparison.

8—27.   *Using budget data to analyze performance.* The Rocky Mountain Sweatshirt Company makes heavy sweatshirts which they advertise as providing significantly more warmth than the average garment of that type. The company has produced the following data describing performance for the past year.

	BUDGET	ACTUAL	PERSON RESPONSIBLE
Sweatshirts sold	400,000	410,000	Vice-president—sales
Revenues	$ 6,000,000	$ 6,150,000	Vice-president—sales and president
Cost of goods manufactured and sold:			
Direct materials	$ 856,000	$ 897,900	Vice-president—mfg. and purchasing agent
Direct labor	960,000	984,000	Vice-president—mfg.
Variable overhead	440,000	442,000	Vice-president—mfg.
Fixed mfg. overhead	928,000	928,000	Vice-president—mfg. and president
Total	$ 3,184,000	$ 3,251,900	
Variable selling expenses:			
Commissions	300,000	307,500	Vice-president—sales
Advertising	400,000	415,000	Vice-president—sales
Fixed selling expenses:			President
Salaries	150,000	156,000	
Depreciation	50,000	50,000	
Administrative expenses:			President
Salaries	200,000	210,000	
Utilities	28,000	26,500	
Depreciation	89,000	89,000	
Insurance and other	16,000	18,900	
Total expenses	$ 4,417,000	$ 4,524,800	
Income before taxes	$ 1,583,000	$ 1,625,200	
Assets	$11,583,000	$10,965,000	President

Additional information:

1. The president is responsible for revenues to the extent that she sets selling prices.
2. The amount of direct materials used is the responsibility of the vice-president of manufacturing, while the cost of those raw materials is the responsibility of the purchasing agent. Raw materials costing $4,100 were unaccounted for in the manufacturing process at the end of the period and were either lost, stolen, or spoiled.
3. The president controls fixed manufacturing overhead to the extent that this figure includes things such as depreciation on the facilities and the salary of the vice-president of manufacturing. Approximately 30% of the total figure can be significantly influenced by the vice-president of manufacturing. The actual cost of those items controllable by the vice-president of manufacturing was $275,000.
4. Raw materials used in the manufacturing process this period were purchased this period. The units sold this period were manufactured this period.

REQUIRED: Evaluate the performance of each of the individuals listed as having responsibility for the data given. Support your evaluation with appropriate figures.

8—28. *Analysis of performance, return on investment and residual income.* The Natural Ingredients Food Company produces a number of different products which are prepared with what the company terms "all natural ingredients." The company is broken down for cost-control purposes into business units based on different product lines. Data for the Bakery Product business unit and the Beverages business unit are given below. Each of these business units is treated as an investment center, and managerial performance is evaluated on the basis of return on investment on the assets controlled by the business unit.

	BAKERY PRODUCTS		BEVERAGES	
	Budget	Actual	Budget	Actual
Units produced and sold	500,000	500,000	800,000	800,000
Average selling price	$1.61	$1.60	$0.73	$0.75
Average full costs:				
Variable production costs	$ .40	$ .43	$ .110	$ .105
Fixed production costs	.13	.12	.076	.080
Variable selling expenses	.25	.26	.140	.120
Fixed selling and administrative	.22	.20	.100	.100
Total costs	$1.00	$1.01	$ .426	$ .405
Assets controlled by the business unit	$2,400,000	$2,400,000	$1,350,000	$1,350,000

Additional information:

The minimum desired long-term return on assets controlled by the business units is 10% for Bakery Products and 15% for Beverages.

REQUIRED:

1. Prepare a variance report which shows the variance between budgeted income and actual income for each item on the income statement. Calculate for each item on the income statement the percent of each variance relative to the budget. Which variances appear significant?
2. Calculate ROI for each business unit based on budgeted results and actual results.
3. Calculate residual income for the two business units based on budgeted and actual results.
4. Evaluate the performance of each business unit. How well did each perform and what affected performance?
5. By what amount would the ROI of the Bakery Products business unit have changed if fixed costs were at their actual level for the period and 520,000 units could have been produced at the actual variable cost per unit and sold at the actual selling price?

8—29. *Transfer pricing.* Cowpersons, Inc., is a large producer of western-style clothing and accessories for men and women. One of its divisions produces denim and another produces jeans. Each division is considered a profit center. Relevant data for these two divisions for a monthly period are shown below:

	DENIM DIVISION	JEANS DIVISION
Full capacity	120,000 yards	10,000 pairs
Actual capacity	90,000 yards produced and sold	10,000 pairs produced and sold
Manufacturing costs:		
Variable	$.50 per yard	$8.00 per pair[a]
Fixed	$.25 per yard based on actual capacity	$3.00 per pair based on actual capacity
Selling price	$1.50 per yard	$25.00 per pair
Selling and administrative (all fixed)	$42,000	$98,000

[a] Includes material cost of $1.45 × 3 yd = $4.35.

The Jeans Division is currently purchasing all its denim yardage external to the firm at $1.45 per yard. It takes 3 yards of denim to make each pair of jeans. The Denim Division would like to operate at full capacity and has offered to supply the 30,000 yards of denim needed each month by the Jeans Division at the same price which that division is currently paying externally.

REQUIRED:

1. Prepare income statements which show the effects on each division and the company as a whole of:

   a. A continuation of the current situation.

   b. The transfer of the 30,000 yards to the Jeans Division from the Denim Division at $1.45 per yard.

2. Suppose that all 120,000 yards of denim which the Denim Division can produce can be sold externally at $1.50 and the Jeans Division has a contract with an external source to provide its denim needs at $1.45. Is this contract in the best interest of the company, or should the yardage needed by the Jeans Division be transferred by the Denim Division at some appropriate transfer price? Support your answer with computations.

3. Suppose that the Denim Division is currently making 90,000 yards and would like to make an additional 30,000 yards to transfer to the Jeans Division. The manager of the Jeans Division says that the highest acceptable transfer price to him is something less than the external price which he is currently paying. Should the transfer take place at a price of less than $1.45. Who will benefit? Support your answer with appropriate computations.

8—30. *Investment disincentive with ROI.* The following budgetary data for the coming year relate to the operations of three of the eight divisions of the Shape-Up America Company—the Diet Foods Division, Diet Beverages, and the Exercise Clothing Division.

	DIET FOODS	DIET BEVERAGES	EXERCISE CLOTHING
Estimated operating income	$1,150,000	$ 962,000	$ 416,600
Estimated assets	$6,500,000	$7,400,000	$6,300,000

Each of the divisions is considering a major capital expenditure for the coming year for equipment. Assume that the size of the expenditure in the case of each division would be $800,000 and would generate a return of $96,000. Neither the asset investment nor the return generated has been included in the estimated income and asset figures given above. The overall rate of return of Shape-Up America is estimated at 10% for the coming year.

REQUIRED: 1. Calculate ROI for each of the divisions, assuming:

   a. The investment is made.

   b. The investment is not made.

   2. Based on the results you have calculated in part 1, which divisions, if any, can be expected to make the investment if performance is evaluated on the basis of ROI?

   3. Is it in the best interest of the company as a whole that each of the divisions make the investment? Support your answer with appropriate figures.

   4. Calculate residual income for each of the three divisions using the company's overall anticipated rate of return for the coming year of 10%, assuming:

   a. The investment is made.

   b. The investment is not made.

   5. Based on your solution to part 4, which divisions, if any, can be expected to invest in the new equipment if performance is measured by residual income?

chapter nine

Using Flexible Budgets and Standard Costs for Controlling Direct Material and Direct Labor

OBJECTIVES

After you have completed this chapter, you should be able to answer the following questions:

- How does a static budget differ from a flexible budget?
- What are the benefits of preparing a flexible budget?
- How does a standard cost system differ from an actual cost system used in conjunction with a budget?
- How are direct material and direct labor standards set?
- For what kinds of operations is a standard cost system feasible?
- How are the total variance, the price variance, and the usage variance calculated for direct materials and direct labor?
- How does breaking a total variance between budget (or standard) and actual costs into price and usage components aid in the control process?
- How do the journal entries for direct materials and direct labor inputs differ between an actual cost system and a standard cost system?

The budget schedules we prepared in Chapter 7 were based on one level of activity—a *static budget*. In Chapter 8 we discussed briefly the need to adjust the budgeted activity level to the actual activity level to aid in interpreting variances. In this chapter we shall discuss this need for adjustment more fully and the way the adjustment can be made using the concept of a *flexible budget*—a budget which describes costs and revenues at various levels of activity.

Let's look first at the problem which arises when the budget is based on one level of activity and actual performance is on another level. Consider the data presented for Handicrafts, Limited, which manufactures a number of different decorative items. The data presented are for the production of a line of large woven baskets (Basket #679), used primarily for holding plants.

HANDICRAFTS, LIMITED
Cost of Goods Manufactured Budget—Basket #679
for the Year Ended December 31

Budgeted Unit Production: 20,000 Baskets

	PER UNIT	TOTAL
Variable Manufacturing Costs:		
Simulated bamboo, 10 feet per basket @ $.20 per foot	$2.00	$ 40,000
Direct Labor, .75 hour per basket @ $6 per hour	4.50	90,000
Variable Overhead:		
Indirect Materials	.50	10,000
Other	.25	5,000
Total Variable Manufacturing Cost	$7.25	$145,000
Fixed Manufacturing Overhead Costs:		
Indirect Labor		25,000
Depreciation		10,000
Utilities		7,000
Other		3,000
Total Fixed Manufacturing Costs		$ 45,000
Cost of Goods Manufactured		$190,000
Budgeted Cost Per Unit for 20,000 Units		$9.50

Let us assume that Handicrafts uses a standard cost system and bases its standards on normal efficiency as reflected in its budget estimates. We'll describe fully what is meant by a standard cost system later in this chapter. Handicrafts uses an applied overhead system based on direct labor hours. A standard cost card—a document which describes what costs

should be for a particular item—Basket #679—for the budget period is
shown below:

Standard Costs—Decorative Basket #679

Direct materials: 10 feet of simulated bamboo @ $.20 per foot	$2.00
Direct labor: .75 hour for each basket @ $6 per hour	4.50
Manufacturing overhead applied on the basis of direct labor hours:	
Variable overhead: $15,000/15,000 hours* = $1 per direct labor hour × .75 hour per unit	.75
Fixed overhead: $45,000/15,000 hours* = $3 per direct labor hour × .75 hour per unit	2.25
Standard Cost Per Unit	$9.50

* Cost as reflected in the budget divided by direct labor hours required for the production of 20,000 units.

Based on the expectations reflected in the budget for Handicrafts
and the standard cost card, consider Illustration 9-1, which shows budgeted
(also standard) costs compared with actual costs. Note the series of
unfavorable variances. Only one variance is favorable—supplies and other.
Why aren't these variances meaningful? The answer is that the budget
was based on an anticipated production volume of 20,000 units, while
21,000 units were actually made. Even if production was done exactly
consistent with the cost and usage standards as defined on the standard

ILLUSTRATION 9-1

HANDICRAFTS, LIMITED
Comparison of Actual and Budgeted Cost of Goods Manufactured
for the Year Ended December 31

	BUDGET— STANDARD COSTS	ACTUAL		VARIANCE
Units of Production	20,000		21,000	1,000
Direct Materials—simulated bamboo	40,000	214,200 ft @ $0.19 per foot	40,698	698 U
Direct Labor	90,000	168,000 hr @ $6.25 per hour	105,000	15,000 U
Variable Manufacturing Overhead:				
Indirect Materials	10,000		11,000	1,000 U
Supplies and Other	5,000		4,800	200 F
Total Variable Overhead	15,000		15,800	800 U
Fixed Manufacturing Overhead:				
Indirect Labor	25,000		26,000	1,000 U
Depreciation	10,000		10,000	—
Utilities	7,000		7,302	302 U
Other	3,000		3,100	100 U
Total Fixed Overhead	45,000		46,402	1,402 U
Total Manufacturing Overhead	60,000		62,202	2,202 U
Cost of Goods Manufactured	190,000		207,900	17,900 U
Unit Cost	9.50		9.90	$0.40 U

cost card, a series of unfavorable variances could be anticipated for all the variable cost inputs because more units were made than had been anticipated. For example, to make 20,000 units, 15,000 direct labor hours represent the standard input. Operating with equal efficiency, to produce the 21,000 units, 15,750 hours (21,000 units × .75 hours per unit) are the standard, thus causing actual costs to exceed budgeted (standard) costs even if labor costs per hour were equal to the standard of $6 per hour.

THE FLEXIBLE BUDGET

To make a comparison of actual results with budget results meaningful when actual activity differs from the budgeted activity, the budget needs to be adjusted consistent with the actual activity level. Many companies prepare a flexible budget—a budget which describes budgeted amounts consistent with the company's most likely levels of activity.

To illustrate, let's assume that the costs which Handicrafts has defined for the production of Basket #679 are valid for production levels ranging from 19,000 to 21,000 baskets. This level of activity is Handicrafts' relevant range—the range of production for which variable cost relationships (cost per unit) and the total amounts of fixed costs are not expected to change. A flexible budget for Handicrafts, Limited, is depicted in Illustration 9-2.

ILLUSTRATION 9-2

HANDICRAFTS, LIMITED
Flexible Budget—Basket #679
for the Period Ended December 31

	UNIT COSTS	PRODUCTION VOLUME IN UNITS		
		19,000	20,000	21,000
Variable Manufacturing Costs:				
Direct Materials	$2.00	$ 38,000	$ 40,000	$ 42,000
Direct Labor	4.50	85,500	90,000	94,500
Overhead:				
Indirect Materials	.50	9,500	10,000	10,500
Supplies and Other	.25	4,750	5,000	5,250
Total Variable Manufacturing Costs	$7.25	$137,750	$145,000	$152,250
Fixed Manufacturing Overhead:				
Indirect Labor		$ 25,000	$ 25,000	$ 25,000
Depreciation		10,000	10,000	10,000
Utilities		7,000	7,000	7,000
Other		3,000	3,000	3,000
Total Fixed Manufacturing Overhead		$ 45,000	$ 45,000	$ 45,000
Total Manufacturing Costs		$182,750	$190,000	$197,250
Budgeted Cost per Unit		$9.62	$9.50	$9.39

There is no general agreement as to whether fixed costs should be included in a flexible budget. As you can see from Illustration 9-2, if the flexible budget is prepared for a company's relevent range of activities, the fixed costs should not change between different volume levels. For this reason, they are not meaningful when applying the concept of flexible budgeting.

COMPARING ACTUAL WITH THE FLEXIBLE BUDGET

Illustration 9-3 is a comparison of actual results with budget results. However, it differs from Illustration 9-1 in that the actual production level has been used for the budget figures. That is, the budget figures which are being used for comparative purposes represent those costs which should have been incurred in producing 21,000 units with normal efficiency.

Comparing the variances in Illustration 9-1 with those in 9-3, actual performance was not up to expectations as represented by the budget and the standard unit costs. However, the amount of the overall variance was cut from $17,900 to $10,650. The direct materials variance became favorable rather than unfavorable, and the size of all unfavorable variable cost variances was reduced when the flexible budget comparison was made. There was no difference in the amount or sign of the fixed cost variances. This is because fixed costs do not change with volume changes, hence the budgeted level of fixed cost remained the same.

ILLUSTRATION 9-3

	BUDGET	ACTUAL		VARIANCE
HANDICRAFTS, LIMITED Comparison of Actual and Flexible Budget Costs for the Year Ended December 31				
Units of Production	21,000		21,000	0
Direct Materials	$ 42,000	214,200 ft @ $.19	$ 40,698	$ 1,302 F
Direct Labor	94,500	16,800 hr @ $6.25	105,000	10,500 U
Variable Manufacturing Over- head:				
Indirect Materials	10,500		11,000	500 U
Supplies and Other	5,250		4,800	450 F
Total Variable Manufacturing Costs	$152,250		$161,498	$ 9,248 U
Fixed Manufacturing Overhead:				
Indirect Labor	25,000		26,000	1,000 U
Depreciation	10,000		10,000	—
Utilities	7,000		7,302	302 U
Other	3,000		3,100	100 U
Total Fixed Manufacturing Overhead	$ 45,000		$ 46,402	1,402 U
Total Manufacturing Costs	$197,250		$207,900	$10,650
Unit Costs	$9.39		$9.90	$0.51 U

EXPLAINING PRODUCTION-VOLUME DIFFERENCES

The data which we prepared in Illustration 9-3 using the flexible budget does not give us any insights into why 21,000 units were produced rather than the 20,000 originally scheduled. We would have to look for the cause of this change in plans somewhere else. What Illustration 9-3 tells us is whether we produced the units which we actually made in keeping with our expectations as expressed in the budget and in our standard unit cost. In contrast, when we originally compared budget data for 20,000 units with actual cost figures for 21,000 units, we were unable to determine whether our productive efforts had been efficient.

Differences between the budgeted production volume and actual production volume are often caused by changes in the sale forecast made during the budget period. For example, Handicrafts, Limited, as we shall see in the next chapter, originally forecast sales of 17,000 baskets. Demand exceeded this expectation and triggered an increase in production. By the same token, if, when a periodic reading of budget and actual results is made, sales are less than budgeted, this may cause a cutback in production.

There are numerous other reasons why the budgeted production volume and the actual production volume may differ. Other common reasons are employee strikes, failure of productive equipment, and lack of raw materials.

In summary, using a flexible budget does not mean that we should ignore differences in actual levels of activity and what our expectations were when the original budget was set. We should, if these differences are significant, attempt to find the cause and determine whether corrective action is required.

VARIANCE ANALYSIS FOR DIRECT MATERIALS AND DIRECT LABOR

Now that we have generated a series of meaningful variances, we can attempt to find the cause of each one that is deemed significant because of its size or because it indicates potential problems. However, we can refine our variance analysis procedures for direct materials and direct labor by further classifying these variances between that part which is caused by usage factors and that part which is caused by price factors. Before doing this, since the type of analysis with respect to direct materials and direct labor is the same whether we are dealing with a company which used a budgetary system but not a standard cost system or with a company which used both a standard cost system and a budgetary system, let's first discuss standard costs.

THE PURPOSE OF STANDARD COST SYSTEMS

Standard cost accounting systems are used in an effort to control costs and make operations more efficient. The concept behind a standard cost system is that what represents an efficient amount of inputs, both in usage and price terms, for various kinds of activities can be specified. With a standard cost system, differences between standard costs and actual costs are generated by the accounting system, thus highlighting for the responsible manager areas which may need attention.

To illustrate, the amount of raw material needed to produce a unit of product can be determined and the cost of that raw material estimated. This becomes the standard material input. If actual raw material usage or costs differ from the standard, that difference will show up as a variance in a report to the responsible manager. When the size of the variance is significant, an investigation will be triggered to determine if corrective action is required.

THE RELATIONSHIP OF STANDARD COSTS AND BUDGETS

This topic of standard costs could have been included in our discussion of cost accumulation systems, because a standard cost system is a way of attaching dollar amounts to outputs. However, it is treated here instead because it is a control tool and is closely related to the concepts of and procedures used in budget preparation.

Standard costs and budgetary systems are alike in a number of ways, which include:

1. Expected costs of output—products or services—are specified in advance based on the amount of input and the price of those inputs
2. Actual results are compared with expected results at periodic intervals, and significant variances are investigated to determine if corrective actions are needed.
3. Planning, coordinating, motivating, and controlling are facilitated.
4. Problems arise related to the quantification of expectations and the use of these quantifications as a control device.

Differences Between a Budgetary System and a Standard Cost System

In at least two ways a true standard cost system differs from a budgetary system:

1. With a standard cost system, standard costs are actually incorporated into the company's accounts.
2. Standard cost systems do not encompass an organization's entire operations.

Each of these differences is discussed below.

Incorporating standards into the accounts. Budget amounts are outside of the company's accounts. The budget is prepared and actual costs are compared with the budget, but neither the budgeted amounts nor the results of this comparison, variances, are debited and credited into the company's accounts. In contrast, with a standard cost system, the company's ledger accounts are debited and credited for standard amounts. For example, if a standard cost system is in use, the work-in-process inventory account is charged with the standard direct labor input at the standard rate rather than with actual labor costs. In addition, units transferred into finished goods are transferred at standard costs, not actual costs.

Since actual costs are also being captured by the accounting system, the differences between actual and standard will appear in the accounts as a series of variances. Returning to the example of direct labor, wages payable will reflect actual earnings, while work-in-progress is charged with standard amounts for direct labor. The balancing difference is recorded in variance accounts—accounts which are part of the entity's general ledger.

Limited use of standard costs. A budgetary system tends to be comprehensive. When a company prepares a budget, it generally does so for the entire organization. Standard costs are limited in their application to costs and do not include revenues. In other words, a company may have a standard cost system but will not enter in the records a revenue figure based on what they expected to sell at expected selling prices. Standard cost systems, as the name implies, are limited to controlling costs.

Even with costs, while we may say that a company has a standard cost system, in reality this means that they have a standard cost system for some of their operations, most commonly manufacturing operations. In contrast, with a budgetary system costs have generally been estimated for the entity's total operations. The reason for the more limited use of standard costs as opposed to budgetary costs is explained next.

THE USE OF STANDARD COSTS

Standard costs can be used for an operation where realistic quantifications of expected inputs can be made in terms of both amounts and prices. It is easiest, perhaps, to see this in a manufacturing application. Consider a company which is making metal tables suitable for office use. There are two operations—the stamping out of the pieces and the assembly. This company could use a standard cost system for the manufacturing cost of its product because it could determine (a) how much metal is required for each table and at what cost, and (b) how much time is required for each operation and the rate at which persons who are performing those operations should be working. In addition, if it uses a predetermined overhead rate, the company has already specified an overhead rate for each unit of output.

While standard cost systems are used most often by companies which manufacture products as a way of controlling manufacturing costs, this is just one type of possible application. In an office setting where repetitive operations are being done, such as typing forms, time and cost inputs can be specified and a standard cost system adapted. The key to the application of a standard cost system is repetitive operations. Standard cost systems are not suitable in situations where a variety of different kinds of tasks are being done. Here, budgetary control rather than standard cost control is generally used.

SETTING STANDARDS

Setting Standards for Direct Material and Direct Labor Usage

Standards, in both usage and dollar terms, are generally defined on the basis of requirements per unit of output. That is, the organization develops a standard cost for a unit of production.

Direct materials usage. The standard amount of material for a unit of output is usually set by logic, observation, measurement, or engineering estimate. One of the major problems in standard-setting for materials is raw material waste and spoilage. How much loss of materials is consistent with efficient operations? There is no easy answer, and the amount incorporated into the standard is a combination of historical experience and judgment.

Occasionally firms set a standard, called an *ideal standard*, which requires calculation of costs assuming operations at maximum efficiency— i.e., no inefficiency. With an ideal standard, any variation from perfect use of productive inputs is reflected as a variance. Most firms do not use an ideal standard but rather a *normal standard*, which represents costs consistent with the amount of efficiency which can generally be expected. The use of a normal standard tends to be more useful. The reason is that, in interpretation of variances from an ideal standard, consideration must be given to what part of the total variance may be preventable. With a normal standard system the variance calculated needs no additional analysis to determine what part may be preventable. An ideal standard system does emphasize the costs of *all* inefficiency.

Direct labor usage. A well-designed direct labor usage standard requires that the various operations required in the production of an item be isolated and the time required to complete each be determined. This is work which is done by time-and-motion-study experts. Because workers resent being studied as a basis for setting standards, and because some union contracts prevent such a study, direct labor usage standards frequently evolve based on historical experience. These standards are changed only when operations are materially changed by production requirements or technological innovation.

Setting Standards for Direct Material and Direct Labor Costs

Besides usage, the other element of a standard cost system is cost or price. For direct material costs, once the types of materials have been specified, vendors' price lists or price quotations are obtained. The process for attaching standard costs to standard units is the same as coming up with costs for the budgetary process.

Wage rates for standard cost purposes are obtained from current contracts or agreements with workers or from their anticipated level if these are being renegotiated for the period for which the standard is being developed. Because workers who are doing the same thing may be earning different amounts, owing to seniority or other factors, the standard wage rate is usually an average rate for persons performing a particular operation.

UPDATING STANDARDS

A standard is useful as a control tool only so long as it is relevant. Out-of-date standards produce variances which have no meaning. Standards should be reviewed annually and revised consistent with changed conditions. Material usage standards and labor usage standards may remain static for periods of time. However, both material and labor cost standards tend to change from period to period or even within a period.

For either a budget representation or a standard cost, the question arises as to what should be done if circumstances change during the period so that the standard or budget representation is no longer appropriate. Should the budget or standard be changed immediately, or should the original representation for the period continue to be used? It is at management's discretion to decide which strategy is most appropriate. The tendency seems to be to continue to use the old budget or standard cost and interpret variances in light of the difference between it and what it would be if it were revised immediately.

ILLUSTRATION FROM PRACTICE: THE USE OF MONTHLY FORECASTS AT AMERICAN CAN COMPANY

American Can Company's operations have been described in a previous chapter. This company has devised an interesting response to the question of whether or not a budget figure should be revised during the period as conditions change.

American Can does not change its budget figures for changed conditions. However, responsible managers must prepare and submit with their actual results for the past month a forecast of the level of revenues and expenses for the coming month, quarter, and full year based on changed conditions. Then, actual results for that next month are compared not only with the original budget level but with the manager's forecast. The manager is held responsible for those deviations from his or her forecast.

CALCULATION OF VARIANCES—GENERAL MODEL

The procedures illustrated here can be used to calculate variances from either a standard or from budget if a company does not use a standard cost system.

Variances for direct material and direct labor costs are based on two factors: price and usage. Whether we are analyzing variances for direct materials or for direct labor, our process is the same.

The total variances between actual costs and standard or budgeted costs for material and labor and the component parts of those total variances—price and usage variances—are found as follows:

total variance = (standard usage × standard cost) − (actual usage × actual cost)

price variance = actual usage × (standard costs − actual costs)

usage variance = standard costs × (standard usage − actual usage)

Graphically these calculations of variance can be shown as follows:

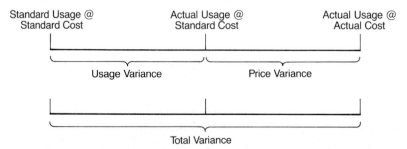

ILLUSTRATIVE EXAMPLE OF VARIANCE CALCULATIONS

To illustrate the actual calculation of price and usage variances for direct materials and direct labor, refer back to the actual and budget data for Handicrafts, Limited, in Illustration 9-3 and the standard cost card shown on p. 354.

We can see from that illustration that production costs exceeded budget and standard by $10,650 or almost $.51 per unit. We will now analyze each variance to try to obtain further information as to its cause. For the direct material and direct labor costs each variance will be broken down into a price and usage component, as explained earlier.

Direct Materials

Before we get lost in the mechanics of calculation, let's look logically at what happened with respect to direct materials. The budget called for 10 feet per unit of output or 210,000 feet (21,000 units × 10 feet). Actually 214,200 feet were used, so we can see immediately that we will have an unfavorable usage variance; i.e., 4,200 more feet were used than was called for by the standard and the budget.

With respect to price, the budget and standard called for a unit cost for each foot of bamboo of $.20. Handicrafts actually paid $.19 per foot. The cost was less than anticipated, and the result will be a favorable price variance.

The graphic calculation of the total variance, price variance, and usage variance for direct materials is as follows:

Standard Usage @ Standard Cost	Actual Usage @ Standard Cost	Actual Usage @ Actual Cost
210,000 ft @ $.20 = $42,000	214,200 ft @ $.20 = $42,840	214,200 ft @ $.19 = $40,698

Usage Variance = $840 U	Price Variance = $2,142 F

Total Variance = $1,302 F

Using the general formulas shown previously, the variance would be calculated as follows:

$$Total\ variance = \left(\begin{array}{c}\text{standard usage}\\ \times\\ \text{standard cost}\end{array}\right) - \left(\begin{array}{c}\text{actual usage}\\ \times\\ \text{actual cost}\end{array}\right)$$

$$\underline{\$1,302}\ \text{F} = (210,000\ @\ \$.20) - (214,200\ @\ \$.19)$$

$$Usage\ variance = (\text{standard costs})(\text{standard usage} - \text{actual usage})$$

$$-\underline{840}\ \text{U} = (\$.20)(210,000 - 214,200)$$

$$Price\ variance = (\text{actual usage})(\text{standard cost} - \text{actual cost})$$

$$\underline{\$2,142}\ \text{F} = (214,200)(\$.20 - \$.19)$$

Direct Labor

The direct labor usage (sometimes called an efficiency variance) and the price variance (sometimes called a rate variance) are calculated the same way as are the direct materials variances. Before we do any calculation, we can use the same logical analysis to get a feel for what the variances will look like.

In terms of usage, our budget and standard called for using 15,750 hours to produce the 21,000 baskets which Handicrafts made this period (21,000 units × .75 hours per unit = 15,750 hours). According to our actual data, 16,800 hours were used, which translates into an unfavorable usage variance.

The standard and budget called for an average rate of $6 per direct labor hour. The actual data show that, instead, costs were $6.25 per hour. The result will be an unfavorable price variance.

A graphical illustration of the direct labor variances is as follows:

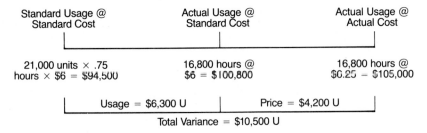

Standard Usage @ Standard Cost	Actual Usage @ Standard Cost	Actual Usage @ Actual Cost
21,000 units × .75 hours × $6 = $94,500	16,800 hours @ $6 = $100,800	16,800 hours @ $6.25 = $105,000
Usage = $6,300 U	Price = $4,200 U	

Total Variance = $10,500 U

By formula, the direct labor variance calculations would be made as follows:

$$Total\ variance = \left(\begin{array}{c} standard\ usage \\ \times \\ standard\ cost \end{array}\right) - \left(\begin{array}{c} actual\ usage \\ \times \\ actual\ cost \end{array}\right)$$

$$-\underline{\$10,500}\ U = \left(\begin{array}{c} 21.000\ units \times .75 \\ hours\ @\ \$6\ per\ hour \end{array}\right) - (16,800\ @\ \$6.25)$$

$$Usage\ variance = (standard\ cost)(standard\ usage - actual\ usage)$$

$$-\underline{\$6,300}\ U = (\$6)(15,750\ hours - 16,800\ hours)$$

$$Price\ variance = (actual\ usage)(standard\ cost - actual\ cost)$$

$$-\underline{\$4,200}\ U = (16,800)(\$6 - \$6.25)$$

INTERPRETING DIRECT MATERIAL AND DIRECT LABOR VARIANCES

The only reason to go a step beyond a comparison of actual and budget (or standard) and calculate, in addition to the total variance, price and usage variances is to enhance control. Control can be enhanced by being able to isolate probable causes of the variance and by being able to determine the person who exercises the greatest amount of control over the variance.

Direct Materials

Look at the total direct materials variance—a $1,302 favorable variance. Without a further refinement of this variance into its price and usage components, it could appear that no corrective actions are necessary. Possibly, however, certain actions on the part of the manager could reduce direct material costs even further.

The fact that the total direct materials variance is favorable masks the fact that more raw materials were used than should have been. When we compute the usage variance, the above-normal usage is apparent and the cost of that usage. Although in our example the usage variance is small ($840), a much larger usage variance could have been offset by a favorable price variance.

Knowing that usage was unfavorable, what reasons can we find? The following list is not exhaustive but illustrates some avenues which the responsible manager could explore.

1. Raw materials are being spoiled because of poorly trained workers or because of machines which are operating poorly or are set improperly.
2. Raw materials are being wasted because of employee carelessness.
3. Raw materials are being taken from the premises by workers.
4. The quality of the raw materials is such that the usage standards cannot be met.
5. The estimate of raw materials usage represented by the budget and standard was improperly set.

All of these reasons are subject to corrective action. For example, if pilferage by workers appears to be the problem, inspections can be made as workers leave the premises. For any corrective action, however, the cost must be weighed against the benefits.

Not only can the breakdown of a total direct material or direct labor variance into its component parts make isolating the cause easier, but it also gives the manager who is using variances as a way of evaluating performance more insight as to where the locus of control is. If the production vice-president were reviewing the direct materials variance and saw the $1,302 favorable amount, he or she would not know by whom this variance was generated because it might be related to the work of two different people. The usage portion is related to whoever supervises the production effort. However, the price component is associated with the work of the person purchasing raw materials.

To illustrate more clearly this idea of the locus of control, assume that the apparent cause of the unfavorage usage variance was the poor quality of the raw materials. This can be controlled, but not by the person who oversees production. Instead, it is part of the data which will be used in evaluating the performance of the person responsible for raw materials purchases. Here we see a case where price and usage variances may be related. The reason for the lower-than-standard acquisition cost for raw materials may be the purchase of raw materials of a lower quality. We then confront the question whether this lower purchase price is a true saving for us and consistent with the quality standards of our product.

Other reasons that might cause direct material price variances include:

1. Purchases are being made in lot quantities different from those envisioned when the budget was prepared.
2. New vendors are being used.
3. More favorable terms have been obtained through making a longer-term commitment to the supplier.
4. Supply and demand factors may have changed prices.
5. The standard or budgeted price may have been improperly set.
6. The inflation (deflation) rate may be different from that anticipated when the budget was prepared.

Direct Labor

The direct labor variance was the most significant variance of the period, $10,500 unfavorable. If we did not look at the usage and price parts of this variance, we would be less likely to know what types of corrective actions, if any, are possible.

Our analysis reveals that both the usage and the price variance were unfavorable. The usage variance, which was responsible for $6,300 of the amount by which actual costs exceeded budget and standard, could be caused by one of the following factors:

1. The quality of the raw materials required a greater input of worker time.
2. Productive equipment was not operating efficiently or was broken down during the period.
3. Workers are poorly trained.
4. Workers are not motivated to work efficiently.
5. Because of production bottlenecks, units of product were not available, thus causing idle time.
6. The standard time input may not have been properly measured.

The cause of the unfavorable direct labor price variance could be:

1. The average hourly wage exceeded the budgeted and standard rate because more highly paid workers were used than was anticipated.

2. Contracts or agreements with workers were negotiated at higher than anticipated levels.

3. Workers are not being assigned to the production effort consistent with the skills required; for example, low-skill labor is being performed by higher-skilled workers who command a higher hourly rate.

4. The average hourly rate may have been affected by more than the anticipated amount of overtime.

5. Cost-of-living adjustments were higher than anticipated because of increasing inflation rates.

Again, as with the direct materials, our investigation of the price and usage variances may steer us toward a corrective action and also help us determine responsibility. If, for example, workers are being hired who do not have skills consistent with the job requirements, this may be caused by (a) an improper job description, (b) the unavailability of more skilled workers, or (c) poor practices by the individuals responsible for hiring. In cases (a) and (c) immediate steps can be taken to prevent a recurrence. In the case of the unavailability of skilled workers, this may require a longer-run solution, such as instituting a training program.

JOURNAL ENTRIES—STANDARD COST SYSTEM VERSUS ACTUAL COST

Remember our earlier discussion of standard costs and budgets. A company may have a budgetary system but not use a standard cost system. On the other hand, a company may have both a standard cost system and a budgetary system. The thing which is unique with a standard cost system is that production is charged with standard costs rather than actual costs. Units are transferred into finished goods at standard costs rather than actual cost. In other words, with a standard cost system, debits and credits relative to production are made based on standard rather than actual costs.

How standards are incorporated into the accounts through journal entries and how these entries differ from those under an actual cost system will be illustrated using the data for Handicrafts, Limited. As with the calculation and explanation of variances, the illustration will cover direct materials and direct labor only. A discussion of overhead will be deferred to Chapter 10.

Transaction: During the period 214,200 feet of simulated bamboo was put into production which resulted in an output of 21,000 units. The cost of each foot was $.19. The standard input was 10 feet per unit at a cost of $.20.

Standard Cost System		Actual Cost System	
(a) Work-in-Process			
Inventory		(a) Work-in-Process	
(21,000 × 10 ft ×		Inventory	
$.20)	42,000	(214,200 ft × $.19)	40,698
Materials usage		Raw Materials	
variance	840[a]	Inventory	40,698
Raw Materials			
Inventory			
(214,200 ft ×			
$.19)	40,698		
Raw Materials			
Price Variance	2,142[b]		

[a] $.20 (210,000 ft − 214,200 ft).
[b] 214,200 ft ($.20 − $.19).

Transaction: During the period, 16,800 direct labor hours were used to make the 21,000 baskets. The average cost of each direct labor hour was $6.25. The standard and budget called for .75 hour per unit of production (21,000 × .75 = 15,750 hours) at an average cost of $6 per hour.

(b) Work-in-Process		(b) Work-in-Process	
Inventory		Inventory	
(21,000 × .75 hr × $6)	94,500	(16,800 hr × $6.25)	105,000
Direct labor usage			
variance[a]	6,300	Wages Payable	105,000
Direct labor price			
variance[b]	4,200		
Wages Payable			
(16,800 × $6.25)	105,000		

[a] $6 (15,750 hr − 16,800 hr).
[b] 16,800 hr ($6 − $6.25).

Compare the journal entries under the two systems and note the following:

1. With the actual cost system, variances are calculated outside of the general ledger accounts. With the standard cost system, the variances are produced as part of the debit and credit process.
2. With the actual cost system, the actual costs being incurred are attached to products produced. Using a standard cost system, the output is charged with costs which represent a normal level of efficiency, not actual costs. What this means is that inefficiencies as defined by the predetermined standard will not be carried over into subsequent periods as part of inventory.

The entries shown above are given in T-account form in Illustration 9-4. Looking at the entries, you can see that unfavorable variances are

ILLUSTRATION 9-4

Product Cost Flows—Standard Cost Systems versus Actual Cost Systems, Direct Materials, and Direct Labor

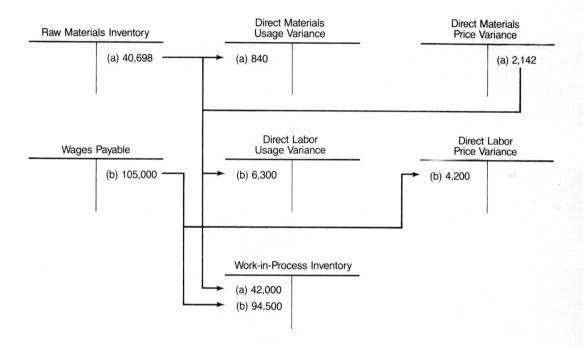

STANDARD COST SYSTEM

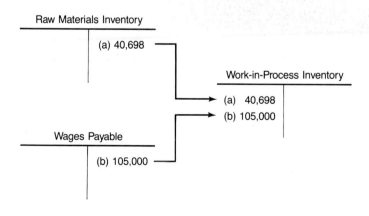

ACTUAL COST SYSTEM

debits while favorable variances are credits. This assignment of debits and credits is consistent with the fact that expenses are debits and reductions in expenses (or revenues) are credits. When a company is inefficient and has an unfavorable variance, this decreases its profit potential. If a company operates more efficiently than the standard it has set, it is enhancing its profit potential through reduced costs.

CALCULATING THE DIRECT MATERIALS PRICE VARIANCE AT TIME OF PURCHASE

We demonstrated the calculation of the raw materials price variance at the time raw materials were put into process based on the quantities put into production. From a control point of view, if the purchasing function is done by a person other than the manager who oversees production, a more meaningful price variance is calculated at the *time materials are purchased* based on the quantities actually purchased.

To illustrate, assume the following:

Standard purchase price, raw materials	$5 per pound
Actual purchase price, raw materials	$5.50 per pound
Pounds purchased during the period	100,000
Pounds put into production during the period	60,000

If the raw materials price variance is calculated at the time of purchase, it is calculated as follows:

$$\text{Price variance} = \text{Actual quantity purchased (standard price} - \text{actual price)}$$
$$= \quad 100,000 (\$5 - \$5.50) = -\$50,000 \text{ U}$$

Raw materials, with this system, are put in inventory and will be withdrawn from inventory at the standard price. The entry to record purchases for the period is:

Raw materials inventory (100,000 × $5)	$500,000	
Price variance (100,000 × $.50)	50,000	
Accounts payable (100,000 × $5.50)		$550,000

If the raw materials price variance is calculated at the time raw materials are put into production, the initial charge to inventory is at actual cost and the price variance would be recorded when the units are put into process through the following entry:

Work-in-process (60,000 × $5)	$300,000	
Price variance (60,000 × $.50)	30,000	
Raw materials inventory (60,000 × $5.50)		$330,000

The shortcoming with the latter approach is that the unfavorable variance shown, $30,000, does not reflect the total deviation from standard for the period for which the manager in charge of purchasing should be held responsible. The purchasing price variance associated with that manager's performance for the period is $50,000 unfavorable.

DISPOSAL OF VARIANCES

With a standard cost system, direct material and direct labor variances from standards are recorded in the accounts. The most commonly used method of disposing of these variances is to treat them as adjustments to cost of goods sold, just as was done with over- or underapplied overhead. An alternative would be to allocate them between work-in-process, finished goods inventory, and cost of goods sold on a pro rata basis.

ILLUSTRATION FROM PRACTICE:
A REPORT COMPARING ACTUAL DIRECT LABOR COSTS
WITH STANDARD DIRECT LABOR COSTS
FOR AMERICAN THREAD

The operations of American Thread were described in a previous chapter. Illustration 9-5 shows the type of performance report generated for one of the mills maintained by the company. This report relates to direct labor (termed productive labor in the report) and compares actual costs and standard costs. Although standard costs are not shown in the report itself, the variance is based on a comparison of actual and standard costs.

An additional column shows actual costs as a percent of standard. If anything in this column is at 100%, this means there was no variance between actual and standard. Amounts exceeding 100% indicate unfavorable variances and amounts less than 100% favorable variance.

The report shows a total productive labor variance $6,666 unfavorable and then indicates what part of that is due to rate factors. The remainder is related to efficiency. Comparisons between actual and standard are made for the month covered by the report and on a year-to-date basis.

ILLUSTRATION 9-5
Illustration from Practice: A Report for American Thread Comparing Actual and Standard Labor Costs

MILL OPERATING STATEMENT

Location _____Sylvan_____   Operation _____Cotton Mfg._____

Month _____June_____   Y T D 6 months

COST ELEMENT	Actual	Variance (Unf)	% Act. to Std.	Actual	Variance (Unf)	% Act to Std.
Productive Labor						
Open& Picking						
Card operator	2 548	8	100	13 549	(1 446)	112
#1 Draw Operator	2 308	(8)	100	11 438	(124)	101
Lapper Operator	2 113	(25)	101	10 841	(657)	106
Comber Operator	4 164	(64)	102	20 676	(721)	104
Finish Draw Operator	2 236	(125)	106	11 296	(1 096)	111
Roving Operator	8 222	(1 766)	127	41 566	(9 268)	129
Spinning Operator	23 238	(2 293)	111	116 157	(10 706)	110
Spinning Doffer	12 089	(635)	105	64 698	(4 674)	108
Spooler Operator	26 345	53	100	132 124	197	100
Doubler Operator	8 563	(356)	104	42 332	(1 119)	103
Twister Operator	15 181	1 250	92	80 176	213	100
Twister Doffer	8 407	(1 865)	129	39 682	(9 335)	131
Winder Operator	12 692	(840)	107	61 370	(3 631)	106
Subtotal Productive Labor	128 906	(8 000)	105	645 905	(42 367)	107
Wage Rate Variance		9 778			48 280	
Total Productive Labor	128 906	3 112	98	645 905	5 913	99

---

chapter highlights

If a static budget—a budget based on just one level of activity—is prepared, variance calculations are difficult to interpret when actual activity differs from the budget level. With a flexible budget, a budget is prepared for the different levels of activity at which a company may operate.

If a flexible budget is used, the budget level consistent with actual activity is used for comparative purposes. Thus, variances indicate whether the production (or other activity) which took place was done efficiently.

In addition to having a budgetary system for control purposes, some companies also use standard cost systems. If the standards are set at the normal level of efficiency, standard costs are consistent with costs as shown in the budget. The difference between a standard cost system and a budgetary system used without standard costs is that with a standard cost system, expectations in the form of standards are actually debited and credited into the accounts. That is, work-in-process is charged with standard costs inputs rather than actual costs inputs. In addition, units of product are transferred into finished goods at standard rather than actual costs.

With either a budgetary system or a standard cost system, variances for actual direct material and actual direct labor costs can be further analyzed. This is done by breaking the total variance down into a price variance—the amount of the total variance caused by price (cost) factors, and a usage variance—the amount of the total variance caused by the amount of direct materials or direct labor used.

questions

1. When a budget is based on one activity level and actual performance is at another level, what problem arises in comparing the two results?
2. What part does the concept of a relevant range play in a budgetary system?
3. What is meant by a flexible budget?
4. What are the advantages of a flexible budget relative to a static budget?
5. Some people say that fixed costs have no relevance to a flexible budget. Why do they make this statement?
6. Differences between budgeted production *volume* and actual production *volume* are not explained by using a flexible budgeting system. Why not?
7. Contrast a standard cost system with a budgetary system. How are they alike and in what ways do they differ?
8. Differentiate between "normal" and "ideal" standards. Which is used most commonly?
9. Describe how a direct labor standard might be determined.
10. What purpose is served by breaking direct material and direct labor variances into their component parts—price and usage? Give an example.
11. What different methods can be used to dispose of direct material and direct labor variances?
12. Contrast the costs which attach to units as they flow through production when a standard cost system is used with those which attach to units when a standard cost system is not in use.

13. The total direct labor variance for a particular period was not of a significant size. Should the variance still be broken down into usage and rate variances? Why or why not?

14. An account entitled Direct Labor Efficiency had a debit balance at the end of the accounting period. What does this mean?

15. What factors should a manager consider in deciding whether a variance is significant and warrants further investigation?

16. When can standard cost systems be used effectively?

17. The factory manager stated that he should not be held responsible for the direct material variance because he is not responsible for the purchase of these materials and hence cannot control their costs or their quality. Do you agree? Why or why not?

18. Give two examples, not related to manufacturing, in which standard cost systems might be effectively used.

19. How often should a standard which is used with a standard cost system be revised?

20. The purchasing agent for a company stated: "There is no way my performance can be effectively judged with the standard purchase prices which were set for this period. Inflation has made those standards meaningless. Since top management decided not to revise the standards during the year, the purchase-price variances are not my responsibility." Do you agree? Why or why not?

exercises

9—1. The Walcott Machinery Company prepared the following budget for one of its product lines:

Anticipated production in units	300,000
Direct material cost	$ 600,000
Direct labor costs, 1½ hours per unit	2,700,000
Variable manufacturing overhead:	
Supplies and indirect materials	150,000
Utilities and other	90,000
Fixed manufacturing overhead:	
Indirect labor	180,000
Depreciation	80,000
Other	100,000
Total budgeted production costs	$3,900,000
Budgeted production cost per unit	$13.00

REQUIRED: 1. Assuming that the company's normal range of production is from 280,000 units to 320,000 units, prepare a flexible budget for these two additional levels of production.

2. Calculate variable costs per unit at the 280,000-unit, 300,000-unit, and 320,000-unit levels and explain your results.
3. Calculate fixed costs per unit at each of the three production levels and explain your results.

9—2. Last year Huffmire Industries incurred the following unit costs when its production volume was 800,000 units:

Direct materials	$1.50
Direct labor	2.00
Variable manufacturing overhead:	
Indirect materials	.30
Supplies	.10
Utilities and other	.20
Fixed manufacturing overhead:	
Indirect labor	.80
Depreciation	.50
Other	.10
Actual production cost per unit	$5.50

For the coming budget period, Huffmire Industries anticipates that both direct and indirect material costs will increase 10% per unit. Depreciation will increase by $10,000 per year because of the addition of new equipment. Although direct labor costs will rise per hour, because of more efficient equipment, less direct labor will be used, thus keeping these costs at the past year's level. No other cost changes are estimated for the budget period.

REQUIRED: Prepare a flexible budget for the coming year for Huffmire based on production levels of 750,000 units, 800,000 units, and 850,000 units. Show as part of your flexible budget the fixed cost for each level of production.

9—3. The Steel Blade Knife Company's records show the following data for the production of one of its product lines for the quarter just ended:

	STANDARD INPUT PER UNIT	ACTUAL INPUT FOR 200,000 KNIVES
Direct materials:	1 blade @ $1	203,000 blades @ $213,150
	2 wood handle pieces @ $.30 each	404,000 wood handle pieces @ $109,080
Direct labor:	30 minutes per unit @ $6 per hour	98,000 hours @ $6.05 per hour

REQUIRED: Calculate the total variance between standard costs and actual costs, the price variance, and the usage variance for each of the direct materials inputs and for direct labor. Label each variance either favorable or unfavorable.

9—4. Refer to the information in Exercise 9—3.

REQUIRED: Prepare the journal entries which The Steel Blade Knife Company would make to record its actual results, assuming it uses a standard cost system for direct materials and direct labor. The company puts raw materials into inventory at actual costs.

9—5. The Natural Way Chemical produces a product for which the following standard inputs for direct materials and direct labor have been developed:

Standard Inputs per Bottle Produced

Direct materials:	1 pound of chemicals @ $1.50 per pound
Direct labor:	2 hours @ $5.50 per hour

During the current period Natural Way produced 50,000 bottles of its product and the following variances between actual and standard were recorded:

Raw materials price variance:	$ 1,560 favorable
Raw materials usage variance:	$ 3,000 unfavorable
Direct labor price variance:	$10,200 unfavorable
Direct labor usage variance:	$11,000 unfavorable

Actual direct materials usage was 52,000 pounds and actual direct labor costs were $5.60 per hour.

REQUIRED: Calculate the following amounts:

1. The total cost of direct materials used.
2. The actual price of a pound of direct materials used.
3. The total actual cost of direct labor used.
4. The actual number of direct labor hours used.

9—6. The incomplete flexible budget for one product of Baker Inc. is given below:

	PRODUCTION VOLUME IN UNITS		
	5,000	6,000	7,000
Variable Manufacturing Costs:			
Direct Materials	?	?	21,000
Direct Labor	25,000	?	?
Overhead	?	6,000	?
Fixed Manufacturing Costs:			
Indirect Labor	7,500	?	?
Depreciation	?	?	4,300
Utilities	?	750	?
Total Manufacturing Costs:	?	?	?

REQUIRED: Supply the missing information in the flexible budget.

9—7. The Scott Stapler Manufacturing Company produces industrial staples which require a high-grade steel in their manufacture. During the past month,

Scott manufactured 5,500 lots of staples, using 6,755 lb of steel in the process. The steel cost them $27,020. The company's standards for one lot of staples are 1.10 lb of steel per lot at a cost of $4.15 per lb.

REQUIRED: 1. What direct materials cost should have been incurred by Scott during the past month? What is the total direct materials variance?

2. Break the total direct materials variance into usage and price variances, indicating whether they are favorable or unfavorable.

9—8.   The Word Processing Division of Central Bank and Trust uses standard costs to control labor time and costs. The standard time for processing a will is 30 minutes and the average standard rate related to wills is $6.50 per hour. During the past week, the division processed 78 wills and required 43.5 hours to complete them, including 5 hours of overtime at $10 per hour. Nonovertime hours costs $6.50 per hour.

REQUIRED: 1. Compute the labor usage and price variances that resulted from the division's processing of wills last week.

2. Prepare journal entries to record direct labor activities for the week.

9—9.   Blaine Products, Inc., produces industrial vacuum cleaning machinery and employs a standard cost system. The standard time to produce a cleaning machine is 3.6 hours. Owing to a fire, the records showing total production hours for the past month were destroyed. It is known, however, that 65 machines were completed during the period and the total labor variance was $21 favorable. Standard labor cost is $10.75 per hour, and the production foreman remembers that there was a $92 unfavorable labor rate variance.

REQUIRED: 1. Compute the actual number of hours spent on production during the last month and any labor usage variance.

2. Compute the actual labor cost per hour.

3. Recreate the missing journal entries to record the labor activities during the past month.

9—10.   The Apco Chemical Company has developed a new product to be marketed for use in swimming pools. The raw material components needed to produce 1 gallon of the new product include: 3 quarts of chlorine, 2.5 pounds of a cleaning detergent, and 2 quarts of water. The purchase prices associated with the raw materials are:

Chlorine—$2.25 per 5-gallon container. Average shipping charges of $60 are incurred by Apco per delivery of 100 containers. Apco purchases in lot sizes of 100 containers.

Cleaning Detergent—$65 per 100-pound lot. Shipping charges are paid by the supplier, who offers a 10% discount for orders over 500 pounds. Apco plans to order 8 lots at a time.

Water—Apco has its own water supply and the cost is considered insignificant.

REQUIRED: Compute the standard raw material quantities and costs per gallon of the new product.

9—11.   The Suffolk Bicycle Company produces a racing bicycle which requires extruded aluminum in its manufacture. Standard cost data and actual cost data related to the product include:

	STANDARD PER UNIT		ACTUAL PER UNIT	
	Direct Materials	Direct Labor	Direct Materials	Direct Labor
Quantity per unit	?	2.5 hr	?	?
Price per square foot or hour	?	$10.50	?	?

The aluminum raw material is purchased by the square foot. During the last quarter, the company paid $12,132.50 in direct labor costs incurred to produce 500 bicycles. The company paid $4,805 for raw materials, all used in production during the period, representing 1,550 square feet of aluminum. In addition, the following variances were incurred:

Total materials variance	$80.00	U
Material price variance	$77.50	F
Labor usage variance	$1,050	F

REQUIRED: **1.** Determine the materials usage variance.
2. Determine the labor price variance.
3. Compute the missing amounts for standard and actual cost data.

9—12.   The Rustic Manufacturing Company makes picnic tables which appear to have been carved from a tree. Standard and actual costs for the period during which 10,000 tables were made are as follows:

Standard direct materials:	10 square feet of lumber at $2.30 per foot
Standard direct labor:	3 hours per table at $5.50 per hour
Standard overhead:	$250,000
Actual direct materials:	98,000 feet having an actual cost of $220,500
Actual direct labor:	33,000 hours costing $183,150
Actual overhead:	$250,000

Purchases of lumber totaled 100,000 feet at $225,000 and were recorded at actual costs. The 10,000 tables were all transferred to finished goods inventory.

REQUIRED: **1.** Prepare the general journal entries to record the information given, assuming the company uses an actual cost system.
2. Prepare the general journal entries to record the information given, assuming the company uses a standard cost system.
3. Calculate the cost of a picnic table put into finished goods inventory if the company uses:

  a. An actual cost system.
  b. A standard cost system.

9—13. Walker Manufacturing makes leather soccer balls. A comparison of actual and budget data for the past month is given below. Unfavorable variances are indicated by parentheses.

	BUDGET	ACTUAL	VARIANCE
Balls produced	50,000	55,000	5,000
Revenues	$1,250,000	$1,347,500	$97,500
Cost of Goods Mfg. and Sold:			
Direct Materials	100,000	115,500	(15,500)
Direct Labor	250,000	269,500	(19,500)
Variable Overhead	50,000	55,000	(5,000)
Fixed Overhead	200,000	206,000	(6,000)
Variable Selling Exp.	75,000	71,500	3,500
Fixed Selling Exp.	120,000	117,000	3,000
Fixed Admin. Exp.	180,000	185,000	(5,000)
Total Expenses	$ 975,000	1,019,500	(44,500)
Operating Income	$ 275,000	$ 328,000	$53,000

REQUIRED: Prepare a flexible budget which will better describe the results of operations for the period.

9—14. Contented Children Manufacturing makes tree swings for which the following standard direct material and direct labor costs have been developed:

Standard Cost per Swing

Direct materials:	
12 feet of rope at $.10 per foot	$1.20
Plastic seat, 1 per swing @ $1	1.00
Direct labor:	
½ hour per swing at $6 per hour	3.00
Standard direct material and labor costs per swing	$5.20

During the month, Contented Children made 20,000 swings and incurred the following costs:

260,000 feet of rope used costing $31,200.
20,300 plastic seats used costing $19,285.
9,800 hours of direct labor costing $59,780.

REQUIRED:
1. What were the actual direct material and direct labor costs per swing for the period? (Round to the nearest cent.)
2. Assuming Contented Children uses a standard cost system and standard overhead cost per swing amounted to $4, give the journal entry to record the transfer of swings to Finished Goods Inventory during the period.
3. For each type of direct material and for direct labor calculate the following variances:
   a. Total.
   b. Price.
   c. Usage.

9—15. The following data relate to the operations of the Big-Pop Popcorn producing company for a production volume of 100,000 cans of popcorn.

	ACTUAL COST OF JAR OF POPCORN	STANDARD COSTS OF JAR OF POPCORN
Popcorn	$.10	$.09
Can	.035	.03
Direct Labor	.16	.15
Overhead	.075	.08
Total	$.37	$.35

During the month, of the 100,000 cans of popcorn produced, 90,000 were sold for $1 per can. Selling and administrative costs amounted to $43,000.

REQUIRED:

1. Assuming the use of a standard cost system, give the entry to record the sale of the 90,000 cans of popcorn. The company uses a perpetual inventory system and updates inventory and records Cost of Goods Sold at the time of sale.
2. Assuming the use of a standard cost system and that variances are treated as adjustments to Cost of Goods Sold, calculate the gross margin for the company for the month.
3. Assuming the use of a standard cost system, what will be the carrying value of the 10,000 cans of popcorn in ending inventory?
4. Assuming the use of an actual cost system, give the entry to record the sale of the popcorn. The company uses a perpetual inventory system.
5. Assuming the use of an actual cost system, calculate the gross margin for the company for the year.
6. Assuming the use of an actual cost system, calculate the carrying value of the ending finished goods inventory.
7. Explain any differences you got between the two gross margin figures and the two ending inventory valuations which you have calculated.

problems

9—16. *Preparation of a flexible budget.* Soft Soap Manufacturing reported the following cost of production for the accounting period just ended:

Containers of soap produced	1,000,000
Direct material costs	$200,000
Direct labor	150,000
Variable manufacturing overhead:	
Indirect materials	50,000
Supplies	20,000
Utilities and other	30,000
Fixed manufacturing overhead:	
Indirect labor	80,000
Depreciation	30,000
Insurance and property taxes	10,000
Other	12,000
Cost of goods manufactured	$ 582,000

For the coming budget period, Soft Soap has made the following projections:

1. The cost of *all* materials will increase by 10%.
2. Direct labor costs will increase by 8%.
3. Utility and "other" variable costs will increase by 15%.
4. Indirect labor costs will be reduced by $5,000.
5. Insurance and property taxes will increase by 10%.
6. All other costs will remain at the same level as for the period presented.

REQUIRED:
1. Prepare a flexible production budget for volumes of 950,000 units, 1,000,000 units, and 1,050,000 units. Include fixed costs in your budget presentation. Carry unit cost to four decimal places.
2. Calculate the variable manufacturing cost per unit, the fixed manufacturing cost per unit, and total cost per unit at each of the three levels of production. Explain differences in these costs for the different production levels. Use four decimal places.

9—17. *Straightforward variance problem.* Reliable Manufacturing Company, which uses a standard cost system, makes molded plastic chairs with metal bases. Data for the accounting period relevant to the manufacture of this product line are as follows:

Standard Direct Material and Direct Labor Inputs per Chair

Direct materials: 1 molded plastic piece @ $6	$ 6.00
1 metal base @ $8	8.00
Direct labor: ½ hour per chair @ $5.80 per hour	2.90
Standard direct material and direct labor cost per chair	$16.90

Actual inputs for the period to manufacture 300,000 chairs

Direct materials: 303,000 molded plastic pieces	$1,787,700
301,200 metal bases	2,454,780
Direct labor: 125,000 hours	750,000
Direct material and labor costs for the period	$4,992,480
Actual material and labor cost per chair	$16.6416

REQUIRED:
1. Calculate the actual cost per unit for plastic used in the chairs.
2. Calculate the actual cost per unit of input for metal bases used in the chairs.
3. Calculate the actual direct labor cost per unit of output.
4. Calculate the total variance, price variance, and usage variance for each of the two direct material components and for direct labor.
5. Assume that the company had no beginning finished goods inventory. What will be the carrying value of its ending inventory, assuming 280,000 chairs were sold, variances are treated as adjustments to cost of goods sold, and standard overhead cost per chair was $7?

9—18. *Difference between accounting for direct material and direct labor inputs with a standard cost system and an actual cost system.* Two companies engaged in identical transactions during the accounting period. The first company, General Products, Inc., has a budgetary system but does not use a standard cost system to control direct material and direct labor costs. The other company, American Products Company, has a budgetary system and a standard cost system for direct material and direct labor inputs. Data for the two companies are as follows:

Budget (General Products) and Standard (American Products) Inputs per Unit Produced

Direct materials:	2 units @ $5 per unit
Direct labor:	3 hours @ $7 per hour

Actual inputs for each company which produced 100,000 units

Direct materials:	205,000 units @	$1,014,750
Direct labor:	298,000 hours @	$2,094,940

Additional data:

1. Neither company had any variance between budgeted or standard and actual overhead. Each charged $1,800,000 of overhead to work-in-process.
2. Neither company had a beginning work-in-process inventory. All 100,000 units started during the period were completed and transferred to finished goods.
3. Of the 100,000 units transferred to finished goods, 70,000 were sold at $100 per unit.

REQUIRED:

1. Prepare general journal entries for the two companies for the period to record the following (round all amounts to the nearest cent):
   a. The inputs into work-in-process.
   b. The transfer of units to finished goods.
   c. The sale of the completed units, assuming the company uses a perpetual inventory system.
   d. The closing of any variance accounts to cost of goods sold.
2. Calculate finished goods inventory (assuming the companies had no beginning finished goods inventory) for the two companies and explain any differences in your figures.
3. Calculate the gross margin for the companies, assuming that American Products adjusts cost of goods sold for any standard cost variances. If the gross margins differ, explain why.

9—19. *Comprehensive variance analysis.* The standard cost card for a bookcase produced by the Anderson Office Furniture Company, which uses a flexible budgeting system, follows:

STANDARD COSTS—BOOKCASE #200

Direct materials: 30 feet of white pine @ $.80 per foot
Direct labor: 1½ hours per bookcase @ $7.50 per hour
Manufacturing overhead (applied on the basis of direct labor hours):
  Variable overhead: $1,005 for budget period*
                            or $1.34 per direct labor hour
  Fixed overhead: $2,500 for budget period*

* The budget for the quarter reflects expected production of 500 bookcases.

Additional data from the past quarter:

Actual production	560
Materials purchased and used	18,800 ft
Price of white pine	$.90 ft
Direct labor cost incurred	$6,513
Direct labor rate	$7.80
Variable overhead cost incurred	$1,345
Fixed overhead incurred[a]	$2,450

[a] Fixed overhead is not expected to change between output levels from 400–700 units.

REQUIRED:
1. Compute the standard cost per bookcase.
2. Compute direct materials total variance, usage and price variances.
3. Compute direct labor total variance, usage and price variances.
4. Based on this information, what are possible causes for the variances?

9—20. *Standard costs—equivalent units.*   Davis Corporation manufactures a single product under a process costing system. Davis uses standard costs to improve internal control, basing these on equivalent units of production. Standard costs are:

Raw materials	2 gal @ $5 per gal per unit
Direct labor	3 hr @ $6 per hr per unit
Factory overhead	1 hr @ $2 per hr per unit

Results of the last quarter revealed:

1. Beginning work-in-process inventory consisted of 1,500 units, 100% complete for raw materials and 50% complete for direct labor.
2. An additional 8,000 units were started during the quarter.
3. Ending work-in-process inventory consisted of 1,000 units, 100% complete for raw materials and 50% complete for direct labor.

4. Actual costs (including costs in beginning work-in-process inventory) included $96,000 for 20,000 gallons of raw materials used and $183,000 for 30,000 hours of direct labor worked.

REQUIRED: 1. Compute actual costs per equivalent unit of production for materials and labor. (Round to the nearest penny.)
2. Compute standard costs per equivalent unit of production.
3. Determine applicable variances.

9—21.   *Standard costs—flexible budgets.*   The Filer Refrigeration Products Company uses a standard cost system and flexible budgets. During February, Filer completed 12,000 units of a particular product and incurred direct labor costs of $55,719. An unfavorable labor usage variance of $600 resulted. Because of the ratification of a new labor contract, the average wage rate was $.20 higher than the standard wage rate of $8. For this product, Filer purchases the unit outside and simply performs all assembly and finishing work. Direct material units purchased and used during the month cost $276,000. Raw material prices declined unexpectedly from a budgeted $25 per unit to $23 per unit. There were no beginning raw materials or finished goods inventories. One unit of direct material is required for each unit of output.

REQUIRED: 1. Determine the following amounts:
    a. Actual direct labor hours for February.
    b. Direct labor price variance.
    c. Standard direct labor hours.
    d. Materials usage variance.
    e. Materials price variance.
2. Prepare a flexible budget for variable material and direct labor costs at 10,000, 12,000, and 14,000 units of production.

9—22.   *Variance calculations; two ways to calculate material price variance.*   (CMA adapted) Eastern Company manufactures special electrical equipment and parts. Eastern employs a standard cost accounting system with separate standards established for each product. A special transformer is manufactured in the Transformer Department. Production volume is measured by direct labor hours in this department, and a flexible budget system is used to plan and control department overhead. Standard costs for the special transformer are determined annually in September for the coming year. The standard cost of a transformer was computed at $67 as shown below.

Direct materials:			
Iron	5 sheets	@ $2	$10
Copper	3 spools	@ $3	9
Direct labor	4 hours	@ $7	28
Variable overhead	4 hours	@ $3	12
Fixed overhead	4 hours	@ $2	8
Total			$67

Variable overhead costs are expected to vary with the number of direct labor hours actually used.

During January of the year for which the standards were developed, 800 transformers were produced. This was below expectations because a work stoppage occurred during contract negotiations with the labor force. Once the contract was settled, the department scheduled overtime in an attempt to catch up to expected production levels.

The following costs were incurred in January for direct materials:

DIRECT MATERIAL	DIRECT MATERIALS PURCHASED	MATERIALS USED
Iron	5,000 sheets @ $2.00/sheet	3,900 sheets
Copper	2,800 spools @ $3.10/spool	2,600 spools

Other costs incurred during January were

Direct labor:	2,000 hours @ $7.00
	1,400 hours @ $7.20
Variable overhead:	$10,000
Fixed overhead:	$ 8,800

REQUIRED:

1. Determine the materials price and usage variances. Assume materials are put into inventory at standard costs.
2. Determine the labor price and efficiency variances.
3. Calculate the materials price variance, assuming materials are put into inventory at actual costs.
4. What is the advantage of putting materials into inventory at standard costs?

9—23. *Variance analysis—working backward to find inputs.* (AICPA adapted) On May 1 Bovar Company began the manufacture of a new mechanical device known as "Dandy." The company installed a standard cost system in accounting for manufacturing costs. The standard costs for a unit of "Dandy" are as follows:

Raw materials, 6 lb at $1 per lb	$ 6.00
Direct labor, 1 hour at $4 per hour	4.00
Overhead, 75% of direct labor costs	3.00
	$13.00

The following data were obtained from Bovar's records for the month of May:

	UNITS
Actual production of "Dandy"	4,000
Units sold of "Dandy"	2,500

	DEBIT	CREDIT
Sales		$50,000
Inventory (26,000 pounds)	$26,000	
Material price variance	2,600	
Material quantity variance	1,000	
Direct labor rate variance	760	
Direct labor efficiency variance		800

The amount shown above for material price variance is applicable to raw material *purchased* during May.

REQUIRED: Compute each of the following items for Bovar for the month of May. Show computations in good form.

1. Standard quantity of raw materials allowed (in pounds).
2. Actual quantity of raw materials used (in pounds).
3. Standard hours allowed.
4. Actual hours worked.
5. Actual direct labor rate.
6. Actual cost per pound of raw materials purchased.

9—24. *Variance analysis—process cost accounting.* Minerva Corporation is a manufacturing company that produces a single product. The company uses the average process costing method for both financial statement and internal management reporting. A standard costs system is used. The standards, which are based upon equivalent units of production, are as follows:

Raw material per unit	1 pound at $10 per pound
Direct labor per unit	2 hours at $4 per hour

Data for the month of April are presented below:

There were no beginning work-in-process inventories.
An additional 10,000 units were started during the month.
The ending inventory consisted of 2,000 units which were 100% complete as to raw material and 40% complete as to direct labor and factory overhead.
Costs applicable to April production are as follows:

	ACTUAL COST
Raw material purchased and used (11,000 lb)	$121,000
Direct labor (18,480 hr actually worked)	$ 75,768

REQUIRED: **1.** For each element of production for April (raw material and direct labor) compute the following:

a. Equivalent units of production.
b. Cost per equivalent unit of production at actual and at standard.

Show supporting computations in good form.

2. Prepare a schedule analyzing for April production the following variances. Indicate whether each is favorable or unfavorable.

   a. Total materials.
   b. Materials price.
   c. Materials usage.
   d. Total labor.
   e. Labor rate.
   f. Labor efficiency.

9—25. *Standard costs with job order costing.* (CMA adapted) The Justin Company has recently installed a standard cost system to simplify its factory bookkeeping and to aid in cost control. The company makes standard items for inventory, but because of the many products in its line, each is manufactured periodically under a production order. Prior to the installation of the system, job order cost sheets were maintained for each production order. Since the introduction of the standard costs system, however, they have not been kept.

The Fabricating Department is managed by a general supervisor who has overall responsibility for scheduling, performance, and cost control. The department consists of four machine/work centers. Each work center is manned by a four-person work group or team and the centers are aided by a 12-person support group. Departmental practice is to assign a job to one team and expect the team to perform most of the work necessary to complete the job, including acquisition of materials and supplies from the Stores Department and machining and assembling. This has been practical and satisfactory in the past and is readily accepted by the employees.

Information regarding production cost standards, products produced, and actual costs for the Fabricating Department in March is presented below:

Analysis of the Fabricating Department Account for March

Debits		
Materials:		
Job No. 307-11	$ 5,200	
Job No. 307-12	2,900	
Job No. 307-14	9,400	$17,500
Labor charges:		
Job No. 307-11	$ 4,000	
Job No. 307-12	2,100	
Job No. 307-14	6,200	
Indirect labor	12,200	24,500
Variable overhead costs (e.g., supplies, electricity, etc.)		18,800
Fixed overhead costs (e.g., supervisor's salary, depreciation,		
property tax, insurance, etc.)		7,000
Total charges to department for March		$67,800

Credits

Completed jobs:		
Job No. 307-11,		
2,000 units part A7A at $7.25	$14,500	
Job No. 307-12,		
1,000 units part C6D at $10.00	10,000	
Job No. 307-14,		
6,000 units part C7A at $5.00	<u>30,000</u>	$54,500
Variances transferred to the factory variance account:		
Materials[a]	$ 1,500	
Direct labor[b]	1,300	
Variable overhead	9,000	
Fixed overhead	<u>1,500</u>	<u>13,300</u>
Total credits		<u>$67,800</u>

[a] Material price variances are isolated at date of purchase and charged to the Purchasing Department.
[b] All direct labor was paid at the standard wage rate during March.

Unit Standard Costs

	PART		
	A7A	C6D	C7A
Material	$2.00	$ 3.00	$1.50
Direct labor	1.50	2.00	1.00
Overhead (per direct labor dollars):			
Variable	3.00	4.00	2.00
Fixed	<u>.75</u>	<u>1.00</u>	<u>.50</u>
	<u>$7.25</u>	<u>$10.00</u>	<u>$5.00</u>

REQUIRED: 1. Justin Company assumes that its efforts to control costs in the Fabricating Department would be aided if variances were calculated by jobs. Management intends to add this analysis next month. Calculate all the variances other than those related to overhead by job that might contribute to cost control under this assumption.

2. Do you agree with the company's plan to initiate the calculation of job variances in addition to the currently calculated departmental variances? Explain your answer.

9—26. *Labor variances.*   Larson Manufacturing Company uses a standard cost system and a flexible budget. The standard direct labor rates used in the flexible budget are established each year at the time the annual plan is formulated and held constant for the entire year. The standard direct labor rates in effect for the year and the standard hours allowed for the output for the month of April are shown below:

	STANDARD DIRECT LABOR RATE PER HOUR	STANDARD DIRECT LABOR HOURS ALLOWED FOR OUTPUT
Labor Operation 1	$8.00	500
Labor Operation 2	$7.00	500
Labor Operation 3	$5.00	500

The wage rates for each labor class increased on April 1 under the terms of a new union contract. The standard wage rates were not revised to reflect the new contract. The actual direct labor hours worked and the actual direct labor rates per hour experienced for the month of April were as follows:

	ACTUAL DIRECT LABOR RATE PER HOUR	ACTUAL DIRECT LABOR HOURS
Labor Operation 1	$8.50	550
Labor Operation 2	$7.50	650
Labor Operation 3	$5.40	375

REQUIRED:
1. Calculate the total direct labor variance for the month of April.
2. Calculate the labor usage (efficiency) and labor rate variances.
3. Discuss the advantages and disadvantages of a standard cost system in which the standard direct labor rates per hour are not changed during the year to reflect events such as a new labor contract.

9—27. (CMA adapted) Harden Company has experienced increased production costs. The primary area of concern identified by management is direct labor. The company is considering adopting a standard cost system to help control labor and other costs. Useful historical data are not available because detailed production records have not been maintained. Harden Company has retained Finch & Associates, an engineering consulting firm, to establish labor standards. After a complete study of the work process, the engineers recommended a labor standard of one unit of production every 30 minutes or 16 units per day for each worker. Finch further advised that Harden's wage rates were below the prevailing rate of $7 per hour. Harden's production vice-president thought this labor standard was too tight and the employees would be unable to attain it. From his experience with the labor force, he believed a labor standard of 40 minutes per unit or 12 units per day for each worker would be more reasonable.

The president of the Harden Company believed the standard should be set at a high level to motivate the workers, but he also recognized that the standard should be set at a level to provide adequate information for control and reasonable cost comparisons. After much discussion, the management decided to use a dual standard. The labor standard recommended by the engineering firm of one unit every 30 minutes would be employed in the plant as a motivation device, and a cost standard of 40 minutes per unit would be used in reporting. Management also concluded that the workers would not be informed of the cost standard used for reporting purposes. The production vice-president conducted several sessions prior to implementation in the plant, informing the workers of the new standard cost system and answering questions. The new standards were not related to incentive pay but were introduced at the time wages were increased to $7 per hour.

REQUIRED: 1. Discuss the impact of different types of standards on motivation and specifically discuss the effect on motivation in Harden Company's plant of adopting the labor standard recommended by the engineering firm.
2. Evaluate Harden Company's decision to employ dual standards in their standard cost system.

9—28. *Standard costs, journal entries, and income statement.*   The File 13 Company makes wastebaskets in a variety of bright colors. The company uses a standard cost system to control manufacturing costs and has developed the following standards:

Metal per wastebasket, ½ sheet at $4 per sheet	$2.00
Direct labor, ¾ hour @ $8 per hour	6.00
Manufacturing overhead	1.50[a]
Standard costs per wastebasket	$9.50

[a] Based on anticipated production of 600,000 wastebaskets.

Actual results for the period during which 600,000 wastebaskets were produced, of which 550,000 were sold for $14.50 each, were:

Metal sheets used	306,000 sheets
Direct labor, 440,000 hours	$3,696,000
Manufacturing overhead	$ 900,000

During the period 350,000 metal sheets were purchased for $4.20, all at the same unit price. All the sheets put into production this period were purchased during the period. Selling and administrative expenses for the period were: variable selling expenses, $1.35 per wastebasket; fixed selling and administrative expenses, $950,000. The company's tax rate is 46%. *Materials price variances are recorded at the time units are acquired.* All expenses except $100,000 of manufacturing-related depreciation and $250,000 of nonmanufacturing depreciation were paid in cash during the period. Sales were for cash. There was no Finished Goods Beginning Inventory.

REQUIRED: 1. Prepare all the journal entries for the period, based on the data provided.
2. The company disposes of any standard cost variances as an adjustment to cost of goods sold. Prepare an Income Statement for the period.
3. Calculate the carrying value of the Ending Finished Goods Inventory.
4. What would the carrying value of the Ending Finished Goods Inventory have been, assuming the use of an actual cost system rather than a standard cost system?
5. Explain the difference between the inventory valuations you have computed with the two costing systems.

9—29. *Preparation of a flexible budget.*   The Golden Glow Company manufactures a suntan lotion designed to give the skin a healthy bronze glow
after a short period in the sun. Their estimated *full* cost of producing an
8-ounce plastic tube of lotion is:

Lotion	$ .15
Plastic tube	.06
Direct labor	.11
Variable manufacturing overhead	.04
Fixed manufacturing overhead	.06[a]
Variable selling expenses	.25
Fixed selling and administrative expenses	.37[a]
Full cost per tube	$1.04

[a] Based on anticipated production and sale of 840,000 tubes.

Although the company has prepared the figures given above based on
the anticipated production of 840,000 tubes, they believe they could
produce as few as 800,000 tubes or as many as 880,000. Within this
relevant range of production, the level of fixed costs would not be affected.
The anticipated selling price of a tube of suntan lotion is $1.50.

REQUIRED: 1. Prepare income statements for the anticipated production range, applying the
concepts of flexible budgeting.

   2. Calculate the cost of manufacturing a tube of lotion (carry your answer to three
decimal places) under each production assumption. Explain any differences in
results.

   3. Calculate the profit margin on sales (operating income divided by sales) at each
level of production and sales, carrying your answer to three decimal places.
Which level yields the highest profit margin and why?

9—30. *Explanation of variances.*   Assume you are the production manager
of a department in the Fileno Manufacturing Company, which makes bed
comforters. You have just received the following report on your performance for the past month with a comment from your supervisor: "You
really had a bad month and are going to have to shape things up down
there. Please send me a memo immediately giving me your explanation
of this performance."

Budgeted Production:	8,000 comforters	( ) indicates unfavorable variances
Actual Production:	8,800 comforters	
Standard Cost Variances:		
Price variance, cotton covering fabric		$ (3,432)
Price variance, filler		(6,450)
Usage variance, cotton covering fabric		(3,248)
Usage variance, filler		(3,000)
Rate variance, direct labor		(6,160)
Efficiency variance, direct labor		(2,560)
Total material and labor standard cost variances		($24,850)

Additional information:

Wage rates are set by union contract. A new three-year contract was in effect for the current month. You are not a part of Fileno Manufacturing's labor negotiating team.

Each comforter has a standard material input of 8 yards of cotton fabric; actual usage for the month amounted to 68,640 yards at $.75 per yard.

The standard amount of filler put into each comforter is 5 pounds @ $1 per pound. During the period 43,000 pounds were used.

Each comforter has a standard direct labor input of 1½ hours. During the period 12,320 hours of direct labor were used at an average cost of $8.50 per hour.

All raw materials are purchased by the company's purchasing department.

REQUIRED: Prepare your response to your supervisor. Support your response with appropriate calculations.

chapter ten

Using Flexible Budgets and Standard Costs for Controlling Manufacturing Overhead

OBJECTIVES

After you have completed this chapter, you should be able to answer the following questions:

- How can a flexible budget formula for manufacturing overhead be calculated?
- What three cost systems can be used for charging work-in-process with product costs?
- When a standard cost system is used, how are the total variable overhead variance, the spending variance, and the efficiency variance calculated?
- How should spending and efficiency variances for variable overhead be interpreted?
- When a standard cost system is used, how are the total fixed overhead variance, the spending variance, and the volume variance calculated?
- How should spending and volume variances for fixed overhead be interpreted?
- How do the calculation of overhead variances from budget differ if an actual/applied cost system is used rather than a standard cost system?
- What problems arise in the interpretation of overhead variances?

In the previous chapter we looked at the use of flexible budgets, standard costs, and variance analysis in controlling direct material and direct labor costs. In this chapter we shall continue the discussion of those same control tools and how they can be applied to manufacturing overhead. We shall use the same data for Handicrafts, Limited, which we developed in the last chapter. Remember the original budget for overhead looked like this:

Budgeted Unit Production		20,000 baskets
	Per Unit	**Total**
Variable Manufacturing Overhead:		
Indirect Materials	$.50	$10,000
Other	.25	5,000
Total Variable Manufacturing Overhead	$.75	$15,000
Fixed Manufacturing Overhead:		
Indirect Labor		$25,000
Depreciation		10,000
Utilities		7,000
Other		3,000
Total Fixed Manufacturing Overhead		$45,000
Total Manufacturing Overhead for 20,000 units		$60,000
Manufacturing Overhead Per Unit for 20,000 units		$3.00

Handicrafts uses a standard cost system and applies overhead on the basis of direct labor hours. Recall that the labor usage envisioned when a budget was prepared for 20,000 units was 15,000 direct labor hours (20,000 units × .75 hour per unit = 15,000 direct labor hours).

We now have what we need in order to come up with a rate for applying manufacturing overhead: (a) an estimate of manufacturing overhead costs for a given volume and (b) an input measure, direct labor hours. Handicrafts' application rate can be broken down into a variable rate and a fixed rate as follows:

$$\text{Variable overhead rate} = \$15,000/15,000 \text{ direct labor hours}$$
$$= \$1 \text{ per direct labor hour}$$
$$\text{Fixed overhead rate} = \$45,000/15,000 \text{ direct labor hours}$$
$$= \$3 \text{ per direct labor hour}$$

The overhead section of the standard cost card prepared for a unit of production by Handicrafts, Limited, was as follows:

Manufacturing overhead applied on the basis of direct
  labor hours:
  Variable overhead: $15,000/15,000 hours = $1 per
    direct labor hour × .75 hour per unit $0.75
  Fixed overhead: $45,000/15,000 hours = $3 per
    direct labor hour × .75 hour per unit   2.25
  Standard manufacturing overhead cost per unit $3.00
  Standard rate per direct labor hour $4.00

PREPARATION OF THE FLEXIBLE OVERHEAD BUDGET

Using the original budget data given for manufacturing overhead, we can develop a flexible budgeting formula which will enable us to calculate what manufacturing overhead should be at relevant ranges of volume. Variable manufacturing overhead costs are expected to be $1 per direct labor hour ($15,000/15,000 hours = $1).

Fixed costs are not expected to vary in total within a relevant range of production. Thus, for flexible budget purposes we anticipate $45,000 of fixed overhead. Combining the variable rate per direct labor hour of $1 with the level of fixed overhead expected, we have a flexible budget formula for calculating manufacturing overhead:

Manufacturing overhead = $1 per direct labor hour + $45,000

Using this formula, we can calculate expected manufacturing overhead for various direct labor inputs. For example, if we anticipated production requiring 16,000 direct labor hours, the budgeted manufacturing overhead costs would be:

Manufacturing overhead = $1 (16,000 direct labor hours) + $45,000

= $61,000

In Illustration 9-2 in Chapter 9 we showed flexible budget amounts for three different levels of production: 19,000, 20,000, and 21,000 baskets. The manufacturing overhead portion of those flexible budgets was as follows:

	19,000	20,000	21,000
Units of Production	19,000	20,000	21,000
Direct Labor Hours	14,250	15,000	15,750
Variable Manufacturing Overhead:			
Indirect Materials	9,500	10,000	10,500
Supplies and Other	4,750	5,000	5,250
Total Variable Overhead	$14,250	$15,000	$15,750
Fixed Manufacturing Overhead:			
Indirect Labor	$25,000	$25,000	$25,000
Depreciation	10,000	10,000	10,000
Utilities	7,000	7,000	7,000
Other	3,000	3,000	3,000
Total Fixed Overhead	$45,000	$45,000	$45,000
Total Manufacturing Overhead	$59,250	$60,000	$60,750

USE OF THE FLEXIBLE OVERHEAD BUDGET

As with direct materials and direct labor, variances from a static budget for variable manufacturing overhead are difficult to interpret if the budget is prepared for one volume level and actual volume is at another level. If a static budget is used, variances do not necessarily mean inefficiency or more than expected efficiency. Rather they may be simply the result of volume differences.

As discussed in the previous chapter, fixed manufacturing overhead or any other fixed costs are not relevant for flexible budgeting. So long as the flexible budget is prepared for relevant ranges of volume, any budgeted fixed costs should not change. This was reflected in the flexible budgeting formula we developed for overhead, which showed $45,000 (the fixed overhead for Handicrafts) as a constant unaffected by volume changes.

DIFFERENT METHODS OF ASSIGNING OVERHEAD TO OUTPUT

With direct materials and direct labor we have two basic approaches for assigning these costs to the units produced—an *actual cost system* and a *standard cost system*. With an actual cost system, work-in-process is charged with actual direct material and direct labor costs. These costs are attached to units as they are transferred to finished goods. With a standard cost system, the standard costs (what costs should have been) for direct materials and direct labor are charged to work-in-process and attached to units as they are transferred to finished goods.

For manufacturing overhead, first we have the alternative of absorption costing versus variable (direct) costing. Recall that with absorption costing, which is required by generally accepted accounting principles, all units of output are charged with both variable and fixed manufacturing overhead. With a variable costing system, only variable overhead costs are attached to the units being produced. Fixed manufacturing overhead is treated as a period cost, rather than a product cost, and expensed out in the period incurred. Since variable costing is not in keeping with generally accepted accounting principles, we shall assume the use of absorption costing.

Not only do we have the question of whether to use absorption costing or variable costing in assigning overhead to production, but once this decision is made, there are three different ways of applying overhead to units produced. Looking at all factors of production—direct materials, direct labor, and manufacturing overhead—we can describe three different costing systems.

1. *An actual cost system:* Work-in-process is charged with actual costs for direct materials, direct labor, and manufacturing overhead.
2. *An actual/applied cost system* (sometimes called a "normal" cost system): Work-in-process is charged with actual costs for direct materials and direct labor and with overhead based on a predetermined rate. With an actual/applied system, the amount of overhead charged to work-in-process is based on the predetermined rate × *actual input.* For example, if the predetermined overhead rate is based on direct labor hours, work-in-process will be charged with: predetermined overhead rate × actual direct labor hours used.
3. *A standard cost system:* Work-in-process is charged with standard costs for direct materials, direct labor, and manufacturing overhead. For manufacturing overhead the charge to work-in-process is based on a standard overhead rate × *the standard input for the production level achieved.* For example, Handicrafts produced 21,000 units, which should have required 15,750 direct labor hours; instead 16,800 were used. With an actual/applied overhead system, work-in-process would have been debited for $67,200 (16,800 hours × $4 overhead rate per hour). With a standard cost system, work-in-process would be debited for $63,000 (15,750 hours × $4 overhead rate per hour).

In assigning direct materials and direct labor to production we use either actual costs or standard costs. For manufacturing overhead, we have three alternatives: actual overhead, predetermined overhead based on *actual inputs,* and standard overhead (standard rate × *standard input).* Because we have two types of overhead, variable and fixed, even more combinations are possible. This point will be discussed later in the chapter.

The different inputs to work-in-process which result from different cost systems is illustrated in T-account form below:

Actual Cost System   Actual/Applied Cost System

Work-in-Process		Manufacturing Overhead		Work-in-Process	

Actual direct
  materials
Actual direct
  labor
Actual
  manufacturing
  overhead
		Actual
		overhead
			Applied
			  overhead:
			  Predetermined
			  rate ×
			  actual input
				Actual direct
				  materials
				Actual direct
				  labor
				Predetermined
				  overhead
				  rate × actual
				  input	

Standard Cost System

Manufacturing Overhead		Work-in-Process	

Actual overhead	Applied overhead:
	  Standard rate ×
	  standard input for
	  volume level
	  achieved
		Standard direct
		  materials
		Standard direct labor
		Standard overhead
		  rate × standard
		  input for volume
		  achieved	

Note that when an actual cost system is used, there is by definition no over- or underapplied overhead. With an actual/applied cost system or with a standard cost system, overhead is over- or underapplied if the amount of actual overhead costs incurred differs from the amount charged to work-in-process.

BUDGET VARIANCES VERSUS STANDARD COST VARIANCES

Variance calculation and analysis is not limited to a company which uses a standard cost system. Any company which prepares a budget can calculate variances—the difference between expectations as expressed in the budget and actual. For direct materials and direct labor, as well as for other factors, these variances can be broken down into price and usage components.

Direct Materials and Direct Labor

If a company uses a standard cost system and bases its standard on normal efficiency, figures which represent standards and budgeted amounts are developed the same way and will generally be the same amounts. For example, to calculate its standard costs for direct materials *or* the proper amount to include in the budget, a company will have to estimate usage and price based on normal efficiency. What this means is that the standard direct materials costs and the budgeted direct materials costs will probably be the same. Therefore, variances from standard or from budget, if the company does not use a standard cost system, will be the same for the total variance as well as for price and usage factors. This is also true for direct labor.

To make this point clearer, remember that based on the flexible budget, Handicrafts should have spent $42,000 for direct materials (21,000 units @ $2 per unit). They actually spent $40,698. If they use a budgetary system and don't use a standard cost system, there is a $1,302 favorable variance, which can be broken down into price and use components. If they use a standard cost system, they will be comparing identical figures. The only difference is that with the standard cost system, the variances are actually recorded in the accounts through debits and credits.

Manufacturing Overhead

With manufacturing overhead, the amounts and calculation of variances differ depending on whether the company is using a standard cost system with the standards reflected in the budget or whether it is simply using a budget without a standard cost system. This is true because although the total manufacturing overhead variance under either approach is measured by comparing overhead costs applied to units produced with actual overhead costs, the amounts applied differ.

In the case of a company which does not have a standard cost system, overhead will be applied to production on the basis of *actual inputs*. With a standard cost system, overhead will be applied to production on the basis of *standard inputs* for the volume achieved. Hence, unless actual and standard input is the same, the total manufacturing overhead applied will differ with a standard cost system from the amount applied using an actual/applied cost system. This difference and its effect on the calculation of overhead variances is discussed fully later in the chapter.

OVERHEAD VARIANCE ANALYSIS WITH A STANDARD COST SYSTEM

Let's look again at the actual results for Handicrafts, Limited, versus the flexible budget with respect to overhead:

	FLEXIBLE BUDGET	ACTUAL	VARIANCE
Units Produced	21,000	21,000	
Direct Labor Hours	15,750	16,800	1,050 U
Variable Manufacturing Overhead:			
Indirect Materials	$10,500	$11,000	$ 500 U
Supplies and Other	5,250	4,800	450 F
Total Variable Overhead	$15,750	$15,800	$ 50 U
Fixed Manufacturing Overhead:			
Indirect Labor	$25,000	$26,000	$1,000 U
Depreciation	10,000	10,000	—
Utilities	7,000	7,302	302 U
Other	3,000	3,100	100 U
Total Fixed Overhead	$45,000	$46,402	$1,402 U
Total Manufacturing Overhead	$60,750	$62,202	$1,452 U

Variable Manufacturing Overhead Variances

In calculating variances we shall analyze variable overhead and then fixed overhead. We are assuming Handicrafts uses a standard cost system. Here is what has happened:

1. The company has charged to work-in-process $15,750 of variable overhead. This is based on the $1 standard predetermined rate × 15,750 direct labor hours, which represent the standard labor usage for the 21,000 units completed.
2. The company's actual variable overhead costs amount to $15,800.
3. Based on the 16,800 of direct labor hours actually used, $16,800 of variable overhead costs would have been expected. This assumes that since overhead is applied on the basis of direct labor hours, there is a cause-and-effect relationship between the two. That is, the use of direct labor hours causes variable overhead costs to be incurred.

We can take these three pieces of data and calculate variances which we shall call (1) an efficiency variance and (2) a spending variance.

Graphically the calculation of the variable manufacturing overhead variances is described below:

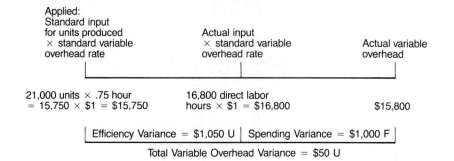

In formula form, the calculation of variances for variable manufacturing overhead is described as follows:

$$\left(\begin{array}{c}\text{Total variable manufacturing}\\ \text{overhead variance}\end{array}\right) = \left(\begin{array}{c}\text{standard variable}\\ \text{overhead rate}\end{array} \times \begin{array}{c}\text{standard input for}\\ \text{units made}\end{array}\right) - \left(\begin{array}{c}\text{actual variable}\\ \text{overhead}\end{array}\right)$$

$$-\$50\,\text{U} = \$15{,}750 - \$15{,}800$$

$$\left(\begin{array}{c}\text{Efficiency}\\ \text{variance}\end{array}\right) = \left(\begin{array}{c}\text{standard variable}\\ \text{overhead rate}\end{array}\right) \times \left(\begin{array}{c}\text{standard input for}\\ \text{units made}\end{array} - \text{actual input}\right)$$

$$-\$1{,}050 = \$1 \times (15{,}750 - 16{,}800)$$

$$\left(\begin{array}{c}\text{Spending}\\ \text{variance}\end{array}\right) = \left(\text{actual input} \times \begin{array}{c}\text{standard variable}\\ \text{overhead rate}\end{array}\right) - \left(\begin{array}{c}\text{actual variable}\\ \text{overhead}\end{array}\right)$$

$$= (16{,}800 \times \$1) - \$15{,}800$$

$$+\$1{,}000\,\text{F} = \$16{,}800 - \$15{,}800$$

Why is our efficiency variance unfavorable? The answer is that with the 16,800 direct labor hours used by Handicrafts they should have produced 22,400 baskets (16,800 direct labor hours ÷ .75 hour per basket) rather than the 21,000 which they actually produced.

Consider the fact that if our direct labor usage variance is unfavorable and we apply overhead on the basis of direct labor hours, our efficiency variance for variable manufacturing overhead will also be unfavorable. The nature of the variable manufacturing overhead efficiency variance—favorable or unfavorable—will be the same as that of the input component to which it is related.

The spending variance is based on the assumption of a causal relationship between variable overhead and direct labor hours used. Since

Handicrafts used 16,800 hours, the expectation was that each of these hours would have caused $1 of variable overhead. Our actual overhead was only $15,800, meaning that we did not spend at the rate per direct labor hour which was anticipated.

Note that if we look at the flexible budget relative to actual variable manufacturing overhead on p. 399, the $50 difference is reflected here. For variable manufacturing overhead with a standard cost system, these amounts will be the same:

1. The difference between the flexible budget amount and the actual amount of variable manufacturing overhead *equals*
2. The total variance for variable manufacturing overhead *equals*
3. The amount by which variable manufacturing overhead is over- or underapplied.

In the case of Handicrafts, items 1, 2, and 3 above were all equal to $50. These relationships do not hold true for fixed manufacturing overhead, as is explained later.

Price and Usage Variances
Versus Spending and Efficiency Variances

You may wonder why we don't account for each item of variable manufacturing overhead the same way we do the other variable cost inputs—direct materials and direct labor. Why don't we set a standard (or budgeted) usage and price figure for each item of variable overhead, determine actual usage and costs, and then compute an overall, a price, and a usage variance. In other words, rather than having only one set of variances to describe the difference between standard (or budgeted) variable overhead and actual overhead, we would have a whole series of overall, price, and usage variances—for example, a set for indirect materials, a set for supplies, and a set for repairs.

The answer is we could and should do this for any variable manufacturing overhead cost which is a significant part of the cost of units which we are manufacturing. However, companies tend to have a number of variable overhead costs, none of which is significant taken alone. Thus, rather than keep track of a series of variances, these overhead elements are combined into one figure, and only one set of variances is calculated.

Your next question might be, for control purposes, why do we apply variable overhead on the basis of some other input factor such as direct labor? Why don't we just come up with an overall standard usage figure and an overall standard rate figure which encompasses all the parts of variable manufacturing overhead and use this directly in attaching variable overhead costs to production? The answer is that it would be a time-consuming and a difficult if not impossible job to develop such a standard usage and price figure.

To illustrate, suppose we had just two variable manufacturing overhead components and we collected the following data when 21,000 units were produced:

	STANDARD	ACTUAL
Indirect materials	1 per unit of output @ $.50	21,200 units @ $.53
Supplies	2 per unit of output @ $.10	41,000 units @ $.11

First look at the detail that has to be collected. Second, if we wanted a single set of variances for variable manufacturing overhead, how would we combine different factors. What would be standard usage or standard price?

Because of the difficulties described above, many companies instead relate variable overhead to other inputs. Handicrafts, for example, bases variable overhead estimates on an assumed causal relationship between that production input and direct labor hours. In reality, for certain items of variable overhead, this relationship may not exist. But what is lost in accuracy should be offset by the lack of materiality or by cost savings.

There are two outcomes when variable manufacturing overhead is applied to production on the basis of some other manufacturing input. First, anytime there is a difference between the standard level of the input which is being used as a basis for applying overhead and the actual level of that input, we will have an efficiency variance. For example, since Handicrafts' standard direct labor hours for 21,000 units was 15,750 hours and 16,800 hours were used, there was an unfavorable variance.

Second, when an applied overhead rate is used in a standard cost system, a spending variance is based on an *indirect causal* relationship—units produced caused the use of direct labor hours which caused the incurrence of variable overhead. Variances for direct materials and direct labor are based on a *direct causal* relationship—units produced caused direct labor hour or direct material inputs. The spending variance we calculated of $1,000 is favorable. This occurred because we assume a causal relationship existed between direct labor hours and variable overhead—each hour would cause $1 of variable overhead. The favorable spending variance indicates that this relationship did not hold. By labeling this a spending variance, we are indicating that we spent less (in the case of a favorable variance) per direct labor hour than was expected. Realistically, this may not be true. Instead, the variance may result from a faulty assumption—that variable overhead is caused by direct labor.

What all this means is that for variable overhead items of significant size, additional analysis on an individual basis is required to determine whether that item is being properly controlled. Opportunities for control may be lost if only overall variances for variable manufacturing overhead are examined.

FIXED MANUFACTURING OVERHEAD VARIANCES

For fixed overhead, Handicrafts set a standard rate of $3 per direct labor hour. This means that:

1. Work-in-process has been charged for $47,250 of fixed overhead ($3 rate × 15,750 standard hours for the 21,000 units produced). In other words, fixed overhead has been treated as if it were a variable cost in applying it to units produced.
2. Actual fixed overhead costs amounted to $46,402.
3. Budgeted or standard fixed overhead was $45,000.

Fixed overhead variances can be calculated as follows:

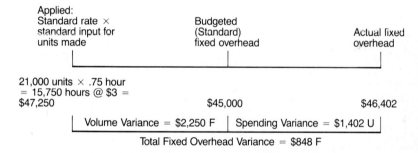

In formula form, these fixed overhead variances can be expressed as:

$$\left(\begin{array}{c}\text{Total fixed}\\\text{overhead variance}\end{array}\right) = \left(\begin{array}{c}\text{standard fixed overhead}\\\text{rate} \times \text{standard input} \quad - \quad \text{actual fixed overhead}\\\text{for units produced}\end{array}\right)$$

$$\$848 \text{ F} = (15,750 \text{ hr @ } \$3) - \$46,402$$

$$\text{Volume variance} = \left(\begin{array}{c}\text{standard fixed overhead} \qquad \text{budgeted or standard}\\\text{rate} \times \text{standard input} \quad - \quad \textit{total dollar} \text{ amount of}\\\text{for units produced} \qquad \text{fixed overhead}\end{array}\right)$$

$$\$2,250 \text{ F} = (15,750 \text{ hr @ } \$3) - \$45,000$$

$$\text{Spending variance} = \left(\begin{array}{c}\text{budgeted or standard total}\\\text{dollar amount of fixed} \quad - \quad \text{actual fixed overhead}\\\text{overhead}\end{array}\right)$$

$$-\$1,402 \text{ U} = \$45,000 - \$46,402$$

Interpreting Fixed Overhead Variances

Unlike the spending variance we calculated with respect to variable overhead, the spending variance for fixed overhead means just what the name implies. We had anticipated spending at one level but actually spent at another. Overhead should not have varied with changes in production; thus differences are due entirely to the level of spending.

The volume variance results from treating fixed overhead as if it were variable when an applied overhead rate is used. If we had actually used the number of direct labor hours on which we based our rate calculation—in the case of Handicrafts, 15,000—there would have been no volume variance. The volume variance is favorable because we had more units over which to spread our fixed costs than we anticipated when the rate was calculated—21,000 actual versus 20,000 expected. If standard inputs had been less than those on which the fixed overhead rate was based, this would imply the production of fewer units than had been anticipated, and an unfavorable volume variance.

Recall that for variable overhead, the total overhead variance was equal to (a) the difference between the flexible budget and the actual costs and (b) the amount of over- or underapplied overhead. That is, for variable manufacturing overhead, comparison of the flexible budget with actual on p. 399 shows a difference of $50 U. Comparing actual variable manufacturing overhead of $15,800 with applied overhead of $15,750 shows that overhead was underapplied by $50. Finally, the total variable overhead variance as calculated on p. 399 is also $50.

In the case of fixed manufacturing overhead, these relationships do not hold. Look at the comparison of the flexible budget with the actual fixed overhead shown on p. 399. This difference is $1,402 U. Compare actual overhead $46,402 with applied overhead of $47,250 and we can see that overhead was overapplied by $848. This $848 is also the total fixed overhead variance. The difference between the flexible budget and actual is equal to one part of the overall overhead variance, the spending variance of $1,402.

The reason why the difference between budgeted overhead and actual overhead is not the same as the total fixed overhead variance and the amount by which overhead is over- or underapplied is that overhead is fixed but, in applying it, it was being treated as if it were a variable cost. The total anticipated fixed overhead level did not change when more units were produced—it remained at $45,000.

OVERHEAD ANALYSIS WITH AN ACTUAL/APPLIED COST SYSTEM

In our discussion of different systems for attaching costs to units produced, we pointed out that with an actual/applied cost system, work-in-process was charged for actual direct material and direct labor costs. In addition, it was debited with manufacturing overhead on the basis of a predetermined rate applied to the *actual inputs* on which the rate was based.

If Handicrafts used an actual/applied cost system rather than a standard cost system, this means that work-in-process would have been debited for $16,800 of variable manufacturing overhead and $50,400 of fixed manufacturing overhead, determined as follows:

Variable manufacturing overhead = $1 per direct labor hour × 16,800 direct labor hours actually used

Fixed manufacturing overhead = $3 per direct labor hour × 16,800 direct labor hours actually used

Variable Manufacturing Overhead Variances

With an actual/applied system, an efficiency variance for variable manufacturing overhead cannot be calculated. Consider the graphical calculation of variable overhead variance when a standard cost system was used:

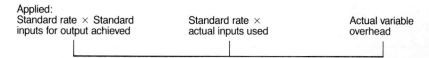

With an actual/ applied system, the amount of overhead applied will be equal to the budgeted rate × actual inputs used, eliminating the efficiency variance. Thus, with an actual/applied system we have only a spending variance for variable overhead which we can calculate—the differences between the actual inputs at the predetermined overhead rate and the actual variable overhead:

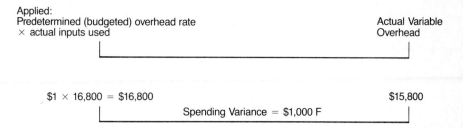

Fixed Manufacturing Overhead Variances

For fixed manufacturing overhead we can still calculate a total variance, a volume variance, and a spending variance as we did when a standard cost system was used. This can be done because again, as with a standard cost system, for product costing purposes we are treating fixed overhead as it if were a variable item.

Using the data for Handicrafts in conjunction with an actual/applied cost system, the following variances would be generated:

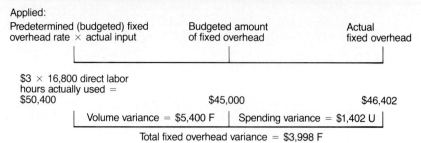

Applied:
Predetermined (budgeted) fixed   Budgeted amount   Actual
overhead rate × actual input   of fixed overhead   fixed overhead

$3 × 16,800 direct labor
hours actually used =
$50,400 $45,000 $46,402

| Volume variance = $5,400 F | Spending variance = $1,402 U |

Total fixed overhead variance = $3,998 F

The spending variance indicates that Handicrafts has higher costs for its fixed overhead items than it had anticipated when it set the budget. The volume variance is a result of the fact that the rate was based on an assumed use of 15,000 direct labor hours. Actual direct labor hours were 16,800. The implication is that productive facilities were utilized more fully than had been anticipated when the predetermined overhead rate was set, resulting in a favorable volume variance.

JOURNAL ENTRIES FOR DIFFERENT COST SYSTEMS

In the previous chapter we looked at the journal entries which Handicrafts would have made for an actual cost system in contrast with a standard cost system for direct materials and direct labor. With regard to overhead, we will have to consider three alternatives: (1) the charging of actual overhead to work-in-process; (2) the use of a predetermined overhead rate applied on the basis of actual inputs, and (3) the use of a standard cost system with overhead charged to work-in-process on the basis of a standard rate applied to the standard input for the volume achieved.

These entries are shown in Illustration 10-1 and are based on the following data for Handicrafts:

1. Actual variable overhead = $15,800. Actual fixed overhead = $46,402.
2. The predetermined and standard rate for applying overhead was: for variable overhead, $1 per direct labor hour; for fixed overhead, $3 per direct labor hour. These rates were based on an assumed volume of 20,000 units requiring 15,000 direct labor hours.
3. Handicrafts produced 21,000 units using 16,800 direct labor hours. The standard direct labor input for this level of production was 15,750 direct labor hours (21,000 × .75 hour = 15,750).

Observe the differences in the recording of overhead under the three cost systems, as shown in Illustration 10-1.

1. With the actual cost system, work-in-process is charged with actual overhead. As a result there are no variances and no under- or overapplied overhead.
2. With the actual/applied cost system:
   a. Work-in-process is charged with the predetermined rate × the direct labor hours actually worked.

b. The balances in the two overhead summary accounts represent over- or underapplied overhead. For Handicrafts, overhead was overapplied (too much was charged to units produced) by $4,998 ($62,202 of actual overhead less $67,200 debited to work-in-process). This overapplication occurred because the rate was based on an anticipated use of 15,000 direct labor hours but was applied to the 16,800 hours actually worked.

c. No variances accounts are set up.

3. When a standard cost system is used:

a. Work-in-process is charged with the predetermined rate × the standard direct labor hours for the volume achieved.

b. The sum of the variances represents the over- or underapplication of overhead. In the case of Handicrafts, overhead was overapplied by $798, calculated as follows:

− $1,050	unfavorable variable overhead efficiency variance
$1,000	favorable variable overhead spending variance
− $1,402	unfavorable fixed overhead spending variance
$2,250	favorable fixed overhead volume variance
$ 798	net favorable variance and overapplied overhead

Or, it can be calculated by comparing actual of $62,202 with the $63,000 charged to work-in-process.

DISPOSAL OF OVERHEAD VARIANCES

With an actual/applied cost system and with a standard cost system over- or underapplied overhead may arise. There will be a balance in the overhead summary account(s) when an actual/applied cost system is used if overhead is over- or underapplied. If a standard cost system is used, over- or underapplied overhead will be recorded in the various overhead variance accounts. In either case, the alternatives for disposing of the over- or underapplied overhead are (1) dispose of it in the current period as an adjustment to cost of goods sold, (2) allocate it between work-in-process, finished goods inventory, and cost of goods sold, or (3) carry it over on the balance sheet. These alternatives were discussed in more detail in a previous chapter. The most commonly used alternative is to treat it as an adjustment to cost of goods sold, which is the treatment used throughout this text.

A COMBINED VARIANCE FOR VARIABLE AND FIXED OVERHEAD

Rather than computing an overall variance and then two components of that variance for variable overhead and for fixed overhead, some companies analyze differences between expected overhead and actual overhead

ILLUSTRATION 10-1

Journal Entries and T-Accounts for Overhead, Assuming the Use of Different Cost Systems

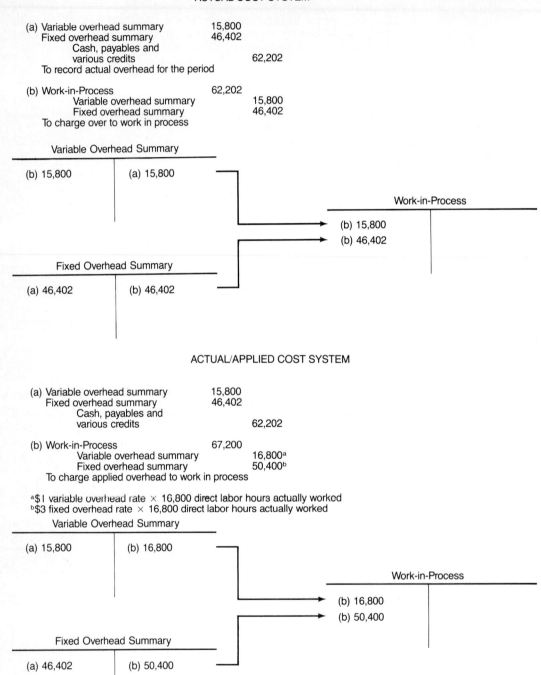

ACTUAL COST SYSTEM

(a) Variable overhead summary	15,800	
Fixed overhead summary	46,402	
Cash, payables and various credits		62,202
To record actual overhead for the period		

(b) Work-in-Process	62,202	
Variable overhead summary		15,800
Fixed overhead summary		46,402
To charge over to work in process		

Variable Overhead Summary

(b) 15,800	(a) 15,800

Work-in-Process

(b) 15,800	
(b) 46,402	

Fixed Overhead Summary

(a) 46,402	(b) 46,402

ACTUAL/APPLIED COST SYSTEM

(a) Variable overhead summary	15,800	
Fixed overhead summary	46,402	
Cash, payables and various credits		62,202

(b) Work-in-Process	67,200	
Variable overhead summary		16,800[a]
Fixed overhead summary		50,400[b]
To charge applied overhead to work in process		

[a]$1 variable overhead rate × 16,800 direct labor hours actually worked
[b]$3 fixed overhead rate × 16,800 direct labor hours actually worked

Variable Overhead Summary

(a) 15,800	(b) 16,800

Work-in-Process

(b) 16,800	
(b) 50,400	

Fixed Overhead Summary

(a) 46,402	(b) 50,400

ILLUSTRATION 10-1 (cont.)

STANDARD COST SYSTEM

(a) Variable overhead summary   15,800
     Fixed overhead summary   46,402
        Cash, payables and
          various credits   62,202
     To record overhead for the period

(b) Work-in-Process   63,000[a]
     Variable OH efficiency variance   1,050
     Fixed OH spending variance   1,402
        Variable overhead summary   15,800
        Fixed overhead summary   46,402
        Variable overhead spending variance   1,000
        Fixed overhead volume variance   2,250
     To charge work-in-process with standard overhead for
     the period and record overhead variances

[a]$1 standard rate × 15,750 standard hours for 21,000 units + $3 standard
fixed overhead × 15,750 standard hours for 21,000 units = $63,000

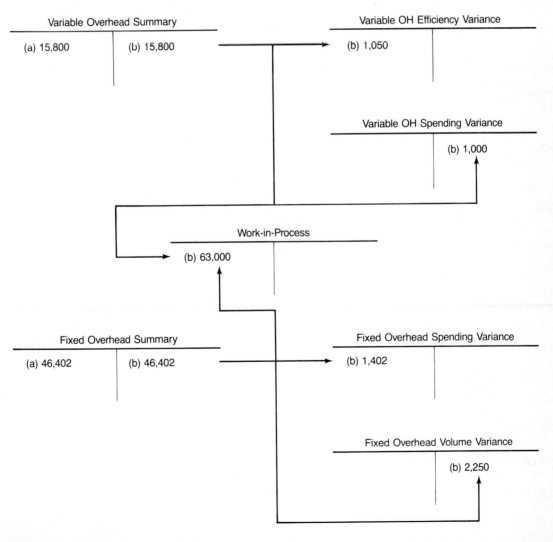

for variable and fixed overhead combined. That is, they have an overall overhead variance and then break that variance down into a spending and a volume variance.

The calculation of variances assuming the use of a standard cost system when variable and fixed overhead are combined is done as follows and illustrated using data for Handicrafts, Limited.

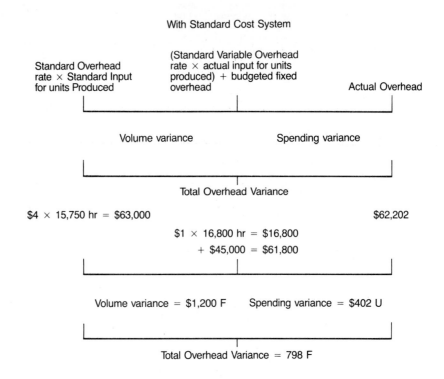

The favorable volume variance results from the fact that more baskets were produced over which to spread the fixed overhead costs than were anticipated when the overhead rate was set. Overhead was overapplied by the total overhead variance of $798 for the same reason.

If a combined set of overhead variances for variable and fixed overhead is desired and the company uses an actual/applied costing system, variances are calculated as follows and again illustrated using the data for Handicrafts, Limited.

Note that the spending variance is the same with the use of a standard cost system and with an actual/applied system because the computations are identical. The volume variance is related solely to fixed overhead because the amount of variable overhead applied is equal to the predetermined overhead rate times the actual hours used.

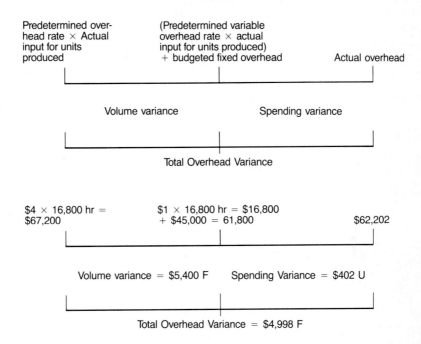

With an Actual/Applied Cost System

Illustration shows overhead variance analysis diagram with:

Predetermined overhead rate × Actual input for units produced | (Predetermined variable overhead rate × actual input for units produced) + budgeted fixed overhead | Actual overhead

Volume variance | Spending variance

Total Overhead Variance

$4 × 16,800 hr = $67,200 | $1 × 16,800 hr = $16,800 + $45,000 = 61,800 | $62,202

Volume variance = $5,400 F | Spending Variance = $402 U

Total Overhead Variance = $4,998 F

ILLUSTRATION FROM PRACTICE: STANDARD VERSUS ACTUAL COST REPORTS FOR AMERICAN THREAD

Illustration 10-2 shows the type of report which American Thread prepares on a monthly basis for each of its mills to describe the difference between standard overhead costs and actual results. Note the items which are assumed to vary with production versus those which are described as period overhead and are assumed to be fixed. For variable costs the report indicates the use of flexible budgeting, meaning the budgeted costs have been adjusted to the output level achieved.

Rather than calculating variances for variable overhead and for fixed overhead separately, the company follows the practice of calculating an overall spending variance and a volume variance for both types of overhead.

Illustration 10-3 is a summary report for the month for one of American Thread's mills. It summarizes the data provided in detailed schedules for materials, direct labor, and overhead. In addition, the company treats fringe benefits as a special cost component, reporting it as a part neither of direct labor nor of overhead. From the bottom line of this report, you will note that for this mill for the month actual costs exceeded standard costs by $52,913, or, stated another way, actual costs were 105% of the standard.

ILLUSTRATION 10-2

Illustration from Practice:
A Comparison of Actual and Standard Overhead for American Thread

MILL OPERATING STATEMENT

OVERHEAD   Cotton & Syn. Mfg.

MONTH   June   YEAR-TO-DATE   5 months

COST ELEMENT	ACTUAL	VARIANCE (UNF)	% ACT. TO STD.	ACTUAL	VARIANCE (UNF)	% ACT. TO STD.
VARIABLE OVERHEAD:						
Routine Repair Labor	11,791	2,843	81	60,516	12,574	83
Other Overhead Labor	8,761	995	90	42,855	5,872	88
Mill Supplies	2,652	(297)	113	13,844	(2,082)	118
Processing Supplies	7,548	(4,857)	280	19,796	(6,355)	147
Ticketing & Labeling						
Pack & Ship Supplies	976	706	58	4,488	3,913	53
Routine Repair and Supplies	63,118	(13,330)	127	244,174	4,498	98
Electricity	98,660	(12,540)	115	389,983	40,153	91
Fuels		168		600	241	71
All Other	773	237	77	4,861	180	96
TOTAL VARIABLE OVERHEAD	194,279	(26,075)	116	781,117	58,994	93
PERIOD OVERHEAD:						
Overhead Salaries	45,130	(6,463)	117	203,506	(10,171)	105
Overhead Labor	1,655	1,320	56	9,589	(5,286)	64
Period Fringe Benefits	8,549	(132)	102	43,701	(1,616)	104
Office & Mill Supplies	4,727	(2,410)	204	11,897	188	98
Production Supplies	40	460	08	2,747	(747)	79
R&R and Gen. Mill Rep. Sup.	4,931	5,565	47	18,458	34,022	35
Travel, Enter., etc.	556	36	94	2,601	359	88
Industrial Relations	527	1,124	32	4,738	3,517	57
Taxes	6,384	(46)	101	30,576	1,114	96
Insurance	2,147	1	100	10,735	2	100
Depreciation	26,917	2,250	92	134,400	11,437	92
Telephone & Telegraph	613	145	81	4,081	(290)	108
Electricity (Demand)	13,805		100	69,025		100
All Other	3,354	2,836	54	26,705	4,245	43
TOTAL PERIOD OVERHEAD	119,335	4,686	96	572,759	47,346	92
TOTAL SPENDING VARIANCE	313,614	(21,389)		1,353,876	106,340	
VOLUME VARIANCE		6,335			27,337	
TOTAL VARIANCE		(15,054)			133,677	

ILLUSTRATION 10-3

Illustration from Practice:
A Summary Comparison of Standard and Actual Production Costs

MILL OPERATING STATEMENT SUMMARY

LOCATION   Sylvan

OPERATION   Cotton & Rayon Mfg.

MONTH   June

YEAR-TO-DATE   5 months

MATERIALS

	Actual	Variance (Unf)	% Act. To Std.	Actual	Variance (Unf)	% Act. to Std.
Cotton	525,828	(14,397)	103	2,462,848	(39,515)	102
Synthetics	14,850	(510)	104	149,527	(504)	100
Grey Yarn						
Total Raw Materials	540,678	(14,907)	103	2,612,375	(40,019)	102
Finishing	67	1,184	05	4,683	968	83
Put-up, pack & ship	3,789	(16)	100	11,251	1,268	90
Total Materials	544,534	(13,739)	103	2,628,309	(37,783)	101

DIRECT LABOR

	Actual	Variance (Unf)	% Act. To Std.	Actual	Variance (Unf)	% Act. to Std.
Productive labor	128,906	(6,666)	105	645,905	(42,367)	107
Service labor	85,995	(5,922)	107	426,929	(25,638)	106
Overtime premium	11,510	(6,676)	238	35,728	(11,712)	149
Training, etc.	8,353	1,162	88	37,289	9,968	97
Total Direct Labor	234,764	(18,102)	108	1,145,851	(69,749)	106

FRINGE BENEFITS

	Actual	Variance (Unf)	% Act. To Std.	Actual	Variance (Unf)	% Act. to Std.
Fringe Benefits	62,586	(200)	100	313,919	(4,059)	101

OVERHEAD

	Actual	Variance (Unf)	% Act. To Std.	Actual	Variance (Unf)	% Act. to Std.
Variable	194,279	(26,075)	116	781,117	58,994	93
Period: Spending	119,335	4,686	96	572,759	47,346	92
Volume	XXXX	6,335		XXXX	27,337	
Total Overhead	313,614	(15,054)	105	1,353,876	133,677	91

TOTAL OPERATING COST BEFORE ADJUSTMENTS

	Actual	Variance (Unf)	% Act. To Std.	Actual	Variance (Unf)	% Act. to Std.
Total Operating Cost	1,155,498	(47,095)	104	5,441,955	22,086	100

ADJUSTMENTS AND TOTAL PROFIT VARIANCE

	Actual	Variance (Unf)	% Act. To Std.	Actual	Variance (Unf)	% Act. to Std.
Matl. price var.		(18,785)			(31,075)	
Wage rate variances		16,183			80,383	
Adj. to Avg. Std.		(6,350)			(11,064)	
Adj. to mchdse. std.		3,134			8,298	
Total Profit Variance	1,155,498	(52,913)	105	5,441,955	68,628	99

VARIABLE COSTING AND STANDARD COSTS

In an earlier chapter we discussed the concept of variable costing. With variable costing, only variable production costs—direct materials, direct labor, and *variable* manufacturing overhead—are treated as product costs and inventoried. Fixed manufacturing overhead is expensed in the period incurred. While this costing method is not in keeping with generally accepted accounting principles, it can be and is used for internal accounting purposes.

Variable costing, like absorption costing, can be used in combination with standard costs. With a standard variable costing system, units passing through work-in-process and into finished goods inventory are costed at standard variable production costs. Actual fixed manufacturing overhead is expensed as a period cost.

SUMMARY OF PRODUCT COSTING SYSTEMS

Our discussion of different product costing systems is now complete. We have described the following types:

Actual absorption costing
Actual/applied absorption costing.
Standard absorption costing.
Actual variable costing.
Actual/applied variable costing.
Standard variable costing.

The differences between the methods are described in Illustration 10-4.

HYBRID COST SYSTEMS

In discussing the assignment of costs to products produced we described three alternatives: an actual cost system; an actual/applied cost system, where materials and labor are recorded at actual and overhead is charged into process using a predetermined rate; and a standard cost system. In reality, other combinations of these systems also can occur.

For example, the concepts of standard costs are most clearly related to direct materials and direct labor, productive inputs for which usage and price factors can be most easily estimated. In the case of variable manufacturing overhead, because of the multitude of items which may be encompassed in this category, cost and usage factors are not generally

	ELEMENTS OF PRODUCT COST		
	Actual Product Costing	Actual/Applied Product Costing	Standard Product Costing
Absorption Costing			
Direct materials	Actual costs	Actual costs	Standard costs
Direct labor	Actual costs	Actual costs	Standard costs
Variable overhead	Actual costs	Applied on the basis of *actual inputs* at a predetermined rate	Applied on the basis of *standard inputs* for units produced at a standard rate
Fixed manufacturing overhead	Actual costs	Same as variable overhead	Same as variable overhead
Variable Costing			
Direct materials	Actual costs	Actual costs	Standard costs
Direct labor	Actual costs	Actual costs	Standard costs
Variable manufacturing overhead	Actual costs	Applied on the basis of *actual inputs* at a predetermined rate	Applied on the basis of *standard inputs* for units produced at a standard rate
Fixed manufacturing overhead	None	None	None

estimated but instead standards are set on the basis of some assumed causal relationship. Very commonly, in the case of variable manufacturing overhead, direct labor is assumed to be the cause of variable overhead. The shortcomings of this assumption have already been discussed. For fixed manufacturing overhead, the concept of a usage factor is generally not relevant, as these costs do not vary with volume changes.

Because the concept of standard costs is less meaningful for items other than direct materials and direct labor, some companies use standard costs only for these two elements or prime cost. Another variation found in practice is to use standard costs for all variable productive inputs, but not for fixed manufacturing overhead. What this means is that companies should and do use standard costs selectively for whatever items they believe can best be controlled by this means. When standard costs are not used, reliance is instead placed on the budget as a primary control tool.

STANDARD COSTS AND NONMANUFACTURING ORGANIZATIONS

As stated in the previous chapter, standard costs systems can be used by any kind of organization. They are suitable for repetitive operations where usage and price factors can be reasonably estimated. Service organizations generally do not have operations of this type or have only limited ones.

Instead of using standard costs as part of their control system, service organizations generally rely on budgetary control alone.

Consider the case of a CPA firm which performs an audit for a company. When the CPA firm quotes a fee, they have estimated the number of hours and the level (and hence costs) of the persons expected to perform those hours of service. Rather than having a standard cost for each hour required by the audit, they will have a budget for the job. The lack of a standard cost system, as emphasized in the two chapters on this topic, does not preclude the calculation of an overall variance or the further analysis of that variance into price and usage factors. The CPA firm can look at the actual hours of service performed by persons who did the job and compare these with the budget levels, calculating not only an overall variance but also price and usage variances.

chapter highlights

Direct material and direct labor costs may be attached to products being produced on the basis of actual costs or standard costs. For manufacturing overhead, three alternatives exist for charging work-in-process: actual costs, a predetermined rate applied to actual inputs, or a standard rate applied on the basis of standard input for the volume level actually achieved.

When a standard cost system is used for assigning overhead to production, variances for variable overhead can be calculated as follows:

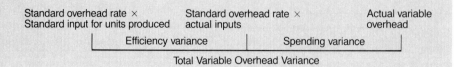

Standard overhead rate × Standard input for units produced	Standard overhead rate × actual inputs	Actual variable overhead
Efficiency variance	Spending variance	

Total Variable Overhead Variance

The efficiency variance reflects whether the amount of the input measure used (for example, direct labor hours), on which the predetermined overhead rate was based, was more or less than the standard input for the units produced. The spending variance is based on an assumed causal relationship between the input measure on which the predetermined rate was based and variable overhead.

Fixed overhead variances when a standard cost system is used are calculated as follows:

Standard overhead rate × Standard input for units produced	Budgeted (standard) overhead	Actual fixed overhead
Volume variance	Spending variance	

Total Fixed Overhead Variance

The volume variance reflects whether facilities were used as fully as was anticipated when the standard rate was set. If the actual input is the same as that on which the fixed overhead rate was based, there will be no volume variance. If actual overhead differs from the total amount of fixed overhead anticipated at the time the budget or standard was set, a spending variance is generated. This is assumed to be due to cost factors, since fixed overhead should not vary with volume.

When an actual/applied cost system is used rather than a standard cost system, there will be no efficiency variance for variable overhead, as overhead is applied on the basis of actual input rather than on some other basis. The spending variance will be the same as if a standard cost system were in use.

When an actual/applied system is used for fixed overhead, a total variance and a volume and spending variance can be calculated. The total variance and the volume variance will differ from what is calculated with a standard cost system, because overhead is applied on the basis of actual input rather than standard input for the volume achieved. The spending variance will be the same as with a standard cost system.

Remember that the overhead variances calculated summarize what happened with respect to a number of different items ranging from indirect materials to depreciation. Since they are aggregate measures, they may not adequately indicate problem areas and areas where efficiency can be improved. Instead, for material items of overhead, each should be reviewed on an individual basis to determine if corrective actions are required.

questions

1. Why are fixed manufacturing overhead costs not relevant in flexible budgeting?
2. Name the three basic costing systems and describe how manufacturing overhead is treated in each.

3. In which of the systems in question 2 does under- or overapplied overhead occur?

4. When an unfavorable direct labor usage variance exists and overhead is applied on the basis of direct labor hours, what can be said about the variable manufacturing overhead efficiency variance?

5. Define a fixed manufacturing overhead volume variance. When does it occur?

6. Contrast a standard cost system with an actual/applied system in terms of the variable overhead variances which result from the two systems. How are they alike and how do they differ?

7. How are overhead variances recorded and disposed of in (a) a standard cost system and (b) an actual/applied system? Assume that overhead was overapplied by $200 in each case and give the journal entries to record its disposal.

8. For overhead, we generally summarize all elements of overhead as being either variable or fixed and calculate a set of variances for the variable component and for the fixed component. What are the problems with this approach to analyzing overhead?

9. Assume that manufacturing overhead was underapplied for the month of June. What does this imply about the nature of the total overhead variance for June?

10. The chapter states that when an applied overhead rate is used, a spending variance is based on an indirect causal relationship, while variances for direct materials and direct labor are based on a direct causal relationship. What does this mean?

11. What is meant by a flexible budgeting formula for manufacturing overhead?

12. Variable manufacturing overhead costs were $5 per unit and fixed manufacturing overhead costs were $3 per unit when 150,000 units were produced. Give the flexible budgeting formula implied by this information. Use the formula you have prepared to estimate overhead when 180,000 units are made.

13. How does a standard variable costing system differ from a standard absorption costing system?

14. How are the total variance, the spending variance, and the volume variance computed for fixed manufacturing overhead when a standard cost system is used?

15. How are the total variance, the efficiency variance, and the spending variance for variable manufacturing overhead computed when a standard cost system is used?

16. The standard *fixed* manufacturing overhead rate was set based on the assumption that 24,000 units would be produced, each requiring 1 hour of direct labor. Actually, 26,000 units were produced, each of which used 1 hour of direct labor. Overhead is applied on the basis of direct labor hours. What, if anything, do we know about the fixed overhead *volume* variance based on these data?

17. The standard *variable* manufacturing overhead rate was set based on the assumption that 24,000 units would be produced, each requiring 1 hour

of direct labor. Actually, 26,000 units were produced, each of which used 1 hour of direct labor. Overhead is applied on the basis of direct labor hours. What, if anything, do we know about the variable overhead efficiency variance based on these data?

18. The variable overhead variance for the period totaled $8,000 favorable. What else do we know about overhead and the relationship of the flexible budget to actual costs based on this information?

19. How do the debits for manufacturing overhead which are made to the work-in-process account differ when a company is using a standard cost system versus when they are using an actual/applied or an actual system?

20. A company developed an overhead rate based on the assumption that they would produce 120,000 units, each of which required 2 standard hours of direct labor. Actually they produced 125,000 units and used 256,000 direct labor hours. Overhead is applied on the basis of direct labor hours. If the company has a standard costing system, how many direct labor hours will they use in applying overhead to production this period?

exercises

10—1. The Boardman Company uses a standard cost system and has established the following overhead standards for the production of its product:

Standard production volume	10,000 units
Standard direct labor inputs	40,000 hours
Variable manufacturing overhead: $80,000/40,000 hours = $2 per direct labor hour × 4 hours per unit	$ 8 per unit
Fixed manufacturing overhead: $240,000/40,000 hours = $6 per direct labor hour × 4 hours per unit	$24 per unit
Standard manufacturing overhead cost per unit based on standard volume of 10,000 units	$32 per unit

REQUIRED:

1. Calculate the amount of overhead which will be applied to production in each of the following cases:

   a. 10,000 units were produced using 44,000 hours of direct labor time.

   b. 12,000 units were produced using 46,000 direct labor hours.

   c. 9,000 units were produced using 40,000 direct labor hours.

   d. 11,000 units were produced using 46,000 direct labor hours.

2. How would your answer have differed in case 1b above, if the data given were for a company which used a budgetary system and applied overhead on the basis of direct labor hours, rather than a company which uses a standard cost system? Show the relevant calculation.

10—2. The Melady Corporation uses a standard cost system and applied overhead on the basis of direct labor hours. The company's standard cost card for a unit of production shows the following data:

Variable manufacturing overhead	$2 per unit
Fixed manufacturing overhead	$3 per unit
Standard manufacturing cost per unit based on the use of 200,000 direct labor hours and the production of 100,000 units	$5 per unit

REQUIRED:

1. Prepare a flexible budget formula for the company based on the data given above and the estimated use of 200,000 direct labor hours.
2. Prepare a *flexible budget formula* for the company, assuming the use of 210,000 direct labor hours and the production of 105,000 units.
3. Assume that the company produced 110,000 units and used 212,000 direct labor hours. How much overhead did they apply to production, based on the use of a standard cost system?
4. Assume that Melady Corporation does not use a standard cost system and that the data given are budget data rather than standard cost data. Recompute your answer to part 3.

10—3.   Stone Corporation uses a standard cost system and a flexible budget in accounting for manufacturing overhead. The company developed the following flexible budget formula for manufacturing overhead:

Manufacturing overhead = $5 per direct labor hour + $200,000

Stone estimated that for the budget period it would manufacture 50,000 units, each of which required 2 direct labor hours, and applied overhead to the units produced on this basis. Actual data for the period were as follows:

Units produced	52,000
Direct labor hours used	103,000
Variable manufacturing overhead	$518,000
Fixed manufacturing overhead	$197,000

REQUIRED:

1. How much overhead was charged to work-in-process this period?
2. For variable manufacturing overhead calculate:

   a. The total variance between actual and standard.
   b. The efficiency variance.
   c. The spending variance.

3. For fixed manufacturing overhead calculate:

   a. The total variance between actual and standard.
   b. The volume variance.
   c. The spending variance.

10—4.   Prestige Products developed the following flexible budget formula for its manufacturing overhead:

Total manufacturing overhead = $1 per direct labor hour + $300,000

The company estimated that it would produce 100,000 units of its product, each of which would require 1 hour of direct labor.

REQUIRED: Calculate the overhead applied to the units produced under each of the following independent assumptions:

1. The company uses an applied overhead rate but does not have a standard cost system. During the period it produced 100,000 units using 101,000 hours of direct labor time.
2. The company uses an applied overhead rate but does not have a standard cost system. During the period it produced 95,000 units using 94,000 direct labor hours.
3. The company uses an applied overhead rate and has a standard cost system. During the period it produced 100,000 units using 101,000 hours of direct labor time.
4. The company uses an applied overhead rate and has a standard cost system. During the period it produced 95,000 units using 94,000 direct labor hours.

10—5. Evergreen Turf Builder Inc. based its overhead rate for the period on an assumed production level of 500,000 units, each of which requires 2 pounds of raw materials. The company uses a standard cost system and applies overhead on the basis of raw material usage. The overhead rates used in applying overhead for the period were:

Variable manufacturing overhead	$.80 per pound of raw materials
Fixed manufacturing overhead	$.50 per pound of raw materials

Actual raw material usage for the 500,000 units produced amounted to 1,040,000 pounds.

Actual variable manufacturing overhead	$842,400
Actual fixed manufacturing overhead	$509,600

REQUIRED:
1. How much variable overhead was applied to units produced during the period?
2. Calculate the following variances between actual and standard costs for variable manufacturing overhead:
   a. Total variance.
   b. Efficiency variance.
   c. Spending variance.
3. How much fixed overhead was applied to units produced during the period?
4. Calculate the following variances between actual and standard costs for fixed manufacturing overhead:
   a. Total variance.
   b. Volume variance.
   c. Spending variance.
5. Explain the figure you got for fixed overhead volume variance.

10—6. Bayview Industrial Parts Company uses an actual/applied cost system and applies overhead to production on a machine-hour basis in their machining department and on a direct-labor-hour basis in their assembly department. The following *budget data* are available for the two departments for the upcoming *quarter*, January through March. Production inputs and costs are spread evenly over the three-month period.

	MACHINING DEPARTMENT	ASSEMBLY DEPARTMENT
Direct labor cost	$345,000	$750,000
Manufacturing overhead, variable	$216,000	$ 56,000
Manufacturing overhead, fixed	$180,000	$ 90,000
Direct labor hours	50,000	100,000
Machine hours	180,000	36,000

Actual costs incurred in January were:

	MACHINING DEPARTMENT	ASSEMBLY DEPARTMENT
Direct labor cost	$120,000	$255,000
Machine hours	58,000	12,000
Direct labor hours	17,000	34,000
Manufacturing overhead, variable	$ 65,500	$ 20,000
Manufacturing overhead, fixed	$ 55,700	$ 29,500

REQUIRED: 1. Determine what overhead costs (variable and fixed) would have been charged to work-in-process during January.

2. What variances result, if any, and are they favorable or unfavorable?

10—7.   Refer to the information in Exercise 10-6. Assume that the Bayview Company uses a standard cost system rather than an actual/applied system and that their quarterly budget reflects standards. Production for January was equal to that budgeted.

REQUIRED: 1. Determine what overhead costs (variable and fixed) would have been charged to work-in-process in January.

2. Calculate any variances, indicating how they differ from those calculated in Exercise 10—6.

10—8.   The Benson Company manufactures one product, metal wastebaskets, and uses a standard costing system. The *flexible overhead budget is based on normal capacity of 15,000 units* and allows the following standard rates and amounts:

Baskets produced per direct labor hour	2.5
Manufacturing overhead:	
Fixed	$22,500
Variable	$5 per direct labor hour

In September the number of baskets was 10% less than normal capacity. Direct labor hours used were 5,500. Actual overhead incurred during the month included $26,000 variable and $20,500 fixed.

REQUIRED: 1. Calculate variable overhead and fixed overhead applied to production.
2. Calculate all overhead variances.

10—9. The following incomplete overhead cost information has been obtained for the Ridgeway Company during March. Ridgeway uses a standard costing system and flexible budgeting system.

Budgeted fixed overhead	?
Standard fixed overhead rate per direct labor hour	$2.50
Actual total variable overhead	?
Standard total variable overhead	?
Fixed overhead spending variance	?
Standard variable overhead rate per direct labor hour	?
Standard direct labor hours allowed for actual production	30,000
Actual total overhead incurred	184,300

The volume variance for the month was 6,000 unfavorable and the total fixed overhead variance was 2,000 favorable. The *total* (both variable and fixed) overhead variance was $8,300 unfavorable.

REQUIRED: Compute the missing numbers.

10—10. The flexible budget formula for the Brown Company, which uses a standard cost system, was:

$$\text{overhead} = \$2 \text{ per direct labor hours used} + \$50,000$$

Anticipated production for the budget period is 50,000 units, each of which require 2 hours of direct labor. During the year 48,000 units were made using 85,000 direct labor hours. The variable overhead spending variance was $2,000 unfavorable, while the fixed overhead spending variance was $1,000 favorable.

REQUIRED: 1. Calculate the rates at which both variable and fixed overhead were charged to production (debited to work-in-process) during the period. They are applied on the basis of direct labor hours.
2. Compute both variable and fixed overhead applied to production for the period.
3. Compute actual variable and actual fixed overhead incurred during the period.

10—11. The following information was obtained from the cost control records of Hubex Company, which uses a standard cost system:

Variable overhead costs per standard hour	$2.25
Fixed overhead total variance	225 F
Total actual variable and fixed costs	39,500
Volume variance	430 F
Spending variance—variable cost	600 U
Efficiency variance	450 F
Standard hours for activity level achieved	12,500

REQUIRED: Compute:

1. Actual hours used.
2. Actual variable costs.
3. Actual fixed costs.
4. Fixed overhead applied to production.
5. Budgeted fixed overhead.

10—12.   (CMA adapted) Standard Company has developed standard overhead costs based on a capacity of 180,000 direct labor hours as follows:

Standard cost *per unit*:

Variable portion, 2 hours @ $3	$ 6
Fixed portion, 2 hours @ $5	10
	$16

During April 85,000 units were scheduled for production; however, only 80,000 units were actually produced. The following data relate to April:

Actual direct labor cost incurred was $644,000 for 165,000 actual hours of work. Actual overhead incurred totaled $1,378,000—$518,000 variable and $860,000 fixed.

All inventories are carried at standard cost.

REQUIRED: Calculate for April:

1. The variable overhead spending variance.
2. The variable factory overhead efficiency variance.
3. The fixed overhead spending variance.
4. The fixed overhead volume variance.

10—13.   The following data relate to the operations of the Sharpex Pen Company, which applies overhead to the units it produces on the basis of direct labor hours:

Budget data	
Budgeted production:	900,000 pens
Budgeted and standard direct labor hours per pen	1.25 hours
Budgeted variable overhead rate	$.90 per direct labor hour
Budgeted fixed overhead rate	$1.20 per direct labor hour
Actual data	
Actual production	920,000 pens
Actual direct labor hours	1,100,320 hours
Actual variable overhead	$1,069,500
Actual fixed overhead	$1,300,000

REQUIRED: 1. What was the flexible overhead formula for the period?
2. Based on the formula you have developed, how much overhead should have been incurred for the period when 920,000 pens were produced?
3. Assume the company used an actual absorption cost system. How much overhead will be attached to each pen produced? (Round to the nearest cent.)

4. Assume the company uses an actual/applied absorption costing system. How much overhead will be attached to each pen produced? (Round to the nearest cent.)
5. Assume the company uses a standard absorption costing system and the budgeted overhead rates are the standard rates. How much overhead will be attached to each pen produced? (Round to the nearest cent.)
6. Assume the company uses a standard variable costing system. How much overhead will be attached to each pen produced?

10—14. Refer back to the information in Exercise 10—13.

REQUIRED: 1. Give the journal entries to charge work-in-process with overhead under each of these assumptions (absorption costing is used):

  a. The company uses an actual costing system.
  b. The company uses an actual/applied costing system.
  c. The company uses a standard costing system.

2. For each of the approaches you have used to charge overhead to production in part 1 above, calculate the amount by which overhead is over- or underapplied. For standard costing, calculate over- or underapplied overhead two ways.

10—15. Refer back to the information given in Exercise 10—13.

REQUIRED: 1. Calculate overhead variances for both variable and fixed overhead combined, assuming the use of a standard cost system. (In other words, you will calculate only three variances.)
2. Calculate overhead variances from budget for both variable and fixed overhead combined, assuming the use of an actual/applied costing system.

problems

10—16. *Straightforward/variance analysis.* The Doplinger Company makes wheelbarrows. For the period under consideration, they had budgeted at a production level of 100,000 wheelbarrows. The company uses a standard cost system, and manufacturing overhead is applied on the basis of direct labor hours. Each wheelbarrow has a standard direct labor usage of 2 hours. Based on the budgeted production level, the following standard manufacturing overhead rates were developed by Doplinger:

Standard variable manufacturing overhead rate	$3 per direct labor hour
Standard fixed manufacturing overhead rate	$2.50 per direct labor hour

Actual data for the period were as follows:

Wheelbarrows produced	97,000
Direct labor hours used	191,100
Variable manufacturing overhead	$590,000
Fixed manufacturing overhead	$480,000

REQUIRED: 1. Calculate the amount of variable manufacturing overhead which was applied to the units produced for the period.

2. Calculate the following standard cost variances for variable manufacturing overhead:

   a. Total variance.

   b. Efficiency variance.

   c. Spending variance.

3. Calculate the amount of fixed manufacturing overhead which was applied to the units produced for the period.

4. Calculate the following standard cost variances for fixed manufacturing overhead:

   a. Total variance.

   b. Volume variance.

   c. Spending variance.

10—17. *Straightforward manufacturing overhead variance analysis.* Cycle Incorporated manufactures bicycles and uses a standard cost system for its manufacturing operations. Each bicycle requires 3 hours of direct labor time. Manufacturing overhead is applied on the basis of direct labor hours. The standard manufacturing overhead rate is $4 per direct labor hour. Of this rate, $1 is fixed overhead, the remainder is variable. The manufacturing overhead rate was based on the assumption that 150,000 bicycles would be manufactured during the year. Actual data for the period were as follows:

Bicycles produced	160,000
Direct labor hours used	488,000
Variable manufacturing overhead	$1,450,000
Fixed manufacturing overhead	$ 500,000

REQUIRED: 1. Calculate the amount of variable manufacturing overhead applied to the units produced during the period.

2. Calculate the following standard cost variances for variable manufacturing overhead:

   a. Total variance.

   b. Efficiency variance.

   c. Spending variance.

3. Calculate the amount of fixed manufacturing overhead applied to the bicycles produced this period.

4. Calculate the following standard cost variances for fixed manufacturing overhead:

   a. Total variance.

   b. Volume variance.

   c. Spending variance.

10—18. *Development of a flexible budget formula for overhead, application of overhead, and variance analysis.* Grand Reproductions, which makes statues of flamingos for use on lawns and in gardens, developed the following estimated unit costs for overhead based on an anticipated production of 100,000 statues. Overhead is applied on the basis of the number of pounds of molding materials used in each unit. The average unit requires 5 pounds of such materials. Grand Reproductions uses a standard cost system in accounting for its manufacturing costs.

Standard Overhead Cost per Unit Based on the Production of 100,000 Statues Using 500,000 Pounds of Raw Materials

Variable manufacturing overhead	$ 5.00
Fixed manufacturing overhead	$ 7.50
Standard manufacturing overhead per unit at a volume of 100,000 units	$12.50

REQUIRED:

1. Develop a flexible budget formula based on direct material usage for manufacturing overhead.

2. Calculate estimated overhead costs for each of these levels of production, using the formula you developed in part 1:

   a. 150,000 statues.

   b. 90,000 statues.

3. Assume that the initial data given represented the company's expected volume for the period and that standard overhead was applied on the basis of the use of 500,000 pounds of raw materials. What is the standard overhead rate per pound of direct materials? What part of this rate is related to variable overhead and what part to fixed?

4. Assume that overhead was applied to production on the basis of an anticipated production level of 100,000 units but 90,000 were actually produced which used 470,000 pounds of raw materials.

   a. How much total overhead was applied to the 90,000 units produced, assuming the use of a standard cost system for applying overhead?

   b. Assume actual variable manufacturing overhead was $450,000 and actual total fixed manufacturing overhead was equal to the total amount originally budgeted. By what amount was overhead over- or underapplied?

   c. Without doing any computations, will the variable manufacturing overhead efficiency variance be favorable or unfavorable? How do you know?

   d. Without doing any computations, will the fixed manufacturing overhead volume variance be favorable or unfavorable. How do you know?

5. Assume that overhead was applied to production on the basis of an anticipated production level of 100,000 units but 110,000 were actually produced which required the use of 540,000 pounds of raw materials. Actual variable manufacturing overhead was $535,000 and actual fixed manufacturing overhead was $800,000.

a. Give the journal entries to charge work-in-process with standard overhead, and record any variances between standard overhead costs and actual overhead costs.

b. By what amount was overhead over- or underapplied? Compute this amount two ways.

10—19. *Different methods for charging work-in-process with manufacturing overhead.* Budnick Manufacturing Company makes rocking chairs. For the coming period they anticipated producing 50,000 rocking chairs, each of which required 5 hours of direct labor time. The company estimated that their variable manufacturing overhead would amount to $750,000 for the period and fixed manufacturing overhead would be $250,000. Budnick Manufacturing actually produced 48,000 rocking chairs using 235,200 direct labor hours. Actual variable manufacturing overhead cost amounted to $729,600, while actual fixed manufacturing overhead cost amounted to $248,000. The company accumulates overhead costs in two separate summary accounts—one for variable manufacturing overhead and the other for fixed manufacturing overhead.

REQUIRED:

1. Assume that the company uses an actual overhead system in charging production with overhead cost. Prepare the journal entries to record actual overhead (use "various credits" for the credit part of this entry) and to charge production with the appropriate amount of overhead.

2. Assume that the company uses an actual/applied costing system and has developed an overhead rate based on the estimated data given. Prepare the journal entries to record actual overhead and to charge production with the appropriate amount of manufacturing overhead. Overhead is applied on the basis of direct labor hours.

3. Assume that the company uses a standard cost system and has developed its standard overhead rate on the basis of the estimated data provided. Give the journal entries to record actual overhead and to charge production with the appropriate amount of overhead. Overhead is applied on the basis of direct labor hours.

4. Compare the amount by which overhead was over- or underapplied under each of the three methods for charging production with overhead cost. Why do your results differ when an applied system is used in conjunction with a standard cost system from your results when an applied system is used without a standard cost system?

10—20. *Manufacturing overhead variance analysis—calculating unknowns.* Selected data from the records of Atlas Manufacturing Company, which uses a standard cost system in costing its production, are as follows:

Budgeted production in units	200,000
Direct labor hours to produce 200,000 units	400,000
Budgeted variable manufacturing overhead	$600,000
Budgeted fixed manufacturing overhead	?

Actual production in units	205,000
Actual direct labor hours used to produce 205,000 units	?
Actual variable manufacturing overhead	?
Actual fixed manufacturing overhead	$795,000
Total variable overhead variance	?
Variable overhead efficiency variance	7,500 U
Variable overhead spending variance	17,500 F
Total fixed overhead variance	25,000 F
Fixed overhead spending variance	?

Overhead is applied on the basis of direct labor hours.

REQUIRED: Calculate the following:

1. Actual direct labor hours used to produce the 205,000 units.
2. Actual variable manufacturing overhead.
3. Total variable overhead variance.
4. Rate at which fixed overhead was applied to production.
5. Fixed overhead spending variance.

10—21. *Comprehensive overhead variance problem.* At the time its budget was prepared, the Food Preparation Department of Oakmont Hospital anticipated serving 360,000 meals using 180,000 direct labor hours. Its variable overhead costs were budgeted at $1.30 per direct labor hour and its fixed overhead was estimated at $540,000 for the period. These budget estimates were adopted as standards for the Department, which uses a standard cost system. Overhead is applied on the basis of direct labor hours. During the period the Food Preparation Department actually served 380,000 meals using 178,000 direct labor hours. Its variable costs amounted to $250,000 and its fixed costs were $525,000.

REQUIRED:
1. Calculate the total variance, the efficiency variance, and the spending variance for variable overhead.
2. At what rate was fixed overhead applied during the period?
3. For fixed overhead, calculate the total variance, the volume variance, and the spending variance.
4. Prepare journal entries to record actual and applied overhead for the period. You may assume that, except for $120,000 of depreciation, all overhead costs were paid in cash.
5. Prepare a journal entry to close out the overhead variances to the "Food Preparation Expense" account.

10—22. *Comprehensive standard cost problem with journal entries.* The following actual information is available for Smith and Company for the first quarter of the year: Smith and Company manufacture only one product, an industrial fan.

Sales	$250,000
Selling price per unit	25
Direct materials used (11,200 units @ $7.50)	84,000
Direct labor cost incurred ($6.25/hr)	97,300
Variable manufacturing overhead incurred	18,900
Fixed manufacturing overhead incurred	18,150
Variable selling and administrative expenses	19,700
Fixed selling and administrative expenses	13,150

Smith and Company use a standard costing system, and one unit of direct materials is standard input for each finished unit. Standard costs for materials are $8 per unit. Based on normal production of 10,000 fans, 15,000 direct labor hours are used. The standard cost of a direct labor hour is $6. Standard variable overhead is $18,750, while standard fixed overhead is $15,750. Overhead is applied to production on the basis of standard direct labor hours for the number of units produced. Of the fans produced during the period, 1,000 were put into inventory; the remainder were sold. When raw materials are purchased, they are put into inventory at their actual cost. There were no beginning or ending work-in-process inventories.

REQUIRED:
1. Prepare all journal entries for the period, based on the data provided. If an entry would actually require a credit to a number of different accounts, simply use the term "various credits" for the credit part of the entry. Assume that all variances from standard are closed to cost of goods sold.
2. Prepare the work-in-process T-account, showing all debits and credits during the period, assuming the company uses:

   a. A standard cost system.

   b. An actual cost system (disregard the data describing standards).

3. Calculate the cost of a fan put into inventory, assuming the use of standard costs and assuming the use of actual costs. How do you explain the difference between the amounts you have calculated?

10—23. *Calculations of materials, labor, and overhead variances.* (AICPA adapted) The Terry Company manufactures a commercial solvent that is used for industrial maintenance. This solvent is sold by the drum and generally has a stable selling price. The following information is available regarding Terry's operations for the month of December.

1. Standard cost per drum of product manufactured were as follows based on estimated production of 60,000 drums.

Materials:		
10 gallons of raw material	$20	
1 empty drum	1	
Total materials	$21	
Direct labor:		
1 hour	$ 7	
Factory overhead (fixed):		
Per direct labor hour	$ 4	
Factory overhead (variable):		
Per direct labor hour	$ 6	

2. Actual costs incurred during December, when 60,000 drums were produced, were:

> Raw materials: (carried in inventory at standard cost)
>   600,000 gallons were purchased at a cost of $1,150,000.
>   700,000 gallons were used, 100,000 of which were taken
>   from beginning inventory.
> Empty drums:
>   85,000 drums were purchased at a cost of $85,000.
>   60,000 drums were used.
> Direct labor:
>   65,000 hours were worked at a cost of $470,000.
> Factory overhead:
>   Variable, $396,500.
>   Fixed, $270,000.

REQUIRED: Prepare a schedule computing the following variances for the month of December:

1. Materials price variance (computed at time of purchase).
2. Materials usage variance.
3. Labor rate variance.
4. Labor usage (efficiency) variance.
5. Factory overhead using a four-variance method. Each of the four variances should be appropriately titled. (Calculate two variances for variable overhead and two for fixed overhead.) Indicate whether each variance was favorable or unfavorable.

10—24. *Manufacturing overhead variance analysis—calculating unknowns.* Aster Inc., uses a standard cost system in costing its product. The following information is available:

Budgeted production in units	7,500
Direct labor hours to produce 7,500 units	1,500
Budgeted variable overhead	$5,100
Budgeted fixed overhead	$3,000
Actual production in units	7,000
Actual direct labor hours to produce 7,000 units	?
Actual variable overhead	?
Actual fixed overhead	$3,500
Total variable overhead variance	$ 197 F
Variable overhead efficiency variance	?
Variable overhead spending variance	$ 707 F
Total fixed overhead variance	$ 700 U
Total fixed volume variance	?
Fixed overhead spending variance	?

Overhead is applied on the basis of direct labor hours.

REQUIRED: Calculate:

1. Standard overhead applied.
2. Total overhead variance.
3. Actual variable overhead.
4. Actual direct labor hours used.
5. Variable overhead efficiency variance.
6. Fixed overhead volume variance.
7. Fixed overhead spending variance.

10—25. *Manufacturing overhead variance analysis—calculating unknowns.* Williams Manufacturing Co. uses a standard cost system to cost its production. Incomplete cost data for the quarter include:

Budgeted:	
Production in pounds	57,000
Direct labor hours per lb	1.9 hr per lb
Variable overhead rate	$2.25 per direct labor hour
Fixed overhead rate	$ .65 per direct labor hour
Actual:	
Production in pounds	51,800
Direct labor hours used	b
Manufacturing overhead (20% fixed)	$297,650
Variances:	
Total manufacturing overhead	$12,232 U
Total variable overhead	a
Total fixed overhead	d
Variable overhead efficiency	$11,655 U
Variable overhead spending	c
Fixed overhead volume	e
Fixed overhead spending	f

REQUIRED: Calculate the unknowns, *a–f*.

10—26. *Journal entries, comprehensive standard cost problem.* Mantuck Manufacturing makes unicycles, for which the following standard costs have been developed:

Steel for the frame, 2 units per unicycle @ $5	$10.00
One seat per unicycle @$2	2.00
One wheel per unicycle @ $3.50	3.50
Direct labor, 2 hours per unicycle @ $5 average cost	10.00
Variable manufacturing overhead, applied on the basis of $1 per direct labor hour	2.00
Fixed manufacturing overhead, applied on the basis of $1.70 per direct labor hour based on a production level of 100,00 unicycles	3.40
Standard cost per unicycle at a volume of 100,000 cycles	$30.90

Actual results for the period were as follows:

Unicycles produced	90,000
Unicycles sold (LIFO costing)	80,000
Steel used	178,000 units
Seats used[a]	90,500 seats
Wheels used	90,000 wheels
Direct labor, 171,000 hours	$846,450
Variable overhead	$185,000
Fixed overhead	$325,000

[a] All unicycles have a seat, but some are lost or spoiled in production.

The selling price for a unicycle was $55. All sales were for cash. Assume that all expenses were paid in cash except for depreciation of $90,000, which was a part of fixed overhead. Purchases of inventory for cash were as follows:

Units of steel	220,000 @ $4.90
Unicycle seats	130,000 @ 2.15
Unicycle wheels	130,000 @ 3.55

All transfers from raw materials inventory to production are on a LIFO basis, and the raw materials purchase-price variances are recorded when units are acquired.

REQUIRED:
1. Record all the transactions described in the data above, assuming the use of a standard cost system.
2. Prepare a partial income statement through the gross margin section for the period, assuming standard costs variances are accounted for as adjustments to cost of goods sold.
3. Calculate over- or underapplied overhead two ways.
4. Assume Mantuck had a beginning inventory of 2,000 unicycles @ $30. Calculate the ending finished goods inventory valuation.

10—27. *Different product costing systems.* Use the information provided in Problem 10—26 to answer the questions given below.

REQUIRED:
1. Assume that the figures given for standard costs are budget figures and the company uses an actual/applied absorption costing system for product costing purposes. Calculate the following amounts:
   a. The cost of a unicycle put into inventory during the period.
   b. Variable overhead applied to production for the period.
   c. Fixed overhead applied to production for the period.
   d. All variable overhead variances for the period.
   e. All fixed overhead variances for the period.
   f. Over- or underapplied overhead.

2. Assume that the company uses a standard variable costing system for product costing purposes. Calculate the following amounts:

    a. The cost of a unicycle put into inventory during the period.

    b. Total overhead applied to units produced during the period.

10—28. *Combined overhead variances versus separate overhead variances for variable and fixed overhead.* Weed-Away Manufacturing makes a device commonly known as a weedeater, which cuts weeds using a string that rotates at a very rapid rate. Information regarding manufacturing overhead for this device for the period is given below:

STANDARD OVERHEAD COSTS		ACTUAL DATA	
Variable manufacturing overhead applied on the basis of direct labor hours, $1.30 × 4 direct labor hours per unit	$5.20	Variable manufacturing overhead	$590,240
		Fixed manufacturing overhead	$328,000
Fixed manufacturing overhead applied on the basis of direct labor hours, $0.80 × 4 direct labor hours based on labor inputs of 400,000 hours	3.20	Units produced	108,000
		Direct labor hours used	434,000 hr
Standard overhead per unit at a volume of 400,000 hours	$8.40		

REQUIRED:

    1. Calculate all standard cost variances for variable manufacturing overhead.

    2. Calculate all standard cost variances for fixed manufacturing overhead.

    3. Calculate one set of variances which describes the difference between standard and actual for variable and fixed overhead combined.

10—29. *Journal entries, different product costing systems.* One of the products which Handiperson Manufacturing makes is a snow shovel called "the back-saver." The handle is curved to facilitate the pushing of snow with less strain on the back. The following data have been gathered with respect to the back-saver:

Standard or Budgeted Costs per Unit—Production Level of 200,000 Shovels	
Aluminum blade, 1 per shovel @ $4.50	$4.50
Wooden handle, 1 per shovel @ $1.10	1.10
Direct labor hours, 1/2 hour per shovel @ $6	3.00
Variable overhead applied on the basis of direct labor hours, $1 per direct labor hour	.50
Fixed manufacturing overhead applied on the basis of direct labor hours, $2.20 per direct labor hour	1.10
Standard (budgeted) cost of a "back-saver" at a production level of 200,000 shovels	$10.20

Actual Data for the Period at a Production Level of 200,000 Shovels	
Aluminum blades, 203,000 costing	$964,250[a]
Handles, 210,000 costing	$210,000
Direct labor hours, 98,000	$568,400
Variable overhead costing	$ 92,000
Fixed overhead	$227,000

[a] All back-savers have a blade and handle, but some materials are either lost in process or spoiled. Workers have a tendency to take handles because they have found them useful for staking-up plants in their gardens.

REQUIRED: **1.** Give the entries to charge work-in-process with all manufacturing inputs assuming the use of:

a. A standard cost system.

b. An actual/applied cost system.

c. An actual cost system.

d. An actual variable cost system.

Assume all materials are taken from inventory and these materials were put into inventory at actual, rather than standard, costs. Direct labor is accrued, and manufacturing overhead except for $40,000 of depreciation was paid in cash.

2. Give the entries to record actual manufacturing overhead under each system. You may label the credit part of the entry "cash and various credits."

3. Give the entries to close any over- or underapplied overhead to cost of goods sold under each system.

4. Calculate the cost of a snow shovel which was put into inventory this period based on each of the product costing systems listed under part 1 above.

10—30. *Analysis of overhead and flexible budgeting.* Gandhi, Inc., produces carrying chests made from styrofoam. The chests can be used to keep food or beverages cold. The company uses a standard cost system to control manufacturing costs. Data for overhead costs for the past year were:

	BUDGET	ACTUAL
Variable manufacturing overhead:		
Bonding material	$ 16,000	$ 19,000
Handles and screws to attach handles	240,000	220,000
Other variable costs	48,000	43,000
Fixed manufacturing overhead:		
Indirect labor	320,000	328,000
Depreciation on factory building and equipment	480,000	475,000
Repairs and maintenance	100,000	106,000
Utilities	160,000	158,000
Other fixed costs	92,000	89,000

When Gandhi, Inc., set the budget, it anticipated making 800,000 chests. Actual production totaled 750,000 chests, and 1,505,000 sheet of styrofoam were used. The company uses the budget data to develop standard overhead rates based on raw materials—sheets of styrofoam used. Each chest requires an input of 2 sheets of styrofoam. The standard overhead rates are then used to apply overhead to production.

REQUIRED: 1. What were the standard overhead rates per piece of styrofoam for variable and for fixed overhead for the period?

2. What was the flexible budget formula for the period?

3. Apply flexible budgeting concepts and restate each item of budgeted overhead consistent with the actual production level of 750,000 chests. Compare the figures with actual, and calculate variances.

4. Calculate variable manufacturing overhead variances from standard costs for the period. Compare your results with the differences between the flexible budget you prepared in part 3 and actual costs. What do you observe?

5. Calculate fixed manufacturing overhead variances from standard costs for the period. Compare your results with the differences between the flexible budget and actual results. What do you observe?

6. Calculate over- or underapplied overhead for the period by two methods.

chapter eleven

CONTROLLING REVENUES, EXPENSES, AND INVESTMENT

OBJECTIVES

After you have completed your study of this chapter, you should be able to answer the following questions:

- How can the concepts of flexible budgeting and variance analysis be applied to revenues and to variable operating expenses?
- What types of standards other than budgetary standards can be used as a basis for control and in evaluating performance?
- What are common size statements and how can they be used?
- What are commonly calculated ratios which can assist in the control of operations and evaluation of performance?

FLEXIBLE BUDGETS FOR RESULTS OF OPERATIONS

In the previous two chapters we considered the use of flexible budgets in conjunction with manufacturing costs. The problems that pertained to the use of a static budget and to the interpretation of the difference between budget and actual also exist with respect to revenues and all nonmanufacturing variable expenses.

Illustration 11-1 shows the budgeted income statement and the actual income statement for Handicrafts, Inc. As you can see from this exhibit, Handicraft had budgeted for sales of 17,000 baskets but actually sold 18,000. For the variable expenses, a series of unfavorable variances have been generated. As explained in the previous chapter, these variances cannot be interpreted as meaning that Handicrafts operated inefficiently. Rather, since variable expenses are expected to vary with volume, the higher level of actual expenses relative to budgeted expenses could be due solely to the increased volume.

Illustration 11-2 depicts the results of applying flexible budgeting

ILLUSTRATION 11-1

<table>
<tr><td colspan="6" align="center">HANDICRAFTS, LIMITED
Comparison of Actual and Budgeted Income Statements
for Period Ended December 31</td></tr>
<tr><td></td><td colspan="2" align="center">Budget</td><td colspan="2" align="center">Actual</td><td align="center">Variance</td></tr>
<tr><td align="center">Unit Sales</td><td></td><td align="center">17,000</td><td></td><td align="center">18,000</td><td align="center">1,000 F</td></tr>
<tr><td>Sales</td><td>17,000 @ $25</td><td>$425,000</td><td>18,000 @ $23</td><td>$414,000</td><td>$11,000 U</td></tr>
<tr><td>Cost of Goods Sold (LIFO)</td><td>17,000 @ $9.50</td><td>161,500</td><td>18,000 @ $9.90</td><td>178,200</td><td>16,700 U</td></tr>
<tr><td>Gross Margin</td><td></td><td>$263,500</td><td></td><td>$235,800</td><td>$27,700 U</td></tr>
<tr><td>Other Variable Expenses:</td><td></td><td></td><td></td><td></td><td></td></tr>
<tr><td> Sales Comissions</td><td>5% of sales</td><td>$ 21,250</td><td></td><td>$ 20,700</td><td>$ 550 F</td></tr>
<tr><td> Other Variable
    Expenses</td><td>10% of sales</td><td>42,500</td><td></td><td>39,000</td><td>3,500 F</td></tr>
<tr><td> Total Variable Operating
    Expenses</td><td></td><td>$ 63,750</td><td></td><td>$ 59,700</td><td>$ 4,050 F</td></tr>
<tr><td>Contribution Margin</td><td></td><td>$199,750</td><td></td><td>$176,100</td><td>$23,650 U</td></tr>
<tr><td>Fixed Selling and
  Administrative:</td><td></td><td></td><td></td><td></td><td></td></tr>
<tr><td> Salaries</td><td></td><td>$ 80,000</td><td></td><td>$ 83,000</td><td>$ 3,000 U</td></tr>
<tr><td> Depreciation</td><td></td><td>25,000</td><td></td><td>25,000</td><td>—</td></tr>
<tr><td> Utilities</td><td></td><td>10,000</td><td></td><td>8,600</td><td>1,400 F</td></tr>
<tr><td> Insurance</td><td></td><td>9,000</td><td></td><td>9,200</td><td>200 U</td></tr>
<tr><td> Supplies</td><td></td><td>5,600</td><td></td><td>5,000</td><td>600 F</td></tr>
<tr><td> Other</td><td></td><td>5,000</td><td></td><td>$ 6,000</td><td>1,000 U</td></tr>
<tr><td> Total Fixed Expenses</td><td></td><td>$134,600</td><td></td><td>$136,800</td><td>$ 2,200 U</td></tr>
<tr><td>Net Income</td><td></td><td>$ 65,150</td><td></td><td>$ 39,300</td><td>$25,850 U</td></tr>
</table>

ILLUSTRATION 11-2

HANDICRAFTS, LIMITED
Comparison of Actual and with Budgeting Income Statement
for Period Ended December 31

	Budget		Actual		Variance
Unit Sales		18,000		18,000	—
Sales	18,000 @ $25	$450,000	18,000 @ $23	$414,000	$36,000 U
Cost of Goods Sold (LIFO)	18,000 @ $9.50	171,000	18,000 @ $9.90	178,200	7,200 U
Gross Margin		$279,000		$235,800	$43,200 U
Other Variable Expenses:					
Sales Comissions	5% of sales	$ 22,500		$ 20,700	$ 1,800 F
Other	10% of sales	45,000		39,000	6,000 F
Total Variable Operating Expenses		$ 67,500		$ 59,700	$ 7,800 F
Contribution Margin		$211,500		$176,100	$35,400 U
Fixed Selling and Administrative:					
Salaries		$ 80,000		$ 83,000	$ 3,000 U
Depreciation		25,000		25,000	—
Utilities		10,000		8,600	1,400 F
Insurance		9,000		9,200	200 U
Supplies		5,600		5,000	600 F
Other		5,000		$ 6,000	1,000 U
Total Fixed Expenses		$134,600		$136,800	$ 2,200 U
Net Income		$ 76,900		$ 39,300	$37,600 U

concepts to the budgeted income statement. Sales revenues, cost of goods sold, and related variable expenses have been adjusted consistent with the 18,000 units actually sold. The variances generated when the flexible budget is compared with the actual results for Handicrafts are quite different from those which appeared when the static budget comparison was made. Sales revenues with the flexible budget shows an unfavorable variance of $36,000 rather than an unfavorable $11,000 variance. The cost of goods sold variance is still unfavorable, but the size has been reduced, because the budgeted unit price was applied to the 18,000 units actually sold rather than to the 17,000 which provided the basis for the static budget shown in Illustration 11-1.

In the original comparison of budget and actual, when the budget was based on an anticipated volume of 17,000 units, there were unfavorable variances for sales commissions and other variable expenses, the level of which varies with sales. Comparing actual for these two items with the flexible budget, the variances are favorable. When the static budget was used, the gross margin variance was unfavorable in the amount of $27,700. In comparison with the flexible budget, this unfavorable margin has become larger.

Because fixed selling and administrative expenses, like fixed manufacturing expenses, do not vary with volume changes, there is no difference in the fixed expense variances when a static budget was used and when the flexible budget was used.

VARIANCE ANALYSIS FOR RESULTS OF OPERATIONS

When we were doing variance analysis for manufacturing costs, we assumed that changes in the production volume were triggered by changes in the anticipated sales volume. For Handicrafts, when units produced were increased from the originally contemplated level of 20,000 to 21,000, we assumed that this was done because of changes in selling activity which were not the responsibility of the managers who were charged with controlling direct material, direct labor, and manufacturing overhead costs.

Now that we are looking at the income statement for Handicrafts (or for some part of that organization), we have reached the level at which the manager whose performance is being judged by income is responsible for the sales volume. Thus, in our variance analysis we want to look at the results of volume changes as well as revenue and expense variances. This can be done by comparing three amounts for sales revenues and for all variable expenses which vary with sales. Those amounts are: (a) the static budget, (b) the flexible budget for the sales volume actually attained, and (c) the actual results.

Sales Revenue Variances

Consider the sales revenue figure. *When the flexible budget is compared with the actual sales revenue figure, the variance has no volume component.* It is solely the result of the fact that Handicrafts' average selling price of $23 was $2 less than the budgeted selling price of $25. The selling-price variance can be computed as follows:

$$\text{Selling-price variance} = (\text{actual unit sales}) \times \left(\begin{array}{c} \text{budgeted selling} - \text{actual selling} \\ \text{price} \qquad\qquad \text{price} \end{array} \right)$$

$$\$36,000\,\text{U} = (18,000\,\text{units})(\$25 - \$23)$$

The sales-volume variance is generated by a comparison of the static budget with the flexible budget:

$$\text{sales-volume variance} = (\text{budgeted selling price}) \times \left(\begin{array}{c} \text{budgeted unit} - \text{actual unit} \\ \text{sales} \qquad\quad \text{sales} \end{array} \right)$$

$$\$25,000\,\text{F} = (\$25)(17,000\,\text{units} - 18,000\,\text{units})$$

Market-Share Variance

If appropriate industry data are available, the sales-volume variance can be analyzed further. To illustrate assume the following data:

	ESTIMATED	ACTUAL
Total demand for baskets of the type produced by Handicraft as provided by industry sources	100,000 baskets	115,000 baskets
Handicraft's market share	17,000 or 17%	18,000 or 15.7%

Although Handicraft's volume was greater than anticipated, the company did not maintain its market share, which would have been 19,550 baskets (115,000 actual demand × 17% estimated market share). The $25,000 favorable volume computed in the preceding section is accounted for entirely by a larger demand for baskets, not because Handicraft obtained a bigger market share. In fact, they lost a part of their market share.

We can compute the dollar cost of having lost market share as follows:

Sales-volume variance (computed in the previous section)	$25,000 F
Portion of variance due to increased demand for baskets based on Handicraft's anticipated market share at budgeted selling price, (19,550 − 17,000) = 2,550 × $25	63,750 U
Cost of not maintaining market share	$38,750 U

or

Demand based on 17% market share	19,550
Less: Actual volume (18,000)	18,000
Volume lost based on market share	1,550
Cost of market share lost: 1,550 units × $25 budgeted selling price	$38,750

A General Approach to Variances for Revenues, Cost of Goods Sold, and Operating Expenses

Rather than trying to break each variance down into price in the case of revenues (or cost in the case of expenses) and volume components, by the use of formulas similar to those shown for analyzing sales, we can instead generate these variances by a direct comparison of the three amounts referred to previously: (a) the static budget, (b) the flexible budget amounts, and (c) the actual amounts.

We shall designate the results of comparing these three amounts as: the income variance, the volume variance, and the flexible budget variance, computed as follows:

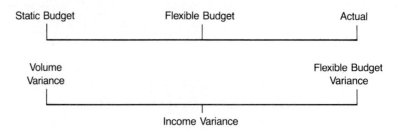

The *volume variance* is due solely to differences between the volume anticipated when the static budget was set and the actual volume which was achieved. The *flexible budget variance* is due to the fact that budgeted selling prices and actual selling prices differ and the budgeted costs of expense items differed from the actual cost. This flexible budget variance is sometimes called a price variance but we have called it a flexible budget variance to distinguish it from the price variances we previously described for direct materials and direct labor. The variances which result from comparing the static budget, the flexible budget, and actual results for Handicrafts, Limited, are shown in Illustration 11-3.

What Illustration 11-3 tells us is that if we could have had the 18,000-unit volume without any changes in selling prices or in the level of our costs and expenses, our profits would have increased by $11,750. This amount could have been calculated another way based on the concept of contribution margin—the difference between revenues and all variable costs. The contribution margin, based on budgeted amounts for Handicrafts, can be calculated as follows:

Budgeted sales price per unit		$25.00
Budgeted variable cost:		
Cost of goods sold	$9.50	
Sales commissions, $25 × 5%	1.25	
Other, $25 × 10%	2.50	13.25
Budgeted contribution margin per unit		$11.75

Based on the budgeted contribution margin, if sales volume increased by 1,000 units, the net income would be expected to increase by $11,750. The fixed costs are irrelevant in this analysis because they are not expected to change with the increase in volume.

The flexible budget and the actual results are based on the same volume assumptions. Variances between these two indicate that revenues, costs, and expenses were not at the levels contemplated when the budget was prepared. This fact had a negative impact on income in the amount of $37,600. The major reasons for this relate to the sales price, which was $2 less than the budget level, and the cost of producing the units which were sold this period. Handicrafts had anticipated producing baskets at a cost of $9.50 each; instead the cost was $9.90. This resulted in an

ILLUSTRATION 11-3

Price and volume variances for income statement amounts

	(1) STATIC BUDGET	(2) [(1) − (3)] SALES VOLUME VARIANCE	(3) FLEXIBLE BUDGET	(4) [(3) − (5)] FLEXIBLE BUDGET VARIANCE	(5) ACTUAL	(6) [(1) − (5)] IMPACT ON INCOME
Unit Sales	17,000	1,000 F	18,000	—	18,000	
Sales	$425,000	$25,000 F	$450,000	$36,000 U	$414,000	$11,000 U
Cost of Goods Sold	161,500	9,500 U	171,000	7,200 U	178,200	16,700 U
Gross Margin	$263,500	$15,500 F	$279,000	$43,200 U	$235,800	$27,700 U
Other Variable Expenses:						
Sales Commissions	$ 21,250	$ 1,250 U	$ 22,500	$ 1,800 F	$ 20,700	$ 550 F
Other	42,500	2,500 U	45,000	6,000 F	39,000	3,500 F
Total Other Variable Expenses	$ 63,750	$ 3,750 U	$ 67,500	$ 7,800 F	$ 59,700	$ 4,050 F
Contribution Margin	$199,750	$11,750 F	$211,500	$35,400 U	$176,100	$23,650 U
Fixed Selling and Administrative Expenses:						
Salaries	80,000	—	80,000	3,000 U	83,000	3,000 U
Depreciation	25,000	—	25,000	—	25,000	—
Utilities	10,000	—	10,000	1,400 F	8,600	1,400 F
Insurance	9,000	—	9,000	200 U	9,200	200 U
Supplies	5,600	—	5,600	600 F	5,000	600 F
Other	5,000	—	5,000	1,000 U	6,000	1,000 U
Total fixed S & A	$134,600	$ —	$134,600	$ 2,200 U	$136,800	$ 2,200 U
Net Income	$ 65,150	$11,750 F	$ 76,900	$37,600 U	$ 39,300	$25,850 U

Sales-volume variance = $11,750 F   Flexible budget variance = $37,600 U
Income variance = $25,850 U

unfavorable variance in cost per basket of $.40 for 18,000 baskets produced and sold, or $7,200.

SUMMARY—BUDGETS AND STANDARD COSTS AS CONTROL TOOLS

We can now summarize the steps in using budgets and standard costs in the control process:

1. Adjust the static budget to the actual level of performance, that is, prepare a flexible budget.
2. Calculate variances.
   a. Decide how detailed the variance calculations will be.
   b. Determine how often the variance calculations should be made, which is influenced by: (1) the time span for control and (2) the impact of a variance on efficient operations.

3. Analyze the variances.

    a. Decide which variances are significant and should be investigated.

    b. Determine which variances are controllable.

    c. Assign responsibility for controllable variances.

Each of these steps, other than the first one which has already been discussed in detail, are more fully described below.

Calculate Variances

Two major issues in variance calculation must be confronted: (1) how much variance analysis should be done and (2) how often should a variance be computed. With respect to the first issue, suppose that an ice cream maker had estimated originally that 100,000 gallons of ice cream would be sold for $3 per gallon. Actually, 85,000 gallons were sold for $3.10 per gallon. We could do the following levels of variance analysis:

First level: Compare the original budget with the actual results.

Second level: Prepare a flexible budget and separate the first level budget variance into the components owing to volume and those owing to price.

Third level: Analyze the volume variance to determine what part is due to industry factors.

Additional levels: Calculate variances by flavor of ice cream, by type of customer, by type of container, etc.

Before variances are calculated, a decision must be made as to what levels of analysis are appropriate. For the ice cream manufacturer, management must decide whether analysis such as by flavor or container will help the company in operating more efficiently.

The second issue in calculated variances relates to timing. Not all variances should be calculated on the same time schedule. Some variance may be appropriately calculated daily, others weekly and still others only annually. The critical factors to consider in deciding how often a variance or set of variances should be computed are (1) the time span within which the variance is controllable, and (2) the implication of the variance with respect to the overall operations of the company. In terms of the time span for control, if, for example, unfavorable raw materials usage variances tend to be related to machines which are improperly set, corrective actions can be taken immediately and hence variance calculations for usage should be done frequently. On the other hand, a cost such as factory depreciation or property taxes is controllable only in the long run and a frequent analysis of differences between budget (or standard) and actual does not yield useful information to management.

Some variances are important because of what they indicate about the state of a process and thus should be looked at frequently. For example, if a favorable usage variance for raw materials indicates that insufficient materials are being used to insure the quality of the product, the implications for the future may be very serious. In the case of our ice cream maker, if significant favorable usage variances for nuts and flavorings are occurring, the quality of the product may be deteriorating and will have an impact on future sales. Hence, a frequent calculation of the variances relating to nuts and flavorings may be desirable.

Analyze the Variances

Once the variances have been calculated, a decision must be made as to which are significant and warrant further study. This decision is based on managerial experience and judgment. Management policy defining the dollar level or percentage amount which will trigger investigation of a particular variance may be needed.

The reason for variance computation and analysis is to better control operations. This means that we must determine what variances are controllable and assign responsibility for the control of those variances to a specific manager or managers. Our tendency in the classroom is to treat the computation of a variance as the critical factor. Instead, the critical factor is using variances to better control performance. Responsibility is not always easy to assess. For example, an unfavorable labor usage variance may mean lack of motivation, poor training, or lack of product on which to work. In each case, a different manager may be responsible for the unfavorable variance.

ALTERNATIVE STANDARDS OF COMPARISON FOR RESULTS OF OPERATIONS

In Chapter 8 we discussed the concept of responsibility accounting and expense centers, revenue centers, profit centers, and investment centers. Remember that for an expense center, the responsible manager is held accountable only for inputs in the form of costs over which he or she can exert significant control. At the profit center level, the head of the responsibility center is judged on the basis of income—the differences between the revenues and expenses which are deemed to be controllable by that manager. The greatest amount of responsibility is vested in the head of an investment center, who is held accountable for both income and the assets used to earn that income.

A budget is a suitable control device for all levels of the organization. It, along with standard cost systems, is an important combination of control tool and a primary source of the information used in evaluating a manager's performance in responsibility centers that are expense centers. In responsibility centers that encompass both revenues and expenses and also those that extend to cover investment, perspectives other than those provided by a budget and actual comparison and variance analysis become useful.

We are going to look at two alternative standards of comparison in addition to the budget which can be used to evaluate a responsible manager's performance and give that manager additional insights into areas where inefficiencies exist. The first of these standards is that of historical performance; the second is represented by the industry of which an entity is a part.

Historical Standards

Let us assume that Handicrafts is organized in such a way that a vice-president is in charge of the production and sale of the product line represented by the large decorative baskets for which data have been provided in the preceding two chapters. In other words, this vice-president is head of a profit center and is held accountable for both revenues from the sale of the basket and the cost of making and selling these baskets. Our vice-president has the data provided in Illustration 11-4—income statements for the past two years and the current year.

A comparison for the three-year period shows that:

1. Sales volume in units and dollars has been increasing.
2. The gross margins and contribution margins for the three-year period have been almost stable.
3. Profits have been declining and are currently almost half of what they were two years ago.

Common Size Statements

To gain additional insights into the reason for the declining profits despite rising sales, the income statements expressed in dollars could be recast into percent terms, with each item on the income statement expressed as a percent of sales revenues. For example, to find what part of the sales dollar is absorbed by cost of goods sold, we would make the following calculation:

$$\$178,000 \text{ cost of goods sold}/\$414,000 \text{ sales} = 43\%$$

If we do this for the other two years, we see that while in dollar terms the gross margin is relatively constant, in relationship to sales, more of Handicrafts' sales dollars are being absorbed by cost of goods sold.

Illustration 11-5 gives the three comparative income statements for Handicrafts expressed in common size dollar form. Looking at this statement, the manager can see that two areas are causing the segment income to decline—a rising cost of goods sold, indicating rising costs for

ILLUSTRATION 11-4

HANDICRAFTS, LIMITED—BASKET #679 Comparative Income Statements for the Years Ended December 31	CURRENT YEAR	LAST YEAR	TWO YEARS AGO
Unit Sales	18,000	16,000	15,000
Sales	$414,000	$384,000	$360,000
Cost of Goods Sold (LIFO)	178,200	149,800	126,000
Gross Margin	$235,800	$234,200	$234,000
Other Variable Operating Expenses:			
Sales Commissions	$ 20,700	$ 19,200	$ 18,000
Other	39,000	38,400	39,600
Total Variable Operating Expenses	$ 59,700	$ 57,600	$ 57,600
Contribution Margin	$176,100	$176,600	$176,400
Fixed Selling and Administrative:			
Salaries	$ 83,000	$ 69,000	$ 57,600
Depreciation	25,000	25,000	23,000
Utilities	8,600	7,700	3,600
Insurance	9,200	7,800	7,200
Supplies	5,000	3,800	3,600
Other	6,000	3,600	7,000
Total Selling and Administrative	$136,800	$116,900	$102,000
Segment Income	$ 39,300	$ 59,700	$ 74,400

ILLUSTRATION 11-5

HANDICRAFTS, LIMITED—BASKET #679 Common Size Comparative Income Statements for the Year Ended December 31	CURRENT YEAR	LAST YEAR	TWO YEARS AGO
Unit Sales	18,000	16,000	15,000
Sales	100%	100%	100%
Cost of Goods Sold (LIFO)	43	39	35
Gross Margin	57%	61%	65%
Other Variable Operating Expenses:			
Sales Commissions	5%	5%	5%
Other	10	10	11
Total Variable Operating Expenses	15%	15%	16%
Contribution Margin	42%	46%	49%
Fixed Selling and Administrative:			
Salaries	20%	18%	16%
Depreciation	6	6	6
Utilities	2	2	1
Insurance	2	2	2
Supplies	1	1	1
Other	1	1	2
Total Selling and Administrative	32	30%	28%
Segment Income	10%	16%	21%

the units being produced, and increasing selling and administrative salaries. The manager knows where to look in an attempt to control cost. This does not mean that the manager will be able to cut costs, but at least he or she is aware of the major places where increasing costs are cutting into the segment's income.

We have shown this analysis done on the basis of year-end data. A shorter control horizon may be appropriate. This information could be computed on a monthly or quarterly basis to give the responsible manager guidance throughout the period as to where past relationships between income-statement items are not holding true for the current period. Some of these changed relationships may be beyond the manager's control; others may be controllable only over a longer time span, and some may indicate the need for immediate action. For example, the increasing cost of goods sold may be caused by rising raw materials costs which cannot be controlled by the manager. On the other hand, the increasing amount of the sales dollar being used to cover selling and administrative salaries could indicate that employees are not being used efficiently and hence the number of employees has gone up more than it should have.

Industry Standards

One problem with using historical performance as a way of evaluating current performance is that past standards may have been based on inefficient operations. For example, salaries may have remained at 16% of sales revenue for the three-year period. Yet, this segment of the organization may have more employees than it needs to accomplish the necessary work.

Industry standards provide an outside perspective against which performance can be measured. Illustration 11-6 shows the performance of Handicrafts' large decorative basket segment compared with that of other companies which manufacture and sell a similar product line. The comparison for Handicrafts shows that the cost of goods sold percentage and selling and administrative salaries are high relative to the industry, just as they were in a historical comparison. These offer areas to which the responsible manager will want to give some attention.

There are difficulties in using industry statistics. One problem is finding comparable data. We have made the simplifying assumption that industry data are available for companies which manufacture a product line similar to the Handicrafts line which we are attempting to analyze. In reality, data this specialized may not be available. Common souces of industry statistics are investment services such as Standard & Poor's and Moody's. Dun & Bradstreet is also a common source. In addition, trade associations and trade publications frequently publish statistics for the industry which they serve. Illustration 11-7 shows some of the statistics published by Dun & Bradstreet which may be useful to an entity in

ILLUSTRATION
11-6

HANDICRAFTS, LIMITED—BASKET #679
Comparison of Operating Performance with Industry
for the Year Ended December 31

	CURRENT YEAR	
	Handicrafts	Industry
Sales	100%	100%
Cost of Goods Sold	43%	39%
Gross Margin	57%	61%
Other Variable Operating Expenses:		
Sales Commissions	5%	5%
Other	10	8
Total Variable Operating Expenses	15%	13%
Contribution Margin	42%	48%
Fixed Selling and Administrative:		
Salaries	20%	17%
Depreciation	6	7
Utilities	2	2
Insurance	2	3
Supplies	1	1
Other	1	2
Total Selling and Administrative	32%	32%
Income	10%	16%

evaluating its performance. Computer-accessed data sources are in frequent use today, as discussed in an earlier chapter.

In addition, the accounting principles chosen by a company can have an impact on what is shown in its financial statements and the statement amounts. For example, we know that Handicrafts uses LIFO in costing its inventory. If this is not typical of the industry of which Handicrafts is a part, the cost-of-goods-sold figure differences may be attributable to the use of different accounting methods.

Another problem with using industry statistics is that the statistics may just provide a mean average value. If the industry is made up of companies of different sizes, this average representation may be misleading. The large companies in the industry may not exhibit the same characteristics as the small ones; yet they are included as part of the averaging process.

ANALYTICAL TECHNIQUES FOR INVESTMENT CENTERS

In the first part of this chapter we assumed that the manager was responsible for revenues and expenses; that is, he or she was the head of a profit center. Performance evaluation was based on profitability. In this section we shall discuss analytical techniques which can be used to control operations and evaluate performance for investment centers—responsi-

ILLUSTRATION 11-7

Example of operating statistics available from published sources

INDUSTRY	Total Number of Returns Filed	Cost of Goods Sold %	Gross Margin %	SELECTED OPERATING EXPENSES								
				Compensation of Officers %	Rent Paid on Business Property %	Repairs %	Bad Debts %	Interest Paid %	Taxes Paid %	Amortization Depreciation Depletion %	Advertising %	Pension & Other Employee Benefit Plans %
ALL INDUSTRIES	2,082,200	71.70	28.30	1.90	1.34	0.78	0.41	4.01	2.76	2.97	0.91	1.80
CONTRACT CONSTRUCTION	195,933	81.08	18.92	3.55	0.65	0.57	0.24	1.24	2.16	1.94	0.25	0.92
General Building Contractors & Operative Builders	78,115	86.79	13.21	2.67	0.41	0.34	0.19	1.64	1.52	1.27	0.27	0.55
Heavy Construction Contractors	16,533	79.59	20.41	2.25	0.87	1.07	0.21	1.19	2.12	3.56	0.10	1.20
Special Trade Contractors	101,285	74.91	25.09	5.42	0.82	0.55	0.31	0.78	2.97	1.81	0.30	1.21
RETAILERS & WHOLESALERS	635,540	78.76	21.24	1.63	1.32	0.33	0.20	0.80	1.42	0.91	0.92	0.51
RETAIL TRADE	407,666	72.39	27.61	1.74	2.16	0.45	0.20	0.87	1.80	1.18	1.52	0.59
Building Materials, Garden Supplies, & Mobile Home Dealers	30,988	73.10	26.90	2.98	1.26	0.47	0.46	1.03	1.93	1.15	1.08	0.60
General Merchandise Stores	9,322	64.79	35.21	0.43	2.69	0.50	0.37	1.48	2.44	1.47	2.59	0.87
Food Stores	31,370	78.08	21.92	0.60	1.49	0.49	0.05	0.32	1.25	0.96	1.00	0.81
Automotive Dealers & Service Stations	70,693	84.63	15.37	1.54	0.90	0.24	0.12	0.90	1.13	0.73	0.76	0.27
Motor Vehicle Dealers	33,449	86.19	13.81	1.32	0.75	0.20	0.11	0.94	0.87	0.64	0.81	0.27
Gasoline Service Stations	15,861	84.75	15.25	1.44	1.13	0.34	0.11	0.44	2.22	0.93	0.16	0.14
Other Automotive Dealers	21,383	72.23	27.77	3.44	1.75	0.40	0.23	1.17	1.85	1.19	1.15	0.43
Apparel & Accessory Stores	38,497	59.41	40.59	3.33	6.02	0.36	0.25	0.71	2.23	1.15	2.26	0.60
Furniture & Home Furnishings Stores	33,410	64.45	35.55	4.14	3.11	0.40	0.52	1.04	2.09	0.91	3.37	0.52
Eating & Drinking Places	84,964	44.23	55.77	3.43	4.93	1.26	0.08	1.28	3.89	2.96	1.86	0.56
Drug Stores & Proprietary Stores	19,950	70.78	29.22	2.74	2.66	0.29	0.09	0.47	1.66	0.79	1.14	0.61
Liquor Stores	11,593	79.45	20.55	2.91	2.12	0.33	0.07	0.58	1.87	0.91	0.54	0.20
Other Retail Stores	108,422	67.75	32.25	3.24	2.64	0.39	0.27	0.72	1.99	1.33	1.83	0.56

WHOLESALE TRADE	**84.47**	**15.53**	**1.52**	**0.57**	**0.23**	**0.19**	**0.75**	**1.08**	**0.67**	**0.38**	**0.43**
226,857	84.47	15.53	1.52	0.57	0.23	0.19	0.75	1.08	0.67	0.38	0.43
Groceries & Related Products — 20,292	87.84	12.16	0.98	0.47	0.25	0.13	0.40	0.71	0.55	0.24	0.37
Machinery, Equipment & Supplies — 49,849	74.99	25.01	2.84	0.74	0.28	0.28	1.08	1.22	1.09	0.46	0.66
Motor Vehicles & Automotive Equipment — 18,974	78.49	21.51	1.90	0.89	0.18	0.17	0.97	1.13	0.65	1.17	0.44
Drugs, Chemicals & Allied Products — 6,483	81.22	18.78	1.14	0.54	0.16	0.18	0.43	0.74	0.57	0.44	0.45
Apparel, Piece Goods & Notions — 9,623	76.87	23.13	2.96	1.03	0.11	0.30	0.90	1.69	0.42	0.53	0.59
Farm-Product Raw Materials — 9,076	94.36	5.64	0.36	0.19	0.25	0.06	0.66	0.32	0.58	0.09	0.14
Electrical Goods — 14,104	76.21	23.79	2.09	0.78	0.14	0.32	0.76	1.23	0.57	1.12	0.59
Hardware, Plumbing & Heating Equipment — 10,357	76.72	23.28	3.00	0.92	0.20	0.34	0.76	1.33	0.62	0.30	0.83
Alcoholic Beverages — 4,042	78.22	21.78	1.40	0.56	0.23	0.11	0.43	5.42	0.59	0.52	0.58
Lumber & Construction Materials — 10,322	82.40	17.60	2.01	0.58	0.30	0.41	0.97	1.07	0.75	0.31	0.42
Metals & Minerals, except Petroleum & Scrap — 4,843	88.40	11.60	1.28	0.34	0.17	0.15	0.94	0.23	0.61	0.09	0.44
Petroleum & Petroleum Products — 9,898	95.83	4.17	0.62	0.45	0.22	0.13	0.50	1.27	0.67	0.11	0.25
Paper & Paper Products — 4,233	80.94	19.06	2.22	0.29	0.46	0.24	0.57	0.89	0.59	0.19	0.56
Other Wholesale Trade, Durable & Nondurable Goods Combined — 54,761	84.22	15.78	1.71	0.65	0.24	0.22	0.98	1.02	0.69	0.44	0.43
MANUFACTURING — 212,333	**73.23**	**26.77**	**0.89**	**0.81**	**1.23**	**0.19**	**1.55**	**2.77**	**2.96**	**1.06**	**2.00**
Food & Kindred Products — 15,478	77.43	22.57	0.59	0.64	0.83	0.11	0.98	2.51	1.78	2.33	1.07
Meat Products — 2,292	86.66	13.34	0.42	0.52	0.55	0.11	0.80	1.02	1.29	0.73	0.82
Dairy Products — 1,983	82.02	17.98	0.41	0.72	0.87	0.11	0.68	1.35	1.57	1.23	1.13
Canned & Preserved Fruits & Vegetables — 1,066	73.80	26.20	0.56	0.79	0.96	0.11	1.61	2.02	1.90	2.97	1.22
Grain Mill Products — 1,495	78.29	21.71	0.51	0.64	1.12	0.13	1.00	1.25	1.64	3.28	1.06

bility centers in which the manager is responsible not only for revenues and expenses but also for investment or some part of investment.

Let us assume that the data we have for Handicrafts and basket #679 relate to operations of a division which is headed by a manager. This manager is responsible for generating profits and controlling the level of investments.

In this situation we can use many of the same control tools and performance standards which we have just described for a profit center. Additional financial data will be added to that used for a profit center—a balance sheet or partial balance sheet for the division. Now the responsible manager will be evaluated in terms of both income and investment.

Common Size Balance Sheets

Balance sheets, like income statements, can be converted into common size statements. The current year's balance sheet for Handicrafts is shown in Illustration 11-8. This balance sheet and those for the preceding two

ILLUSTRATION 11-8

HANDICRAFTS, LIMITED
Balance Sheet
for the Year Ended December 31

Assets

Current Assets:		
Cash		$ 10,200
Accounts Receivable (Net)		72,500
Inventories:		
Raw Materials	$15,600	
Work-in-Process	—	
Finished Goods	25,500	
Total Inventories		41,100
Prepaid Expenses		1,700
Total Current Assets		$125,500
Property, Plant and Equipment (Net)		155,300
Total Assets		$280,800

Liabilities

Current Liabilities:	
Accounts Payable	$ 48,100
Salaries Payable	4,000
Interest Payable	2,200
Total Current Liabilities	$ 54,300
Mortgage Payable	72,000
Total Liabilities	$126,300

Stockholders' Equity

Capital Stock	$ 80,000
Paid-in Capital in Excess of Par	22,300
Retained Earnings	52,200
Total Stockholders' Equity	$154,500
Total Liabilities and Stockholders' Equity	$280,800

ILLUSTRATION
11-9

HANDICRAFTS, LIMITED Common Size Comparative Balance Sheets for the Years Ended December 31			
	CURRENT YEAR	LAST YEAR	TWO YEARS AGO
Assets			
Current Assets:			
Cash	4%	6%	7%
Accounts Receivable (Net)	26	22	20
Inventories:			
Raw Materials	5	7	5
Work-in-Process	—		
Finished Goods	9	6	6
Total Inventories	14%	13%	11%
Prepaid Expenses	1	1	1
Total Current Assets	45%	42%	39%
Property Plant and Equipment (Net)	55	58	61
Total Assets	100%	100%	100%
Liabilities			
Current Liabilities:			
Accounts Payable	17%	15%	15%
Salaries Payable	1	1	1
Interest Payable	1	2	3
Total Current Liabilities	19%	18%	19%
Mortgage Payable	26	28	30
Total Liabilities	45%	46%	49%
Stockholders' Equity			
Capital Stock	28%	29%	27%
Paid-in Capital in Excess of Par	8	7	6
Retained Earnings	19	18	18
Total Stockholders' Equity	55%	54%	51%
Total Liabilities and Stockholders' Equity	100%	100%	100%

years have been converted into common size statements in Illustration 11-9. Total assets and total liabilities and stockholders' equity have been set equal to 100%, and each line on the balance sheet is expressed in terms of these totals. For example, the current year's cash represents 4% of total assets. This calculation is made as follows:

$$\$10,200 \text{ cash}/\$280,800 \text{ total assets} = 4\%$$

We can see from the comparative common size balance sheets that Accounts Receivable and Finished Goods Inventory have been increasing as a percent of total assets, However, sales have also been increasing, so this increase may be related primarily to the increased sales.

Looking at the liability/stockholders' equity side of the balance sheet, the balance in accounts payable has risen slightly, while long-term liabilities as a percentage of total liabilities has been decreasing. If we look at the part of the total equities of the company that has been provided by creditors as opposed to shareholders, we note that an increasing percentage of the investment is provided by the shareholders.

Industry Comparisons

Handicrafts may wish to view its balance sheet in the context of similar companies in the same industry. They might not be able to find complete balance-sheet information, but the sources previously listed (in the discussion of the income statement) often provide certain balance-sheet relationships, such as:

Accounts Receivable/Total Assets
Inventories/Total Assets
Current Assets/Total Assets
Debt/Equity

We encounter the same kinds of problems in making balance-sheet comparisons that we do in making income-statement comparisons: the lack of detailed data, the use of different accounting principles, and the existence of firms of different size within the same industry.

RATIO ANALYSIS

Many companies compute certain key ratios on a regular basis—monthly or quarterly—to give them an indication of how they are doing. They may have set certain goals in these areas and make the calculation to see if they are meeting these goals. The calculation and meaning of some commonly used ratios are shown in Illustration 11-10. These ratios are further described below.

Activity Ratios

The following ratios, described collectively as activity ratios, relate the income statement and the balance sheet.

1. Accounts receivable collection period. Cash is a vital part of the operations of organizations. While sales may be made, if these are on account, cash is not flowing in until the receivables are collected. Many firms which sell on account keep a close watch on the period of time it

ILLUSTRATION 11-10

Commonly calculated ratios for controlling operations and evaluation of performance

RATIO NAME	COMPUTATION	INTERPRETATION
Activity Ratios 1. Average collection period for accounts receivable	$\dfrac{\text{Average Accounts Receivable}}{\text{Net Credit Sales/360 days}}$	The average length of time that it takes the company to collect for its sales on account
2. Inventory turnover	$\dfrac{\text{Cost of Goods Sold}}{\text{Inventory}}$	Indicates the number of times the inventory was sold during the year
3. Total asset turnover	$\dfrac{\text{Net Sales}}{\text{Total Assets}}$	Measures the number of dollars of sales produced by each dollar of assets
Liquidity and Debt Capacity 1. Current (working capital) ratio	$\dfrac{\text{Current Assets}}{\text{Current Liabilities}}$	Measures short-term solvency by indicating to what extent claims of short-term creditors are covered by assets which are expected to be converted to cash in a period roughly corresponding to the maturity of the claims
2. Acid test (quick) ratio	$\dfrac{\text{Cash + Acc. Rec. + Marketable Sec.}}{\text{Current Liabilities}}$	A more stringent test of short-term solvency than the current ratio
3. Debt/equity ratio	$\dfrac{\text{Total Debt}}{\text{Total Stockholders' Equity}}$	Indicates the number of dollars of debt for each dollar of shareholders' equity
Profitability Measures 1. Profit margin on sales	$\dfrac{\text{Net Income (or Operating Income)}}{\text{Net Sales}}$	Indicates the percentage of each sales dollar which is ultimately realized as net income (or operating income)
2. Return on investment	$\dfrac{\text{Net Income (or Operating Income)}}{\text{Total Assets}}$	Measures the return on the total investment in the company

takes them to collect a receivable. This is measured by the following ratio:

$$\text{Accounts receivable collection period} = \frac{\text{Accounts Receivable}}{\text{Credit Sales/360 days}}$$

We can calculate this ratio for Handicrafts:

$$\text{Accounts receivable collection period} = \frac{\$72,500}{\$414,000/360} = \underline{63 \text{ days}}$$

This ratio, like others we have discussed, is meaningless unless viewed in some context. It can be compared with this statistic for previous years, with the anticipated collection period as represented in the budget, and with an industry average. Let's assume that we have the data given in Illustration 11-11 for this and other key ratios which Handicrafts calculates.

Handicrafts shows an unfavorable trend with respect to the time it takes them to collect an account receivable. There are a number of common reasons for this, some of which management can control and others which it cannot. These include:

1. Granting credit to companies that don't pay or take a long time to pay. A review of its credit-granting policies may be in order.
2. Failure to bill or send out overdue account notices on a timely basis.
3. Failure to write off uncollectible accounts or to make an adequate provision for them.
4. Failure to exert pressure when an account becomes overdue.
5. Depressed economic conditions in the area or industry in which the company does business. (Based on the industry statistic, in our example, the slow collection period does not appear to be related to overall industry conditions.)
6. Disputes with customers regarding the type or quality of merchandise sent to them.

In addition to the accounts receivable collection period some companies calculate the accounts receivable turnover ratio:

$$\frac{\text{Accounts receivable}}{\text{turnover ratio}} = \frac{\text{Net Credit Sales}}{\text{Accounts Receivable}}$$

For Handicrafts, the turnover would be:

$$\frac{\text{Accounts receivable}}{\text{turnover ratio}} = \frac{\$414,000}{\$72,500} = 5.7 \text{ times}$$

ILLUSTRATION 11-11

Handicrafts, Limited, key ratios

RATIO	INDUSTRY	CURRENT YEAR	LAST YEAR	TWO YEARS AGO
Activity Ratios				
Accounts receivable collection period	50 days	63 days	55 days	52 days
Inventory turnover	7×	7×	6.8×	7×
Total asset turnover	2.00	1.47	1.40	1.70
Liquidity and Debt Capacity				
Current (working capital) ratio	1.85:1	2.3:1	2.5:1	2.2:1
Acid test ratio	1:1	1.5:1	1.8:1	1.8:1
Debt/equity ratio	1.5	.82	.92	1.02
Profitability Measures				
Profit margin on sales	16%	9%	16%	21%
Return on investment	18.5%	14%	18%	19%

The faster this ratio, the shorter the collection period for the accounts receivable. The accounts receivable turnover ratio can also be used in an alternative method of calculating the accounts receivable collection period:

$$\text{Accounts receivable collection period} = \frac{360 \text{ days}}{\text{Accounts receivable turnover ratio}}$$

Using this approach, the accounts receivable collection period for Handicrafts would be calculated as follows:

$$\text{Accounts receivable collection period} = \frac{360 \text{ days}}{5.7} = \underline{\underline{63 \text{ days}}}$$

ILLUSTRATION FROM PRACTICE: THE USE OF A RATIO AS A CONTROL DEVICE BY BRAND REX

Some information about Brand Rex and its operations was given in a previous chapter. Brand Rex has set as a standard for its divisions a 41-day collection period for accounts receivable. As monthly reports received in corporate headquarters show slippage in this area, the chief financial officer checks with division managers to determine the nature of the problem. Procedures such as calls on the customer by the division manager along with the chief financial officer and sending someone in person to pick up a check which the creditor says is ready are procedures which are used to impress on the customer and the division manager how important controlling this item is.

---

2. Inventory Turnover. This statistic measures how many times during a period, in our case a year, the company sold its inventory. The ratio is calculated as follows:

$$\text{Inventory turnover} = \frac{\text{Cost of Goods Sold}}{\text{Inventory}}$$

For Handicrafts, the inventory turnover is:

$$\frac{\$178,200 \text{ cost of goods sold}}{\$25,500 \text{ finished goods inventory}} = 7 \text{ times}$$

This ratio is equal to that of the industry and historically is relatively stable. Low inventory turnovers may be related to factors such as:

1. A declining demand for the company's products or certain product lines.
2. Failure to write off obsolete inventory.

Conversely, a high inventory turnover could indicate that the company is not producing enough inventory and runs the risk of not being able to meet customer demands. In addition, a company which uses LIFO in a period of rising prices will have a high turnover relative to a FIFO company because (1) the cost of goods sold will be high relative to FIFO and (2) inventory valuation will be low (older prices are carried in inventory) relative to FIFO (current prices are carried in inventory).

3. Total asset turnover.   This ratio answers the question: How many dollars of sales are generated by each dollar of assets? The general formula and the calculation for Handicrafts are:

$$\text{Total asset turnover} = \frac{\text{Sales}}{\text{Total Assets}}$$

$$1.47 = \frac{\$414,000 \text{ sales}}{\$280,800 \text{ total assets}}$$

Unique problems are involved in this computation and in any other ratio which requires the use of assets. We are faced with the problem of the impact of depreciation and depreciation methods on asset valuation. If, for example, sales were at the same level for a number of years and no new assets were being acquired the asset turnover could be increasing, not because of more efficient use of assets in generating sales but rather because the asset base is declining owing to depreciation. This would happen if there were not a constant pattern of reinvestment in depreciable assets.

In addition, in comparing performance of divisions within an entity or in comparing industry statistics, problems arise because of the use of different depreciation methods—accelerated versus straight-line, for example. Also, the size of the asset base, net of depreciation, is affected by the age of the assets. Without replacement, the older the assets being depreciated, the smaller the asset base.

Because of these problems, some companies, when they calculate statistics requiring the use of total assets, use gross assets. In other words, they include depreciable assets in the asset base at their original cost before deducting any depreciation. Their approach was discussed in a previous chapter.

The use of average figures in calculating activity ratios.   In calculating the activity ratios for Handicrafts, we use the end-of-the-period balance-sheet figure for accounts receivable and inventories. Realistically, for the company which is calculating these ratios on an annual basis, an average for the year for these two items may be appropriate. Consider, for example, the retailing firm which does a large Christmas business. If it uses a year-end fiscal period and calculates accounts receivable collection period and inventory turnover on year-end balances in the receivables and inventory account, the resulting ratios will not be descriptive of the period as a whole. This is true because such a firm will have its receivables at a year high and its inventories at a year low at the conclusion of the Christmas season. In other words, the basis used to calculate the measures of activities will not be typical of the period as a whole.

Liquidity and Solvency Ratios

Three measures often are computed to indicate a company's short-term debt-paying abilities and its capacity to increase its debt.

1. Current (working capital) ratio. This ratio purports to measure the company's ability to liquidate its short-term obligations. The general formula and the calculation for Handicrafts is as follows:

$$\text{current ratio} = \frac{\text{Current Assets}}{\text{Current Liabilities}}$$

$$\$2.3 = \frac{\$125,000 \text{ current assets}}{\$54,300 \text{ current liabilities}}$$

This ratio, which is frequently expressed in the form $2.3:$1, tells us that for every dollar of current liabilities which Handicrafts has on its balance sheet it has $2.30 of current assets. This interpretation is based on the assumption that the current assets or working capital assets of the company are quite liquid and will be converted into cash within a relatively short period. Actually, this may not be true. If inventories consist of items which are not highly salable and receivables include amounts which are difficult or impossible to collect, the company's liquidity may be severely limited.

This ratio is also called the *working capital ratio* because it compares the company's working capital accounts, current assets, and current liabilities. These accounts are termed working capital accounts because they are related to its daily operations—making and selling inventory.

2. Acid test ratio. If a company wants a more stringent measure of liquidity or if some of its current asset accounts are not quite liquid, it may calculate the so-called *acid test ratio*, which compares cash and near cash assets (marketable securities and accounts receivable, typically) with current liabilities using the following formula:

$$\text{Acid test ratio} = \frac{\text{Cash} + \text{Accounts Receivable} + \text{Marketable Securities}}{\text{Current Liabilities}}$$

Handicrafts acid test ratio is:

$$1.5 = \frac{\$82,700 \text{ cash and receivables}}{\$54,000 \text{ current liabilities}}$$

3. Debt/equity ratio.   This statistic describes the investment of the creditors in the assets of the business relative to the investment of the shareholders or owners. A company does not have an infinite ability to expand its borrowing. Lenders keep an eye on this relationship and may refuse to lend if they believe it is "out of line." What "out of line" means is a matter of judgment affected by the industry, overall economic conditions, and the perceived abilities of the company's management. The general method of calculation and the computations for Handicrafts are as follows:

$$\text{Debt/equity ratio} = \frac{\text{Debt (Liabilities)}}{\text{Shareholders' Equity}}$$

$$.82 = \frac{\$126,300 \text{ total liabilities}}{\$154,500 \text{ total shareholders' equity}}$$

For every dollar of investment by shareholders, creditors have an investment of $.82. Another way of viewing this is that the creditors' investment is more than covered by that of the shareholders. This ratio is significantly less than for the industry, which may indicate that Handicrafts has available borrowing capacity or that it has failed to use debt as much as it should. Whether or not it should have used more debt to finance its structure, as the industry has done, depends on what can be earned by the additional funds borrowed relative to their cost.

MEASURES OF PROFITABILITY

How well a company, or a profit center or investment center of that company, is doing is measured in part by the amount by which revenues exceed expenses. However, we can more fully develop the meaning of this figure by looking at it in at least two ways: (1) in relationship to sales and (2) in relationship to investment. The first of these can be used for a company as a whole or a profit center; the second is reserved for investment centers or the company as a whole.

Profit Margin on Sales

This statistic is found by the following calculation:

$$\text{Profit margin on sales} = \frac{\text{Operating Income (Net Income)}}{\text{Sales}}$$

For Handicrafts the profit margin is: [1]

$$9\% = \frac{\$39{,}300 \text{ income}}{\$414{,}000 \text{ sales}}$$

A company or a responsibility center of that company could have a very large amount of sales as expressed in dollar terms but not be doing well. This occurs when the company is unable to realize the results of its selling activities on the bottom line in the form of profits. A declining profit margin and a margin which is low relative to expectations or industry standards could indicate one of the following problems:

1. The sales price is not set at a proper level.
2. Expenses are not being controlled as effectively as they should be.
3. For multi-product-line entities, selling activities may be centered around the less profitable products.

Return on Investment

In evaluating a company or any part thereof, a key question about return is how much was required to earn that return. If we know that one of our investment centers earned $100,000 while another earned $200,000, we can't say that the one which earned $200,000 did twice as well as the other. One reason is that we don't know what level of investment was required to earn the returns shown. By relating return to investment, we have a better *indication* of which division operated most efficiently. *Indication* is italicized to stress the fact that knowing the amount of the investment is just one aspect of evaluating performance of one investment center, or one company, relative to another.

The key to using ROI properly is to base the standard against which measurement is to be made on the *potential* of the investment center or the company as a whole. Generally, not all investment centers have the same potential.

For example, the performance of the manager of an investment center generating a 10% return may be superior to that of the manager of an investment center earning 15% because of the nature of the products or services which are being produced and sold by the two centers. Geographical location and numerous other factors could also affect the size of an investment center's return on assets.

---

[1] Note the 9% figure differs from that given in the common size income statements shown earlier, which gave profit margin of 10%. This difference is due to rounding. On the common size statements, when revenues expressed as a percent were compared with expenses expressed as a percent, the difference was 10%.

The calculation of ROI, the problems with this calculation, and the use of residual income as a substitute measure of performance for investment centers were discussed in Chapter 8.

ILLUSTRATION FROM PRACTICE: UNIROYAL'S METHOD FOR ASSESSING THE POTENTIAL OF SUBCOMPONENTS OF THE ORGANIZATION

The Uniroyal name is familiar to most of us because of its production of automobile tires. However, tires and related products account for less than 50% of Uniroyal's revenues. The company also produces natural and synthetic rubber; specialty agricultural chemicals such as miticides and growth regulants; vinyl coated fabrics; and plastics and reinforced rubber products such as conveyor belts and belts for power transmission. Sales are more than $2 million and it employs approximately 23,000 people.

One of the methods Uniroyal uses to analyze its businesses is a system developed by the Boston Consulting Group. Each business unit is classified as to its potential using a four-quadrant grid with these classifications: (1) business units which are star performers and which have the best potential for generating future returns, (2) new products and other units about which there is uncertainty, (3) those parts of the company which are cash generators for the company (sometimes referred to as "cash cows"), and (4) those parts of the organization which are being made ready to be sold or disposed of (harvested). The quadrant appears as follows:

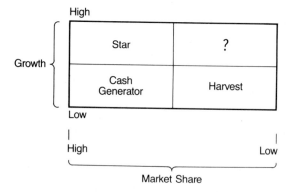

Uniroyal uses circles transcribed on the quadrant to represent each of its business units and the size of the circle represents the amount of the investment. What is expected of a business unit is dependent on its classification. An interesting twist on Uniroyal's approach is that the managers of the business units are not told what their rate of return should be. The corporation does not dictate to units in order to motivate the manager to generate the highest return possible. It is felt that if the manager knows the expected return in advance, this will probably be the highest return which will be generated by the business unit which he or she heads.

USING RATIO FORMULAS TO PROJECT OTHER VARIABLES

The formulas we used in calculating the ratios for Handicrafts can also be used to project various components of those formulas. For example, recall that the accounts receivable collection period is calculated by the following formula:

$$\text{Accounts receivable collection period} = \frac{\text{Accounts Receivable}}{\text{Net Credit Sales}/360\text{ days}}$$

Based on the data for Handicrafts, the accounts receivable collection period was 63 days. The industry average was 50 days.

Suppose that Handicrafts would like to know at what level it would have to maintain its accounts receivable next year to conform to the industry average. Suppose, further, that Handicrafts projects its credit sales for the coming year as $504,000. The amount of receivables it could support and meet the industry standard based on its projected net credit sales would be calculated as follows:

$$50\text{ days (industry standard)} = \frac{x}{\$504,000/360\text{ days}}$$

where x = accounts receivable. Completing the calculations, we find that Handicrafts would have to maintain its accounts receivable balance at $70,000:

$$50\text{ days} = \frac{x}{\$1,400}$$
$$x = \$70,000$$

We can use any of our ratio formulas the same way and find the various component parts based on different assumptions. Microcomputers make these calculations very easy to perform for a wide variety of assumptions.

chapter highlights

The concepts of flexible budgeting are applicable not only to variable manufacturing costs but also to revenues and variable operating expenses. For these items, if a static budget is used, variances are more difficult to interpret because the variances may be related solely to volume as opposed to efficiency.

For income-statement accounts, the difference between the most likely results which were incorporated into the income-statement budget and actual results can be labeled an income variance. This variance is based on all income-statement accounts and shows the amount by which income expected based on volume, selling price, and cost expectations differed from actual income.

This income variance can be broken down into a sales-volume variance by comparing the static budget with a flexible budget—a budget in which amounts have been adjusted consistent with actual volume. The other component of the income variance is the flexible budget variance, which is found by comparing the flexible budget income-statement amounts with actual results.

Expectations as expressed in the budget are just one standard which can be used as a control tool and as a way of evaluating performance. Especially for responsibility centers which are organized as either profit or investment centers, historical standards and industry standards are commonly used. A comparison of the actual income statement produced by a profit center with income statements for prior years may indicate problem areas which the manager should investigate. Rather than compare dollar amounts directly, common size statements may be more helpful, as they express each income-statement item as a percentage of sales and show past and present relationships. Common size comparisons of the investment base of an investment center may also reveal problems which require the manager's attention.

A comparison of operating results and some key ratios with industry results and ratios may help the manager see where operations are less efficient or problems are developing. The use of industry standards as a control tool and a way of evaluating performance is not without problems. Some of the difficulties include (1) finding statistics for comparable operations in terms both of outputs produced and size of the entity and (2) the use of different accounting methods by companies within the same industry.

questions

1. When analyzing the performance of a manager of a profit or investment center, why must sales-volume changes be considered and how may sales-volume changes be analyzed?

2. How does the volume assumption made in preparing a flexible budget differ from that used in preparing a static budget?

3. How are the following income-statement variances calculated: volume variance, flexible budget variance, and income variance?

4. The sales manager of a company performed in such a way that sales exceeded budget levels. The president of the company, however, was not happy, because he said the company had lost "market share." What did the president mean?

5. What standards, in addition to budgetary standards, can be used to measure performance?

6. What is a major problem in the use of historical data as a measure of performance?

7. The Wong Department Store's accounts receivable collection period had historically been 48 days. For the current period it has risen to 56 days. What are some possible causes of this increase in the collection period?

8. Gleason Products has an inventory turn of 4 times per year; the industry average is 7 times per year. What are some possible reasons for this difference?

9. Conglomerates, International, has a current ratio of 2:1. Is this good? Explain your answer.

10. What does profit margin on sales measure?

11. How does the acid test or quick ratio differ from the current ratio?

12. In what type of responsibility center is a budgeting system used in conjunction with a standard cost system the most important combination of control tools?

13. Define the term "common size dollar form" and describe when it might be used.

14. The use of industry standards provides what benefits and problems in control and evaluation of performance?

15. Describe what control tools might be used for evaluating an investment center. How does evaluation of the investment center differ from evaluation of a profit center?

16. Identify problems involved in computing ratios which include assets in their computation. How can such problems be counteracted?

17. The Smith Department Store uses calendar year-end balance-sheet figures to compute various activity ratios, which are then used to evaluate Smith's results for the year. Comment on any problems involved.

18. The Klein Company's sales have increased over the past three years, until presently they have the largest share of sales for two of their products in the region. The company president, however, is perplexed by a falling profit margin in light of the high sales. Comment on its meaning and possible causes.

19. Division 1 and Division 2 of a large manufacturing firm are investment centers, evaluated on return on investment. Net income and net assets are used in computing the ratio. In the last period, Division 1 suffered extensive plant damage due to a tornado. In addition, Division 2 uses an accelerated depreciation method while Division 1 does not. Comment on

the usefulness of ROI as calculated in comparing results for the two divisions and how it might be improved.

20. Aside from problems related to the numerator and denominator calculation for the return-on-investment computations, what other critical problems arise when ROI is used to compare the performance of managers of different investment centers?

exercises

11—1. The Super Strength Concrete Company's records show the following data:

	BUDGET	ACTUAL	VARIANCE[a]
Unit sales in bags	2,500,000	2,400,000	(100,000)
Sales revenues	$25,000,000	$24,360,000	$ (640,000)
Cost of goods sold	18,750,000	17,520,000	1,230,000
Gross margin	6,250,000	6,840,000	590,000
Selling expenses—variable	1,250,000	1,248,000	2,000
Selling expenses—fixed	800,000	788,000	12,000
Administrative expenses—variable	625,000	552,000	73,000
Administrative expenses—fixed	1,500,000	1,580,000	(80,000)
Total operating expenses	$ 4,175,000	$ 4,168,000	$ 7,000
Net income	$ 2,075,000	$ 2,672,000	$ 597,000

[a] Parentheses indicate an unfavorable variance.

REQUIRED: Using flexible budgeting concepts, calculate a more appropriate budget figure to use for comparative purposes and calculate variances of budget from actual based on your revised budget representations.

11—2. Use the data provided in Exercise 11—1 for Super Strength Concrete Company.

REQUIRED: For *each item* listed and for the company as a *whole*. Calculate:

1. The variance due to volume factors.
2. The flexible budget variance.
3. The impact of both the flexible budget variance and volume variance on income.

11—3. Perkins Electrical Circuitry has accumulated the following data for the accounting period just ended:

	BUDGET	ACTUAL
Unit sales	800,000	820,000
Sales revenues	$4,000,000	$4,059,000
Cost of goods sold	2,160,000	2,132,000
Gross margin	$1,840,000	$1,927,000
Variable selling expenses	640,000	639,000
Fixed selling expenses	100,000	103,000
Variable administrative expenses	400,000	451,000
Fixed administrative expenses	500,000	505,000
Total operating expenses	$1,640,000	$1,698,000
Net income	$ 200,000	$ 229,000

The president of Perkins states that he knows the company put into effect some expense-cutting measures in an attempt to improve net income. However, because the actual volume and the budgeted volume are not the same, he does not know how much of the improvement in the bottom line is due solely to the increased volume sold.

REQUIRED: Prepare some data for the president which will show the effects of the volume increase only on the results of operations for the period.

11—4. The manager of the Construction Toys Division of Thor Toys, Inc., has the following data for December of the current year and December of last year.

	DECEMBER CURRENT YEAR	DECEMBER LAST YEAR
Sales	$6,700,000	$5,300,000
Cost of goods manufactured and sold:		
Direct materials	1,005,000	689,000
Direct labor	1,675,000	1,060,000
Manufacturing overhead	670,000	583,000
Total	$3,350,000	$2,332,000
Gross margin	$3,350,000	$2,968,000
Operating expenses:		
Advertising	804,000	424,000
Sales salaries and commissions	469,000	371,000
Administrative salaries	1,005,000	530,000
Depreciation	536,000	424,000
Utilities	670,000	371,000
Other	201,000	106,000
Total operating expenses	$3,685,000	$2,226,000
Net income (loss)	($ 335,000)	$ 742,000

He asks you to prepare a statement for him which will help him pinpoint the areas where *costs relationships have changed* for the current December relative to the past December. He believes that this will help him determine why his division showed a loss despite an increased volume and aid him in finding where costs may be controlled more effectively.

REQUIRED: Prepare a statement which will provide the division manager with the information he has requested.

11—5. Selected data for Gomez Wood and Pulp Company are given below along with industry statistics for companies with similar product lines and of similar size.

	GOMEZ	INDUSTRY
Average accounts receivable	$ 850,000	$ 700,000
Average finished goods inventory	272,500	334,000
Sales (assume all are credit sales)	5,450,000	5,580,000
Cost of goods sold	2,180,000	2,340,000
Operating income	436,000	725,000
Average investment	4,100,000	4,530,000

REQUIRED:
1. Calculate the following ratios for Gomez and for the industry:
   a. Average collection period for accounts receivable.
   b. Inventory turnover.
   c. Profit margin on sales.
   d. Return on investment.
2. Which areas represent possible trouble spots for Gomez, based on a comparison with industry results?
3. Gomez's sales forecast for the next period is $6,012,000. To what level would its average balance of accounts receivable have to be reduced so that Gomez would have a collection period of the same length as that of the industry?

11—6. (CMA adapted) If a company changed its inventory measurement method from FIFO to LIFO, just prior to a period of rising prices, what effect would this have on the current ratio and inventory turnover in the next period? If the company also eased enforcement of its credit terms, what effect would this have on the accounts receivable turnover ratio (Calculated as: Net Sales/ Average Receivables)?

11—7. (CMA adapted) Mr. Sparks, the owner of School Supplies, Inc., is interested in keeping control over accounts receivable. He understands that the accounts receivable collection period will give a good indication of how well receivables are being managed. School Supplies, Inc., does 70% of its business during June, July, and August. The terms of sale are 2/10, net/60. Net sales for the year ended December 31, and the receivables balance, are given below:

Net sales	$1,512,000
Receivables, at Dec. 31	$ 273,000

REQUIRED:
1. Calculate the accounts receivable collection period from the data above based on a 360-day period.
2. What does this result indicate to Mr. Sparks?

11—8. (CMA adapted) The financial statements for Johanson Co. are reproduced below.

JOHANSON CO.
Statement of Financial Position
December 31
($000 omitted)

	LAST YEAR	CURRENT YEAR
Assets		
Current assets:		
Cash and temporary investments	$ 380	$ 400
Accounts receivable (net)	1,500	1,700
Inventories	2,120	2,200
Total current assets	$4,000	$4,300
Long-term assets:		
Land	$ 500	$ 500
Building and equipment (net)	4,000	4,700
Total long-term assets	$4,500	$5,200
Total assets	$8,500	$9,500
Liabilities and Equities		
Current liabilities:		
Accounts payable	$ 700	$1,400
Current portion of long-term debt	500	1,000
Total current liabilities	$1,200	$2,400
Long-term debt	4,000	3,000
Total liabilities	$5,200	$5,400
Stockholders' equity		
Common stock	$3,000	$3,000
Retained earnings	300	1,100
Total stockholders' equity	$3,300	$4,100
Total liabilities and equities	$8,500	$9,500

JOHANSON CO.
Statement of Income and Retained Earnings
for the Year Ended December 31, Current Year
($000 omitted)

Net sales		$28,800
Less: Cost of goods sold	$15,120	
Selling expenses	7,180	
Administrative expenses	4,100	
Interest	400	
Income taxes	800	27,600
Net income		$ 1,200
Retained earnings January 1		300
Subtotal		$ 1,500
Cash dividends declared and paid		400
Retained earnings December 31		$ 1,100

REQUIRED: **1.** Calculate for Johanson for the current year the:

    a. Acid test ratio.

    b. Current ratio.

    c. Accounts receivable collection period based on *average* receivables and a 360-day year.

$$\text{Average receivables} = \frac{\text{Beginning balance} + \text{ending balance}}{2}$$

    d. Asset turnover based on year-end figures.

    e. Inventory turnover based on year-end figures.

    f. Profit margin on sales.

    g. Return on investment based on year-end figures.

  2. What problems do you have in interpreting the ratios which you have calculated?

11—9. Fragrances So Sweet produces perfume. The following data for the past period have been accumulated for the company.

	BUDGET	ACTUAL
Bottles of perfume sold	500,000	520,000
Revenues	$5,000,000	$5,304,000
Cost of goods manufactured and sold	1,550,000	1,560,000
Variable selling expenses	1,000,000	1,196,000
Fixed selling expenses	450,000	455,000
Fixed administrative	1,210,000	1,214,000
Total expenses	$4,210,000	$4,425,000
Operating income	$ 790,000	$ 879,000

REQUIRED: For each item shown on the income statement and for the company as a whole, calculate the variances due to volume factors, the variances from the flexible budget which are due to price and cost factors, and the income variance—that is, the impact of each variance on income.

11—10. The following information relates to the operations of the Authentic Tomato Catsup Company and the industry of which it is a part:

Estimated sales: 2,800,000 bottles of catsup @ $1.25
Actual sales: 3,000,000 bottles of catsup for $3,870,000
Historical share of the catsup market: 40%
Industry sales of catsup for the period: 8,200,000 bottles

REQUIRED: **1.** Calculate the difference between estimated sales revenues and actual sales revenues.

  2. What part of the difference between actual and estimated sales revenues was accounted for by:

    a. Volume factors?

    b. Price factors?

  3. What actual share of the market did Authentic have for the period?

  4. What was the cost to Authentic of loosing market share?

11—11. Given below are some data for Winnetka Fur Products, Inc., and for the industry of which it is a part:

	WINNETKA
Average accounts receivable	$ 600,000
Average inventory	480,000
Sales	3,600,000
Average assets	3,000,000
Cost of goods sold	1,440,000
Net income	432,000

	INDUSTRY STATISTICS
Accounts receivable collection period	50 days
Inventory turnover	4 times
Profit margin on sales	15%
Asset turnover	2 times
Return on investment	18%

REQUIRED: 1. Calculate for Winnetka the same statistics which have been provided for the industry. Use a 360-day year.

2. Assume that Winnetka's level of sales, cost of goods sold, and average assets for the current year are typical for the company.

   a. To what balance would accounts receivable have to be reduced for Winnetka to have a collection period equal to that of the industry?

   b. To what balance would inventory have to be reduced for Winnetka to have an inventory turnover equal to that of the industry?

   c. How much net income would Winnetka have to generate to have a profit margin on sales equal to that of the industry?

11—12. The Yaeger Gumdrop Company's records show the following information:

	BUDGET	ACTUAL	VARIANCE
Cost of packages of gumdrops manufactured and sold	$879,000	$900,000	21,000 U

The only *manufacturing variances* from standard costs which Yaeger had for the period were for raw materials used. These amounted to a $23,000 unfavorable price variance and a $12,000 favorable usage variance or a net variance from standard cost of units manufactured of $11,000 unfavorable.

REQUIRED: Give all the reasons you can suggest for the fact that the net variance from standard cost of units manufactured is not the variance shown above when budgeted and actual results were compared.

11—13. Income-statement data for a three-year period are given below for the Cashin Appliance Repair Center.

	CURRENT YEAR YEAR 3	YEAR 2	YEAR 1
Revenues	$200,000	$150,000	$100,000
Operating expenses:			
Salaries	74,000	43,500	30,000
Parts and supplies	46,000	28,500	20,000
Rent	20,000	20,000	15,000
Depreciation of equipment	16,000	16,000	12,000
Utilities	8,000	7,500	5,000
Accounting Services	6,000	6,000	—
Insurance	4,000	6,000	2,000
Miscellaneous	6,000	4,500	1,000
Total expenses	$180,000	$132,000	$ 85,000
Operating income	$ 20,000	$ 18,000	$ 15,000

REQUIRED:

1. Based on the data given, how well did the company do in the current year relative to the prior two years?

2. Convert the income statements for the three years to common size statements. Comment on the performance of Cashin Appliance based on these calculations.

3. Comment on the extent to which each expense is subject to the control of the company.

11—14. The performance of the Sunshine Bicycle Manufacturing Company has been disappointing to the company's management. As a result they have hired you as a business consultant and are seeking your help in improving the company's performance. You have been provided with the following information regarding the company's performance relative to that of the bicycle industry. Sunshine believes that the industry statistics are typical and represent a realistic standard for the company.

	SUNSHINE	INDUSTRY
Accounts receivable collection period	73 days	65 days
Inventory turnover	3 times	8 times
Asset turnover	.9 times	1.2 times
Profit margin on sales	4%	12%
Return on investment	5%	14%

REQUIRED: For each of the statistics, draft some key questions which you will want to have answered as part of your study of Sunshine's operations.

11—15. The Clean-Sweep Electric Broom Company has assembled the following information:

Budgeted sales: 400,000 electric brooms @ $42
Actual sales: 350,000 electric brooms for $13,300,000
Estimated industry sales: 2,000,000 electric brooms
Actual industry sales: 1,400,000 electric brooms

REQUIRED: 1. Calculate the differences between budgeted sales revenues and actual sales revenues which are caused by volume differences and those which are caused by price factors.
2. Prepare an analysis which shows how well the company did relative to industry performance.

---

problems

11—16. *Calculation of volume, flexible budget, and income variances for operations.* The Chang Glass Company's records show the following for the period just ended for one of its divisions:

	BUDGET	ACTUAL
Sales in units	500,000	470,000
Revenues	$3,000,000	$2,805,900
Cost of goods sold	1,500,000	1,433,500
Gross margin	$1,500,000	$1,372,400
Variable selling expenses	500,000	488,800
Fixed selling expenses	200,000	197,000
Variable administrative expenses	150,000	150,400
Fixed administrative expenses	350,000	349,000
Total operating expenses	$1,200,000	$1,185,200
Net income	$ 300,000	$ 187,200

In a conference with the president of Chang Glass, the division manager stated that sales volume had been adversely affected by the price-cutting actions of one of the division's major competitors. However, she pointed out that the division had really performed well, because, with the exception of an insignificant difference between actual variable administrative expenses and budgeted, all the division's costs and expenses were less than budget.

REQUIRED: 1. Do you agree with the division manager's statement about the performance of the division with respect to cost control? Why or why not?
2. Using flexible budget concepts, prepare a budget presentation consistent with actual sales.
3. Prepare a schedule which shows the impact of volume variance, flexible budget

variance, and the total income-statement impact of these variances for each income-statement item.

11—17. *Calculation of volume, flexible budget, and income variances for operations.*   The General United Corporation has a division which manufactures and sells electric fans. The controller of the Fan Division prepared a report for Larry Jones, the division's manager, which describes the divisions's performance. The report is shown below:

	BUDGET	VARIANCE[a]
Unit sales	2,000,000	100,000
Sales	$60,000,000	$ 5,100,000
Cost of goods sold	36,000,000	(6,000,000)
Gross margin	$24,000,000	$ (900,000)
Variable selling expenses	6,000,000	(90,000)
Fixed selling expenses	8,000,000	(50,000)
Variable administrative expenses	1,000,000	(8,000)
Fixed administrative expenses	3,000,000	(100,000)
Total operating expenses	$18,000,000	$ (248,000)
Net income	$ 6,000,000	$(1,148,000)

[a] Parentheses indicates an unfavorable variance.

After reviewing the report, Jones commented that he didn't find it very helpful. In most instances he could not tell by looking at the report whether costs were higher because of volume changes or because of actual increases in prices and costs. He asked the controller to re-do the report in some way so that the effects of volume changes were separated from those of price changes.

REQUIRED: 1. Generate a report of the type requested by Jones which will segregate volume effects from effects not related to volume for each income-statement item.
2. Based on the revised report which you have prepared, what are the major problem areas for the Fan Division?
3. Jones believes that next year the cost of materials used in the manufacture of fans, which represents 50% of the cost of each unit produced, will be 10% greater than actual cost for the current period. He believes all other costs will remain unchanged and that next year's volume will be approximately 2,100,000 fans. Jones would like to make a profit of $4,000,000. To make this profit, by what amount will the sales price have to be increased over the current year's actual selling price? Assume the company uses a LIFO inventory costing system and that sales volume is equal to production volume.

11—18. *Common size statement preparation.*   Bruhn Chemical Company manufactures a variety of pain relievers which are sold over-the-counter.

The results of its operations for the past two years and for the current year are shown below (000 omitted):

	CURRENT YEAR	LAST YEAR	TWO YEARS AGO
Revenues	$12,500	$10,500	$9,800
Cost of Goods Manufactured and Sold:			
Direct Materials	1,250	1,050	980
Direct Labor	3,125	2,100	1,764
Variable Manufacturing Overhead	500	420	490
Fixed Manufacturing Overhead	750	840	686
Total	$ 5,625	$ 4,410	3,920
Gross Margin	$ 6,875	$ 6,090	$5,880
Variable Operating Expenses:			
Sales Commissions	625	315	294
Supplies	125	105	98
Advertising	1,125	420	294
Total	$ 1,875	$ 840	$ 686
Fixed Operating Expenses:			
Salaries	2,500	2,100	2,450
Depreciation	625	630	588
Utilities	500	315	196
Insurance	250	420	294
Other	125	210	98
Total	$ 4,000	$ 3,675	$3,626
Total Operating Expenses	$ 5,875	$ 4,515	$4,312
Net Income	$ 1,000	$ 1,575	$1,568

Although they are packaged differently and have different brand names, all the products produced and sold by Bruhn are very similar and entail similar costs.

The president of Bruhn has asked you to prepare a statement which shows what happens to the sales dollar and why more of it is not realized in the form of profit. She points out that while volume increased significantly during the three-year period, net income has dropped, with a very material drop occurring when the current year is compared to the previous year.

REQUIRED: 1. Prepare common size income statements for Bruhn Chemical for the three-year period.
2. In what areas have costs increased significantly, and where would you suggest the company look in an effort to improve its profit margin?
3. If direct labor costs and the salaries shown under fixed operating expenses could have been held at last year's dollar levels, what percentage of the sales dollar for the current year would have been realized as net income?

11—19. *Calculation and use of ratios.* Arm-Chair Sports, which manufactures video games, prepared the three-year comparative financial statements shown below:

ARM-CHAIR SPORTS
Comparative Income Statements
for the Years Ended December 31

	CURRENT YEAR	LAST YEAR	TWO YEARS AGO
Revenues	$900,000	$840,000	$750,000
Cost of Goods Sold	270,000	269,000	248,000
Gross Margin	$630,000	$571,000	$502,000
Selling Expenses	225,000	194,000	150,600
Administrative Expenses	252,000	252,000	245,000
Total Operating Expenses	$477,000	$446,000	$395,600
Net Income	$153,000	$125,000	$106,400

ARM-CHAIR SPORTS
Comparative Balance Sheets
as of December 31

	CURRENT YEAR	LAST YEAR	TWO YEARS AGO
Current Assets:			
Cash	$ 50,000	$ 13,500	$13,000
Accounts Receivable (net)	112,500	110,000	90,000
Raw Materials Inventory	80,000	65,000	70,000
Finished Goods Inventory	30,000	29,000	31,000
Other	20,000	5,000	6,000
Total Current Assets	$292,500	$222,500	$210,000
Property, Plant and Equipment (net)	$507,500	$557,500	$600,000
Total Assets	$800,000	$780,000	$810,000
Curent Liabilities	$160,000	$100,000	$122,000
Long-Term Liabilities	250,000	367,000	380,000
Total Liabilities	$410,000	$467,000	$502,000
Stockholders' Equity:			
Common Stock (no par)	$208,000	$208,000	$208,000
Retained Earnings	182,000	105,000	100,000
Total Stockholders' Equity	$390,000	$313,000	$308,000
Total Liabilities and Stockholders' Equity	$800,000	$780,000	$810,000

Some key statistics for the current period for the video game industry are shown below:

Accounts receivable collection period	38 days
Inventory turnover	6 times
Profit margin on sales	15%
Return on investment	18%

REQUIRED: 1. Calculate the following ratios for Arm-Chair Sports for each of the three years for which data have been provided. Arm-Chair Sports uses year-end balances in calculating the collection period and inventory turnover.

    a. Accounts receivable collection period.

    b. Inventory turnover.

    c. Profit margin on sales.

    d. Return on investment.

2. Looking at the ratios you have computed, comment on the trend of Arm-Chair Sports' ratios and on its current set of ratios relative to those shown for the industry. (In other words, how well do you think the company is performing?)

3. Are there any suggestions you would make in terms of the way the company calculates its ratios?

4. Return on investment may be calculated two ways: Income/Investment, or Asset turnover × Profit margin on sales. Calculate return on investment by the latter method based on current-year data.

11—20. *Analyzing performance against objectives.* (CMA adapted) Tablon Inc. is a wholly-owned subsidiary of Marbel Co. The philosophy of Marbel's management is to allow the subsidiaries to operate as independent units. Corporate control is exercised through the establishment of minimum objectives for each subsidiary, accompanied by substantial rewards for success and penalities for failure. The time period for performance review is long enough for competent managers to display their abilities.

Each quarter the subsidiary is required to submit financial statements. The statements are accompanied by a letter from the subsidiary president explaining the results to date, a forecast for the remainder of the year, and the actions to be taken to achieve the objectives if the forecast indicates that the objectives will not be met. The Marbel management in conjunction with Tablon management had set the objectives listed below for the year ending May 31, 1984. These objectives are similar to those set in prior years.

Sales growth of 20%.
Return on investment of 10%.
A *long-term debt-to-equity* ratio of not more than 1.00.
Profit margin on sales of 8%.

Tablon's controller has just completed preparing the financial statements for the six months ended November 30, 1983, and the forecast for the year ending May 31, 1984. The statements are presented below. After a cursory glance at them, Tablon's president concluded that all objectives would not be met. At a staff meeting of the Tablon management the president asked the controller to review the projected results and recommend actions that could be taken during the remainder of the year that would enable Tablon to more nearly meet their objectives.

TABLON INC.
Income Statement
($000 omitted)

	YEAR ENDED MAY 31, 1983	SIX MONTHS ENDED NOV. 30, 1983	FORECAST FOR YEAR ENDING MAY 31, 1984
Sales	$25,000	$15,000	$30,000
Cost of Goods Sold	$13,000	$ 8,000	$16,000
Selling Expenses	5,000	3,500	7,000
Administrative Expenses and Interest	4,000	2,500	5,000
Income Taxes (40%)	1,200	400	800
Total Expenses and Taxes	$23,200	$14,400	$28,800
Net Income	$ 1,800	$ 600	$ 1,200
Dividends Declared and Paid	600	0	600
Income Retained in the Business	$ 1,200	$ 600	$ 600

TABLON INC.
Statement of Financial Position
($000 omitted)

	MAY 31, 1983	NOV. 30, 1983	FORECASTED FOR MAY 31, 1984
Assets			
Cash	$ 400	$ 500	$ 500
Accounts Receivable (net)	4,100	6,500	7,100
Inventory	7,000	8,500	8,600
Plant and Equipment (net)	6,500	7,000	7,300
Total Assets	$18,000	$22,500	$23,500
Liabilities and Equities			
Accounts Payable	$ 3,000	$ 4,000	$ 4,000
Accrued Taxes	300	200	200
Long-term Borrowing	6,000	9,000	10,000
Common Stock	5,000	5,000	5,000
Retained Earnings	3,700	4,300	4,300
Total Liabilities and Equities	$18,000	$22,500	$23,500

REQUIRED: **1.** Calculate the projected results for each of the four objectives established for Tablon Inc. State which results will not meet the objectives by year-end.

2. From the data presented, identify the factors which seem to contribute to the failure of Tablon Inc. to meet all its objectives.

3. Explain the possible actions the controller could recommend in response to the president's request.

11—21. *Calculating ratios to analyze performance; forecasting cash flows.* (CMA adapted) Warford Corporation was formed five years ago through a public subscription of common stock. Lucinda Street, who owns 15% of the common stock, was one of the organizers of Warford and is its current president. The company has been successful but currently is experiencing a shortage of funds. On June 10, Street approached the Bell National Bank, asking for a 24-month extension on two $30,000 notes, which are due on June 30 and September 30 of the current year. Another note of $7,000 is due on December 31 of next year, but she expects no difficulty in paying this note on its due date. Street explained that Warford's cash flow problems are due primarily to the company's desire to finance a $300,000 plant expansion over the next two fiscal years through internally generated funds. The Commercial Loan Officer of Bell National Bank requested financial reports for the last two fiscal years. These reports are reproduced below.

WARFORD CORPORATION
Statement of Financial Position
March 31

	LAST YEAR	CURRENT YEAR
Assets		
Cash	$ 12,500	$ 16,400
Notes Receivable–Current	104,000	112,000
Accounts Receivable (net)	68,500	81,600
Inventories (at cost)	50,000	80,000
Plant and Equipment (net of depreciation)	646,000	680,000
Total Assets	$881,000	$970,000
Liabilities and Owners' Equity		
Accounts Payable	$ 72,000	$ 69,000
Notes Payable–Current	54,500	67,000
Accrued Liabilities	6,000	9,000
Common Stock (60,000 shares, $10 par)	600,000	600,000
Retained Earnings[a]	148,500	225,000
Total Liabilities and Owners' Equity	$881,000	$970,000

[a] Cash dividends were paid at the rate of $1.00 per share last year and $1.25 per share in the current year.

WARFORD CORPORATION
Income Statement
for the Fiscal Years Ended March 31

	LAST YEAR	CURRENT YEAR
Sales	$2,700,000	$3,000,000
Cost of Goods Sold[b]	1,720,000	1,902,500
Gross Margin	$ 980,000	$1,097,500
Operating Expenses	780,000	845,000
Net Income Before Taxes	$ 200,000	$ 252,500
Income Taxes (40%)	80,000	101,000
Income After Taxes	$ 120,000	$ 151,500

[b] Depreciation charges of $102,500 are included in Cost of Goods Sold for the current year. The depreciation charge is expected to remain at this level for the following two years.

REQUIRED:

1. Calculate the following items for Warford Corporation for the two years:

   a. Current ratio.
   b. Acid test (quick) ratio.
   c. Inventory turnover based on year-end balances.
   d. Return on assets (ROI).
   e. Percentage change in sales, cost of goods sold, gross margin, operating expenses, and net income after taxes from last year to the current year.

2. Assume that the percentage changes experienced in the current year as compared with last year for sales, cost of goods sold, and operating expenses, will be repeated in each of the next two years. Is Warford's desire to finance the plant expansion from internally generated funds realistic? Support your answer by estimating cash flows for the next two years. Assume that all revenues represent cash inflows and that all expenses except depreciation represent cash outflows. Further assume that the bank extends the current loans and that the plant expansion will be paid in equal amounts during the next two years. Warford plans to pay dividends at the current rate.

3. Should Bell National Bank grant the extension on Warford's notes, considering Street's statement about financing the plant expansion through internally generated funds? Explain your answer.

11—22. *Issues in investment-center evaluation—nonquantitative problem.* (CMA adapted) The Notewon Corporation is a highly diversified company which grants its divisional executives a significant amount of authority in operating the divisions. Each division is responsible for its own sales, pricing, production, costs of operations, and the management of accounts receivable, inventories, accounts payable, and use of existing facilities. Cash is managed by corporate headquarters; all cash in excess of normal operating needs of the divisions is transferred periodically to corporate headquarters for redistribution or investment.

The divisional executives are responsible for presenting requests to corporate management for investment projects. The proposals are analyzed and documented at corporate headquarters. The final decision to commit funds to acquire equipment, to expand existing facilities, or for other investment purposes rests with corporate management. This procedure for investment projects is necessitated by Notewon's capital allocation policy.

The corporation evaluates the performance of division executives by the return-on-investment (ROI) measure. The asset base is composed of fixed assets employed plus working capital exclusive of cash. The ROI performance of a divisional executive is the most important appraisal factor for salary changes. In addition, the annual performance bonus is based on the ROI results, with increases in ROI having a significant impact on the amount of the bonus.

The Notewon Corporation adopted the ROI performance measure and related compensation procedures about ten years ago. The corporation did so to increase the awareness of divisional management of the importance of the profit/asset relationship and to provide additional incentive to the divisional executives to seek investment opportunities. The corporation seems to have benefited from the program. During its first years the ROI for the corporation as a whole increased. Although the ROI has continued to grow in each division, the corporate ROI has declined in recent years. In the past three years the corporation has accumulated a sizable amount of cash and short-term marketable securities. The corporation management is concerned about the increase in the short-term marketable securities. A recent article in a financial publication suggested that the use of ROI was overemphasized by some companies with results similar to those experienced by Notewon.

REQUIRED:
1. Describe the specific actions division managers might have taken to cause the ROI to grow in each division but decline for the corporation. Illustrate your explanation with appropriate examples.
2. Explain, using the concepts of goal congruence and motivation of divisional executives, how Notewon Corporation's overemphasis on the use of the ROI measure might result in the recent decline in the corporation's ROI and the increase in cash and short-term marketable securities.
3. What changes could be made in Notewon Corporation's compensation policy to avoid this problem? Explain your answer.

11—23. *Ratio calculation and analysis.* Rodriquez Products manufactures child safety restraints for automobiles. Comparative financial statements for two years follow:

RODRIQUEZ PRODUCTS
Comparative Income Statements
for the Year Ended Dec. 31

	(CURRENT YEAR) YEAR 2	YEAR 1
Revenues (net)	$212,000	$212,250
Cost of Goods Sold	177,000	176,000
Gross Margin	$ 35,000	$ 36,250
Selling Expenses	11,000	15,750
Administrative Expenses	9,000	8,500
Total Operating Expenses	20,000	24,250
Net Income (before taxes)	$ 15,000	$ 12,000

RODRIQUEZ PRODUCTS
Comparative Balance Sheet
as of Dec. 31

	(CURRENT YEAR) YEAR 2	YEAR 1
Current Assets		
Cash	$ 12,720	$ 8,000
Accounts Receivable (net)	23,650	20,400
Raw Materials Inventory	17,200	15,700
Finished Goods Inventory (LIFO)	6,100	5,300
Marketable Securities	4,000	2,000
Total Current Assets	$ 63,670	$ 51,400
Property, Plant and Equipment (net)	125,700	131,000
Total Assets	$189,370	$182,400
Liabilities		
Current Liabilities	37,500	25,700
Long-term Liabilities	78,000	86,500
Total Liabilities	$115,500	$112,200
Stockholders' Equity		
Common Stock (no par)	$ 40,000	$ 40,000
Retained Earnings	33,870	30,200
Total Stockholders' Equity	$ 73,870	$ 70,200
Total Liabilities and Stockholders' Equity	$189,370	$182,400

REQUIRED: 1. Calculate the following ratios for Rodriquez Products for Year 1 and for Year 2:

    a. Accounts receivable collection period.

    b. Inventory turnover.

    c. Total asset turnover.

    d. Current ratio.

    e. Quick ratio.

    f. Debt/equity ratio.

    g. Profit margin on sales.

    h. Return on investment.

2. Assuming that Rodriquez is a new firm, comment on their first two years of operations, based on the ratios computed. If industry statistics show an accounts receivable collection period of 30 days, based on year-end accounts receivable, and inventory turnover, based on year-end inventory, of 20 times, what actions should Rodriquez contemplate?

11—24. *Common size statements, ratio analysis, and projection of future results.* Magna Motors, Inc., manufactures motors which are used in small appliances. They have collected the following data relative to their own performance and the industry of which they are a part.

	MAGNA MOTORS	INDUSTRY DATA EXPRESSED IN PERCENTS
Sales	$8,500,000	100%
Cost of goods manufactured and sold:		
Direct materials	$1,530,000	15%
Direct labor	1,275,000	10
Manufacturing overhead:		
Variable	510,000	8
Fixed	255,000	5
Total	$3,570,000	38%
Gross margin	$4,930,000	62%
Selling expenses:		
Salaries	$ 850,000	10%
Supplies	340,000	2
Advertising	1,020,000	7
Other	85,000	1
Total	$2,295,000	20%
Administrative expenses:		
Salaries	$1,700,000	8%
Supplies	850,000	5
Utilities	340,000	6
Depreciation and other	680,000	9
Total	$3,570,000	28%
Total operating expenses	$5,865,000	48%
Net income (loss)	($ 935,000)	14%

Additional selected data for Magna:

Average balance in accounts receivable	$1,204,000
Average finished goods inventory	$ 714,000
Year-end asset total	$9,000,000

Additional industry data:

Accounts receivable collection period	40 days
Inventory turnover	8 times
Return on investment	18%

Magna Motors has hired you as a consultant to help them turn the company around and make it profitable. Your first step is to do some additional financial analysis.

REQUIRED:
1. Convert Magna Motor's Income Statement into a common size statement so that it can be compared with the industry statistics available.
2. Calculate the same ratios for Magna that are shown above under additional industry data.
3. Magna believes that they will sell $9,000,000 next year. They want to show a profit margin of 14% consistent with that of the industry for the current year.

   a. To show the 14% profit margin, how much net income must Magna make for next year?

   b. After a careful review of its manufacturing costs, Magna believes that the cost of goods manufactured and sold can be reduced next year to 40% of sales. Magna would like to keep its average finished goods inventory at a level which will give it the same inventory turnover—8 times—as that of the industry. What is the average amount of inventory which Magna can have on hand?

   c. Next period Magna would also like to have an accounts receivable collection period equal to or less than that of the industry. What is the average amount of accounts receivable for the next period which Magna must maintain to equal the industry collection period?

   d. Magna plans to cut salaries of those perons whose salaries are described as part of administrative expenses by 10% next year and reduce expenditures for supplies $100,000. In addition, it believes that utility cost will be 5% higher than they are during the current period. All the other administrative expenses are expected to remain at the current level. To show the 14% profit margin on sales, how much can Magna spend for selling expenses, considering the data given in part (b) above?

   e. To report a return on investment consistent with that of the industry and assuming a 14% profit margin on sales, what level of investment in assets must Magna maintain for the coming period?

11—25. *Common size statements for a bank.*   The People's Bank's income statements for a three-year period are shown below (000,000 omitted):

	CURRENT YEAR YEAR 3	YEAR 2	YEAR 1
Interest Revenue:			
On loans	$274	273	229
On investment securities	25	31	32
On time deposits in other banks	21	3	17
Miscellaneous	10	13	6
Total interest revenue	$330	$320	$284

	CURRENT YEAR YEAR 3	YEAR 2	YEAR 1
Noninterest Revenues:			
Trust and agency fees	23	24	26
Customer service fees	19	15	11
Other	12	14	10
Total noninterest revenue	54	53	47
Total revenues	$384	$373	$331
Interest Expenses:			
Interest on savings	24	23	24
Interest on money market accounts	1	—	—
Interest on time deposits	108	103	75
Interest on borrowings	57	70	70
Total interest expenses	$190	$196	$169
Provision for possible losses on loans	6	4	5
Noninterest Expenses:			
Compensation	66	58	52
Employee benefits	14	12	11
Occupancy expense	13	12	11
Equipment expense	14	13	11
Other	39	35	30
Total noninterest expense	146	130	115
Total expenses	$342	$330	$289
Income before taxes	$ 42	$ 43	$ 42

REQUIRED:
1. Convert the income statements for the People's Bank into common size statements. Design your statement in such a way that total revenues = 100%.
2. What areas, if any, do you believe deserve special attention from management? Justify any areas you have selected.

11—26. *Calculating volume and flexible budget variances for a service organization; analyzing performance.* Budget and actual data for Jennifer's Jiffy Car Wash are given below:

	BUDGET	ACTUAL
Number of cars washed	10,800	12,000
Number of cars given a hot wax application	3,600	2,500
Revenues from washing	$40,500	$48,000
Revenues from waxing	7,200	5,000
Total revenues	$47,700	$53,000
Operating expenses:		
Variable:		
Water	4,320	5,040
Detergent	1,620	2,040
Wax[a]	900	625
Electricity	1,080	1,320
Fixed:		
Salaries	15,000	16,200
Depreciation	6,000	6,000
Insurance	2,000	2,300
Other	1,500	1,400
Total expenses	32,420	34,925
Operating income	$15,280	$18,075

[a] Varies with number of cars waxed. All other variable expenses vary with cars washed.

REQUIRED:
1. Prepare a statement which compares the original budget, a flexible budget, and actual results and show a volume variance, flexible budget variance, and income variances for each item of revenue and expense. Prepare the statement in a format which shows contribution margin. (Remember: Contribution margin = revenues less all variable expenses.)

2. Suppose that the cost of the wax itself is the only major cost of waxing a car as it passes through the car wash. The original budget was prepared on the assumption that one-third of the cars washed would be waxed. If Jennifer's Car Wash had been able to provide waxing for one-third of the actual cars washed, at the actual waxing cost per car, by what amount would operating income have increased.

3. Budgeted and actual assets of Jennifer's Jiffy Car Wash total $139,000. How was actual return on investment affected by *volume* differences? Show the percent effect. How was actual return on investment affected by revenue and cost differences between budget and actual results? Calculate the percent effect.

4. Suppose that Jennifer's Jiffy Car Wash has the capacity to wash 14,000 cars without increasing its fixed expenses. Based on washing the cars alone, if the company could reach this volume, by what amount would operating income increase over its current actual level? Use actual costs data in your analysis.

11—27. *Calculation and use of ratios.*   Financial data for Zeigler Soft Drink Company are given below:

Average accounts receivable	$ 250,000
Average inventory	90,000
Average assets	1,440,000
Sales	1,800,000
Cost of goods sold	540,000
Net income	144,000
Other expenses which vary with sales	630,000

As one of its goals Zeigler's management seeks to perform at the level of the industry for certain key ratios. Those industry ratios which have been adopted as objectives of Zeigler are:

Accounts receivable collection period	45 days
Inventory turnover	10 times
Asset turnover	3 times
Profit margin on sales	15%
Return on investment (assets)	12%

REQUIRED:
1. Calculate the ratios for Zeigler which have been provided for the soft drink industry. Use 360 days = 1 year.

2. For the coming year, Zeigler has made the following projections:

Sales	$2,000,000
Cost of goods sold	600,000
Other variable expenses	700,000

Based on these projections, calculate the average balance of accounts receivable and inventory which Zeigler would have to maintain to meet industry standards for the collection period and inventory turnover. Also, calculate the net income

Zeigler would have to make and the level of investment the company could maintain to meet industry standards for profit margin on sales and return on investment.

11—28. *Calculating the effects of changes in market share.* Feathered Friends, Inc., produces and sells sunflower seeds which are used primarily to feed birds. The following information about the company is available:

Budgeted sales: 360,000 fifty-pound bags of seed at $12 per bag.
Actual sales: 400,000 fifty-pound bags of seed, $4,900,000.
Estimated industry demand: 1,000,000 bags.
Actual industry sales: 1,200,000 bags.

In a conversation with the president of the company, the sales manager points out that he has had a particularly good year, since he and his staff sold 40,000 more bags than had been anticipated at the time the budget was set.

REQUIRED:

1. Calculate the difference between actual revenues and budgeted revenues, the part of that difference which is due to volume factors, and the part of that difference which is due to selling-price differences.
2. Analyze the volume difference further, showing what part of the volume change in dollar terms is due to industry demand changes and what part is not.
3. Suppose that actual industry sales amounted to 900,000 bags. Analyze the volume difference between actual and budgeted results to determine what part of the volume change in dollars is due to industry factors and what part is not.
4. Based on the original data provided, do you believe the sales manager did a good job? Why or why not?

11—29. *Comparing performance with historical and industry standards.* The accountant for Connaway's Chuckwagon Bar-B-Que has provided its owner with the following performance data for the past two months, which were the first two months of the restaurant's operations:

	JANUARY	FEBRUARY
Revenues	$150,000	$130,000
Expenses:		
Food	58,500	46,800
Food servers	22,500	15,600
Linen service and accessories	3,000	2,600
Other	1,500	1,300
Salaries	24,000	24,000
Depreciation	7,500	7,500
Utilities	4,500	4,000
Advertising	15,000	5,000
Insurance	1,500	1,500
Other	6,000	6,000
Total expenses	$144,000	$114,300
Operating income	$ 6,000	$ 15,700

Industry data for restaurants of similar size and type are given below:

Revenues	100%
Food costs	33%
Food servers	10%
Linen and accessories	2%
Other variable costs	1%
Fixed salaries	16%
Depreciation	7%
Utilities	3%
Advertising	5%
Insurance	2%
Other	4%
Total expenses	83%
Operating income	17%

REQUIRED:

1. Convert Connaway's income statements to a common size basis and compare the restaurant's monthly performance to that of the industry.

2. Based on your computations in part 1, give some likely reasons for differences between the two months. Comment on the behavior of fixed costs when stated in percent terms.

3. Compute Connaway's performance for the two-month period as a whole and compare it to that of the industry.

4. Give some possible explanations for significant differences between Connaway's performance and that of the industry.

11—30. *Comprehensive variance-analysis problem.* Data for Imperial Chocolates, the manufacturer of an expensive line of boxed chocolate candies, are as follows:

	BUDGET	ACTUAL
Sales volume in 1-lb boxes	500,000	520,000
Production volume in 1-lb boxes	600,000	610,000
Revenues	$3,500,000	$3,770,000
Variable selling	$ 200,000	$ 223,600
Fixed selling	$ 500,000	$ 493,000
Fixed adminstrative	$ 700,000	$ 702,000

Standard Cost for 1 Pound of Chocolates

1 ounce of ingredients for each ounce of candy at a cost of $.05 per ounce	$ .80
Direct labor, $\frac{1}{4}$ hour for each pound of chocolates @ $6 per hour	1.50
Variable overhead applied on the basis of direct labor hours at a rate of $1 per direct labor hour	.25
Fixed overhead applied on the basis of direct labor hours at a rate of $2 per direct labor hour at a volume of 600,000 boxes	.50
Standard cost for a 16-ounce box of candy at a volume of 600,000 boxes	$3.05

Actual Production Costs

Ingredients, 9,600,000 ounces	$432,000
Direct labor, 148,000 hours	947,200
Variable overhead	136,500
Fixed overhead	283,800

The company costs its finished goods inventory on a LIFO basis. The company uses a standard cost system in costing its products.

REQUIRED: 1. Calculate all standard cost variances for direct material, direct labor, variable manufacturing overhead, and fixed manufacturing overhead.

2. Prepare a schedule which shows revenues and expenses based on the static budget, the flexible budget, and actual results along with volume, flexible budget, and income variances for each revenue and expense item. Prepare this schedule in a contribution-margin format.

chapter twelve

COST-VOLUME-PROFIT ANALYSIS

OBJECTIVES

After you have completed this chapter, you should be able to answer the following questions:

- How is the break-even point both in unit and in dollar terms calculated, and what does the break-even point mean?
- How is the contribution-margin percent calculated and how is it used in cost-volume-profit analysis?
- How can the volume required to meet a profit objective, either before or after taxes, be computed?
- How can cost-volume-profit relationships be described graphically?
- How do changes in selling price, variable expenses, sales volume, and/or the level of fixed costs affect break-even and profit expectations?
- What are some ways in which cost-volume-profit analysis can aid in decision making?
- What major limiting assumptions underlie cost-volume-profit analysis?
- How can mixed costs be divided into their variable and fixed components?
- Why does a change in sales mix affect break-even and profit expectations?

CONCEPTS UNDERLYING COST-VOLUME-PROFIT ANALYSIS

Cost-volume-profit analysis is used to determine (1) break-even for a product, a group of products, or a company as a whole and (2) how profits will change if changes are made in price, volume, costs, or any combination of these factors. This technique is based on the following relationships:

1. Revenues are equal to the number of units sold (volume) times the selling price per unit.
2. Variable expenses for a period are equal to the variable expenses per unit times the number of units sold.
3. The selling price per unit minus variable expenses per unit is the contribution margin, which is available to cover fixed costs and generate a profit.
4. Fixed costs are fixed in total for the period within a relevant activity range and do not vary with changes in sales volume.
5. If the contribution margin exceeds fixed costs, a profit is generated; if the contribution margin is less than fixed costs, a loss results.

The same relationships may be described in an income statement prepared in the contribution format as follows:

Sales price × units sold	= Sales revenue
Less: Variable expenses per unit × units sold	= Variable expenses
(Selling price per unit − variable expenses per unit) × units sold	= Contribution margin
Less: Expenses which are fixed in total and do not vary with sales volume	= Fixed expenses
Contribution margin − fixed expenses	= Profit (Loss)

Note the four factors which determine profit: *sales volume, selling price per unit, variable expenses per unit*, and *total fixed costs*. A change in any or all of these components of profit will change a company's profit margin.

BREAK-EVEN ANALYSIS

A company may wish to determine for the company as a whole or for a particular product line, line of services, or group of product and service lines how much volume it has to generate before it will be profitable. For example, if an insurance company is thinking about adding a new type of policy, part of the decision to go or not go with the policy may be based on how much volume would have to be generated before that particular type of policy would contribute to the company's overall profitability. That point at which revenues and expenses are exactly equal is known as the *break-even point*. Volume beyond that at the break-even point is required to generate a profit.

Thinking about the relationships described three paragraphs above, we can see the following relationship:

Profit = [(selling price − variable expenses) × units sold] − fixed expenses

or

Profit = contribution margin − fixed expenses

The break-even point is thus that point where the contribution margin and fixed expenses are exactly equal. There are two ways in which break-even can be expressed—in volume terms or in dollar terms. To illustrate the calculation of the break-even point, assume the following data for Collegiate Gym Bag Company:

Selling price per unit	$25
Variable expenses per unit sold	$15
Total fixed cost for the period	$500,000

Break-even Volume

The break-even point expressed in volume terms can be found by the following calculation:

$$\text{Break-even volume} = \frac{\text{fixed expenses}}{\left(\begin{array}{c}\text{selling price} \\ \text{per unit}\end{array}\right) - \left(\begin{array}{c}\text{variable expenses} \\ \text{per unit}\end{array}\right)}$$

or

$$\text{Break-even volume} = \frac{\text{fixed expenses}}{\text{contribution margin per unit}}$$

Before applying the formula, let's see why it works. The data provided tell us that every time a gym bag is sold, $10 is generated to cover fixed expenses and contribute to profits ($25 selling price − $15 variable expenses). With a contribution margin of $10 per unit sold, how many units have to be sold before all the fixed costs are covered? This is the concept of break-even. Using our formula, we can see that the break-even point is 50,000 units:

$$\text{Break-even} = \frac{\$500,000 \text{ fixed expenses}}{\$10 \text{ contribution margin per unit}} = \underline{\underline{50,000}} \text{ units}$$

We can prove that our calculation of the break-even volume is correct by preparing an income statement for this volume of activity. That income statement would appear as follows:

Sales: 50,000 units × $25 $1,250,000
Variable expenses: 50,000 units × $15   750,000
Contribution margin: 50,000 units × ($25 − $15) $ 500,000
Fixed expenses   500,000
Profit   -0-

Break-even in Dollars

If we wish to have the break-even point expressed in dollars of sales revenues rather than in the number of units which have to be sold, we can do so in either of two ways. First, we can simply take the break-even volume in units we calculated and multiply it times the selling price per unit:

$$\text{Break-even in sales dollars} = \text{break-even volume} \times \text{selling price per unit}$$

For Collegiate Gym Bags, the break-even in sales dollars is $1,250,000, computed as follows:

$$\text{Break-even in sales dollars} = 50,000 \text{ break-even volume} \times \$25 \text{ selling price}$$
$$= \underline{\$1,250,000}$$

The other way to calculate the break-even in sales dollars is to calculate the contribution-margin percentage—that is, what percent of the sales dollar is left after variable expenses are covered:

$$\text{Contribution-margin percent} = \frac{\text{contribution margin}}{\text{sales revenues}}$$

For Collegiate Gym Bags the calculation of the contribution-margin percent is as follows:

$$\text{Contribution-margin percent} = \frac{\$10 \text{ contribution margin per unit}}{\$25 \text{ selling price per unit}}$$
$$= \underline{40\%}$$

This calculation tells us that 40% of every sales dollar is available to cover fixed expenses and make a contribution to profits.

Using the contribution-margin percent, we can find the break-even point in dollars by the following formula:

$$\text{Break-even point in sales dollars} = \frac{\text{fixed expenses}}{\text{contribution-margin percent}}$$
$$= \frac{\$500,000}{40\%} = \underline{\$1,250,000}$$

CHANGES IN THE BREAK-EVEN POINT

The break-even volume, either in dollars or in the units we calculated above, is valid only so long as:

1. We have defined the underlying relationships correctly, and
2. Those relationships do not change.

To calculate the break-even point we had to (1) estimate the selling price per unit, (2) classify all related expenses as either variable or fixed, (3) estimate the variable expense rate per unit, and (4) estimate the total level of fixed expenses. If in the company's actual activities our estimates for any of these items are significantly inaccurate, then the break-even point which we estimated will not be correct. For example, the Collegiate Gym Bag Company has estimated that they could sell their product for $25 each; suppose that, owing to heavy competition, they were forced to cut the selling price to $23. Obviously, this will increase the volume at which the product becomes profitable. The new break-even point for Collegiate Gym Bag will be:

$$\text{Break-even volume in units} = \frac{\$500,000 \text{ fixed costs}}{\$23 \text{ selling price} - \$15 \text{ variable expenses}}$$

$$= \frac{\$500,000}{\$8 \text{ contribution margin}} = \underline{\underline{62,500}} \text{ bags}$$

We can summarize the effects of any changes in the relationships on which break-even volume is calculated as follows:

Changes which cause break-even volume to increase:
1. Decrease in selling price.
2. Increase in variable expenses per unit.
3. Increase in level of total fixed expenses.
4. All combinations of changes 1, 2, and 3.

Changes which cause break-even volume to decrease:
1. An increase in selling price per unit.
2. A decrease in variable expenses per unit.
3. A decrease in the level of total fixed expenses.
4. Any combination of changes 1, 2, and 3.

It should be clear that a change in one component of break-even analysis can be offset by a change in another, so that the break-even volume remains unchanged. For example, if selling prices were decreased by $2 per unit and variable expenses could be cut by the same amount, there would be no effect on the break-even volume.

DETERMINING VOLUME TO ACHIEVE PROFIT OBJECTIVES

If a company wants to stay in business and is a profit-making entity, it cannot be satisfied with simply breaking even. Instead, it will have profit objectives, and the firm's management will want to know what type of volume must be generated to meet those profit objectives. We can modify the analysis we did to determine the break-even point and provide this information for management.

Referring back to the basic data for the Collegiate Gym Bag Company, let us assume that the company's investment is $2,000,000 and the company's objective is to earn a 20% return on this investment. Their profit objective is to earn $400,000 ($2,000,000 investment × 20% desired rate of return). How many gym bags would they have to sell to meet this profit objective? We can answer this question by using our break-even formula and treating the profit as a fixed element to be covered by the contribution margin. In other words, we can rewrite our formula as follows:

$$\text{Volume in units to achieve profit objective} = \frac{\text{fixed expenses} + \text{desired profit}}{\left(\begin{array}{c}\text{selling price}\\\text{per unit}\end{array}\right) - \left(\begin{array}{c}\text{variable expenses}\\\text{per unit}\end{array}\right)}$$

Thus we can calculate the volume for Collegiate consistent with its profit objective as follows:

$$\text{Volume to achieve profit objective} = \frac{\$500,000 \text{ fixed expenses} + \$400,000 \text{ desired profit}}{\$25 \text{ unit selling price} - \$15 \text{ unit variable expenses}}$$

$$= \underline{90,000} \text{ gym bags}$$

So long as the selling price per unit, variable expenses per unit, and total fixed expenses stay at the levels shown in the calculation above, Collegiate will earn $400,000 when 90,000 gym bags are sold.

MARGIN OF SAFETY

Some companies like to compute a margin of safety—the difference between their break-even volume and their actual volume. The margin of safety can be expressed in two forms: (a) a simple numerical difference between break-even and actual volume or (b) in percentage terms: [(actual volume − break-even volume)/actual volume]. Assume that Collegiate Gym Bag did achieve its volume sales objective of 90,000 units. Since its break-even volume was 50,000 bags, its margin of safety and margin-of-safety percentage are:

$$\text{Margin of safety in units} = \text{actual volume} - \text{break-even volume}$$

$$= 90{,}000 \text{ units} - 50{,}000 \text{ units} = \underline{\underline{40{,}000}} \text{ units}$$

$$\text{Margin-of-safety percentage} = \frac{\text{volume difference}}{\text{actual volume}}$$

$$= \frac{40{,}000}{90{,}000} = \underline{\underline{44.4\%}}$$

These figures tell us that volume can decline by 40,000 units or by 44.4% from the current actual level before the break-even point is reached.

INCOME TAXES AND PROFIT OBJECTIVES

If we wish to determine how much volume we would have to attain to generate a desired after-tax profit, our calculations will have to be modified. Taxes are generally stated as a percent of income before taxes. Hence, our calculation of the required volume would take the following form:

$$\begin{array}{c}\text{Volume in units to}\\ \text{achieve profit}\\ \text{objective}\end{array} = \frac{\text{fixed expenses} + \left(\dfrac{\text{desired after-tax net income}}{1 - \text{tax rate}}\right)}{\text{selling price per unit} - \text{variable expenses per unit}}$$

Suppose that the $400,000 profit which Collegiate Gym Bag Company wants to earn is an after-tax figure and the effective tax rate for the company is 50%. The volume required to earn this level of profits would be 130,000 bags:

$$\begin{array}{c}\text{Volume in units to}\\ \text{achieve profit}\\ \text{objective}\end{array} = \frac{\$500{,}000 \text{ fixed expenses} + \dfrac{\$400{,}000}{1 - .50}}{\$25 \text{ selling price} - \$15 \text{ variable expenses}}$$

$$= \underline{\underline{130{,}000}} \text{ bags}$$

The logic of this computation is as follows: Since $.50 of each dollar of before-tax income will be taken by taxes, twice as much before-tax income will have to be generated to accomplish the profit objective. While the profit objective is $400,000, based on the tax rate, enough units will have to be sold to earn $800,000 before-tax dollars.

The proof of our volume estimate can be shown as follows:

Sales, 130,000 bags @ $25	$3,250,000
Variable expenses, 130,000 @ $15	1,950,000
Contribution margin, 130,000 @ $10	$1,300,000
Fixed expenses	500,000
Income before taxes	800,000
Taxes @ 50%	400,000
Net income	$ 400,000

GRAPHIC PRESENTATIONS OF COST-VOLUME-PROFIT CONCEPTS

Sometimes information can be digested more easily if it is presented in a visual form such as a graph or a chart. Cost-volume-profit relationships and the break-even point are often presented in a graphic form.

The basic assumptions which underlie cost-volume-profit analysis are shown in Illustration 12-1. As the graph shows, revenues and variable expenses are assumed to be a direct function of volume changes. Both of these lines originate at zero, based on the idea that if there is no volume there will be no revenues nor variable expenses. Each unit sold raises the revenue line and the variable-cost line by an equal amount. Fixed costs, on the other hand, do not change with volume changes and are assumed to exist whether or not production takes place. The total-expense line is the fixed cost plus the variable costs.

Keep in mind that these behaviors of revenues and expenses are tempered by the concept of the relevant range. Fixed costs will not stay fixed over all ranges of productive activity, nor can we expect to sell an infinite amount of units at a given selling price. Our ability to sell, as well as the price at which we can sell an additional unit, is affected by demand. The relationships on which cost-volume-profit analysis is based exist only within certain volume limits—those volume limits are called the *relevant range*.

The break-even point and the profit or loss potential for different volumes can be determined and illustrated graphically by the combination of lines shown in Illustration 12-1. Graphic presentation of this data can be accomplished in numerous forms; two of these are shown in Illustrations 12-2 and 12-3, which are based on the data previously provided for the Collegiate Gym Bag Company.

The total-cost line for any volume is found as follows:

Total cost = fixed costs + (variable cost per unit × units sold)

For example, when no units are assumed to be sold, total costs are equal to fixed costs of $500,000. When 30,000 units are sold, total costs for the

ILLUSTRATION 12-1

Graphic description of behavior of revenues and expenses

Revenue Behavior

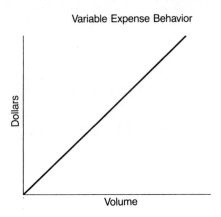
Variable Expense Behavior

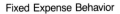
Fixed Expense Behavior

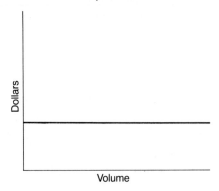

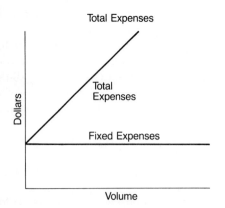
Total Expenses

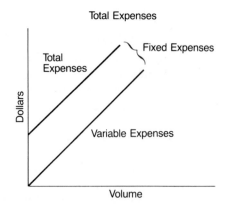
Total Expenses

ILLUSTRATION 12-2

Cost-Volume-Profit
Graph for Collegiate
Gym Bag Company

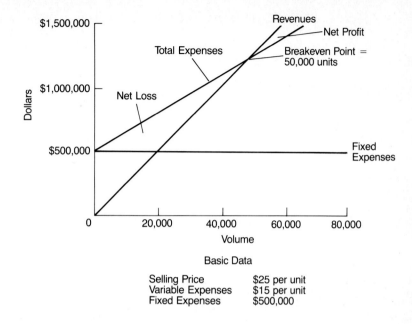

Basic Data

Selling Price	$25 per unit
Variable Expenses	$15 per unit
Fixed Expenses	$500,000

ILLUSTRATION 12-3

Cost-Volume-Profit
Graph for Collegiate
Gym Company:
Alternate Method
of Plotting
Total-Cost Line

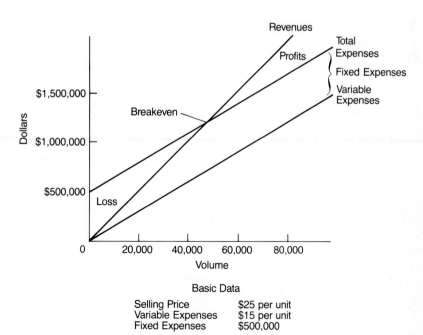

Basic Data

Selling Price	$25 per unit
Variable Expenses	$15 per unit
Fixed Expenses	$500,000

Collegiate Gym Bag Company are calculated as follows:

Total cost = $500,000 fixed costs + ($15 variable cost per unit × 30,000 units)

= $950,000

We now have two points on the graph for total expenses and can draw the total-expense line:

VOLUME	TOTAL EXPENSES
0	$500,000
30,000 units	$950,000

The revenue line is plotted by taking the selling price times the units sold:

Total sales revenue = unit selling price × units sold

For Collegiate, if 30,000 units were sold, revenues would be:

Total sales revenue = $25 selling price × 30,000 units

= $750,000

Since we know the following, we can graph the revenue line:

VOLUME	REVENUE
0	0
30,000	$750,000

The break-even point for the company is that point where the revenue and total-expense lines intersect—in our example, at a volume of 50,000 bags. Any volume less than that amount results in a loss, which can be read from the graph. Any volume greater than the break-even volume results in profits, which can also be determined by looking at the graphs.

"WHAT IF" ASSUMPTIONS

Cost-volume-profit analysis is useful not only in developing break-even or the necessary volume for a desired level of profits but also in seeing what will happen if any of the four determinants of profits are changed. Recall what those four determinants of profits are: sales volume, selling price per unit, variable expenses per unit, and total fixed costs. Managers sometimes refer to exercises involving variations in these four determinants of profits as making "what if" assumptions.

For example, the Collegiate Gym Bag Company might generate three different forecasts of volume—a pessimistic level, a most likely level, and an optimistic level. The company's management may wish to see what the profits would be at each of these three different levels. This is an example of using "what if" assumptions in conjunction with cost-volume-profit analysis.

To illustrate, suppose that Collegiate does make the following sales forecasts:

Pessimistic	80,000 bags
Most likely	90,000 bags
Optimistic	100,000 bags

The three different income statements which would result, based on the previously defined relationships for Collegiate, are shown in Illustration 12-4 along with the related rates of return based on Collegiate's assumed investment of $2,000,000. Break-even volume for Collegiate remains at 50,000 bags, since the "what if" assumptions are based on volume changes rather than changes in cost relationships.

Let's assume instead that Collegiate's management believes their volume will be 90,000 units and wants to know what profits, return on investment, and break-even volume would be based on the following assumptions: (1) variable costs increase 10%, (2) variable costs remain unchanged, and (3) variable costs can be cut by 10%. The data resulting from these assumptions are shown in Illustration 12-5.

Illustration 12-6 shows the effects of a full range of changes on net income, return on investment, and break-even volume. First the effects of a volume change are shown, then the effects of a selling-price change, an increase in variable costs, an increase in the level of fixed costs, and finally a combination of all these elements.

ILLUSTRATION 12-4

THE COLLEGIATE GYM BAG COMPANY
Forecasted Income Statements
for the Year Ended December 31

Volume Assumptions in Units	80,000	90,000	100,000
Sales Revenue, $25 per unit	$2,000,000	$2,250,000	$2,500,000
Variable Expenses, $15 per unit	1,200,000	1,350,000	1,500,000
Contribution Margin, $10 per unit	$ 800,000	$ 900,000	$1,000,000
Fixed Expenses	500,000	500,000	500,000
Net Income	$ 300,000	$ 400,000	$ 500,000
Return on Investment (assumed investment $2,000,000)	15%	20%	25%

ILLUSTRATION 12-5

THE COLLEGIATE GYM BAG COMPANY
Forecasted Income Statements for Changing Levels of Variable Expenses
for the Year Ended December 31
(Assumed Volume—90,000 units)

	VARIABLE EXPENSES INCREASE 10% TO $16.50 PER UNIT	VARIABLE EXPENSES REMAIN AT $15 PER UNIT	VARIABLE EXPENSES DECREASE TO $13.50
Sales Revenue, $25 per unit × 90,000 units	$2,250,000	$2,250,000	$2,250,000
Variable Expenses	1,485,000	1,350,000	1,215,000
Contribution Margin	$ 765,000	$ 900,000	$1,035,000
Fixed Expenses	500,000	500,000	500,000
Net Income	$ 265,500	$ 400,000	$ 535,000
Return on Investment (assumed investment $2,000,000)	13.3%	15%	26.8%
Break-even Volume in units	58,824[a]	50,000[b]	43,478[c]

[a] Break-even = $\dfrac{\$500,000}{\$25 - \$16.50} = 58,824$ bags

[b] Break-even = $\dfrac{\$500,000}{\$25 - \$15} = 50,000$ bags

[c] Break-even = $\dfrac{\$500,000}{\$25 - \$13.50} = 43,478$ bags

**ILLUSTRATION
12-6**

Changing the
components of
cost-volume-
profit analysis,
Collegiate Gym
Bag Company

Base case		
Volume, 90,000 bags	Sales	$2,250,000
Selling price, $25	Variable expenses	1,350,000
Variable expenses, $15	Contribution margin	$ 900,000
Fixed costs, $500,000	Fixed expenses	500,000
Investment, $2,000,000	Net income	$ 400,000

ROI = $400,000/$2,000,000 =   20%

Break-even = $500,000/$25 − $15 =   50,000 bags

Assumption 1:   Volume increases 10%; all other assumptions remain unchanged from base case.

Sales (90,000 × 1.10) = 99,000 bags × $25 =	$2,475,000
Variable expenses: 99,000 × $15 =	1,485,000
Contribution margin	$ 990,000
Fixed costs	500,000
Net income	$ 490,000

ROI = $490,000/$2,000,000 =   24.5%

Break-even = $500,000/$25 − $15 =   50,000 bags

Assumption 2:   Sales prices increase 10%; all other assumptions are unchanged from the base case.

Sales: 90,000 × ($25 × 1.10) = 90,000 × $27.50 =	$2,475,000
Variable expenses: 90,000 × $15	1,350,000
Contribution margin	$1,125,000
Fixed expenses	500,000
Net income	$ 625,000

ROI = $625,000/$2,000,000 =   31.3%

Break-even = $500,000/$27.50 − $15 =   40,000 bags

Assumption 3:   Variable expenses increase 10%; all other assumptions are unchanged from the base case.

Sales: 90,000 × $25	$2,250,000
Variable expenses ($15 × 1.10) = $16.50 × 90,000 =	1,485,000
Contribution margin	$ 765,000
Fixed expenses	500,000
Net income	$ 265,000

ROI = $265,000/$2,000,000 =   13.3%

Break-even = $500,000/$25 − $16.50 =   58,824 bags

Cont.

**ILLUSTRATION
12-6—Cont.**

Assumption 4: Fixed expenses increase 10%; all other assumptions are unchanged from the base case.

Sales: 90,000 × $25 =	$2,250,000
Variable expenses: 90,000 × $15 =	1,350,000
Contribution margin	$ 900,000
Fixed expenses: 500,000 × 1.10 =	550,000
Net income	$ 350,000
ROI = $350,000/$2,000,000 =	17.5%
Break-even = $550,000/$25 − $15 =	55,000 bags

Assumption 5: Volume increases 10%; selling prices, variable expenses, and fixed expenses increase 10%.

Sales: 90,000 × 1.10 = 99,000 × ($25 + 1.10) = 99,000 × $27.50 =	$2,722,500
Variable expenses: 99,000 × ($15 × 1.10) = 99,000 × $16.50 =	1,633,500
Contribution margin	$1,089,000
Fixed expenses: 500,000 × 1.10 =	550,000
Net income	$ 539,000
ROI = $539,000/$2,000,000 =	27%
Break-even = $550,000/$27.50 − $16.50 =	50,000 bags

COMPUTER TECHNOLOGY AND "WHAT IF" ASSUMPTIONS

Computer software packages have made "what if" assumptions very easy to use. For example, with these software packages, just one change in one item of variable expense could be forecast and the effects of this change could be mirrored in the income statement.

To be more specific, remember that we have taken lots of different items of cost and expense and summarized them in the categories of variable expenses and fixed expenses. Suppose that a company has generated a forecasted statement of income, assuming an inflation rate of 10% that was reflected directly in increased direct material costs, indirect material costs, supplies, and utility costs. Before computer technology became more advanced, if the company making the forecast wanted to change its inflation assumption from 10% to 12% or down to 9%, each item affected by the rate of inflation would have had to be carefully recomputed and all summarizing figures—such as cost of goods sold, manufacturing overhead, contribution margin, and operating profits—would have had to be recalculated.

Software packages that cost just a few hundred dollars and can be run on micro (personal) computers could handle the type of change in the rate of inflation described and display or print out very rapidly the resulting income statements. We have described just one change. Any combination of changes could be made and rapidly translated by the computer into income-statement (and/or balance-sheet) effects.

ADDITIONAL APPLICATIONS OF COST-VOLUME-PROFIT ANALYSIS

Three additional examples of the use of cost-volume-profit analysis are described below.

Example 1. Competition in the personal computer field has intensified greatly. The Trend Setter Company has accumulated the following data with respect to its TSC #50 model:

Current selling price	$2,500
Estimated variable expenses—next year	$1,500
Estimated fixed expenses—next year	$50,000,000
Estimated volume—next year	55,000 units
Estimated investment in assets—next year	$15,000,000

Trend Setter believes that it cannot raise its selling price for the coming year and to accomplish its volume objective must spend more for advertising. If the company wants to earn a 15% before-tax return on investment, how much can it afford to spend on advertising?

Solution: Contribution margin ($2,500 − $1,500) × 55,000 units ... $55,000,000

Less: Fixed expenses	$50,000,000	
Desired profit ($15,000,000 investment × 15%)	$ 2,250,000	52,250,000
Available to spend for advertising		$ 2,750,000

Example 2. Quality Paperbacks has always paid its sales staff on a straight salary basis. They are considering switching to a commission basis. The following estimated data are available for the coming period:

Average selling price per book	$2.50
Average variable expenses per book	.75
Fixed expenses	$500,000

Included in the fixed expenses is $100,000 of salaries paid to the sales staff. At what volume is Quality Paperbacks indifferent between these two alternatives: (1) pay the sales staff at a fixed rate of $100,000 per year or (2) pay them on a commission basis at the rate of 10% of selling price?

Solution: The question is, at what point will costs under the alternatives be the same? If the commission rate is 10% of the selling price, it is $.25, which would increase the variable expenses per book to $1.00 ($.75 current level + $.25 commission) but would decrease the fixed expenses to $400,000 ($500,000 current level − $100,000 sales salary expense). Thus we can find the volume at which the two alternatives will give equal results as follows. Let X = unit sales; then

$$\frac{\text{Pay a Commission}}{(\$2.50 - \$1.00)X - \$400,000} = \frac{\text{Fixed Salary}}{(\$2.50 - \$.75)X - \$500,000}$$

$$\$1.50X - \$400,000 = \$1.75X - \$500,000$$

Collecting like terms on the same side of our equation, we have

$$\$.25X = \$100,000$$

$$X = \underline{400,000}$$

We can see that if units sales are 400,000, the company is indifferent between the two alternatives. At higher volumes it is better off with a fixed salary, because additional volume will not cause any increase in expenses. At volumes less than 400,000 the company is better off with the commission basis, because its selling costs will be less than $100,000, which under a fixed-salary basis it would have to pay out.

Example 3. Martino Beverages is considering the acquisition of a small wine producer. There are two companies which Martino could acquire. The acquisition cost of each is the same. Data for each are as follows:

	FINEST WINES	SUPERIOR WINES
Revenues, 500,000 @ $6	$3,000,000	$3,000,000
Variable expenses	1,250,000	625,000
Contribution margin	$1,750,000	$2,375,000
Fixed expenses	750,000	1,375,000
Operating income	$1,000,000	$1,000,000

Because of its management and reputation, Martino believes that if it acquired either company it could increase volume by 10% or 50,000 bottles over the present level without changing any of the present cost relationships. If this projection of volume increase is true, which company should Martino acquire?

Solution: The fixed costs for both companies are already covered, so the investment should be made in the one which has the highest contribution margin per unit. Variable expenses for each company are as follows:

$$\text{Finest's variable expenses} = \$1,250,000/500,000 \text{ units} = \$2.50$$

$$\text{Superior's variable expenses} = \$\ \ 625,000/500,000 \text{ units} = \$1.25$$

Contribution margins are thus:

	FINEST WINES	SUPERIOR WINES
Selling price	$6.00	$6.00
Variable expenses	2.50	1.25
Contribution margin	$3.50	$4.75

Since Superior contributes an additional $1.25 per bottle, profits on the new volume would be $62,500 greater (50,000 bottles × $1.25) with an investment in this company compared to an investment in Finest.

LIMITATIONS OF COST-VOLUME-PROFIT ANALYSIS

A number of limiting assumptions that underlie cost-volume-profit analysis must be kept in mind.

1. The selling price per unit, variable cost per unit, and total fixed costs can be *accurately specified* and *behave in a linear fashion* over the relevant range.
2. All costs can be accurately classified as being either fixed or variable.
3. The method is applicable to the production and sale of a single product or, if applied to a group of products, an assumption is made that the sales mix does not change.
4. There are no significant changes in the level of inventories.
5. Volume is the only factor which affects costs and revenues.

Each of these assumptions is discussed below.

Specification of Relationships and Linear Behavior of Revenues and Costs

When we use cost-volume-profit relationships as a way of forecasting results, we have summarized an entity's total operations in terms of four factors: volume, selling price per unit, variable expenses per unit, and total fixed costs. If any one of the factors varies from our expectations, the results of our projections will be affected.

To illustrate by a simple example, assume that we have two products for which we have developed the following data:

	PRODUCT A	PRODUCT B
Selling price	$20	$20
Variable expenses	9	10
Contribution margin	$11	$10

All things being equal, we would try to maximize the sales of Product A because it provides a greater contribution margin. Each unit of A will provide an extra dollar to cover fixed costs and make a contribution to profits beyond that of Product B. If, however, our specified relationships do not prove accurate, our decision to maximize sales of Product A may be incorrect. For example, if because of increased competition we find that we must decrease the selling price of Product A from $20 to $18, our projections of break-even, contribution margin, and profit margin will not hold true.

Cost-volume-profit analysis assumes not only that we can accurately describe the relationships between volume and revenues and costs, but also that revenues and cost are linear over some range of volume which we call the relevant range. Referring back to the data for Product A, we assume that every unit sold will be sold for $20 and move the revenue line upward by $20. In addition, each additional unit will cause variable expenses to increase by $9 while fixed costs are unaffected. These assumptions simply may not be true.

Classification of Costs as Variable or Fixed

One of the assumptions underlying cost-volume-profit analysis is that all costs can be classified as fixed or variable. For some costs this is not a problem. Direct raw materials clearly are a variable cost, while depreciation computed on the straight-line basis is a fixed cost. However, other kinds of costs may have a variable and a fixed component and are called semivariable (or semifixed) or mixed costs. To use cost-volume-profit analysis, we must break such mixed costs down into their fixed and variable parts.

A number of methods exist for determining what part of a cost is fixed and what part is variable. Three that we shall consider briefly are the high-low method, the use of a scattergraph, and the least-squares method. Each of these methods assumes that the user has available a set of observations of the data to be analyzed.

To illustrate the use of these three methods, suppose a company believes that the utility cost (basically electricity) incurred in its factory is a mixed cost. Part is incurred in simply lighting, heating, and cooling the factory; the other portion is related to the use of machinery. The following data are available:

UNITS PRODUCED	UTILITY COSTS
100	$1,500
130	1,800
150	2,300
200	2,000
220	2,300
270	2,700
300	2,800
330	2,700
350	2,900
400	3,000

With the high-low method we compare the high and low values and simply take the change in costs relative to the change in units produced to determine a variable cost rate per unit. Based on the data provided, our calculation is:

$$\text{Variable rate} = \frac{\text{highest cost} - \text{lowest cost}}{\text{volume at highest cost} - \text{volume at lowest cost}}$$

$$\begin{array}{l}\text{Variable utility}\\ \text{rate per unit}\\ \text{produced}\end{array} = \frac{\$3{,}000 \text{ (highest cost)} - \$1{,}500 \text{ (lowest cost)}}{400 \begin{array}{c}\text{(volume at which}\\ \text{cost was highest)}\end{array} - 100 \begin{array}{c}\text{(volume at which}\\ \text{cost was lowest)}\end{array}}$$

$$= \$5 \text{ variable utility cost per unit}$$

This indicates that every time a unit is produced we have $5 of variable utility cost. We can find the fixed component in the following manner:

$$\text{Fixed cost} = \text{total cost} - \text{total variable cost}$$

Substituting in the data for a production level of 100 units, we estimate fixed utility cost at $1,000 as follows:

$$\text{Fixed cost} = \$1{,}500 - (100 \text{ units} \times \$5 \text{ variable cost})$$
$$= \underline{\underline{\$1{,}000}}$$

Note that the high-low method yields an estimate of the variable and fixed relationship based on two observations. If we had chosen a level of production other than the 100 units which was our low point, our estimate of fixed cost could have been different. For example, assume that we calculated fixed cost when production was 130 units. Substituting into our fixed-cost equation, we would have:

$$\text{Fixed cost} = \$1{,}800 \text{ total cost} - (130 \text{ units} \times \$5 \text{ per unit})$$
$$= \underline{\underline{\$1{,}150}}$$

This difference in fixed cost when a production level other than one of those used in the high-low computation is used can occur because the relationship of variable cost to fixed cost does not hold perfectly for all levels of production.

The scattergraph method for dividing mixed costs into their fixed and variable components and the use of the least-squares method are based on the same concept. We are finding the equation of the straight line which best describes the relationship of our data. With a scattergraph, the observations are plotted on a graph and the equation of the line is determined visually. With the least-squares method, the equation for the straight line is determined statistically.

The scattergraph for the relationship of volume and utility costs is shown in Illustration 12-7. A line which attempts to describe the points plotted has been drawn in Illustration 12-8. Looking at that line, we can

**ILLUSTRATION
12-7**
Scattergraph
for Utility Costs
and Units
Produced

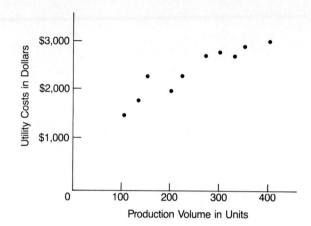

see that it intercepts the axis of the graph on which utility costs have been plotted at $1,000. This tells us that when no units are produced, costs are $1,000. These are the costs which are independent of volume; that is, these are our fixed costs.

Once we have read the fixed-costs amount from our graph, we can calculate variable costs as follows:

$$\text{Variable costs} = \text{total cost} - \text{fixed cost}$$

When 100 units are produced, solving for our variable costs, we find that they total $500:

$$\text{Variable costs} = \$1,500 - \$1,000$$
$$= \underline{\underline{\$500}}$$

To express variable costs on a per-unit basis, we can simply divide the

**ILLUSTRATION
12-8**
Line Describing
Relationship
of Utility Costs
and Units
Produced

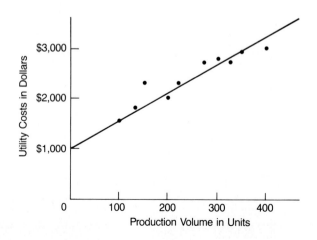

total variable costs by the volume basis:

$$\frac{\$500 \text{ total variable cost}}{100 \text{ units of production}} = \$5 \text{ variable cost per unit}$$

Now we have an equation which describes what portion of the utility cost varies with production and what portion is fixed. Remember the equation of a straight line:

$$y = a + bx$$

Writing the equation we have developed in this form, we can project total costs for various levels of production:

Total utility costs = \$1,000 fixed cost + (\$5 variable cost per unit × units)

Look again at Illustration 12-7. Take a ruler (or something with a straight edge) and try to decide where a line should be drawn which would best fit the set of observations given. It should be clear that a number of different lines could be drawn, and it would be difficult to tell which is the best fit. The difference between using a visually fitted line and using the equation of a line developed by the least-squares method is that the latter gives a unique answer: there is one line which best fits the set of observations. While two different people fitting a line visually could easily get different results, if they used the least-squares method they would get the same results.

Consider Illustration 12-9. Notice that not all the observations lie on the line which has been drawn. However, the line developed by the least-squares method will have the least amount of overall deviation between the line and the observations it is supposed to describe; this is what makes it the best line to describe the set of observations. Illustration 12-9 also shows how the equation for that line was developed. Although the number of observations was small, a great deal of manual calculation was involved. Fortunately, computer softwear for developing the equation of a line using the least-squares method is readily available. In fact, many readers probably own hand-held calculators which will do the job.

Changes in Sales Mix

For the one-product entity, cost-volume-profit analysis is easy because there is only one item to which all costs and revenues relate. If we are trying to do cost-volume-profit analysis for a firm which has more than one product, we must take care in applying the method, because the mix of products which is sold may be different from that which was sold in the past.

ILLUSTRATION 12-9

Scattergraph for utility costs and units produced—line fitted using the least-squares method

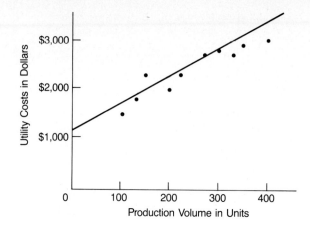

Supporting calculations for the least-squares line are as follows. Variable costs = b; fixed costs = a; n 5 the number of observations.

x	y	y^2	x^2	xy
100	1,500	2,250,000	10,000	150,000
130	1,800	3,240,000	16,900	234,000
150	2,300	5,290,000	22,500	345,000
200	2,000	4,000,000	40,000	400,000
220	2,300	5,290,000	48,400	506,000
270	2,700	7,290,000	72,900	729,000
300	2,800	7,840,000	90,000	840,000
330	2,700	7,290,000	180,900	891,000
350	2,900	8,410,000	122,500	1,015,000
400	3,000	9,000,000	160,000	1,200,000
2,450	24,000	59,900,000	692,100	6,310,000

The equations for solving for a and b in the equation $y = a + bx$ are:

$$b = \frac{xy - \frac{(x)(y)}{n}}{x^2 - \frac{(x)^2}{n}}$$

$$b = \frac{6,310,000 - \frac{(2,450 \times 24,000)}{10}}{692,100 - \frac{(2,450)^2}{10}} = \underline{\$4.68} \text{ variable cost per unit}$$

$$a = \frac{1}{n}[y - b(x)]$$

$$a = \frac{1}{10}[24,000 - (\$4.68)(2,450)] = \underline{\$1,253.40} \text{ total fixed cost}$$

To illustrate, let's use the information shown previously for Products A and B and extend it by the addition of volume assumptions and an assumed level of fixed costs of $54,000. Illustration 12-10 shows the company's contribution-margin percentage based on two different assumptions about the sales mix. If the company's fixed expenses are $54,000, break-even based on a sales mix which is 80% Product A (8,000 out of total sales of 10,000) and 20% Product B would be:

$$\text{Break-even in sales dollars} = \frac{\$54,000 \text{ fixed expenses}}{.54 \text{ contribution margin for present sales mix}}$$

$$= \$100,000$$

This break-even volume of $100,000 is valid only when the company sells a product mix consisting of 80% of the unit volume in Product A and 20% in Product B. Since the selling price of $20 per unit is assumed to be the same for both products, the number of units which would have to be sold is 5,000 ($100,000/$20 selling price per unit).

Using the company's overall contribution margin to forecast profits is valid also only when the 80%/20% sales mix holds. Suppose the company anticipates a sales volume of $240,000 next year and that fixed costs will

Assumption 1: 8,000 units of Product A were sold and 2,000 units of Product B

	PRODUCT A		PRODUCT B		TOTAL
Sales	8,000 @ $20	$160,000	2,000 @ $20	$40,000	$200,000
Variable expenses	8,000 @ $ 9	72,000	2,000 @ $10	20,000	92,000
Contribution margin		$ 88,000		$20,000	$108,000
Contribution-margin percent: contribution margin sales		55%		50%	54%

Assumption 2: 2,000 units of Product A were sold and 8,000 units of Product B

	PRODUCT A		PRODUCT B		TOTAL
Sales	2,000 @ $20	$ 40,000	8,000 @ $20	$160,000	$200,000
Variable expenses	2,000 @ $ 9	18,000	8,000 @ $10	80,000	98,000
Contribution margin		$ 22,000		$ 80,000	$102,000
Contribution-margin percent		55%		50%	51%

remain at $54,000. The forecasted profits will be:

Contribution margin, $240,000 × 54% $129,600
Less: Fixed expenses   54,000
Operating income $ 75,600

This profit level can be proved as follows:

$$\frac{\$240,000 \text{ sales}}{\$20 \text{ per unit}} = 12,000 \text{ units}$$

Sales of each product based on current sales mix:

Product A: 12,000 units × 80% = 9,600 units
Product B: 12,000 units × 20% = 2,400 units

	PRODUCT A		PRODUCT B		TOTAL
Sales	9,600 @ $20	$192,000	2,400 @ $20	$48,000	$240,000
Variable expenses	9,600 @ $9	86,400	2,400 @ $10	24,000	110,400
Contribution margin		$105,600		$24,000	$129,600
Less: Fixed expenses					54,000
Operating income					$ 75,600

To illustrate that cost-volume-profit relationships stay the same only when the sales mix is unchanged, consider Assumption 2 in Illustration 12-10. If the sales mix reverses and 20% of the units sold are Product A while 80% are Product B, profits of the company will be adversely affected. This should be obvious from a comparison of the contribution-margin percents on the two products and the overall contribution margin for the two different sales mixes. Based on sales of $240,000, using the second assumption as to sales mix, profits will drop from $75,600 to $68,400, since the overall contribution margin declined from 54% to 51%.

Contribution margin: $240,000 × 51% $122,400
Fixed expenses   54,000
Operating income $ 68,400

No Changes in the Inventory Level

Cost-volume-profit analysis is based on the assumption that there will be no significant changes in the level of finished goods and work-in-process inventory. While all the ramifications of changes in the inventory level are beyond the scope of this text, a brief illustration of the effects of inventory changes on break-even analysis is given below.

Consider a company for which the following data are relevant:

Selling price per unit	$1
Variable manufacturing expenses per unit	$.35
Fixed manufacturing expenses	$30,000
Variable selling and administrative expenses per unit	$.15
Fixed selling and administrative	$15,000

Calculating in the usual way, the break-even volume in units is 90,000:

$$\text{Break-even volume in units} = \frac{\$30,000 + \$15,000 \text{ (total fixed expenses)}}{\$1 \text{ selling price} - (.35 + .15 \text{ variable expenses})}$$

$$= \underline{\underline{90,000}} \text{ units}$$

If we assume that all units produced will be sold, the break-even volume *is* 90,000 units, as can be shown below:

Sales, 90,000 @ $1		$90,000
Cost of goods sold (90,000 @ $.35 variable mfg. + 30,000 fixed mfg. expenses)		61,500
Gross margin		$28,500
Operating expenses:		
Variable selling and administrative (90,000 units @ $.15)	$13,500	
Fixed selling and administrative	15,000	28,500
Net income		0

Remember what happens with absorption costing. If more units are produced than are sold, some of the fixed manufacturing overhead is carried over into inventory and would not appear on the income statement of the period. Suppose that 90,000 units were sold but 100,000 were produced. The break-even point would no longer be 90,000 units, as can be seen from the following income statement and calculation of unit manufacturing cost.

$$\text{Unit manufacturing cost at a 100,000-unit volume} = \$.35 \text{ variable} + \$30,000/100,000 \text{ units}$$

$$= \$.\underline{\underline{60}}$$

Sales		$90,000
Cost of goods sold, 90,000 @ .65		58,500
Gross margin		$31,500
Variable selling and administrative	$13,500	
Fixed selling and administrative	15,000	28,500
Net income		3,000

When the production exceeded the sales, rather than showing no profits when 90,000 units were sold, a profit of $3,000 emerged because of fixed costs carried over into inventory on the 10,000 unsold units.

We can approximate a break-even point when there are changes in inventory by assuming that inventory changes carry the same ratio of fixed costs as units which are currently being manufactured and sold.

To illustrate, fixed costs are currently assumed to be $30,000 and production 100,000 units. Each unit, whether it is going to be sold or going into inventory, will carry $.30 of fixed costs. To calculate break-even if 10,000 units are going into inventory, we would reduce fixed costs which have to be covered this period by $3,000 (10,000 units × .30 fixed cost). Break-even volume would become 84,000 units.

$$\text{Break-even in units} = \frac{(\$30,000 \text{ fixed mfg.} - \$3,000 \text{ into inventory} + \$15,000 \text{ fixed S \& A})}{\$1 \text{ selling price} \quad (\$.35 + .15 \text{ variable expenses})}$$

$$= \frac{\$42,000}{\$0.50 \text{ contribution margin}} = \underline{\underline{84,000}} \text{ units}$$

If sales exceeded production (units were being taken out of inventory), to calculate break-even we would have to make some assumption about the additional fixed costs reaching the income statement attached to those units being drawn out of inventory.

Effect of Volume

A final limitation of cost-volume-profit analysis is its assumption that volume is the only relevant factor affecting revenue and cost. It is clear that volume cannot be the only thing which affects revenues. This would imply an infinite demand for a product at a stated selling price. Realistically, demand regulates volume and the price at which a product can be sold.

Variable expenses are not just a function of the level of production or sales. They are affected by factors such as management's attitude toward them (tight control versus loose control), worker morale, worker efficiency, and supply and demand.

In the case of fixed expenses, these are assumed to be independent of volume. As pointed out previously, this is true only within a relevant range of activity. If activity is outside that range, fixed costs will increase (for example, in the case of added facilities) or decrease (for example, facilities can be closed or partially closed).

chapter highlights

Cost-volume-profit analysis is based on the assumption that selling price per unit, variable expenses per unit, sales volume, and the level of fixed expenses can be accurately specified. The calculation of the break-even point is an application of cost-volume-profit analysis and describes the volume of activity in either unit or dollar terms at which revenues and expenses are exactly equal.

Variation in any one of the four components on which cost-volume-profit analysis is based—selling price, variable expenses, volume, and fixed expenses—can change the break-even point and profit expectations. Computer technology eliminates the drudgery of making "what if" assumptions and permits managers to make changes in any or all of these items and see the effects.

The assumptions which underlie cost-volume-profit analysis should be kept in mind. The major assumptions are:

1. The selling price per unit, variable cost per unit, and total fixed costs can be accurately specified and behave in a linear fashion over the relevant range.
2. All costs can be accurately classified as being either fixed or variable.
3. When more than one product line is involved, the sales mix does not change.
4. There are no significant changes in the level of inventories.
5. Volume is the only factor which affects costs and revenues.

If reality departs materially from these assumptions, the results of cost-volume-profit analysis may be misleading.

questions

1. Explain the meaning of the break-even point.
2. If you know that the contribution margin for a firm is 30%, what does this indicate to you?

3. What pieces of information must you have before you can calculate a company's break-even volume in units? in dollars?

4. What factors can cause a company's break-even volume to change?

5. What are the major limiting assumptions on which break-even analysis is based?

6. Assume a firm wishes to achieve a $100,000-dollar profit after taxes. How could break-even analysis be used to determine the volume necessary to achieve this objective?

7. Assume that you have prepared a cost-volume-profit graph which has a line for fixed costs, one for variable costs, a total-cost line, and a revenue line. If the fixed costs can be decreased, how would each line on the graph and the break-even point be affected?

8. Assume that you have prepared a cost-volume-profit graph which has a line for fixed costs, a line for variable costs, a total-cost line, and a revenue line. How would each line on the graph and the break-even point be affected by an increase in volume?

9. In what way has computer technology been helpful to management in cost-volume-profit analysis.

10. What are mixed costs and how are they treated in cost-volume-profit analysis?

11. What methods can be used to break a mixed cost down into its variable and fixed components?

12. In trying to break a mixed cost down into its variable and fixed components, what advantage does the least-squares method have over other methods? What is its major disadvantage for this purpose?

13. Why can a change in sales mix affect break-even and profit expectations?

14. What is meant by the term "margin of safety"?

15. A company had a volume of 9,000 units, fixed costs of $20,000, and a contribution margin per unit of $4. What was the company's margin of safety, if any?

16. Using the information in question 15, calculate the margin-of-safety percentage.

17. In determining the volume necessary to achieve a particular after-tax profit objective, part of the equation used is:

$$\frac{\text{desired profit}}{1 - \text{tax rate}}$$

Why does the desired profit have to be divided by (1 − tax rate) to obtain the after-tax profit?

18. What is a scattergraph and how is it used in cost-volume-profit analysis?

19. Why does a change in the level of inventory affect a firm's break-even point?

20. Assume a company has calculated its break-even point as 50,000 units. State whether each of the following changes, *taken independently*, would

cause break-even to increase, decrease, or remain unchanged:

a. The selling price per unit increases.
b. Variable costs per unit increase.
c. Variable costs per unit decrease.
d. The sales volume decreases.
e. Fixed costs decrease.
f. The selling price per unit decreases.
g. The sales volume increases.
h. Fixed costs increase.

exercises

12—1. Futures, Inc., is a consulting group which helps companies with their long-range planning. Futures charges $200 per hour for such service and estimates its variable costs as $120 per hour. Fixed costs on an annual basis are estimated as $480,000.

REQUIRED:

1. How many billable hours of consulting will Futures, Inc., have to render before it breaks even?
2. Suppose the company wants to make a profit after taxes of $120,000 and the tax rate is 40%. How many billable hours of service will Futures, Inc., have to provide to reach its profit objective?
3. If Futures, Inc., can render 7,200 billable hours of service, what will its margin of safety be? What does the margin of safety you calculated mean?

12—2. The Sunshine Company would like to make an after-tax profit of $165,000. Its tax rate is 45%. Management also wants to know the break-even volume. The company believes that one of the following outcomes is likely:

Outcome 1: Selling price $7.50, variable expenses $4, fixed costs, $700,000.
Outcome 2: Selling price $8, variable expenses $3, fixed costs, $700,000.
Outcome 3: Selling price $7, variable expenses $3, fixed costs, $700,000.

REQUIRED: For each of the possible outcomes for Sunshine described above, calculate the volume required to (a) achieve its after-tax profit objectives and (b) break even. Round all amounts to the nearest number of pairs of sunglasses which would have to be sold.

12—3. The following information relates to expected revenues and expenses for the Quirk Blind Company's best-selling window blind:

	PER UNIT
Selling price	$20.00
Cost of each item (variable)	8.00
Monthly fixed expenses:	
Rent	$1,300
Wages	5,600
Other fixed expenses	700
Total fixed expenses per month	$7,600

REQUIRED:
1. Calculate the break-even point in number of units and in dollar sales for Quirk's next month of operations. (Round to the nearest unit or dollar.)
2. Assuming Quirk wished to realize income *before taxes* of $4,500 for the month, calculate the required volume in units and dollars. (Round to the nearest unit or dollar.)
3. Assume rent was doubled and calculate break-even volume in units and in dollars. (Round to the nearest unit or dollar.)
4. Assume the selling price drops to $18 per unit and the original variable and fixed expenses remain the same. Calculate the monthly break-even point in number of units and dollar sales. (Round to the nearest unit or dollar.)

12—4. Blaustone Publishers recently published a special edition of poetry with illustrations by well-known contemporary artists. The book sells for $150 per copy. Fixed period costs related to the issue are $34,000 and variable costs per unit $70.

REQUIRED:
1. If Blaustone pays taxes at a 40% rate and wishes to earn an $18,000 profit after taxes, how many books must it sell? (Round to the nearest book.)
2. To achieve its profit objective, how many dollars of sales will Blaustone have to generate?
3. Calculate the sales volume in units which would give Blaustone a 20% margin of safety.
4. If variable and fixed costs each increase by 5%, what will be the effect on its present break-even volume?

12—5. The Sharp Scissor Company manufactures two types of industrial scissors, used primarily by clothing manufacturers. Budgeted data for Scissor #1 and Scissor #2 include:

	SCISSOR #1	SCISSOR #2
Selling price	$15	$21
Variable expenses	7	12

Annual fixed expenses, based on anticipated annual sales of 10,000 units of Scissor #1 and 7,500 units of Scissor #2, have been assigned as follows:

Scissor #1	$16,000
Scissor #2	$27,000

REQUIRED: 1. Compute the break-even point in units for each of the two products individually; i.e., the break-even for Scissor #1 and then the break-even for Scissor #2.

2. Compute the break-even point in units for each product, assuming that anticipated sales change from 10,000 to 15,000 units for Scissor #1 and fall from 7,500 to 7,200 units for Scissor #2. Fixed cost will be unaffected by the volume changes.

3. Compute the required sales volume in units for Scissor #1, assuming Sharp discontinues production of Scissor #2, pays tax at a 35% rate, and wishes to realize a $13,000 profit after taxes. Assume that $11,000 of fixed costs associated with Scissor #2 can be eliminated; the other portion will have to be covered by sales of Scissor #1.

12—6. Use the data in Exercise 12—5.

REQUIRED: 1. Based on anticipated sales volumes of 10,000 units for Scissor #1 and 7,500 units for Scissor #2, calculate the company's projected before-tax profits.

2. Assume that the actual volumes for the two products were the reverse of those anticipated—7,500 units of #1 and 10,000 units of #2 were sold. Calculate the company's actual profits.

3. Compute the company's break-even volume in sales dollars under each of the two different volume assumptions described in parts 1 and 2 above.

12—7. The Tate House Maintenance Firm offers four basic services. Revenues and variable costs for the past month for each of the services were:

	REVENUES	VARIABLE COSTS
Lawn mowing	$ 6/hr—1,200 hr	$ 5/hr
House cleaning	$ 7/hr— 800 hr	$ 5/hr
Chimney cleaning	$15/hr— 200 hr	$10/hr
Leaf raking	$ 4/hr— 900 hr	$ 3.50/hr

Its fixed costs for the period were $3,500. Tate is contemplating a stronger concentration on chimney cleaning, owing to the increased use of wood stoves for household heating and the onset of cold weather.

REQUIRED: 1. Assume the product mix and hours remain the same as in the past month. Compute break-even sales in dollars for the coming month. Round your contribution-margin percent to the nearest whole percent. Round the break-even volume to the nearest dollar.

2. Assume the services *revenue mix* changes to the ratio of 10% of revenues from lawn mowing, 35% of revenues from house cleaning, 40% from chimney cleaning, and 15% from leaf raking. The hourly revenue rate is unchanged. Variable expenses per hour remain at their previous rates. Compute the break-even point in sales dollars. Round your contribution-margin percent to the nearest whole percent and the break-even volume to the nearest dollar.

12—8. Reliable Products currently incurs fixed costs of $17,550 and variable costs of $13 per unit. Their product, a squirrel-resistant bird feeder, sells for $26.50. Taxes are paid at a 40% rate.

REQUIRED: 1. Compute the break-even point in units and in dollars.

2. Assume Reliable can raise its selling price by 10% while keeping its fixed and variable costs at the present level. How will the break-even point be affected? (Round to the nearest unit.)

3. If Reliable wishes to maintain a 15% safety margin, compute the required volume in units based on the original selling price.

4. If Reliable wishes to achieve a $5,400 profit, how many units must it sell based on a $26.50 selling price? (Round to the nearest unit.)

12—9.   The Dawson Sugar Company produces refined sugar. Dawson's fixed costs are anticipated to be $3,500 for the coming month and variable costs are $1.60 per *ten pounds* of sugar produced. Demand for Dawson's product is sensitive to the selling price. Dawson estimates the following demand based on different selling prices:

1. 18,000 lb @ $1 *per 5 lb.*
2. 15,000 lb @ $1.05 *per 5 lb.*
3. 12,000 lb @ $1.10 *per 5 lb.*
4. 10,000 lb @ $1.15 *per 5 lb.*

Dawson's fixed costs will not change within the volume range being considered.

REQUIRED: What selling price would you suggest to Dawson? Support your answer with appropriate computations.

12—10.   The Reliable Watch Company believes that the electricity costs which they incur are partially variable and partially fixed. So that they may perform various kinds of financial analysis, they would like to determine what part of these costs are fixed and which part are variable. The company's electricity costs for several months are given below along with production data.

ELECTRICITY COSTS	WATCHES PRODUCED
$740	1,000
$780	1,200
$810	1,500
$760	1,300
$750	1,100
$790	1,400

REQUIRED: 1. Using the high-low method, estimate the amount of fixed electricity costs and the variable cost per watch incurred by Reliable Watch each period.

2. Write a formula for projecting total electricity costs at different volume levels.

3. Using the costs you have developed in part 1, project costs when 1,100 watches are produced. Compare your solution with actual costs when 1,100 watches were produced. Why do your results differ?

12—11.   Assume the following data:

Selling price per unit	$50
Variable costs per unit	$30
Fixed expenses	$400,000

REQUIRED:
1. Calculate the break-even point in units.
2. Calculate the break-even point in units under each of the following *independent* assumptions. (Round all answers to the nearest whole unit.)
   a. Selling price increased 10%.
   b. Selling price decreased 10%.
   c. Variable costs increased 10%.
   d. Variable costs decreased 10%.
   e. Fixed costs increased 10%.
   f. Fixed costs decreased 10%.
   g. Sales volume increased 10%.
   h. Sales volume decreased 10%.
3. Based on your computations in part 2, summarize your findings as to the effect of different kinds of changes on the break-even point.

12—12. Dallas Corporation wishes to market a new product for $15 per unit. Fixed costs to manufacture this product are $90,000 for less than 100,000 units. For production over 100,000 units fixed costs will increase by $140,000; that is, for production levels above 90,000 units, fixed costs will total $240,000. Dallas wants to earn a 20% contribution margin on its product and a before-tax profit of $300,000.

REQUIRED:
1. What are the variable costs per unit which Dallas can incur to meet its contribution-margin objective?
2. To meet its profit-margin objective, how many units will Dallas have to manufacture?
3. What is Dallas's break-even volume in dollars?

12—13. The Green World Company makes two types of garden hose; one is made from plastic, the other from rubber. Cost and revenue figures associated with each line are as follows:

	PLASTIC HOSE	RUBBER HOSE
Selling price per 50 feet	$8	$16
Variable costs per 50 feet	$4	$12
Fixed costs associated with each product line	$287,500	$200,000

REQUIRED:
1. Calculate the break-even volume in sales dollars and in units for both product lines.
2. Calculate the break-even volume in sales dollars for the company as a whole, assuming current volume for plastic hose is 200,000 units and for rubber hose is 100,000 units.
3. Which product line should Green World try to push (put the most sales effort behind)? Justify your answer with appropriate computations.

12—14. The World Facts Reference Book Company compensates its salespersons on a commission basis equal to 20% of the selling price, or $40 for every set of reference books sold. Other variable costs per set of books total $10. The company's fixed costs are $500,000. The company is considering changing its compensation plan and paying its sales persons a flat salary of $20,000 per year. The company currently employs a sales staff of 10.

REQUIRED: 1. Assume the company's volume is currently 8,000 sets of books. Would its profits increase or decrease if salaries became a fixed rather than a variable expense?

2. At what sales volume is the World Facts Reference Book Company indifferent between paying a sales commission and compensating its employees on a fixed-salary basis?

3. What do you see as the major disadvantage of changing the salary payments to a fixed amount per year?

12—15.   The Security Insurance Company of Europe has a new life insurance product for which the following data have been projected:

Annual premium	$500
Variable cost per policy	$100
Fixed costs	$800,000
Invested assets	$2,000,000

The company's profit objective is to earn a 20% after-tax return on the invested assets associated with this policy. The current tax rate is 50%.

REQUIRED: 1. How many insurance policies will the company have to sell to reach its profit objective?

2. Suppose the company wants to spend any funds generated beyond the 20% return on an institutional advertising program promoting the name of the insurance company. At a volume of $2,500,000 sales, how much, if any, will be available for the advertising program?

problems

12—16.   *Straightforward calculation of break-even; effects of cost and volume changes.*   The Executive Products Company makes a simulated leather briefcase for which the following data have been assembled:

Selling price per briefcase	$80
Variable costs per unit	$30
Annual fixed costs	$500,000

REQUIRED: 1. Calculate the break-even point for Executive Products both in unit and in dollar terms.

2. Assume that Executive Products wishes to earn an after-tax profit of $600,000 and its earnings are taxed at a 40% rate. How many units will the company have to produce to reach its profit objective?

3. Assume that the data provided are for the past year. Executive Products estimates that variable costs will increase 20% over last year's level. The company plans to spend an additional $50,000 for advertising because of increasing competition. It will not be able to raise its selling price.

   a. What will be the projected break-even for the company for the coming year.
   b. If it wants to increase last year's after-tax profits of $600,000 by 10%, how many briefcases will it have to sell?

12—17. *Cost-volume changes—impact on net income.* Exton Products anticipates selling 300,000 units of its main product, plant stands, during the coming year. The selling price is expected to be $10.75 per unit and variable expenses will account for 60% of the price. Fixed expenses are budgeted at $525,000.

REQUIRED: Calculate the following (consider each assumption independently):

1. Projected net income.
2. Projected net income if variable expenses decrease by 10% from their current level.
3. Projected net income if the sales price increases to $11 and sales volume decreases by 20%. Variable expenses will be 60% of the *new* selling price.
4. Projected net income if fixed expenses decrease by 15%.
5. Projected net income if fixed expenses increase by $50,000 and variable expenses decrease by 15% from their current level.

12—18. *Break-even point and earnings under different alternatives.* The Goshen Museum has been suffering declines in attendance and in order to increase attendance has been considering two alternatives:

1. Spend $15,000 per year on advertising without changing their present admission charge of $3 per person.
2. Decrease the admission charge to $2 per person.

The first alternative is expected to increase attendance by 15%. The second alternative is expected to increase attendance by 40%.

Currently, the museum incurs variable costs of $.50 per visitor, which will not change with either alternative, and $175,000 in annual fixed costs. During the current year attendance averaged 5,000 visitors per month. In addition, the museum has revenue from an endowment which amounts to $50,000 per year. A local manufacturing firm has agreed to underwrite $5,000 of the advertising expense if that alternative is chosen.

REQUIRED:
1. Compute the museum's current break-even point in terms of attendance.
2. Compute the break-even point in terms of attendance under each of the two alternatives.
3. Compute expected earnings under each of the two alternatives.

4. Which alternative would you recommend? If the expected increase in attendance was less certain under the first alternative, would that change your recommendation?

12—19. *Mixed costs—two methods of determining component costs: high/low; scattergraph.* The Jackson Trucking Firm incurs mixed costs in operating its fleet of rental trucks. Actual data relating to the mixed costs for the past twelve quarters include:

YEAR	QUARTER	MILES DRIVEN	COST
1984	1	10,500	$6,150
	2	12,700	7,064
	3	9,400	6,102
	4	10,900	6,706
1983	1	10,300	6,605
	2	10,950	6,942
	3	11,400	7,218
	4	12,200	7,636
1982	1	12,500	7,875
	2	13,100	8,240
	3	12,600	8,166
	4	11,800	8,074

Other fixed costs not included in the mixed costs were $15,000 for the period.

REQUIRED: **1.** Use the high-low method to determine the total amount of fixed costs and the per-unit variable cost. (Round variable cost to the nearest cent.)

2. Based on your calculations for part 1, develop an equation which Jackson Trucking can use in projecting its operating costs.

3. Use the equation you developed in part 2 to predict expenses when 11,000 miles are driven.

4. Would the equation you developed in part 2 be relevant if 25,000 miles were driven? Why or why not?

5. Prepare a scatter diagram and visually fit a line to the points on the graph. Based on this procedure, estimate fixed costs and the variable cost per mile driven.

6. What is a major shortcoming of the scattergraph with a visually fitted line as a means of breaking mixed costs into their variable and fixed components?

12—20. Gourmet Foods, Inc., offers four basic catering services. Revenues and variable costs for the past quarter are given below. In addition, fixed costs for the period were $28,000 and are expected to rise 20% in the upcoming quarter.

	REVENUES	VARIABLE COSTS
Buffets—dinner	$30,000	$ 8/person
Buffets—cocktails	$24,500	$ 4/person
Dinners—four-course	$32,000	$17/person
Picnics—carry-out	$20,000	$ 7.50/person

Nancy Knickerbocker, Gourmet's president, believes that meals served during the coming quarter will be distributed between the different types of services as follows:

	NUMBER OF MEALS ESTIMATED TO BE SERVED NEXT QUARTER
Buffets—dinner	2,000
Buffets—cocktails	4,500
Dinners—four-course	1,000
Picnics—carry-out	3,500

She also plans to raise the present rates, which are $12 per person for dinner buffets, $7 per person for cocktail buffets, $20 per person for four-course dinners, and $10 per person for carry-out picnics, by $2 each in order to offset an expected 10% increase in variable expenses in all categories.

REQUIRED:
1. Compute the contribution margin and the contribution-margin percent for the past quarter for each class of meal and for the company as a whole. (Round the contribution margins which you compute to the nearest whole percent.)
2. Calculate the break-even volume in sales dollars for the company as a whole for the past quarter. (Round your answer to the nearest whole dollar.)
3. Calculate the contribution margin and the contribution-margin percent based on anticipated changes for the coming quarter for each class of meals and for the company as a whole. Also, calculate the anticipated income for the company as a whole for the coming quarter. (Round the contribution-margin percents you calculate to the nearest whole percent.)
4. What is the break-even volume in sales dollars for the coming quarter. (Round your answer to the nearest whole dollar.)
5. The contribution-margin percentage you calculated for the company as a whole in part 3 should have been larger than the one you calculated in part 1. What two factors are responsible for the increase?

12—21. *Determining the most profitable level of service.* Travelers' Delights packs meals which travelers on airlines can purchase and eat on the plane in lieu of the regular airline fare. Travelers' Delights believes that the demand for its meals is sensitive to the price charged. They estimate the following monthly volumes based on the prices shown.

ALTERNATIVE NUMBER	ESTIMATED NUMBER OF MEALS	PRICE PER MEAL
1	2,500	$13.00
2	2,750	12.50
3	3,000	11.75
4	4,000	10.25
5	5,200	9.50

SECTION III Using Accounting Data in Special Analysis for Decision Making

Variable costs are $8.75 per meal, which includes a bottle of wine. Fixed costs per month for the company are estimated at $4,125, and its earnings are taxed at a 40% rate.

REQUIRED:

1. Calculate the most profitable level of service for Travelers' Delights.
2. Assume that the company decides to charge $12.50 per meal. What are their anticipated after-tax profits?
3. Based on a charge of $12.50 per meal, by what amount can volume decline before the company sustains a loss on its operations?
4. Variable costs could be reduced to $8 if the bottle of wine was not included with the meal. The price per meal could also be dropped by $.75 from $12.50 to $11.75 with the anticipated change in volume shown in the original data. Would this change increase or decrease profits? By what amount?

12—22. *Calculating selling price; taking a special order.* Friedman, Inc., makes medical products, primarily a blood sampling kit which can be used in the field to detect malaria. The management of Friedman, Inc., has performed cost studies and projected the following annual costs on *40,000 units* of production and sales.

	TOTAL ANNUAL COSTS	VARIABLE PORTION OF TOTAL ANNUAL COSTS
Direct material	$400,000	100%
Labor	360,000	75%
Other manufacturing overhead	300,000	40%
Selling and administrative	200,000	25%

REQUIRED:

1. Compute Friedman's unit selling price that will yield a projected 10% profit before taxes, based on sales of 40,000 units.
2. Assume that Friedman, Inc., decides to set its selling price at $40 per kit. If it wants to make an after-tax profit of $90,000, how many units must it sell? Friedman's earnings are taxed at a 40% rate.
3. If the company makes a "gift" to a foreign official, the country which the official represents will place an order for 10,000 of the kits at the regular selling price of $40 per kit. Production would have to be raised by 10,000. This could be done without changing any of the fixed costs. There would be no variable selling and administrative expenses relative to this order. The 40,000 units currently being sold would still be sold. What amount can Friedman give as a gift if it wants to improve overall company profits by $50,000 as a result of the gift?
4. Should the gift be made? Why or why not?

12—23. *Break-even point and earnings under different alternatives.* The Jackson Movie Theater is attempting to attract larger audiences. Three alternatives have been presented to the theater's manager toward this end:

1. Spend $5,000 more per year on acquiring more up-to-date first-run movies.
2. Increase their present minimal advertising policy to include some newspaper coverage. This is anticipated to cost $500.

3. Combine the above two alternatives and spend $2,000 on movies and $300 more on advertising.

The theater at present incurs fixed costs of $62,500 per year and, although it fluctuates, monthly attendance has averaged 4,800 viewers. In addition, variable costs incurred per viewer are $1.10. The theater charges a $2.50 admission charge for adults and $1 per child. (Approximately 20% of monthly viewers are children and most are accompanied by adults.)

REQUIRED:
1. Determine the number of annual viewers necessary to break even.
2. If it is anticipated that alternative 1 will increase attendance by 15%, alternative 2 by 5%, and alternative 3 by 10%, compute the earnings and break-even point in terms of attendance under each alternative. Under any of the alternatives, the audience is expected to be 80% adults and 20% children.
3. Which alternative would you recommend and why?

12—24. *Calculating break-even under different assumptions.* In a recent period the Pleasant Dreams Company, which makes sleeping bags good for temperatures down to 40 below zero, had the following experience:

Sales (10,000 units @ $200)			$2,000,000
Costs:			
	FIXED	VARIABLE	
Direct material	$ —	$ 200,000	
Direct labor	—	400,000	
Factory overhead	160,000	600,000	
Administrative expenses	180,000	80,000	
Other expenses	200,000	120,000	
Total costs	$540,000	$1,400,000	$1,940,000
Income before taxes			$ 60,000

REQUIRED: Each item below is independent.

1. Calculate the break-even point for Pleasant Dreams in terms of units and sales dollars.
2. Based on current results, what is the company's margin of safety in units?
3. What sales volume would be required to generate a before-tax income of $96,000?
4. What is the break-even point if management makes a decision which increases fixed costs by $18,000?
5. Referring back to the original data, if Pleasant Dreams could increase their sales volume by 2,000 units without a change in the level of fixed costs, calculate:
   a. The net income before taxes.
   b. The break-even volume in units.

12—25. *The high-low and least-squares methods for analyzing mixed costs.* Data relating to the mixed costs incurred by Leeds Printers in operating their printing machines for the past 10 months are presented below:

MONTH	HOURS, x	TOTAL MIXED COSTS, y	xy	x^2
1	480	$ 1,752	$ 840,960	230,400
2	500	1,800	900,000	250,000
3	475	1,750	831,250	225,625
4	503	1,820	915,460	253,009
5	481	1,765	848,965	231,361
6	477	1,763	840,951	227,529
7	492	1,800	885,600	242,064
8	495	1,807	894,465	245,025
9	483	1,794	866,502	233,289
10	501	1,811	907,311	251,001
	4,887	$17,862	$8,731,464	2,389,303

REQUIRED: 1. Use the high-low method to determine the total amount of fixed costs and the per-unit variable cost.

2. Use the least-squares method ($y = a + bx$, where a is the fixed component and b is the variable cost rate) to determine the total fixed and per-unit variable costs for the data above.

3. Compare the two methods at the 500-machine-hour level. Which method would you recommend using and why?

12—26. *Break-even for a hospital.* The Oakdale Hospital is a 200-bed health facility which derives revenues both from patient care and from the use of the hospital as a teaching facility for a local medical school. Oakdale's monthly expenses include:

Wages of nurses (variable) costs based on 100% capacity	$300,000
Administrative salaries (fixed)	$315,000
Supplies (variable) costs based on 100% capacity	$120,000
Utilities (fixed)	$ 35,000
Other expenses (fixed)	$ 54,000
Food service (average cost per meal per day)	$4

Each patient is served three meals each day. The standard patient charge is $200 per day and the average stay is 5 days per patient. Average volume is 85% of capacity. The medical school contributes $50,000 per month.

REQUIRED: 1. Calculate the variable cost per day for a patient staying in Oakdale Hospital. Assume a 30-day month for your analysis.

2. Calculate break-even for Oakdale in terms of how many beds must be occupied each month. At what percent of capacity must they operate to break even?

3. Calculate break-even for Oakdale in terms of the number of patients who must be cared for each month to break even.

4. The medical school which uses Oakdale is supported by state funds. Owing to strained economic conditions in the state, the medical school has asked Oakdale to contribute the use of its facilities to the school on a no-cost basis. To maintain its current profit level, by what amount would Oakdale have to raise the cost per patient per day if it no longer received the contribution from the medical

school? Assume the average volume would remain at 85% of capacity. (Round your answer to the nearest dollar.)

12—27. *The effects on profits of high versus low contribution margins.* Walter and Freda Thompson own a restaurant which specializes in fried chicken. They plan an expansion by acquiring a second restaurant. They are considering two possibilities: one which is a steak house and the other which specializes in Chinese food. The acquisition cost of each is the same. Financial results for the two restaurants, which are typical of the performance of each, are shown below:

	STEAK HOUSE	CHINESE FOOD
Revenues, 50,000 meals served	$350,000	$350,000
Variable expenses	175,000	105,000
Fixed expenses	115,000	185,000
Total expenses	$290,000	$290,000
Income before taxes	$ 60,000	$ 60,000

REQUIRED:
1. Calculate break-even for each acquisition which is being considered. Round to the nearest meal. Explain any differences in your results.
2. Suppose the Thompsons believe that the reputation for fine food and service which their current restaurant enjoys would carry over to the new acquisition and increase volume by 15% over the current level. If this projection can be realized without any change in fixed costs, which restaurant should they acquire? Support your answer with appropriate computations.
3. Assume that the economy is expected to be extremely depressed in the area where the restaurants are located, and it is likely that volume could decrease 30% from its current level in either restaurant which the Thompsons acquire. Fixed costs in either could be cut by about $12,000. If this projection is realized, which restaurant should be acquired? Support your answer with appropriate computations.

12—28. *The effects of changes on profits.* The Lima Company manufactures file cabinets. The company is projecting the following results for the coming year:

Sales, 100,000 units @ $150			$15,000,000
Expenses:			
	FIXED	VARIABLE	
Direct materials		$4,000,000	
Direct labor		3,000,000	
Manufacturing overhead	$1,000,000	600,000	
Selling expenses	1,500,000	500,000	
Administrative expenses	2,000,000		
Total expenses	$4,500,000	$8,100,000	12,600,000
Income before taxes			$ 2,400,000
Taxes @ 50%			1,200,000
Net income			$ 1,200,000

REQUIRED: 1. Calculate the break-even point for Lima Company. (Round to the nearest unit.)

2. How would after-tax profits be affected if, by spending an additional $5 per unit on advertising, Lima could increase volume by 10% without any change in fixed costs?

3. By lowering its selling price to $125, Lima estimates that it could increase volume by 10% without any change in fixed costs. What impact would this have on profits?

4. Lima currently pays its advertising agency $200,000 per year for the advertising it places. Lima has received an offer from a competing agency which would take over the advertising on a commission basis. The agency is suggesting that they receive a commission of 1% of gross sales.

   a. Based on the current volume, should the company change its advertising agency?

   b. If volume is expected to decline in the future by about 15%, should the company change its advertising agency?

   c. At what volume level is Lima indifferent between the two advertising alternatives? (Round to the nearest unit.)

12—29.   *Effects of changes in the product mix.*   Good Life, Inc., manufactures redwood hot tubs. They have two basic models, one for outside use and the other for inside. Sales and cost information for the two product lines are as follows:

	INSIDE TUBS	OUTSIDE TUBS	COMPANY TOTALS
Revenues:			
1,000 @ $800	$800,000		
2,000 @ $500		$1,000,000	$1,800,000
Cost of goods manufactured and sold	500,000	400,000	900,000
Other variable expenses	100,000	200,000	300,000
Fixed expenses	150,000	200,000	350,000
Total expenses	$750,000	$ 800,000	$1,550,000
Income before taxes	$ 50,000	$ 200,000	250,000
Taxes @ 40%			100,000
Net income			$ 150,000

REQUIRED: 1. Calculate the contribution-margin percent for each product line and for the company as a whole. (Round to the nearest whole percent.)

2. Calculate the dollar volume at which the company as a whole will break even. (Round to the nearest dollar.)

3. Assume that Good Life, Inc., would like to make an after-tax profit of $300,000 next year. It does not expect any changes in selling prices, unit variable costs, total fixed costs, or the sales mix. What dollar volume of sales will it have to generate next year to meet this objective? (Round to the nearest dollar.)

4. Good Life, Inc., is expanding its marketing efforts into states with colder climates. They believe that as a result, volumes for the coming year will be 3,000 outside tubs and 3,000 inside tubs. The price of inside tubs will remain at $800; the price for outside tubs will be increased to $570. Variable unit costs

will be unchanged. Total fixed costs will increase by $80,000 for advertising, divided equally between the two product lines.

a. Compare profits with the anticipated sales mix with what profits would have been if the current sales mix had been maintained in the new markets.

b. Compute the dollar volume at which the company will break even with the sales mix anticipated for next year. (Round the contribution margin to the nearest whole percent and the sales volume to the nearest dollar.)

12—30. *Impact of changes on profits.* The Lighter Way Company produces standard light bulbs of various wattages. Results for the company for the past year are summarized below:

Revenues, 8,000,000 bulbs at an average price of $.80	$6,400,000
Variable costs	2,560,000
Fixed costs	3,200,000
Total costs	$5,760,000
Income before taxes	$ 640,000

REQUIRED: *Consider each of the following cases independently unless otherwise stated.*

1. The company presently has a return on investment based on income before taxes of 10%. Its objective for the coming year is to raise that to 12%. The investment base next year is expected to remain at the current year's level. Next year's contribution margin percent will be the same as that for the current year. Calculate the sales-dollar volume which Lighter Way must generate to meet this objective. (Round to the nearest dollar.)

2. Lighter Way anticipates that variable costs will increase by 2 cents per bulb next year. With a well-organized cost-cutting program, the company believes it can reduce fixed costs by 8%. Volume will increase 8%. To realize the same before-tax profits next year as they had for the past year, at what amount can they set the selling price? (Round to the nearest cent.)

3. The inflation rate is projected as being 10% next year and will cause variable expenses to increase $.03 per unit and fixed costs to rise by 10%. The company plans to raise its selling price by 10% to reflect the inflation rate. Based on these changes, what are projected before-tax profits for next year? Volume is expected to be adversely affected and will drop by 5%.

4. Increased competition is forcing Lighter Way to cut its selling price for next year to an average of $.75 per bulb. Volume will be at the past year's level. Fixed costs are expected to increase by 8%, while variable costs will be held at the past year's unit amount. What are the anticipated before-tax profits for next year?

chapter thirteen

ANALYSIS FOR SHORT-TERM, NONROUTINE DECISION MAKING

OBJECTIVES

After you have completed this chapter, you should be able to answer the following questions:

- What are the steps in the decision-making process?
- What costs are relevant in choosing between alternatives and why?
- Why are sunk costs irrelevant to the decision-making process?
- Why are cash flows the important decision variables rather than accounting numbers based on an accrual accounting system?
- What distinguishes short-term, nonroutine decisions from long-term nonroutine decisions?
- What are some common types of short-term nonroutine decisions which a manager is likely to encounter?

ROUTINE VERSUS NONROUTINE DECISIONS

Routine decisions are those which are recurring and a result of normal operations. These include decisions such as setting the selling price for a product, deciding where to place an order for raw materials, and evaluating a subordinate's performance. *Nonroutine decisions* are those which occur less frequently and include decisions such as whether to take a special order, drop a product line, buy a part rather than make it, or build a new factory.

This chapter is concerned with decisions that are treated as having a short time horizon—usually an annual period. "Having a short time horizon" means that by focusing on the immediate or short-run cash consequences of an alternative we can make a decision. In contrast to short-term nonroutine decisions, other nonroutine decisions have a long time horizon with cash flows affecting multiple future periods. This latter type of decision we characterize as a *long-term* decision.

To clarify the different time perspectives for short- and long-term nonroutine decisions, let us consider some examples. A company is trying to decide whether it should take a special order at a price less than its normal selling price. The cash consequences of this decision will be experienced by the company in a relatively short period.

On the other hand, suppose that a company is trying to decide whether it should build a new factory. The cash consequences of this decision will affect a number of future periods. This type of long-term decision, which has a capital investment component, we refer to as a capital budgeting decision—a topic which will be discussed in the next two chapters.

PROCESS FOR MAKING NONROUTINE DECISIONS

The steps in the nonroutine decision-making process are as follows:

1. Define the problem or opportunity.
2. Determine what alternatives exist.
3. Eliminate any alternatives which are not acceptable or those which are less desirable.
4. Quantify to the extent possible and evaluate the effects of acceptable alternatives or opportunities.
5. Consider factors which cannot or have not been quantified.
6. Make a decision.

1. Define the Problem or Opportunity

Management often becomes aware that a problem exists when quantitative measures of performance are adversely affected—for example, productivity goes down, down-time on a machine increases, labor turnover is high, or profit margins decrease. However, problems can be indicated by less tangible conditions such as low morale.

Decisions also have to be made when opportunities exist for expansion or change. Good management is always alert to new markets, new products, and new technologies. Once these come to the attention of management, a decision must be made as to whether the opportunities are in keeping with the organization's goals.

Once a problem or opportunity has come to the attention of a manager, that manager must make an initial investigation. This usually leads to a definition of the problem or opportunity. For example, if the president of a company notes that overall profits are down, the next step he or she may take is to look at performance figures which are more refined, such as sales by product lines. This could lead to the observation that a particular product line is performing poorly. Then the manager looks for reasons, and these could include a number of things such as high production costs or decreasing demand. If the production costs are the culprit, further investigation will be required to determine whether these costs are related to direct material cost and usage, unskilled workers, inefficient equipment, or some other reasons.

In other words, defining the problem means pursuing results which management finds unacceptable or which it believes need improvement until a problem or series of problems to which alternative solutions are available emerge. Until we have defined a problem to the extent that alternative solutions can be considered, we have not sufficiently defined the problem. For example, if we have decided that production costs are too high, this does not give us a set of possible solutions, because the problem definition is still too broad. If, however, we have decided that direct labor costs are too high, we can immediately see a number of possible solutions: replace workers with machines, use workers who command lower wage rates, improve worker productivity, or stop producing the product.

For opportunities, defining the opportunity means taking an idea and investigating it to the extent that the manager can decide whether to proceed to step 4, quantification of the effects of taking the action implied by the opportunity. To illustrate, assume that a manager is considering the addition of a new product line. Defining the opportunity would require further investigation to answer questions such as (1) What is the demand for the product? and (2) Can the resources (materials, labor) be obtained at prices and in locations which make it practical for the company to produce the product?

2. Determine What Alternative Solutions Exist

Determining a set of alternative solutions to a defined problem can be very difficult for the manager for a number of reasons, including difficulty in (a) seeing anything beyond the status quo and (b) considering solutions which would adversely affect the manager's own well-being.

With respect to status quo, it is very hard for most of us to imagine a home, world, or work environment radically different from what we are accustomed to. For example, in considering program cutbacks, university faculty members frequently offer as a prelude to their argument, "But all universities must have a _____ (you supply the name: accounting, psychology, etc.) department." Creative solutions are often blocked by our inability to think beyond the current state of the organization of which we are a part.

Another problem is that sometimes viable alternatives adversely affect the position of the manager who is making a decision, hence these alternatives are automatically eliminated. A partial solution to this problem is a routine review of the alternative solutions to significant problems by a management level which is removed from the impact of the decision.

3. Elimination of Alternatives

For some problems a large number of possible alternatives may be identified. However, taking the next step—quantifying the results of the alternatives—can be a costly process. For this reason, some preliminary screening is usually required. This screening process is designed to eliminate all but the most likely sets of alternatives. Which alternatives are less desirable and should be screened out is largely a matter of managerial judgment, and we have the same problems that we did in developing a set of possible solutions. Those alternatives which may be screened out first are those which represent significant departures from the status quo and those which would adversely affect the manager responsible for the part of the organization where the problem exists.

Another difficulty in elimination of alternatives is to decide on the relevant time range. If we are considering, for example, dropping a product or service line or discontinuing a department, what time perspective is relevant? Thinking of the university setting, demand for liberal arts degrees in areas such as history and philosophy is currently very low. On this basis, should these departments be eliminated or cut back and resources shifted to high demand areas such as business, engineering, and computer science? The answer may depend on the time perspective adopted—today versus a few years in the future when demand may have shifted.

There are no answers to the issues being raised with respect to sifting through alternatives and retaining only the most likely ones. While we have raised issues to be considered, the final classification of alternatives as viable or nonviable is largely a matter of managerial judgment.

4. Quantification of the Results of Alternatives or an Opportunity

After an alternative, a set of viable alternatives, or an opportunity has been defined, the next step is to quantify the results. That is, an attempt is made to translate into dollar terms the consequences of different courses of action. This quantification of results is important for both profit-making and nonprofit organizations. For the profit-making entity, management is always concerned with the impact of decisions on profits. For the nonprofit organization, quantification is important because most organizations of this type have limited resources for accomplishing their objectives. This issue of quantification will be discussed in more detail in the next section of this chapter.

5. Consider Qualitative Factors

Often, after the results of different courses of action have been quantified to the extent possible, consideration should be given to those factors which cannot be quantified or which were too difficult or costly to quantify. On the basis of dollars and cents only, we may conclude that one course of action is most appropriate, but after factoring in considerations that were not quantified, our actual decision may be to pursue another course of action.

6. Make a Decision

The final decision reached should be based on a consideration of both the quantitative analysis and the significant variables which have not been quantified. It should be the decision which is most likely to move an organization toward its major goals—more profits, better service, or whatever else has been defined as a major goal.

Managerial judgment is the critical factor when one alternative is not clearly superior. Having to make such choices is what distinguishes a manager from a nonmanager. If a decision is not made among alternatives, in effect a decision has been made—to maintain the status quo.

In making decisions, the manager should be conscious of the time perspective of the alternatives being considered. Is the best solution for today also best in the long run for the organization? Unfortunately, because of managerial mobility and the tying in of management compensation packages to what happens today, managers may not be motivated to think in anything other than short-run terms.

Another problem with certain types of nonroutine decisions is that it is often difficult to evaluate the merit of a particular decision based on what happens in the future. That is, it is difficult to determine in retrospect whether a decision was "good" (in the best interest of the organization) or "bad." Once an alternative is forgone, generally we no longer track its outcomes.

To demonstrate, think about two decisions: a decision by a profit-making organization to drop a product line and a decision by a university to drop intercollegiate football. If the other decision had been made, the organization would have been different—in what ways we don't know, because those data are not a part of the organization's information system.

QUANTIFICATION OF ALTERNATIVES

In attaching dollar outcomes to different courses of action, the relevant amounts are those which are (1) different between alternatives and (2) future, rather than past, cash amounts. In other words, two types of amounts are not relevant when trying to choose between alternatives:

1. Those which will be the same between two alternatives.
2. Past amounts.

The word "amounts" is used here rather than costs because alternative decisions can have three dimensions: a revenue dimension, a cost dimension, and an investment dimension. What is relevant in a decision-making context is the same for all three dimensions—cash amounts which differ between alternatives and cash amounts which relate to the future.

Amounts Which Do Not Differ Between Alternatives

To illustrate that costs which do not differ between alternatives are not relevant in the decision-making process, consider this simple situation. The Sandahl Company is considering whether to sell a line of combination bookcase and desk units as an unfinished (unpainted) product or in finished form. Consider the following data with respect to *prime* costs of a single unit:

	UNPAINTED UNITS	PAINTED UNITS
Wood costs	$60	$60
Direct labor—cutting and assembly	18	18
Painting and finishing materials		5
Direct labor—painting and finishing	—	8
Total prime costs	$78	$91

Whether the units are sold as unfinished or as finished units, the basic wood costs and direct labor costs of cutting and assembly will still have to be incurred. These costs are not relevant to the decision. What is relevant is the $13 of additional costs incurred in the painting and finishing process. If the selling-price differential between the two different products does not exceed the additional costs incurred in the finishing and painting process, which includes not only prime costs but all other additional costs, further processing beyond the unpainted stage cannot be justified on a quantitative basis.

Past Amounts

On the one hand this is a very straightforward and simple concept. Looking back at Sandahl, the data which the manager evaluates should relate to the future. If the costs and revenue figures which he or she is studying are historical figures rather than estimates for the future, an incorrect decision may be made.

The other aspect of past amounts and their lack of relevance is more difficult to appreciate. This relates to what accountants call sunk costs. *Sunk costs* are defined as costs which have already been incurred and which therefore cannot be avoided regardless of future courses of action which management may take.

The sunk costs most often related to a decision-making process of the type we are considering are those incurred in the acquisition of depreciable assets. To illustrate the conflicts that managers have with respect to the relevancy of such expenses, let's look at a simple example. The Sigma Pi Delta professional fraternity, a nonprofit organization, owns a Roxing copying machine. The copier is located in the Sigma Pi Delta office in the School of Business Building and is available for student use at the cost of $.05 per copy. The fraternity has been approached by the salesperson of another company which rents MIB copying machines. The salesperson offers the fraternity a contract which would entail the installation of a coin-operated MIB copier. The company would provide all paper and maintenance and pay the fraternity $.025 for each copy made on the machine.

The treasurer of Sigma Pi Delta collected data and made an analysis as follows. The Roxing copier was acquired at a cost of $8,000 and is being depreciated over a four-year life. At present it has an estimated remaining life of two years. At the end of that period the machine will be donated to the School of Business library. If an agreement is signed with MIB, the old machine will be turned over to the library immediately.

Alternative 1: Continue Using Roxing Machine

	YEAR 1	YEAR 2
Revenues, 240,000 copies per year @ $.05	$12,000	$12,000
Paper cost, 240,000 copies per year @ $.025	6,000	6,000
Service contract	400	400
Depreciation on equipment	2,000	2,000
Total operating costs	8,400	8,400
Operating income	$ 3,600	$ 3,600

Alternative 2: Sign a Two-Year Contract with MIB

	YEAR 1	YEAR 2
Revenues, 240,000 copies per year @ $.025	$ 6,000	$ 6,000
Loss on retirement of old machine	4,000	0
Operating income	$ 2,000	$ 6,000

The sunk cost involved in this decision is that of the old copier. Under either alternative the $4,000 of costs will be charged against revenues and will have no effect on cash flows. Thus in the decision whether or not a contract should be signed with MIB, the cost of the old copier is irrelevant. If Sigma Pi Delta were not a tax-exempt organization, the loss of the depreciation expense and the retirement could have an impact on cash flows because of taxes.

In our simple example, the fraternity should accept the contract with MIB because it results in cash flows of $6,000 in both years, while continuing to use the Roxing machine results in cash flows of only $5,600 (operating income + depreciation which does not require any cash) in each of the two years. To understand the fact that, ignoring taxes, neither depreciation nor the write-off of the loss on the retirement of the equipment has any cash consequences, recall the bookkeeping entries which are made to record these transactions:

	Year 1		Year 2	
Depreciation Expense	2,000		2,000	
Accumulation Depreciation		2,000		2,000
Loss on Retirement	4,000			
Copier		4,000		

Neither transaction affects cash.

Looking at the data displayed, you should be able to appreciate why a manager may have difficulties accepting the fact that the sunk cost—the cost of the Roxing machine—is irrelevant. If this were a profit-making entity and you as manager were being judged on the basis of operating income, your accountant could talk about sunk cost endlessly and not convince you that you would want to go with the MIB because of the negative impact on results in Year 1—operating income of $3,600 if we continue to use the Roxing machine versus $2,000 if we don't. Although the second-year results are improved if the MIB agreement is signed, that doesn't help the manager who is being evaluated this year on this year's results. This demonstrates the problem we discussed earlier: managers may be encouraged to make dysfunctional decisions because their performance tends to be evaluated on a short-run basis.

Another important point to remember is that sunk costs cannot be dismissed as irrelevant if they have tax consequences. In our example we had a tax-exempt organization, so sunk costs truly were irrelevant. With an organization for which taxes are a reality, the tax impact of the sunk costs must be factored into the decision-making process. Based on the example involving the copier, there are two parts to the tax issue: (1) What will be the impact of losing the tax-deductible depreciation? (2) What will be the tax effect of retiring the old machine? These issues will be explored in detail later.

DIRECT COSTS AND SEGMENT MARGINS

Remember in managerial accounting that we measure costs for various purposes. The purpose for which we measure costs is called the *cost objective*. When we studied product costing, our cost objective was to assign costs to output—either goods or services. In discussing budgeting, we measured costs in terms of responsibility centers. Now, when we are trying to choose between alternatives, we will assign costs between alternatives.

Direct costs are those which can be specifically identified with our cost objectives. In the context of making alternate choices, direct costs associated with an alternative are those which can be specifically related to that alternative. Or, putting it another way, direct costs of an alternative are those which would be eliminated if that alternative were forgone.

For alternatives with which we can also associate revenues, we shall use the term *segment margin* to describe the difference between the revenues from that alternative and the direct costs of that alernative. For example, assume that a jewelry store is considering closing its watch repair department. The following data have been accumulated with respect to the watch repair department:

Revenues		$20,000
Repairperson's salary	$14,000	
Supplies	3,000	
Allocated overhead	5,000	22,000
Income of watch repair department		($ 2,000)

Thinking in terms of direct costs and segment margin, we could rearrange the data as follows:

Revenues		$20,000
Repairperson's salary	$14,000	
Supplies	3,000	17,000
Segment margin		$ 3,000

Note the following:

1. Segment margin and contribution margin are not synonomous terms. *Contribution margin* is the result of comparing revenues with variable expenses. *Segment margin* is the result of comparing revenues with all costs which can be specifically

identified with the segment. The repairperson's salary is probably a fixed expense. Yet it is deducted from revenues to find the segment margin because it is a cost which can be specifically identified with the watch repair department.

2. A *segment*, in a decision-making context, can be defined in whatever way is appropriate to the decision being made. A segment might be a department; instead it could be a product line. For financial reporting purposes, what constitutes a segment is defined by generally accepted accounting principles, so the term is not being used the same way here as it is for those purposes.

ACCOUNTING INCOME VERSUS CASH FLOW

In the example above involving the replacement of the copier, the treasurer developed data in the format of accrual-basis income statements. Yet we stated that the fraternity should accept the contract with MIB because the *cash flows* (rather than accounting income) were greatest when that alternative was accepted. Two questions may come to your mind: (1) What is the difference between cash flow and accrual income? (2) Which should we consider in weighing alternative courses of action—accrual income or cash flow?

The distinction between cash flow and accrual income is based on how we recognize revenues and expenses under an accrual accounting system. Accrual accounting recognizes a revenue when that revenue is earned (generally at point of sale), not when cash flows in, and recognizes an expense when it is incurred, not when cash is paid out. When the cash flows from an alternative are quantified, the cash inflows rather than accrual income are compared with the cash outflows rather than with accrual-based expenses. In the example involving the copier, when we looked at cash flows from the alternatives, we ignored depreciation even though it was an expense on an accrual basis. We also ignored the loss on retiring the old copier even though it adversely affected accounting income.

Theoretically what is relevant in choosing between alternatives is cash flows rather than accrual income. Over the life of an organization, cash income and accrual income should be equal. However, an organization cannot spend or invest accrual income; what has value here is *cash*. This fact should be recognized in choosing between alternatives. The selection of an action should be based on the size and timing of cash flows rather than on the size and timing of accrual income.

For two reasons, however, practice may depart from the principle that cash flows are what is relevant in the decision-making process. The first departure relates to short-term decision making and can be financially and logically justified. Because the time horizon is short, often accrual figures are used as surrogates for cash figures because the timing difference between the recognition of an expense or revenue on an accrual basis is assumed not to differ greatly from that on a cash basis. For example, think about the data given for the watch repair department. Not all the revenues, the repairperson's salary, and the supplies may represent cash flows—some part of them may actually be receivables or payables. However, the cash flows are assumed to be so immediate that the accrual figures can be substituted. To clarify, while some of the watch repairs may have been done on account, collection is assumed to take place shortly, hence there is no significant difference between revenues on an accrual basis and revenues on a cash basis.

This use of accrual figures for cash figures cannot be defended when the time horizon lengthens. To use an oversimplified illustration, assume that a piece of equipment with a life of three years and no salvage value can be obtained by paying $12,000 today to buy it or by paying $4,000 at the beginning of each of the next three years to lease it. In the context of financial accounting, which is based on accrual concepts, these alternatives may look identical:

First alternative—buy: Depreciation expenses, $4,000 per year
Second alternative—lease: Rent expenses, $4,000 per year

In managerial accounting, the two alternatives differ because of the cash flows—$12,000 immediately versus $4,000 immediately and the deferral of $8,000 of cash outflows to future years. The differences between these cash flows for decision-making purposes will be discussed more fully when we introduce the concept of present value in the next chapter.

The second departure from the use of cash flows in decision making cannot be financially or logically justified. It arises because of (1) the way managers believe decisions are made external to the firm and (2) the way managers are evaluated within the firm.

Profit-making firms put a great deal of emphasis on the "bottom line." The reason is that external users of financial statements—stockholders, creditors, and society in general—receive data developed on an accrual basis. If a manager believes that the firm is being evaluated by those external to the firm on the basis of accrual accounting figures, then in making a decision the manager will be conscious of and may be influenced by the accrual-basis impact of that decision. This may not lead to the best decision. The write-off of old equipment in replacing it with more efficient equipment may, for example, have a significant impact on accrual income, an impact which management believes will be detrimental to the way those external to the firm evaluate it. Yet, as we saw in the example involving the copier, the cost of the old machinery is a sunk cost and should not influence the replacement decision.

As discussed previously, if accrual-based income figures are used internally to evaluate managers and the time perspective used for evaluation is short-run, a manager may fail to make the optimal decision because of the immediate negative impact of that decision on the figures by which his or her performance is judged.

COMPREHENSIVE ILLUSTRATION—
DROPPING A DEPARTMENT

In this chapter we are dealing with decisions that are assumed to have a short time horizon. To illustrate in detail what is involved in a decision of this type, we shall consider The Contemporary Prints Gallery (The Gallery). This is a profit-making gallery which handles the work of selected artists on a consignment basis—when a print is sold, the gallery keeps 40% and submits the balance to the artist. On the basement floor, which opens into a small courtyard, of the four-story building, the company operates a tearoom where beverages, light snacks, and desserts are available during the hours the gallery is open.

The Gallery is organized as two responsibility centers—the gallery itself and the tearoom. The following data for the past year have been accumulated and are typical of the results of operations for the two previous years.

	GALLERY	TEAROOM	TOTAL
Revenues	$900,000	$300,000	$1,200,000
Cost of food and beverages		165,000	165,000
Salaries	200,000	35,000	235,000
Supplies	80,000	15,000	95,000
Shipping and packing costs	98,000	—	98,000
Insurance	30,000	10,000	40,000
Utilities	24,000	8,000	32,000
Rent	225,000	75,000	300,000
Depreciation of furniture and fixtures	7,500	7,500	15,000
Accounting and data processing costs	4,500	1,500	6,000
Total expenses	$669,000	$317,000	$ 986,000
Operating income (loss)	$231,000	($ 17,000)	$ 214,000

1. Define the Problem

Sarah Lawrence, the owner and operator of The Gallery, noted the current-year results and stated, "I'm tired of operating a tearoom which continues to pull down my overall profitability."

"Before you do anything hasty," Martin Smith, her accountant, cautioned, "let's think about alternatives and analyze the effects." Smith had just graduated with a major in business and a minor in fine arts; he had worked for the gallery for less than a month.

2. Determine What Alternatives Exist

Smith suggested three possibilities:

1. Renting the space to someone else and letting them run the tearoom.
2. Turning the space into a gallery which displayed popular inexpensive prints by well-known artists, such as Picasso, Grandma Moses, and Renoir, and which could be purchased either framed or unframed.
3. Adding additional artists to those whose work The Gallery already displayed and using the basement space as additional gallery area.

3. Eliminate Any Alternatives Which Are Not Acceptable

Lawrence responded that alternative 1 was too much trouble and she didn't want to share the building with someone else. She didn't believe that either of the other two alternatives was economically feasible. With respect to alternative 2, the local college bookstore did this already and even allowed people to rent such prints. As to alternative 3, Lawrence stated that she already had sufficient space to display the work of additional artists if she chose to. In addition, a great deal of money would be required to redecorate and light the basement in a manner suitable for displaying prints.

Finally, Lawrence maintained that she saw only one viable alternative—closing the tearoom and using the basement for office space for Smith, a clerical assistant, and for storage. No major renovations would be required and the necessary office equipment could simply be moved from its current third-floor location to the basement.

"Ms. Lawrence," Smith countered, "before we do anything drastic, let's take a look at the figures your previous accountant put together. Sometimes in choosing between alternatives, numbers which are used for general accounting and responsibility accounting purposes are not relevant. Give me two days to develop the pertinent data before you make a decision."

4. Quantify the Effects of Acceptable Alternatives

Smith decided to classify the figures provided between direct expenses—those which could be specifically traced to the two responsibility centers—gallery operations and the tearoom—and indirect expenses which had been allocated between the two. For those expenses which had been allocated, he decided to determine the basis of the allocation.

The data Smith gathered are described below:

1. *Direct expenses for the tearoom:* Salaries, supplies, and cost of food and beverages. These expenses were directly traceable to the operations of the tearoom.
2. *Indirect expenses allocated to the tearoom:*

   a. *Insurance, utilities, and rent:* These expenses were allocated 75% to the gallery operations and 25% to the tearoom on the basis that this was the breakdown of space occupied between the two operations. The gallery used three floors, the tearoom one floor.

b. *Depreciation on furniture and fixtures:* In the gallery itself furniture and fixtures were minimal, consisting of a few benches, chairs, desks, and office equipment. The tearoom had kitchen equipment, tables, and chairs. The depreciation, which was not a very large amount, was divided equally between the two operations on the basis that each had about 50% of the total equipment of the business.

c. *Accounting and data processing costs:* These items were allocated on the basis of sales revenues—one-third to the tearoom, two-thirds to the gallery.

Smith prepared the following schedule, which matched direct cash expenses of the two operations with cash revenues generated by each to show the cash-basis segment margin—the contribution of each operation to the indirect expenses of the business. The analysis revealed that the tearoom contributed $85,000 of cash flows toward meeting the company's indirect costs, which on a cash basis totaled $378,000. In other words, the tearoom made a significant contribution to the Gallery's overall cash flows.

	GALLERY	TEAROOM	TOTAL
Revenues	$900,000	$300,000	$1,200,000
Direct expenses:			
Cost of food and beverages		165,000	165,000
Salaries	200,000	35,000	235,000
Shipping and packing costs	98,000	—	98,000
Supplies	80,000	15,000	95,000
Total direct expenses	$378,000	$215,000	$ 593,000
Segment margin—cash basis	$522,000	$ 85,000	$ 607,000
Indirect cash expenses:			
Insurance			$ 40,000
Utilities			32,000
Rent			300,000
Accounting and data processing			6,000
Total indirect expenses			$ 378,000
Operating income—cash basis			$ 229,000

In further analysis of costs Smith determined the following:

1. Insurance coverage could be reduced at an approximate savings of $5,000.

2. Rent would not change, and any reduction in utilities would not be significant.

3. Accounting and data processing costs paid to outside vendors for special payroll records and tax reports could be reduced by $500.

4. The equipment used by the tearoom could be sold for its book value of approximately $25,000.

Smith then prepared the following report, which shows the cash results from (1) continuing to operate the tearoom, (2) closing the tearoom and converting the space to offices and storage, and (3) operating the gallery without a tearoom.

	CASH FLOWS BASED ON CURRENT OPERATIONS	CASH DIFFERENTIAL AMOUNT RELATED TO THE OPERATION OF THE TEAROOM	CASH FLOWS FROM BUSINESS *WITHOUT* THE TEAROOM
Revenues	$1,200,000	$300,000	$900,000
Cost of food and beverages	165,000	165,000	—
Salaries	235,000	35,000	200,000
Supplies	95,000	15,000	80,000
Shipping and packing costs	98,000	—	98,000
Insurance	40,000	5,000	35,000
Utilities	32,000	—	32,000
Rent	300,000	—	300,000
Accounting and data processing	6,000	500	5,500
Total cash expenses	$ 971,000	$220,500	$750,500
Cash income from operations	$ 229,000	$ 79,500	$149,500
Cash flow from sale of tearoom equipment—one time only			25,000

In a meeting with Ms. Lawrence, Smith pointed out the following:

1. The relevant decision variables are the cash flows.
2. The cash differential of closing the tearoom is $79,500. That is, the cash revenues which would disappear if the tearoom were closed exceed the cash expenditures which would be eliminated by $79,500. The Gallery's recurring cash flows would be diminished by $79,500.

Ms. Lawrence asked, "What did you do about the depreciation on the tearoom equipment? Your report talks about cash differentials. Why wouldn't you consider the $7,500 reduction in depreciation which would occur if I closed the tearoom?"

Smith explained that the cost of the tearoom equipment was a sunk cost and was based on an expenditure which had already been made. The tearoom equipment was relevant only to the extent that its sale would generate a *one-time only* cash flow of $25,000 in the period of sale.[1]

"How should I factor the one-time-only $25,000 cash flow into my decision process?" Ms. Lawrence asked.

"You would have to make some assumptions about how you would invest it and then view the lost cash flows as being net of the assumed cash return from that investment. For example, Ms. Lawrence, suppose that you assume you could invest the $25,000 to earn a simple annual return of 12% or $3,000 per year. Your net cash-flow loss from closing the tearoom would be $79,500 minus $3,000 or $76,500. In a case such as this you can view the lost cash flow relative to the cash which would be

---

[1] To the extent that the loss of the depreciation deduction will increase taxable income, there is a cash impact. This will be discussed in detail in the next chapter.

freed to see what rate of return you would have to earn to compensate for those lost cash flows. In our present situation that would be an impossible (or at least highly unlikely) return, as you can see from these calculations:

$$\frac{\text{lost cash flow} = \$79,500}{\text{one-time cash inflow} = \$25,000} = 318\%$$

In other words, you would have to earn a simple annual return of 318% to compensate for the lost cash flow which would result from closing the tearoom."

"I can't imagine where I could earn that kind of return," Ms. Lawrence replied. "My banker seems to like to look at The Gallery's income statement. Although you've told me that I should be concerned only with cash flows in making my decision, how would my income statement look if I closed the tearoom?"

Smith pointed out that if Ms. Lawrence wanted to see how an income statement prepared on an *accrual basis* would look, assuming the closing of the tearoom, she could take the cash income from operations, assuming the closing of the tearoom, and subtract from it any noncash expenses which would still be incurred by the remaining segment of the business.

"Here," Smith said, "is how that calculation would look:

Cash income if the tearoom is closed	$149,500
Less: Depreciation on the equipment used by the gallery operation	7,500
Income before taxes, assuming the closing of the tearoom	$142,000

Since the tearoom equipment would be sold at its book value, its sale would not have any impact on the income statement."

"Well, since I'm showing income of $214,000 with it open, my income statement certainly wouldn't look any better if I closed it," sighed Ms. Lawrence.

5. Consider Factors Which Cannot or Have Not Been Quantified

"Martin," Ms. Lawrence remarked, "now that I think about the issue a little more, I realize that the tearoom also serves another useful purpose. It brings people into the gallery who might not otherwise come, as we are so conveniently located in the heart of downtown. There's a certain glamor in getting together at a gallery for coffee or a light lunch. Who knows how often the tearoom brings someone in who later buys a print?"

6. Make a Decision

"That was a good piece of analysis. We'll definitely keep the tearoom open," Ms. Lawrence stated.

"Don't forget, Ms. Lawrence," Smith pointed out, "that we looked at only one of a number of possible alternatives. If you should change your mind about the acceptability of any of those plans I suggested for using the tearoom space, I'll make an analysis of the consequences. In addition, now that I'm on the scene, I can take a look at all our costs and see if some of them can be reduced. For example, if you would purchase a microcomputer for me, there would be no need to use an outside vendor for any accounting and data processing. If you think that sounds like a good idea, I'll do the analysis on whether we should purchase the micro right away."

"Martin," Ms. Lawrence sighed, "I'm an artist at heart, and numbers always give me a splitting headache. Why don't you just do the routine things and we'll get together and talk some more in six or eight months."

ADDITIONAL SHORT-TERM, NONROUTINE DECISIONS

The type of decision which we have just considered can be broadly called "operation versus shutdown." In our case it related to an operation (or department) within an organization. Analysis of this type can also be applied to a line of products or services, to a particular plant or operation within that plant, or to a division or subsidiary.

Additional classes of nonroutine decisions which organizations often encounter include:

1. *Make-or-buy decisions.* Should an organization buy an item in a ready-to-use state or should it make it?
2. *Special-order decision.* Should a company accept a special order which may either use some of the organization's excess capacity or displace some of the productive activity which is currently taking place?
3. *Sell versus additional processing.* If the outputs of products in various stages have a market, at which stage should a sale be made?

Each of these three types of decisions is illustrated below.

MAKE-OR-BUY DECISIONS

Precisions Electronics, Inc., makes a hand-held calculator for business applications such as regression analysis and calculation of present value and compound interest. Projected financial data for this product line for the coming year are shown below:

Sales, 500,000 units @ $35		$17,500,000
Cost of goods manufactured and sold:		
Direct materials @ $4	$2,000,000	
Direct labor @ $8	4,000,000	
Variable factory overhead @ $1	500,000	
Fixed factory overhead @ $3[a]	1,500,000	
Total		8,000,000
Gross margin		$ 9,500,000
Operating expenses:		
Variable selling expenses @ $1.50	$ 750,000	
Fixed selling expenses	1,250,000	
Administrative expenses—all fixed	2,500,000	
Total operating expenses		$ 4,500,000
Operating income		$ 5,000,000

[a] $3 at a volume of 500,000 units.

Each calculator takes an electronic component which Precision cstimates accounts for $1 of direct materials costs, $3.55 of direct labor, and $.35 of variable overhead cost per completed calculator.

Eden Electronic has approached Precision with an offer to make the electronic component for $5 each. If Precision accepts Eden's offer, they estimate that could cut their fixed manufacturing overhead by the following amounts:

1. Supervisory salaries and fringe benefits, $45,000.
2. Heating and lighting costs, $18,000, because they would no longer use the section of the building in which the component is now being manufactured.
3. Depreciation, $12,000, as they would stop using certain equipment. They would simply abandon the equipment, because there is no ready market for it because of its age.

The relevant comparison is of the cost of purchase with those costs which will be eliminated if the part is no longer made. The $12,000 depreciation should not be considered in making the decision, as it has no cash consequences and will reach the income statement either as depreciation, if manufacture continues, or as a write-off of a loss on retirement if the equipment is abandoned.

The analysis of the alternatives—continuing to make the electronic component or buying it from Eden—is shown below:

Cost of purchasing 500,000		
components @ $5		$2,500,000
Cost avoided by purchasing:		
Direct materials @ $1 per unit	$ 500,000	
Direct labor @ $3.55	1,775,000	
Variable manufacturing overhead		
@ $.35 per unit	175,000	
Supervisory salaries and fringes	45,000	
Heating and lighting	18,000	2,513,000
Advantage of purchasing parts		$ 13,000

Based on the analysis, there is an advantage in purchasing the parts from Eden. At this point, Precision Electronics should consider some factors which have not been quantified; some of the more important of these include:

1. How long will Eden be willing to supply the part at $5?
2. Will Eden be able to deliver the parts at the time and in the quantities needed by Precision?
3. Is the quality of Eden's product the same as that of Precision's?

To keep our make-or-buy illustration relatively simple, we have assumed that the space currently being used to make the electronic component would no longer be used. If alternative uses of the space and/or equipment do exist, these could also be factored into the decision. The excess of revenues from the alternative use relative to the costs would be the other part of the quantitative data we would consider.

To illustrate, assume that Precision can let a food and beverage vendor use the space formerly used for manufacturing. Any cost of preparing the area will be the responsibility of the vendor, who will give Precision a percentage of its revenues in exchange for the use of the space. Precision estimates that its share of revenues from the vendor would be approximately $25,000.

The advantage of purchasing the parts as computed will have to be revised to factor in this additional variable. The results of the analysis would be as follows:

Advantage of purchasing (as previously computed)	$13,000
Add: Revenues from food vendor	25,000
Total	$38,000
Less: Heating and lighting which no longer would be avoided	18,000
Advantage of purchasing the part and letting vendor use the space	$20,000

SPECIAL-ORDER DECISIONS

Refer to the basic data provided for Precision Electronics and assume that the company has idle capacity. This means that the company could raise its level of production without increasing its fixed manufacturing overhead.

A large fast food chain, Hearty Burgers, has approached Precision with a special order. Hearty Burgers is going to have a national contest and would like to award as prizes 20,000 calculators. A vendor has offered to supply the calculators to Hearty at a cost of $14 each. The costs of packing each calculator so it can be sent out to the winners by Hearty and of shipping the packaged calculators to Hearty Burgers would be paid by the vendor.

The company which has made the bid to Hearty is not well known in this country; thus, Hearty Burgers would prefer to distribute Precision's product and offers the business to Precision on the same basis as the bid it has received. Hearty will pay Precision $14 per calculator, and Precision will have to pay the cost of packing each calculator individually and shipping them to Hearty's headquarters at an approximate cost of $5,000. Should Precision take the order?

If Precision looks at the full production cost of producing the calculator, it will compare revenues of $14 per unit with manufacturing cost per unit of $16:

Direct materials	$ 4
Direct labor	8
Variable factory overhead	1
Fixed factory overhead	3
Full production cost	$16

What Precision should look at instead is the differential costs of accepting the order relative to the revenue it will generate:

Revenues 20,000 @ $14			$280,000
Differential costs:			
Direct materials	$ 4		
Direct labor	8		
Variable factory	1		
overhead	$13		
Differential production cost			
per unit, $13 × 20,000			
units		$260,000	
Additional packing and			
shipping costs		5,000	265,000
Advantage of accepting			
the special order			$ 15,000

Accepting the order will provide Precision with an additional $15,000 of revenues. The fixed manufacturing overhead costs were irrelevant to the decision because they would not change with the acceptance of the order.

Factors which have not been quantified and which should be considered in this decision include:

1. Will this undermine Precision's regular pricing structure; that is, will other customers demand a lower price?
2. Will legal difficulties result from price discrimination between customers?

SELL-VERSUS-PROCESS-FURTHER DECISIONS

Quality Wood Products produces a line of bookcases which are sold unassembled and unpainted. The company is considering further processing the bookcases and selling them as assembled and finished. Estimated cost for the coming year for the manufacture of unassembled bookcases is as follows:

	ESTIMATED DATA, UNASSEMBLED BOOKCASES
Selling price per unit	$60
Volume	20,000 units
Unit variable costs:	
Direct materials	$20
Direct labor	10
Variable manufacturing overhead	3
Fixed manufacturing overhead for the year:	
Indirect labor	$30,000
Rent of factory space	48,000
Utilities	18,000
Depreciation on factory equipment	36,000
Insurance and other	12,000

The data given below are relevant to further processing of the bookcases:

Selling price	$100 per unit
Unit variable costs incurred by further processing:	
Direct materials	$ 6
Direct labor	12
Other variable manufacturing expenses	4
Total additional variable manufacturing costs	$ 22

Other data:

1. Quality Wood Products has sufficient space available to accommodate the assembly and finishing operation.
2. An additional supervisor would have to be added at a cost to the company, including fringe benefits, of $23,000.
3. Packing and shipping costs will increase by $4 per unit for the assembled product.
4. The tools needed to do the assembling and finishing are treated as supplies by the company, and their costs are included in the variable manufacturing expenses shown above.

The answer to whether further processing should take place is based on a comparison of the incremental revenues which will result versus the incremental costs:

Increased revenues: $40 per unit × 20,000 units
   ($100 selling price for assembled product − $60
   selling price for unassembled product) $800,000
Increased costs:
  Additional variable manufacturing costs:
    $22 per unit × 20,000 units $440,000
  Increase in shipping and packing costs: $4 per unit
    × 20,000 units   80,000
  Additional supervisory costs   23,000   543,000
Incremental revenue from further processing $257,000

Based on the data assembled by Quality Wood Products, they would increase their revenues by $257,000 if they sold the bookcase in an assembled and finished form rather than as an unfinished, unassembled product.

One important factor which should be noted is that Quality did not forecast any change in demand with the change in the product and the increased selling price. Certainly before a decision is made to further process, the effects of this decision on demand must be carefully weighed.

PROBLEMS IN AND BENEFITS OF QUANTIFYING ALTERNATIVES

In textbook examples, it is hard to convey the difficulties of quantifying alternatives. Consider for a moment what is needed. First, we must be able to predict future amounts with a reasonable degree of accuracy. The shorter the time horizon, the better our chances of doing this. As you will see when we discuss capital budgeting, the decision models we use require the projection of costs, revenues, and investments for a number of years into the future. This is often an extremely difficult process.

Second, we must be able to determine which costs will change between alternatives. In the examples in this chapter this is easy, because you are told which costs will change. But in a real-world decision-making process, each significant element of relevant variables must be analyzed and the amount of change, if any, projected. Will we need additional supervisors? Will utilities costs go up significantly? How will our volume be affected?

Third, for a number of types of short-term decisions, such as the one illustrated on selling versus further processing, we must be able to separate variable costs from fixed costs.

Finally, in other situations, we need to distinguish direct from indirect costs of a particular cost objective. In the comprehensive example in this chapter when we were considering the dropping of the tearoom, we had to decide which costs were specifically identified with our cost object— measuring the cost of operating the tearoom.

Despite these difficulties, an organization is generally better off when it attempts to quantify the effects of alternatives rather than making a decision without having gone through this process. One big benefit of quantification is that it forces the decision-making manager to think through the outcomes of an alternative completely. He or she must do an analysis sufficient to allow the attaching of dollars to possible actions.

chapter highlights

The steps in the nonroutine decision-making process are as follows:

1. Define the problem of opportunity.
2. Determine what alternatives exist.
3. Eliminate the less desirable or unacceptable alternatives.
4. Quantify and evaluate acceptable alternatives or opportunities.
5. Consider factors which have not been quantified.
6. Make a decision.

This chapter focuses on short-term, nonroutine decisions. Some examples of such decisions which managers are likely to confront include (a) continue operations versus shut down, (b) make or buy, (c) accept or reject a special order, and (d) sell versus additional processing.

What distinguishes short-term from long-term nonroutine decisions is that in short-term decision making we analyze the cash consequences which are assumed to occur within a relatively short period. Long-term nonroutine decisions have multiple-period cash consequences which must be analyzed before a decision can be made.

The components of an alternative which may require quantification include revenues, costs, and investment. In considering these three components, the only amounts which are relevant are future amounts and amounts that differ between the alternatives being considered. Costs which have already been incurred, known as sunk costs, should not influence a choice between alternatives.

Cash flows from alternatives rather than accounting numbers based on accrual accounting should be used in the decision-making process. While accrual accounting numbers may be perceived as having significance in the evaluation of performance by those external to the firm, what is relevant in decision making is the size and timing of cash flows which a particular alternative will generate.

Quantification of the effects of alternatives is difficult but fosters a logical and thorough approach to decision making. Once the effects of an alternative have been quantified, factors which cannot be or were not quantified must also be considered before a final decision is made.

questions

1. Define routine and nonroutine decisions and give examples of each in a manufacturing and nonmanufacturing setting.

2. What are the steps in the nonroutine decision-making process?

3. When quantifying alternatives, which amounts are relevant and which are not? Give an example of each.

4. Define the term "sunk costs." Give two examples of such costs.

5. Contrast cash-basis accounting with accrual-basis accounting. Which should be used in the decision-making process?

6. A company carries in inventory obsolete parts which cost it $50,000 to manufacture and is deciding whether to remachine the parts for $10,000 and then sell them for $25,000 or simply scrap them for $5,000. Which amounts are relevant to the decision?

7. Define the term "segment margin" in a decision-making context.

8. Give two factors which may hinder a manager in determining the full range of alternative solutions which may exist for a particular problem.

9. How do incremental costs and opportunity costs differ?

10. Describe what the term "direct costs" means with respect to product costing as opposed to its use in nonroutine decision making.

11. A company has done a quantitative analysis and found that taking a special order it is considering would cause an increase in profits. The selling price on the special order would be less than the normal selling price which the company gets for its product. Before making a final decision on taking the order, what nonquantitative factors should the company consider? List at least two.

12. A company has on its books a machine which has a book value of $20,000

and a remaining life of two years. If a certain alternative is accepted, the company will have to scrap the machine and will receive nothing for it. If the alternative is not accepted, it will continue to use the machine and depreciate it at the rate of $10,000 per year. Ignoring taxes, why is the $20,000 book value of the old machine irrelevant in considering the alternative?

13. Colby Manufacturing makes a product and incurs the following manufacturing costs per unit:

Direct materials	$ 3
Direct labor	5
Variable manufacturing costs	2
Fixed manufacturing costs	4
Total unit costs	$14

Which of the above costs, if any, are *most likely* to be irrelevant in a non-routine decision-making context? Explain why.

14. What distinguishes short-term nonroutine decisions from long-term nonroutine decisions?

15. The text states that one difficulty in eliminating alternatives is deciding on a time range which is relevant. What is meant by this statement?

16. A manager declares that trying to quantify alternatives is a waste of time: managerial intuition is a better approach. How would you respond in refuting this position?

17. When are sunk costs relevant to the decision-making process?

18. Under what circumstances can the use of some accrual accounting figures in a short-term nonroutine decision-making situation, rather than cash flows, be justified?

19. What are some commonly encountered problems in trying to quantify the impact of alternatives?

20. What type of cost may be relevant in a decision-making context but is not generally recorded by a company's accounting system?

exercises

13—1. Claybourgh's Fine Foods is a grocery store. The delicatessen department is treated as a profit center and has been showing a loss rather than a profit. As a result, the store's management is considering dropping this department. The following data have been accumulated to aid management in its decision:

	DELICATESSEN	OTHER PROFIT CENTERS	COMPANY AS A WHOLE
Sales	$160,000	$1,300,000	$1,460,000
Cost of goods sold	$112,000	$ 520,000	$ 632,000
Salaries	36,000	260,000	296,000
Heating and light	4,000	96,000	100,000
Maintenance	7,000	68,000	75,000
Depreciation on plant equipment	9,000	100,000	109,000
General administrative and other costs, excluding depreciation	19,000	132,000	151,000
Total expenses	187,000	1,176,000	1,363,000
Income or (loss) before taxes	($ 27,000)	$ 124,000	$ 97,000

Other data:

1. If the department is discontinued, all the cost of goods sold and $15,000 of salaries will be eliminated.
2. Heating and light and maintenance will not change and will have to be absorbed by other departments.
3. The depreciation is for equipment used exclusively by the delicatessen department. If the department is closed, it will be transferred to other departments.
4. The general administrative and other costs will be allocated to other profit centers.

REQUIRED:

1. Determine the amount by which cash flows for the company as a whole would change if the Delicatessen Department were closed. Would you recommend closing this department?
2. What nonquantitative factors should be considered in making this decision?

13—2. Hardesty Manufacturing Company makes bits which are used in industrial drills. The company is operating at 80% capacity. The following information has been gathered with respect to the company's operations:

Revenues, 10,000 drill bits @ $300	$3,000,000
Manufacturing costs:	
Variable	$1,500,000
Fixed	500,000
Selling and administrative:	
Variable	100,000
Fixed	700,000
Total expenses	$2,800,000
Income before taxes	$ 200,000

Hardesty has been approached by a small African country with a request to supply 1,000 drilling bits at a contract price of $190,000. Since variable selling and administrative expenses consist of sales commission and advertising, there will be none of this type of cost if this order is taken. There will, however, be additional shipping and packing charges of $15 per bit.

REQUIRED: 1. Calculate the *full* cost (*all* costs) per bit based on current volume.
2. Calculate the current cost of manufacturing a drill bit at the current volume. Should this order be taken? Support your answer by comparing the effect of taking the order to the effect of rejecting it on Hardesty's profits.

13—3.   The Playmate Company makes a jungle-gym type item which has bars for climbing, ropes, for swinging, and other features which young children enjoy. At present the company sells these at its premises and buyers must assemble them at home. The company is considering selling the jungle gym at a price which would include assembly by the company on the customer's premises. They would no longer sell unassembled sets. The following data are available to help Playmate's management in deciding whether it should change the nature of its operations:

Current selling price, unassembled	$ 400 per unit
Cost of producing a jungle gym set	$ 200 per unit (at a volume of 4,000 units)
Selling expenses, total	$162,000 (fixed)
Administrative expenses, total	$348,000 (fixed)
Cost of assembling the product	$ 100 per unit variable
	$ 78,000 fixed

Additional data:

1. If the company sells the jungle gym and assembles it for the customer, it can eliminate one of the current salespersons, who receives an annual salary of $18,000. This is possible because salespersons currently spend a significant amount of time demonstrating how the set should be assembled.
2. The company does not produce any units for inventory.

REQUIRED: 1. Assume that the current sales and production volume is 4,000 units per year and that this volume will not be affected by the change being considered. What selling price will the company have to set for the installed jungle gym to maintain their current before-tax income level?
2. Suppose that all selling and administrative expenses are fixed and that 80% of the manufacturing costs at a volume of 4,000 units are variable. Further assume that the company sets the price of an installed unit at $550 and, because of this increase, anticipates a 20% decline from its current 4,000-unit level and will also cut production by 20%. Will profits increase or decrease from the current level if the units are sold installed under the conditions just described?

13—4.   The King Company manufactures cotton rope. At present, King's cost is $25 per pound to manufacture 20,000 lb of cotton cord, which is then processed further into the rope. The president of King is considering purchasing the cord instead of manufacturing it and renting the space currently used in its manufacture for $20,000 per year. Assume that cord of equal quality can be purchased with no problems related to availability. Cost data related to the present manufacturing process follow:

Variable costs:	
Raw materials	$13/lb
Direct labor	$ 7/lb
Overhead	$ 1/lb
Fixed manufacturing overhead costs:	
Utilities	$30,000 per year
Depreciation	$50,000 per year

If the company buys the cord rather than manufacturing it, neither the utility costs nor depreciation costs will be eliminated, since these are allocated costs. They will simply have to be absorbed by other operations.

REQUIRED:
1. How much can King Company pay per pound for cord and be as well off as if it continues to make the cord itself?
2. What factors that have not been quantified should King consider in making its decision?

13—5. (CMA adapted) The Bodine Company produces a single product which currently sells for $5. Fixed costs are expected to amount to $60,000 for the year, and all variable manufacturing and administrative costs are expected to be incurred at a rate of $3 per unit. Bodine has two salesmen who are paid strictly on a commission basis. Their commission is 10% of the sales dollars they generate. These commissions are the only variable selling expenses the company has.

REQUIRED:
1. If Bodine alters its current plans by spending an additional amount of $5,000 on advertising and increases its selling price to $6 per unit, what will its before-tax profit be on 60,000 units?
2. The Sorde Company has just approached Bodine to make a special one-time purchase of 10,000 units. These units would not be sold by the salesmen, so no commission would have to be paid. If Bodine wants to earn a before-tax profit of $14,000 on this special order, how much will it have to charge for each unit? Assume that Bodine has idle capacity sufficient to produce the additional 10,000 units and that present demand will not be affected by this special order.

13—6. (CMA adapted) The Cum-Clean Corporation produces a variety of cleaning compounds and solutions for both industrial and household use. While most of its products are processed independently, a few are related. "Grit 337" is a coarse cleaning powder with many industrial uses. It costs $1.60 a pound to make and has a selling price of $2 a pound. A small portion of the annual production of this product is retained for further processing in the Mixing Department, where it is combined with several other ingredients to form a paste which is marketed as a silver polish selling for $4 per jar. This further processing requires $\frac{1}{4}$ pound of Grit 337 per jar. Other ingredients, labor, and variable overhead associated with this further processing cost $2.50 per jar. Variable selling costs amount to $.30 per jar. If the decision were made to cease production of the silver polish, $5,600 of fixed Mixing Department costs could be avoided.

REQUIRED: What is the minimum number of jars of silver polish that would have to be sold to justify further processing of Grit 337? Assume that all Grit produced could be sold outside at $2 per pound.

13—7. (CMA adapted) Moorehead Manufacturing Company produces two products, for which the following data have been tabulated. Fixed manufacturing cost is applied at a rate of $1 per machine hour.

PER UNIT	XY-7	BD-4
Selling price	$4.00	$5.00
Variable manufacturing cost	2.00	2.50
Fixed manufacturing cost	.75	.20
Variable selling cost	1.00	2.00

The Sales Manager has had a $160,000 increase in his budget allotment for advertising and wants to apply the money to the most profitable product. In the eyes of the company's customers the products are not substitutes for one another.

REQUIRED: 1. Assume the Sales Manager chose to devote the entire $160,000 to increased advertising for XY-7. What would be the minimum increase in sales *units* and *dollars* of XY-7 required to offset the increased advertising?

2. Assume the Sales Manager chose to devote the entire $160,000 to increased advertising for BD-4. What would be the minimum increase in sales *units* and *dollars* of BD-4 required to offset the increased advertising?

13—8. (AICPA adapted) Boyer Company manufactures basketballs. The forecasted income statement for the year before any special orders is as follows:

	AMOUNT	PER UNIT
Sales	$4,000,000	$10.00
Manufacturing cost of the goods sold	3,200,000	8.00
Gross profit	800,000	2.00
Selling expenses	300,000	.75
Operating income	$ 500,000	$ 1.25

Fixed costs included in the above forecasted income statement are $1,200,000 in manufacturing cost of goods sold and $100,000 in selling expenses.

A special order offering to buy 50,000 basketballs for $7.50 each was made to Boyer. There will be no additional selling expenses if the special order is accepted. Assume Boyer has sufficient capacity to manufacture 50,000 more basketballs.

REQUIRED: By what amount would *operating income* be increased or decreased as a result of taking the special order?

13—9. The Martinez Company makes magnetic tape units. The costs and revenues from its normal volume of 50,000 tapes each month are shown below:

Revenues, 50,000 tapes	$600,000
Cost of goods manufactured and sold:	
Direct materials	$ 90,000
Direct labor	210,000
Variable overhead	30,000
Fixed overhead	72,000
Total	402,000
Variable selling and administrative	60,000
Fixed selling and administrative	120,000
Total expenses	582,000
Income before taxes	$ 18,000

The company currently makes the plastic case in which the tapes are housed. Of the costs stated above, 10% of the direct material costs, 15% of the direct labor, and 8% of the variable overhead are related to the manufacture of this case. If the case were no longer manufactured, fixed manufacturing overhead could be reduced by $5,100. The company has an offer from Plastics, Inc., to supply the case for $1.05 per unit.

REQUIRED: 1. Should Martinez purchase the plastic case from Plastics, Inc., assuming it has no alternative use for the facilities now being used to produce the case internally?

2. At what volume level, if any, would buying outside be preferable to making inside? (Round your answer to the nearest whole unit.)

13—10. Tony Nixson, the owner of Tasty Doughnuts, wants to expand his business and offer something other than doughnuts to his customers. He is considering two possible expansions: (1) making three varieties of cookies—chocolate chip, peanut butter, and sugar, or (2) baking dinner rolls. The costs of producing a dozen units of each product line, together with the quantities in which the products will be sold, are shown below:

	COST PER DOZEN	
	Cookies	Rolls
Ingredients	$.80	$.45
Direct labor	.50	.35
Other direct costs of production that are variable	.28	.10

Cookies would be sold for $2.50 per dozen, rolls for $1.50 per dozen. Tony believes that if he makes cookies, $200 of his total overhead costs should be allocated to this product. If he makes rolls, he would allocate $50 of his total overhead to their production. Adding either product line will not increase Tony's total overhead.

REQUIRED: 1. Suppose that Tony believes he could sell equal volumes of the two products each month. Which line of baked goods should he produce? Support your answer with appropriate calculations.

2. Assume that Tony believes he could sell and could get orders from a local restaurant for some of his rolls and hence could sell 1,000 dozen rolls each month, while cookies sales would be 800 dozen each month. Which product should he make? Support your answer with appropriate computations.

13—11. The CPA Training Institute of America offers special short courses to help people prepare for the Certified Public Accountant (CPA) examination. The course meets 3 hours, 5 evenings each week, for a period of 6 weeks. The CPA Training Institute is trying to decide whether it should offer the course in a new location. The rental fee for the facility it wants to use is $50 per evening. Materials for participants, which the Institute orders from a publisher and provides to the people in the course, cost $50 per copy. An instructor would receive $8 per session to cover his or her costs of driving to and parking at the facility where the course will be located. Visual aids and other equipment for the course must be rented each day at a cost of $10 per day. Advertising for the course would cost $600. Participants are provided with coffee and a sweet roll halfway through each session at a cost of $.90 per person to the Institute. The instructor receives a fee of $80 per hour. The Institute's other costs would not change as a result of offering this course.

REQUIRED:
1. If the Institute wants to make a profit of $8,000 on the course, what will it have to charge each participant, assuming it estimates an enrollment of 80?
2. What amount of profits, if any, would the Institute make if only 50 people signed up for the course in its initial offering and the Institute charged $300 per person?
3. Assume fifty people did sign up for the course at $300 each. Even though the Institute did not reach its profit objective the first time it offered the course, should it offer the course again? Why or why not? As part of your answer, calculate the company's break-even volume.

13—12. (AICPA adapted) Relay Corporation manufactures batons. Relay can manufacture 300,000 batons a year at a variable cost of $750,000 and a fixed cost of $450,000. Based on Relay's predictions, 240,000 batons will be sold at the regular price of $5 each. In addition, a special order was placed for 60,000 batons to be sold at a 40% discount off the regular price.

REQUIRED: By what amount would operating income be increased or decreased as a result of taking the special order?

13—13. The Scenic Travel Bus Company maintains a snack bar in one of its terminals. The snack bar serves sandwiches, beverages, and desserts. Costs and revenues are estimated to be:

Revenues (normal volume, 1,500 customers)	$ 3.50 per customer
Foods costs	$ 1.40 per customer
Salaries and fringe benefits of 2 persons who operate the snack bar	$2,000 per month
Depreciation of furniture (tables and chairs)	$ 400 per month
Miscellaneous	$ 150 per month

A vending-machine company has approached Scenic Travel and would like to replace the snack bar with a series of vending machines. The vendor would pay Scenic Travel 10% of its revenues, which it estimates at $8,000 per month. It would do all maintenance, and there would be no additional costs to Scenic.

If Scenic closed the snack-bar section of its terminal, it would leave the tables and chairs for people using the vending machines. Kitchen equipment has no significant resale value and would probably be donated to some charitable organization. It is fully depreciated, and no additional depreciation is being recorded on it.

REQUIRED:
1. Prepare an income statement for Scenic Travel for its snack bar based on current operations.
2. Prepare a schedule of cash flows relevant to the operations of the snack bar.
3. Should the vendor's offer be accepted? Justify your answer.

13—14. Alma Connaway owns a large acreage of heavily wooded land. She is in the process of starting a wood-cutting business. Alma is trying to decide whether she should offer wood cut into 4-foot lengths or cut into 2-foot lengths which are split and ready for immediate use. She is also trying to decide whether customers should pick the wood up at her barn or whether she should deliver it. Alma has assembled the following figures:

Time required to cut a cord of wood and saw it into 4-foot lengths	3 hours
Additional time required to cut 4-foot lengths into 2-foot lengths and split	2 hours
Hourly wage earned by wood cutters	$10
Cost of delivering a cord of wood	$15 per cord

REQUIRED:
1. What minimum additional charge per cord must Alma make to justify (a) splitting it and (b) delivering it?
2. Assume that Alma wants to offer all wood (a) either in 4-foot lengths or in 2-foot, split lengths and (b) either picked up or delivered. She assesses demand as follows:

4-foot lengths, picked up	500 cords @ $100
4-foot lengths, delivered	450 cords @ $120
2-foot lengths, picked up	380 cords @ $150
2-foot lengths, delivered	330 cords @ $175

Should 4-foot or 2-foot lengths be offered? Should they be offered on a pickup basis or delivered? Support your answer with pertinent calculations.

13—15. The Wellington Historical Society offers a tour of historical sites in the area each spring. Relevant costs to the Society are:

Bus rental (bus accommodates 50 persons including tour guide)	$100 per bus
Tour guide, one per bus, token honorarium	$ 20 for the day
Cost of printing 500 tickets	$ 25
Advertising	$235
Box lunches served on the buses	$ 6 per person

The Society wants to make $1,000 as a result of the tour and has set ticket prices at $15. Tour guides are given a free lunch and do not have to pay for their tickets. For safety reasons bus drivers are not permitted to eat.

REQUIRED: 1. What volume of demand will the Society have to generate to meet its profit objective? [*Hint:* Figure out the profit contribution per bus to cover other costs and the profit objective.]

2. Suppose that sufficient tickets were sold to cover the profit objective and there was additional demand. What minimum number of tickets should be sold before hiring an additional bus?

problems

13—16. *Special order.* Masaba Manufacturing makes electric shavers which are carried by many retail establishments. Projected data for the company's operations for the coming year are shown below:

Revenues, 300,000 shavers @ $20		$6,000,000
Cost of goods manufactured and sold:		
Direct materials	$ 900,000	
Direct labor	1,200,000	
Variable manufacturing overhead	300,000	
Fixed manufacturing overhead	600,000	3,000,000
Gross margin		$3,000,000
Operating expenses:		
Selling expenses (5% sales commission is variable;		
remainder is fixed)		840,000
Administrative expenses—fixed		1,050,000
Total operating expenses		1,890,000
Income before taxes		$1,110,000
Taxes @ 46%		510,600
Net income		$ 599,400

Masaba has been approached by a well-known retailer which would like to purchase 30,000 shavers from Masaba on a special-order basis at $15 per shaver. The retailer would put its brand name on the shaver. There would be no variable selling expenses on this order. Masaba can take the order without increasing its fixed costs.

REQUIRED: 1. Calculate the *full* costs (including all elements of cost except taxes) of a shaver based on the projections.

2. Show the *relevant* costs which should be considered in deciding whether or not the special order should be taken. If your answer differs from what you calculated in part 1, explain why.

3. By what amount will net income increase or decrease if the special order is taken? Support your answer with computations.
4. Calculate the contribution margin of a shaver sold at the regular price and one sold at the special-order price.
5. Suppose that Masaba's capacity is limited to the production of 300,000 shavers each year. The special order will displace current business. Should Masaba take the order? Support your answer with appropriate calculations.
6. *Assume* that you found, based on a quantitative analysis, that Masaba *should not* take the special order if it displaces some of its current business. What additional factors should be considered before the order is rejected?

13—17. *Make or buy.* Use the projected income-statement data for Masaba given in Problem 13—16. *Ignore information regarding the special order.*

Part of the cost of the shaver which Masaba makes is a plug-in recharging unit. It is currently made by Masaba and accounts for the following part of their variable manufacturing costs:

Direct materials	$.70
Direct labor	.90
Variable manufacturing overhead	.10

If the unit is no longer made, the supervisor of that department, who is earning a salary of $23,000, will be terminated. All other fixed manufacturing costs associated with the manufacture of the recharging unit, amounting to $67,000, will have to be absorbed by other parts of the company. Equipment used in the manufacture of the recharging unit will be left idle. Mohawk Electric has made a bid to Masaba for the manufacture of the recharging unit. Mohawk will supply the 300,000 units which Masaba needs for $1.85 per unit.

REQUIRED:
1. Prepare an analysis to assist the management of Masaba in deciding whether the recharging unit should be purchased from Mohawk.
2. Based on quantitative factors only, at what volume will Masaba be indifferent between the two alternatives of making versus buying? (Round your answer to the nearest full unit.)
3. Assume the $1.85 bid price from Mohawk. If Masaba buys the part, it can convert the facilities used for making the recharging unit and use them to make 6-foot extension cords. The supervisor will be retained. The labor costs would be the same as those incurred in making the recharging unit. Direct material costs would be reduced to $.35 and variable overhead to $.08 per extension cord. Masaba could make 300,000 extension cords, which have a selling price to retailers of $1.50. Based on this alternative use of facilities, should Masaba continue to make the recharging unit or buy it? Calculate the effects of the alternative use of facilities.

13—18. The Farmington School operates approximately ten months each year as a preparatory school for children in grades 10–12. All students are boarding students. For the past two years it has been operating an eight-week summer school for day students–students who do not stay overnight at the school. The following data show the performance of the regular session of the school, the summer program, and the school as a whole.

	REGULAR SESSION	SUMMER SESSION	TOTAL
Tuition:			
300 students @ $7,000	$2,100,000		
100 students @ $1,000		$100,000	$2,200,000
Endowment-fund revenue	60,000	—	60,000
Total revenues	$2,160,000	$100,000	$2,260,000
Expenses:			
Salary of instructional staff	$ 425,000	$ 45,000	$ 470,000
Food and lodging costs	1,400,000	4,000	1,404,000
General administration	102,000	34,000	136,000
Insurance and property taxes	28,000	5,600	33,600
Depreciation	92,000	18,400	110,400
Books and supplies	45,000	5,000	50,000
Total expenses	$2,092,000	$112,000	$2,204,000
Operating income (loss)	$ 68,000	($ 12,000)	$ 56,000

Additional information:

1. Teachers are given special contracts for the summer session. If the session were not held, these instructional costs would not be incurred.
2. Students in the summer session are given a sandwich at noon. This cost varies directly with the number of students enrolled and would be eliminated if the session were not held.
3. Since one-fourth of the total number of students enrolled in the school are summer-session students, one-fourth of the general administration costs are allocated to this session. These would not decrease in total if the summer session were not held.
4. Insurance and property taxes and depreciation are allocated on the basis of months the facilities are used by each program. Thus two-twelfths or one-sixth of these costs are assigned to the summer session. These costs would not decrease in total if the summer session were not held.
5. Books and supply costs vary directly with the number of students enrolled in the summer session and would not be incurred if the session were canceled.

Noting the results shown above, the school's trustees have asked its chief financial officer to prepare an analysis to help them decide whether to continue to offer the summer program.

REQUIRED:
1. Prepare an analysis showing the cash contribution of the summer session to covering the costs of the school.
2. Prepare an income statement showing operating income for the school if the summer session were discontinued.
3. Suppose that by adding another teacher at a cost of $5,000 the school could add 15 students in the summer session. How would the school's overall profitability be affected?

4. Do you believe that the bases used to allocate general administration, insurance and property taxes, and depreciation between the regular session and the summer session were appropriate. Defend your answer.

13—19. *Selling versus further processing.* The Brand Bleach Company makes a bleach which is used for domestic purposes and also has some industrial applications. At present, the company sells its monthly output of 100,000 gallons to other companies in 1,000-gallon returnable containers. The purchasing companies repackage the bleach and sell it to retailers or end users. Monthly revenue and cost figures for Brand Bleach are shown below:

Revenues, 100,000 gallons @ $.60 per gallon	$60,000
Direct materials	$11,000
Direct labor	18,000
Variable manufacturing overhead	5,000
Fixed manufacturing overhead	7,000
Fixed selling and administrative expenses	14,000
Total expenses	$55,000
Income before taxes	$ 5,000

Rather than continuing to sell all its output in 1,000-gallon containers, Brand Bleach is considering packaging half its output in gallon containers, labeling it, and selling it directly to retailers. It estimates that packaging half its output will entail the following incremental costs:

Container costs and labeling	$.04 per gallon
Labor	$.02 per gallon
Variable overhead	$.03 per gallon
Monthly rental of bottling equipment	$800
Supervisory costs per month	$1,200

Selling and administrative expenses would not be affected by adding the bottling operation.

REQUIRED: *Treat each part independently.*

1. If Brand Bleach wants the bottling operation to make an incremental contribution to income before taxes of $1,000 per month, at what amount will it have to sell its bottled and labeled bleach?

2. Based on a selling price of $.90 per gallon for the bottled product, and current volume levels, should Brand Bleach add the bottling operation? Show the impact on company cash flows.

3. Brand Bleach has idle capacity and believes that it could sell 80,000 bottles of labeled bleach and continue to produce and sell 50,000 gallons in the large vats. Brand believes the 80,000 bottles of bleach could be sold for $.80 per gallon. If Brand can increase its capacity without increasing its fixed costs, except for the rental of the bottling equipment and the supervisory costs for the bottling operation, prepare an income statement which will show its income before taxes with the increased production.

4. Calculate the cost of producing a gallon of bleach based on the production of 100,000 gallons and the cost based on the production of 130,000 gallons. Round your answer to the nearest cent. Do not include bottling costs. Why do your answers differ?

13—20. *Make-or-buy decision; alternative use of facility.* The Sloan Company manufactures shovels. Sloan produces the metal shovel as well as the wooden handle used in the final assembly of the finished product. During the past year Sloan sold 15,000 units at $26 per unit. Cost data for the year follow:

	COSTS RELATED TO	
	Metal Shovel	Wooden Handle
Variable costs:		
Direct materials	$165,000	$11,250
Direct labor	75,000	30,000
Variable mfg. overhead	22,500	7,500
Other variable costs	15,000	500
Sales commissions	30,000	—
Fixed costs:		
Separable[a]	23,000	3,500
Common (allocated)	8,000	2,000

[a] Directly traceable to the production of shovels or handles, and all representing cash outflows.

REQUIRED:

1. Assume that Sloan had the opportunity to purchase the wooden handles from another manufacturer for $3.54 each. Had Sloan done so, the separable fixed costs of the handles would have been avoided. What would have been the effect on cash flows if Sloan had purchased rather than manufactured the handles during the year?

2. Assume that, if Sloan had purchased the handles for $3.54 each, they could have used the facilities presently used to manufacture the handles to produce a special commemorative shovel instead to be sold for use in ceremonies dedicating new buildings. Sloan estimates that they could have made and sold 3,500 of these deluxe shovels at $35 per unit, in addition to the regular 15,000 units. Costs associated with the new unit are:

	PER UNIT
Variable (excluding sales commission)	$22.50
Sales commissions	10% of sales

Handles would also have had to be purchased for the commemorative shovels at $3.54 each. The $3,500 of separable costs incurred when the wooden handles were manufactured would have been incurred in the manufacture of the commemorative shovels. What would have been the advantage/disadvantage of making the deluxe units? What would have been the effect on Sloan's operating income under this alternative? (Prepare an income statement for the period, using the contribution-margin format.)

3. In purchasing the handles outside, what other factors should be considered?

13—21. *Special-order decision.* Olsen, Inc., manufactures ceramic coffee mugs and during the last year produced 1,500,000 mugs. Olsen's fixed manufacturing costs were $750,000, and fixed selling and administrative costs were $730,000, including sales commissions which were 4% of sales. Olsen's income statement for the year included:

Sales	$3,000,000
Manufacturing cost of goods sold	2,175,000
Gross profit margin	825,000
Selling and administrative expenses	750,000
Operating income	$ 75,000

During the year, Olsen's president had considered and rejected a special order offer from a well-known retailer of kitchen equipment and housewares to manufacture 200,000 mugs to the retailer's specifications for $300,000. Although Olsen had excess capacity, the president determined that the offer was too low. He estimated that additional costs of $.30 per mug would be incurred to comply with the size, color, and design format requested, and therefore Olsen's present policy of pricing at $.05 per unit above full unit cost could not be maintained. No sales commission would be paid on the special order.

REQUIRED:
1. Do you agree with the president's decision to reject the special order? Why or why not? Prepare an analysis, showing Olsen's results under each of the two alternatives. Indicate the relevant factors in your decision.
2. What nonquantifiable factors may have influenced the president's decision?
3. Assume that the president decides to reconsider the special-order offer during the next year. Assume the same production cost and sales data as for the preceding year, with the exception that fixed manufacturing costs are expected to increase by 10%. What should be the lowest per-unit price at which Olsen would be willing to accept the same special order? (Ignore nonquantifiable considerations.)

13—22. *Dropping product line/segment.* A large department store in a busy center-city area maintains a small bakery close to a street-level entrance. The bakery is supplied by a local distributor. Sales and cost information for the store's major product divisions during the last month follows:

	CLOTHING	HOUSEWARES	FURNITURE	COSMETICS AND DRUGS	BAKERY
Sales	$550,000	$325,000	$210,000	$105,000	$55,000
Less variable expenses	220,000	175,000	98,000	56,000	42,000
Contribution margin	330,000	150,000	112,000	49,000	13,000
Less fixed expenses:					
Salaries	150,000	90,000	75,000	25,000	11,500
Advertising	45,000	10,500	6,000	4,300	750
Utilities	5,000	1,875	1,875	625	625
Depreciation—fixtures	4,000	2,500	1,500	3,000	500
Administrative (general)	22,000	13,000	8,500	4,000	2,000
Rent	17,600	10,400	6,800	3,200	1,600
Total fixed expense	$243,600	$128,275	$ 99,675	40,125	$16,975
Segment income (loss)	$ 86,400	$ 21,725	$ 12,325	$ 8,875	$ 3,975

Salaries, advertising and depreciation expenses represent expenses of the product divisions involved. For the bakery, depreciation relates to two display cases, a microwave oven, and a refrigerator. The two display cases would be used in other parts of the store, and the oven and refrigerator would be placed in the employees' lounge if the bakery were closed. Utilities, rent, and administrative expenses represent costs of the entire store. The utility cost is allocated on the basis of space occupied. The rent and administrative expenses are allocated to all departments on the basis of sales. All variable expenses are cash costs.

The new general manager of the department store has determined that the bakery should be discontinued because it is operating at a loss. He reasons that the effect of dropping the two bakery employees and eliminating the bakery's advertising expense will improve overall net income. He anticipates that the space presently occupied by the bakery will be used by the adjoining, cramped Housewares Department at no additional expense to Housewares.

REQUIRED:
1. Prepare an analysis of cash flows which compare keeping the bakery department open with the alternative of closing it.
2. What nonquantifiable factors should also be considered in the manager's decision?
3. Recast the income-statement data into a cash-basis segment-margin-format statement. How does this facilitate your analysis?

13—23.   *Sell or process further.*   Eaton Chemicals Co. produces two chemical products, Ultra A and Ultra B. They are produced jointly in a process that costs $175,000 and yields 750,000 liters of Ultra A and 300,000 liters of Ultra B simultaneously. Both products are sold to the rubber industry to be used in various rubber products. At present both products are sold at the end of the joint production process (split-off point) when they become individually identifiable. Ultra A is sold for $.52 per liter and Ultra B for $.37 per liter. Management at Eaton recently determined that they could process Ultra B beyond the split-off point to produce Ultra B-2, which they could sell to the petroleum industry. It would cost an additional $.07 per liter to process Ultra B further, and the product could be sold for $.50 per liter.

REQUIRED:
1. Assuming that management will sell Ultra A at the split-off point for $.52 per liter, should they also sell Ultra B at this point for $.37 per liter or process it further and sell it as Ultra B-2 for $.50 per liter?
2. Assume that there is no market for Ultra B-2 and that Ultra B should be sold at split-off. However, there is a market for Ultra A-2, which can be produced by further processing Ultra A at a cost of $.22 per liter. Ultra A-2 will sell for $.72 per liter. Should Ultra A-2 be processed further or sold at split-off?

13—24.   *Dropping a segment.*   Jane Seymour owns Seymour Art Supplies which carries a full line of art supplies, as well as a line of posters and prints and a line of framing supplies. She is considering dropping the framing department and concentrating on the poster and print department, which could use the additional space. The fixtures and personnel currently used by the framing department would be used by the poster and print department. Income by department follows:

SEYMOUR ART SUPPLIES
for the Year Ending December 31

	ART SUPPLIES	POSTERS AND PRINTS	FRAMING
Sales	$840,000	$180,000	$36,000
Less:			
Cost of merchandise sold	300,000	120,000	13,200
Sales personnel	120,000	46,800	12,000
Rent	6,000	1,320	1,080
Insurance on inventory (1% of cost of sales)	3,000	1,200	120
General and administrative costs	17,640	5,280	1,080
Depreciation on fixtures	3,600	1,800	1,800
Income by department	$389,760	$ 3,600	$ 6,720

REQUIRED:

1. If the poster and print department was expanded as a result of the elimination of the framing department, how much additional cash would it need to generate in order to justify the change?
2. Recast the data above into a segment-margin format which shows the cash contribution of each department to the common cash expenses of the business.

13—25. *Pricing decision.* (CMA adapted) Stac Industries is a multiproduct company with several manufacturing plants. The Clinton Plant manufactures and distributes two household cleaning and polishing compounds, regular and heavy-duty, under the Cleen-Brite label. The forecasted operating results for the first six months of the year, when 100,000 cases of each compound are expected to be manufactured and sold, are presented in the following statement.

CLEEN-BRITE COMPOUNDS—CLINTON PLANT
Forecasted Results of Operations
for the Six-month Period Ending June 30
($000 omitted)

	Regular	Heavy Duty	Total
Sales	$2,000	$3,000	$5,000
Cost of sales	1,600	1,900	3,500
Gross profit	$ 400	$1,100	$1,500
Selling and administrative expenses:			
Variable	$ 400	$ 700	$1,100
Fixed[a]	240	360	600
Total selling and administrative expenses	$ 640	$1,060	$1,700
Income (loss) before taxes	$ (240)	$ 40	$ (200)

[a] The fixed selling and administrative expenses are allocated between the two products on the basis of dollar sales volume on the internal reports.

For the first six months of the year actual results were exactly equal to the forecast. During this period the regular compound sold for $20 a case and the heavy-duty for $30 a case. The manufacturing costs by case of product are presented in the schedule below. Each product is manufactured on a separate production line. Annual normal manufacturing capacity is 200,000 cases of each product. However, the plant is capable of producing 250,000 cases of regular compound and 350,000 cases of heavy-duty compound annually.

	COST PER CASE	
	Regular	Heavy-Duty
Raw materials	$ 7	$ 8
Direct labor	4	4
Variable manufacturing overhead	1	2
Fixed manufacturing overhead[a]	4	5
Total manufacturing cost	$16	$19
Variable selling and administrative costs	$ 4	$ 7

[a] Depreciation charges are 50% of the fixed manufacturing overhead of each line.

The schedule below reflects the concensus of top management regarding the price/volume alternatives for Cleen-Brite products for the last six months of the year. These are essentially the same alternatives management had during the first six months.

REGULAR COMPOUND		HEAVY-DUTY COMPOUND	
Alternative Prices (per case)	Sales Volume (in cases)	Alternative Prices (per case)	Sales Volume (in cases)
$18	120,000	$25	175,000
20	100,000	27	140,000
21	90,000	30	100,000
22	80,000	32	55,000
23	50,000	35	35,000

Top management believes the loss for the first six months reflects a tight profit margin caused by intense competition. Management also believes that many companies will be forced out of this market by next year and profits should improve.

REQUIRED: 1. What unit selling price should Stac Industries select for each of the Cleen-Brite compounds (regular and heavy-duty) for the remaining six months of the year? Support your selection with appropriate calculations.

2. Without prejudice to your answer to part 1, assume the optimum price/volume alternatives for the last six months were a selling price of $23 and volume level of 50,000 cases for the regular compound and a selling price of $35 and volume of 35,000 cases for the heavy-duty compound.

a. Should Stac Industries consider closing down its operations for the remainder of the year in order to minimize its losses? Support your answer with appropriate calculations.

b. Identify and discuss the qualitative factors which should be considered in deciding whether the Clinton Plant should be closed down during the last six months of the year.

13—26. *Decision alternatives.* (CMA adopted) Auer Company had received an order for a piece of special machinery from Jay Company. Just as Auer Company completed the machine, Jay Company declared bankruptcy and defaulted on the order. Auer's manufacturing manager identified the costs already incurred in the production of the special machinery for Jay as follows:

Direct materials used		$16,600
Direct labor incurred		21,400
Overhead applied:		
Manufacturing.		
Variable	$10,700	
Fixed	5,350	16,050
Fixed selling and administrative		5,405
Total cost		$59,455

Another company, Kaytell Corp., would be interested in buying the special machinery if it were reworked to Kaytell's specifications. Auer has offered to sell the reworked special machinery to Kaytell as a special order for a net price of $68,400. Kaytell has agreed to pay the net price when it takes delivery. The additional identifiable costs to rework the machinery to Kaytell's specifications are as follows:

Direct materials	$ 6,200
Direct labor	4,200
	$10,400

A second alternative available to Auer is to convert the special machinery to the standard model. The standard model lists for $62,500. The additional identifiable costs to convert the special machinery to the standard model are:

Direct materials	$ 2,850
Direct labor	3,300
	$ 6,150

A third alternative for the Auer Company is to sell, as a special order, the machine as is (e.g., without modification) for a net price of $52,000. The following additional information is available regarding Auer's operations:

Sales commission rate on sales of standard models is 2%, while on special orders it is 3%. All sales commissions are calculated on net sales price (i.e., list price less cash discount, if any).

Normal credit terms for sales of standard models are 2/10, net/30. Customers take the discounts except in rare instances. Credit terms for special orders are negotiated with the customer and usually do *not* include a discount.

The application rates for manufacturing overhead and the fixed selling and administrative costs are as follows:

Manufacturing:
  Variable   50% of direct labor cost
  Fixed   25% of direct labor cost
Selling and administrative:
  Fixed   10% of the total of direct material,
                    direct labor, and manufacturing
                    overhead costs

Auer normally sells a sufficient number of standard models to allow it to operate at a volume in excess of the break-even point.

REQUIRED:
1. Determine the dollar contribution margin that each of the three alternatives will add to the Auer Company's before-tax profits.
2. If Kaytell makes Auer a counteroffer, what is the lowest price Auer should accept for the reworked machinery from Kaytell? Explain your answer.
3. Discuss the influence fixed factory overhead cost should have on the sales prices quoted by Auer for special orders when:
   a. A firm is operating at or below the break-even point.
   b. A firm's special orders constitute efficient utilization of unused capacity above the break-even volume.

13—27. *Alternative payment methods.*   (CMA adapted) Weldon's Bike Shop has been in business for five years. The shop buys medium- to high-quality bicycles and related bike accessories for resale to customers. The Bike Shop has shown profits for the past four years. The projected results for the current year are presented below.

WELDON'S BIKE SHOP
Projected Statement of Income
for the Year Ended December 31
(000 omitted)

	DOLLARS	PERCENT
Sales revenues	$300	100%
Cost of goods sold	180	60
Gross margin	$120	40%
Operating expenses:		
Sales commissions	$ 15	4%
Fixed expenses:		
Advertising	9	3
Salaries	21	7
Rent	18	6
General administration	12	4
Total operating expenses	$ 75	25%
Net income before taxes	$ 45	15%
Income taxes (40%)	18	6
Net income	$ 27	9%

The sales figure results from strict cash sales only. No personal checks are accepted, nor are credit or credit-card sales made. Ann Weldon, the owner, is now considering accepting the following modes of payment in addition to strict cash:

Personal checks only.
Bank credit cards only.
Both personal checks and bank credit cards.

Ann believes that sales will increase if she accepts other modes of payment in addition to strict cash. She also realizes that some cash customers will change to a different mode of payment if alternatives are available. The schedule below presents her estimates of how sales will increase under each of the proposed three modes of payment and how total sales will be collected under each:

ALTERNATIVES	PERCENTAGE INCREASE IN SALES	PERCENTAGE OF TOTAL SALES PAID BY		
		Cash	Check	Credit Card
Payment by check	10%	60%	40%	—
Payment by bank credit card	20%	50%	—	50%
Payment by check and bank credit card	25%	20%	40%	40%

If checks are accepted as a mode of payment, approximately 10% of all check sales can be expected to be returned for nonsufficient funds (NSF). One-half of the NSF checks (5% of total sales) would be collectible through a collection agency at a cost of 25% of the amount collected; the remaining NSF checks would never be collected. In addition, the merchandise paid for by NSF checks would not be recovered. Bank credit-card sales can be deposited daily as if they were cash. However, the bank charges a 4% discount fee when credit-card sales are deposited. The behavior patterns of the existing costs and expenses are expected to be unchanged regardless of the mode of payment.

REQUIRED: Prepare an analysis which shows the effect each of the proposed modes of payment being considered by Weldon's Bike Shop would have on the shop's net income. Based upon your analysis, identify and explain whether Weldon's Bike Shop should accept any of the proposed modes of payment in addition to strict cash; if so, identify the mode which should be selected.

13—28. *Special order.* Nubo Manufacturing, Inc., is presently operating at 50% of practical capacity, producing about 50,000 units annually of a patented electronic component. Nubo recently received an offer from a company in Yokohama, Japan, to purchase 30,000 components at $6 per unit, FOB Nubo's plant. Nubo has not previously sold components in Japan. Budgeted production costs for 50,000 and 80,000 units of output follow:

Units	50,000	80,000
Costs:		
Direct material	$ 75,000	$120,000
Direct labor	75,000	120,000
Factory overhead	200,000	260,000
Total costs	$350,000	$500,000
Costs per unit	$7.00	$6.25

The sales manager thinks the order should be accepted, even if it results in a loss, because he feels the sales may build up future markets. The production manager does not wish to have the order accepted, primarily because the order would show a loss of $.25 per unit when computed on the new average unit cost. The treasurer has made a quick computation indicating that accepting the order will actually increase gross margin.

REQUIRED: **1.** Explain what apparently caused the drop in cost from $7 per unit to $6.25 per unit when budgeted production increased from 50,000 to 80,000 units. Show supporting computations. Estimate the variable component of factory overhead.

2. a. Explain whether either the production manager or the treasurer or both are correct in their reasoning.

b. Explain why the conclusions of the production manager and the treasurer differ.

3. Explain why each of the following may affect the decision to accept or reject the special order.

a. The likelihood of repeat sales and/or sales to be made at $6 per unit.

b. Whether the sales are made to customers operating in two separate, isolated markets or to customers competing in the same market.

13—29. In-Touch, Inc., produces telephones in various styles. The president of the company, Catherine Phillips, believes that one of the product lines—black dial telephones—is no longer producing a profit. The company's accounting staff has assembled the following information for Ms. Phillips:

IN-TOUCH, INC.
Income Statement for the Year Ended 12/31

Sales	$6,000,000
Cost of goods manufactured and sold	$2,300,000
Selling expenses	947,000
Administrative expenses	1,334,000
Total expenses	$4,581,00
Income before taxes	$1,419,000
Taxes @ 46%	652,740
Net income	$ 766,260

Additional information:

1. Ten percent of the revenues are accounted for by sales of black dial telephones. Unit sales amounted to 40,000 phones.
2. Fifteen percent of the cost of goods manufactured and sold represents the cost of black dial telephones. Of this amount 50% is variable and 50% is fixed. Of the fixed manufacturing overhead, $70,000 in cash expenditures could be eliminated if the company quit manufacturing black dial telephones. All the variable costs would be eliminated.
3. For each phone sold, the company spends $.50 for advertising and pays a sales commission of 10% of the selling price. These are the only variable selling expenses. None of the fixed selling expenses could be avoided by no longer making and selling the black dial telephone. Fixed selling expenses are allocated to product lines on the basis of sales revenues. One half of the company's selling expenses are fixed.
4. Administrative expenses are all fixed and are allocated to product lines on the basis of employees associated with each. The black dial telephone line has 12% of all employees associated with its activities. Allocated administrative expenses would have to be absorbed by other parts of the organization if the black dial phone product line were discontinued.

REQUIRED:

1. Prepare an income statement which shows income before taxes for the black dial telephone product line based on the data provided.
2. Calculate the cash consequences of dropping the black telephone line.
3. On the basis of your analysis in parts 1 and 2, make a recommendation to Ms. Phillips concerning the elimination of the black dial telephone product line.
4. What factors which have not been quantitified should be considered in deciding whether the line should be discontinued?

13—30. *Special order and other alternatives.* The Faculty Center at Southwestern University serves a special International Dinner one night each month which features a menu from a different country. The Center has been approached by the Senior Citizens Club, which would like to make the dinners available to its members. The accountant at the Faculty Center has assembled the following data with regard to the International Dinners:

Charge per person	$ 12.50
Food cost per person	$ 5.00
Waiters (see additional information)	
Linen, flowers, special favors, and other supplies per table, 4 persons each table	$ 10.00 per table
Allocated costs:	
Salaries	$4,000
Utilities	1,200
Depreciation	3,000
Other	2,400

Additional information:

1. Waiters are hired especially for these dinners at extra costs to the Faculty Center, and each is paid $50 for the evening. The Center maintains a ratio of 1 waiter to 16 people (or 1 waiter to 4 tables).

2. All the allocated costs will continue whether or not International Dinners are held and will not increase if the Senior Citizens patronize the dinners.

3. Linen and other supply costs shown above would not be incurred if the International Dinners were not held.

REQUIRED:

1. Assume that regular attendance at International Dinners averages 160 people. What do these dinners contribute to the Center's profits?

2. If the Senior Citizens can guarantee attendance of 12 tables or 48 of their members at each dinner, to give the Center a contribution margin of $3 per person, what price will the Center have to charge the Seniors? (Round to the nearest half-dollar.)

3. Some members have suggested that on International Dinner evenings an orchestra should be available. Assume that the cost of hiring a small orchestra for an evening is $500 and that attendance by members would increase to 208. To maintain the contribution you calculated in part 1, what price increase, if any, would be required? Because of the increased attendance by members, the Senior Citizens could not be accommodated. (Round to the nearest half-dollar).

chapter fourteen

CAPITAL BUDGETING PRELIMINARIES:

Present-Value Concepts and Income Tax Implications of Investment Decisions

OBJECTIVES

After you have completed this chapter, you should be able to answer the following questions:

- What is meant by "present value"?
- How is the concept of present value relevant to investment decisions?
- What is meant by the term "present value of an annuity"?
- Why is depreciation considered a "tax shield"?
- How does Accelerated Cost Recovery System depreciation, which is required for tax purposes, work?
- What is an investment tax credit and how does it differ from a tax-deductible expense?
- What impact does an investment tax credit have on investment decisions?
- How may cash outflows for taxes be affected by the disposal or exchange of a depreciable asset?

What distinguishes short-term nonroutine decisions from long-term non-routine decisions is that, for the latter, selecting the optimal alternative requires the analysis of cash flows for multiple future periods. For many long-term decisions, not only must the cash costs and revenues of alternatives be considered but they must be looked at in the context of the required investment. The term *capital budgeting* is used to describe these nonroutine decisions which require capital expenditures—investment in capital (long-term) assets.

Before we look at different ways to evaluate proposed capital budgeting projects, we must firmly grasp certain concepts. These include:

1. The meaning of present value.
2. The tax implications of capital investment decisions.

Both of these items are discussed in this chapter as a preliminary to the discussion of capital budgeting decision models in Chapter 15.

THE MEANING OF PRESENT VALUE

Present value is based on a simple idea—money has value. If you have a sum of money, you have the potential for making additional money through investment. That investment may be as simple as putting the sum you have in a savings account and letting it earn interest. Assume that you have $10,000 and you put it in a savings account which pays interest at the rate of 7% per year. At the end of one year your investment will have grown to $10,700. When we look at sums today, assume a certain rate of earnings, and determine how much we will have at some date in the future, we are dealing with future amounts—a context which most of us have no difficulty in understanding.

Present value has a different time orientation. Instead of looking at a sum today and asking to what amount it will accumulate in the future, given a defined rate of return, with present value we are asking the question:

Given a specified rate of return, what is the equivalent amount today of some amount which is payable or receivable in the future?

To clarify, suppose that someone asked you, "Would you prefer to have $10,000 today or $10,000 one year from today?" Your answer would obviously be "today," because $10,000 today will be worth more than $10,000 one year from now, assuming that you invest it at some rate of return. Ten thousand dollars today and $10,000 one year from today are not equivalent sums.

The pertinent question is: "What could I accept today and be as well off as if I received $10,000 one year from today?" Think about this question. Should your answer be greater or smaller than $10,000? Remembering that money has value, the answer is a sum less than $10,000. What the sum is depends on the assumed rate at which you think you could invest the money received.

Let's suppose that you believe you could invest any funds received at a rate of 10% per year. Now we are ready to answer the question: "What sum today is equivalent to $10,000 received one year in the future?"

Look at Table A in the appendix to this chapter. Table A gives the present value of $1 received at some time in the future. We are interested in a 10% rate and one year into the future. Reading the value for one period at 10%, you should see .909. This tells us that if we had $.909 today and invested it at 10%, we would have $1 one year in the future:

Principal	$.909
Interest: $.909 × 10%	.09
Sum one year from today	$.999

Our answer varies from $1 only because the present-value table is carried to three decimal places. Now we can answer the question about the present value of $10,000. The sum that we would need to have in hand today and invest at a 10% rate to be as well off as if we received $10,000 one year in the future is $9,090. If the present value of $1 is $.909, the present value of $10,000 of those dollars must be $9,090. In other words, we took the value in the table and multiplied it by the relevant number of dollars. To prove our answer we can develop this computation:

Received today	$9,090
One year's interest at 10%, $9,090 × 10%	909
Amount one year from today	$9,999

Again our sum differs from $10,000 simply because of rounding to three decimals in the present-value table.

Our analysis has shown that $9,090 invested today at 10% and $10,000 receivable one year from today are equivalent sums. If we are offered either alternative, we should be indifferent between the two, based on an annual earning rate of 10%.

PRESENT VALUE OF AN AMOUNT AND PRESENT VALUE OF AN ANNUITY

In capital budgeting we will be looking at single sums (amounts) which are payable or receivable in the future and sometimes at series of payments which are payable or receivable in the future. Table A (in the appendix to this chapter), the present value of $1, is designed for single sums. Table

B, the present value of an annuity of $1, is designed for an annuity. An *annuity* means equal sums of money equally spaced over time.

To illustrate the relationship between Tables A and B, let's consider an investment which will pay us $5,000 one year from today and $5,000 two years from today. The question we want to answer is, what can we afford to pay for those returns if we want to earn a return of 10%? We can answer our question by using Table A as follows:

$5,000 × present value of $1 for 1 year = $5,000 × .909	$4,545
$5,000 × present value of $1 for 2 years = $5,000 × .826	4,130
Present value of the two cash flows	$8,675

We can pay $8,675 today for an investment which will return $5,000 at the end of the next two years. This investment will give us our desired 10% rate of return. Graphically, the discounting of future cash flows to the present can be shown as follows:

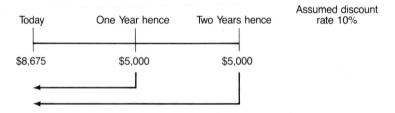

Since our investment decision deals with two equal sums of money equally spaced in time, we can, rather than using Table A and discounting each payment individually, use Table B directly:

$5,000 × present value of an annuity of $1 at 10% for 2 periods $8,680
= $5,000 × 1.736

Our two answers differ simply because of rounding errors.

Note that if the anticipated returns from our investment were unequal amounts or the returns were not equally spaced over time, we could not use Table B, which is based on the assumption of equal payments equally spaced. For example, if our $10,000 return were timed to give cash flows of $4,000 at the end of year 1 and $6,000 at the end of year 2, we would have to use the present value of $1 (Table A) and discount each anticipated cash receipt individually.

To test your understanding of present value and the basic concept that money has time value, answer this question: If you were offered two investment alternatives, one which paid $5,000 at the end of each of the next two years and one which paid $4,000 at the end of year 1 and $6,000 at the end of year 2, assuming the same 10% desired rate of return, which would you prefer and why?

If your answer was the one which paid $5,000 at the end of each of the two years, you would be correct. With this alternative you would have an extra $1,000 more at the end of year 1 to invest than you would with the second alternative.

We can compare the present values of the two alternatives as follows:

Alternative 1: Make an investment which pays $5,000 at the end of each of the next two years:

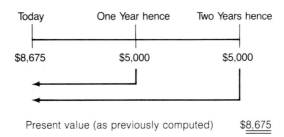

Present value (as previously computed)   <u>$8,675</u>

Alternative 2: Make an investment which pays $4,000 at the end of year 1 and $6,000 at the end of year 2:

Present value of $4,000 @ 10% for 1 period
    = $4,000 × .909 (from Table A) $3,636
Present value of $6,000 @ 10% for 2 periods
    = $6,000 × .826 (from Table A)   <u>4,956</u>
Present value   <u>$8,592</u>

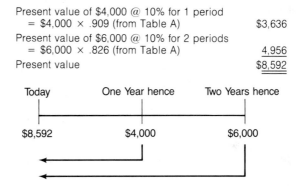

What our calculations tell us is that the further the cash flow from our investment is into the future, the smaller the present value—that is, the smaller is the sum required today which would represent an equivalent amount.

ILLUSTRATIONS USING PRESENT-VALUE CONCEPTS

To further clarify the meaning of present value and the use of present-value tables, a series of examples is provided below.

Examples 1: Lump Sum Versus Future Payments

A nonprofit organization needs to acquire a piece of equipment. This equipment has a three-year life and at the end of that period will have to be discarded as junk. (We use a nonprofit organization in this example to avoid the effects of taxes on the decision—an issue which is considered later in the chapter.) There are two ways the company can acquire the equipment: buy it with a $10,000 cash payment today or lease it for three years with a lease payment of $4,000 at the end of each year. Should the organization buy the equipment or lease it?

If we ignore the time value of money, the analysis looks like this:

Buy	$10,000
Lease: $4,000 × 3 years	12,000
Advantage of buying	$ 2,000

This presentation ignores the facts that money has time value and that, if the organization can defer paying out all or part of the $10,000, it will have this money to use. To make the alternatives comparable we must bring all cash flows to the same point in time. In other words, we must look at the present value of the three lease payments relative to the immediate $10,000 purchase price.

Let's assume that the organization believes a 12% interest (discount) rate is appropriate. The new analysis would appear as follows:

Buy	$10,000
Lease: Present value of an annuity of $4,000 for 3 periods @ 12% = $4,000 × 2.402 (from Table B)	9,608
Advantage of leasing	$ 392

Consider what would happen if the organization used an 8% discount rate rather than a 12% rate:

Buy	$10,000
Lease: Present value of an annuity of $4,000 for 3 periods @ 8% = $4,000 × 2.577 (from Table B)	10,308
Advantage of buying	$ 308

Previously we pointed out that the further the sum is into the future, the smaller its present value. Now you should be aware that the higher the assumed interest rate, the smaller the present value. This may seem confusing, but think about it for a moment. The higher the rate you assume you can earn if you had cash in hand immediately, the smaller the amount must be in order to be equivalent to a sum receivable in the future. The selection of an appropriate discount rate is discussed later in the chapter.

Example 2: Annuities with Immediate Cash Flows

In Example 1 we assumed that the first lease payment was due at the end of Year 1. A more realistic assumption would probably be that lease payments are due at the beginning of each year. Graphically the two assumptions about lease payment would appear as follows:

Assumption 1: Lease payments are due at the end of each of the next three years.

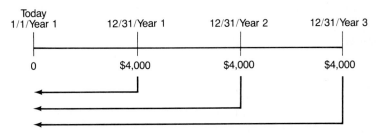

Assumption 2: Lease payments are due at the beginning of each of the three years.

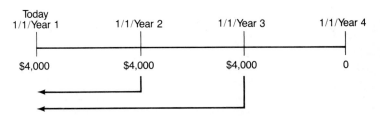

When Assumption 1 was adopted, we could use Table B directly, because it is based on the assumption of cash flows at the end of the period. If instead we wanted to use Assumption 2, under which an immediate payment of one of the installments is made, we would have to modify the way in which we use Table B as follows:

The first payment is made immediately, so there is no reason to discount it	$4,000
The second payment is made one year into the future and the third payment two years into the future. These payments can be discounted by using the factor from Table B for two periods @ 12%: $4,000 × 1.69	6,760
Present value of alternative 2—payments at the beginning of each of the three years	$10,760

We can generalize regarding the use of the present-value-of-an-annuity table when a cash flow is immediate:

Add "1" to the present-value factor to recognize that the payment which is immediate is already stated in present-value terms	1.000
To discount additional cash flow, use the Table B value for one less than the number of periods over which the cash flow will be accumulated. (In our example, there were three cash flows, so we used the table value for two periods at a 12% rate)	1.690
Sum the two amounts to find the discount factor. Present-value factor to be used in discounting an annuity of three cash flows, the first of which is an immediate cash flow	2.690

Multiplying this factor by the size of the payments, we find the same present value which we computed previously:

$$\$4{,}000 \times 2.690 = \underline{\$10{,}760}$$

Example 3: Salvage Value

Let's change our example just a little and assume that the immediate purchase price is still $10,000 versus three payments at the end of each of the next three years of $4,000 each. However, let us add another piece of data: the equipment, if purchased, will have a resale value (salvage value) at the end of Year 3 of $800.

Cash flows if the purchase is made can be shown graphically as follows:

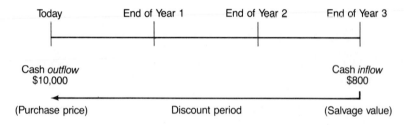

In the first example, we calculated the present value of the lease payments:

$$\$4{,}000 \times \text{present value of annuity @ 12\% for} \qquad \underline{\$9{,}608}$$
$$\text{3 periods} = \$4{,}000 \times 2.402$$

With the buy alternative we have a future cash inflow to discount and offset against the immediate cash outlay of $10,000

Purchase price today	$10,000
Less: Cash anticipated from resale at end of 3 years discounted to the present: $800 × present value of $1 for 3 periods @ 12% = $800 × .712 (Table A)	570
Net present value of purchasing	$ 9,430
Net present value of leasing	9,608
Advantage of purchasing	$ 178

Example 4: Finding the Future Cash Flows

A tax-exempt organization needs a piece of equipment which costs $20,000. It is short on cash and would like to offer the vendor of the equipment an alternative pay plan which would extend over the next four years. In other words, the tax-exempt organization would like to acquire the equipment on the installment plan. It is willing to pay an interest rate of 10% for the privilege of deferring cash payments.

The piece of equipment has an expected life of four years and no salvage value. What is the size of the installments which the organization should offer to make to the vendor, assuming such payments come at the end of each of the next four years?

In the other examples, we had future cash flows and had to discount them back to the present:

$$\text{Cash flows} \times \text{present-value factor} = \text{present value}$$

In this example, we know the present value—the immediate purchase price. We know the period and the interest rate, so we can find the present-value factor. Then we can find the cash flows. The calculation would have to be done as follows:

$$\frac{\text{present value}}{\text{present-value factor}} = \text{cash flows}$$

$$\frac{\$20,000}{\substack{\text{present value of an annuity} \\ \text{for 4 periods @ } 10\% = 3.170}} = \$6,309 \text{ (rounded)}$$

The organization would have to offer the vendor four payments of $6,309.

CHOOSING AN APPROPRIATE DISCOUNT RATE

In doing analysis using present-value concepts, we must have a discount (interest) rate to use to discount future payments back to the present time. Financial theory states that the minimum discount rate should generally be the company's cost of capital—that is, a combination of the cost of debt capital and the cost of capital provided by owners. The combined cost of capital is found by weighting each component part—debt and owners' equity—by the proportion of each in the capital structure.

To illustrate, let's assume that a company had the following capital structure:

	AMOUNT	COST BEFORE TAXES
Debt	$20,000,000	14%
Equity	80,000,000	15%

Since interest paid on debt is generally tax deductible, the cost before taxes will have to be adjusted to an after-tax cost before the cost of capital is calculated. Assuming a 50% tax rate, the cost of debt is 7%. Now we can calculate the weighted average cost of capital, which is the minimum return the company given in our illustration should earn on its investments:

	AFTER-TAX COST	×	WEIGHT—PERCENT OF CAPITAL STRUCTURE	=	WEIGHTED COST
Debt	7% ×		$\left(\dfrac{\$20,000,000}{\$100,000,000} = 20\% \right)$	=	1.4%
Equity	15% ×		$\left(\dfrac{\$80,000,000}{\$100,000,000} = 80\% \right)$	=	12.0%
Weighted average cost of capital					13.4%

This company should invest only in projects which will return more than 13.4%.

While the cost of debt capital can usually be estimated realistically, the cost of equity capital is difficult to estimate. This subject is usually examined in detail in finance texts.

Practically, many companies set a target rate of return, and this is used as the discount rate or as the rate with which project returns are compared in capital budgeting applications. A company should know its cost of capital and set the target rate for capital projects at not less than that cost of capital.

SUMMARY OF PRESENT-VALUE ANALYSIS

Present value involves the discounting of future inflows or outflows of cash to the present time. The objective is to state future cash flows in terms so that they can be compared with cash flows today. Present-value analysis requires knowledge of three things:

1. The amount(s) of cash flows.
2. The timing of cash flows.
3. A discount rate.

The further in the future a cash flow is, the smaller its present value will be. The higher the discount rate used, the smaller the present value of the amount being discounted will be.

TAX ASPECTS OF DECISION MAKING

In decision making, both short- and long-run, cash flows rather than accounting amounts based on accrual concepts are the relevant numbers. Because taxes have an effect on cash flows, we need to understand some of the major ways in which cash flows are affected by the tax structure. While state taxes are also relevant to cash flows, in this text we shall deal only with the impact of the federal income tax regulations. Specifically, we shall consider the relationship of (1) depreciation, (2) the investment

tax credit, and (3) asset disposal and retirement to cash flows for an organization which is subject to federal income taxes.

Depreciation as a Tax Shield

As you are aware, depreciation is a noncash expense; that is, it does not represent a cash outflow in the period in which it is recorded. Recall the way depreciation is recorded by a general journal entry:

Depreciation	XXXX	
Accumulated Depreciation		XXXX

When this expense is put on the books, there is no related cash outflow.

If only cash flows are relevant in decision making, why then do we need to concern ourselves with depreciation? If we lived in a tax-free environment or if we were operating a tax-exempt organization, depreciation would be totally irrelevant to our decision-making process, because there is no cash flow involved.

However, for federal income tax purposes, depreciation is an expense which can be deducted in calculating taxable income. Thus, it affects cash flows because it decreases the cash flows required for tax purposes.

To illustrate why depreciation is relevant in calculating cash flows, consider the income statement for Mansfield Associates, a firm which does site-preparation work using heavy equipment such as bulldozers and payloaders:

Revenues		$9,750,000
Operating expenses:		
Salaries	$2,000,000	
Supplies	1,000,000	
Depreciation	4,000,000	
Utilities	500,000	
Insurance	800,000	
Other	650,000	8,950,000
Income before taxes		$ 800,000
Taxes @ 48%		384,000
Net income		$ 416,000

We will assume that there are no differences between the amounts reported above and those reported for tax-paying purposes. Just how much is the $4,000,000 of depreciation worth in terms of tax savings? To answer this question, let's assume for a moment that depreciation is not a tax-deductible expense and recompute Mansfield Associates' income before taxes and the related taxes:

Revenues	$9,750,000
Operating expenses less depreciation	
(8,950,000 − $4,000,000)	4,950,000
Income before taxes	$4,800,000
Taxes @ 48%	2,304,000
Net income	$2,496,000

Consider the difference in cash flows for taxes which would be required: $2,304,000 − $384,000 (when depreciation was deducted) = $1,920,000. Because depreciation is a tax-deductible expense, it provides Mansfield Associates with what is often termed a *tax shield*. That is, it shelters part of Mansfield's earnings from a tax liability. The amount of the tax shield of an item such as depreciation can be found by taking the amount and multiplying it by the tax rate. Thus we can find the tax savings inherent in the depreciation deduction without having to prepare another income statement as follows:

$4,000,000 depreciation × .48 tax rate = $1,920,000

What this means is that while depreciation itself has no impact on cash flows, we must consider it in computing one of our cash flows—that required for taxes. Assuming that the other items listed on Mansfield Associates' income statement do not differ significantly from what they would be on a strictly cash basis, Mansfield Associates' cash flows are estimated as follows:

Cash inflows from revenues		$9,750,000
Cash outflows for expenses:		
Salaries	$2,000,000	
Supplies	1,000,000	
Utilities	500,000	
Insurance	800,000	
Other	650,000	
Federal income taxes	384,000	5,334,000
Cash flow from operations		$4,416,000

BOOK DEPRECIATION VERSUS DEPRECIATION FOR TAX PURPOSES

As you will recall from financial accounting, companies may elect to use one depreciation method in reporting to shareholders (for financial accounting or book purposes) and another method in computing taxable income. The method used for calculating depreciation for book purposes has no relevance to decision making. It is the depreciation method used for tax purposes which affects taxes payable and hence cash flows of the organization.

Depreciation Methods for Tax Purposes

Prior to 1981, companies could use a number of depreciation methods in computing taxable income. These included double-declining-balance depreciation, sum-of-the-years'-digits depreciation, and straight-line depreciation based on an asset's estimated useful life. With the passage of the

Economic Recovery Tax Act (ETRA) of 1981, the methods available for depreciating most assets were limited to straight-line depreciation and depreciation calculated according to an accelerated cost recovery system (ACRS) which eliminates the use of the useful life as the period over which depreciation can be recognized. Instead, under ACRS, recovery periods which are ordinarily shorter than the existing useful life of an asset are used in computing tax-deductible depreciation.

ACRS Depreciation recognizes the following classes of assets and the related period over which depreciation should take place:

MAJOR TYPES OF PROPERTY	LENGTH OF THE DEPRECIATION PERIOD
Autos, light-trucks, equipment used in connection with research and experimentation	3 years
Machinery, equipment, furniture and fixtures, single-purpose agricultural structures and petroleum storage facilities not included in the three-year category described above	5 years
Public utility property which under old tax laws had an asset depreciation range (ADR) midpoint life greater than 18 but not greater than 25 years, railroad tank cars, and real property with an ADR midpoint life of 12.5 years or less	10 years
Public utility property not included in the 10-year category described above and real property with an ADR life of more than 12.5 years	15 years

Depreciation rates on these types of property are specified by the tax laws and are as follows:

YEARS OF RECOVERY	DEPRECIATION LIFE RECOVERY PERIOD			
	3-year	5-year	10-year	15-year
1	25%	15%	8%	5%
2	38	22	14	10
3	37	21	12	9
4	—	21	10	8
5	—	21	10	7
6	—	—	10	7
7	—	—	9	6
8	—	—	9	6
9	—	—	9	6
10	—	—	9	6
11	—	—	—	6
12	—	—	—	6
13	—	—	—	6
14	—	—	—	6
15	—	—	—	6
	100	100	100	100

Note that in reports to shareholders, depreciation will continue to be based on the useful life of the asset. In addition, for tax purposes *the first-year rate shown in the table is used regardless of when, in the year, the asset was acquired.* A three-year asset which was acquired January 1 will be depreciated 25%; a three-year asset acquired October 31 will be depreciated 25%. Finally, *in applying ACRS depreciation rates, any anticipated salvage value is ignored.*

Illustration of Effects of ACRS Depreciation on Cash Flows

Assume that a company is considering the purchase of a machine costing $100,000, for which the following data are relevant:

Estimated annual cash savings in labor cost with machine	$8,000(Net of taxes)
Estimated annual utility and other cash savings with machine	3,000(Net of taxes)
Life for tax purposes based on ACRS depreciation	5 years
Estimated salvage value	0
Company's tax rate	48%

The annual cash flows relevant to the acquisition of this machine would be as follows:

YEAR	SAVINGS IN CASH OPERATING COSTS (NET OF TAXES)	TAX SAVINGS PROVIDED BY DEPRECIATION SHIELD	TOTAL CASH FLOWS
1	$11,000	$100,000 × 15%[a] × 48% = $7,200	$18,200
2	$11,000	$100,000 × 22%[a] × 48% = $10,560	$21,560
3	$11,000	$100,000 × 21%[a] × 48% = $10,080	$21,080
4	$11,000	$100,000 × 21%[a] × 48% = $10,080	$21,080
5	$11,000	$100,000 × 21%[a] × 48% = $10,080	$21,080

[a] Rates as provided by the ACRS tax tables.

Because of the changing percentage rates in the ACRS depreciation tables, cash flows for years when the rates change must be calculated individually. Although we shall defer the actual calculation to a subsequent chapter, in deciding whether or not the company should buy the machine described above, we would apply the concept of present value and discount the cash flows. They are not of equal value, even though those for years 3–5 are of equal amounts, because they are not all receivable at the same time. The further into the future a cash flow is, the smaller is its present value.

THE INVESTMENT TAX CREDIT

To encourage companies to invest in productive assets, the United States Congress has from time to time legislated an investment tax credit. A tax credit is just what the name implies. *Taxes payable are calculated and then any tax credits are subtracted from these taxes to come up with the actual amount which must be paid.* To illustrate, assume that a company had accumulated the following data:

Taxable revenues	$1,000,000
Tax-deductible expenses	750,000
Investments eligible for investment tax credit	50,000
Investment tax credit rate	10%
Tax rate	50%

The amount of taxes which this company would actually have to pay is $120,000, calculated as follows:

Revenues		$1,000,000
Expenses		750,000
Taxable income		250,000
Taxes payable ($250,000 × 50%)	$125,000	
Less: Investment tax credit ($50,000 × 10%)	5,000	120,000
Net income		$ 130,000

If there were no investment in items eligible for the investment tax credit or if there had been no provision in the tax laws for an investment credit, the company's taxes would have been $5,000 higher.

Sometimes there is confusion as to a tax credit versus a tax-deductible expense. The latter is an amount which is deducted from taxable revenues to determine how much income is subject to taxes. Depreciation is an example of a tax-deductible expense. A tax-deductible expense, as we saw earlier, results in a savings in taxes equal to the amount of the expense times the tax rate. In contrast, with a tax credit, taxable income is calculated and the tax rate is applied to this amount. After the taxes payable have been calculated, the credit is offset directly against this amount. A tax credit reduces taxes by the full amount of the credit.

Currently, qualified assets—generally assets used by businesses for productive purposes—are eligible for an investment tax credit. For property which has a recovery period of three years using ACRS depreciation, the amount of the investment tax credit is 6%. For qualified assets with longer recovery periods, the amount of the tax credit is 10%.

Under the Tax Equity and Fiscal Responsibility Act of 1982 (TEFRA) taxpayers must reduce the cost recovery (depreciable) basis of fixed-asset acquisitions after December 31, 1982, by one-half of the investment tax credit allowable. For assets acquired prior to that date, the investment tax credit did not reduce the depreciable basis of the fixed asset. To illustrate, assume the following data:

	ASSET A	ASSET B
Acquisition date	1/1/82	1/1/83
ACRS recovery period	5 years	5 years
Cost	$100,000	$100,000
Investment tax credit rate	10%	10%

For Asset A taxes payable for 1982 would be reduced by $10,000. In calculating taxable income, the full $100,000 of cost would be deductible as depreciation over the 5-year period at the rate shown in the ACRS table.

In contrast, for Asset B, while the taxable income for 1983 would be reduced by the full $10,000 investment tax credit, only $95,000 ($100,000 cost minus half of $10,000 investment tax credit) of depreciation could be recognized for tax purposes over the 5-year recovery period.

In addition, the amount of investment tax credit that can be used to reduce income taxes payable is limited to $25,000 plus 85% of the remaining federal income taxes payable. Thus if a company had taxes payable of $100,000, the total amount of investment tax credit they could take in that year would be:

$$\$25,000 + .85\ (\$100,000 - \$25,000) = \underline{\$88,750}$$

Illustration of the Effects of the Investment Tax Credit on Cash Flows

In investment decisions, the investment tax credit will have an impact on cash flows through an immediate reduction of taxes payable in the year in which assets eligible for the investment tax credit are acquired. In addition, it will have an impact on cash flows over the cost recovery period of the asset for tax purposes, because the amount of cost which can be written off as depreciation for tax purposes is reduced by half of the investment tax credit.

To clarify the impact of the investment tax credit on cash flows assume the following information:

Cost of the investment	$200,000
Cost recovery period for tax purposes	5 years
Investment tax credit percent	10%
Cash revenues generated by the investment less cash expenses caused by the investment for Years 1–5	$100,000
Tax rate	50%

A table of cash flows for this investment for its five-year life (with outflows being indicated by parentheses) is given in Illustration 14-1.

ILLUSTRATION 14-1

Impact of the Investment Tax Credit on Cash Flows

	YEAR 1	YEAR 2	YEAR 3	YEAR 4	YEAR 5
Calculation of Taxable Income					
Revenues less expenses other than depreciation	$100,000	$100,000	$100,000	$100,000	$100,000
Tax depreciation (rates are from the ACRS table on p. 593)[a]	28,500	41,800	39,900	39,900	39,900
Taxable income	$ 71,500	$ 58,200	$ 60,100	$ 60,100	$ 60,100
Cash Flows					
Taxes payable @ 50% of taxable income	($ 35,750)	($ 29,100)	($ 30,050)	($ 30,050)	($ 30,050)
Less: Investment tax credit ($200,000 × 10%)	20,000	—	—	—	—
Net cash outflow for taxes	($ 15,750)	($ 29,100)	($ 30,050)	($ 30,050)	($ 30,050)
Cash inflow: cash revenues less cash expenses	100,000	100,000	100,000	100,000	100,000
Net cash flows from investment	$ 84,250	$ 70,900	$ 69,950	$ 69,950	$ 69,950

[a] Depreciable base = $200,000 − ½ ($200,000 × 10%) = $190,000.
Year 1: $190,000 × 15% = $28,500.
Year 2: $190,000 × 22% = $41,800.
Years 3, 4, 5: $190,000 × 21% = $39,900.

How the company accounts for the investment tax credit for book purposes or what method of depreciation it chooses for book purposes is irrelevant to the cash flows. The entire impact of the investment tax credit is felt on cash flows in Year 1, the year in which the qualified investment was made. Note the reduction in taxes payable in Year 1 as shown in Illustration 14-1. In addition, note that the total amount of depreciation which can be written off for tax purposes and thus has an impact on cash flows is $190,000—the cost of the investment reduced by half the investment tax credit.

TAX IMPACT OF ASSET RETIREMENT OR EXCHANGE

When an asset has lost utility for an organization, it may be sold, abandoned, or exchanged for another asset. Any of these actions may have a tax impact and hence influence cash flows from the investment in the asset. A comprehensive treatment of the many outcomes of ceasing to use an asset is beyond the scope of this text; however, a summary description is given below.

If an asset is sold, the undepreciated basis (book value *for tax purposes*) is compared with the proceeds of the sale, and a gain or loss is determined. For example, if an asset had an undepreciated basis of $10,000 for tax purposes and was sold for $12,000, a gain of $2,000 would result. Such gains will be treated for tax purposes in one of two ways: (1) recognized as ordinary income or (2) recognized as a capital gain. If a gain is classified as "ordinary," this means that it is treated as any other taxable revenue. No special tax rates apply.

To illustrate, if the $2,000 gain previously described were an ordinary gain, it would increase the company's tax payments by $2,000 × tax rate and its net-of-tax cash inflow by $2,000 × (one − tax rate).

On the other hand, if a gain on sale of an asset qualifies for capital gains treatments, this means that the amount received for the asset is taxed at a rate which currently would not exceed 28%. Thus a $2,000 gain would cost the company only $560 in taxes and would result in net cash flows of $1,440.

An ordinary loss results if an asset is sold for less than its undepreciated basis or is abandoned before its cost is fully written off for tax purposes. For example, if the asset which had an undepreciated basis of $10,000 were sold for $8,000, a $2,000 tax-deductible loss would result. Since the loss is deemed "ordinary," its effect will be to reduce taxes by $2,000 × tax rate.

If one asset is exchanged for another of a similar nature, under the tax laws a "like-kind exchange" may have taken place. If so, the undepreciated basis of the old asset is added to the depreciable basis of the new asset. No gain or loss on the exchange is recognized. For example, if the asset described previously which had an undepreciated basis for tax purposes of $10,000 were given along with $100,000 in cash to acquire a new asset of a like-kind, the new asset, for tax purposes, would be recorded on the entity's books at $110,000, and this amount would be written off as depreciation for tax purposes.

SUMMARY OF AFTER-TAX IMPACT OF REVENUES, EXPENSES, AND TAX CREDITS

It is frequently difficult to keep straight the after-tax impacts of revenues, expenses, and tax credits. The following summary should be helpful:

1. The after-tax impact of revenue =

revenue × (1 − tax rate)

Example: A before-tax revenue is $10,000; the tax rate is 46%. What is its after-tax impact on net income? It will increase net income by

$10,000 × (1 − 46%) = $5,400

Looking at it another way, you can see that this is true.

Revenue	$10,000
Tax @ 46%	4,600
Revenue after taxes	$ 5,400

2. The additional taxes caused by a revenue =

revenue × tax rate

Example: Using the information in Example 1, without the $10,000 of revenues, the $4,600 of taxes would not have been incurred.

3. The tax shield provided by a tax-deductible expense =

expense × tax rate

Example: A company had revenues of $10,000 and tax-deductible expenses of $8,000. Its tax rate was 46%. The tax shield provided by those expenses was

$8,000 × 46% = $3,680

This can be proved by the following illustration:

	TAXES WITHOUT EXPENSES	TAXES WITH EXPENSES
Revenues	$10,000	$10,000
Expenses	0	8,000
Taxable income	$10,000	$ 2,000
Taxes @ 46%	4,600	920
Net income	$ 5,400	$ 1,080

The tax-deductible expenses caused taxes to be $3,680 less.

4. The after-tax cost of an expense =

$$\text{expense} \times (1 - \text{tax rate})$$

Example: Refer to Example 2 above. Without the tax-deductible $8,000 of expenses, taxes would have been $3,680 more. Thus the after-tax cost is $8,000 − $3,680 = $4,320, or

$$\$8,000 \times (1 - 46\%) = \$4,320$$

5. An investment tax credit's impact on taxes is to reduce taxes by the full amount of the credit and increase net income by the same amount:

$$\text{impact of investment tax credit on income} = \text{tax credit} \times 1$$

Example: A company is entitled to a $500 investment tax credit. Its taxable revenues are $10,000, its tax-deductible expenses $8,000, and the tax rate 46%.

Revenues		$10,000
Expenses		8,000
Taxable income		$ 2,000
Taxes @ 46%	$920	
Less: ITC	500	420
Net income		$ 1,580

chapter highlights

Most decision models used in making capital budgeting decisions are based on the cash flows which an investment will require and generate. Since these cash flows may extend over a number of years, and money has time value, the present value of the cash flows should be calculated. The present value of a future cash flow is the sum which has equivalent value today. Present-value analysis involves the discounting of sums of cash which are receivable or payable in the future so that they may be compared with amounts receivable or payable today.

Federal income taxes reduce cash flows from businesses which are not tax exempt. Depreciation of fixed assets is a tax-deductible expense and should be considered in estimating the cash flows from an investment. Present tax laws specify a recovery period (period over which depreciation for tax purposes is recognized) which is not based on the useful life of an asset. It is the recovery period and depreciation rates specified by the tax laws which are relevant to cash flows rather than the depreciation recorded for bookkeeping purposes.

An investment tax credit is currently available for investments in certain types of productive assets. Since an investment tax credit reduces the cash flows required for taxes, it has an impact on investment decisions. Under existing tax law, for depreciable assets which are currently being acquired, the cost of the asset which can be written off as depreciation for tax purposes is reduced by one-half of the investment tax credit.

When assets are exchanged or disposed of through either sale or abandonment, there may be an impact on cash flows because of the tax treatment of these actions. Gains on disposals of assets may be subject to ordinary tax rates or may be taxed at lower rates if they qualify as capital gains. Losses on disposal are generally tax-deductible. If a "like-kind" asset exchange takes place, the depreciable base of the new asset for tax purposes is increased by the book value of the old asset. This results in higher depreciation charges which can be deducted in computing taxable income and hence a lower cash flow for taxes.

chapter fourteen appendix

Table A, the present value of $1 received at some time in the future, is designed for single sums. Table B, the present value of an annuity of $1, is designed for annuities.

TABLE A
Present Value of $1

YEARS HENCE	1%	2%	4%	6%	8%	10%	12%	14%	15%	16%
1	0.990	0.980	0.962	0.943	0.926	0.909	0.893	0.877	0.870	0.862
2	0.980	0.961	0.925	0.890	0.857	0.826	0.797	0.769	0.756	0.743
3	0.971	0.942	0.889	0.840	0.794	0.751	0.712	0.675	0.658	0.641
4	0.961	0.924	0.855	0.792	0.735	0.683	0.636	0.592	0.572	0.552
5	0.951	0.906	0.822	0.747	0.681	0.621	0.567	0.519	0.497	0.476
6	0.942	0.888	0.790	0.705	0.630	0.564	0.507	0.456	0.432	0.410
7	0.933	0.871	0.760	0.665	0.583	0.513	0.452	0.400	0.376	0.354
8	0.923	0.853	0.731	0.627	0.540	0.467	0.404	0.351	0.327	0.305
9	0.914	0.837	0.703	0.592	0.500	0.424	0.361	0.308	0.284	0.263
10	0.905	0.820	0.676	0.558	0.463	0.386	0.322	0.270	0.247	0.227
11	0.896	0.804	0.650	0.527	0.429	0.350	0.287	0.237	0.215	0.195
12	0.887	0.788	0.625	0.497	0.397	0.319	0.257	0.208	0.187	0.168
13	0.879	0.773	0.601	0.469	0.368	0.290	0.229	0.182	0.163	0.145
14	0.870	0.758	0.577	0.442	0.340	0.263	0.205	0.160	0.141	0.125
15	0.861	0.743	0.555	0.417	0.315	0.239	0.183	0.140	0.123	0.108
16	0.853	0.728	0.534	0.394	0.292	0.218	0.163	0.123	0.107	0.093
17	0.844	0.714	0.513	0.371	0.270	0.198	0.146	0.108	0.093	0.080
18	0.836	0.700	0.494	0.350	0.250	0.180	0.130	0.095	0.081	0.069
19	0.828	0.686	0.475	0.331	0.232	0.164	0.116	0.083	0.070	0.060
20	0.820	0.673	0.456	0.312	0.215	0.149	0.104	0.073	0.061	0.051
21	0.811	0.660	0.439	0.294	0.199	0.135	0.093	0.064	0.053	0.044
22	0.803	0.647	0.422	0.278	0.184	0.123	0.083	0.056	0.046	0.038
23	0.795	0.634	0.406	0.262	0.170	0.112	0.074	0.049	0.040	0.033
24	0.788	0.622	0.390	0.247	0.158	0.102	0.066	0.043	0.035	0.028
25	0.780	0.610	0.375	0.233	0.146	0.092	0.059	0.038	0.030	0.024
26	0.772	0.598	0.361	0.220	0.135	0.084	0.053	0.033	0.026	0.021
27	0.764	0.586	0.347	0.207	0.125	0.076	0.047	0.029	0.023	0.018
28	0.757	0.574	0.333	0.196	0.116	0.069	0.042	0.026	0.020	0.016
29	0.749	0.563	0.321	0.185	0.107	0.063	0.037	0.022	0.017	0.014
30	0.742	0.552	0.308	0.174	0.099	0.057	0.033	0.020	0.015	0.012
40	0.672	0.453	0.208	0.097	0.046	0.022	0.011	0.005	0.004	0.003
50	0.608	0.372	0.141	0.054	0.021	0.009	0.003	0.001	0.001	0.001

18%	20%	22%	24%	25%	26%	28%	30%	35%	40%	45%	50%
0.847	0.833	0.820	0.806	0.800	0.794	0.781	0.769	0.741	0.714	0.690	0.667
0.718	0.694	0.672	0.650	0.640	0.630	0.610	0.592	0.549	0.510	0.476	0.444
0.609	0.579	0.551	0.524	0.512	0.500	0.477	0.455	0.406	0.364	0.328	0.296
0.516	0.482	0.451	0.423	0.410	0.397	0.373	0.350	0.301	0.260	0.226	0.198
0.437	0.402	0.307	0.341	0.328	0.315	0.291	0.269	0.223	0.186	0.156	0.132
0.370	0.335	0.303	0.275	0.262	0.250	0.227	0.207	0.165	0.133	0.108	0.088
0.314	0.279	0.249	0.222	0.210	0.198	0.178	0.159	0.122	0.095	0.074	0.059
0.266	0.233	0.204	0.179	0.168	0.157	0.139	0.123	0.091	0.068	0.051	0.039
0.225	0.194	0.167	0.144	0.134	0.125	0.108	0.094	0.067	0.048	0.035	0.026
0.191	0.162	0.137	0.116	0.107	0.099	0.085	0.073	0.050	0.035	0.024	0.017
0.162	0.135	0.112	0.094	0.086	0.079	0.066	0.056	0.037	0.025	0.017	0.012
0.137	0.112	0.092	0.076	0.069	0.062	0.052	0.043	0.027	0.018	0.012	0.008
0.116	0.093	0.075	0.061	0.055	0.050	0.040	0.033	0.020	0.013	0.008	0.005
0.099	0.078	0.062	0.049	0.044	0.039	0.032	0.025	0.015	0.009	0.006	0.008
0.084	0.065	0.051	0.040	0.035	0.031	0.025	0.020	0.011	0.006	0.004	0.002
0.071	0.054	0.042	0.032	0.028	0.025	0.019	0.015	0.008	0.005	0.003	0.002
0.060	0.045	0.034	0.026	0.023	0.020	0.015	0.012	0.006	0.003	0.002	0.001
0.051	0.038	0.028	0.021	0.018	0.016	0.012	0.009	0.005	0.002	0.001	0.001
0.043	0.031	0.023	0.017	0.014	0.012	0.009	0.007	0.003	0.002	0.001	
0.037	0.026	0.019	0.014	0.012	0.010	0.007	0.005	0.002	0.001	0.001	
0.031	0.022	0.015	0.011	0.009	0.008	0.006	0.004	0.002	0.001		
0.026	0.018	0.013	0.009	0.007	0.006	0.004	0.003	0.001	0.001		
0.022	0.015	0.010	0.007	0.006	0.005	0.003	0.002	0.001			
0.019	0.013	0.008	0.006	0.005	0.004	0.003	0.002	0.001			
0.016	0.010	0.007	0.005	0.004	0.003	0.002	0.001	0.001			
0.014	0.009	0.006	0.004	0.003	0.002	0.002	0.001				
0.011	0.007	0.005	0.003	0.002	0.002	0.001	0.001				
0.010	0.006	0.004	0.002	0.002	0.002	0.001	0.001				
0.008	0.005	0.003	0.002	0.002	0.001	0.001	0.001				
0.007	0.004	0.003	0.002	0.001	0.001	0.001					
0.001	0.001										

TABLE B

Present value of an ordinary annuity of $1 received annually for N years

YEARS (N)	1%	2%	4%	6%	8%	10%	12%	14%	15%	16%
1	0.990	0.980	0.962	0.943	0.926	0.909	0.893	0.877	0.870	0.862
2	1.970	1.942	1.886	1.833	1.783	1.736	1.690	1.647	1.626	1.605
3	2.941	2.884	2.775	2.673	2.577	2.487	2.402	2.322	2.283	2.246
4	3.902	3.808	3.630	3.465	3.312	3.170	3.037	2.914	2.855	2.798
5	4.853	4.713	4.452	4.212	3.993	3.791	3.605	3.433	3.352	3.274
6	5.795	5.601	5.242	4.917	4.623	4.355	4.111	3.889	3.784	3.685
7	6.728	6.472	6.002	5.582	5.206	4.868	4.564	4.288	4.160	4.039
8	7.652	7.325	6.733	6.210	5.747	5.335	4.968	4.639	4.487	4.344
9	8.566	8.162	7.435	6.802	6.247	5.759	5.328	4.946	4.772	4.607
10	9.471	8.983	8.111	7.360	6.710	6.145	5.650	5.216	5.019	4.833
11	10.368	9.787	8.760	7.887	7.139	6.495	5.988	5.453	5.234	5.029
12	11.255	10.575	9.385	8.384	7.536	6.814	6.194	5.660	5.421	5.197
13	12.134	11.343	9.986	8.853	7.904	7.103	6.424	5.842	5.583	5.342
14	13.004	12.106	10.563	9.295	8.244	7.367	6.628	6.002	5.724	5.468
15	13.865	12.849	11.118	9.712	8.559	7.606	6.811	6.142	5.847	5.575
16	14.718	13.578	11.652	10.106	8.851	7.824	6.974	6.265	5.954	5.669
17	15.562	14.292	12.166	10.477	9.122	8.022	7.120	6.373	6.047	5.749
18	16.398	14.992	12.659	10.828	9.372	8.201	7.250	6.467	6.128	5.818
19	17.226	15.678	13.134	11.158	9.604	8.365	7.366	6.550	6.198	5.877
20	18.046	16.351	13.590	11.470	9.818	8.514	7.469	6.623	6.259	5.929
21	18.857	17.011	14.029	11.764	10.017	8.649	7.562	6.687	6.312	5.973
22	19.660	17.658	14.451	12.042	10.201	8.772	7.645	6.743	6.359	6.011
23	20.456	18.292	14.857	12.303	10.371	8.883	7.718	6.792	6.399	6.044
24	21.243	18.914	15.247	12.550	10.529	9.985	7.784	6.835	6.434	6.073
25	22.023	19.523	15.622	12.783	10.675	9.077	7.843	6.873	6.464	6.097
26	22.795	20.121	15.983	13.003	10.810	9.161	7.896	6.906	6.491	6.118
27	23.560	20.707	16.330	13.211	10.935	9.237	7.943	6.935	6.514	6.136
28	24.316	21.281	16.663	13.406	11.051	9.307	7.984	6.961	6.534	6.152
29	25.066	21.844	16.984	13.591	11.158	9.370	8.022	6.983	6.551	6.166
30	25.808	22.396	17.292	13.765	11.258	9.427	8.055	7.003	6.566	6.177
40	32.835	27.355	19.793	15.046	11.925	9.779	8.244	7.105	6.642	6.234
50	39.196	31.424	21.482	15.762	12.234	9.915	8.304	7.133	6.661	6.246

18%	20%	22%	24%	25%	26%	28%	30%	35%	40%	45%	50%
0.847	0.833	0.820	0.806	0.800	0.794	0.781	0.769	0.741	0.714	0.690	0.667
1.566	1.528	1.492	1.457	1.440	1.424	1.392	1.361	1.289	1.224	1.165	1.111
2.174	2.106	2.042	1.981	1.952	1.923	1.868	1.816	1.696	1.589	1.493	1.407
2.690	2.589	2.494	2.404	2.362	2.320	2.241	2.166	1.997	1.849	1.720	1.605
3.127	2.991	2.864	2.745	2.689	2.635	2.532	2.436	2.220	2.035	1.876	1.737
3.498	3.326	3.167	3.020	2.951	2.885	2.759	2.643	2.385	2.168	1.983	1.824
3.812	3.605	3.416	3.242	3.161	3.083	2.937	2.802	2.508	2.263	2.057	1.883
4.078	3.837	3.619	3.421	3.329	3.241	3.076	2.925	2.598	2.331	2.108	1.922
4.303	4.031	3.786	3.566	3.463	3.366	3.184	3.019	2.665	2.379	2.144	1.948
4.494	4.192	3.923	3.682	3.571	3.465	3.269	3.092	2.715	2.414	2.168	1.965
4.656	4.327	4.035	3.776	3.656	3.544	3.335	3.147	2.752	2.438	2.185	1.977
4.793	4.439	4.127	3.851	3.725	3.606	3.387	3.190	2.779	2.456	2.196	1.985
4.910	4.533	4.203	3.912	3.780	3.656	3.427	3.223	2.799	2.468	2.204	1.990
5.008	4.611	4.265	3.962	3.824	3.695	3.459	3.249	2.814	2.477	2.210	1.993
5.092	4.675	4.315	4.001	3.859	3.726	3.483	3.268	2.825	2.484	2.214	1.995
5.162	4.730	4.357	4.033	3.887	3.751	3.503	3.283	2.834	2.489	2.216	1.997
5.222	4.775	4.391	4.059	3.910	3.771	3.518	3.295	2.840	2.492	2.218	1.998
5.273	4.812	4.419	4.080	3.928	3.786	3.529	3.304	2.844	2.494	2.219	1.999
5.316	4.844	4.442	4.097	3.942	3.799	3.539	3.311	2.848	2.496	2.220	1.999
5.353	4.870	4.460	4.110	3.954	3.808	3.546	3.316	3.850	2.497	2.221	1.999
5.384	4.891	4.476	4.121	3.963	3.816	3.551	3.320	2.852	2.498	2.221	2.000
5.410	4.909	4.488	4.130	3.970	3.822	3.556	3.323	2.853	2.458	2.222	2.000
5.432	4.925	4.499	4.137	3.976	3.827	3.559	3.325	2.854	2.499	2.222	2.000
5.451	4.937	4.507	4.143	3.981	3.831	3.562	3.327	2.855	2.499	2.222	2.000
5.467	4.948	4.514	4.147	3.985	3.834	3.564	3.329	2.856	2.499	2.222	2.000
5.480	4.956	4.520	4.151	3.988	3.837	3.566	3.330	2.856	2.500	2.222	2.000
5.492	4.964	4.524	4.154	3.990	3.839	3.567	3.331	2.856	2.500	2.222	2.000
5.502	4.970	4.528	4.157	3.992	3.840	3.568	3.331	2.857	2.500	2.222	2.000
5.510	4.975	4.531	4.159	3.994	3.841	3.569	3.332	2.857	2.500	2.222	2.000
5.517	4.979	4.534	4.160	3.995	3.842	3.569	3.322	2.857	2.500	2.222	2.000
5.548	4.997	4.544	4.166	3.999	3.846	3.571	3.333	2.857	2.500	2.222	2.000
5.554	4.999	4.545	4.167	4.000	3.846	3.571	3.333	2.857	2.500	2.222	2.000

questions

1.   In nonroutine long-term decisions, what factors must be considered? How is this different from short-term decision making?

2.   Describe the relationship which exists between the distance a sum to be received is in the future and its present value.

3.   What can you say about the size of the interest rate and the present value of sums which are discounted using that rate? In other words, do high interest rates result in large present values?

4.   Why should present-value concepts be used in evaluating or comparing investment alternatives?

5.   Describe briefly how a company's cost of capital is determined.

6.   How should a company's cost of capital be used in making investment decisions?

7.   Explain the meaning of the term "depreciation tax shield." How does it affect capital investment decisions?

8.   In making investment decisions, why is it important to consider any investment tax credit?

9.   How do asset retirements or exchanges influence investment decisions?

10. How does Accelerated Cost Recovery System depreciation, which may be required for tax purposes, differ from other depreciation methods?

11. What is an annuity?

12. Why does salvage value have to be considered in evaluating investments?

13. To find the present value of the cash flows from an investment, what three things must be known or estimated?

14. How does depreciation differ from most expenses? What is the implication of this difference in analyzing investment decisions?

15. How does an investment tax credit differ from a tax-deductible expense?

16. Why is it necessary to know whether an item is classified as ordinary income or as a capital gain for tax purposes?

17. Under current tax law, how does the investment tax credit affect tax-deductible depreciation?

18. A company is considering two different investments. One has a cash return of $10,000 at the end of Year 2. The other has two equal returns of $5,000 at the end of each of the next two years. If all other things are equal, which is preferable and why?

19. A company may use straight-line depreciation in reporting to its investors and accelerated cost system depreciation in reporting to the Internal Revenue Service. In investment analysis, which type of depreciation is significant and why?

20. A company is trying to analyze an investment decision. The cash flows from the investment will be received over the next four years, and during that period the inflation rate is estimated to be rising sharply. One of the

managers involved in the decision states that if present-value concepts are applied, the effects of inflation will be recognized in the resulting calculations. Is the manager correct?

exercises

14—1. Two new alternative business activities are available to the King Company, which operates in northern Maine. King's average cost of capital is 12%. Cash flows from each activity are shown below.

	CASH FLOWS ON ANNUAL BASIS	
	Logging	Potato Farming
Year 1	$12,000	$ 4,000
Year 2	10,000	6,000
Year 3	8,000	8,000
Year 4	6,000	10,000
Year 5	4,000	12,000

REQUIRED: 1. Which plan would you advise King to follow? Support your answer with appropriate present-value calculations.

2. Assume King's cost of capital is 8%. Would your answer to part 1 change? Support your answer with appropriate present-value calculations.

14—2. The Mapa Company has the following capital structure:

Debt $270,000
Equity $630,000

The cost of debt before taxes is 15%, and the cost of equity before taxes is 13%. Mapa pays taxes at the rate of 40%.

REQUIRED: 1. Calculate Mapa's weighted average cost of capital.

2. Assume that the cost of debt before taxes was 13% and cost of equity was 15%. How does that change your answer in part 1?

3. Assume that Mapa had the opportunity to invest in a project with a return of 12%. Would they accept the opportunity given the capital structure in parts 1 and 2? Why?

14—3. Realco Incorporated would like to purchase a computer which costs $80,000. Because of their current cash position, it is not possible to pay that amount at present. The salesman for the computer has suggested an alternative payment schedule of $25,000 per year on an installment basis for five years. The payment would be made at the end of each year.

REQUIRED: 1. Assuming that a fair interest rate for deferring cash payments is 14%, would you, as Realco's president, accept the salesman's offer? Why or why not? If not, what alternative payment schedule would you propose? (Ignore taxes.)
2. What rate of interest is implied in the salesman's offer? Approximate the rate; you do not have to interpolate.

14—4.   You have learned that you are the winner in a state lottery. The state has offered you three options related to the receipt of the winnings:

1. Receive $150,000 at the end of four years.
2. Receive $100,000 immediately.
3. Receive $25,000 at the end of each year for six years.

REQUIRED: Assume that you expect a 12% rate of return on your winnings. Which option would you choose?

14—5.   (CMA adapted) A businessman wants to withdraw $3,000 (excluding principal) from the investment fund at the end of each year for five years.

REQUIRED: 1. How much should he invest at the beginning of the first year if the fund earns 6% compounded annually?
2. How much should he invest at the beginning of the first year if the fund earns 10% compounded annually?
3. Assume that the businessman wants to invest a certain sum of money at the end of each year for five years, and he will need a total accumulation of $30,000 at the end of the five-year period. If the investment earns 8% compounded annually, how much should he invest annually to meet his requirement?

14—6.   (CMA adapted) The Sanch Company plans to expand its sales force by opening several new branch offices. Sanch has $5,200,000 in capital available for new branch offices. Sanch will consider opening only two types of branches: 10-person branches (Type A) and 5-person branches (Type B). Expected initial cash outlays are $650,000 for two Type A branches and $335,000 for three Type B branches. Expected annual cash inflow, net of income taxes, is $46,000 for a Type A branch and $18,000 for a Type B branch. Sanch expects to receive a return of 8% on the new branches and expects them to operate for 12 years.

REQUIRED: Which type of branch should Sanch open? Support your answer with appropriate present-value calculations.

14—7.   (AICPA adapted) Ludington, Inc., purchased a new machine on January 1 for $350,000. The machine is expected to have a useful life of eight years and no salvage value. Straight-line depreciation is to be used. The present value of the cash flow, net of taxes, generated by the machine was calculated to be $371,120 using a 14% rate of return.

REQUIRED:
1. What was the annual cash inflow, net of income taxes, expected from the new machine?
2. Assume the machine was expected to have a useful life of only seven years and a $15,000 salvage value, with the other facts unchanged. Calculate the annual cash inflow associated with the new machine.

14—8. Radmore Inc. is planning a project that will cost $57,500 and expects the annual cash inflow (before taxes) associated with the project to be $12,300 a year for seven years.

REQUIRED:
1. If Radmore expects a rate of return of 12%, what is the value of the cash flows generated by the project today? Should Radmore accept it?
2. If the cash flows of the project, discounted to the present, were equal to $60,000, what is the rate of return associated with the project?
3. If Radmore plans to invest $5,000 at the beginning of each of the next 12 years at an annual rate of 16% compounded semiannually, what is the value of the total investment today?

14—9. The Zlatkovich Company has the following capital structure:

Debt	$494,000
Equity	$806,000

The cost of debt before taxes is 12% and the cost of equity before taxes is 14%. Zlatkovich pays taxes at the rate of 55%.

REQUIRED:
1. Calculate Zlatkovich's weighted average cost of capital. (Round your final results to three decimal places.)
2. Assume that the cost of debt was 18% and the cost of equity was 10%. How does that change your answer to part 1? (Round your final results to three decimal places.)
3. Assume Zlatkovich is considering selling a $200,000 bond issue which has an interest rate of 10%. Based on the original data, how will this affect Zlatkovich's cost of capital? (Round your results to three decimal places.)

14—10. A company reported income before taxes of $400,000 to its shareholders. There was only one difference between income for book purposes and income for tax purposes. This difference was due to depreciation. The company purchased a new piece of equipment, costing $100,000. For book purposes the equipment is being depreciated on a straight-line basis over ten years. It is expected to have no salvage value because it will be obsolete at the end of that period. For tax purposes it is being depreciated using ACRS depreciation, a five-year life, and no salvage value. The company's earnings are taxed at a 46% rate.

REQUIRED:
1. What are the company's cash outflows for taxes in the first year of the equipment's life?
2. What is the value of the depreciation tax shield in the second year of the equipment's life?
3. What is the value of the depreciation tax shield in the eighth year of the equipment's life?

14—11.   Refer to the information in Exercise 14—10 and assume that the equipment purchase will provide the company with a 10% investment tax credit which reduces the depreciable base for tax purposes by one-half of the investment credit.

1. What are the company's cash outflows for taxes in the first year of the equipment's life?
2. Under current tax law, what is the value of the depreciation tax shield in the second year of the equipment's life?

14—12.   The Schuster Construction Company began operations on the first day of the current year. On that date they purchased equipment costing $800,000, which has a useful life for financial reporting purposes of ten years. The results of operations, *excluding depreciation* for the first two years of the company's operations, are as follows:

	YEAR 1	YEAR 2
Revenues	$1,300,000	$1,600,000
Expenses	800,000	950,000

For tax purposes, Schuster's equipment is depreciated using accelerated cost recovery system depreciation over a 5-year life. Schuster is entitled to a 10% investment tax credit in the year the equipment was purchased. Under current tax law, the depreciable base of property is reduced by one-half of the investment tax credit. Schuster's earnings are taxed at a 46% rate.

REQUIRED: 1. Calculate the income before taxes which Schuster will report for financial reporting purposes for the two-year period.
2. Calculate taxes payable for the two-year period.

14—13.   Kupperman Industries is considering the purchase of some coal-mining equipment. Data relevant to the equipment are as follows:

Cost of the equipment	$500,000
Cost recovery period for tax purposes	5 years
Investment tax credit in year of acquisition	10%
Cash revenues generated by the investment less *cash expenses* caused by the investment for Years 1–5	$300,000 per year
Tax rate	45%

Assume that the depreciable base of the asset for tax purposes is reduced by one-half of the investment tax credit.

REQUIRED: Calculate the net-of-taxes cash flow for the investment for Years 1–5. (Round taxes payable to the nearest dollar.)

14—14.   Tamarkin, Inc., plans to purchase ten delivery trucks costing $30,000 each. Information regarding the investment is summarized below:

Cost recovery period of trucks for tax purposes	3 years
Investment tax credit in years of acquisition	6%
Cash revenues generated by the investment less *cash expenses* caused by the investment for Years 1–3	$200,000 per year
Tax rate	30%
Anticipated taxable gain from sale of the trucks at the end of three years, subjected to taxes at ordinary income rates	$5,000 each

Tamarkin plans to retire at the end of three years and will dispose of the delivery trucks at that time. The depreciable base of the trucks is reduced by one-half of the investment tax credit.

REQUIRED: Calculate the net-of-taxes cash flows for the investment in the trucks for Years 1–3.

14—15. Priscilla Douglas is considering two investment alternatives for which the following data have been assembled:

	INVESTMENT A	INVESTMENT B
Initial investment	$500,000	$ 500,000
Cash returns:		
Year 1	$200,000	$ 400,000
Year 2	$300,000	$ 200,000
Year 3	$350,000	$ 400,000
Total	$850,000	$1,000,000
Rate at which returns will be taxed	30%	50%

Ms. Douglas wants to earn an after-tax return of 12% on all her investments.

REQUIRED: Applying present-value concepts, evaluate the two investments. Which investment, if either, should Ms. Douglas make?

problems

14—16. *Present-value calculations.* Kalm, Inc., has determined that it requires major equipment purchases which involve a large outlay of cash. Kalm has the option, if it purchases the equipment from one particular company, of choosing from different payment plans outlined below:

1. $800,000 cash immediately.
2. $100,000 down payment immediately, $150,000 for Years 1–2, beginning with the current year, and $165,000 for Years 3–5. All payments except the down payment are made at the end of the year.
3. $165,000 now and at the beginning of each of the next four years.
4. $160,000 down payment immediately and $140,000 per year for five years, beginning with the current year. All payments other than the down payment are made at year-end.

REQUIRED:
1. If the expected effective interest rate during the period in question is 8%, determine which payment plan you would recommend to Kalm's management.
2. If the expected effective interest rate was 7%, which payment plan would Kalm choose? Note the present-value factors at a rate of 7%.

PERIOD	PRESENT VALUE OF $1	PRESENT VALUE OF AN ORDINARY ANNUITY
1	.935	.935
2	.873	1.808
3	.816	2.624
4	.763	3.387
5	.713	4.100

3. If the expected effective interest rate was 12%, would your recommendation change? If so, what is the reasoning behind any change?

14–17. *Finding present values.* Lindquist Copper Mining Company is going to expand its operations by investing in either one of two mines—one in Dry Gulch, the other in Sandy Bend. Estimated net-of-taxes cash flows from the two mines for the next five years, after which both will be depleted, are shown below. The cost of both mines is the same. Lindquist uses a 12% after-tax rate of return in evaluating investments.

YEAR	DRY GULCH	SANDY BEND
1	$ 500,000	$ 200,000
2	$1,500,000	$1,200,000
3	$1,500,000	$1,200,000
4	$1,800,000	$2,000,000
5	$ 300,000	$1,000,000
Totals	$5,600,000	$5,600,000

REQUIRED:
1. Which mine should Lindquist buy? Support your answer with appropriate present-value computations.
2. If Lindquist lowered its desired after-tax rate of return to 10%, would your answer to part 1 change? Explain your answer.

14—18. *Using present values to equate alternatives.* Pryor's Department Store believes that it can increase its revenues by beginning a free delivery service within 25 miles of the store. It will need three trucks to provide the service. Pryor's is considering three alternatives:

Alternative 1: Purchase the three trucks for an immediate cash outlay of $120,000. At the end of five years the trucks will be sold for a total of approximately $20,000, net of taxes.

Alternative 2: Lease the three trucks for a five-year period. Lease payments of $28,000 are due at the beginning of each year.

Alternative 3: Lease the three trucks for five years. An immediate lease payment of $15,000 is due January 1 of the first year of the lease. Annual lease payments of $25,000 are due at the end of each year, including the first year of the lease agreement, for five years.

Assume that the after-tax cash operating costs will be the same under all three alternatives. Pryor's believes a 12% discount rate should be used in evaluating the alternatives. No investment tax credit is available with any alternative.

REQUIRED:
1. Which alternative should Pryor's select? Support your answer with computations.
2. Assume that if Pryor's purchases the truck, it will receive a 6% investment tax credit at the end of Year 1. Further assume that the investment tax credit does not reduce the depreciable base of the asset and that after-tax cash operating costs remain the same under the three alternatives. Would your answer to part 1 change?

14—19. *The impact of interest rates on present values.* Virginia Bean has $800,000 to invest. She has examined the literature relevant to investment offerings by a number of different companies and has narrowed her choice down to the following two:

	ESTIMATED YEAR-END CASH FLOWS	
Year	Alternative 1	Alternative 2
1	$ 150,000	$ 200,000
2	$ 200,000	$ 600,000
3	$ 600,000	$ 800,000
4	$ 600,000	$ 600,000
	$1,550,000	$2,200,000

Ms. Bean believes that Alternative 2 is a higher-risk investment than Alternative 1. As a result she would be satisfied with a return on Alternative 1 of 8% but would want a 12% return on Alternative 2.

REQUIRED: **1.** Applying present-value concepts, which investment is best?

2. Assume that Alternative 1 is more risky than Alternative 2. Reverse the rates used and recalculate the present value of the two alternatives. What does this process tell you about the impact of interest rates on present values?

14—20.   *Calculating the cost of capital; finding the implicit interest rate.*   The Superior Portfolios Investment Company has the following capital structure:

Debt	$3,000,000
Equity	$7,000,000

The weighted average interest rate on the debt is 15%; the estimated cost of equity capital is 12%. Superior Portfolios is taxed at a 40% rate. The company's management has two investment alternatives, both of which have guaranteed annual returns as follows:

Alternative 1: Annual cash flows, $200,000 for five years. Initial investment, $686,600.

Alternative 2: Annual cash flows: $100,000 for nine years. Initial investment, $624,700.

REQUIRED: **1.** Calculate the company's weighted average cost of capital.

2. Find the interest rates implicit in each of the investment alternatives.

3. Based on quantitative factors only, should Superior Portfolios make either investment? Justify your answer.

14–21.   *Finding present values of alternatives, no taxes.*   The Pomfret Military Academy needs a computer to keep student records and to facilitate its accounting system. The Academy's business manager has assembled the following information:

Purchase cost for cash	$20,000
Annual lease payment due the first day of each year for five years	$4,400
Installment purchase:	
Down payment due immediately	$5,000
Annual installment due at the end of the year for five years including the first year	$3,500

Under any of the alternatives, Pomfret Military Academy would pay all costs of operating and maintaining the computer. The business manager believes that a computer obtained today will be obsolete at the end of five years and will have to be replaced with a new computer. If the computer is purchased under either of the purchase alternatives, the estimated resale value at the end of five years is estimated to be $2,000. Pomfret's cost of capital is 12%.

REQUIRED: Assume that Pomfret Military Academy is a tax-exempt organization. Which alternative should be selected? Support your answer with appropriate present-value calculations.

14—22. *Finding the cash flows from alternatives when taxes are a factor.* Use the information provided for Pomfret in Problem 14—21. Assume that Pomfret Military Academy is not a tax-exempt organization but instead is taxed at a 40% rate. For tax purposes, if it acquires the computer it will depreciate it using accelerated cost recovery system depreciation and a five-year life. Other expenses incurred in connection with the computer will not vary between alternatives. Lease payments are fully tax-deductible. The resale value will be taxed at ordinary income rates.

If the computer is acquired, the Academy will receive an investment tax credit at the end of the year of acquisition of 10%. Assume that tax laws have been revised and the tax credit does *not* reduce the asset's depreciable base for tax purposes. Under the lease agreement, Pomfret is not entitled to any investment tax credit.

REQUIRED: Which alternative for acquiring the computer should be selected? Support your answer with appropriate present-value computations. (Round all calculations to the nearest dollar.)

14—23. *Calculating after-tax cash flows from an investment.* The Delhi Mill is contemplating the purchase of some new spinning equipment. If it does purchase the equipment, it believes that it will have cash savings in labor, material spoilage, electricity, and other items amounting to $8,000 per year. The equipment will cost $20,000, have a life of five years and an estimated resale value of $3,000. For tax purposes five-year accelerated cost recovery system depreciation will be used, which ignores salvage value. The equipment will produce an investment tax credit of 10% in the year of acquisition. The depreciable base of the equipment for tax purposes will be reduced by one-half of the investment tax credit. Delhi's tax rate is 40%.

REQUIRED: Prepare a schedule which shows the annual net-of-tax cash flows from the investment in the equipment.

14—24. *Finding the present value of after-tax cash flows from alternatives.* Software, Unlimited, plans to provide its five vice-presidents with a Corvette, which it believes is in keeping with the image the company wants to create. Software is considering two alternatives: purchasing the autos or leasing them. If they purchase the cars, they will be subjected to three-year-life accelerated cost recovery system depreciation for tax purposes. Software will receive a 6% investment tax credit at the end of the year of acquisition. This investment tax credit will reduce the depreciable basis of the cars for tax purposes by one-half of the investment tax credit. At the end of three years the cars will be sold at an amount which will produce a taxable gain of $5,000 each. The resale value will be taxed at a capital gains rate of 28%. The purchase price of each Corvette is $28,000.

If the five cars are leased, lease payments will be $36,000, due on the last day of each year. The lessor will retain any investment tax credit. Lease payments are tax-deductible. Under either alternative additional cash operating costs paid by the company in conjunction with the cars will be the same. Software, Unlimited, uses a 14% discount rate in finding the present value of alternatives. Its earnings are taxed at a 45% rate.

REQUIRED: Based on the present value of the after-tax cash flows from the two alternatives, which should Software, Unlimited, accept? (Round all amounts to the nearest dollar.)

14—25.   *Testing alternatives for sensitivity to estimation errors.*   Hal Abrahamson is considering the purchase of a small timber logging operation. For the first two years of operations he would use only one wood cutter; for the next two years he would try to double the size of his operation. Because of weather conditions, logging cannot be done each day throughout the year. Based on the experience of the previous owner, Abrahamson has made the following estimates:

Average number of trees which can be cut each day by one logger	25 logs per day
Average number of days per year when logging can be done	200 days
Cost of hiring a logger who will provide his/her own equipment and transport logs to the sawmill as they are cut	$100 per day
Average selling price per tree cut	$7

Abrahamson feels that the actual results may vary significantly from the estimates given above. Abrahamson wants a 16% before-tax return on his investment and wants to recover his investment in four years. Assume all cash flows come at year-end.

REQUIRED: **1.** What could Abrahamson afford to pay for the logging operation, based on the data provided?
2. If timber could be logged 250 days instead of 200 days, how much could Abrahamson afford to pay?

14—26.   *Calculating the cost of capital; finding the present value of cash flows.*   Barkowski Realty has the following capital structure:

Long-term debt	$6,000,000
Stockholders' equity	$4,000,000

The average cost of the long-term debt is 12% before taxes while that of stockholders' equity is 18%. Barkowski pays taxes at a 30% rate.

Barkowski Realty is trying to decide whether it should invest in a condominium project which would require an estimated investment of $3,000,000 and for which cash flows are estimated to be as follows for the next three years:

Year 1	$ 800,000
Year 2	$1,500,000
Year 3	$1,600,000

The company decides whether or not it should invest in a project by comparing the present value of the cash flows from the project with the initial cost of the investment using its cost of capital as the discount rate. If the discounted present values equal or exceed the initial investment, they consider the project acceptable.

REQUIRED:
1. Is the condominium project which Barkowski is considering an acceptable investment based on the criteria it has set? (Round the cost of capital to the nearest whole percent.)
2. Suppose that the capital structure was the reverse of that given—$4,000,000 long-term debt and $6,000,000 stockholders' equity. Would the investment be acceptable, based on Barkowski's criteria?

14—27. *Present-value concepts.* Ray Bopp purchased a large farm, which he has been paying for through an annual payment of $15,000 on December 31 of each year. As of January 1 of the current year, he still owed three installments of $15,000. He is paying interest on the unpaid balance at a rate of 10% per year. Interest and principal payments are made each December 31.

Ray recently inherited some money from his grandmother. He would like to liquidate the farm loan. With what is left over he wants to purchase a new tractor and invest the remainder. One of his neighbors has told Ray that he probably should buy the tractor on the installment plan and invest the whole sum which remains after paying off his farm in a mutual fund. If Ray buys the tractor on the installment plan, he will have to make five annual year-end payments of $10,000. If he buys the tractor outright, he can purchase it for a lump-sum payment of $34,330. The mutual fund is currently generating an annual return of 12%. Ignore taxes.

REQUIRED:
1. From a financial point of view, should Ray use any of the money he has inherited to liquidate the loan on his farm? Why or why not?
2. If Ray does decide to liquidate the loan, what amount should he offer the lender, assuming the lender believes the money received could be reinvested at 12%?
3. What interest rate is implicit in the installment purchase of the tractor?

4. Should Ray purchase the tractor outright and invest only the remainder in the mutual fund, or should he buy the tractor on the installment plan and invest the remainder in the mutual fund?

14—28. *Account income versus cash flows.* Marla Brim is considering the purchase of a bakery. Revenues from the bakery are estimated as $28,000, $32,000, and $35,000, respectively over Years 1, 2, and 3. Salaries, utilities, and other cash expenses, excluding interest, are expected to be $15,000 in Year 1 and to increase by 10% over the previous year in each of the next two years. Bakery equipment included in the purchase will cost $9,000 and be depreciated on a straight-line basis over a three-year period. For tax purposes, accelerated cost recovery system depreciation and a three-year life will be used. Marla would receive a 6% investment tax credit, for which she would use the flow-through method for financial accounting purposes. (Remember, with the flow-through method, the entire benefit of the investment tax credit is recognized in the year the asset is acquired, which is consistent with the tax treatment.) Assume the investment tax credit does *not* reduce the depreciation basis of the asset.

Marla would have to finance the purchase of the bakery by giving a note for $20,000 with interest at 12% payable December 31 of each year. The note will be due in three years. Marla's expected tax rate is 30%. The loan will be made January 1.

REQUIRED:
1. Prepare an income statement for each year of the three-year period.
2. Prepare a schedule which shows the cash flows from the investment for each year of the three-year period.
3. In making the decision as to whether or not she should acquire the bakery, which set of information—accounting income or cash flows—should Marla use? Justify your answer.

14—29. *Quantifying cash flows from an income statement; calculating taxes payable.* The income statement of Securities Transport, Inc., showed the following information for a two-year period:

	YEAR 1	YEAR 2
Revenues	$600,000	$700,000
Operating expenses:		
Salaries	$450,000	$465,000
Depreciation on vehicles	30,000	30,000
Utilities	5,000	5,600
Rent	18,000	18,000
Goodwill amortization	6,000	6,000
Insurance	4,000	5,000
Gain on sale of equipment	—	2,000
Total expenses	$513,000	$531,600
Income before taxes	$ 87,000	$168,400

All the vehicles were purchased at the beginning of Year 1 and are being depreciated on a straight-line basis, assuming no salvage and a five-year life. Land was sold on December 31 of Year 2 for $8,000 and had a book value of $6,000. The gain on its sale is taxed at a 28% capital gains rate. For tax purposes, the vehicles are subjected to accelerated cost recovery system depreciation using a three-year life. The company received a 6% investment tax credit in the year of acquisition which did *not* reduce the depreciable base for tax purposes. Goodwill amortization is not tax-deductible. The ordinary income tax rate is 46%.

REQUIRED: Using the information given, estimate the after-tax cash flows from operations of Security Delivery Service for the two-year period. Remember, you must recompute income to calculate taxes.

14—30. *Calculating cash flows.* Camera Equipment and Supplies' cash revenues less cash expenses for a three-year period were:

Year 1	$320,000
Year 2	$380,000
Year 3	$410,000

It began operations in Year 1 and purchased equipment costing $200,000 with an expected life of ten years, having no expected salvage value, and on which straight-line depreciation was being recorded for financial reporting purposes. The equipment was being depreciated over a five-year period using accelerated cost recovery system depreciation for tax purposes. Camera Equipment and Supplies had received a 10% investment tax credit on the equipment in the year of acquisition which did not reduce the equipment's depreciable base for tax purposes.

At the beginning of Year 3 the company purchased a delivery vehicle at a cost of $30,000 with an estimated useful life of seven years and an immaterial salvage value. It is being depreciated for tax purposes over a three-year life using accelerated cost recovery system depreciation. The company received an investment tax credit of 6%. The depreciable base of the asset for tax purposes was reduced by one-half of the investment tax credit. Camera Equipment and Supplies is taxed at a 40% tax rate.

REQUIRED: **1.** Calculate taxes payable for each of the three years.
2. Calculate after-tax cash flows for the company for each of the three years.

chapter fifteen

EVALUATION OF CAPITAL EXPENDITURE PROJECTS

OBJECTIVES

After you have completed this chapter, you should be able to answer the following questions:

- How does the capital budgeting process work?
- How is the accounting rate-of-return method applied in analyzing capital projects, and what are its shortcomings?
- What problems arise in computing the accounting rate of return for a project?
- Despite its limitations, why do managers compute the accounting rate of return for projects?
- How are the cash-payback and the discounted cash-payback methods applied, and what are their limitations?
- How is the net-present-value method used; what are the problems with it?
- How is the internal rate-of-return method applied; what are its shortcomings?
- Why should the net-present-value method or the internal rate-of-return method be used in determining whether a project is justified?
- Why do managers use methods other than the net-present-value method and the internal rate-of-return method?
- What problems arise in evaluating any capital project?

INTRODUCTION

A critical managerial issue for many organizations is, "Where shall we make future investment?" Managers look for data which will help them in this decision-making process, which is critical to the future of the organization.

Among other information, a manager considers quantitative data which attempt to measure the benefits to the organization of a particular investment. Suppose that a company has two divisions, and each division wants to have a long-term capital investment project financed. Should both projects be financed or both rejected? Quantitative data provided by capital budgeting techniques are one important source of information. One problem with these techniques is they measure what is "best" for the organization in different ways.

In this chapter we shall first discuss the capital budgeting process and then describe and evaluate four techniques which are used to assist in making capital investment decisions. These techniques are the (1) accounting rate of return, (2) cash payback, (3) net present value, and (4) internal rate of return. An illustrative example is used to show how each method works. In addition, the advantages and disadvantages of each technique are discussed.

THE CAPITAL BUDGETING PROCESS

Large companies usually have a formal process through which requests for capital projects must pass. Not all capital expenditures must pass through a capital expenditures approval process. Limits are set on the size of expenditures which can be made without additional approval at various managerial levels throughout the organization. The amount varies a great deal, depending on the managerial level and also on the company philosophy. Some organizations allow managers to spend large sums of money without additional approval; others are quite restrictive in terms of spending autonomy.

If a project must pass through the capital approval process, the manager requesting the project prepares a description of the project including quantitative data. Most companies have a prescribed form for this. One used by Emhart Corporation is shown in Illustration 15-1.

The exact nature of the capital expenditures approval process varies from company to company. The process used by Uniroyal and described here as an Illustration from Practice is a typical kind of process used by large companies.

ILLUSTRATION FROM PRACTICE:
EMHART'S MODEL CAPITAL PROJECT
INFORMATION REQUEST FORM

Emhart's annual revenues are close to $2 billion. These revenues come from a wide variety of industrial and consumer products, which include shoe machinery and materials, glass containers, electronic components, door hardware, locks, smoke detectors, adhesives, and fasteners. Emhart employs approximately 30,000 people and has operations in many locations around the world.

Illustration 15-1 shows a model form used by Emhart as a means of obtaining information on capital project requests.

ILLUSTRATION FROM PRACTICE:
UNIROYAL'S CAPITAL PROJECT APPROVAL PROCESS

A brief description of Uniroyal was given in a previous chapter. The following is a simplified description of the company's capital project approval process.

All capital requests are generally funneled through a corporate department or committee which is charged with making an initial review of the capital request, seeing if the data it contains is accurate and complete and asking the requesting manager to make any clarifications required. As you can see from Illustration 15-2 at Uniroyal, a part of the corporate headquarters called "Corporate Finanacial Analysis" makes this initial review, logs in the requests received, and distributes them to the Capital Appropriations Review Board.

The Capital Appropriations Review Board, now an amorphous group that renders its opinions by mail, rather than meeting formally, reviews requests, keeping in mind corporate strategies, capital plans, and the performance of the manager and unit he or she heads. For example, if corporate strategies have indicated that a particular section of the company is a declining business segment, it is unlikely that the Capital Appropriations Review Board would look favorably upon a request for expansion.

Projects which are approved by the Capital Appropriations Review Board are then reviewed by the highest level corporate officers. The written request is generally supplemented by an oral presentation by a representative of the part of the organization making the request.

Projects which are approved by the corporate officers are ready for submission to the Board of Directors. These project requests are first reviewed by the finance committee of the Board, which recommends them to the whole board for final approval. Approved projects become part of Uniroyal's capital budget.

ILLUSTRATION 15-1

Illustration from Practice: Model Capital Budgeting Request Form—Emhart

LINE NO.		DESCRIPTION	REF. PG. NO.	TOTAL	0 19	1 19	2 19	3 19	4 19	5 19	6 19	7 19	8 19	9 19	10 19	11 19
ECONOMIC JUSTIFICATION			(000)		REQUESTING UNIT					C.E.A. NUMBER						
					ANNUAL CASH INFLOW (OUTFLOW)											
1	INVESTMENT	CAPITAL AMOUNT														
2		ALLOWANCES & CREDITS														
3		ASSOCIATED EXPENSES														
4		LESS INCOME TAXES														
5		INVESTMENT AVOIDED														
6		WORKING CAPITAL														
7		OTHER														
8	TOTAL INVESTMENT AFTER TAXES															
9	NET SALES															
10	Costs & Expenses Related To Add'l Sales Volume	DIRECT MATERIAL														
11		DIRECT LABOR														
12		INDIRECT LABOR														
13		FRINGE BENEFITS														
14		MFG OVERHEAD														
15		OPERATING EXPENSES														
16		OTHER COSTS														
17																
18																
19		TOTAL COSTS														
20	ADDITIONAL INCOME															
21	COST SAVINGS															
22	ADD'L INCOME/COST SAVINGS															
23	INCOME TAX @ ___%															
24	NET SAVINGS AFTER TAX															
25	TAX SHELTER	ANNUAL DEP ACCELERATED														
26		ANN DEP ACC × TAX @ ___%														
27	ANNUAL CASH FLOW															
28	DISCOUNT FACTOR @ ___%															
29	R	NET PRESENT VALUE = ___														
30	O	INTERNAL RATE OF RETURN ___%														
31	I	YEARS PAYBACK ___														
32	MEMO ITEMS	ANNUAL OPERATING HOURS														
33		WORKING SHIFTS														
34		EMPLOYEE CHANGES (+ −)														

ILLUSTRATION 15-2

Illustration from practice: capital projects approval process—Uniroyal

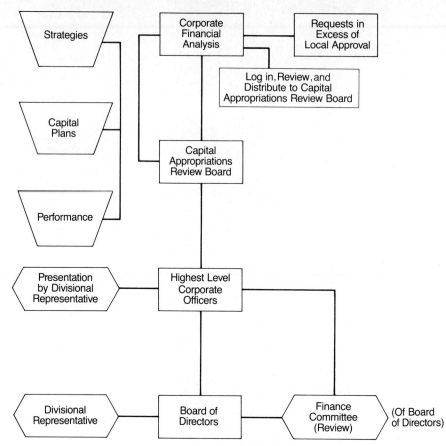

MONITORING PROGRESS OF PROJECTS

As projects are begun, progress is monitored through accumulation of cost and performance data. Many companies now have a postcompletion audit process which looks at projects after they are operational and compares actual results with what was anticipated at the time the project was undertaken. The postcompletion audit allows management to see where actual results have departed from anticipated results and to seek reasons for this difference. This information may trigger corrective action to bring project results closer to expectations. The results of the postcompletion audit are also used when future requests from a particular manager are being evaluated. The postcompletion audit results represent a particular manager's track record. Most organizations tend to look more favorably on managers whose past projects have lived up to expectations as opposed to projects of managers whose forecast results departed materially from actual results.

DATA FOR ILLUSTRATIVE EXAMPLE

The Berney Machine Company is considering the replacement of an old lathe. Over the past year this lathe has not been performing properly and has been down three times for costly repairs. Further, it does not seem to be providing the tolerances necessary for the work required.

A salesperson for Garstka Lathe advised the Company that it could replace the old lathe with a new Garstka Lathe which would do all the machining that the old lathe did with higher tolerances and lower waste. It was also faster. The cost of the Garstka Lathe would be $20,000 installed. Under existing tax laws (Accelerated Cost Recovery System depreciation) the cost recovery period for the lathe would be 5 years; its useful life is estimated as 6 years. At the end of 6 years it would have no material salvage value. For book purposes the machine would be depreciated on a straight-line basis over 6 years.

The lathe currently being used by Berney has 2 years of life left and a book value of $3,000. Although Garstka Lathe will not take it in trade, its estimated current resale value is $2,000, net of any removal costs. For tax and book purposes, the old lathe is being written off on a straight-line basis down to a zero salvage value. The loss on disposal is fully tax-deductible.

The estimated annual savings from the new machine are $5,000 in wages and $4,500 in elimination of wasted materials because of the new machine's higher tolerances.

The Berney Machine Company wants to earn a return on any investment of at least 15%. The company's marginal tax rate is 46%. The lathe qualifies for a 10% investment tax credit, which reduces its depreciable base by one-half the investment tax credit.

CALCULATION OF THE IMPACT OF REPLACEMENT ON NET INCOME

One method which is used to evaluate capital projects—the accounting rate-of-return method—uses the change in net income as part of the input for evaluation. Thus, to provide the relevant data for this model, we shall first calculate the impact of replacement on net income. These calculations are shown in Illustration 15-3. Based on *accounting numbers*, not cash flows, this investment would cause an increase in net income in Year 1 of $5,140, $4,140 in Year 2, and $3,330 in Years 3–6. In all six years, to get the income-before-taxes figure, the wage and materials savings are compared to depreciation. The assumed tax rate of 46% for our example is directly applied. However, while we record book depreciation on the $20,0̸

ILLUSTRATION
15-3

Impact of
replacement
on net income

	YEAR 1	YEAR 2	YEARS 3–6
Factors increasing net income before taxes:			
Wage savings	$5,000	$5,000	$5,000
Material savings	4,500	4,500	4,500
Total increases	$9,500	$9,500	$9,500
Factors decreasing net income before taxes:			
Depreciation on new lathe, $20,000 cost/ 6-year life	$3,333	$3,333	$3,333
Less: Depreciation on old lathe, $3,000 book value/2-year remaining life	1,500	1,500	—
Net increase in depreciation expense	$1,833	$1,833	$3,333
Loss on retirement of old lathe, $3,000 book value − $2,000 resale	1,000	—	—
Total decreases	$2,833	$1,833	$3,333
Impact on income before taxes	$6,667	$7,667	$6,167
Income tax expense at 46%	$3,067	$3,527	$2,837
Less: Investment tax credit, ($20,000 × 10%) less $460	(1,540)	—	—
Net income tax expense	$1,527	$3,527	$2,837
Increase in income from investment	$5,140	$4,140	$3,330

investment, $1,000 of that amount ($20,000 cost of asset × 10% investment tax credit × ½) will never be deductible for tax purposes. It represents a timing difference between book and taxable income. In effect, it reduces the value of the investment tax credit by the lost depreciation (the lost tax shield) times the tax rate ($1,000 of non-tax deductible depreciation × 46%) or $460.

The Financial Accounting Standards Board requires that the impact of the additional taxes which will have to be paid because of the lost depreciation be recognized as tax expense in the year the asset is acquired. Taxes which the company must actually pay are based on income reported for tax purposes and are shown for the Berney Machine Company in Illustration 15-4. Differences between income taxes which will actually be paid and those which are reported for financial purposes are reconciled through the deferred taxes payable account as shown below:

	YEAR 1	YEAR 2	YEAR 3–5	YEAR 6
Debit Tax Expense (based on income for financial reporting purposes from Illustration 15-3)	$1,527	$3,527	$2,837	$2,837
Credit Taxes Payable (based on taxable income from Illustration 15-4)	1,289	3,137	2,535	4,370
Debit (Credit) Deferred Taxes Payable	($ 238)	($ 390)	($ 302)	$1,533*

* Credits exceed debits by $1 because of rounding

In Year 1, an additional item appears on the income statement for financial reporting purposes. The loss on the sale of the old lathe of $1,000 is assumed to be fully deductible for tax purposes.

CALCULATION OF THE IMPACT OF REPLACEMENT ON CASH FLOWS

The other three methods for evaluating proposed investment require the use of cash flows. We shall do this calculation in two steps: we shall calculate (1) the tax impact of replacement and (2) the impact on cash flows.

Cash Flows for Taxes

To find the impact on taxes, we shall determine taxable income. We cannot use the numbers we generated in Illustration 15-3, because they are based on how we shall determine income for book purposes. The tax figure we have calculated is what would be reported to shareholders, not what would be paid to the Internal Revenue Service. The difference between the two is based on different depreciation systems for book and tax purposes and any other reporting differences. In calculating cash flows, we must use ACRS depreciation.

This illustration of the calculation of cash flows for taxes, resulting from the replacement decision, shows the three potential impacts of investment decisions on taxes described in the previous chapter. (1) Depreciation on the new asset will provide a tax shield. (2) There is an investment tax credit which reduces taxes payable in the year the qualified asset is acquired, and in keeping with the current law reduces the basis of the asset for depreciation in future years. (3) There is a loss on the retirement of the old asset which is fully deductible for tax purposes.

Look at the calculation of cash flows for taxes for Year 1 in Illustration 15-4 relative to the cash flows for subsequent years. Because the loss on retirement of the old lathe can be deducted and because the investment tax credit directly reduces the taxes which have to be paid, the amount due in Year 1 is significantly smaller than that due in other years. In contrast, taxes are significantly higher in Year 6 than in Years 2–5, because for tax purposes the machine is fully depreciated at the end of Year 5 and there is no depreciation to shield income in Year 6.

Cash Flows from Replacement

Illustration 15-5 depicts the cash flows which will arise from the replacement. Cash savings in operating costs will result from wage and materials savings. However, these reductions in expense levels will also cause taxable income to increase. The impact of taxes, as calculated in Illustration 15-4, is subtracted from the cash savings from operations. In Year 1 there will be an additional cash flow—the $2,000 resulting from the resale of the old lathe. Because of the cash flowing from the sale of the old lathe and the lower taxes of Year 1, this is the year in which the greatest amount of cash flows will result from the replacement of the old lathe with the new lathe. Because there is no depreciation shield for any of the cash savings of Year 6, cash flows will be at their lowest level in this year. If there had been a resale value for the new lathe at the end of Year 6, this would have resulted in an additional cash flow in that year.

Now we have all the data we need to apply four techniques which a manager may use in deciding whether or not to make an investment. Each of the four techniques—accounting rate of return, cash payback, net present value, and internal rate of return—is described below.

ILLUSTRATION 15-4

Impact of replacement on cash flows for taxes

	YEAR 1	YEAR 2	YEAR 3–5	YEAR 6
Factors increasing taxable income:				
Wage savings	$5,000	$5,000	$5,000	$5,000
Material savings	4,500	4,500	4,500	4,500
Total	$9,500	$9,500	$9,500	$9,500
Factors decreasing taxable income:				
Depreciation on new lathe[a]	$2,850	$4,180	$3,990	0
Less: Depreciation on old lathe, $3,000 book value/2 years	1,500	1,500	—	—
Net increase in depreciation	$1,350	$2,680	$3,990	$ 0
Loss of retirement of old lathe, $3,000 book value − $2,000 resale	1,000	—	—	—
Total decreases	$2,350	$2,680	$3,990	$ 0
Impact on taxable income	$7,150	$6,820	$5,510	$9,500
Income taxes at 46%	$3,289	$3,137	$2,535	$4,370
Less: Investment tax credit, $20,000 × 10%	2,000	—	—	—
Cash flows for taxes	$1,289	$3,137	$2,535	$4,370

[a] The rates used below are taken from the ACRS table on p. 593 of Chapter 14 and are applied to the cost of the asset less one-half of the investment tax credit as currently required by tax law.

$$[\$20,000 \text{ cost} - \tfrac{1}{2}(20,000 \times 10\%)] = \$19,000 \text{ depreciable base}$$

Year 1:	19,000 × 15%	= $2,850
Year 2:	19,000 × 22%	= $4,180
Years 3–5:	19,000 × 21%	= $3,990
Year 6:	0	= 0

ILLUSTRATION
15-5

Cash flows from
replacement of
old lathe with
new lathe

	YEAR 1	YEAR 2	YEARS 3–5	YEAR 6
Cash savings from operations				
Wage savings	$ 5,000	$ 5,000	$ 5,000	$ 5,000
Material savings	$ 4,500	$ 4,500	$ 4,500	$ 4,500
Total cash savings from operations	$ 9,500	$ 9,500	$ 9,500	$ 9,500
Less: Cash flows for taxes (Illustration 15-4)	1,289	3,137	2,535	4,370
Net cash flows from operations	$ 8,211	$ 6,363	$ 6,965	$ 5,130
Add: Cash from resale of old lathe	2,000	—	—	—
Cash flows from replacement	$10,211	$ 6,363	$ 6,965	$ 5,130

ACCOUNTING RATE-OF-RETURN METHOD

When the accounting rate-of-return method is used, accounting numbers, based on accrual concepts, are used to determine how good a potential investment is. That is, income-statement numbers rather than cash flows are used in the evaluation of investment proposals.

The calculation of accounting rate of return is based on the return-on-investment formula (ROI), which looks at income relative to investment:

$$\text{Accounting rate of return} = \frac{\text{increase in income due to investment}}{\text{increase in required investment}}$$

However, as is true with return on investment, with accounting rate of return the two components of the formula—income and investment—can be defined a number of ways. For example, the numerator could be:

1. The increase in income for each separate year of the investment proposal's life, resulting in six different rates of return.
2. An average increase in income for the life of the investment, yielding one rate of return for the project's life.

The investment base could be calculated a number of ways, including:

1. The initial increase in investment required for the project.
2. The end-of-the-year book values of the investment, resulting in six different rates of return.
3. The average-for-the-year book values of the investment, yielding six different rates of return.
4. An average book value of the investment for the project life.

You can see that a large number of combinations is possible.

In addition, it is not clear what represents an appropriate definition of "investment" as a starting point for all four of the investment bases

630 SECTION III   Using Accounting Data in Special Analysis for Decision Making

described above. The conflict arises in part because of uncertainty as to whether we should look at the investment alone or whether we should determine what happens to the company's overall asset base as a result of the investment. To illustrate this conflict, consider the lathe that the Berney Machine Company is thinking of purchasing. If we want to look at the impact on accounting numbers, what should be defined as investment? Three among a number of possible approaches are:

1. Recording basis for book purposes of the new asset:

New lathe $20,000

2. Cash outlay required by the new investment:

Cost of new lathe		$20,000
Less: Investment tax credit	$2,000	
Cash inflow from sale of old lathe	2,000	
Tax savings from loss on sale of old lathe, $1,000 × 46%	460	4,460
Initial investment		$15,540

3. Increase in book value of Berney's total asset base as a result of replacement:

Cost of new lathe		$20,000
Deduct: Write-off of old lathe		3,000
		$17,000
Add: Cash inflow from sale of old lathe	$2,000	
Tax savings from loss on old lathe	460	
Tax savings from investment tax credit	2,000	4,460
Initial change in asset base of Berney due to replacement		$21,460

There are problems with any of the three definitions of initial investment shown above. With the first, the number being used has no economic significance, in that it does not represent what the company would give up to acquire the new lathe. However, using this accounting number at which the lathe would be recorded is consistent with the use of accounting income as the numerator of the accounting rate-of-return fraction.

The second definition of initial investment—cash outlay—does have an economic meaning in that it describes the resources which would be used if the investment were made. However, if it is used as the denominator of the accounting rate-of-return ratio, we are looking at cash flows relative to income, which is based on accrual accounting concepts.

The last number, the increase in book value of Berney's total asset base as a result of replacement, fits the project into the context of the firm's total asset structure. It attempts to depict how the asset base will change when replacement takes place. Generally, rather than taking this approach, companies considering investments prefer to consider the project isolated from the firm's existing asset base.

Any of the three figures described above captures "investment" at a single point in time. The investment changes over the life of the asset. For example, the $20,000 cost of the new asset will be adjusted over the life of the project for book purposes as depreciation is recorded.

There is no one acceptable answer as to how the accounting rate of return should be calculated. Any company which wants to use the model must specify how the income and investment components will be calculated.

Companies which do calculate accounting rate of return tend to generate a number which attempts to describe return over the life of the project rather than computing a separate rate of return for each year of the project's life. For this there are at least two reasons. First, if they calculate a different return for each year of a project's life, the choice of accounting methods will influence the results. For example, the accounting income generated by a project on a year-by-year basis would differ, depending on whether any investment credit was accounted for by the flow-through method or by the deferred method.

Second, if a company calculates a different return for each year of a project's life using as the investment base the book value of the asset, the rate of return will tend to rise each year. This happens because the book value of the asset decreases each year owing to depreciation.

There appear to be two commonly used methods of calculating accounting rate of return for the life of a project:

$$\frac{\text{Accounting rate}}{\text{of return}} = \frac{\text{average increase in income over project's life}}{\text{initial recording basis of investment}}$$

$$\frac{\text{Accounting rate}}{\text{of return}} = \frac{\text{average increase in income over project's life}}{\text{average book value of the investment over project's life}}$$

The calculations required to apply these two methods, based on the data for the Berney Machine Company, are as follows:

$$\frac{\substack{\text{Average increase in income} \\ \text{over project's life} \\ \text{(Illustration 15-3)}}}{} = \frac{\text{income for each year of the project's life}}{\text{project life}}$$

$$= \frac{\substack{\$5,140 + \$4,140 + \$3,330 + \$3,330 \\ + \$3,330 + \$3,330}}{6 \text{ years}}$$

$$= \underline{\underline{\$3,767}}$$

$$\frac{\text{Initial recording basis}}{\text{of asset}} = \underline{\underline{\$20,000}}$$

$$\begin{array}{rl} \text{Average book value of the} \\ \text{investment over the} & = \dfrac{\text{beginning-of-the-year book value for each year}^2}{\text{project life}} \\ \text{project's life} \end{array}$$

$$or \quad = \dfrac{\left(\begin{array}{c}\text{initial recording}\\ \text{basis of asset}\end{array}\right) + \left(\begin{array}{c}\text{book value at beginning of}\\ \text{last year of asset's life}\end{array}\right)}{2}$$

$$= \dfrac{\$20,000 + \$16,667 + \$13,334 + \$10,001 \\ + \$6,668 + \$3,335}{6 \text{ years}}$$

$$= \underline{\$11,667}$$

$$or$$

$$= \dfrac{\$20,000 + \$3,335}{2}$$

$$= \underline{\$11,667}$$

The first computation of accounting rate of return *using the initial recording basis of the asset* would be:

$$\text{Accounting rate of return} = \dfrac{\$3,767}{\$20,000} = 18.8\%$$

Using the average book value of the investment over the project's life would result in a return almost double that shown above:

$$\text{Accounting rate of return} = \dfrac{\$3,767}{\$11,667} = 32.3\%$$

The first method of making the calculation looks at the investment as being a commitment over the life of the project. The second method recognizes that the investment will be recovered in part on a year-by-year basis through cash flows related to the fact that the depreciation expense recorded does not represent a cash outlay. Note, however, that the figures used are book figures and do not represent cash committed to the project.

With these two alternatives for calculating rate of return, there is no right or wrong. The rates generated must be viewed in the context of how they were generated. If the average book value is used, the cut-off rate

---

[2] Book value = cost less accumulated depreciation; thus, book value for the beginning of year 2 would be:

$$\begin{array}{rl} \$20,000 & \text{original cost} \\ -3,333 & \text{accumulated depreciation} \\ \hline \$16,667 & \text{book value} \end{array}$$

in deciding whether a project is acceptable should be significantly higher than the rate based on the use of initial investment.

Why Accounting Rate of Return Is Calculated

After thinking about the difficulties of computing an accounting rate of return and the many results which may be obtained, you may wonder why companies use this method to evaluate capital investments. From an economic point of view, cash flows rather than accrual income should be used in evaluating an investment alternative. However, for the reasons cited below, managers may try to assess the impact of an investment on income as measured by accounting principles.

First, a firm may calculate an account rate of return because they believe it approximates how the investment will impact on numbers which are *externally* circulated. Assume that a company's return on investment based on externally circulated numbers has been increasing each year and currently stands at 18%. In determining whether a particular investment should be made, management will want to know how that 18% figure will be affected by a proposed investment if the investment is of a significant size. If the accounting rate of return indicates that the return on the investment proposal being considered is higher than 18%, the investment is expected to have a positive impact on the company's overall rate of return. On the other hand, if the project has a rate of return of less than 18%, it will have a negative impact on the company's overall rate of return.

Second, remember that return on investment may be used internally to measure the performance of part of the organization which is treated as an investment center and/or to evaluate the performance of the manager who heads that investment center. If return on investment is used to evaluate performance of either the investment center or its manager, that manager will want to know the impact of a particular investment on return on investment for the investment center which he or she manages. Thus, the manager will probably use the accounting rate-of-return model to approximate that impact.

In addition, the higher-level managers to whom the heads of investment centers report may want to know the accounting rate of return on a particular investment as a check to determine whether those heads of investment centers are making decisions which are dysfunctional for the company as a whole. Consider an investment center which has a rate of return of 20%. If a proposed project would earn less than that amount, the manager of the investment center will be likely to turn it down because it would have a negative impact on the performance of the organization *segment* which he or she heads. However, if the rate which the proposed project can earn is more than the overall company's cost of capital and there are no competing projects with better rates of return, the *company's* rate of return will be enhanced by the investment which the investment center manager did not find satisfactory.

Shortcomings of Accounting Rate of Return

While the accounting rate of return attempts to approximate for the manager the impact of a particular investment decision on accounting numbers, it does not describe the economic essence of the transaction. Cash, not accounting income, has value to a company, because it can be invested and earn a rate of return. Since the accounting rate-of-return method does not depict the cash impact of an investment decision, it cannot aid managers in making decisions which will enhance the cash inflows of the company.

Since the year-by-year return for an investment is measured in accrual income terms rather than cash, we cannot find the present value of those returns. Hence, income which is earned in Year 5 is treated similarly to income earned in Year 1.

CASH-PAYBACK METHOD

The cash-payback method for evaluating possible investments is based on the concept that the shorter the period required to recover an investment, the better the investment is. Cash payback for projects which have even cash flows can be calculated as follows:

$$\text{Cash payback} = \frac{\text{cash investment}}{\text{annual cash flow}}$$

Assume that an investment cost $40,000 and generates $10,000 of cash flow each year. The payback period would be four years. That is, in four years the investor will have recovered the full amount of his or her investment.

If cash flows are not even, the cash-payback period is found by accumulating cash flows until the investment is recovered. Using the cash-flow figures for Berney Machine Company given in Illustration 15-5, we should first calculate what the cash investment is. We can calculate it in a number of ways, including the following two:

Cash investment		$20,000
Cash investment		$20,000
Less: Tax savings from investment tax credit	$ 2,000	
Cash from sale of old lathe	2,000	
Tax savings from loss on sale of old lathe	460	4,460
Cash investment		$15,540

If we are not discounting cash flows, as is frequently the case when the cash-payback method is used, it doesn't matter whether items such as the tax savings from the investment tax credit are considered a reduction in the cash investment or a part of the stream of cash inflows from the investment. What does matter is that they not be counted both places.

Using $20,000 as the cash investment, we would calculate the payback as follows:

	ANNUAL CASH FLOW	CUMULATIVE CASH FLOW
Year 1	$10,211	$10,211
Year 2	6,363	16,574
Year 3	6,965	23,539

We can see that the investment is recovered sometime during Year 3.

If we assume that cash flows are distributed evenly over the year, we can approximate when in Year 3 payback is reached by making the following calculation:

Cash investment	$20,000
Cumulative cash flow at end of Year 2	16,574
Unrecovered Investment at end of Year 2	$ 3,426

$3,426/$6,965 cash flows for Year 3 = 49%.

Thus we could approximate the payback as being approximately $2\frac{1}{2}$ years.

If, using Method 2, we defined the cash investment as $15,540, we would calculate the payback as follows:

	ANNUAL CASH FLOW		CUMULATIVE CASH FLOW
Year 1	$10,211 − ($2,000 investment tax credit + $2,000 from selling old lathe + $460 tax savings from loss on sale of old asset) =	$5,751	$ 5,751
Year 2		$6,363	$12,114
Year 3		$6,965	$19,079

We took out of annual cash flows those items which we used to reduce the cash investment in the asset. The resulting payback comes sometime in the third year. Again, we can approximate where if we assume that cash flows are distributed evenly during the third year:

Cash investment	$15,540
Cumulative cash flow at end of Year 2	12,114
Unrecovered investment at the end of Year 2	$ 3,426

$3,426/$6,965 cash flows for Year 3 = 49%

Our results will be the same whether we calculate our investment by Method 1, Method 2, or something in between.

Shortcomings of the Cash-Payback Method

Two criticisms are frequently made of the payback method as a tool for evaluating capital expenditures. The first is that if the decision rule, "Choose the investment with the shortest payback" is applied indiscriminately, poor decisions *may* be made. For example, assume that there are two projects with the following annual cash flows, cash investment requirements, and project lives:

	ANNUAL CASH FLOW	CASH INVESTMENT	PROJECT LIFE
Project A	$10,000	$20,000	3
Project B	$12,000	$36,000	5

Paybacks for the two projects would be:

$$\text{Project A} = \$20,000/\$10,000 = 2 \text{ years}$$
$$\text{Project B} = \$36,000/\$12,000 = 3 \text{ years}$$

A simplistic application of payback would result in the selection of Project A with a payback of 2 years. This ignores the fact that Project A is expected to generate $10,000 per year for only 3 years, while Project B is expected to generate $12,000 for 5 years. Within a 2-year period, cash flows from Project A will be only $20,000, while those from Project B will be $24,000.

Another criticism frequently made of the cash-payback method is that the traditional calculation of this statistic ignores the time value of money. To illustrate, we could have two projects with the following cash flows:

	INVESTMENT	ANNUAL CASH FLOWS	
		Year 1	Year 2
Project A	$10,000	$5,000	$5,000
Project B	$10,000	$7,000	$3,000

The payback for both projects is 2 years. However, because Project B returns greater cash flows earlier in the investment's life, all other things being equal, it is superior to Project A.

Companies have overcome this problem by discounting the cash flows before making the cash-payback calculation. If we do this, we cannot be indifferent to whether a cash flow for something such as the selling of an old asset is considered a reduction in the cash investment or a cash flow for the period. We should consider as reduction in the cash investment only those cash flows which will occur at approximately the same time as the cash outlay for the new asset.

Applying the idea of a discounted cash payback to the Berney Machine Company example, assume that the cash from the sale of the old lathe will be realized immediately and that the tax savings resulting from the investment tax credit and the loss on the sale of the old asset will be realized at the end of Year 1. Remember that Berney wanted to earn a 15% return on any investments.

Cash investment	$20,000
Less: Proceeds from sale of old lathe	2,000
Net cash investment to be recovered	$18,000

ANNUAL CASH FLOW (Illustration 15-5)	DISCOUNT FACTOR AT 15%[a]	DISCOUNTED CASH FLOW	CUMULATIVE DISCOUNTED CASH FLOW
Year 1 $10,211 − $2,000 from sale of old lathe = $8,211	.870	$7,144	$ 7,144
Year 2 $6,363	.756	4,810	11,954
Year 3 $6,965	.658	4,583	16,537
Year 4 $6,965	.572	3,984	20,521

[a] From Table A in the appendix to Chapter 14, p. 602.

As you can see from the cumulative cash flows shown above, when cash flows are discounted, the payback period is extended from $2\frac{1}{2}$ years to approximately $3\frac{1}{3}$ years.

THE NET-PRESENT-VALUE METHOD

When the net-present-value method is applied, cash flows from a project discounted at a predetermined rate are compared with the investment. If the discounted cash flows equal or exceed the required investment, the project is acceptable. To apply this method we must have:

1. The cash investment required.
2. The amount and timing of the cash flows from the project.
3. The desired rate of return for the project which will be used as the rate at which cash flows are discounted.

Based on our discounted cash-payback analysis given above, we already know that the project is acceptable based on Berney's desired rate of return of 15%, because in the fourth year the cash investment is recovered. However, to illustrate the method, we shall do the complete analysis:

YEAR	ANNUAL CASH FLOW (Illustration 15-5)	DISCOUNT FACTOR AT 15%	DISCOUNTED CASH FLOW
1	$8,211	.870	$ 7,144
2	6,363	.756	4,810
3	6,965	.658	4,583
4	6,965	.572	3,984
5	6,965	.497	3,462
6	5,130	.432	2,216
	Total discounted cash flows from project		$26,199
	Cash investment required for project ($20,000 − $2,000 from sale of old lathe)		18,000
	Net present value		$ 8,199

Any net present value of zero or greater indicates that the project is acceptable based on the discount rate which is being used. Remember our discussion of present value in relationship to the Berney example. If we had used a lower discount rate, the project's net present value would have been even greater. Using a higher discount rate, the project would have yielded a lower net present value.

Shortcoming of the Net-Present-Value Method

The most frequent criticism of the net-present-value method is that, while it tells you whether or not a project is acceptable, it does not tell you what discounted rate of return is actually earned by that investment. This problem is overcome when the internal rate-of-return method is used.

INTERNAL RATE-OF-RETURN METHOD

To calculate the internal rate of return on a project, we must have two of the same things we need to calculate net present value: cash investment and cash flows from the project. What we don't have to specify is any desired rate of return. What the method does, instead, is determine what discounted rate of return is inherent in a specific investment and a specified series of cash flows. We are looking for the rate of return which equates a series of cash flows with the cash investment.

Assume that we have an investment proposal which will require a cash investment of $33,520, has a life of 5 years, and will generate a cash flow of $10,000 at the end of each of those next 5 years. Because we want to take into consideration the fact that money has time value, we cannot simply look at the cash flows relative to the investment to get a rate. All of the cash flows do not come at the same point in time. To see the logic of how we shall make the computation, remember how we compute present value when we have cash flows and a discount rate:

$$\text{Present value of investment} = \text{cash flows} \times \left(\begin{array}{l} \text{present-value factor for} \\ \text{life of project at desired} \\ \text{rate of return} \end{array} \right)$$

With our example, we have a different set of pieces of information. We know the present value of the investment—$33,520, the required cash investment. We know the cash flows—$10,000—and also the life of the project. What we don't know is the rate.

Plugging what we do know into the formula given above, we have:

$$\$33,520 = \$10,000 \times R \text{ (the unknown rate for 5 years)}$$

Going through the algebraic manipulations, we have:

$$\$33,500 = \$10,000R$$

Dividing each side of our equation by $10,000, we then have:

$$\frac{\$33,520}{\$10,000} = R$$

and finally

$$\underline{\underline{3.352}} = R$$

What we have found is the present-value factor. We must now check our present-value-of-an-annuity table (Table B in the appendix to Chapter 14, p. 604) to see what rate is implied with this number. We shall read across the 5-period line until we find something close to 3.352. We find this under the rate column for 15%. In other words, if a project has a life of 5 years, returns $10,000 at the end of each of those years, and costs $33,520, its internal rate of return is 15%. We can prove this result by applying our present-value formula in the normal manner:

$$\begin{aligned} \text{Present value} &= \text{cash flows} \times \text{present-value factor} \\ &= \$10,000 \times 3.352 \text{ (discount rate at 15\% for 5 years)} \\ &= \underline{\underline{\$33,520}} \end{aligned}$$

The mechanics of the process become more complex if our cash flows are not equal, as is true with the Berney example. Fortunately, computer programs are readily available to do the mechanics for you. Some hand-held calculators will also enable you to determine the internal rate of return rapidly.

To further enhance our understanding of the conceptual basis of internal rate of return, let's assume that we have no computer program and the battery on our hand-held calculator has died. How would we calculate internal rate of return?

Recall what our objective is—to find the rate of return which will equate a series of cash flows with the cash investment. We will proceed as follows:

1. Estimate the internal rate of return by looking at cash investment relative to cash flows from the investment. Since our cash flows using the Berney Machine Company data are not equal, we shall find our average cash flow (using yearly cash flows from Illustration 15-5):

$$\text{Average cash flow} = \frac{\$8,211 + \$6,363 + \$6,965 + \$6,965 + \$6,965 + \$5,130}{6 \text{ years}}$$

$$= \underline{\underline{\$6,767}}$$

$$\frac{\text{cash investment}^3}{\text{average cash flows}} = \frac{\$18,000}{\$6,767} = \underline{\underline{2.660}}$$

2. Look in the present-value-of-an-annuity table along the row which is equal to the life of the project and read across that row until you find the present-value factors which bracket (the present value falls between these values) the one you computed in Step 1.

In the case of Berney, we read across the 6-period row, and we find that the present-value factor of 2.660 which we computed in Step 1 is bracketed by a return of 28%[4], which has a present-value factor of 2.759, and 30%, which has a present-value factor of 2.643. Actually, the 2.660 present-value factor which we computed is so close to the present-value factor for 30% that we could stop right here and say that the return on the new lathe is approximately 30%. However, to demonstrate fully the way internal rate of return is computed, we shall continue and come up with a more exact rate.

3. Test the rates selected by multiplying the present value of $1 for the factors selected by each of the cash flows. Note that while we use the present value of an annuity table to estimate the rate, since the cash flows are of uneven sizes, the actual discounting will have to be based on the present-value-of-$1 table (Table A, p. 603).

Using the data from the Berney Machine Company example, our calculations would appear as follows:

YEAR	CASH FLOW	PRESENT-VALUE FACTOR FOR 28%	CASH FLOWS DISCOUNTED AT 28%	PRESENT-VALUE FACTOR FOR 30%	CASH FLOWS DISCOUNTED AT 30%
1	$8,211	.781	$ 6,413	.769	$ 6,314
2	6,363	.610	3,881	.592	3,767
3	6,965	.477	3,322	.455	3,169
4	6,965	.373	2,598	.350	2,438
5	6,965	.291	2,027	.269	1,874
6	5,130	.227	1,165	.207	1,062
		Total discounted cash flows	$19,406		$18,624

---

[3] Cash investment = $20,000 − 2,000 from resale of old lathe = $18,000.
[4] If our present-value-of-an-annuity table had 29%, we would have used this rather than 28%.

Since our cash investment is $18,000 ($20,000 − $2,000 from sale of old lathe), we can see that the rate is very close to 30%. We are looking for the rate that will equate the cash flows with the cash investment.

Unfortunately, when we apply the trial rates we selected to the cash flows, the total discounted cash flows range from $19,606 to $18,624. The true rate does not lie within this interval but must be something more than 30%. Using our present-value tables, the next highest rate we have is 35%. We'll test this rate as follows:

YEAR	CASH FLOW	PRESENT-VALUE FACTOR FOR 35%	CASH FLOWS DISCOUNTED AT 35%
1	$8,211	.741	$ 6,084
2	6,363	.549	3,493
3	6,965	.406	2,828
4	6,965	.301	2,096
5	6,965	.223	1,553
6	5,130	.165	846
			$16,900

Based on our total discounted cash flows, we know that the true rate of return lies somewhere between 30% and 35%.

RATE	DISCOUNTED CASH FLOW
30%	$18,624
35%	16,900
Difference	$ 1,724
Cash Investment	$18,000
Discounted cash flow @ 30%	18,624
Difference	$ 624

$$\frac{\$624}{\$1,724} = 36\%$$

Thus, the true rate lies approximately at (.36)(.05) beyond 30%—.05 being the difference between 30% and 35%. By interpolation the internal rate of return is:

Internal rate of return = .30 + (.36)(.05) = .30 + .018 = 31.8%

We added the increment to 30% because we could tell by looking at the total discounted cash flows that the rate was higher than 30%.

Berney's required rate of return on investments was 15%, so the return from replacing the lathe far exceeds this standard. The decision rule would tell Berney that the replacement should be made.

UNDERLYING ASSUMPTIONS AND SENSITIVITY ANALYSIS

It is apparent that for complex projects a multitude of estimates must be made, some of them fairly accurate, others resting on certain assumptions about the future. As part of any capital budgeting request the major assumptions which underlie the request should be stated. This requirement forces the preparer of the capital expenditure analysis to clarify the assumptions on which a proposal is based.

It also helps a reviewer to understand the numbers in the request. In addition, in terms of follow-up, reality can be compared with assumptions that were made when the request was initially made and approved.

Another advantage of stating the underlying assumptions is that doing so facilitates sensitivity analysis. With sensitivity analysis we are trying to determine the effects on a project, and its acceptability, of variations in the basic assumptions. Berney, for example, might vary his cash savings estimates by 5% to 10% to compensate for estimation errors and reassess the acquisition of the lathe on this basis.

Sensitivity analysis tends to be used in two contexts. First, as with the Berney example given above, it is used as a way to compensate for errors in estimates which underlie a project. Thus cash flows from a project are varied by some amount and the impact noted. Rather than taking this approach, some companies prepare a worst-case and best-case senario and analyze the impact on capital project proposals.

ILLUSTRATION FROM PRACTICE: GENERAL ELECTRIC APPROACH TO SENSITIVITY ANALYSIS AND THE DEVELOPMENT OF STATEMENTS OF UNDERLYING ASSUMPTIONS FOR CAPITAL PROJECT REQUESTS

Most of us are familiar with the General Electric name because of its well-known home appliance line and its light bulbs. However, GE produces a wide range of products, including aircraft engines, natural resources, communication systems, and plastics. In addition, it owns the General Electric Credit Corporation and the General Electric Venture Capital Corporation, which represent part of its financial services line of business. Its earnings are almost $2 billion, and it employs almost 300,000 people around the world.

Illustration 15-6 shows the forms which GE uses to obtain supporting data for capital project requests. As you can see, key alternatives must be listed and evaluated. In addition the key assumptions underlying the proposal and its alternatives must be stated. Finally the form requests information relative to sensitivity of the assumptions, especially to downside risk.

ILLUSTRATION
15-6

Illustration
from practice—
General Electric

Key Assumptions, Evaluation of Alternatives, and Sensitivity Analysis

1. *Brief description of major alternatives*

   This Request –

   Alternative I –

   Alternative II –

   Alternative III –

2. *Principal advantages/disadvantages and reasons for rejecting alternatives*

   This Request –

   Alternative I –

   Alternative II –

   Alternative III –

3. *Key assumptions basic to achieving project objectives upon which
   This Request is based*

   a.

   b.

   c.

   d.

   e.

4. *Key assumptions upon which individual alternatives are based*

   Alternative I   a.

                    b.

                    c.

   Alternative II   a.

                    b.

                    c.

ILLUSTRATION 15-6—Cont.

Alternative III a.

         b.

         c.

5. *Sensitivity Analysis* – Evaluate the project *downside risk* by identifying "worst case" changes in key variables. The project's upside potential, if relevant, may also be identified here, or in the text of the appropriation.

VARIABLE (SELLING PRICES, MARKET SHARE, MATERIAL COSTS, ETC.)	ASSUMPTION REFLECTED IN PROJECT FUNDS FLOW	MANAGEMENT ASSESSMENT OF "WORST CASE" RESULTS	DOWNSIDE DCRR	
			Reported	Inflation adjusted

SIMPLIFIED ILLUSTRATIVE EXAMPLES

In the comprehensive example, you saw how to develop the data needed for any of the four capital budgeting techniques described. Although the data developed were related to a project involving asset replacement, the income-statement effects, effects of taxes, and cash-flow information would be developed the same way regardless of the type of project involved. Following are two simplified examples of capital expenditure decisions which are commonly encountered—a capital project involving expansion and a lease-or-buy decision. The data needed for the decision models used have already been developed for you.

Expansion Project

The Quality Paperback Company is considering adding a new line of paperbacks. It currently prints the following lines: mystery, romantic fiction, and science fiction. It would like to add a series of "how-to" books, including diet books, cookbooks, popular psychology, and home repair books. Quality Paperbacks has a cost of capital of 16% and will use the net-present-value method in evaluating the proposed expansion.

Quality Paperbacks has accumulated the following data:

Initial cash investment in equipment and other capital assets	$50,000
Anticipated annual revenues from sales	$38,000
Anticipated annual cash expenses	$15,000
Annual taxes	$ 8,300
Investment time horizon	5 years

As with the previous example involving asset reduction, Quality would have to make many estimates to develop the data given above—cost and salvage value of the capital assets, sales volume, and the level of all expenses related to the new production. In addition, an expansion project of this type requires the use of a time horizon. With the asset replacement example, the time horizon was provided by the life of the new equipment. With Quality Paperbacks they can continue to print "how-to" books for an infinite period of time, although equipment would have to be replaced. Also, the capital assets required may have different lives. In projects of this type, management frequently develops a policy as to what time horizon should be used. Five years, the time period used by Quality, is a period frequently used.

Based on a 16% rate of return, the project has a negative net present value and cannot be economically justified, as shown below:

Cash revenues	$38,000
Cash expenses	15,000
Cash income before taxes	$23,000
Less: Taxes	8,300
Annual cash flow	$14,700

Discounted cash flow from project:	
$14,700 × present value of an annuity @ 16% for 5 years (Table B)	
= $14,700 × 3.274	$48,128
Cash investment	50,000
Net present value	($ 1,872)

Lease versus Buy

The Olsen Electrical Supply Company wants to obtain a copying machine. They can either buy the machine or lease it. Under either alternative Olsen will have to pay for repairs and maintenance and supply the necessary paper. Olsen uses the net-present-value method in evaluating capital projects and wants any investment to earn a return of 20%. Lease payments will be made on the first day of each year of the lease agreement. If the copying machine is purchased, Olsen anticipates it will have a life of six years and at the end of that period a salvage value of $500. The cost of buying the machine is $7,000, while annual lease payments are $1,800. To simplify, taxes are ignored in this example.

ILLUSTRATION 15-7

Illustration from Practice: EMHART CORPORATION BUY VERSUS LEASE ANALYSIS

	0	1	2	3	4	5	6	7	TOTAL
				$000 YEARS					
BUY CASE MAINTENANCE (a)									
PROPERTY TAX & INSURANCE		(20)	(20)	(20)	(20)	(20)			(100)
OTHER COSTS									
SUBTOTAL		(20)	(20)	(20)	(20)	(20)			(100)
LESS INCOME TAX @ 50%		10	10	10	10	10			50
AFTER TAX COSTS		(10)	(10)	(10)	(10)	(10)			(50)
PURCHASE COST OF ASSET (b)	(500)								(500)
INVESTMENT TAX CREDIT OR ALLOWANCE (c)	50								50
AFTER TAX PROCEEDS FROM SALE OF ASSET (d)						25			25
DEPRECIATION TAX SHIELD (e)	38	55	52	53	52				250
NET CASH FLOW—BUY	(412)	45	42	43	42	15			(225)
LEASE CASE ANNUAL LEASE COST (f)		(176)	(176)	(176)	(176)	(176)			(880)
OTHER COSTS									
LESS INCOME TAX @ 50%		88	88	88	88	88			440
NET CASH FLOW—LEASE		(88)	(88)	(88)	(88)	(88)			(440)
RELATIVE CASH FLOW	(412)	133	130	131	130	103			215
IMPLICIT INTEREST RATE 16% (after tax)									

CEA 11C

Assuming the after tax borrowing rate is 8%, this analysis shows that asset should be purchased not leased, as the implicit after tax interest rate included in the lease is 16.4%.

ACRS Depreciation

Year	%	Amount	× Tax rate	= Tax Shield (e)
0*	15	$ 75	50%	$ 38
1	22	110	50%	55
2	21	105	50%	52
3	21	105	50%	53
4	21	105	50%	52
	100	$500		$250

* Recorded in year 0, as ACRS depreciation for personal property includes the ½ year convention. Note that the ½ year convention does not apply to real property.

FORM CEA-11C

a. Maintenance is excluded because it will be incurred whether asset is leased or purchased.
b. Purchase cost of assets excluded freight and installation, as these costs would be incurred whether the assets were leased or purchased.
c. In some lease contracts, the lessee is granted the investment tax credit or allowance. In such cases the credit or allowance is to be omitted, as it applied whether the asset is leased or purchased.
d. Assumption made that assets sold at end of 5th year for $50 which after providing for income taxes at 50% results in cash proceeds of $25.
f. Initial lease contract covers a 3 year term. Assumption is made that lease will be renewed for 2 additional years so that the lease period corresponds to asset's estimated useful life of 5 years.

Using Olsen's discount rate, the machine should be purchased, as this alternative results in the lowest present value—$6,832 versus $7,184, calculated as follows:

Discounted cash flows for Lease Payments:
$1,800 × present value of an annuity for 5 periods @ 20% +
"1"[a] (Table B) = $1,800 × (2.991 + 1) $7,184

Cash investment   7,000

Less: Present value of salvage = $500 × present value of $1 @
20% for 6 years (Table A) = $500 × .335   (168)

Net investment   6,832

Net-present-value differential $ 352

---

[a] Since the payments are made at the beginning of the year, the first payment is not discounted and we have only 5 payments to be discontinued.

ILLUSTRATION FROM PRACTICE: EMHART'S BUY-OR-LEASE ANALYSIS

A more elaborate illustration of how the cash-flow data for a buy-versus-lease analysis is developed is shown in Illustration 15-7. This example is taken from the instructions which Emhart Corporation provides to its managers who are involved in capital project requests and analysis. Emhart's operations were described earlier in this chapter.

CHOICE OF AN EVALUATION METHOD

We have looked at how four different tools for evaluating capital projects are applied and discussed the shortcomings of each. At this point you may feel confused and be asking yourself, "Which method should be used?" One problem with managerial accounting is that often there is no one answer to such questions.

A company should not invest in a project which will not return an amount greater than its cost of capital. The techniques which will allow a company to determine whether a project will generate a positive return are the net-present-value method, the internal rate-of-return method, and the discounted cash-payback method. For this reason, projects should be evaluated using one of these techniques.

However, managers may wish to supplement the information obtained from using those methods by looking at undiscounted cash payback and/or accounting rate of return. The manager may want to know not only whether the project is justified taking into consideration the time value of money and the company's cost of capital (net-present-value and internal rate-of-return methods) but how soon the cash investment will be recovered (cash payback) and how the income statement will be affected (accounting rate of return).

In addition, managers may choose to use different methods or combinations of methods in different situations. At least three variables may affect the choice of a method: (1) the type of capital request being considered, (2) the dollars being committed, and (3) the part of the organization which is requesting the project. Below we give some examples of the effect of these variables.

ILLUSTRATION FROM PRACTICE: UNIROYAL'S CAPITAL PROJECTS CLASSIFICATION SYSTEM

The classes of capital project requests used by Uniroyal are shown in Illustration 15-8. As you can see, they basically recognize projects related to the maintenance of business (replacement), cost reduction, expansion of existing business, or introduction of new products.

ILLUSTRATION 15-8

Illustration from Practice: Uniroyal

Capital Project Classification System Used by Uniroyal

1. CLASS I—MAINTENANCE OF BUSINESS
   A—Funds necessary to maintain operation.
   B—Funds necessary to remain in business.
   C—Funds necessary for OSHA, Safety or Environmental products or processes to remain in current business activities.
   CLASS I-S—Same as IA, B, C, but with savings.

2. CLASS II—COST REDUCTIONS
   Funds which would generate a positive economic savings to current operating costs based on the most recent full-year actual performance.

3. CLASS III—EXPANSION
   Funds requested to expand current production capacity or to debottleneck existing systems.

4. CLASS IV—NEW PRODUCTS
   A—To establish production of new products for commercial sale.
   B—*New Products:* Funds requested to establish pilot or laboratory investment.
   C—*Acquisition of Joint Venture:* Funds required to purchase, either wholly or partially, a business, product line, customer list, etc.

Example 1. Remember that some companies break their business down into subcomponents and then classify these components as to whether (a) the business unit is a high-growth and high-profit unit, (b) the future of the business unit is uncertain, (c) the business unit is primarily a generator of cash, or (d) the business unit is in a declining area and is getting ready for harvest (sale or discontinuance).

Such a company may look primarily at payback for projects requested by the part of the organization ready for harvest, as they want to limit investments to projects which will be realized in a short period.

Example 2. If a project is extremely large, its impact on the income statement seen by external investors may be a prime consideration of management. As a result, those making the capital investment decision may give added weight to the accounting rate of return.

Example 3. A company may wish to impose different standards for projects of different types and different sizes.

ILLUSTRATION FROM PRACTICE: UNIROYAL'S MATRIX FOR EVALUATING CAPITAL PROJECTS

Uniroyal, a company whose operations were previously described, has developed the matrix shown below for viewing projects. They set a different standard in terms of payback and rate of return for different classes of projects with different investment requirements. For example, cost reduction projects are expected to have a quicker payback and a higher rate of return than new projects, thus encouraging the manager to think in terms of new projects and also have more "patience" with a new product than in a case where the motive is only cost reduction economics. If the matrix shown below were completed, a cut-off payback and return rate would be included in each of the cells.

DOLLARS (in thousands)	CLASS I AND CLASS II: COST REDUCTION AND MAINTENANCE		CLASS III: EXPANSION		CLASS IV: NEW PRODUCTS	
	Payback	Return	Payback	Return	Payback	Return
$ 50–100						
$100–250						
$250–500						
$500–1,000						
over $1,000						

PROJECT CLASSIFICATIONS AND CORPORATE STRATEGY

As you saw in Illustration 15-8, Uniroyal uses four basic classes for its capital projects: maintenance of business, cost reduction, expansion, and new products. One reason is to allow applying different decision rules to different types of projects. Such classification also is useful in integrating capital budgeting with corporate strategy. For example, suppose that a company does use Uniroyal's four classes. They can then look at what they are committing into each category relative to the overall goals of the company.

A company might develop a matrix of the following type:

CAPITAL PROJECT CLASS	PRESENT PERCENT OF CAPITAL EXPENDITURES	CAPITAL INVESTMENT OBJECTIVES
Maintenance of business	70%	50%
Cost reduction	10%	20%
Expansion of existing business	10%	10%
New product	10%	20%

This matrix indicates that the company is going to shift some of its resources away from maintenance and into cost reduction and the development of new products—an expression of corporate strategy.

PROBLEMS AND REWARDS OF CAPITAL BUDGETING

It is easy to see why the quantitative analysis of capital projects is often difficult. This analysis requires the estimation of many variables for future periods. These include estimation of future revenue and expense streams in accrual-accounting or cash-flow terms, the life of depreciable assets, and tax rates. Despite a company's best efforts, significant differences may occur between actual results and estimates made as part of the capital project evaluation process.

On the positive side, the capital budgeting process requires that a manager think through a capital expenditure request, considering its costs and benefits and the period of time which will be affected by the project. This process of trying to quantify expectations and subjecting those expectations to review enhances the likelihood that investments will be made in projects in keeping with the goals of the company.

In addition, the data required as part of the capital budgeting process serve as a benchmark against which actual results can be measured. Significant variances should trigger an investigation and can lead to corrective actions.

LINKAGE OF THE CAPITAL EXPENDITURES BUDGET TO OTHER BUDGETS

The quantitative techniques for looking at capital expenditure projects described in this chapter enable a company to apply predetermined criteria and decide what projects are acceptable, given those criteria. Once quantitative factors have indicated that a project is acceptable, nonquantitative factors are considered.

If it is decided to make a project operational, it becomes a part of the organization's capital budget and its impact must be incorporated into other budgets which make up the master budget. If, for example, as the result of capital project analysis a decision is made that a piece of equipment will be purchased, the impact of that purchase must be factored into other budgets.

Raw materials usage and direct labor budgets may be affected and thus the budgeted income statement and cash flows. Any interest costs which will be incurred as a result of the purchase must be factored into the budgeted income statement and, to the extent the interest is paid, into the cash budget. The budgeted balance sheet will reflect the anticipated cost of the equipment and related depreciation.

chapter highlights

A recurring problem which organizations face is where to make long-term investment commitments. A number of techniques have been developed to aid managers in determining what capital projects should be undertaken. These techniques include the accounting rate of return, cash payback, net present value, and internal rate of return.

The accounting rate-of-return method tries to look at accounting income based on accrual concepts relative to investment to determine whether a project is justified. It attempts to depict the income-statement impact of a capital investment. Managers may want this information because it shows them how an investment would affect externally circulated financial statements or internally generated statistics which are used in performance evaluation.

The other three techniques substitute cash flows for accounting income and investment. The cash-payback method attempts to tell the manager how long it will be before the required cash investment is recovered. The discounted cash-payback method, the net-present-value method, and the internal rate-of-return method all recognize that money has time value and discount cash flows related to a project.

With the net-present-value method, a desired rate of return, which should not be less than the company's cost of capital, must be selected. If the discounted cash flow from a project using that desired rate of return is equal to or exceeds the required investment, the project is economically justified.

The net-present-value method does not tell the user the actual rate of return being earned by a project. This information is provided by the internal rate-of-return technique.

In choosing among the four techniques described, the user should keep in mind that only three—net present value, internal rate of return, and discounted cash payback—will indicate whether a project is generating a time-adjusted rate of return which exceeds the firm's cost of capital. The cash-payback and the accounting rate-of-return methods provide supplemental data which may be helpful to the manager in making capital expenditure decisions.

questions

1. Give a brief description of how the capital budgeting process works.
2. What is the purpose of a postcompletion audit of capital projects?
3. What are two commonly used ways of calculating accounting rate of return? What are the problems involved in using the accounting rate-of-return method?
4. If, from an economic point of view, cash flows rather than accrual income should be used in evaluating an investment alternative, why do companies use the accounting rate-of-return method to evaluate investment alternatives?
5. Should an investment with the shortest payback be chosen? Why?
6. If actual cash flows are used in the payback model, what problem may arise and how might it be corrected?
7. To apply the net-present-value method, what three inputs are necessary? What disadvantage is associated with the method, and how may it be overcome?
8. How should an evaluation method be chosen? What variables should be considered in the choice?
9. Although the capital budgeting process is time-consuming, often difficult, and sometimes results in estimates which are significantly different from actual results, what positive attributes are associated with it?
10. How does the internal rate-of-return method for evaluating capital projects differ from the net-present-value method?
11. When the net-present-value method for evaluating a capital project is used, which projects are acceptable?

12. Which methods for evaluating capital projects ignore the time value of money?

13. Students are frequently confused in looking at amounts on an after-tax basis as to whether they should multiply an amount by the tax rate or by (1 − tax rate). Describe the circumstances when each is appropriate.

14. Why is the depreciation method used for tax purposes the relevant method for depreciation, as opposed to the book method of recording depreciation, when cash flows are being calculated?

15. A company is considering the acquisition of an asset which will cost $50,000. It is anticipated that five years from the date of acquisition the asset will be sold for a gain of $3,000, which will be taxed at the capital gains rate of 28%. If the company is using either the net-present-value method or the internal rate-of-return method to evaluate capital projects, how will the information given above be used?

16. How does the information that is required in applying the internal rate-of-return method to capital project evaluation differ from that required when the net-present-value method is used?

17. Based on the use of a discount rate of 10%, an investment had a net present value of negative $100. If the discount rate had been 8%, would this project have been acceptable? Explain your answer.

18. A project has a cash acquisition cost of $100,000 and will return $40,000 of cash flow for each of the next three years. *In word terms*, explain what the internal rate of return for this project will be. No computations are necessary.

19. Why is finding the internal rate of return for a project which does not have equal cash flows equally spaced over time so difficult without the use of a computer or a calculator which will compute the rate?

20. When a project has equal cash flows, payback is found by cash investment/annual cash flows. If cash flows are not equal, can this method be used? How?

exercises

15—1. The Clean Write Corporation makes typewriter and computer ribbons. It is contemplating the purchase of some robotic equipment to use in its production process. The following data have been prepared with respect to the equipment:

Estimated annual cash operating savings (primarily from reduced labor costs and material spoilage)	$13,000
Cash cost of the equipment	$40,000
Estimated useful life	5 years

Straight-line depreciation will be used for both tax and financial reporting purposes. No significant salvage value for the equipment is anticipated because of technological obsolescence. The equipment is not subject to an investment tax credit. Clean Write pays taxes at the rate of 40%.

REQUIRED:

1. Calculate the cash payback for the equipment based on after-tax cash flows. (Round to one decimal place.)

2. Calculate the accounting rate of return (rounded to the nearest whole percent) for the equipment based on:

   a. $\dfrac{\text{average increase in income over the project's life}}{\text{initial recording basis of the investment}}$

   b. $\dfrac{\text{average increase in income over the project's life}}{\text{average book value of the investment over project's life}}$

3. What other information do you need before you can determine whether the project is acceptable under any of the evaluation methods you have used?

4. What is the major shortcoming of the methods you have used to evaluate the investment?

15—2.   Refer to the information in Exercise 15—1.

REQUIRED:

1. Find the net present value of the investment, assuming the company uses a discount rate of 16% in evaluating projects of this type. Is the project acceptable? Round all amounts to the nearest dollar.

2. Assume that the equipment had an estimated salvage value of $6,000 at the end of five years. Find the net present value using a 16% discount rate. Is the project acceptable? (Round to the nearest dollar.)

15—3.   The Medford Mop and Broom Company is considering the purchase of a piece of equipment which they use in making mops. Data relevant to the acquisition follows:

Cash acquisition cost	$300,000
Estimated annual cash savings from the new equipment	$200,000
Depreciation method for book purposes: straight-line, 6-year life, no salvage value	
Depreciation method for tax purposes: accelerated cost recovery system, 5-year life, no salvage	
Tax rate	45%
Investment tax credit	None

REQUIRED: Calculate the after-tax cash-payback period. (Interpolate to the nearest month.)

15—4.   Use the information provided for Medford Mop and Broom Company in Exercise 15—3.

REQUIRED:

1. Assuming Medford wants to earn a discounted rate of return after taxes on all investments of 18%, calculate the discounted cash payback. (Round all calculations to the nearest dollar. Interpolate to the nearest month.)

2. In what way is the discounted cash-payback method superior to the nondiscounted cash-payback method?

3. *Without doing any calculations,* if the net-present-value method of evaluating investments were being used and a cut-off rate of 18% were used, would this be an acceptable investment? How do you know?

15—5. Refer to the information provided for Medford Mop and Broom Company in Exercise 15—3.

REQUIRED: Calculate the accounting rate of return before taxes based on:

1. $$\frac{\text{average increase in before-tax income over the project's life}}{\text{initial recording basis of the investment}}$$

2. $$\frac{\text{average increase in before-tax income over the project's life}}{\text{average book value of the investment over the project's life}}$$

15—6. Ye Old English Electric Tea Kettle Company is thinking about expanding its operations from the northeast area of the United States into the West Coast area, where it believes the number of hot-tea drinkers is expanding. It estimates its cash revenues after expenses and taxes from the expansion to be as follows:

Year 1	$ 300,000
Year 2	500,000
Year 3	800,000
Year 4	900,000
Year 5	1,000,000

The cash investment required to finance the expansion is $2,000,000. Ye Old English wants to recover that investment plus a 16% after-tax return on any expansion programs within five years.

REQUIRED: 1. Using the net-present-value method, is the expansion justified based on the criteria the company has set?

2. Suppose the Ye Old English believes cash flows for each year may be over-estimated by as much as 10%. If the estimates are off by this amount, is the expansion still acceptable based on the use of the net-present-value method?

15—7. *Part A:* An investment has an after-tax cash flow per year of $50,000 for four years and requires an initial cash investment of $129,450.

REQUIRED: Calculate the internal rate of return generated by the investment.

Part B: An investment generates the following after-tax cash flows and requires an initial investment of $1,553,100.

Year 1	$500,000
Year 2	300,000
Year 3	800,000
Year 4	700,000

REQUIRED: Provide calculations to prove that the internal rate of return on this investment is 16%.

15—8. The Jarston Crafts Exchange is considering the purchase of a new heating unit, which is expected to save $7,500 in cash per year for five years. The heater has an estimated useful life of five years with a residual value of $5,000. The unit will cost Jarston $30,000, plus $2,000 in installation costs. Jarston expects all investments to earn 10%. Assume Jarston is a tax exempt organization.

REQUIRED:
1. Determine if the investment should be made, using the net-present-value method.
2. Assume that there is *no* residual value. Calculate the investment's internal rate of return using interpolation techniques.
3. Assume Jarston has an alternative investment opportunity which will produce the same annual cash savings (*excluding salvage value*) and have a net present value of $1,200. Calculate the cost of the investment.

15—9. Given the following incomplete data:

PROJECT LIFE (YEARS)	INITIAL INVESTMENT	ANNUAL CASH FLOWS	REQUIRED RETURN ON INVESTMENT	NET PRESENT VALUE	INTERNAL RATE OF RETURN
6	(a)	$25,000	18%	(b)	16%
11	$750,000	(c)	18%	(d)	14%
7	$385,920	(e)	16%	(22,410)	(f)

REQUIRED: Complete the missing amounts, (a)–(f). Annual cash flows for each are of equal amounts for each year of a project's life.

15—10. Handyman Tool Company makes a large number of tools commonly used around the home, such as pliers and screwdrivers. The company is considering the purchase of a fleet of cars for their salespersons to use. Presently, salespersons are reimbursed for the use of their personal automobiles. Handyman estimates that cash savings of purchasing the cars will be $100,000 annually. Ten cars will be needed at a cost of $150,000. For book purposes, the cars will be depreciated over a three-year life and are expected to have salvage values totaling $20,000. For tax purposes, the cars will be depreciated using a three-year life, no salvage value, and accelerated cost recovery system depreciation. Handyman will receive a 6% investment tax credit at the end of the year of purchase, which will reduce the depreciable base of the auto fleet for tax purposes by half of the investment tax credit. The investment tax credit is accounted for by the flow-through method for financial reporting purposes; i.e., it is taken into income in its entirety in the year received. The $20,000 salvage value will not represent a gain or loss for financial reporting purposes but will simply be a recovery of book value. For tax purposes, it will be a gain taxed at a capital gains rate of 25%.

In calculating net income for financial reporting purposes, the tax rate is simply applied to book income to get the tax expense. Handyman's rate is 40%.

REQUIRED: **1.** Assume that the company wants to make investments which have an undiscounted cash payback of two years or less. Is this an acceptable investment?

2. Assume that the company wants to make investments which have a discounted cash payback of two years or less based on a discount rate of 10%. Is this an acceptable investment? (Round all calculations to the nearest dollar.)

15—11. Use the information provided for the Handyman Tool Company in Exercise 15—10.

REQUIRED: Handyman wants to make investments only if they can earn at a discounted rate of 12%. The company uses the net-present-value method in evaluating investment alternatives. Should the company buy the fleet of cars for its salespersons? (Round all calculations to the nearest dollar.)

15—12. Use the information provided for the Handyman Tool Company in Exercise 15—10.

REQUIRED: Based on the average income from an investment over the initial investment required (average income/initial investment), Handyman wants an accounting rate of return on all investments of 30%. Based on this criterion, should Handyman make the investment?

15—13. The Jackson Shoe Company is contemplating the purchase of a new machine to be used in the cutting process. The following data have been compiled by the manager of operations:

OLD MACHINE		NEW MACHINE	
Acquisition cost	$18,000	Cash price	$21,000
Remaining book value	$15,000	Expected life	3 years
		Disposal value in three	
Remaining life	3 years	years	0
		Annual variable operating	
Disposal value at present	$15,000	expenses	$21,500
		Annual revenue from	
Disposal value in 3 years	0	sales (cash inflows)	$65,000
Annual variable operating expenses, cash outflows	$25,000		
Annual revenue from sales (cash inflows)	$65,000		

Jackson Shoe would not receive an investment tax credit for the investment in the new machine. The disposal value of the old machine would be realized at the time the new machine was acquired. The company pays taxes at a 40% rate. Straight-line depreciation is being used for both book and tax purposes.

REQUIRED: **1.** Calculate the difference in taxes payable if the old machine is kept versus the purchase of the new machine. The $15,000 current disposal value of the old machine is not taxable.

2. Calculate the differential cash flows from the two alternatives. Assume that Jackson wants to earn an 8% return on all investments, using the net-present-value method, should the old machine be replaced?

15—14.   Children's Hospital of New England is a tax-exempt organization. It is considering investing in some cardiac monitoring equipment which would have a cost of $180,000 and an installation cost of $2,000. The installation cost would be capitalized (treated as part of the cost of the asset). The installation of this new equipment would permit the rearrangement of one department within the hospital, and staff could be reduced. Resulting cash operating cost savings would be $60,000 annually over the anticipated four-year life of the equipment. The equipment would be obsolete at the end of four years and would probably have no resale value. Depreciation is recorded on a straight-line basis.

REQUIRED:
1. Calculate the cash payback for the equipment to the nearest half-year.
2. Calculate the accounting rate of return for the equipment based on average income over initial investment.
3. Find the net present value of the equipment assuming a discount rate of 10%.
4. Estimate the internal rate of return on the investment. Do not interpolate.
5. Which, if any, of the above measures should Children's Hospital use in deciding whether or not the new equipment should be purchased?
6. What factors which have not been quantified should be considered in deciding whether or not the new equipment should be purchased?

15—15.   Yale, president of Hotchkiss, Inc., your client, recently attended a seminar at which a speaker discussed planning and control of capital expenditures, which he referred to as "capital budgeting." Yale tells you that she is not quite sure she understands that concept.

REQUIRED:
1. Explain the nature of and identify several uses of capital budgeting.
2. What are the basic differences between the payback method and the net-present-value method of capital budgeting? Explain.
3. Define "cost of capital."
4. Financial accounting data are not entirely suitable for use in capital budgeting. Explain.

problems

15—16.   *Different methods for evaluating capital budgeting expenditures; simple data, no taxes.*   The First Church is a tax-free organization. It has recently received a large donation of $1,124,000 from the estate of one of its members. It is considering an investment which is expected to generate the following cash flows over a five-year period:

Year 1	$ 300,000
Year 2	200,000
Year 3	400,000
Year 4	300,000
Year 5	500,000
	$1,700,000

REQUIRED: **1.** Calculate the cash payback for the investment. Interpolate to the nearest month.

2. Calculate the accounting rate of return based on:

$$\frac{\text{average increase in income over the project's life}}{\text{initial investment}}$$

(Round to the nearest whole percent.) Assume that the cash-flow figures are equal to accounting income from the investment.

3. Calculate the net present value of the investment based on a discount rate of 12%.

4. Present calculations to prove that the internal rate of return on the project is 14%.

15—17. *Net-present-value method; taxes, no investment tax credit.* The Superior Metal Works Company is considering the purchase of a new piece of equipment which would enable the company to produce a new product—door hinges. Data relevant to the purchase are shown below:

Annual cash revenues from sale of door hinges	$ 90,000
Cash operating expenses	$ 40,000
Cost of the new machinery	$100,000

Additional information:

1. For financial reporting purposes the machinery will be depreciated over a five-year period using straight-line depreciation and is expected to have no salvage value.

2. For tax purposes the machinery will be depreciated over a five-year life based on accelerated cost recovery system depreciation and no salvage value. There is no investment tax credit.

3. Earnings of Superior Metal Works are taxed at a rate of 40%.

4. The company wants to earn an after-tax return on all investments of 16%.

REQUIRED: **1.** Calculate taxes payable for the company on an annual basis over the five-year period as a result of the investment.

2. Using the net present value and the criteria the company has set, should the new product be produced? (Round all calculations to the nearest dollar.)

15—18. *Accounting rate of return.* Use the data provided in Problem 15—17. Income taxes for financial reporting purposes are based on before-tax book income.

REQUIRED: 1. Calculate the accounting rate of return based on:

$$\frac{\text{average increase in income over the project's life}}{\text{initial investment}}$$

2. Calculate the accounting rate of return based on:

$$\frac{\text{average increase in income over the project's life}}{\text{average investment over the project's life}}$$

3. What are the major shortcomings of this method as a way of evaluating capital expenditures?

15—19. *Cash-flow methods for ranking alternatives.* Carson Products is faced with two investment alternatives: (1) expand their existing facilities, which will resolve their immediate growth crisis, or (2) build a completely new plant, which will allow them to accommodate immediate as well as future growth. If the present plant is expanded, the initial cost will be $500,000 and it is expected to be usable for ten more years. At the end of that period it would have no salvage value. The expected net cash inflow associated with this investment is $100,000 per year. If a new plant is built, the initial cost is expected to be $1,200,000 with a ten-year expected life and no residual value. Production can be doubled with a new plant as compared with an expansion of the old. As a result, expected annual net cash inflows would be $200,000. Carson expects a return of 14% on investments. Assume the cash inflows are stated on an after-tax basis.

REQUIRED: 1. Rank the two alternatives using the undiscounted cash-payback method.
2. Rank the two alternatives using the net-present-value method.
3. Rank the two alternatives using the internal rate-of-return method. Interpolation of your results is not necessary.
4. Do the three capital budget techniques you used give the same ranking? Can you always expect the results you got in parts 1 through 3?

15—20. *Cash payback, discounted cash payback; taxes, investment tax credit.* Sally Sanders is thinking about starting a truck rental service. The truck would cost $50,000 and have an estimated useful life of five years. For tax purposes the truck would be depreciated over a three-year life using accelerated cost recovery system depreciation. The investment in the truck would qualify for an investment tax credit of 6%, which would *not* reduce the depreciable base of the truck for tax purposes. Sally estimates that the cash operating revenues and expenses for a five-year period would be:

YEAR	CASH REVENUES	CASH EXPENSES
1	$45,000	$15,000
2	52,000	17,000
3	58,000	20,000
4	60,000	23,000
5	62,000	25,000

Cash flows from revenues and for expenses and for the investment credit can be assumed to come at year-end. Sally estimates her tax rate to be 30%.

REQUIRED:
1. Calculate taxes payable for each of the five years.
2. Calculate after-tax cash flows for each of the five years.
3. Determine the undiscounted cash-payback period for the truck. (Interpolate to the nearest month.)
4. Determine the discounted cash-payback period for the truck using a discount rate of 12%. (Do not interpolate. Round all amounts to the nearest dollar.)

15—21. *Net-present-value method; taxes, investment tax credit.* Use the data presented in Problem 15—20.

REQUIRED: Using the net-present-value method and a desired rate of return of 20%, determine whether Sally should buy the delivery truck. (Round all amounts to the nearest dollar.)

15—22. *Net present value, differential amounts, taxes, investment tax credit.* The Pearson Sandbox Company is considering the replacement of a precision cutting machine with a newer, more sophisticated model. The new machine would cost $40,000. Under the accelerated cost recovery system, the machine will be depreciated for five years, which is also its useful life. Pearson uses straight-line depreciation for book purposes. Pearson's present cutting machine has a book value of $15,000 and five remaining years of useful life. It is being written off to a zero salvage value using straight-line depreciation for book and tax purposes. Estimated annual savings associated with the new machine are $15,000, 80% of which represents a labor savings and the remainder a savings in materials.

Additional information:

Pearson pays taxes at a 50% rate.
The machine qualifies for a 10% investment tax credit.
The investment tax credit reduces the depreciable base for tax purposes by one-half the investment tax credit.
Pearson requires a return of 10% on investments of this type.
Present resale value of the old machine is $5,000 (fully taxable at ordinary income rates).

REQUIRED:
1. Calculate the increase in differential taxes payable which would result if the new machine were acquired. (Round all amounts to the nearest dollar.)
2. Find the after-tax differential cash flows which would result from the purchase of the new machine. Using the net-present-value method, determine whether the investment should be made, based on the company's 10% return criterion. (Round all amounts to the nearest dollar.)

15—23. *Investment alternatives, net-present-value method.* The Benson Company has decided to install electronic surveillance equipment, which will reduce its present labor costs for security guards. Two models are being investigated:

	MODEL A	MODEL B
Purchase cost	$50,000	$90,000
Annual cash operating cost	$16,000	$12,000
Expected useful life	6 years	12 years

Labor costs eliminated by either model would be $30,000 annually. Benson's cost of capital is 12% and its tax rate is 40%. Straight-line depreciation will be used for tax purposes. Assume Model A would be replaced at the end of Year 6 with the same model, which would cost 20% more at that time.

REQUIRED:

1. Calculate the net present value of having electronic surveillance for a 12-year period. (This means the net present value of installing two Model A units during the period or one Model B.) (Round all amounts to the nearest dollar.)
2. Which model should be selected?
3. What other factors should be considered?

15—24. *Different methods for evaluating capital expenditures; taxes, investment tax credits.*   Robert Lasso Inc. is analyzing the possibility of introducing a new product and believes it could sell 10,000 units per year at $40 per unit for the next five years. To do so would require acquisition of equipment costing $150,000, having a five-year life with no residual value. The equipment is eligible for a 10% investment tax credit and accelerated cost recovery system depreciation. Fixed operating costs associated with the equipment would require annual cash disbursements of $125,000. Variable costs are expected to be $12 per unit. Lasso uses straight-line depreciation and the flow-through method in accounting for the investment tax credit for financial reporting purposes. (With the flow-through method, the investment tax credit is offset against taxes payable in the year the credit is received.) The firm's tax rate is 40%. The depreciable base of the asset for tax purposes is reduced by one-half of the investment tax credit. The firm wants a 20% return on investments of this type. (Round all calculations to the nearest dollar.)

REQUIRED:

1. Calculate Lasso's yearly net income for financial reporting purposes for the five-year period.
2. Calculate Lasso's yearly after-tax cash flows for the five-year period.
3. Calculate the undiscounted payback for the equipment. (Interpolate to the nearest month.)
4. Calculate the net present value of the investment.
5. Based on the analysis you have done, what do you know about the internal rate of return for the project?
6. Calculate the accounting rate of return based on:

$$\frac{\text{average increase in income over the period}}{\text{initial investment}}$$

15—25. *Alternative decisions, no tax consequences.* (CMA adapted) The management of Essen Manufacturing Company is currently evaluating a proposal to purchase a new and innovative drill press as a replacement for a less efficient piece of similar equipment, which would then be sold. The cost of the equipment, including delivery and installation, is $175,000. If the equipment is purchased, Essen will incur costs of $5,000 in removing the present equipment and revamping service facilities. The present equipment has a book value of $100,000 and a remaining useful life of ten years. Owing to new technical improvements, which have made the equipment outmoded, it presently has a resale value of only $40,000.

Management has provided you with the following comparative manufacturing cost tabulation:

	PRESENT EQUIPMENT	NEW EQUIPMENT
Annual costs:		
Labor	$30,000	$25,000
Depreciation (10% of asset book value)	10,000	17,500
Other cash expenses	48,000	20,000
Total expenses	$88,000	$62,500

Both pieces of equipment are expected to have a negligible salvage at the end of ten years. If the new equipment is purchased, the management of Essen would require a 15% return on the investment *before income taxes.*

REQUIRED: **1.** In order to assist the management of Essen in reaching a decision on the proposal, prepare schedules showing the computation of the following:

   a. Net initial outlay before income taxes.

   b. Net present value of investment *before income taxes.*

   2. Would you recommend this investment, and why?

15—26. *Calculating various components of the investment decision.* (CMA adapted) Rockyford Co. must replace some machinery. This machinery has zero book value, but its current market value is $1,800. One possible alternative is to invest in new machinery, which has a cost of $40,000. This new machinery would produce estimated annual pretax operating cash savings of $12,500. The estimated useful life of the new machinery is four years. Rockyford uses straight-line depreciation for book purposes and the double-declining-balance method for tax purposes. If Rockyford accepts this investment proposal, the disposal of the old machinery and the investment in the new equipment will take place on December 31, Year 1. Rockyford is subject to a 40% income tax rate for all ordinary income and capital gains and has a 10% after-tax cost of capital. All operating and tax cash flows are assumed to occur at year-end.

REQUIRED: Calculate the following (for all present-value factors use *only two decimal places*):

1. The present value of the after-tax cash flow arising from the disposal of the machinery in Year 1.
2. The present value of the after-tax cash flows for all four years attributable to operating cash savings.
3. The present value of the tax-shield effect of depreciation at the end of Year 1.
4. The present value of the net effect on the income tax payments related to the project in its second year.

15—27.   *The impact of taxes on cash flows.*   Bygone Products, a new firm, has projected the following cash outflows and inflows for its first five years of operation:

OUTFLOWS		INFLOWS	
End of Year 1	450,000	End of Year 1	500,000
2	310,000	2	510,000
3	440,000	3	520,000
4	400,000	4	540,000
5	425,000	5	540,000

The initial investment in the firm was *$400,000*.

REQUIRED: 1. Find the net present value of the cash flows from the investment, assuming Bygone expects a return of 12% on all investments.
2. What can you determine from the answer in part 1 about the internal rate of return?
3. Calculate the undiscounted cash payback for the investment. (Interpolate to the nearest month.)
4. Assume that the net cash flows from the investment will be taxed at a rate of 45%. Using the net-present-value method and a 12% desired rate of return, is the investment acceptable?
5. Assuming net cash flows are taxed at a 45% rate, find the undiscounted cash payback for the investment based on after-tax cash flows. (Interpolate to the nearest month.)

15—28.   *Differential costs, taxes, investment tax credit.*   Door County Hospital is considering the purchase of a new dialysis machine. The machine will cost $90,000 and is expected to last five years with no salvage value. The hospital expects a rate of return of 6% on investments. The machine which will be replaced is three years old, originally cost $100,000, and has a present book value of $62,500, a remaining life of five years, and a resale value of $45,000. Annual operating costs, exclusive of depreciation, associated with the new and old machine are $24,300 and $37,900, respectively. For tax purposes the old machine is being depreciated using straight-line depreciation, assuming no salvage value. The new machine would be depreciated over a five-year period using accelerated cost recovery system depreciation. The Hospital will receive a 10% investment tax credit, which will not reduce the depreciable base for tax purposes. If the old machine is sold immediately, the proceeds will be realized immediately but will not be taxed until year-end, at which time they are subject to ordinary income tax rates.

REQUIRED
1. Calculate the differences in taxes payable under the two alternatives, assuming a tax rate of 30%. (Round all amounts to the nearest dollar.)
2. Find the net present value of the differential cash flows between the two alternatives—keeping the old machine versus buying the new machine. (Round all amounts to the nearest dollar.)

15—29. *Make-or-buy decision.* Adler Sports Manufacturing Company purchases a part used in the manufacture of its hockey sticks from another company. At present Adler purchases 30,000 parts at $10.90 per part. Dane Roth, an engineer with the firm, has recommended that Adler begin to manufacture the part itself. She has gathered the following information:

1. New equipment necessary to manufacture the part would cost $45,000 and have a five-year life with a salvage value of $3,000. For tax purposes, no salvage value will be recognized in applying accelerated cost recovery system depreciation to the machine on a five-year basis. There is no investment tax credit available. When the $3,000 salvage value is realized at the end of the fifth year, it will be taxed at ordinary income rates.
2. A finishing machine, presently not used by the firm, would also be used to manufacture the part. The machine, which is in storage, was purchased four years ago for $40,000, is being depreciated at $5,000 a year for tax purposes, and is expected to have no salvage value.
3. Adler would incur variable production cost per part as follows:

| Direct labor (.75 hr @ $8 per hr) | $6 |
| Direct materials | $2 |

4. Adler incurs variable cash manufacturing overhead costs of $2 per unit for this part.
5. Adler's cost of capital on an after-tax basis is 16%, and Adler pays taxes at a 40% rate.

REQUIRED:
1. Which costs are not relevant to the decision of making versus buying?
2. Find the net present value of the cash outflows if the part is purchased.
3. Find the net present value of the cash outflows if the part is made.
4. What do you recommend?

15—30. *Lease versus buy with investment tax credit.* The Hodgkiss Winery is considering two alternatives related to the acquisition of a distilling machine. Hodgkiss can either purchase the machine for $280,000 or lease it for five years at $77,000 per year under an ordinary leasing arrangement, where the lease payments are expensed annually and the machine would be returned to the lessor at the end of the lease. Hodgkiss would receive no investment credit from the lease. Lease payments are due January 1 of each year. Hodgkiss anticipates cash savings (excluding lease payments and depreciation) of $100,000 annually with either machine.

The machine is eligible for an investment tax credit and has a five-year life for tax purposes with no salvage value. Hodgkiss uses straight-line depreciation for financial reporting purposes. For tax purposes, accelerated cost recovery system depreciation will be used based on a five-year recovery period. The investment credit is 10%. Assume that the investment tax credit will *not* reduce the depreciable base of the assets for tax purposes.

Hodgkiss wants a return on its investments of 12% and is taxed at a 45% rate. For tax purposes, any unused investment tax credit can be carried forward and offset against taxes payable in future years up to 15 years.

REQUIRED: 1. Calculate the taxes payable as a result of each alternative.
2. Calculate the after-tax cash flows from each alternative.
3. Find the net present value of each alternative.
4. Should the company buy or lease?

chapter sixteen

CASH AND WORKING CAPITAL MANAGEMENT AND THE STATEMENT OF CHANGES IN FINANCIAL POSITION

OBJECTIVES

After you have completed this chapter, you should be able to answer the following questions:

- What are some objectives which govern the management of cash, marketable securities, and accounts payable?
- How can accounts receivable be controlled?
- How can a company decide when to reorder inventory and what size orders to place?
- What are the objectives of the Statement of Changes in Financial Position?
- How does a Statement of Changes in Financial Position prepared in a working capital format differ from one prepared in a cash format?
- How can net income on an accrual basis be converted to either a working capital or a cash basis?
- How is a Statement of Changes in Financial Position in either a working capital or cash format prepared?

Working capital is defined as the difference between a company's current assets and current liabilities. The accounts which make up this group are usually the most active in the company. Unlike fixed assets, they reflect the company's daily activities.

Working capital management has emerged as a major factor in the profitability of business. This has been caused in part by the high cost of funds and the complexities of the business environment. The goal of working capital management is to minimize the cost of working capital while maximizing the firm's profits.

Accounts frequently classified as current assets and current liabilities include:

Current assets

Cash
Marketable securities (short-term investments)
Accounts receivable
Notes receivable—short-term
(or current installments of long-term notes)
Inventory
Prepaid items
Interest receivable

Current liabilities

Accounts payable
Current installments on long-term debt
Salaries payable
Taxes payable
Accrued expenses
Interest payable

From an internal management point of view, the company generally profits when it maximizes the current liability side of working capital accounts and minimizes the nonearning current assets.

To illustrate, compare the working capital structure of two different companies, both having a cost of capital of 12% after taxes. Short-term securities of both firms earn at a 7% after-taxes rate. The working capital structure of each firm represents its typical investment in each working capital account for the period.

	FIRM A	FIRM B
Cash	$ 50,000	$ 10,000
Marketable securities	10,000	30,000
Accounts receivable	100,000	80,000
Inventory	70,000	50,000
Total current assets	$230,000	$170,000
Current liabilities:		
Accounts payable	20,000	70,000
Other short-term		
payables	50,000	40,000
Total current liabilities	70,000	110,000
Working capital	$160,000	60,000

We can approximate the cost to the two firms of their working capital positions as follows:

	FIRM A	FIRM B
Current assets excluding		
marketable securities	$220,000	$140,000
Current liabilities	70,000	110,000
Difference	$150,000	$ 30,000
Cost of capital	12%	12%
Cost of working capital		
before interest on		
marketable securities	$ 18,000	$ 3,600
Less: Return on		
securities:		
$10,000 × 7%	(700)	
$30,000 × 7%		(2,100)
Cost of working capital	$ 17,300	$ 1,500

What our analysis tells us is that Firm A has an implied cost related to its working capital position of $17,300 while Firm B's is $1,500. To be valid, it should be emphasized, the working capital positions shown above should represent the typical working capital position of the firm for the period being analyzed. If, for example, we do our analysis using figures when accounts receivable or inventories are at their yearly high, the costs we have computed will not accurately describe the implicit cost of the company's normal working capital position.

Firm A may be able to improve its profitability by strategies such as:

1. Reducing its accounts receivable.
2. Reducing its inventories.
3. Financing more of its working capital needs on a short-term basis through short-term credit.

CONFLICTING GOALS
IN WORKING CAPITAL MANAGEMENT

While the goal of working capital management is to minimize the investment in working capital, there are many reasons why accomplishing this may be difficult. For example, if a firm wishes to generate new sales, it may have to hold more inventory and relax credit standards. These actions should be taken so long as the increased cost of receivables and inventory is covered by profit from the new business.

Differing objectives of different subcomponents of the same organization also may make minimizing the investment in working capital difficult. For example, production managers want level output and long production runs. They wish to avoid training programs, layoffs, and overtime. Sales managers want as high a level of sales as possible. When customers order, they want the order filled. They want to stimulate new orders and increase market share. These goals of production and sales managers may conflict with efficient working capital management, which would say inventories and account receivable balances should be minimized.

Finally, a firm's ability to minimize its investment in working capital may be limited by (a) actual agreements with creditors, (b) creditors' perceptions of what the working capital structure of a firm should look like, or (c) managers' perceptions of how external users of financial data interpret financial data.

With respect to the first of these, sometimes loan agreements require that a company maintain a certain current ratio, a minimum amount of working capital, or a minimum cash balance. These requirements may preclude a more efficient working capital structure. Companies may also keep a certain working capital structure either because creditors expect it or because managers believe that they (or other providers of capital) do.

CONTROL OF THE COMPONENT PARTS
OF WORKING CAPITAL

While patterns differ from company to company, Illustration 16-1 shows the major components of working capital and where those parts are frequently controlled within a manufacturing organization. This illustration shows a common pattern whereby cash, marketable securities, receivables, and accounts payable are managed centrally. Some companies have departed from this pattern in one or more areas. They are least likely to decentralize control of cash and near-cash securities. The reasons for this have been discussed previously.

ILLUSTRATION 16-1

A typical pattern for controlling working capital accounts

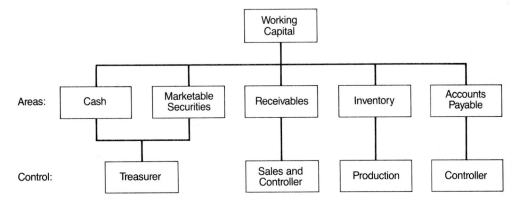

CASH, MARKETABLE SECURITIES, AND SHORT-TERM PAYABLES

Effective controls of cash, marketable securities, and short-term payables are interrelated. Illustration 16-2 describes five objectives that should be kept in mind in managing these accounts and some techniques that can be used in accomplishing each objective. These objectives and techniques are discussed below.

Maximizing the Return on Excess Cash

Profitability is enhanced when the return on excess cash is maximized. A company must know when and how much cash it is going to have available to invest. Two tools are used by companies to provide this information: cash budgets and cash forecasts.

ILLUSTRATION 16-2

Cash, marketable securities, and accounts payable management

1. MAXIMIZING RETURN ON EXCESS CASH	2. MINIMIZING CASH ON HAND	3. MINIMIZING ADVERSE FLOAT	4. MAXIMIZING FAVORABLE FLOAT	5. MINIMIZING REQUIRED CASH
a. Cash budgets b. Cash forecasting	a. Concentration banking b. Zero-balance accounts c. Compensating balance versus fee-for-service	a. Lock boxes b. Electronic funds transfer	Dispursing strategies	a. Borrowing and establishing credit b. Deferring payment until bill is due

The *cash budget* shows estimated cash inflows and outflows from all sources for the budget period. It helps the company determine when cash will be available and for what period. This enables the person responsible for cash management to seek the highest-yielding investments consistent with the company's ability or propensity to take risks.

Some companies prepare cash budgets on a monthly basis. Because funds which are available for as short a period as overnight have earning ability, the time horizon used for the cash budget may be too long for effective management of cash. In addition, conditions may be different from those anticipated at the time the cash budget was prepared. For these reasons cash forecasts are prepared. *Cash forecasts* are short-term projections, sometimes prepared daily, based on prevailing conditions.

Minimizing Cash on Hand

One objective of efficient working capital management is to minimize the amount of cash on hand. This can be done through arrangements such as concentration banking, zero-balance accounts, and replacement of compensating-balance arrangements with fee-for-service arrangements.

When a company uses *concentration banking*, this means that it uses a number of banks close to its customers where deposits are made daily. At periodic intervals, such as at the end of each day, all deposits are transferred from the local banks to a central bank. With the use of *zero-balance* bank accounts, funds are transferred to an account only when checks are presented for payment.

It is not unusual for banks, as part of loan agreements, to require that a company maintain a certain minimum balance in its accounts. This minimum balance is called a *compensating balance*. A business may be able to negotiate loans at slightly higher rates which will be less costly than having to restrict the use of some of its cash balances. In other words, the business may use a *fee-for-service* arrangement. These costs have to be considered on an individual situation basis.

Minimizing Adverse Float and Maximizing Favorable Float

Float refers to the time that elapses from the writing of a check till the check clears the bank and (in the case of a receipt) is added to the customer's account or (in the case of a payment) is subtracted from the customer's account.

Firms should operate to maximize *favorable float*—the interval from the time a check is written until it is subtracted from their checking account. On the other hand, they should attempt to minimize *adverse float*—the amount of time it takes for a cash receipt to be added to their account.

Float can be divided into three parts: *processing float*—the period of time to process a check; *mail float*—the period of time the check is in the mail; and *clearing float*—the period of time the check is in the banking system. Methods are available for using float to the advantage of the business.

One common way to minimize adverse float is to use lock boxes. A *lock box* is a post office box that is located nearest the check mailer. Checks are taken from the lock box and deposited that day in a local bank, then transferred to a regional or concentration bank. On the other hand, a business, to avoid the rapid clearing of checks it has written through the use of lock-box techniques by its creditors, may disburse checks from a series of locations on a random basis or may mail its checks in some obscure location.

Let us look at an example of the use of float. A manufacturing firm's quarterly income tax payment of $50 million was due. The company deposited treasury bills with its disbursing bank in the amount of $50 million and mailed its check to the Internal Revenue Service from a mail box in a remote location furthest from its disbursing bank. The result was approximately seven days of mail float. During this time the firm was earning on the treasury bills which it had deposited and which were not sold until the check cleared the paying bank. The clearing float while the check went through the banking system increased the total float another four days. The result was a profit for the firm of about $210,000 based on a 14% treasury bill rate.

Modern computer technology has made possible electronic funds transfer (EFT). Having funds electronically transferred to the company's checking account, as opposed to having a check written which has to arrive through the mail and then clear the bank system, can speed up cash flows tremendously.

Minimizing Required Cash

By minimizing its cash requirements, a company can maximize the amount of cash it can invest. Cash requirements are minimized primarily through the use of financing from vendors by buying on account. Bills should be paid only when due. In addition, borrowing when cash needs are at a peak may eliminate the need for liquidating long-term investments, which may have high yields which exceed the cost of borrowing. Minimizing the cash required means knowing when cash will be available and when cash will be needed. The primary source of this information is cash budgets and cash forecasts.

ACCOUNTS RECEIVABLE MANAGEMENT

Revenues tied up in the form of receivables are nonearning revenues except to the extent that the company may be able to charge and collect interest on receivable balances. Accounts receivable can be effectively managed in four major ways:

1. Setting appropriate credit standards.
2. Selecting appropriate terms.
3. Monitoring the investment in receivables.
4. Monitoring collection.

Setting Credit Standards

Each company must determine the standards it wants to apply in deciding who gets credit and how much. Consideration must be given to what competitors are doing and the company's objectives, such as increasing market share or entering a new market.

Credit scoring is a popular way to screen applicants for credit. With credit scoring a set of factors is selected to indicate financial ability and stability and given a weight. An applicant for credit fills out a form which includes information about the factors the company considers important. The application form is scored and a number assigned to the applicant. Applicants receiving a score below a certain minimum may be automatically rejected, while those receiving a score above a specified number may receive credit. Additional information may be sought about those in the middle before a credit decision is made. Illustration 16-3 shows some factors which are frequently used in credit-scoring systems.

ILLUSTRATION 16-3

Examples of factors used for credit scoring

Years at the present address
Owns home
Number of bank references
Age of car
Years with present employer
Number of bank credit cards
Years with previous employer
Satisfactory history with the bank

Selecting Appropriate Terms

Whether accounts should become due in 30 days or 60 days can have an important impact on a company's cash flows. In making a decision of this type, a manager must consider factors such as industry practices, economic conditions, and the cash cycle of the company itself. Ideally, credit terms are selected that will complement a company's outflows to its vendors. If a company is buying on a cycle which requires payments to vendors in 30 days, it would not, if it could be avoided, set credit terms for its customers based on a 60-day credit period.

Accounts receivable collections can also be influenced by making discounts available for early payments. All firms have the option of having customers pay in some fixed period, say 30 days, or having dual terms where a customer may pay early, for example in 10 days, and take a discount. The problem is how large the discount should be.

Model building in this area can be very sophisticated. The model presented here exemplifies a relatively simple technique which can be used to determine the appropriate size discount to offer for payment within a defined time. It assumes that customers who do not take advantage of discounts will pay within the same period whether discounts are given or not. In other words, if a customer who *does not plan* to take advantage of discounts would normally pay within 60 days, then if discounts are offered, this customer will still pay in 60 days. The model is

$$D = 1 - (1 + i)^{M - N}$$

where $D =$ the size of the discount
$\quad\quad\quad i =$ interest rate on the company's funds
$\quad\quad\quad M =$ average time in which the discount customers pay
$\quad\quad\quad N =$ average time in which nondiscount customers pay

Let's use the following data and see how the model works:

Interest rate on company's funds, i	12% per year
Average time in which the discount customer pays, M	10 days
Average time in which the nondiscount customer pays, N	60 days

Applying the data to the model, we find that if the company wants to offer a discount for payment within 10 days, the size of that discount should not exceed 1.63%:[1]

$$D = 1 - \left(1 + \frac{.12}{365}\right)^{10 - 60} = 1.63\%$$

Note that the annual interest rate had to be converted to a daily basis (.12/365 days).

Monitoring Investment in Accounts Receivable

In Chapter 11 we discussed the common size balance sheet and also the calculation system for the level of investment in accounts receivable. When a common size balance sheet is prepared, accounts receivable are stated as a percent of either current assets or total assets, depending on how the

---

[1] Raising the term (1 + .12/365) to the 50th power can be done readily on most hand-held calculators by using the y^x key. This model is shown as an example. You will not be expected to solve similar problems. Models of this type are usually discussed in courses specifically devoted to working capital management and are beyond the scope of this course.

statement is designed. This information keeps management aware of changes in the level of assets accounted for by accounts receivable. This level, expressed as a percent of either total assets or current assets, can also be compared with similar statistics of the industry of which the company is a part.

The calculation of the accounts receivable collection period by the formula

$$\text{Collection period} = \frac{\text{average accounts receivable}}{\text{net credit sales/360 or 365 days}}$$

is another way of keeping an eye on the funds tied up in receivables. The application of this formula was demonstrated and discussed in Chapter 11.

If sales vary from one month to another, additional monitoring may be required to determine whether the number of days sales tied up in receivables has changed because of a changing pattern of collections or because of the change in sales volume. Techniques are available to do this but are beyond the scope of this text.

Monitoring Collection

There are no statistical models for monitoring the collection of accounts receivable. A system for monitoring collection consist of the policies the company has developed with respect to such issues as:

1. How soon will the bill be rendered?
2. What period of time is allowed to elapse before any follow-up action is taken after an account becomes overdue?
3. What procedures are used, and in what sequence, when an account becomes overdue—mail reminder, phone call, personal visit, or legal action?

INVENTORY MANAGEMENT

Probably the most widely used methods for controlling working capital investment are models related to inventory control. Inventories frequently constitute a significant proportion of a company's current assets or total assets.

The idea of inventory management is to balance the costs of having too little inventory against those of having too much. There are three components to the cost of inventory: (1) the cost of ordering the inventory or, if the inventory is being manufactured, the cost of setting up for production, (2) the cost of holding or carrying inventory, and (3) the cost of running out of inventory, known as stockout cost. Typical costs in each of these three categories are given in Illustration 16-4.

**ILLUSTRATION
16-4**

Classes and
examples of
inventory costs

Ordering costs
   Preparing the order
   Placing the order
   Following up on the order
Cost of carrying inventory
   Warehousing
   Insurance
   Taxes (property or inventory taxes)
   Clerical costs
   Handling
   Obsolescence or spoilage
   Cost of funds invested in inventory
Cost of stockouts
   Lost sales
   Lost customer goodwill
   Idle production time

Of the three types of costs listed, the most difficult to estimate are those associated with an inventory stockout. These are opportunity costs—the costs of alternatives foregone. Opportunity costs are generally not recorded and measured by accounting systems. They cannot be considered costs for external reporting purposes.

We have two basic questions that the manager must answer to control inventory:

1. When should an order be placed?
2. How big should the order be?

Determining the Reorder Point

How low should inventory be allowed to get before more inventory is ordered? The answer is a function of (1) lead time (how long it takes to receive an order), (2) how much inventory will be sold between the time the order is placed and the time the goods arrive, and (3) the size of the safety stock the company wants to maintain.

Lead time is frequently beyond the control of the ordering company. Lead time may be negotiated as part of the purchase agreement, and a company can change vendors if actual lead time departs materially from what is expected. However, within these limits, the manager's control over lead time is minimal. Reputations of vendors, existing agreements, and historical experience are the sources of information used to develop an estimated lead time for a particular item of inventory.

The next element needed to calculate reorder point is the amount of inventory which will be used or sold during the lead time. This amount must be projected based on historical patterns adjusted for anticipated changes. Let's assume that we have defined the lead time as 10 days and the number of units of inventory which will be sold or consumed during this period as 20 units per day. Thus, assuming the company does not want to maintain any safety stock (stock which would be used if the order did not arrive on a timely basis), the recorder point is 200 (20 units × 10 days). That is, when the level of the inventory reaches 200 units, an order should be placed.

If we cannot project usage or lead time with a high degree of accuracy, we may decide to have safety stock. Assume, for example, that while the daily usage averages 20 units, it may go as high as 30 units per day. In other words, the number of units used during the time it takes an order to arrive may be as much as 300 units (30 units × 10 days). Let's further assume that an item of inventory costs $100.

If we want to insure against running out of inventory while we are waiting for inventory to arrive, we could maintain a safety stock of 100 units. However, the negative aspect of this policy is that we would have $10,000 (100 units × $100 cost per unit) tied up in inventory.

Whether a company has a safety stock or not is a managerial decision. The size of the safety stock is also based largely on judgment. Based on the data we have, the safety stock could range anywhere from 1 to 100 units.

The concept of the reorder point and safety stock is shown in Illustration 16-5. The illustration is built on the assumptions that a safety stock of 100 units will be maintained, the lead time is 10 days, daily usage is 20 units, and 600 units is the normal size of an order. Based on these assumptions, an order will have to be placed each 20 days, calculated as follows:

Order size	600 units
Reorder point	200 units
Units used before reorder	400
400/daily usage of 20 units	20 days

As Illustration 16-5 shows, the order will be placed at the end of 20 days

ILLUSTRATION 16-5

The inventory reorder point

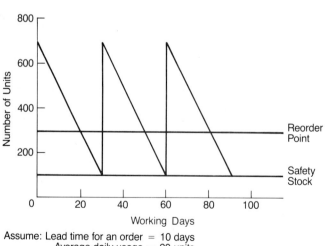

Assume: Lead time for an order = 10 days
Average daily usage = 20 units
Safety stock = 100 units
Normal number of
units ordered = 600 units

when 300 units are still on hand, 100 of which represent the safety stock. During the next 10 days those 200 units will be used and only the 100 units in safety stock will remain. At the end of the 10-day period the 600 units ordered will arrive, bringing the total inventory level to 700 units, the 600 ordered plus the 100-unit safety stock.

Other Ways of Establishing the Reorder Point

Companies use a variety of methods to decide when inventory should be reordered. These include marks on the walls or in bins where inventory is stored. When the mark is reached, it's time to reorder. Another practical approach is called the two-bin system: when one bin of inventory becomes empty, an order for inventory is placed.

Computers have made inventory accounting and control easier. For example, keeping perpetual records of inventory is much easier and less costly. Systems can be installed which will automatically print out a purchase order when inventories reach the reorder point.

Determining the Economic Order Quantity

The next issue which must be resolved is how much inventory should be ordered each time an order is placed. This quantity—the economic order quantity—is a function of the cost of placing an order versus the cost of carrying inventory. We want to order when annual carrying costs and annual purchasing costs are equal, as this will represent the total minimum costs.

Data Used in Calculating the Economic Order Quantity

To find the economic order quantity we must estimate (1) the quantity of inventory which will be used during the period, (2) the cost of placing and ordering, and (3) the annual cost of carrying a unit in stock during the period. The first datum is probably the easiest to obtain; we look to historical demand and budgetary expectations. Calculating the cost of placing an order or the annual cost of carrying a unit in inventory is more difficult, requiring a definition of what items of costs should be included in each. Some elements which could be included in each type of cost were listed in Illustration 16-4.

The Tabular Approach to Calculating Inventory Carrying and Purchasing Costs

Let's use the following data to show how the costs associated with different size order quantities can be determined:

Annual usage	6,000 units
Cost of placing an order	$200
Cost of carrying one unit in stock	$2.40

We'll look at the costs associated with placing orders for 500, 600, 1,000, 1,200, and 1,500 units. The results of these order-size assumptions are shown in Illustration 16-6. We can see that of the order sizes considered, the 1,000-units-per-order size results in the lowest total costs. This same information is presented graphically in Illustration 16-7. You can see from both the tabular presentation and the graphic presentation that the total-cost line becomes relatively flat around the most economical order quantity of 1,000 units. This means that order quantities can be varied somewhat without a material increase in costs. For example, the cost of ordering 1,200 units is only $40 more than that of ordering 1,000 units.

The EOQ Model

The most efficient way to find the economic order quantity is to use a model which has been developed for that purpose:

$$EOQ = \sqrt{\frac{2QP}{C}}$$

where EOQ = economic order quantity
   Q = annual quantity used
   P = the cost of placing an order
   C = cost of carrying a unit in inventory

Using the data previously provided, we could calculate the economic order quantity as follows:

$$EOQ = \sqrt{\frac{(2)(6,000)(\$200)}{\$2.40}} = \sqrt{\$1,000,000} = \underline{1,000 \text{ units}}$$

Using the economic order quantity, we can see that we would have to place six orders each year:

ILLUSTRATION 16-6

Costs associated with different size order quantities

	ORDER SIZE IN UNITS				
	500	600	1,000	1,200	1,500
Average inventory in units[a]	250	300	500	600	750
Number of purchase orders[b]	12	10	6	5	4
Annual carrying cost @ $2.40 per unit[c]	$ 600	$ 720	$1,200	$1,440	$1,800
Annual purchase order cost at $200 per order[d]	$2,400	$2,000	$1,200	$1,000	$ 800
Total annual costs	$3,000	$2,720	$2,400	$2,440	$2,600

[a] Average inventory in units = order size/2; for example, 500 order size/2 = 250.
[b] Number of purchase orders = annual quantity required/order size; for example, 6,000 usage/500 order size = 12 orders.
[c] Annual carrying cost = average inventory × carrying cost per unit; for example, 250 × $2.40.
[d] Annual purchase order cost = number of purchase orders × cost per purchase order; for example, 12 orders × $200 = $2,400.

$$\frac{6{,}000 \text{ annual usage}}{1{,}000 \text{ units per order}} = 6 \text{ orders each year}$$

Using the EOQ Model to Calculate Production Runs

The EOQ model can be applied to the problem of deciding how many units should be made in each production run. We do this by replacing the quantity to be purchased by the quantity to be made and substituting the cost of setting up for a production run for the cost of placing an order. The revised model can be stated as:

$$EPR = \sqrt{\frac{2QP}{C}}$$

where EPR = economic production-run size in units
         Q = quantity of units to be produced each year
         P = production setup costs
         C = cost of carrying one unit in inventory

To illustrate the calculation of the economic production-run size, assume the following data:

Units needed, Q	6,000
Setup costs, P	$120 per production run
Inventory carrying costs, C	$1 per unit

Substituting into the equation, we find that 1,200 units should be made

ILLUSTRATION 16-7

The economic order size

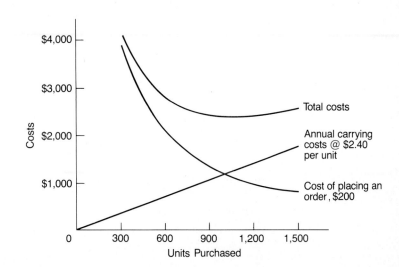

in each production run:

$$EPR = \sqrt{\frac{(2)(6,000)(\$120)}{\$1}} = \sqrt{1,440,000} = \underline{\underline{1,200 \text{ units}}}$$

WORKING CAPITAL MANAGEMENT IN THE FUTURE

Working capital management is an area where additional models and techniques are rapidly being developed to aid the manager. Computer technology and the proliferation of personal computers makes the development and use of models practical for many organizations.

THE STATEMENT OF CHANGES IN FINANCIAL POSITION

Earlier in this chapter we have discussed tools and techniques which managers can use to control working capital. Now we discuss the Statement of Changes in Financial Position, which is used to report externally why

ILLUSTRATION 16-8

| CHRISMAN INTERIORS |
| Statement of Changes in Financial Position, Working Capital Format for the Year Ended December 31, Year 1 |

Financial Resources Generated:
  Working Capital Generated:
    Working Capital from Operations:
      Net Income   59,000
      Add: Depreciation   15,000
      Working Capital from Operations $74,000
    Other Sources of Working Capital:
      Sale of Common Stock   3,000
    Total Working Capital Generated $77,000
  Nonworking Capital Resources Generated:
    Common Stock Exchanged for Land   21,000
  Total Financial Resources Generated $98,000

Financial Resources Applied:
  Working Capital Applied:
    Purchase of Equipment   27,000
    Payment of Dividends   12,000
    Retirement of Long-Term Debt   34,000
    Total Working Capital Applied   73,000
  Nonworking Capital Resources Generated:
    Land Acquired with Stock   21,000
  Total Financial Resources Applied $94,000

Increase in Working Capital $ 4,000

**ILLUSTRATION
16-9**

CHRISMAN INTERIORS
Statement of Changes in Financial Position, Cash Format
for the Year Ended December 31, Year 1

Financial Resources Generated:
  Cash Generated:
    From Operations:

New Income		$59,000
Add: Depreciation	$15,000	
Increase in Accounts Payable	2,000	
Decrease in Supplies	4,000	21,000
Total		$80,000
Deduct: Decrease in Salaries Payable	$ 1,000	
Increase in Accounts Receivable	3,000	(4,000)
Cash from Operations		$ 76,000
Other Sources:		
Sales of Stock		3,000
Total Cash Generated		$ 79,000
Noncash Financial Resources Generated:		
Common Stock Exchanged for Land		21,000
Total Financial Resources Generated		$100,000
Financial Resources Applied:		
Cash Applied to Nonoperating Items:		
Purchase of Equipment		$ 27,000
Payment of Long-Term Notes		34,000
Divident Payments		12,000
Total Cash Applied to Nonoperating Items		$ 73,000
Noncash Resources Applied:		
Land Acquired through Issuance of Common Stock		21,000
Total Financial Resources Applied		$ 94,000
Increase in Cash		$ 6,000

cash, working capital, or some combination of working capital and its components changed during the accounting period.

To be in keeping with generally accepted accounting principles companies must circulate, in addition to an Income Statement and a Balance Sheet, for external reporting purposes, a Statement of Changes in Financial Position, sometimes called a Funds Flow Statement.

The idea behind the preparation of such a statement is to describe for external users of financial information the major investing and financing activities in which a company engaged during the period and the impact of those decisions on the company's working capital, cash, or some combination of current assets such as cash and marketable securities.

For purposes of this book we are going to look at the Statement of Changes in Financial Position expressed in two commonly used formats—the working capital format and the cash format. That is, we will look at statements which show why either working capital (the working capital format) or cash (the cash format) changed.

The Statement of Changes in Financial Position not only describes the company's major financing and investing activities but is the link between beginning-of-the-period balance-sheet account balances and end-of-the-period balance-sheet balances. It explains how and why these account balances changed.

Illustration 16-8 shows a Statement of Changes in Financial Position prepared in a working capital format, which explains the impact of the company's financing and investing activities on working capital. Illustration 16-9 shows a Statement of Changes in Financial Position based on the cash format. These statements are based on data provided by Chrisman Interiors, a company which designs office layouts and interiors. How each statement was developed is explained below.

GENERAL MODEL FOR THE STATEMENT OF CHANGES IN FINANCIAL POSITION

If you examine the statements of changes in financial position prepared by companies and externally circulated as part of their annual reports, you will see a number of different reporting styles used. For our present purposes, so that you have a thorough understanding of what these statements are suppose to contain, you should think of them as taking the following general form. (The numbers and letters are attached to show the relationship of various items in the statement.)

I. Financial Resources Generated
   A. Cash or working capital generated

      1. From operations
      2. From other sources

   B. Noncash or nonworking capital resources generated
   TOTAL FINANCIAL RESOURCES GENERATED
II. Financial Resources Applied (Used)
   A. Cash or working capital applied to nonoperating items
   B. Noncash or nonworking capital resources applied
   TOTAL FINANCIAL RESOURCES APPLIED
   INCREASE OR DECREASE IN CASH OR WORKING CAPITAL

Note that the statement is divided into two major sections: financial resources generated and financial resources applied. The net of these two is the impact of the period's transactions on cash or working capital, depending on the format being used for the statement. The other parts of the statement are described below and are number-consistent with the model statement shown above.

I.A.1. Cash or working capital generated from operations.   Cash or working capital can come from either operations or other sources. It is important that a statement of this type show the impact of operations on cash or working capital. Think about this for a minute. If a company needs funds, what are its sources? The answer is: operations, borrowing, selling additional ownership shares, or liquidating assets. Only one of these sources can be used as a continuing source of funds—operations. The other sources are all limited. As a consequence it is important both to the internal manager and to those external to the firm to know whether operations is generating or using cash or working capital.

I.A.2. Cash or working capital generated from other sources.   This section of the statement should describe sources of cash or working capital other than operations. Common sources are:

Borrowing funds on a long-term basis.
Selling shares of stock, or increased investment by owners.
Liquidating long-term assets, such as property, plant and equipment.

II.A. Cash or working capital applied to nonoperating items.   Cash or working capital applied is limited to that not related to operations, since the impact of operations on cash or working capital should have been totally explained under the section of the statement entitled "Cash or working capital generated from operations." The difference between cash used by operations and cash used for other purposes can be illustrated as follows. Cash used to pay salaries is cash related to operations. It has a direct income-statement impact. Cash used to purchase land is cash used for nonoperating purposes—purposes other than carrying on the usual day-to-day activities of the business. The purchase of the land did not directly affect any income-statement account.

Common nonoperating uses of cash or working capital include:

Liquidating long-term debt.
Repurchasing part of owner's equity—for example, acquisition of treasury stock.
Purchasing long-term assets.
Paying dividends.

I.B and II.B. Noncash or nonworking capital financial resources generated and applied.   If we were preparing a statement which simply explained why working capital or cash changed, we would not need sections for nonworking capital or noncash resources generated and applied. However, generally accepted accounting principles require that the Statement of Changes in Financial Position be prepared on a comprehensive basis to describe *all* major investing and financing activities, not just those which had a cash or working capital impact. Hence, the statement includes these sections.

Transactions which represent noncash or nonworking capital resources *generated* will have an offsetting transaction under the noncash or nonworking capital resources *applied* part of the statement. Think of this transaction—the acquisition of land through issuance of stock. For the company which gave the stock, the stock is the financial resource which was applied to or used for the acquisition of land.

Almost all noncash or nonworking capital entries will be described in this section of the Statement of Changes in Financial Position. An exception is the declaration and distribution of stock dividends. This transaction is not included because it does not change total assets, total liabilities, or total stockholders' equity, but rather is simply a rearrangement of stockholders' equity, as can be seen from the following entry made to record a stock dividend:

Retained Earnings	XXXX	
Common Stock		XXXX
or		
Common Stock		
and		
Additional Paid-in Capital		

PREPARING THE STATEMENT OF CHANGES IN FINANCIAL POSITION—WORKING CAPITAL FORMAT

To demonstrate how the Statement of Changes in Financial Position is prepared in first a working capital format and then a cash format, we shall use the data given for Chrisman Interiors in Illustration 16-10. To take these data and convert them into a statement that also explains what happened to working capital, we will go through the following steps:

1. Prepare a schedule which shows by what amount, if any, working capital changed for the period.
2. Calculate the amount of working capital generated or used by operations.
3. Analyze the changes in the nonworking capital accounts to determine (a) other sources of working capital, (b) nonoperating applications of working capital, and (c) the nature of transactions which occurred but did not affect working capital.
4. Prepare the formal Statement of Changes in Financial Position.

The application of each of these steps to the data provided for Chrisman Interiors is demonstrated below.

Step 1. Prepare a Schedule of Changes in Working Capital

Our first step is to prepare a schedule of changes in working capital for the period. This schedule is shown in Illustration 16-11. When the Statement of Changes in Financial Position is prepared in a working

ILLUSTRATION 16-10

Data used in demonstrating the preparation of the statement of changes in financial position

CHRISMAN INTERIORS
Balance Sheets

	As of 1/1/ Year 1	As of 12/31/ Year 1	Increase or (Decrease) in Account Balances
Current Assets:			
Cash	$ 12,000	$ 18,000	$ 6,000
Accounts Receivable	21,000	24,000	3,000
Supplies Inventory	35,000	31,000	(4,000)
Total Current Assets	$ 68,000	$ 73,000	
Noncurrent Assets:			
Land	—	$ 21,000	$21,000
Buildings and Equipment	277,000	304,000	27,000
Less: Accumulated Depreciation	(35,000)	(50,000)	15,000
Net Buildings and Equipment	$242,000	$254,000	
Total Noncurrent Assets	$242,000	$275,000	
Total Assets	$310,000	$348,000	
Current Liabilities:			
Accounts Payable	$ 18,000	$ 20,000	2,000
Salaries Payable	5,000	4,000	(1,000)
Total Current Liabilities	$ 23,000	$ 24,000	
Noncurrent Liabilities:			
Long-Term Notes Payable	53,000	$ 19,000	(34,000)
Total Liabilities	$ 76,000	$ 43,000	
Stockholders' Equity:			
Common Stock, no par	$200,000	$224,000	24,000
Retained Earnings	34,000	81,000	47,000
Total Stockholders' Equity	$234,000	$305,000	
Total Liabilities and Stockholders' Equity	$310,000	$348,000	

CHRISMAN INTERIORS
Income Statement for the Year Ended 12/31/Year 1

Sales		$180,000
Operating Expenses:		
Salaries	$ 90,000	
Depreciation	15,000	
Supplies	8,000	
Interest	4,000	
Utilities	3,000	
Insurance	1,000	121,000
Net Income		$ 59,000

Additional Data
a. Equipment costing $27,000 was purchased during the period for cash.
b. A piece of land costing $21,000 was obtained by issuing shares of Chrisman Interiors' stock to the land's owner.
c. $34,000 of long-term notes payable were liquidated during the period.
d. Common stock was sold for $3,000.
e. $12,000 of cash dividends were paid.

capital format, generally accepted accounting principles require that it be accompanied by a schedule showing the changes in each working capital account.

Note from Illustration 16-11 that increases in current assets cause working capital to increase, while decreases in current assets cause working capital to decrease. Conversely, increases in current liabilities cause working capital to decrease, while decreases in current liabilities cause working capital to increase. This is because working capital is the net difference between current assets and current liabilities.

We now know what the bottom line of our statement of changes in financial position will show—increase in working capital of $4,000. As a result of preparing the statement, we will know the reasons for this $4,000 increase.

Step 2. Calculate the Amount of Working Capital Generated or Used by Operations

We will take net income and restate it in terms of working capital generated or used by operations. Procedurally, what we do is take net income and adjust it for any items which were listed on the income statement but which did not have a working capital impact.

Let's look at the income statement and re-create the entries which may have been made to record everything on that statement. These entries are:

Cash or Accounts Receivable	180,000	
Sales		180,000
Salaries	90,000	
Cash or Salaries Payable		90,000
Depreciation	15,000	
Accumulated Depreciation		15,000
Supplies	8,000	
Cash, Accounts Payable or Supplies Inventory		8,000
Interest	4,000	
Cash or Interest Payable		4,000
Utilities	3,000	
Cash on Payables		3,000
Insurance	1,000	
Cash, Prepaid Insurance or Payables		1,000

Looking at these entries, we see that the recording of the revenues and the recording of the expenses, with *one exception*, had a working capital impact. For example, in recording the salaries expenses, either cash or salaries payable was credited. In either case, the effect was to decrease working capital.

The transaction which did not have a working capital impact was the recording of depreciation expense. Instead, a contra-asset was affected.

ILLUSTRATION
16-11

	CHRISMAN INTERIORS Schedule of Changes in Working Capital Accounts		
	Balance 1/1/Year 1	Balance 12/31/Year 1	Increase or (Decrease) in Working Capital
Current Assets:			
Cash	$12,000	$18,000	$ 6,000
Accounts Receivable (net)	21,000	24,000	3,000
Supplies Inventory	35,000	31,000	(4,000)
Total	$68,000	$73,000	$ 5,000
Current Liabilities:			
Accounts Payable	$18,000	$20,000	(2,000)
Salaries Payable	5,000	4,000	1,000
Total	$23,000	$24,000	(1,000)
Working Capital	$45,000	$49,000	$ 4,000

Thus, when we want to determine how much working capital was generated or used by operations by Chrisman Interiors, we have just one adjustment to make to it for depreciation. This information would be shown on our Statement of Changes in Financial Position as follows:

Financial Resources Generated:	
Working Capital Generated:	
From Operations:	
Net Income	$59,000
Add or (Deduct) items not affecting working capital:	
Depreciation	15,000
Working Capital from Operations	$74,000

Depreciation add-back is the most common adjustment made to net income to adjust for nonworking capital income-statement items. Other items which may represent adjustments to net income are shown in Illustration 16-12.

ILLUSTRATION
16-12

Items which frequently represent adjustments to net income to convert net income to a working capital basis

Additions to net income
  Depreciation.
  Amortization of goodwill and other intangibles.
  Losses on disposal or liquidation of noncurrent accounts (sale of fixed assets, early retirement of bonds).
  Bond discount amortization.
  Increase in deferred income taxes payable.
  Depletion expense for natural resources.

Deductions from net income
  Income recognized from the equity method of accounting for investments.
  Amortization of bond premiums.
  Decreases in deferred taxes payable.
  Amortization of deferred investment tax credits.
  Gains on disposals or liquidating of noncurrent accounts (sale of fixed assets, early retirement of bonds).

Step 3. Calculate the Change in Each Nonworking Capital Balance-Sheet Account

We simply look at the beginning balance in each nonworking capital account, compare it with the ending balance, and take the difference, noting whether each difference is an increase in the account balance or a decrease.

These changes have already been calculated for Chrisman Interiors in Illustration 16-10; they are:

Land	$21,000 Increase
Building and Equipment	$27,000 Increase
Accumulated Depreciation	$15,000 Increase
Long-Term Notes Payable	$34,000 Decrease
Common Stock	$24,000 Increase
Retained Earnings	$47,000 Increase

Step 4. Analyze the Changes in the Nonworking Capital Accounts to Determine (a) Other Sources of Working Capital, (b) Nonoperating Applications of Working Capital, and (c) the Nature of Transactions Which Occurred but Which Did Not Affect Working Capital

The easiest way to analyze the changes in the nonworking capital accounts is to visualize or reconstruct the general journal entry which was made to support each account balance change.

Based on additional information provided, we can reconstruct the following entries for Chrisman Interiors which account for the balance sheet changes:

a. Equipment was purchased for cash of $27,000.

Equipment	27,000	
Cash		27,000

b. Land costing $21,000 was acquired through the acquisition of stock.

Land	21,000	
Common Stock		21,000

c. $34,000 of long-term notes payable were liquidated.

Long-Term Notes Payable	34,000	
Cash		34,000

d. Common stock was sold for $3,000

Cash	3,000	
Common Stock		3,000

e. $12,000 of dividends were paid.

Retaining Earnings	12,000	
Cash		12,000

    If we examine the transactions which the company engaged in during the period, we can see that all except (b) affected working capital. Transactions (a), (c), and (e) were *nonoperating applications of working capital,* while transaction (d) was a *source of working capital other than operations.* These transactions would fit into the statement of changes in financial position as follows:

Financial Resources Generated:	
Working Capital Generated:	
From Other Sources:	
Sale of Stock	3,000
Nonworking Capital Resources Generated:	
Common Stock Exchanged for Land	$21,000
Financial Resources Applied:	
Working Capital Applied to	
Nonoperating Items:	
Purchase of Equipment	$27,000
Payment of Long-Term Notes	34,000
Dividend Payments	12,000
Total Working Capital Applied to	
Nonoperating Items	$73,000
Nonworking Capital Resources Applied:	
Land Acquired through Issuance of	
Common Stock	$21,000

    At this point you might note that we have not accounted for all of the change in Retained Earnings with the entry shown above, entry (e).

Retained Earnings, Beginning Balance	$34,000
Less: Dividends	12,000
Total	$22,000

The additional change in Retained Earnings is represented by Chrisman Interiors' net income for the period, which, you will recall from financial accounting, is closed out to that account.

Total Retained Earnings from Above	$22,000
Add: Net Income (from the Income	
Statement)	59,000
Retained Earnings, Ending Balance	$81,000

The change in Retained Earnings of $47,000 consisted of a $59,000 increase from net income and a $12,000 decrease for dividend.

We can put together the pieces of the statement which we have developed and prepare the formal Statement of Changes in Financial Position, Working Capital Format, which was shown in Illustration 16-8.

An Internal Perspective on Working Capital Changes Versus an External Perspective

If we were working for Chrisman Interiors or had access to all the company's data, we would have the information given in Illustration 16-10 as "Additional Information." If we were trying to reconstruct what happened during the year as someone external to the firm based on beginning and ending balance-sheet balances, we would simply have to speculate about the most likely reason for some of the balance-sheet changes. To illustrate, look at the transactions labeled (a) and (d). Being internal to the firm, we know these two entries took place:

Land	21,000	
Common Stock		21,000
Cash	3,000	
Common Stock		3,000

If we were external to the firm, we might assume that acquisition of land was for cash and that all the common stock which was issued was for cash, or we might assume that the following entries were made:

Land	21,000	
Cash		21,000
Cash	24,000	
Common Stock		24,000

Working with just balance-sheet information, someone external to the firm could have made these erroneous assumptions as to the nature of transactions which took place. To prevent the user of financial data from making such incorrect assumptions, GAAP accounting requires the reporting of financial information to account for balance-sheet changes in the Statement of Changes in Financial Position.

Mechanical Techniques for Preparing a Statement of Changes in Financial Position

We assembled the Statement of Changes in Financial Position by recreating the entries which were made. For more complex examples it may be easier to do this by using as mechanical aids T-accounts or a worksheet.

The T-account technique.   When working capital changes are being analyzed and a statement of changes in financial position prepared using T-accounts as a method of facilitating this procedure, the steps to be used are:

1. Prepare a schedule analyzing the changes in working capital. We have already prepared such a schedule (see Illustration 16-11) and noted that working capital increased by $4,000.
2. Set up one T-account entitled Financial Resources Generated and Applied and label sections of that T-account consistent with the classifications of amounts on the Statement of Changes in Financial Position as follows:

Financial Resources Generated and Applied	

Financial Resources Generated:
  Working Capital Generated:
    From Operations:
    Other Sources
  Nonworking Capital Resources
    Generated:
	Financial Resources Applied:
	  Working Capital Applied to Non-
	    operating Items:
	
	  Nonworking Capital Resources Ap-
	    plied:

3. Set up T-accounts for all nonworking capital accounts and enter the beginning balances for the period in these accounts.
4. Enter net income (or loss) in the Financial Resources Generated and Applied account and in the Retained Earnings account as shown below:

Financial Resources Generated and Applied		Retained Earnings	

Working Capital Generated:
  From Operations:
  (a) Net Income   59,000
		Beg. Bal. 34,000
		(a) 59,000	

5. Calculate the amount of working capital generated or used by operations and record the impact of any required adjustments in the Financial Resources Generated and Applied account and to other accounts which are affected. We have already determined that the only adjustment to net income to convert it to a working capital basis is to add back the nonworking capital expense, Depreciation. Using the T-account method, after doing this we would find the following information in the accounts:

Financial Resources Generated and Applied		Accumulated Depreciation	

Working Capital Generated:
  From Operations:
  (a) Net Income   59,000
  (b) Depreciation   15,000
		Beg. Bal. 35,000
		(b) 15,000	

6. Analyze each change in the nonworking capital accounts and enter the effects of the changes in the Financial Resources Generated and Applied account and other affected accounts. To demonstrate, consider the purchase of equipment for $27,000 cash.

Financial Resources Generated and Applied		Buildings and Equipment	

	Working Capital Applied to
	  Nonoperating Items:
	  (c) Purchase of
	    Equipment 27,000
		Beg. Bal. 277,000
		(c) 27,000	

After all nonworking capital transactions have been analyzed and recorded, the ending balance in the nonworking capital accounts should agree with that shown on the end of the period balance sheet. For example, looking at the Buildings and Equipment account shown above, the account now shows a balance of $304,000, the ending balance-sheet valuation of that account. You know that you have completed your analysis when you have reconciled all beginning and ending balances and your Financial Resources Generated and Applied account shows a balance consistent with the change in working capital, which you computed in the initial step of this process.

All the T-account entries for Chrisman Interiors are shown in Illustration 16-13. The only unusual thing about the recording in the T-accounts is the treatment accorded transactions which represent both financial resources generated and applied. There will be four parts to these transactions: (1) to record the financial resource generated, (2) to record the financial resource applied in the Financial Resources Generated and Applied account, (3) to record in the nonworking capital accounts the source of the financial resource (in our example, common stock), and (4) to record in the nonworking capital accounts the use of the financial resource (in our example, land).

7. Use the Financial Resources Generated and Applied account and prepare the formal statement of changes in financial position. We have already done this and the statement is presented in Illustration 16-8.

The worksheet technique.   The steps in the worksheet process are as follows:

1. Prepare a schedule which explains the changes in working capital.
2. Set up a four-column worksheet, the first line of which is entitled, "Working Capital." The other lines of the worksheet are used to record nonworking capital account balances. Accounts which have debit balances are shown together, and all accounts with credit balances are grouped together on the worksheet. For example, the Accumulated Depreciation account is a contra-asset but, since it has a credit balance, it will be listed with liability and stockholder equity accounts.
3. Enter beginning-of-the-period balances in the first column of the worksheet; label the next two columns "Changes During the Period." Enter the end-of-the-period balances in the last column. When the worksheet is complete, the figure in the beginning balance column plus or minus what is in the changes columns should equal what is in the last column. In other words, you will have explained all changes in the nonworking capital accounts.
4. At the bottom of the worksheet set up the headings for the Statement of Changes in Financial Position previously outlined. As you are analyzing a change in the nonworking capital accounts, enter the effects in the proper part of the statement of changes. For example, when equipment was purchased for cash, in the changes column of the worksheet a debit of $27,000 to Plant and Equipment will be entered; on the part of the worksheet entitled "Working Capital Applied to Nonoperating Items" a line will be entered: "Purchased Equipment for Cash, $27,000."
5. Enter net income (or loss) on the part of the worksheet designated to collect information as to working capital generated from operations and as a credit (in the case of a loss, as a debit) to Retained Earnings.

ILLUSTRATION 16-13 Using the T-account technique to prepare a statement of changes in financial position, working capital format

Financial Resources Generated and Applied		
Financial Resources Generated:		**Financial Resources Applied:**
Working Capital Generated:		Working Capital Applied to Nonoperating items:
From Operations:		(c) Purchased equip. 27,000
(a) Net Income 59,000		(e) Debt Retired 34,000
(b) Add: Depr. 15,000		(g) Dividends 12,000
Other Sources:		
(f) Sale of Stock 3,000		
		Nonworking Capital Resources Applied:
Nonworking Capital Resources Generated:		(d) Land Acquired with Stock 21,000
(d) Common Stock Issued for Land 21,000		Total Applied 94,000
Total Generated 98,000		Increase in Working Capital 4,000
—		98,000
98,000		

Land

Beg. bal. —	
(d) 21,000	

Building and Equipment

Beg. Bal. 277,000	
(c) 27,000	
Bal 12/31 304,000	

Accumulated Depreciation

	Beg. Bal. 35,000
	(b) 15,000
	Bal. 12/31 50,000

Long-Term Notes Payable

(e) 34,000	Beg. Bal 53,000
	Bal. 12/31 19,000

Common Stock

	Beg. Bal. 200,000
	(d) 21,000
	(f) 3,000
	Bal. 12/13 224,000

Retained Earnings

(g) 12,000	Beg. Bal. 34,000
	(a) 59,000
	Bal. 81,000

Note that the letters used to identify transactions are not those used for some of the transactions described in additional information in Illustration 16-10.

6. Calculate the amount of working capital generated or used by operations and record the impact of any required adjustments in the section of the worksheet designed to show working capital from operations and in other accounts which are affected.

7. Analyze each change in nonworking capital accounts and enter the effects in the proper section of the worksheet representing the Statement of Changes in Financial Position and in the affected accounts. Adding across each line for nonworking capital accounts, you have completed your analysis when the beginning balance has been reconciled to the ending balance. The worksheet is completed by totaling the part of the debit and credit change columns designed to represent the Statement of Changes in Financial Position. The difference between the columns should be the change in working capital which you calculated as the first step in this process and should reconcile beginning and ending working capital on the initial line of your worksheet.

8. Use the bottom half of your worksheet to prepare a formal Statement of Changes in Financial Position, which has already been prepared and is shown in Illustration 16-8.

ILLUSTRATION 16-14

The worksheet technique to preparing a statement of changes in financial position, working capital format, for Chrisman Interiors

ACCOUNTS	BEGINNING BALANCES	CHANGES DURING THE PERIOD DEBIT	CHANGES DURING THE PERIOD CREDIT	ENDING BALANCES
Debit Balances:				
Working Capital	45,000	(h) 4,000		49,000
Land	—	(d) 21,000		21,000
Buildings and Equipment	277,000	(c) 27,000		304,000
Total Debits	322,000			$374,000
Credit Balances:				
Accumulated Depreciation	35,000		(b) 15,000	50,000
Long-Term Notes	53,000	(e) 34,000		19,000
Common Stock	200,000		(d) 21,000 (f) 3,000	224,000
Retained Earnings	34,000	(g) 12,000	(a) 59,000	81,000
Total Credits	322,000	98,000	98,000	374,000
Financial Resources Generated:				
Working Capital Generated:				
From Operations:				
Net Income		(a) 59,000		
Adjustments				
Depreciation		(b) 15,000		
From Other Sources:				
Sale of Stock		(f) 3,000		
Nonworking Capital				
Resources Generated:				
Stock Issued for Land		(d) 21,000		
Financial Resources Applied:				
Working Capital Applied to				
Nonoperating Items:				
Purchase of Equipment			(c) 27,000	
Debt Retired			(e) 34,000	
Dividends			(g) 12,000	
Nonworking Capital				
Resources Applied				
Land Acquired for Stock			(d) 21,000	
		98,000	94,000	
Increase in Working Capital			(h) 4,000	
		98,000	98,000	

The worksheet technique for analyzing working capital changes for Chrisman Interiors is shown in Illustration 16-14.

PREPARING THE STATEMENT OF CHANGES IN FINANCIAL POSITION—CASH FORMAT

The Statement of Changes in Financial Position prepared in a cash format describes the firm's major financing and investing activities and their impact on its cash position. In addition, the statement shows how much cash was generated or used by operations.

The steps required to prepare such a statement are:

1. Determine the change in cash for the period by comparing beginning-of-the-period cash with the end-of-the-period cash balance.
2. Calculate the changes in all other balance-sheet accounts.
3. Calculate the amount of cash generated or used by operations by adjusting net income for changes in the working capital accounts which had an impact on cash generated or used by operations.
4. Analyze the changes in all other accounts to determine (a) other sources of cash, (b) nonoperating applications of cash, and (c) the nature of transactions that occurred which did not affect cash.

The application of these steps to the data provided for Chrisman Interiors is demonstrated below.

Step 1. Determine the Change in Cash

We can get this information from Illustration 16-10, which showed beginning and ending balance-sheet values. This data shows that Chrisman's cash increased by $6,000.

Step 2. Calculate the Changes in All Other Balance-Sheet Accounts

This too was done in Illustration 16-10. Those changes were as follows:

Accounts Receivable	$ 3,000 increase
Supplies Inventory	4,000 decrease
Land	21,000 increase
Buildings and Equipment	27,000 increase
Accumulated Depreciation	15,000 increase
Accounts Payable	2,000 increase
Salaries Payable	1,000 decrease
Long-Term Notes Payable	34,000 decrease
Common Stock	24,000 increase
Retained Earnings	47,000 increase

Step 3. Calculate the Amount of Cash Generated by Operations

This is the difficult part of preparing a cash-basis statement of changes in financial position. We will take net income determined on an accrual basis and convert it to a cash basis. Remember that under accrual accounting, revenues are recognized when earned and expenses when incurred. Under cash-basis accounting, revenues are recognized when cash flows in and expenses when cash flows out.

Let's look again at the entries which could have been made to record the balances shown on the income statement.

Cash or Accounts Receivable	180,000	
Sales		180,000
Salaries	90,000	
Cash or Salaries Payable		90,000
Depreciation	15,000	
Accumulated Depreciation		15,000
Supplies	8,000	
Cash, Accounts Payable, or Supplies Inventory		8,000
Interest	4,000	
Interest Payable or Cash		4,000
Utilities	3,000	
Cash or Payable		3,000
Insurance	1,000	
Cash, Payable, or Prepaid		1,000

When we were converting net income to a working capital basis, most of the transactions above did not result in any adjustment to net income because working capital was affected. With cash, while depreciation is clearly not a cash expense and must be added back to net income to convert net income to a cash basis, the impact of the other transactions on cash from operations is less clear and requires additional analysis as follows:

Sales, assume all were for cash,	$180,000
Assume all beginning-of-the-period accounts receivable were collected	21,000
Potential cash flow	$201,000
Some accounts were not collected, as is shown by the ending balance in accounts receivable	(24,000)
Cash revenues from operations	$177,000

Since we have estimated cash revenues from operations as $177,000 and the net income figure of $59,000 was based on accrual revenues of $180,000, as a first step in converting the net income to a cash basis we will have to subtract the noncash revenues of $3,000 ($180,000 − $177,000).

Supplies Inventory. We want to determine how much we paid in cash for supplies purchased this period. Assume that all accounts payable are related to purchases of supplies. Our analysis will consist of two parts: (1) calculating the amount of supplies purchased during the period and (2) determining how much cash was paid out in conjunction with supplies purchases. This analysis can be done as follows:

Assume all supplies used were purchased during the period	$ 8,000	(from the income statement)
Assume all supplies on hand at the *end* of the period were purchased during the period (from the 12/31 balance sheet)	31,000	
Potential amount of supplies purchased	$39,000	
Not all supplies were purchased during the period because there was a beginning inventory	(35,000)	
Supplies purchased during the period	$ 4,000	
Assume all supplies purchased this period were paid for in cash	$ 4,000	
Add: Cash outflows to pay for supplies which were purchased last period and are on the books as accounts payable	$18,000	
Potential cash outflow for supplies	$22,000	
Less: Supplies which are unpaid for at the end of the period as represented by the ending accounts payable balance	(20,000)	
Cash outflow for supplies	$ 2,000	

To calculate the net income figure on an accrual basis of $59,000, we subtracted $8,000 of supplies expense. On a cash basis, supplies expense was only $2,000. Thus, on a cash basis the cash flow from operations is understated by $8,000 − $2,000 = $6,000, and as a step in converting accrual net income to a cash basis we will add to it $6,000.

Salaries payable. Next, let's calculate how much cash was spent this period which was related to salaries.

		(from the income statement)
Assume all salaries were paid in cash	$90,000	
Assume all beginning-of-the-period slaries payable were paid (1/1 balance sheet)	5,000	
Potential cash flow for salaries	$95,000	
Some salaries were still unpaid at the end of the period, salaries payable, ending balance	(4,000)	
Cash outflow for salaries	$91,000	

We have understated the cash cost of salaries in coming up with the $59,000 net income figure. To convert it to a cash basis we will have to subtract an additional $1,000 ($91,000 cash flow for salaries − $90,000 accrual-based salary expense.

Other items. Since there were no other balance-sheet accounts in the form of prepaids, inventories, receivables, or payables which were related to income-statement representations for the period, it would appear that these other expenses are already in the form of cash flows.

We can thus reconstruct cash from operations as follows:

Cash revenues		$177,000
Cash expenses:		
Salaries	$91,000	
Supplies	2,000	
Interest	4,000	
Utilities	3,000	
Insurance	1,000	101,000
Cash from operations		$ 76,000

Mechanical techniques for converting net income to a cash basis. Our analysis has been lengthy, and it can be shortened through the application of a mechanical approach to converting net income to a cash basis. This technique is based on the following set of rules:

1. Take net income and convert it to a working capital basis, making adjustments of the types shown in Illustration 16-12.
2. After net income has been converted to a working capital basis, adjust it for changes in noncash working capital accounts to convert it to a cash basis by:
   a. Adding to working capital from operations, decreases in current assets and increases in current liabilities and
   b. Deducting from working capital from operations, increases in current assets and decreases in current liabilities.

The logic behind these adjustments is as follows:

Increases in current assets mean that cash is tied up in these accounts—for example, inventories and receivables. Decreases in current assets mean these accounts have been realized in a cash form. Increases in current liabilities mean that income-statement expenses have been financed in part on a short-term basis and no cash has flowed out for these items. Current liabilities decrease because cash flows out in the form of payments.

We can apply the mechanical approach and convert Chrisman Interiors' net income to a cash basis as follows:

Net Income	$59,000
Add: Depreciation	15,000
Working capital from operations	$74,000
Add: Increases in current liabilities:	
Accounts Payable	2,000
Decreases in current assets:	
Supplies Inventory	4,000
Total	$80,000
Deduct: Decreases in current liabilities:	
Salaries Payable	(1,000)
Increases in current assets:	
Accounts Receivable	(3,000)
Cash from operations	$76,000

This mechanical approach does not always work. For example,

suppose that a company had no dividends payable at the beginning of the period but owed $10,000 in dividends (a current liability) at the end of the period. If we applied our mechanical rules, we would note an increase in current liabilities of $10,000 and add this to net income to convert net income to a cash basis. The problem here is that dividends are not an expense, but rather a distribution of earnings, and should not be accounted for as an adjustment to income.

The mechanical approach to converting net income to a cash basis is summarized in Illustration 16-15.

We now have the information to complete the section of our Statement of Changes in Financial Position which shows cash generated or used by operations:

Financial Resources Generated:			
Cash Generated:			
From Operations:			
Net Income			$59,000
Add:	Depreciation	$15,000	
	Increase in		
	Accounts		
	Payable	2,000	
	Decrease in		
	Supplies	4,000	21,000
	Total		$80,000
Deduct:	Decrease in Salaries		
	Payable	$ 1,000	
	Increase in		
	Accounts		
	Receivable	3,000	(4,000)
Cash from Operations			$76,000

ILLUSTRATION 16-15

A mechanical approach to converting net income to a cash basis

Net Income	
Add:	Depreciation
	Amortization of goodwill and other intangibles
	Losses on disposal or liquidation of noncurrent accounts
	Increases in deferred taxes payable
	Depletion
	Bond discount amortization
Deduct:	Income recognized from the equity method
	Amortization of bond premiums
	Decreases in deferred taxes payable
	Amortization of deferred investment tax credit
	Gains on disposals or liquidations of noncurrent accounts
Working Capital from Operations	
Add:	Increases in current liability accounts
	Decreases in current asset account
Deduct:	Decreases in current liability accounts
	Increases in current asset accounts
CASH FROM OPERATIONS	

Step 4. Analyze the Changes in All Other Accounts to Determine
(a). Other Sources of Cash,
(b) Nonoperating Applications of Cash,
and (c) the Nature of Transactions
that Occurred but which Did Not Affect Cash

Recall the other transactions the company had, which are reproduced in general journal form below:

a. Equipment	27,000	
Cash		27,000
b. Land	21,000	
Common Stock		21,000
c. Long-Term Notes Payable	34,000	
Cash		34,000
d. Cash	3,000	
Common Stock		3,000
d. Retained Earnings	12,000	
Cash		12,000

All the transactions except (b) affected cash. Transactions (a), (c), and (e) were nonoperating applications of cash, while transaction (d) was a source of cash other than from operations. Transaction (b) did not affect cash but will be shown in the sections of the statement for noncash resources generated and applied.

We can now construct the other sections of our Statement of Changes in Financial Position prepared in a cash format.

Financial Resources Generated:	
Cash Generated:	
From Other Sources:	
Sale of Stock	$ 3,000
Noncash Resources Generated:	
Common Stock was exchanged for land	$21,000
Financial Resources Applied:	
Cash Applied to Nonoperating Items:	
Purchase of Equipment	$27,000
Payment of Long-Term Notes	34,000
Dividend Payments	12,000
Total Cash Applied to Nonoperating Items	$73,000
Noncash Resources Applied:	
Land acquired through issuance of common	
stock	$21,000

The transactions shown above appeared in the same places on the Statement of Changes in Financial Position prepared using a cash format as they did in the working capital format. Cash is a part of working capital, and generally a large number of items are treated similarly on statements in both formats.

The Statement of Changes in Financial Position, cash format, for Chrisman Interiors was shown in Illustration 16-9.

Mechanical Techniques for Preparing a Statement of Changes in Financial Position, Cash Format

To facilitate the preparation of the Statement of Changes in Financial Position using a cash format we can follow the same two approaches we used in the working capital format.

The T-account technique. A brief description of the application of the T-account technique to preparing a cash-format Statement of Changes in Financial Position is given below. Application of this technique to the data provided for Chrisman Interiors is demonstrated in Illustration 16-16.

1. Calculate the change in cash.
2. Set up one T-account entitled "Financial Resources Generated and Applied" and label sections of that T-account consistent with the classification on the Statement of Changes in Financial Position.
3. Set up T-accounts for all noncash accounts and enter the beginning balances for the period in these accounts.
4. Enter net income (or loss) in the Financial Resources Generated and Applied account and in the Retained Earnings account.
5. Calculate the amount of cash generated or used by operations and record the impact of any required adjustments in the Financial Resources Generated and Applied account and in other accounts which are affected.
6. Analyze each change in the remaining accounts and enter the effects of the changes in the Financial Resources Generated and Applied account and in other affected accounts.
7. Use the Financial Resources Generated and Applied account to prepare the formal statement of changes in financial position.

The worksheet technique. A brief description of the use of a worksheet in preparing a Statement of Changes in Financial Position using a cash format is given below. The application of this technique to Chrisman Interiors is shown in Illustration 16-17.

1. Determine the change in cash.
2. Set up a four-column worksheet, the first line of which is cash. List first all accounts which have a debit balance, then all accounts which have credit balances.
3. Enter beginning-of-the-period balances in the first column of the worksheet. Label the two middle columns the "Changes during the period" column, making the first column the debit column and the second column the credit column. Enter ending account balances in the last column of the worksheet.
4. At the bottom of the worksheet set up the headings of the Statement of Changes in Financial Position.
5. Enter net income (or loss) on the part of the worksheet designated to collect information as to cash generated from operations and as a credit (or a debit, in the case of a loss) to retained earnings.

ILLUSTRATION 16-16

Using the T-account technique to prepare a statement of changes in financial position, cash format, for Chrisman Interiors

Financial Resources Generated and Applied

Financial Resources Generated:		Financial Resources Applied:	
Cash Generated:		Cash Applied to Nonoperating	
From Operations:		Items:	
(a) Net income	59,000	(g) Purchase of Equip.	27,000
(b) Depreciation	15,000	(h) Payment of Long-Term	
(c) Acc. Pay.	2,000	Debt	34,000
(d) Supplies Inv.	4,000	(i) Dividends	12,000
(e) Acc. Rec.	(3,000)		
(f) Salaries Pay.	(1,000)		
Other Sources			
(i) Sale of Stock	3,000		
		Noncash Resources Applied:	
Noncash Resources Generated:		(h) Land Obtained for Common	
(k) Common Stock		Stock	21,000
Exchanged for Land	21,000	Total Applied	94,000
Total Generated	100,000	Increase in Cash	6,000
	100,000		100,000

Accounts Receivable

Beg. Bal.	21,000		
(e)	3,000		
Bal. 12/31	24,000		

Supplies Inventory

Beg. Bal.	35,000	(d)	4,000
Bal. 12/31	31,000		

Land

(k)	21,000		

Buildings and Equipment

Beg. Bal.	277,000		
(g)	27,000		
Bal. 12/31	304,000		

Accumulated Depreciation

		Beg. Bal.	35,000
		(b)	15,000
		Bal. 12/31	50,000

Accounts Payable

		Beg. Bal.	18,000
		(c)	2,000
		Bal. 12/31	20,000

Salaries Payable

(f)	1,000	Beg. Bal.	5,000
		Bal. 12/31	4,000

Long-Term Notes Payable

(h)	34,000	Beg. Bal.	53,000
		Bal. 12/31	19,000

Common Stock

		Beg. Bal.	200,000
		(j)	3,000
		(k)	21,000
		Bal 12/31	224,000

Retained Earnings

(i)	12,000	Beg. Bal.	34,000
		(a)	59,000
		Bal. 12/31	81,000

ILLUSTRATION 16-17

The worksheet technique for preparing a statement of changes in financial position, cash format, for Chrisman Interiors

ACCOUNTS	BEGINNING BALANCES	CHANGES DURING THE PERIOD Debit	CHANGES DURING THE PERIOD Credit	ENDING BALANCES
Debit Balances:				
Cash	12,000	(l) 6,000		18,000
Accounts Receivable	21,000	(f) 3,000		24,000
Supplies Inventory	35,000		(d) 4,000	31,000
Land	—	(h) 21,000		21,000
Buildings and Equipment	277,000	(i) 27,000		304,000
	345,000			398,000
Credit Balances:				
Accumulated Depreciation	35,000		(b) 15,000	50,000
Accounts Payable	18,000		(c) 2,000	20,000
Salaries Payable	5,000	(e) 1,000		4,000
Long-Term Notes Payable	53,000	(j) 34,000		19,000
Common Stock	200,000		(g) 3,000 (h) 21,000	224,000
Retained Earnings	34,000	(k) 12,000	(a) 59,000	81,000
	345,000	104,000	104,000	398,000
Financial Resources Generated:				
Cash Generated:				
From Operations:				
Net Income		(a) 59,000		
Depreciation		(b) 15,000		
Increase in Accounts Payable		(c) 2,000		
Decrease in Supplies		(d) 4,000		
Decrease in Salaries Payable			(e) 1,000	
Increase in Accounts Receivable			(f) 3,000	
Other Sources:				
Sale of Stock		(g) 3,000		
Noncash Resources Generated:				
Common Stock for Land		(h) 21,000		
Financial Resources Applied:				
Cash Applied to Nonoperating Items:				
Purchase of Equipment			(i) 27,000	
Payment of Debt			(j) 34,000	
Divident Payments			(k) 12,000	
Total Cash Applied				
Noncash Resources Applied:				
Land Obtained for Common Stock			(h) 21,000	
		104,000	98,000	
Increase in Cash			(i) 6,000	
		104,000	104,000	

6. Calculate the amount of cash generated or used by operations and record the impact of any requied adjustments in the section of the worksheet designed to show cash from operations and in other accounts affected.
7. Analyze each change in the remaining accounts and enter the effects in the proper section of the worksheet and in the affected accounts.
8. Use the bottom half of your worksheet to prepare a formal Statement of Changes in Financial Position.

CASH VERSUS WORKING CAPITAL FORMAT

You may wonder why some companies prepare the Statement of Changes in Financial Position using the working capital format and others use the cash format. You might reflect, too, that if this statement is supposed to show funds flow, then cash is more consistent with the normal definition of "funds."

Conceptually, the use of working capital to mean funds is based on the idea that noncash working capital accounts are so close to conversion into cash or to requiring an outflow of cash that they can be treated as if they were cash. Some analysts, in trying to calculate the amount of cash generated by operations, will take net income and make only one adjustment—the add-back of depreciation. This approach, too, is based on the assumption that other current accounts are so near to cash or to requiring cash that adjustments do not need to be made for them.

Realistically, accounts receivables and inventories are not liquid. Managers and those external to the firm get a clearer picture of sources and uses of liquid assets when funds is defined as cash.

ILLUSTRATION FROM PRACTICE: GENERAL ELECTRIC'S STATEMENT OF CHANGES IN FINANCIAL POSITION

The Statement of Changes in Financial Position for General Electric (GE) which was included in its 1982 annual report is shown below. Note that GE has used neither the working capital nor cash format but rather an approach which shows the net change in cash, marketable securities, and short-term borrowings. In addition, although it is not labeled, earnings from operations has been converted to a working capital basis. Changes in accounts receivable, inventories, accounts payable, and working capital accounts other than cash, marketable securities, and short-term borrowings are not grouped together in the body of the statement.

Statement of changes in financial position

General Electric Company and consolidated affiliates

For the years ended December 31 (In millions) (note 1)	1982	1981	1980
Source of funds From operations			
Net earnings	$1,817	$1,652	$1,514
Depreciation, depletion and amortization	984	882	707
Income tax timing differences	95	33	63
Investment tax credit deferred — net	44	46	56
Minority interest in earnings of consolidated affiliates	36	46	21
Earnings retained by nonconsolidated finance affiliates	(42)	(27)	(22)
	2,934	2,632	2,339
Reduction in inventories	432	—	—
Disposition of treasury shares	216	169	136
Reduction in current receivables	132	—	—
Increase in long-term borrowings	113	160	122
Increase in current liabilities other than short-term borrowings	—	1,064	498
Other — net	(3)	(78)	143
Total source of funds	3,824	3,947	3,238
Application of funds Additions to property, plant and equipment	1,608	2,025	1,948
Dividends declared on common stock	760	715	670
Reduction in current liabilities other than short-term borrowings	447	—	—
Increase in investments	380	87	129
Purchase of treasury shares	222	176	145
Reduction in long-term borrowings	157	101	69
Increase in current receivables	—	533	692
Increase in inventories	—	118	182
Total application of funds	3,574	3,755	3,835
Net change Net change in cash, marketable securities and short-term borrowings	$ 250	$ 192	$ (597)
Analysis of net change Increase (decrease) in cash and marketable securities	$ 116	$ 270	$ (375)
Decrease (increase) in short-term borrowings	134	(78)	(222)
Increase (decrease) in net liquid assets	$ 250	$ 192	$ (597)

SIGNIFICANCE OF THE STATEMENT OF CHANGES IN FINANCIAL POSITION TO THE MANAGER

While the Statement of Changes in Financial Position is a part of the required external reporting package, its preparation can also have significance for those internal to the firm. Perhaps its greatest value arises when it is prepared in a cash format and it reveals the extent to which a company's operations generated (or failed to generate) cash. As we have noted, the long-run health of a firm may depend on its ability to generate cash through its operations.

In addition, the statement provides a summary of the company's major activities and can be used to answer questions such as the following:

1. How much was invested in productive assets during the period?
2. How does investment in productive assets compare with disinvestment (sale of productive assets)?
3. How much long-term financing did the company require during the period?
4. Were funds provided during the period primarily from borrowing, from owners, or from operations?
5. Did the company pay off any long-term obligations during the period?
6. What amount of funds was raised from shareholders?
7. Was there disinvestment by shareholders through treasury share acquisition (repurchase by the company of its own shares)?
8. What part of the company's liquid resources were used for dividends?
9. Were any major acquisitions financed through the issuance of securities such as stocks or bonds?
10. Were any convertible securities converted during the period?

chapter highlights

The working capital accounts, which are the current asset and current liability accounts of a company, are generally the most active accounts. They can represent a material investment, and their effective management can enhance a firm's profitability.

The objectives of managing cash, marketable securities, and accounts payable can be described as (1) maximizing the return on excess cash, (2) minimizing cash on hand, (3) minimizing adverse float, (4) maximizing favorable float, and (5) minimizing required cash. A series of techniques ranging from the use of electronic funds transfer systems to paying bills only when they become due can aid the manager in accomplishing these objectives.

Accounts receivable can be managed by setting credit controls and credit terms and by monitoring the investment in accounts receivable and collections. Commonly used models to assist a firm in determining its reorder point and establishing economic quantities in which inventory should be purchased have been developed to assist in inventory management.

Generally accepted accounting principles require that a Statement of Changes in Financial Position be prepared for external reporting purposes. These statements may take a number of different formats, all of which show the external user how a company's major investing and financing activities affected working capital or some combination of working capital accounts.

Two commonly used formats for preparing a Statement of Changes in Financial Position are the working capital format and the cash format. These statements are designed to show:

1. How much cash or working capital was generated or used by operations.
2. What other sources provided cash or working capital.
3. Nonoperating applications of cash or working capital.
4. The nature of noncash or nonworking capital transactions which occurred during the period.

Two techniques which can be used to advantage in preparing a Statement of Changes in Financial Position are T-accounts and a worksheet. Both provide an organized method for collecting the information needed to prepare the formal statement.

questions

1. What is working capital and why is it important?
2. What is the underlying objective of working capital management?
3. What are some things a company can do to reduce its working capital?
4. What are some factors which may keep a company from minimizing its investment in working capital?
5. What five objectives should be kept in mind in managing cash, marketable securities, and accounts payable?
6. Describe the three different types of float which may be available to a company.
7. Distinguish between favorable float and adverse float.
8. What is electronic funds transfer, and what effect does it have on float?
9. What are the four ways in which accounts receivable can be managed?
10. What is meant by "credit scoring"?
11. What three kinds of costs have to be kept in mind in managing inventory?
12. What is a stockout? Are the costs of a stockout normally found in the accounting records?
13. Before a reorder point can be determined, what information must you have?

14. What pieces of information must you have to use the economic order quantity (EOQ) formula?

15. What are the objectives of a Statement of Changes in Financial Position?

16. Give two examples of expenses which are commonly found on an accrual-basis income statement but do not have an impact on either working capital or cash.

17. Into what two major sections is a Statement of Changes in Financial Position divided?

18. List a company's major sources of working capital or cash.

19. List four common, nonoperating applications of cash or working capital.

20. Give two examples of transactions which would have to be described in a Statement of Changes in Financial Position but which do not affect either working capital or cash.

exercises

16—1.   The following information is available with respect to blenders, an item of inventory which is carried by Harry's Home Appliance Store.

Economic order quantity	100 units
Maximum weekly use	30 units
Average weekly use	20 units
Lead time	3 weeks
Cost of an item of inventory	$30

REQUIRED: 1. Assuming that no safety stock is carried, what is the reorder point?

2. Assume that Harry wants to stock so that he will not have a stockout of blenders. What is the reorder point?

3. What is the cost to Harry of not wanting to have a stockout of blenders?

4. Assume that Harry wants to maintain a safety stock of five blenders. What is the reorder point?

16—2.   Refer to the information in Exercise 16—1. Assume that the company wishes to maintain a safety stock of ten units.

REQUIRED: Prepare a graph which shows the company's reorder point.

16—3.   Duker Feed and Seed has developed the following information with respect to the dog food which it carries:

Average quantity demanded each year	16,000 bags
Cost of placing an order	$10
Cost of carrying a bag of dog food in inventory for a year	$ 2

REQUIRED:

1. Using the EOQ formula, determine the economic order quantity of bags of dog food for Duker Feed and Seed.
2. Prepare a tabular schedule of the cost of ordering the following quantities: 300 bags, 400 bags, and 500 bags.

16—4. One of the products made by Guttenberg Electronics is an electronic component used in telephones. The company is trying to decide what number of these components it should make in each production run. The following data are available:

Annual demand	4,000 components
Cost of setting up machinery to make a production run	$500
Cost of carrying a component in inventory	$ 4

REQUIRED:

1. Use a variation of the economic order quantity formula to determine how many electronic components should be made in each production run.
2. Assume that Guttenberg has been making production runs of 500 units. By what amount can they reduce their costs by converting to runs of the size you calculated in part 1?

16—5. You have been hired as a summer intern by a small company which makes soft drinks. You were hired from among 400 applicants because you discussed with the company's financial manager some techniques which you believed could help the company better manage their cash, marketable securities, and accounts payable. Now that you have been hired, your first assignment is to write a memo describing those techniques, which the financial manager can discuss with the company's president.

REQUIRED: Draft the memo which you would prepare in response to this assignment.

16—6. Zentner's Department Store has accumulated the information shown below:

Net credit sales	$3,600,000
Accounts receivable—average balance	$ 600,000
Accounts receivable collection period for similar department stores	45 days

REQUIRED:

1. Based on a 360-day year, calculate the accounts receivable collection period for Zentner's and comment on it in comparison to the industry statistic provided.
2. List some actions which Zentner's could take which might improve their collection period.
3. List some factors possibly beyond the company's control which may be affecting Zentner's collection period.
4. If net credit sales for next year are expected to be at about the same level as this year, to have an accounts receivable collection period equal to that of the industry, what average balance of accounts receivable must Zentner maintain?

16—7. Selected balance sheet accounts and balances taken from the records of the Goddard Company are shown below:

	BALANCES	
	January 1	December 31
Cash	$ 10,000	$ 18,000
Long-term notes payable	100,000	100,000
Plant and equipment	850,000	870,000
Inventory	27,000	32,000
Accounts payable	30,000	35,000
Goodwill	10,000	6,000
Common stock	200,000	300,000
Bonds payable	500,000	500,000
Accounts receivable	40,000	35,000
Prepaid rent	18,000	16,000
Salaries payable	12,000	10,000
Accumulated depreciation	60,000	70,000
Retained earnings	150,000	160,000
Short-term notes payable	15,000	19,000
Short-term notes receivable	21,000	17,000
Dividends payable	0	10,000

REQUIRED: Using the information given above, prepare a schedule which shows the change in working capital from January 1 to December 31.

16—8. Selected financial data for Laffette, Inc., are given below:

LAFFETTE, INC.
Income Statement for the Period Ended December 31

Revenues		$110,000
Operating Expenses:		
Salaries	$50,000	
Depreciation Expense	30,000	
Utilities	3,000	
Goodwill Amortization	1,000	
Insurance	1,500	
Bond Premium Amortization	(500)	
Interest Expense	2,000	
Total Operating Expenses		87,000
Income before Taxes		$23,000
Taxes @ 30%		6,900
Net Income		$16,100
Add: Beg. Balance in Retained Earnings		40,000
Total		$56,100
Less: Dividends Paid		14,000
Retained Earnings, Ending Balance		$42,100

Working Capital

	JANUARY 1	DECEMBER 31
Current Assets:		
Cash	$ 5,000	$ 8,000
Accounts Receivable	8,000	9,000
Inventory	10,000	7,000
Prepaid Insurance	600	800
Total Current Assets	$23,600	$24,800
Current Liabilities:		
Accounts Payable	$ 7,000	$ 9,500
Salaries Payable	4,000	3,000
Other Short-Term Payables	2,000	3,000
Total Current Liabilities	$13,000	$15,500
Working Capital	$10,600	$ 9,300

REQUIRED: Using the information given above, calculate the amount of working capital generated from *operations*. (*Note:* You will not be able to explain the total changes in working capital, as you are analyzing only one aspect—that generated by operations.)

16—9. Use the information given in Exercise 16—8.

REQUIRED: Calculate the amount of cash generated by *operations* during the period.

16—10. Use the information in Exercise 16—8. The text of the chapter explains the rationale behind adding and subtracting changes in working capital accounts from net income to convert net income to a cash basis.

REQUIRED: Prepare an analysis similar to those given in your text for accounts receivable and supplies inventory which will explain the following:

1. Why the $200 increase in prepaid insurance should be deducted from net income as part of the process for converting net income to a cash basis.
2. Why the decrease in salaries payable of $1,000 should be subtracted from net income as part of the process for converting net income to a cash basis.

16—11. Consider a statement of changes in financial position which has these major classifications:

A. Items to be added to net income to convert net income to a cash or working capital basis.

B. Items to be deducted from net income to convert net income to a cash or working capital basis.

C. Sources of cash or working capital other than operations.

D. Financial resources generated but not affecting cash or working capital.

E. Cash or working capital applied to nonoperating items.

F. Noncash or nonworking capital financial resources applied.

REQUIRED: Assume that you are preparing a Statement of Changes in Financial Position *using a working capital format.* Number your paper from 1 to 15 and for each item described below, indicate by using the proper letter from the statement classifications given above how that item would appear on the statement you are preparing. If an item would not appear on the Statement of Changes in Financial Position, working capital format, put an "N" on your paper. (*Note: For some items, more than one letter may be required.*) For items which you find difficult, recreate the journal entry which was made to record the transaction.

Example: ___A___ Depreciation expense

1. The exchange of common stock for a piece of land.
2. The purchase of equipment for cash.
3. An increase in accounts receivable during the period.
4. The declaration and payment of a cash dividend.
5. The repurchase of some of the company's own shares of stock.
6. The sale of short-term investments for book value.
7. The purchase of a piece of equipment, giving a *short-term* note payable.
8. The retirement of a bond payable when it matured. Prior to retirement it had not been reclassified as current.
9. A decrease in prepaid insurance.
10. The sale of a piece of equipment with a book value of $10,000 for $12,000.
11. An increase in inventories during the period.
12. The exchange of long-term notes payable for a piece of land.
13. Borrowing through the issuance of long-term notes.
14. The sale of additional shares of the company's stock.
15. A decrease in accounts payable during the period.

16—12. Use the information given in Exercise 16—11 and the transactions described in that exercise.

REQUIRED: Assume that you are preparing a Statement of Changes in Financial Position using the cash format. Number your paper from 1 to 15 and for each item described in the transactions shown in Exercise 16—11, indicate, by using the proper letter from the statement classifications, how that item would appear on the statement you are preparing. If an item would not appear on the Statement of Changes in Financial Position, cash format, put an "N" on your paper. (*Note: For some items, more than one letter may be required.*) For items which you find difficult, recreate the journal entry which was made to record the transaction.

16—13. Beginning-of-the-period and end-of-the-period balance sheets for Carmichael's Fine Furs are shown below along with some additional information describing the company's transactions for the period.

	JANUARY 1	DECEMBER 31
Assets		
Cash	$ 10,000	$ 14,000
Accounts Receivable	14,000	10,000
Inventories	21,000	24,000
Plant and Equipment	240,000	280,000
Less: Accumulated Depreciation	(80,000)	(90,000)
Land	140,000	160,000
Total Assets	$345,000	$398,000
Liabilities		
Accounts Payable	$ 7,000	$ 11,000
Salaries Payable	10,000	7,000
Long-Term Notes Payable	100,000	120,000
Total Liabilities	$117,000	$138,000
Stockholders' Equity		
Common Stock	$200,000	$210,000
Retained Earnings	28,000	50,000
Total Stockholders' Equity	$228,000	$260,000
Total Liabilities and Stockholders' Equity	$345,000	$398,000

Additional information:

1. Land costing $20,000 was obtained by issuing a long-term note payable.
2. Net income for the period was $34,000.
3. Depreciation expense of $10,000 was recorded during the period.
4. Additional plant and equipment costing $40,000 was purchased for cash during the period.
5. Dividends of $12,000 were paid.
6. Common stock was sold for its par value of $10,000.

REQUIRED: 1. Prepare a schedule which shows the changes in each item of working capital and the increase or decrease in working capital for the period.
2. Prepare a Statement of Changes in Financial Position using the working capital format.

16—14. Use the data provided in Exercise 16—13.

REQUIRED: Prepare a Statement of Changes in Financial Position using the cash format.

16—15. Beginning of the period and end of the period balance sheets for the Never-Wet Rainwear Company along with some additional data describing the company's transactions for the period are shown below:

	JANUARY 1	DECEMBER 31
Assets		
Cash	$ 20,000	$ 16,000
Accounts Receivable	15,000	11,000
Inventory	25,000	22,000
Prepaid Insurance	8,000	9,000
Plant and Equipment	200,000	280,000
Accumulated Depreciation	(60,000)	(75,000)
Land	100,000	50,000
Total Assets		
	$308,000	$313,000
Liabilities and Stockholders' Equity		
Accounts Payable	$ 17,000	$ 19,000
Short-Term Notes Payable	8,000	9,000
Salaries Payable	7,000	6,000
Long-Term Notes Payable	50,000	60,000
Bonds Payable (Net of Unamortized Premium)	105,000	104,000
Common Stock, Par Value $10	100,000	102,000
Paid-in Capital in Excess of Par	11,000	12,000
Retained Earnings	10,000	1,000
Total Liabilities and Stockholders' Equity	$308,000	$313,000

Additional data:

1. Net income for the period was $16,000.
2. Depreciation expense for the period was $15,000.
3. Bond premium amortization of $1,000 was recorded.
4. Land costing $50,000 was sold for $70,000. The gain was shown on the income statement as part of ordinary income.
5. 200 shares of common stock with a market value of $15 per share were exchanged for some plant and equipment. The remainder of the plant and equipment purchased this period was purchased for cash.
6. The company borrowed money by giving a long-term note payable of $10,000.
7. Dividends of $25,000 were paid during the period.

REQUIRED: 1. Prepare a schedule which shows the change in each working capital account and in total working capital.

2. Prepare a Statement of Changes in Financial Position using the working capital format.

16—16.   Use the information provided in Exercise 16—15.

REQUIRED: Prepare a Statement of Changes in Financial Position in the cash format.

problems

16—17. *Inventory costs.*   Cook Office Equipment is attempting to determine the maximum number of typewriters it should hold. It costs the firm approximately $24 to order typewriters. Storage costs, insurance, and capital costs are $2 per month per machine. The firm anticipates selling 600 typewriters per year. The average cost of a typewriter is $200.

REQUIRED: **1.** Prepare a tabular presentation which shows the cost of ordering 20 typewriters, 30 typewriters, and 40 typewriters. How do you know that none of these amounts represents the optimal order quantity?
2. Calculate the economic order quantity for typewriters. (Round to the nearest whole unit.)
3. How many orders should the company place for typewriters each year? (Round to the nearest order.)

16—18. *Calculating the optimal size of a production run.*   The Great Outdoors Company makes propane camp stoves. The demand for these stoves is 4,000 per year. It cost $20 to produce a stove, and the carrying cost of warehousing, insurance, and interest on funds amounts to approximately 10% of production cost. To set up the machines for a production run of propane stoves costs $10. Great Outdoors can produce 50 stoves per day.

REQUIRED: **1.** How many propane stoves should be produced per production run? (Round your answer to the nearest whole unit.)
2. What is the length of the production run in days? (Round to the nearest whole day.)
3. The Great Outdoors Company has been making production runs of 100 stoves. What amount will they save by switching to runs of the optimal size which you calculated in part 1?
4. Suppose that demand for the propane stoves fell to 3,000 per year. What effect, if any, would this have on the size of the optimal production run?

16—19.   *Converting net income to a working capital basis.*   The income state-ment for Holderidge Supply and a Schedule of Changes in Working Capital for the company are presented below.

HOLDERIDGE SUPPLY
Income Statement for the Period Ended December 31

Sales		$500,000
Cost of Goods Sold	$200,000	
Salary Expense	150,000	
Depreciation Expense	30,000	
Amortization of Patents	6,000	
Utilities	2,000	
Insurance	1,500	
Loss on Sale of Equipment	2,500	
Interest Expense (net of bond premium amortization of $300)	2,700	
Total Operating Expenses		394,700
Income from Operations		$105,300
Gain on Sale of Land		21,000
Income before Taxes		$126,300
Taxes @ 50%		$ 63,150
Net Income		$ 63,150

Schedule of Changes in Working Capital

	JANUARY 1	DECEMBER 31	INCREASE OR (DECREASE) IN WORKING CAPITAL
Current Assets			
Cash	$ 20,000	$ 25,000	$ 5,000
Accounts Receivable	80,000	87,000	7,000
Inventories	120,000	117,000	(3,000)
Prepaid Insurance	1,200	2,200	1,000
Totals	$221,200	$231,200	$10,000
Current Liabilities			
Accounts Payable	$ 31,000	$ 28,000	$ 3,000
Salaries Payable	11,000	14,000	(3,000)
Taxes Payable	18,000	13,000	5,000
Dividend Payable	—	10,000	(10,000)
Totals	$ 60,000	$ 65,000	($5,000)
Working Capital Increase	$161,200	$166,200	$ 5,000

REQUIRED: Prepare a schedule which will show the amount of working capital, if any, provided by Holderidge Supply's operations. (*Note:* You will not be able to explain the total change in working capital as you are working with only one source—operations.) For items which present you with difficulty, think of the journal entry which was made to record the transaction.

16—20.   *Calculating cash provided by operations.*   Use the data provided for Holderidge Supply in Problem 16—19.

REQUIRED: Prepare a schedule which shows the amount of cash, if any, generated by the operations of Holderidge Supply. (*Note:* You will not be able to explain the total change in cash with your analysis as you are looking at only one possible source—operations.) For items which you find difficult, try to make the journal entry which was made to record the transaction.

16—21. *Explaining the impact of changes in selected working capital accounts on cash generated from operations.* To convert the Net Income of Holderidge Supply, shown in Problem 16—19, to a cash basis we will have to make the following, among other, adjustments for changes in the working capital accounts:

1. Subtract the $7,000 increase in Accounts Receivable from Net Income.
2. Deduct the decrease of $5,000 in Taxes Payable from Net Income.

REQUIRED: 1. Give a written explanation and analysis of why the $7,000 increase in Accounts Receivable must be deducted from Net Income as part of the process used in converting Net Income to a cash basis.
2. Give a written explanation and analysis of why the $5,000 decrease in Taxes Payable must be deducted from Net Income as part of the process of converting Net Income to a cash basis.

16—22. *Preparing a Statement of Changes in Financial Position—working capital format.* Financial information for the operations of the Mazzola Aircraft Company for the past year is presented below (000 omitted):

	BEGINNING-OF-THE-YEAR BALANCES, JULY 1	END-OF-THE-YEAR BALANCES, JUNE 30
Assets		
Cash	$5,000	$8,000
Accounts Receivable	20,000	18,000
Inventories	16,000	27,000
Property, Plant and Equipment	80,000	100,000
Accumulated Depreciation	(10,000)	(25,000)
Patents	3,000	4,000
Total Assets	$114,000	$132,000
Liabilities and Stockholders' Equity		
Accounts Payable	$13,000	$18,000
Salaries Payable	2,000	1,000
Bond Payable (net of unamortized discount)	27,000	27,500
Long-Term Notes Payable	20,000	30,000
Common Stock, no par	40,000	42,000
Retained Earnings	12,000	13,500
Total Liabilities and Stockholder's Equity	$114,000	$132,000

Additional information:

1. Net income for the period was $2,000,000.
2. Depreciation of $15,000,000 was recorded during the year.
3. Patent amortization of $1,000,000 was recorded.
4. Patents costing $2,000,000 were acquired for common stock.
5. Land costing $2,000,000 was sold for $2,000,000.
6. Additional purchases of property, plant and equipment amounted to $22,000,000.
7. Bond discount amortization of $500,000 was recorded.
8. Long-term notes payable in the amount of $10,000,000 were issued.
9. Dividends of $500,000 were paid.

REQUIRED:
1. Prepare a schedule which shows the change in each item of working capital and the total change in working capital.
2. Prepare a Statement of Changes in Financial Position using the working capital format.

16—23. *Preparing a Statement of Changes in Financial Position—cash format.* Use the financial data provided for Mazzola Aircraft in Problem 16—22.

REQUIRED: Prepare a Statement of Changes in Financial Position using the cash format.

16—24. *Preparing a Statement of Changes in Financial Position, working capital format.* The National Auto Parts Distributing Company has assembled the following data:

	BALANCE SHEET DATA AS OF:	
	January 1	December 31
Assets		
Cash	$30,000	$25,000
Accounts Receivable	50,000	58,000
Inventory	89,000	94,000
Prepaid Rent	10,000	3,000
Plant and Equipment	360,000	380,000
Accumulated Depreciation	(90,000)	(110,000)
Land	200,000	150,000
Goodwill	40,000	35,000
Total Assets	$689,000	$635,000

	BALANCE SHEET DATA AS OF:	
	January 1	December 31
Liabilities and Stockholders' Equity		
Accounts Payable	$ 42,000	$ 35,000
Short-Term Notes Payable	70,000	—
Accrued Expenses Payable	19,000	22,000
Long-Term Notes Payable	250,000	300,000
Common Stock,	300,000	250,000
Retained Earnings	8,000	28,000
Total Liabilities and Stockholder's Equity	$689,000	$635,000

Additional information:

1. Net income for the period was $50,000.
2. Dividends of $30,000 were paid.
3. A piece of equipment which had cost $30,000 and on which $10,000 of depreciation had been recorded was sold for $15,000. The loss was shown on the income statement.
4. Depreciation expense of $30,000 was recorded.
5. Goodwill amortization of $5,000 was recorded.
6. Equipment costing $50,000 was purchased during the period.
7. Land costing $50,000 was sold for $70,000 and the gain was recorded on the income statement.
8. Short-term notes payable of $50,000 were converted into long-term notes payable; the remaining balance was paid off in cash. The proceeds of the notes, which were received *last year*, were used to acquire equipment.
9. The company repurchased and retired at its book value $50,000 of common stock.

REQUIRED:

1. Prepare a schedule which shows the change in each item of working capital and the total change in working capital.
2. Prepare a Statement of Changes in Financial Position using the working capital format.
3. Were transactions which caused this company's working capital to increase examples of activities which could be used as recurring sources of working capital? Explain.

16—25. *Preparing a Statement of Changes in Financial Position, cash format.* Use the data provided for The National Auto Parts Distributing Company in Problem 16—24.

REQUIRED: Prepare a Statement of Changes in Financial Position using the cash format.

16—26. *Constructing a Statement of Changes in Financial Position, working capital format, from balance-sheet information; use of the worksheet approach.* You are a business consultant with a nationally known consulting firm. One of your clients has brought you some beginning-of-the-year and end-of-the-year balance-sheet information for a firm in which your client is thinking about making an investment. No income statement or additional information is available. The balance-sheet data are presented below:

READY-MIX PLASTER COMPANY
Balance Sheets

	JANUARY 1	DECEMBER 31
Assets		
Cash	$ 75,000	$ 90,000
Accounts Receivable	98,000	80,000
Inventories	103,000	118,000
Plant and Equipment	800,000	900,000
Accumulated Depreciation	(210,000)	(300,000)
Land	80,000	80,000
Patents	35,000	30,000
Goodwill	100,000	90,000
Total Assets	$1,081,000	$1,088,000
Liabilities and Stockholders' Equity		
Accounts Payable	78,000	98,000
Salaries Payable	30,000	20,000
Rent Payable	12,000	15,000
Long-Term Notes Payable	200,000	180,000
Bonds Payable (less unamortized premium)	306,000	304,000
Common Stock	300,000	310,000
Additional Paid-in Capital in Excess of Par	100,000	105,000
Retained Earnings	55,000	56,000
Total Liabilities and Stockholders' Equity	$1,081,000	$1,088,000

You have discovered that the company paid $60,000 of dividends during the year.

REQUIRED: 1. Prepare a schedule which shows the change in each working capital account and in total working capital.

2. Prepare a four-column worksheet of the type illustrated in the chapter and use the worksheet to analyze the major financing and investing activities in which the company engaged during the year and their impact on working capital.

6—27. *Constructing a Statement of Changes in Financial Position, cash format, from balance-sheet information; use of the worksheet approach.*   Use the information provided in Problem 16—26 above.

REQUIRED: Prepare a four-column worksheet of the type illustrated in the chapter and use the worksheet to analyze the major financing and investing activities in which the company engaged during the year and their impact on cash.

16—28. *Preparing a Statement of Changes in Financial Position, working capital format; use of the T-account technique.* Nolan's Fine Leather Products had the following beginning and ending balances in their balance-sheet accounts:

NOLAN FINE LEATHER PRODUCTS
Balance Sheet

	BEGINNING BALANCES, NOVEMBER 1	ENDING BALANCES, OCTOBER 31
Assets		
Cash	$ 90,000	$ 70,000
Accounts Receivable	100,000	115,000
Inventories	158,000	169,000
Marketable Securities (Short-Term)	70,000	35,000
Plant and Equipment	760,000	910,000
Accumulated Depreciation	(150,000)	(220,000)
Goodwill	60,000	50,000
Total	$1,088,000	$1,129,000
Liabilities and Stockholders' Equity		
Accounts Payable	54,000	69,000
Salaries Payable	18,000	14,000
Taxes Payable	29,000	33,000
Long-Term Mortgage Payable	100,000	80,000
Bonds (net of unamortized discount)	275,000	240,000
Preferred Stock, no par	200,000	220,000
Common Stock, par $1	150,000	175,000
Paid-in Capital in Excess of Par	170,000	195,000
Retained Earnings	92,000	103,000
Total Liabilities and Stockholders' Equity	$1,088,000	$1,129,000

The following additional data are available:

a. Net income for Nolan's was $200,000.
b. Depreciation of $100,000 was recorded.
c. Equipment costing $50,000 with a book value of $20,000 was sold for $10,000.
d. Plant and equipment purchases amounted to $200,000.
e. Goodwill amortization of $10,000 was recorded.
f. $20,000 of the long-term mortgage was extinguished by issuing $20,000 of preferred stock to the mortgage holder.
g. $5,000 of bond discount was amortized. Bonds of $40,000 were retired.
h. A stock dividend to common shareholders was distributed. The entry made to record the dividend was:

Retained Earnings	$15,000	
Common Stock		$ 5,000
Paid-in Capital in Excess of Par		10,000

The remaining changes in the Common Stock and the Paid-in Capital in Excess of Par accounts were due to sales of stock for cash.

i. Cash dividend of $174,000 were paid during the period.

j. Marketable securities were sold at book value.

REQUIRED:

1. Prepare a schedule which shows the change in each working capital account and the total working capital change for the period.
2. Use the T-account technique illustrated in the text to analyze the financing and investing activities of Nolan and their impact on working capital.
3. What transaction(s), if any, in which Nolan engaged are not reported on the Statement of Changes in Financial Position, working capital format?

6—29. *Preparation of a Statement of Changes in Financial Position, cash format; use of the T-account technique.* Use the data presented for Nolan's Fine Leather Products in Problem 6—28.

REQUIRED:

1. Use the T-account technique illustrated in the text to analyze the financing and investing activities of Nolan and their impact on cash.
2. Which transactions, if any, are not reported by Nolan on the Statement of Changes in Financial Position, cash format?
3. Compare the reporting of the change in marketable securities on the Statement of Changes, working capital basis, versus the cash basis.

16—30. *Interpreting a Statement of Changes in Financial Position, cash basis; converting it to a working capital statement.* Presented below is a Statement of Changes in Financial Position, cash basis, for the Universal Cardboard Container Corporation.

UNIVERSAL CARDBOARD CONTAINER CORPORATION
Statement of Changes in Financial Position—Cash Basis
for the Year Ended April 30

Financial Resources Generated:		
Cash Resources Generated:		
From Operations:		
Net Income		$ 90,000
Add: Depreciation	$100,000	
Goodwill Amortization	20,000	
Increase in Accounts Payable	50,000	
Decrease in Prepaid Insurance	8,000	178,000
Deduct: Gain on Sale of Equipment	30,000	
Increase in Accounts Receivable	120,000	
Increase in Inventories	165,000	(315,000)
Cash Generated by Operations		$(47,000)
Other Sources of Cash:		
Sale of Equipment	$200,000	
Sale of Short-Term Investments	110,000	
Issuance of 5-Year Note Payable	320,000	630,000
Total Cash Generated		$583,000
Noncash Financial Resources Generated:		
Common Stock Used to Retire Long-Term Debt		200,000
Total Financial Resources Generated		$783,000

UNIVERSAL CARDBOARD CONTAINER CORPORATION
Statement of Changes in Financial Position—Cash Basis
for the Year Ended April 30
(*Continued*)

Financial Resources Applied:

Cash Applied to Nonoperating Items:		
Dividends	$120,000	
Repurchase of company's stock	<u>290,000</u>	410,000
Noncash Financial Resources Applied:		
Long-Term Debt Retired by Issuing Common Stock		<u>200,000</u>
Total Financial Resources Applied		$610,000
Increase in Cash		$173,000

REQUIRED:

1. Based on the information provided in the Statement of Changes in Financial Position, cash format, comment on the strengths and weaknesses of Universal Cardboard Container.

2. Convert the Statement of Changes into a Statement of Financial Position, working capital format, and prepare an accompanying schedule of changes in working capital accounts.

3. Comparing the statement you were provided with and the one you prepared in part 2, which do you prefer and why?

INDEX